Royal Subjects

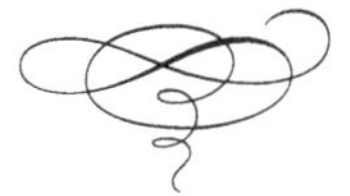

Essays on the Writings of James VI and I

Edited by Daniel Fischlin and Mark Fortier
With a Foreword by Kevin Sharpe

Wayne State University Press
Detroit

06 05 04 03 02 5 4 3 2 1

Library of Congress Cataloging-in-Publication Data

Royal subjects : essays on the writings of James VI and I / edited by
Daniel Fischlin and Mark Fortier ; with a foreword by Kevin Sharpe.
p. cm.
ISBN 0-8143-2877-6 (alk. paper)
1. James I, King of England, 1566–1625—Criticism and interpretation.
2. Politics and literature—Great Britain—History—17th century.
3. Political science—Great Britain—History—17th century. 4. Christian
literature, English—History and criticism. 5. Kings and rulers in
literature. 6. Monarchy in literature. I. Fischlin, Daniel. II.
Fortier, Mark, 1953–
PR2295.Z5 R69 2002
828′.309—dc21

00-012403

Contents

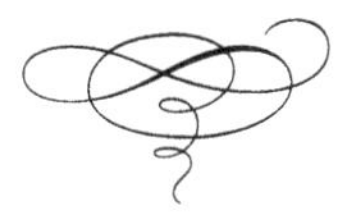

II. Prose, Politics, and Society

III. Writing and Religion

ACKNOWLEDGMENTS

This book has found its way into being thanks to the support of a great many people. Several years ago we began our work on James by preparing a modernized edition of *The True Law of Free Monarchies* and *Basilikon Doron* for the Centre for Reformation and Renaissance Studies (CRRS) at Victoria College (University of Toronto). The support of numerous people at the CRRS as well as the welcome critical reception of that edition gave us impetus to push ahead and address some of the formidable lacunae that exist in Jacobean studies, especially in relation to grasping the extent to which James VI and I's varied writing practices contributed to the literary and political culture of his Scottish and English reigns. We would like to thank the publisher at Wayne State University Press, Arthur Evans, for the care and patience he has shown through the long process of assembling this book. The editors for Wayne State, Kathryn Wildfong and Sandra Williamson, were exemplary in their handling of a large and complicated manuscript. Readers for the press were particularly helpful in their comments, and we would especially like to express our gratitude to Sally Mapstone of St. Hilda's College (Oxford) for her astute observations about how best to shape the diverse material contained in this book. Another anonymous reader was extremely generous in supporting our general sense that the enormous range of James's writings was due for serious and sustained critical attention. Two final readers for the press made invaluable and detailed suggestions that further shaped the form of this project. The contributors, who patiently responded to our many requests over an extended period of time, were a delight to work with—we have learned a great deal from them as the book has taken shape. Colleagues and friends—including Jennifer Ailles, Amy Appleford, Leeds Barroll, Michael Keefer, Maurice Lee Jr., Laura Levine, Mia London, Michael Meredith, David Parkinson, Jim Phillips, Kevin Sharpe, and Jenny Wormald--added a great deal to the intellectual contexts in which this volume was prepared, as have the numerous early modern and Jacobean scholars on whose shoulders we stand. We thank Kevin Sharpe for offering, in spite of an astonishingly busy schedule, to write the foreword, which provides a generous and learned perspective on the many issues that contributors in this book address. An earlier version of chapter eight appeared in *Renaissance Quarterly* 51.4 (Winter 1998).

Students to whom we have taught this material over the years have provided a singular source of enthusiasm and ideas as the material in this volume was honed. Lin Coburn, an honors undergraduate student at the University of Guelph, wrote a particularly distinguished undergraduate thesis on James that she completed just before her untimely death: we dedicate this book to her. Finally, as always, our thanks to our families, who gave us the space in which to undertake and complete a book we felt compelled to do: to Martha, Damian, Hannah, Zoë, and Esmé, and to Debra, Charlotte, and Julia, our belated gratitude and appreciation for the virtues shown when James beckoned.

Contributors

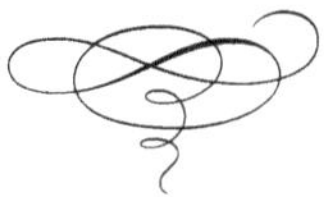

Sandra J. Bell has written and published on James's first collection of poetry, *The Essayes of a Prentise in the Divine Art of Poesie,* and on his long historical poem *Lepanto.* She is currently working on an anthology of sixteenth-century prose and poetry and is an assistant professor of English at the University of New Brunswick (Saint John).

David Bergeron, a widely recognized expert in Jacobean writing, is professor of English at the University of Kansas. He has published *Royal Family, Royal Lovers: King James of England and Scotland* (University of Missouri Press, 1991) and, with the University of Iowa Press, *King James and Letters of Homoerotic Desire* (1999).

James Doelman is currently an assistant professor at Brescia College, University of Western Ontario. His doctoral dissertation on biblical verse paraphrase in the Renaissance led to further research on the circulation and function of religious verse in early seventeenth-century England, which he conducted while on a post-doctoral SSHRCC fellowship at the Centre for Reformation and Renaissance Studies (Victoria College, University of Toronto). His articles have appeared in *ELH, Studies in Philology, Studies in English Literature, Seventeenth Century,* and *The George Herbert Journal.* He has published with Boydell & Brewer a book-length study entitled *James I and the Religious Culture of England* and is currently working on the circulation of epigrams in the early modern period.

Sarah M. Dunnigan received her doctorate in Renaissance poetry from the University of Edinburgh in 1997 and is currently a British Academy Postdoctoral Fellow in the University of Edinburgh's English Literature Department. She has worked extensively and published on the writings of Mary, Queen of Scots and other early modern Scottish women writers. Her book, *Eros and Poetry at the Courts of Mary Queen of Scots and James VI,* is forthcoming from Palgrave, and, with Evelyn S. Newlyn and C. Marie Harker, she is editing a collection of essays entitled *Writing Woman in Medieval and Early Modern Scotland.*

Daniel Fischlin is professor in the School of Literatures and Performance Studies in English at the University of Guelph. He is the author of *In*

Small Proportions: A Poetics of the English Ayre, 1596–1622 (Wayne State University Press, 1998). He has co-edited with Richard Dellamora *The Work of Opera: Genre, Nationhood, and Sexual Difference* (Columbia University Press, 1997) and, with Mark Fortier, *Adaptations of Shakespeare: A Critical Anthology of Plays from the 17th Century to the Present* (Routledge, 2000). He is currently working on a full-length study of early modern monarchic representations entitled *The Sovereignty of Words.*

MORNA FLEMING is presently assistant rector at Beath High School, Cowdenbeath, Fife. In 1997 she completed her D. Phil. at Glasgow University with a dissertation entitled "The Impact of the Union of the Crowns on Scottish Lyric Poetry 1584–1619" under the supervision of Rod Lyall and Theo van Heijnsbergen. In addition to having a number of articles forthcoming—on David Lindsay's *Ane Satyre of the Thrie Estaitis* and on the poetry of the Jacobean court group under James VI and I—she has contributed a commentary on James's *Reulis and Cautelis* to the latest Scotsoun cassette.

MARK FORTIER is associate professor in the English department at the University of Winnipeg. He has published extensively on Shakespeare and has edited, with Daniel Fischlin, two works by James VI and I. He is also the author of *Theory/Theatre: An Introduction* (Routledge, 1997) and co-editor, with Daniel Fischlin, of *Adaptations of Shakespeare: A Critical Anthology of Plays from the 17th Century to the Present* (Routledge, 2000).

PETER C. HERMAN, associate professor at San Diego State University, is the author of *Squitter-wits and Muse-haters: Sidney, Spenser, Milton and Renaissance Anti-poetic Sentiment* (Wayne State University Press, 1996) and the editor of several collections, including *Rethinking the Henrician Era: Essays on Early Tudor Texts and Contexts* (Illinois University Press, 1994), *Opening the Borders: Inclusivism and Renaissance Studies, Essays in Honor of James V. Mirollo* (University of Delaware Press, 1999), and *Day Late, Dollar Short: The Next Generation and the New Academy* (SUNY Press, 2000). He is presently working on early modern historiography.

CAROLYN IVES is a doctoral candidate at the University of Alberta. She is currently working on her dissertation, "Shifting Borders and Fluctuating Margins: The Bannatyne Manuscript and the Construction of Scottish National Identity in the Early Modern Period," under the supervision of Dr. Glenn Burger. The dissertation focuses on the relationship between the politics of nation and the politics of sex and gender in late medieval and early modern Scotland as filtered through the Bannatyne Manuscript. Her previous conference papers and publications include work on Scottish representations of Chaucer, concepts of authorship in the Bannatyne Manuscript, and the politics of scribal editing in the Bannatyne Manuscript.

JOHN N. KING is professor of English at Ohio State University. He is the recipient of major fellowships and grants from the National Endowment for the Humanities, National Humanities Center, American Council of Learned Societies, American Philosophical Society, Andrew Mellon Foundation, Folger Shakespeare Library, and Henry E. Huntington Library. His books include *English Reformation Literature: The Tudor Origins of the Protestant Tradition* (Princeton UP, 1982), *Tudor Royal Iconography: Literature and Art in an Age of Religious Crisis* (Princeton UP, 1989), *Spenser's Poetry and the Reformation Tradition* (Princeton UP, 1990), and *Milton and Religious Controversy: Satire and Polemic in "Paradise Lost"* (Cambridge UP, 2000). The Renaissance English Text Society has published his edition of *The Vocacyon of Johan Bale.* He serves as editor of *Literature and History* and literature editor of *Reformation,* international serials published in the United Kingdom.

LOUIS A. KNAFLA is a professor of history at the University of Calgary, where he has taught early modern English and legal history since 1965. His research and writing have been in this area as well as in legal archives and Canadian legal history. He has written numerous articles and essays on crime, court, judges, and the legal profession; his primary books in this area are *Law and Politics in Jacobean England; Crime Histories and Histories of Crime; Law, Society, and the State;* and *Kent at Law 1602.* Since 1984 he has been the editor of *Criminal Justice History,* and he is also the past-president of the Canadian Law and Society Association. Currently he is working on volume three of the Kent at Law Project (*The Court of Star Chamber*) as well as a full-length biography of the life and times of Sir Thomas Egerton, lord chancellor Ellesmere.

JOSEPH MARSHALL is an assistant curator at the National Library of Scotland. His doctoral thesis "Reading King James VI and I in the Civil War" (University of Edinburgh, 2000), is a study of the appropriation and reworking of James's writings for propaganda, particularly in the 1640s.

DAVID J. PARKINSON, professor of English at the University of Saskatchewan, has published an edition of Gavin Douglas's *Palis of Honoure* and several related essays on poetry and culture in early sixteenth-century Scotland. The Scottish Text Society published his edition of the poems of Alexander Montgomerie (1545?–98) in 2000.

CURTIS PERRY is an associate professor in the Department of English at Arizona State University. He is the author of *The Making of Jacobean Culture: James I and the Renegotiation of Elizabethan Literary Practice* (Cambridge University Press, 1997) as well as several articles on early modern English literature and culture.

KEVIN SHARPE is professor of Renaissance studies in the Department of English at the University of Warwick. His publications include *Reading Revolutions* (Yale University Press, 2000), *Remapping Early Modern England* (Cambridge University Press, 2000), *The Personal Rule of Charles I* (Yale University Press, 1992), *Politics and Ideas* (Pinter, 1989), and *Criticism and Compliment* (Cambridge University Press, 1987). He has also edited *Refiguring Revolutions* (University of California Press, 1998), *Culture and Politics* (Stanford University Press, 1994), and *Politics of Discourse* (University of California Press, 1987). He is currently writing a book entitled *Representations of Authority and Images of Power in England, 1500–1700.*

MALCOLM SMUTS is professor of history at the University of Massachusetts, Boston and president of the North American Society for Court Studies. His publications include *Court Culture and the Origins of a Royalist Tradition in Early Stuart England* (University of Pennsylvania Press, 1987), *The Stuart Court and Europe: Essays in Politics and Political Culture* (Cambridge University Press, 1996), which he edited, and *Culture and Power in England, 1585–1685* (St. Martin's Press, 1999). He has also edited an account of James I's first entry into London on 15 March 1604, which will appear in the *Complete Works of Thomas Middleton,* forthcoming from Oxford University Press in 2001.

JOHANN P. SOMMERVILLE is professor of history at the University of Wisconsin, Madison. He is the author of *Royalists and Patriots: Politics and Ideology in England, 1603–1640,* second edition (Longman, 1999), *Thomas Hobbes: Political Ideas in Historical Context* (Macmillan, 1992), and editor of *James VI and I: Political Writings* (Cambridge University Press, 1994) and Sir Robert Filmer's *Patriarcha* (Cambridge University Press, 1991), both in the *Cambridge Texts in the History of Political Thought* series.

SIMON WORTHAM studied at the University of Sussex and is senior lecturer in English literature at the University of Portsmouth. He has published a number of articles on seventeenth-century literature and culture, as well as on issues in literary and cultural theory. His book *Rethinking the University: Leverage and Deconstruction* was published in 1999 by Manchester University Press.

Foreword

Reading James Writing: The Subjects of Royal Writings in Jacobean Britain

Kevin Sharpe

Royal Subjects is an important and original volume. Indeed its importance is underlined by the remarkable fact that no full study of the writings of James VI and I—or for that matter of any British ruler—has been undertaken before.[1] Historians, predictably, have long cited James's speeches to his parliaments and studied his treatises on kingship, the *Basilikon Doron* and *The True Law of Free Monarchies,* especially after they were collected and edited in Charles McIlwain's *Political Works of James I* (1918). McIlwain, however, was a constitutional historian, interested more in the evolution of the English Parliament and law than in James's own views on church and state; McIlwain's selection of "political" writings was determined by his own notion of what constituted politics. The edition therefore detaches the treatises and speeches from the large body of James's *Workes,* removing them from the contexts in which contemporaries read them and viewed the king.[2] Since 1918 James's other writings gathered in his *Workes*—paraphrases of Scripture, defenses of the oath of allegiance, interventions in European controversy, and his diatribe against tobacco—have been largely ignored. Moreover, his treatises on the Gospel of St. Matthew and the Lord's Prayer, written after the 1616 *Workes,* have scarcely been noticed, presumably because it was assumed they had nothing to offer the historian of politics.

By the same token, historians have ignored the considerable body of James VI and I's poetry and his *Short Reulis and Cautelis to Be Observed and Eschewed in Scottis Poesie.*[3] Our post-Romantic sensibilities have tended to categorize poetry as an aesthetic genre and to view private voice as separate from the business of public and political life. Moreover, for all Sir Philip Sidney's arguments about the truth content of poetry, historians have tended to shy away from reading literature, especially verse, as historical evidence. Though partly a function of lack of training, this reticence is more a consequence of untheorized (indeed unthought) but rigid distinctions between "fact" and "fiction," reliable and unreliable types of sources, and historical "realities" and "representations."[4] As for literary scholarship, critical fashion for long consigned James's writings to obscurity. The New Criticism, which dominated literature departments for half a century, seemed concerned (perhaps understandably in an age of two world wars) to detach great texts from historical circumstance and to focus study on those writers and works that were not for an age but for all time: the great literary geniuses who seemed to provide a refuge from history. James VI and I was not among them. His was a pen and mind manifestly engaged, in verse no less than polemical tract, with his time. For all his importance in forging a literary circle in Scotland and a unique royal representation in England, he earned no place in the canon of eminent writers. Though the Scottish critic James Craigie performed a patriotic act in his excellent editions of James's poetic works, the texts, though now readily available, attracted little more critical than historical interest.[5]

At this point, it would be gratifying to shift from regretful comments about past neglect to praise of more recent historical and critical scholarship. Gratifying but inaccurate. For though revisionist historians redirected close attention to the early Stuart age and rejected the anachronistic perspectives that distorted our view of it, their notion of politics was as attenuated as that of the Whig historians they criticized. While revisionists have—through revisiting the histories of the court and church, faction and Parliament—rehabilitated James, they have shown little interest in his writings, beliefs, and values. If anything, revisionist historians have exhibited more disdain than their predecessors for printed and literary sources, erecting a higher, more rigid barrier between historical facts and representations. Recent studies of the Jacobean church and religion pass over James's scriptural exegeses.[6] In Johann Sommerville's 1994 edition of what are still differentiated as James's "political writings," poetry has no place.

The hope for a new approach lay rather in the revisionist critical movement that soon came to be known as New Historicism. New Historicism's project was to open the category of "literature," to study all "texts"—not just canonical ones—as literary production, and to situate and read texts in their moments of construction, publication, dissemination, and reception. More importantly, New Historicism focused on the relationships of discourse and power, analyzing texts as sites for the constitution of and contest for authority in humanist rhetorical culture.[7] Such scholarship produced dazzling new insights into the politics of Spenser and Shakespeare, Herbert and Milton. But oddly, the most obvious texts of power—the writings of kings and queens—were for the most part ignored. Here the striking and brilliant exception was Jonathan Goldberg. In *James I and the Politics of Literature*, Goldberg combined New Historicist interest in authority with an older historicizing, and traditional close reading with deconstructive criticism, to explore representations not just *of* the king's authority but *as* the king's authority. Goldberg studied not merely James's ideas on kingship but his means of articulating his power. This book was intended to open up new critical/historical agendas and further the study of James's writings. However, historians reviewed Goldberg unfavorably—even, in Jenny Wormald's case, with uncharacteristic hostility—while literary critics remained more at home with canonical texts and authors.[8]

Both critics and historians have missed a rich opportunity. As I discovered while teaching a graduate class, interdisciplinary address to royal writings opens myriad insights into the central issues of historiographical and critical debate: questions of authorship and authority; representation and power; the receptions and appropriations of texts; the politics of genres and material forms; the ambiguities and contradictions inherent in acts of speaking and writing—and ruling; and the negotiations with readers and subjects inherent in both authorial and regal performances. Beyond that, the study of royal writings enables a review of critical theories and historical methods of textual exegesis, offering fruitful suggestions for approaches to other Renaissance texts and other periods. It is to some of the issues raised by the critical and historical conversations in this volume on the writings of James VI and I that I shall now turn.

What several essays make apparent is the extent to which the very subject of this volume—the writings of James, authorship—needs to be problematized.[9] We learn, for example, from Sarah Dunnigan's essay in this volume, that James's *Amatoria*, poems we might consider the most personal of all his writings, were most probably collaborative. To take another case, though James undoubtedly translated some of the Psalms, the volumes of Psalms published in 1631 and 1636 as translated by King James contain the work too of Sir William Alexander and reflect the influence of Charles I, who also edited other of his father's manuscripts.[10] (By contrast, though his name did not appear on the title page, many of James's translations found their way into a 1650 edition.[11]) The fact that, as the title page proclaims, they were *The Psalms of King David* raises larger questions about translation as "authorship," and these merit further examination. Indeed many of James's writings were as much readings of biblical hermeneutics and exegeses as they were also the readings of God's divine decrees and natural laws. Collaboration, translation, exegesis, and paraphrase not only raise the question of who was the author; they also compel consideration of the shifts in the relationship of authoring to authorizing (the two terms were used virtually indiscriminately) and exercising authority.[12] Two contributors here make incisive but undeveloped, and interestingly contradictory, observations. James's 1616 *Workes*, the editors write, marked "a major moment in the history of English authorship"—a moment when the authority of the text resided in the name of the creator.[13] By assisting that development, James furthered the claims of other authors to property, notably Ben Jonson, who gathered his folio works the same year. Thus he may have helped to disperse cultural authority—that is, authority itself—to all writers: writers who were to emerge by the end of the seventeenth century as powerful political agents, not all in the service of the king. Curtis Perry extends the observation about authorship and collaborative writing to politics, stating that "the public persona of a monarch is always produced collaboratively."[14] As with authorship and writing, all representations of monarchy in early modern England were multiple performances and, as we are beginning to see, authority was constructed by several different, often differing, agents.[15]

Whatever the complexities of authorship, what clearly emerges from these essays is James's sense of the centrality of writing to his exercise of rule. As Perry writes, "more than any other monarch, James forged a connection between absolutism and the authority of the printed word."[16] He was not the first monarch to make such a connection. Henry VIII constructed his role as Defender of the Faith and, later, Supreme Head of the Church not least through religious texts written by him and/or published under his own name. Queen Elizabeth, too, authored and authorized volumes of prayers.[17] But where both Tudors are more remembered for their images, James was a monarch of the word. By corollary all his words were regal acts, or, as Peter Herman puts it, "for James no discourse existed separate from sovereignty."[18] In contrast to McIlwain and Sommerville, who address only prose treatises as political writings, Morna Fleming shows that James "used poetry throughout his life as an attempt to control events."[19] He clearly believed the identity of kingship and writing to be ancient and divine. He turned to the Psalms because they were the work of a biblical king, and clearly, in his paraphrases of Revelation and Chronicles, he manifested the belief that it was the duty of God's lieutenant on earth to explain to his subjects the text of the king of kings. For James, scriptural exegesis was part of divine kingship, the fulfillment of the king's obligation to lead his subjects to faith and truth. In turn these writings announced and publicized James as a divine king and claimed scriptural authority for royal words.

James's *Basilikon Doron,* his principal treatise on kingship, was a royal "gift" to his son—and, once published, a gift also to his subjects. Historically the royal word uttered to subjects was (and remains) an especial mark of favor, a priceless gift in the culture of feudal personal relations. As a burgeoning market economy loosened seigneurial ties, gifts too—symbolic capital—became tainted by money and exchange, as contemporaries observed with anguish. Simon Wortham interestingly suggests that James endeavored to preserve the royal word as a priceless gift that could be bestowed exclusively by a sovereign who was positioned above the relations of exchange.[20] But as we shall see, writing partook of and valorized commodity culture. Yet if he could not (as at times he seemed to acknowledge) resist textual exchange, James did reinforce the authority of royal words. As James Doelman shows, the king's intention to produce a new Psalter foreclosed other editions, and in the case of the controversy over tobacco, many were evidently willing to agree with James's (controversial) views about its bad effects simply because he was king.[21] Despite challenges, royal words continued to have special valence. As he grappled against the extraordinary power and popularity of the *Eikon Basilike* of Charles I (which incidentally owed some of its strategy and authority to James's writings), Milton acknowledged how "advantageous it is to a book only to be a king's"; for once "a king is *said* to be the author" (my italics), "there needs no more among the blockish vulgar to make it wise, and excellent, and admir'd, *nay to set it next the Bible.*"[22]

In very obvious ways James set his writings "next the Bible." For as well as containing scriptural paraphrases, the king's 1616 *Workes* adopts some of the material forms of the King James Bible, which was issued as the new "authorised version" five years earlier. Like the 1611 Bible, James's *Workes* was a large folio, with a complex engraved frontispiece that echoes the title page of the Bible. Where in the Bible his majesty's name appears on the slab that bears the title, surrounded by the patriarchs and apostles, the title page of his *Workes,* his own words, is flanked by the figures of religion and peace, presenting James as the biblical Solomon, the embodiment of divine wisdom.[23] The reader of *The Workes of the Most High and Mighty Prince James By the Grace of God King . . . Defender of the Faith* was drawn to recall the text of the king of kings "*revised by his Majesty's special command.*" Daniel Fischlin suggests persuasively that James took trouble over the arrangement of the texts in his volume of writings, and he attaches special significance to its opening with commentaries on Revelation.[24] As the placement of essays on poetry (which is traditionally not read as political) at the start of this collection reminds us, the organization, the material, of books is integral to their performance and reception. James not only attributed importance to arrangement, he excluded sonnets from his verse collections and deployed those arts of authorial influence—prefaces, for example—to direct readings and, in the case of the 1591 edition of *Lepanto,* rereadings.[25] We need to pay more attention than we have to the materiality of James's texts, both manuscript and printed, and especially to frontispieces, title pages, prefaces, and epistles dedicatory. But in doing so we must also come to see how royal books, like all books, could also slip out of their original form, with radical consequences for their performance and reception. Royal texts, as James complained in connection with his *Basilikon Doron,* could be prostituted and corrupted by others.[26] As James Doelman shows, when James's Psalms were published in the 1630s, they were sent to Scotland bound with the new prayer book for the Kirk.[27] As such they became not what James had intended—the Psalter for the new united British church—but part of a text that would script civil war and regicide.[28]

Questions about the material form of texts leads us to another central subject on which these studies of James's writings cast valuable light: the relationship and authority of manuscript and print. Earlier histories, notably Elizabeth Eisenstein's *The Printing Press as an Agent of Change,* were premised on the thesis that print overtook manuscript and gained authority as a more reliable and uniform mode of textual communication—that print in fact authorized texts as reliable and true. Recently, in *The Nature of the Book,* Adrian Johns has questioned these assumptions and argued that manuscripts were, and for a long time were seen to be, more dependable and authoritative. Harold Love, meanwhile, in his *Scribal Publication in Seventeenth Century England,* demonstrates not only the survival of manuscript culture deep into the age of print, but also the two-way textual traffic—from print to manuscript no less than the reverse.[29] Early seventeenth-century England and Scotland were literary and political cultures in which the relative authorities of manuscript and printed forms were unstable, shifting and dependent upon all the circumstances of production and reception. Autolycus in Shakespeare's *The Winter's Tale* sold his ballads as more "true" because "in print" (4.4.260–61), but among court and aristocratic coteries, manuscript carried the cultural authority, and printing and publishing were regarded as vulgar.[30]

James's writings certainly support skepticism about the fixedness of print. Variants of most of James's writings were published in his lifetime, not to mention the obvious differences of Latin, Scottish, and English editions. In the case of the king's *Letter and Directions Touching Preaching and Preachers,* Joseph Marshall argues that different versions, in print and manuscripts, fractured the authority of the royal word, enabling one version to be quoted against another.[31] More generally, James seems to epitomize the ambiguities about manuscript and print. He did not "publish" his early verse, but he clearly intended that it should circulate and influence (which it did); subsequently he gathered some of his poems and his treatise on poetry for publication. When he printed *Basilikon Doron* he issued initially just seven copies, only publishing it more broadly, in a changed version, when he ascended the throne of England.[32] As Simon Wortham puts it, early on James appears to have tried to deploy print as if in the privileged manner of manuscript circulation.[33] It would seem that in England, with the 1603 issues of the *Basilikon Doron* and *True Law* as well as the 1616 *Workes,* James had become firmly converted to "publication as a means of government."[34] Here, however, we must recall the extraordinary poems James penned in the 1620s—to counter criticisms of the Spanish match and the "raylinge rhymes" against his government.[35] Clearly, whether wisely or not, James felt the need to answer squibs circulating in manuscript with manuscript verse from his own hand. Interestingly, too, in 1622 he wrote a mocking poem ordering the nobles to leave London, expressing his hope that a manuscript verse might persuade those to obey and leave whom "scarce a [printed] proclamation can expel."[36] For all the humor (and that was not incidental), it would appear that the king regarded these personal interventions as more authoritative than printed proclamations and statutes. Whatever his belief,

James's acts—acts of printing and not printing—express complexities in the culture and politics of manuscript and print that we are only beginning to address.

The performances of texts were also conditioned in the Renaissance by genres: by the associations and expectations genres aroused and the authority which, from classical antecedents and theory, they conveyed.[37] In the case of James VI and I, scholars have not sufficiently noticed the range of genres in which the king wrote or the relationship of generic election to the purposes, authority, and reception of his writings. Epic, for instance, was regarded as the highest of literary forms. In choosing epic for his poem *The Lepanto,* James selected a genre fitting to a great Christian triumph over the infidel and one that perhaps suited his personal polemical purpose of subjugating the quarrels among Christians to larger ideals of ecumenism and accommodation, which W. B. Patterson has recently documented. Just as translation and exegesis brought to royal texts the authority of divine originals, so epic could evoke global ideals and imperial associations of an age prior to the fissure of Christendom into warring denominational camps. James emerges from the essays in this volume as a writer and ruler sensitive to the cultural power and politics of genre. As Perry effectively demonstrates, James's use of the pastoral for his poem "Off Jacke and Tom" translates the very real and dangerous journey of Prince Charles and the Duke of Buckingham to Spain into the aestheticized balm of pastoral.[38] Moreover it deploys what had been an oppositionist genre to counter criticism of royal policy. The fact that both the king and his critics, however, could deploy pastoral reminds us that genres, because they conveyed expectations, were not the exclusive property of any one writer or group; nor was their meaning fixed.

Indeed the very authority associated with genres resulted in a contest between writers—and readers—to appropriate them. Genres, that is, were multivalent, as Sarah Dunnigan well demonstrates in her essay in this volume on James's love poetry. Love was a privileged discourse of power at the Elizabethan court, and James, as author of sonnets to both Queen Elizabeth and his own Queen Anne, sought to deploy it to construct "a perfect kingdom of sexual authority."[39] But as Dunnigan argues, not only because they dealt with passions "not felt by me," love poems presented James with problems. For love at best implies a reciprocity, and "in the act of desiring, the lover of necessity renounces authority."[40] If James chose not to include love poems in his collected verse, it may be because he did not wish to publicize such submissiveness to his subjects, over whom he frequently claimed to be the "lawful husband."[41] But this ambivalence invites us to consider the problems for James in writing letters as a king and a lover, especially to favorites who were subjects, and for whom sexual love was proscribed by cultural norms and his own declamations against sodomy.[42] Though as a king he could threaten his favorite Carr, as a lover he felt the need to express a willingness to surrender all, his foreign policy objectives and everything, to have his beloved Buckingham "in my arms again."[43] David Bergeron's recent pioneering studies of

James's love letters suggest that letters may be the most revealing sites of the contradictions of genre and, too, of the king's two bodies: contradictions a discourse of authority was meant to conceal.[44] Address to genre will require us to ask again whether when he stepped from the pedestal of his folio *Workes* to write doggerel verse in the strain of the libels circulating against the court, James appropriated a popular genre for his own purposes or was debased by its popularity.

Genres are part of that "interpretive community" that enables writers and readers to communicate, even though they do not construct identical meanings.[45] In recent years literary critics and theorists of textual performance have shifted emphasis from the writers to the readers of texts, and to acts of reading as constituting the meanings that texts enacted. As I argue in a recent book, *Reading Revolutions: The Politics of Reading in Early Modern England,* historians have largely ignored reception theory and the histories of reading, even though there is abundant evidence from the sixteenth and seventeenth centuries that authors acknowledged, even feared, that their fates lay in readers' hands. Though he was a king, as an author James VI and I was no exception. As he acknowledged in publishing *Basilikon Doron,* "this book is now vented and set forth to the public view of the world, and consequently subject to every man's censure."[46] Even in the case of *A Counterblaste to Tobacco* James seemed less than confident about the reception of his work. If his words, he wrote, "carry the force of persuasion with them it is all I can wish, and more than I can expect."[47] For all his deployment of authorial devices for control of interpretation, of the "imaginary of the reader," and for all his investment in his writings as acts of authority, James was right to suspect and fear the independence of readers. In our own day the sharply different interpretations of James's political ideas held by historians such as Johann Sommerville (who categorizes him as an absolutist), Paul Christianson (who sees him as a constitutionalist who changed), and Glenn Burgess (who takes him as a spokesman for a cultural consensus on law and prerogative) speak to the enduring capacity to read the king's words very differently.[48] And James's words were read differently by his contemporaries and seventeenth-century commentators after his death. As we have seen, in the debate over James's *Letter and Directions Touching Preaching and Preachers,* some used variant editions and James's other, earlier texts to claim a meaning quite other than the king's own. As Mark Fortier shows, a text such as the *True Law,* written in the context of James's struggles with the Kirk, might be read quite differently amid English debates over impositions, equity jurisdiction, and royal prerogative.[49] Whatever James's stress on the obligations of rulers, his theory of divine right came, in changed circumstances in his lifetime and after, to arouse concerns, ultimately contributing to the Whig myth of the rise of absolutism. Full understanding of the importance of James VI and I's writings awaits a study, too, of the traces of the readings of the king's works in marginalia and glosses, and, more broadly, a study of the reception of the king's texts—that is, of the king as a text.

The capacity, the opportunity to read the king's works in ways that he had not desired suggests, of course, that the royal texts were less determining, more open than we once assumed such scripts to be. Deconstructive criticism (dismissed by most historians) has theorized and demonstrated the instabilities of meaning in and the self-consuming nature of all texts. For all that royal writing or speech was intrinsic to the exercise of rule in the Renaissance, royal texts could not but reveal the ambiguities and contradictions of a political culture that was wrestling with fundamental issues and debates about faith and obedience, community and individual, stasis and change, traditional values and market relations, power and subjectivity. Indeed, while on the one hand early modern emphases on unity, commonweal, and consensus sought to write over these differences, rhetorical training and habits, arguing in *utrimque partes* or the idea of *discordia concors,* opened any text to alternative readings and writings.[50] Daniel Fischlin writes that "the very textuality that is used as a prop to authoritarian regimes can also serve to subvert the terms by which those regimes enlist textuality in their support."[51] Fischlin discusses James's scriptural exegeses, especially Revelation, which had (and has) a long history of contested hermeneutics. But this collection identifies potentially self-subverting contradiction across all the genres of James's writings. John King reminds us that as well as scriptural validation for divine rule, there was also a "profoundly anti-monarchical strand" in the typology of David appropriated by James and other monarchs.[52] For while the biblical patriarch who united kingdoms may have seemed an ideal model for James—who sought the union of England and Scotland (he recommended David as a pattern to Prince Henry)—David was also a sinner, an adulterer and murderer, who brought disaster on his royal house and suffered reproof from the prophet Nathan.

We have already noticed the contradictions implicit in the *Amatoria*—the ambiguous stances of authority and subjection in the voice of the suitor. But we should note that Dunnigan's study suggests a full recognition of such instabilities by a learned monarch who was "a writer of contradiction and paradox."[53] Indeed, as Fleming shows, in "Two Sonnets to Her M:tie to Show the Difference of Stiles," James plays with Petrarchan conventions to demonstrate how they "could be used for a totally invented statement of emotion."[54] He juxtaposes, that is, honesty and artifice. Such contradictions, and displayed contradictions, situate royal texts in a rhetorical and Reformation culture preoccupied with representation and misrepresentation, truth and what Perez Zagorin has called "ways of lying."[55] Close readings and deconstructive readings of James's writings not only enable us to observe a ruler endeavoring to overwrite challenges to authority, but a king, a thinker, a rhetorician, a lover and man ("As man, a man am I composed all" [BL Add. MS 24195, f.7v; Craigie, *Poems,* 2.71]) participating in those contradictions—personal, social, religious, and political.[56]

A contemporary recognition of contradiction, James's own awareness of the ambiguities of the Davidic, and his contrast (one he made in several speeches) between honesty and dissimulation may, I would suggest, have broader implications for his writing and exercise of authority. In its early manifestation New Historicism tended to study the discourse of authority as controlled and controlling, as hegemonic and willing to license dissent only so as to contain and neuter it in the service of enhanced power.[57] In his later work, Stephen Greenblatt shifted to a more dialogic model of discourse and authority, using in the title of a famous book the term *negotiations.* It is this second model, I believe, that offers more potential insight into early modern political and literary culture, and into the writings of James VI and I.

Throughout this collection we see royal texts as open and multivalent, addressing ambiguity and paradox, airing contradiction, in dialogue within themselves as well as beyond themselves with other texts. Political historians of recent years have characterized James (often in contrast to his son) as a king who excelled in the political arts—flexibility, compromise, and maneuver—a ruler ever willing to adjust to circumstance. For all the sincerity and consistency of his fundamental beliefs, James's writings reveal some of these same qualities—a willingness to discuss, compromise, and negotiate.[58] Though he did famously tear the Commons' Protestation from their journal in 1621, James—as argued by Marshall in this volume—was also willing to abandon one of his own pronouncements, his directions to preachers, "under pressure from his readers."[59] When he penned in kind a verse in response to libels, rather than effecting, as Perry would have it, "a collapse in the relationship between author and reader," James perhaps showed, in difficult circumstances, some willingness to renegotiate that relationship.[60] If my suggestion that an absolute divine king was willing to enter into dialogue and negotiation with subjects itself reads as a paradoxical text, it goes I think to the heart of early modern politics, where authority ultimately rested on consent and cooperation and involved dialogue and negotiation.[61] James's writings may offer us invaluable insights into how a complex set of cultural codes were negotiated in the king's own mind.

Though the last twenty years of scholarship have produced important works on the Jacobean court and church, foreign policy, and political ideas, we await, as Fischlin and Fortier argue in their introduction, a modern biography of King James VI and I.[62] Though James's writings have been neglected hitherto, this volume makes it evident that such a biography must make full use of them; moreover, careful study of these works will refine and revise even recent scholarship. Essays on James's *Amatoria* and Bergeron's evaluation of his love letters open to study a passionate man whose humanity and affective life have been erased or derided by most critics and historians. To say the least they impel a new approach to the history of all James's affective relations and to their significance for politics and the dramatic tensions and clashes between the royal bodies, private and public, within the king's own being and on the public stage. Historians of the "British question" will here see the need to pay attention to James's poetry written in

Scotland and to the relations, as Carolyn Ives and David Parkinson describe them, of "poetic invention" and "national identity"; and perhaps consider the possibilities of a "British" poetic (James carefully anglicized his texts) after 1603.[63] Certainly, Doelman's observation that James hoped for a revised Psalter that "could be a unifying element in all the British churches" suggests the need to explore James's writings as key devices in his project of union.[64] Several essays in this collection, as we have seen, take up James's political ideas and attitudes to the law—subjects of recent monographs and controversy. Here, reading nothing but James's own words, Louis Knafla depicts a monarch who was by no means a threat to the common law but one who, it seems to me, contests the labels of "absolutist" and "constitutionalist" that Sommerville has somewhat anachronistically imposed on seventeenth-century discourse.[65] Whatever our future approach to the "voices" on the early modern constitution, this volume shows they will need to be situated in a broader range of articulations than those privileged as merely "legal" or "political."

It is James's churchmanship that has most benefited from recent scholarship: Patrick Collinson, Peter Lake, Kenneth Fincham, and others have depicted and praised a king able to sustain a peaceful religious settlement by balancing different groups while upholding the "Calvinist consensus" that, they argue, bound those who differed on matters of ceremony and church government.[66] As I have argued elsewhere, and as others have shown, the picture of a Jacobean ecclesiastical peace only disrupted by the Thirty Years War and the "rise of Arminianism" tends to downplay the very real doctrinal divisions that spilled over from Elizabeth's reign to that of the first Stuart.[67] More importantly, much of the new scholarship has left James's own position and faith confusing and unclear—not least because it has paid too little attention to his own works. While Fincham and Lake are right to argue that James's hostility to Puritans was sharpened by their opposition to the Spanish match, that hostility seems evident in all James's writings, from the paraphrase of Revelation to the neglected treatises on the Gospel of St. Matthew and the Lord's Prayer.[68] Here, while underlining both the importance of context for all James's utterances and his enduring suspicion of Catholics, Malcolm Smuts shows how, from his writings in Scotland to the 1620s, "the king's hostility to Protestant radicalism never abated."[69] Importantly, too, Smuts argues that James's (infamous) advocacy of peace was deeply rooted in his providentialist thinking, that his diplomacy, like his domestic government, was taken from his reading of God's divine will and plan. As Fischlin puts it, all James's works, actions, and writings were acts of faith.[70] Ecclesiastical historians need to return to all the writings through which James demonstrated and worked out a faith involving far more than the theological disputes that have dominated our historiography.

Study of James's writings enables a far better understanding of the man and monarch as well as of the nature of Jacobean literary and political culture. Beyond, it points to broader possibilities for elucidating other reigns and representations. Most obviously, James's writings direct us to the discourses of royal predecessors (on which his own drew in ways we have yet to examine) and indeed successors, and to the changes in the genres and circumstances of royal textual performances.[71] Historians of the reign of Henry VIII have briefly noticed Henry's most polemical works—the *Assertio Septem Sacramentorum, A Necessarie Doctrine,* and *The Glasse of Truth*—but they have not subjected them to close rhetorical and critical analysis in order to study the *means* by which Henry endeavored to construct his supremacy. The king's letters, meanwhile, especially his intimate letters, have only recently received critical study—by Seth Lerer—and his songs and love poetry remain little read. Similarly Edward VI's diary calls out for a critical reading that goes beyond the historian's concern with content to study its sparseness, chronicle style, repressions, and emotional distancing as themselves evidence of a politics of representation. Queen Elizabeth's verse, prose translations, and poems are at last being edited, and feminist criticism is adding new perspectives to them as texts of female rule in a patriarchal culture.[72] But we need more extensive editorial and critical work on the prayers written by Elizabeth and/or published under her name, and closer study of the language of female devotion in a Protestant realm and the gendered discourse of the queen's own conscience and faith.[73] Crossing to the other side of the Civil War, Charles II's and others' narratives of his escape from the Battle of Worcester and hiding in an oak tree were widely distributed and popularized, yet only some of the significantly varying texts have been published and edited, and none has been critically analyzed for the deployment of narrative technique and novelistic devices.[74] James II's war memoirs have been ignored by all but military historians, and his devotions are most often referred to merely as texts of Jacobite nostalgia.[75] We must hope that the fertile fruits of these investigations of James VI and I's writings stimulate work on other monarchic texts.

My brief catalogue of royal texts, of course, passed over Charles I. James's son and heir, of his works no less than his crown, seemed before his death, as I have argued, to prefer silence to words—or at least to appear to discern the risk that too much speaking and writing opened the possibility of debate and dispute.[76] In this context it may be revealing that, according to Marshall in his essay in this volume, James I came to think the same. For all his inclination to loquacity, in 1621 James threatened to be silent in future because his words had been turned "like spittle against the wind upon mine own face."[77] James did not keep his resolution, but his experience, and his son's experience, of the vulnerability of the royal text to discursive contest may have helped shape Charles's non-writing—that is, his political—style. And in the end it may have influenced his most powerful textual and political performance, that most "unwriterly" of texts, the *Eikon Basilike.*[78]

Royal writings, however, were only one form of royal representation, and they need to be studied in the context of those other representations—whether visual images, ceremonies, or performances. Fischlin and Fortier's introduction discusses James's writings as "an aestheticization of politics and a politicization of aesthetics." Indeed: in the early modern Renaissance state, aesthetics was politics, and politics involved a set of presentations and representations on canvas as at court, in church and on coin.[79] In Jacobean England, the principal royal patrons of the visual arts were the king's wife and son; James himself was said to dislike sitting for portraits.[80] We may need to return to his writings, with all their rich and evocative figurations, with that reluctance in mind, and consider the importance and reception of texts in what the Tudor arts of representation had made a visual and iconic political culture. But we should also be wary of entirely dissociating King James from the visual, and of detaching words from images. James's coins were the first to depict a monarch imperially wreathed in laurel, and it is clear that he perceived coins, seals, and medals as symbols and enactors of union. Several coins and medals bore the inscription "Nemo separet Quae Deus Coniunxit" and the imperial crown. As we have seen, James's 1616 *Workes* bore an elaborately engraved title page by Renold Elstrack, the complex symbolism of which suggests that James was not unaware of the intricate interdependence of the verbal and visual in an emblematic culture. Interestingly, one of the most powerful representations of James as king of the word is an image—an engraving by William van de Passe—of the family of James I.[81] In this engraving James is enthroned with crown and scepter, surrounded by his family. On his right Prince Charles stands as his heir—to his teaching and words as well as to his crown. Charles extends his right hand to touch an open Bible—the constant text of divine monarchy, as his father had stated in his advice to his sons. Next to it on the table lie other books, only one of which is named: the *Opera Regis,* the writings of King James. King James, the engraving suggests, was his works; but also, he was not. Charles I, I have suggested, followed his father's words almost to the letter, but he did not emulate that other daily representation of monarchy—the king's actions and example. Many venomous and biased accounts of James have undoubtedly distorted our image of his behavior. Yet it cannot be denied that in matters personal and public, he often failed to practice what he preached. And as Marshall puts it, "By fixing his own words in print and enshrining them in his *Workes,* James had given his readers the opportunity to judge his actions against his writings."[82]

Discussion of representation takes us to the heart of Renaissance monarchy. But representation is a term, concept, and subject still neglected by most historians of early modern politics. Revisionist historians such as Conrad Russell write about seventeenth-century politics as though it were as much about ministries and factions as modern politics. He accordingly finds no place in his history for the discussion of a painting or statue, a medal or mausoleum, a play or poem—even a royal poem.[83] The so-called anti-revisionists have taken us no further: Sommerville here adheres to a narrow definition of what counts as "political" writing and to an attenuated notion of politics. But what this collection makes manifest is the pervasiveness of the political and the claim of *all* James's writings to be political texts. Several essays, as we have seen, reclaim poetry for the historian of politics. But perhaps the best demonstration of the need to expand our very idea of the political is Sandra Bell's rich reading in this volume of James's *A Counterblaste to Tobacco*. The subject could hardly appear more removed from politics. However, as Bell shows, in this, the first of his works directed specifically to his new English subjects, James sketched a vision of commonweal and kingship. And in scripting himself as the only "proper physician of his politic body," as the embodiment of and protector of community against disease, foreign invasion, and decadence, he rewrote his authority and the values and ideals that sustained it. Future study of early modern politics must extend to the smoke as well as mirrors of magistrates and to all the leaves in and out of James's books.

A notion of politics that takes in tobacco as well as treatises on law and kingship will require different and rather more approaches than historians in particular have ventured. If the strengths of this volume lie, as I believe they do, in the interdisciplinarity of the contributors, the various essays also clearly mark the great differences in methods and the gulf that divides historians from literary critics and theorists. For instance, Knafla finds more consistency in James's ideas in part because he moves around texts written over decades without close address to the moments and circumstances of their production, which Smuts stresses more. Both approaches are legitimate, but unsurprisingly each influences the "meaning" the historian discovers—and may even decide whether the subject should be characterized as "absolutist" or not. "Absolutist" (I am using language I find unhelpful to explore others' readings) views in Scotland may not be so in England; what seems extreme in 1610 may not appear so in 1621, and so on. Historians, in other words, read and study texts differently. But what they seldom do is read them closely for language, metaphor, and trope, for the means of persuasion and the cultural vocabulary they deploy to persuade. For instance, in Fleming's simple reference to James's "proclivity to natural imagery" lies an important aspect of the naturalization of authority in early modern discourse that awaits full exploration.[84]

Still less do historians address what postmodern criticism has addressed: the repressions and disjunctures in texts that can reveal as much as what they desire to disclose. In this collection, deconstructive, Derridean methods have clearly influenced Fischlin's identification of the fissures and contradictions in James's paraphrase of Revelation—an example as he puts it, of "the arbitrariness of interpretive positionings."[85] Similarly, deconstructive, feminist, and gay criticism inform Ives and Parkinson's and Bergeron's essays, in ways that enable them to illuminate the divided bodies of the writer and his texts. The point is that each of these approaches offers a new perspective, a reading, of James's writings, and *all* are essential to a more complete understanding of those writings (their strategies and style) and of the writer. To argue for such diverse perspectives is to advocate, as I emphatically do, an interdisciplinary practice that early modern studies, especially historical studies, whatever the rhetoric, eschews. Historians may be discomfited by talk of texts "constructing" sovereignty and subjectivity, but this volume underlines how far James exemplifies such an approach and how he must be read and studied in the context of such a discursive theory. *Royal Subjects* has triumphantly demonstrated the importance of the king's texts. If beyond that it leads historians to new approaches, to consider royal authority itself as a set of texts requiring critical exegeses, it will be a larger triumph still.

Notes

1. A related publication that addresses the poetry of early modern monarchs is Herman's forthcoming collection of essays.
2. See McIlwain's *Constitutionalism and The Changing World*, *Constitutionalism Ancient and Modern*, and *The Growth of Political Thought in the West.*
3. See Craigie's and Arber's editions of these texts.
4. See Sharpe, *Remapping Early Modern England*, esp. ch. 1, and Sharpe, *Reading Revolutions*, also ch. 1.
5. When I surveyed the historiography in 1993 no historian had addressed these texts and only Jonathan Goldberg had critically studied them; see now Perry, *The Making of Jacobean Culture.*
6. See, for example, Fincham.
7. For an introduction see Veeser, *New Historicism* and *New Historicism Reader.*
8. See Wormald's review of Goldberg.
9. On the question of authorship see Rose as well as Jazzi and Woodmansee.
10. BL Add. mss. 24195.
11. See Doelman's essay here.
12. See Sharpe, *Reading Revolutions* 27-34.
13. See Fischlin and Fortier's introduction here.
14. See Perry's essay here.
15. See Sharpe, "Representations and Negotiations."
16. See Perry's essay here.
17. See below in this essay.
18. See Herman's essay here; also see Sharpe, "The King's Writ" 123ff.
19. See Fleming's essay here.
20. See Wortham's essay here; see also Peck, esp. chs. 1 and 2.

21. See Doelman's and Bell's essays here.
22. Milton, *Eikonoklastes* 64–65.
23. See Corbett and Lightbown 107–12 and 137–44.
24. See Fischlin's essay here.
25. See Herman's essay here.
26. See Wormald, "James VI and I, *Basilikon Doron* and *The Trew Law.*"
27. See Doelman's essay here.
28. See Donald.
29. See also Marotti.
30. See the comments on manuscript and printed texts in M. A. E. Green's edition of John Rous's diary.
31. See Marshall's essay here.
32. See Wormald, "James VI and I, *Basilikon Doron* and *The Trew Law.*"
33. See Wortham's essay here.
34. See Fischlin and Fortier's introduction.
35. See Bellany.
36. Craigie, *Poems* 2: 179–82.
37. See Colie and Fowler.
38. See Perry's essay here; also see Alpers and A. Patterson.
39. See Dunnigan's essay here.
40. Ibid.
41. See McIlwain, *Political Works* 272, and Kenyon 43.
42. Craigie, *Basilikon Doron* 1: 64.
43. Cited in Bergeron's essay here.
44. See Bergeron and Kantorowicz.
45. See Fish.
46. Craigie, *Basilikon Doron,* "To the Reader" 1: 13.
47. Cited in Bell's essay here.
48. See Sommerville's *Politics and Ideology,* now reissued in a 2nd ed. under the title *Royalists and Patriots,* which I still find crudely schematic; see also Christianson and Burgess.
49. See Fortier's essay here.
50. For the best recent study of Renaissance rhetorical practices see Skinner, pt. 1; on the capacity of language to articulate both consensus and difference, see Sharpe, *Remapping Early Modern England,* esp. ch. 1.
51. See Fischlin's essay here.
52. See King's essay here.
53. See Dunnigan's essay here.
54. See Fleming's essay here.
55. See Zagorin; also see Sharpe, "Private Conscience and Public Duty."
56. See Dunnigan's essay here.

57. Deborah Shuger makes this point in ch. 1 of *Habits of Thought in the English Renaissance.*
58. See Wormald, "James VI and I: Two Kings Or One?," Lee, and Lockyer. Conrad Russell contrasts the political skills of James with the political failings of Charles (see ch. 8 and passim).
59. See Marshall's essay here.
60. See Perry's essay here.
61. See my "Representations and Negotiations" as well as Fox, Griffiths, and Hindle.
62. Professor Glenn Burgess is currently writing this for the Yale UP English Monarchs series.
63. See Ives and Parkinson's essay here.
64. The work on the union has paid little attention to James's writings.
65. See Knafla's essay here; also see Sharpe, *Politics and Ideas* 283–88.
66. See Collinson, *Religion of Protestants* and *Godly People;* also see Lake, "Calvinism and the English Church 1570–1635," and Fincham and Lake, "Ecclesiastical Policies of James I and Charles I" and "Ecclesiastical Policy of King James I."
67. See Sharpe, *Politics and Ideas* ch. 4, and Sharpe, *Personal Rule of Charles I* ch. 6. See also White, J. Davies, and I. M. Green.
68. Fincham and Lake, "Ecclesiastical Policy of James I," 198–202.
69. See Smuts's essay here; I am not persuaded by Peter Lake's view that James changed his definition of who constituted the radicals.
70. See Fischlin's essay here; also, see Pocock.
71. I suggest a greater influence than has been noticed of James's writings on Charles I in "Private Conscience and Public Duty."
72. See Marcus, Mueller, and Rose.
73. See Haugaard; also see Collinson "Windows in a Woman's Soul."
74. See Broadley and Ollard.
75. See Sells and G. Davies.
76. Sharpe, "The King's Writ" 131–38.
77. Cited in Marshall's essay here.
78. After years of critical and historical neglect there is now excellent work on the *Eikon Basilike.* See, for example, Zwicker (ch. 2) and Wheeler.
79. See Sharpe and Zwicker, introduction and passim.
80. See Barroll and Strong.
81. For a discussion, see Goldberg 90–97, and Griffiths 67 and fig. 23.
82. See Marshall's essay here.
83. See ch. 1 in Sharpe's *Remapping Early Modern England.*
84. See Fleming's essay here.
85. See Fischlin's essay here.

Works Cited

Alpers, Paul. *The Singer of the Eclogues: A Study of Virgilian Pastoral.* Berkeley: U of California P, 1979.

Arber, Edward, ed. *The Essayes of a Prentise in the Divine Art of Poesie, 1585 and 1604.* Rpt. New York: Knickerbocker P, 1895.

Barroll, Leeds. "The Court of the First Stuart Queen." *The Mental World of the Jacobean Court.* Ed. Linda Levy Peck. Cambridge: Cambridge UP, 1991. 191–208.

Bellany, A. "'Raylinge Rymes and Vaunting Verse': Libellous Politics in Early Stuart England, 1603–1628." *Culture and Politics in Early Stuart England.* Ed. Kevin Sharpe and Peter Lake. Stanford: Stanford UP, 1993. 285–310.

Bergeron, David M. *King James and Letters of Homoerotic Desire.* Iowa City: U of Iowa P, 1999.

Broadley, Alexander M. *The Royal Miracle. A collection of rare tracts, broadsides, letters, prints, & ballads concerning the wanderings of Charles II. after the Battle of Worcester, September 3–October 15, 1651.* London: S. Paul, 1912.

Burgess, Glenn. *Absolute Monarchy and the Stuart Constitution.* New Haven: Yale UP, 1996.

———. *The Politics of the Ancient Constitution: An Introduction to English Political Thought 1603–1642.* Basingstoke: Macmillan, 1992.

Christianson, Paul. *Discourse on History, Law and Governance in the Career of John Selden, 1610–35.* Toronto: U of Toronto P, 1996.

———. "Royal and Parliamentary Voices on the Ancient Constitution c. 1604–21." *The Mental World of the Jacobean Court.* Ed. Linda Levy Peck. Cambridge: Cambridge UP, 1991. 71–95.

Colie, Rosalie. *The Resources of Kind: Genre Theory in the Renaissance.* Berkeley: U of California P, 1973.

Collinson, Patrick. *Godly People: Essays on English Protestantism and Puritanism.* London: Hambledon P, 1983.

———. *The Religion of Protestants: The Church in English Society, 1559–1625.* Oxford: Clarendon P, 1982.

———. "Windows in a Woman's Soul: Questions about the Religion of Queen Elizabeth I." *Elizabethan Essays.* Ed. Patrick Collinson. London: Hambledon P, 1994. 87–118.

Corbett, Margery, and R. W. Lightbown. *The Comely Frontispiece: The Emblematic Title-page in England 1550–1660.* London: Routledge and Kegan Paul, 1979.

Craigie, James, ed. *The Basilikon Doron of King James VI.* 2 vols. Edinburgh: William Blackwood, 1944–50.

———, ed. *The Poems of James VI of Scotland.* 2 vols. Edinburgh: William Blackwood, 1955–58.

Davies, Godfrey, et al., eds. *Papers of Devotion of James II: being a reproduction of the ms. in the handwriting of James the Second now in the possession of Mr. B. R. Townley Balfour.* Oxford: n.p., 1925.

Davies, Julian. *The Caroline Captivity of the Church: Charles I and the Remoulding of Anglicanism, 1625–1641.* Oxford: Clarendon P, 1992.

Donald, Peter. *An Uncounselled King: Charles I and the Scottish Troubles, 1637–1641.* Cambridge: Cambridge UP, 1990.

Eisenstein, Elizabeth. *The Printing Press as an Agent of Change: Communications and Cultural Transformations in Early-Modern Europe.* 2 vols. Cambridge: Cambridge UP, 1979.

Fincham, Kenneth, ed. *The Early Stuart Church, 1603–1642.* Stanford: Stanford UP, 1993.

Fincham, Kenneth, and Peter Lake. "The Ecclesiastical Policies of James I and Charles I." *The Early Stuart Church, 1603–1642.* Ed. Kenneth Fincham. Stanford: Stanford UP, 1993. 23–50.

———. "The Ecclesiastical Policy of King James I." *Journal of British Studies* 24 (1985): 169–207.

Fish, Stanley. *Is There a Text in This Class?: The Authority of Interpretive Communities.* Cambridge, Mass.: Harvard UP, 1980.

Fowler, Alastair. *Kinds of Literature: An Introduction to the Theory of Genres and Modes.* Cambridge, Mass.: Harvard UP, 1982.

Fox, Adam, Paul Griffiths, and Steve Hindle, eds. *The Experience of Authority in Early Modern England.* New York: St. Martin's, 1996.

Goldberg, Jonathan. *James I and the Politics of Literature.* Baltimore: Johns Hopkins UP, 1983.

Green, Ian M. *The Christian's ABC: Catechisms and Catechizing in England c. 1530–1740.* Oxford: Clarendon P, 1996.

Green, M. A. E., ed. *The Diary of John Rous, Incumbent of Santon Downham Suffolk, 1625–1642.* Camden Society, Old Series, 66, 1856.

Greenblatt, Stephen. *Shakespearian Negotiations: The Circulation of Social Energy in Renaissance England.* Berkeley: U of California P, 1988.

Griffiths, Antony. *The Print in Stuart Britain, 1603–1689.* London: British Museum Press for the Trustees of the British Museum, 1998.

Haugaard, W. "Elizabeth Tudor's *Book of Devotions:* A Neglected Clue to the Queen's Life and Character." *Sixteenth Century Journal* 12 (1981): 79–105.

Herman, Peter C. *Reading Monarchs Writing: The Poetry of Henry VIII, Mary Stuart, Elizabeth I, and James VI/I.* Tempe: Arizona Center for Medieval and Renaissance Studies, forthcoming.

Jaszi, Peter, and Martha Woodmansee, eds. *The Construction of Authorship: Textual Appropriation in Law and Literature.* Durham: Duke UP, 1994.

Johns, Adrian. *The Nature of the Book: Print and Knowledge in the Making.* Chicago: U of Chicago P, 1998.

Kantorowicz, Ernst H. *The King's Two Bodies: A Study in Medieval Political Theology.* Princeton: Princeton UP, 1957.

Kenyon, John P., ed. *The Stuart Constitution, 1603–1688.* 2nd ed. Cambridge: Cambridge UP, 1985.

Lake, Peter. "Calvinism and the English Church 1570–1635." *Past & Present* 114 (1987): 32–76.

Lee, Maurice. *Great Britain's Solomon: James VI and I in His Three Kingdoms.* Urbana: U of Illinois P, 1990.

Lerer, Seth. *Courtly Letters in the Age of Henry VIII: Literary Culture and the Arts of Deceit.* Cambridge: Cambridge UP, 1997.

Lockyer, Roger. *James VI and I.* London: Longman, 1998.

Love, Harold. *Scribal Publication in Seventeenth Century England.* Oxford: Oxford UP, 1993.

Marcus, Leah S., Janel M. Mueller, and Mary Beth Rose, eds. *Elizabeth I: Speeches, Letters, Verses, and Prayers.* Chicago: U of Chicago P, 2000.

Marotti, Arthur. *Manuscript, Print and the English Renaissance Lyric.* Ithaca: Cornell UP, 1993.

McIlwain, Charles H. *Constitutionalism, Ancient and Modern.* Ithaca: Cornell UP, 1940.

———. *Constitutionalism and the Changing World.* Cambridge: Cambridge UP, 1939.

———. *The Growth of Political Thought in the West, from the Greeks to the End of the Middle Ages.* New York: Macmillan, 1932.

———. *The Political Works of James I.* Cambridge, Mass.: Harvard UP, 1918.

Milton, John. *Eikonoklastes.* Vol. 5 of *The Works of John Milton.* General ed. Frank Allen Patterson. New York: Columbia UP, 1931–38.

Ollard, Richard. *The Escape of Charles II after the Battle of Worcester.* London: Hodder and Stoughton, 1966.

Patterson, Annabel. *Pastoral and Ideology: Virgil to Valery.* Berkeley: U of California P, 1987.

Patterson, W. B. *King James VI and I and the Reunion of Christendom.* Cambridge: Cambridge UP, 1997.

Peck, Linda Levy. *Court Patronage and Corruption in Early Stuart England.* London: Unwin Hyman, 1990.

Perry, Curtis. *The Making of Jacobean Culture: James I and the Renegotiation of Elizabethan Literary Practice.* Cambridge: Cambridge UP, 1997.

Pocock, J. G. A. "Texts as Events: Reflections on the History of Political Thought." *Politics of Discourse: The Literature and History of Seventeenth-*

Century England. Ed. Kevin Sharpe and Steven Zwicker. Berkeley: U of California P, 1987. 21–34.

Rose, Mark. *Authors and Owners: The Invention of Copyright.* Cambridge, Mass.: Harvard UP, 1993.

Russell, Conrad. *The Causes of the English Civil War.* Oxford: Oxford UP, 1990.

Sells, A. Lytton, ed. *The Memoirs of James II: His Campaigns as Duke of York 1652–1660.* Bloomington: Indiana UP, 1962.

Sharpe, Kevin. "The King's Writ: Royal Authors and Royal Authority in Early Modern England." *Culture and Politics in Early Modern England.* Eds. Kevin Sharpe and Peter Lake. Stanford: Stanford UP, 1993. 117–38.

———. *The Personal Rule of Charles I.* New Haven: Yale UP, 1992

———. *Politics and Ideas in Early Stuart England.* London: Pinter, 1989.

———. "Private Conscience and Public Duty in the Writings of Charles I." *Historical Journal* 40 (1997): 643–65.

———. "Private Conscience and Public Duty in the Writings of James VI and I." *Public Duty and Private Conscience in Seventeenth-Century England: Essays Presented to G. E. Aylmer.* Ed. John Morrill, Paul Slack, and Daniel Woolf. Oxford: Clarendon P, 1993. 77–100.

———. *Reading Revolutions: The Politics of Reading in Early Modern England.* New Haven: Yale UP, 2000.

———. *Remapping Early Modern England.* Cambridge: Cambridge UP, 2000.

———. "Representations and Negotiations: Texts, Images and Authority in Early Modern England." *Historical Journal* 42 (1999): 853–81.

Sharpe, Kevin, and Steven Zwicker, eds. *Politics of Discourse: The Literature and History of Seventeenth-Century England.* Berkeley: U of California P, 1987.

———, eds. *Refiguring Revolutions: Aesthetics and Politics from the English Revolution to the Romantic Revolution.* Berkeley: U of California P, 1998.

Shuger, Deborah. *Habits of Thought in the English Renaissance.* Berkeley: U of California P, 1990.

Skinner, Quentin. *Reason and Rhetoric in the Philosophy of Hobbes.* Cambridge: Cambridge UP, 1996.

Sommerville, Johann, ed. *King James VI and I: Political Writings.* Cambridge: Cambridge UP, 1994.

———. *Politics and Ideology in England 1603–1640.* London: Longman, 1986. 2nd ed. *Royalists and Patriots: Politics and Ideology in England 1603–1640.* London: Longman, 1999.

Strong, Roy. *Henry, Prince of Wales, and England's Lost Renaissance.* New York: Thames and Hudson, 1986.

Veeser, H. Aram, ed. *The New Historicism.* New York: Routledge, 1989.

———, ed. *The New Historicism Reader.* New York: Routledge, 1994.

Wheeler, E. Skerpan. "Eikon Basilike and the Rhetoric of Self-Representation." *The Royal Image: Representations of Charles I.* Ed. Thomas N. Corns. Cambridge: Cambridge UP, 1999. 122–40.

White, Peter. *Predestination, Policy and Polemic: Conflict and Consensus in the English Church from the Reformation to the Civil War.* Cambridge: Cambridge UP, 1992.

———. "The Rise of Arminianism Reconsidered." *Past & Present* 101 (1983): 34–54.

Wormald, Jenny. "James VI and I, *Basilikon Doron* and *The Trew Law of Free Monarchies:* The Scottish Context and the English Translation." *The Mental World of the Jacobean Court.* Ed. Linda Levy Peck. Cambridge: Cambridge UP, 1991. 36–54.

———. "James VI and I: Two Kings or One?" *History* 68 (1993): 187–209.

———. Rev. of *James I and the Politics of Literature* by Jonathan Goldberg. *History* 70 (1985): 128–30.

Zagorin, Perez. *Ways of Lying: Dissimulation, Persecution, and Conformity in Early Modern Europe.* Cambridge, Mass.: Harvard UP, 1990.

Zwicker, Steven. *Lines of Authority: Politics and English Literary Culture, 1649–1689.* Ithaca: Cornell UP, 1993.

Introduction

"Enregistrate Speech": Stratagems of Monarchic Writing in the Work of James VI and I

Daniel Fischlin and Mark Fortier

I

James VI and I has had a mixed reputation even from his own day. The preacher Andrew Melville called him "God's sillie vassal" to his face, while Henri IV, king of France, labeled him "the most learned fool in Christendom"—an idiot with an education. Among his own cadre he was "Great Britain's Solomon" or, as John N. King shows in this volume, a new King David, wise and divinely inspired, advocate of "a nuanced, moderated absolutism" (Sommerville, *King James* xv). One of the most recent attempts to weigh James's abilities and achievements is that of Roger Lockyer, who asserts that "James was probably the best-educated ruler ever to sit on an English or Scottish throne, and the only one with any claim to be a political philosopher" and that he "achieved the not inconsiderable feat of dying in his bed, unlike his mother, Mary, Queen of Scots, and his son and successor, Charles I, who both met their end on the scaffold" (209).

James had a diverse and interesting reign, and a full evaluation of it would have to take account of many factors. In his Scottish period there are his rather successful dealings with lords and Kirk as well as his adept maneuvers to secure the English throne, including the difficult politics around the execution of his mother. Once he became king of England, there was the failure of the Act of Union of his two kingdoms and his troubled dealings with the English Parliament: his view of kingly prerogative was more expansive than that of many MPs, common lawyers, and judges. There was also the failure of the Great Contract and James's chronic financial problems, whether the product of circumstances or extravagance. In an age of religious conflict, James steered a strained path between papists on the one hand and Puritans and independents on the other. His successful pursuit of peace must be seen in connection with his relative insignificance as a player on the international diplomatic scene, though W. B. Patterson's recent account of his role in the attempt to shape a conciliarist and pacifist approach to religious controversy goes a long way toward revising this view. James's male-centered private and affective life has a long history of commentary, most recently by David M. Bergeron, both in this volume and in a study of James's letters to his male favorites, as well as by Michael B. Young in his recent study of James and the history of homosexuality.

James's place in the history of colonial enterprise is a significant aspect of his complex diplomatic and imperial affiliations, especially in terms of his role in the funding of new world exploration "in areas as widely scattered as Newfoundland and the Amazon" (Willson, *King James VI and I* 330). Also important are his interest in the founding of Jamestown, his relationship to the Virginia Company and the English East India Company, his attempt to establish a trade relationship with Japan (see Willson, *A Royal Request*), and so forth. Moreover, James's influence on religious thought was pronounced, especially through the Authorized Version of the Bible (1611) now better known as the King James Version. Kevin Sharpe has noted how James's Authorized Version "sought to define the parameters of hermeneutic freedom opened by the translation of the Scriptures" and was as a consequence an act of authoritative power more than of piety ("The King's Writ" 118–19). The new translation helped shape English prose style for centuries to come. Finally, it is hard to ignore the flourishing of British culture during his reign: William Shakespeare, John Donne, Ben Jonson, Inigo Jones, Francis Bacon, John Selden, and Edward Coke are a few of the more prominent figures, in such fields as drama, poetry, architecture, and scientific and legal thought, of the Jacobean age. Nor can the formidable influence of James on Scottish court culture be ignored, especially in relation to the important interactive literary context of the poets he surrounded himself with in the 1580s and 1590s—Montgomerie, Polwarth, Stewart of Baldynneis, Fowler—followed by the ongoing interaction with Scottish poets such as Ayton and Alexander after the move to London in 1603.[1]

Even though James continues to be the object of scholarly study in a variety of disciplines, such study is notably inadequate with regard to his literary works. Because of James's unique position as king and writer, his work matters greatly and covers a broad range of issues. As king, James had a concern with his kingdom, which takes him, as he outlined in *Basilikon Doron,* into religious matters, political matters, and even the myriad minutiae of "things indifferent." As king, James took upon himself a central role in church, government, economy, and law. Moreover, his systematic theologico-philosophical position on kingship demonstrates his interest, inter alia, in issues of poetics, politics, theology, and related social issues. Nowhere else in the history of early modern Europe is there a writer and monarch with both a comparable range of interests and such wide-ranging influence. From the substantial 1616 *Workes*[2]—which collected James's political and religious prose, and is itself a major moment in the history of English authorship—to assorted treatises on dueling, sport, tobacco, demonology, various paraphrases and commentaries on religious texts, a massive correspondence with intimates and diplomatic contacts, two published books of poetry characterized by their diversity (translations of other poets, a poetics treatise, different verse forms including a mini-epic), various royal proclamations, speeches, and public pronouncements, unpublished manuscripts (including Curtis Perry's recent discovery of a new British Library ms., Add. 22601, which contains the major *Amatoria* texts) and lost works, James was prolific in a variety of genres.

The chronology of James's written works spans decades and two national contexts, from his early teens in Scotland to late in his life as king of England. Additionally, this chronology is complicated by uncertainty regarding the dating of some of his earliest works, the circulation of his works as part of manuscript culture, the uncertain boundaries between private and public pronouncement, and the hazy sense of authorial identity particular to early modern texts, where silent collaboration and quiet emendation are commonplace. What is clear is that in the 1580s James composed religious prose and verse, biblical paraphrases, verse and a verse treatise, most while still in his teens; he was fifteen when he wrote what is apparently his first poem, "Since Thought Is Free" (see Craigie, *Poems* xii). In the late 1590s, another particularly productive period, James published two widely disseminated political treatises, *The True Law of Free Monarchies* and *Basilikon Doron,* as well as his major intervention on demonological theory, *Daemonologie.* Upon assuming the English throne in 1603 James continued to write and publish, primarily political tracts and speeches seeking to consolidate his position and stave off the threat of Counter-Reformation forces. Works from this period include his *Discourse of the Manner of the Discoverie of the Powder-Treason, Triplici nodo . . . or An Apologie for the Oath of Allegiance, A Premonition,* and various other works that culminated in the 1616 *Workes,* which was reissued in 1620, with changes, in both Latin and English.

There is evidence that James wrote poetry late in his life, though as Craigie notes, it is "a remarkable fact that not a single surviving poem of his can be assigned to the first twelve years after the Union of the Crowns" (*Poems* xiii). James's last significant publication came in 1622 with the *Declaration,* which sets forth his arguments for his dissolution of Parliament in early January of that same year. Posthumously, works continued to be issued in his name, including the *Flores Regii* in 1627, a collection of the king's "bon mots," and his translation of the Psalms, published in 1631. Despite the seemingly inexorable torrent of words he produced, James was no advocate of empty prolixity. His work was subject to careful editorial intervention, as he makes clear in *Basilikon Doron;* here, invoking Horace, he advises withholding publication for at least nine years (Fischlin and Fortier 165–66) in conjunction with having work privately censured by skilled advisers. For James, "virtue" gave words meaning, turned the prolix into something more than empty speech. The *Flores Regii,* for instance, begins with the self-questioning assertion "Wordes are not the difference of good men and bad, for euery man speakes, therefore how noble a thing is *Vertue;* when no man dares professe any thing" (1–2); this suggests that words are one thing, the virtue that gives them meaning quite another.

To study James as a writer is to trace not only the range and subtlety of his subject matter and style over vastly changed political and social contexts, but also the complex ways in which his ideas influenced substantial aspects of public life in Britain as well as the ways in which his subjects reacted to James's pronouncements. *Royal Subjects* is the first book devoted exclusively to these purposes. James's position as a writer is extraordinary for the way in which his political career was intertwined with the texts on which he lavished so much attention. As the monarch ascending to the crown of two distinct court cultures at a moment when humanist literary discourse was profoundly linked with national imaginaries, James's performance as a writer cannot be separated from his performance as embodiment of national identity. It is perhaps in this sense that Jenny Wormald has distinguished James's writings as having a "peculiar, indeed a unique importance. Not since Alfred had a ruler combined the practice and the theory of kingship in his own person" ("James VI and I" 36). In *Royal Subjects,* we see the sovereign as a writer struggling to affirm royal power through the tenuous strategy of linking kingship with the literary and textual forces that also work to contest or subvert sovereign authority. James's unique interventions into various literary genres demonstrate the way in which literary discourses of various sorts were an attribute of power, a mark of an identity without which power, absolutism, and nationhood could not be conceived. *Royal Subjects* explores the contradictory ways in which James's literary output simultaneously enhanced, diminished, and made problematic his position as sovereign.

The general premise of this book, then, is that monarchic writing, oddly enough, is a neglected literary genre and that a specific study of the works of James VI and I would be a sensible place to begin a scholarly dialogue about the genre. There is no question, as much recent scholarship on James has been at pains to elaborate, that James's views on writing form an important backdrop to evaluations of his conduct as monarch. For instance, in discussing James's first published poetry volume, *The Essayes of a Prentise in the Divine Art of Poesie* (1584), David M. Bergeron notes the following: "To refer as James does to the 'divine art of poesie' in the title of his volume of poetry suggests that this young writer took himself and his poetry seriously. In fact, James gathered about him a coterie of poets and served as their patron, even as they assisted him in his writing" (53). Bergeron's observation tags with other recent literary critics and cultural historians—such as Kevin Sharpe, Jenny Wormald, Johann Sommerville, Curtis Perry, and Jonathan Goldberg—who all point to James's literariness and his vast appetite for language, even as they note the critical lacunae that have accrued to James's literary reputation. Bergeron cites two distinguished critics with expertise in sixteenth-century Scottish literature and Jacobean literature generally.

> R. D. S. Jack observes: "What began as part game, part tuition led to James composing verses and having them published. . . . [T]he king's interest resulted in the gathering round him of men of like mind. Gradually James became the accepted leader/patron of a group of poets and musicians styled the Castalian band." This group included Alexander Montgomery, Alexander Hume, John Stewart, William Fowler, and Robert Hudson. As G. P. V. Akrigg notes: "The creation of this literary circle was the more remarkable because at this time there was hardly one of the rough Scots lords who could be regarded as a patron of literature." (ibid.)

What is noteworthy about this early phase in James's literary affairs is the way in which literary patronage slipped into literary accomplishment. If patronage was one of the registers by which a monarch could exercise the influence necessary to an effective deployment of power, then how much more effective for the monarch to engage directly in the practice that his patronage actively supported. As we have noted elsewhere, "For James, textuality was perhaps as much a means to the end of power as was direct political action. James recognized textual representation as crucial to the construction of both the political subject and the sovereign, whose power depended on creating such a subject. The representation of power by literary means, in such a context, was a substantial element in constituting both the self-identity and the public identity of the sovereign" (Fischlin and Fortier 17).

James's early involvement with the Castalian as well as his early literary output as a poet, poetic theorist, and biblical paraphraser anticipate the extent to which he was to imbricate issues of monarchic power with issues of literary representation. As Maurice Lee Jr. points out:

> King James was that most unusual phenomenon among crowned heads, an active and practicing writer. All his life he wrote, from his adolescent poetical lament on the death of his beloved Esmé to the reflections on the passage in Matthew (27: 27–29) in which the soldiers mock Christ, which appeared in 1620. . . . [M]ostly James

> wrote about what he knew best: the business of being a king. Even those writings that superficially appear to have little to do with kingship, such as *Daemonologie,* his tract on witchcraft, and *His Majesty's Declaration against Vorstius,* a diatribe against a man whom James regarded as an atheist, are related to it. Both atheists and witches are enemies of God, whose viceregent the king is; to tolerate either would be to create chaos in the world. (63)

Similarly, Goldberg affirms that "In his writings, James returned again and again to proclaiming his theory of kingship, making announcements about the divinity that hedged the sovereign round. His theme, as it was in his first appearance before the Star Chamber in 1616, was, repeatedly, 'the mysterie of the Kings power'" (56) or of the *arcana imperii.* Moreover, abundant evidence from James's contemporaries supports the notion of James as an inveterate scholar who thoroughly enjoyed disputation, controversy, wit, and the seeking after knowledge. Robert Ashton collects a number of documents relating to this element of James's literariness, an account by John Hacket of James's learned suppers being particularly evocative: "That King's table was a trial of Wits. The reading of some Books before him was very frequent, while he was at his Repast. Otherwise he collected Knowledge by variety of Questions, which he carved out to the capacity of his understanding Writers. . . . He was ever in chase after some disputable Doubts, which he would wind and turn about with the most stabbing Objections that ever I heard" (Ashton 161). When Sir Henry Killigrew met with James in 1574 (as an emissary from Elizabeth), he was impressed enough with eight-year-old James's ability to speak "'the French tongue marvelous well; and that which seems strange to me, he was able *extempore* (which he did before me) to read a chapter of the Bible out of Latin into French, and out of French after into English, so well, as few men could have added anything to his translation'" (cited in Willson 24). The impressive library to which James had access as a young scholar under the tutelage of George Buchanan and Peter Young gives some hint as to the kind of scholarly formation that contributed to James's literary inclinations. Though the library was largely the responsibility of his tutors and had as its nucleus the "wreck of his mother's" (Warner xix) library, the books included Dante in Italian, Plato's *Republic* in French, Froissart, Herodotus in French, Plutarch, Ovid, Petrarch, Cicero, Xenophon, Calvin, and a host of other works representative of the best humanist learning had to offer.

Certainly, scholarship, kingship, and related issues of power and representation are crucial thematic concerns for James. No other early modern monarch has bequeathed as extensive an assemblage of writings on the subject to history. As the essays in this volume show, however, the tenacity with which James sustained his interest in issues of power and literariness found a wide expressive range. And amidst the myriad detail of these writings can be found a range of qualities that James's unique position as both monarch and writer exploited to the full: a prose style at once witty, observant, playful, learned, not afraid of ambiguity or equivocation, balanced between full-blown fustian, scholastic casuistry, and finely-honed rhetorical skills; an eagerness to pronounce—whether on the evils of tobacco or dueling, the appropriate conduct of marriage, or the influence of succubi—where the power of literary assertion is a mark of other forms of empowerment; a strongly developed sense of the performative presence and use of the spoken and written word, and thus the blending in the collected works of 1616 of public speech with writings that take their performative cues from being placed in proximity to published versions of public speeches; an aestheticization of politics and a politicization of aesthetics, especially in relation to how theoretical issues revolving around the monarch's political interests can be tempered, made palatable and persuasive by the literary frame in which they are presented; and, importantly, a sophisticated approach to ethical and moral quandaries that shape the public sphere, or, as Isaac Disraeli puts it at the close of his treatise on James's literary merits: "The character of James I. is a moral phenomenon, a singularity of a complex nature. . . . Warm, hasty, and volatile, yet with the most patient zeal to disentangle involved deception; such gravity in sense, such levity in humour; such wariness and such indiscretion; such mystery and such openness—all these must have thrown his Majesty into some awkward dilemmas" (456). In short, James was a complex character, whose literariness was a symptom of a carefully staged public persona as well as a means to shape the private motivations that gave way to public discourse.

A classic example of the difficulty in ascertaining how James's public presence relied on a private sense of self—if such a thing is even conceivable within the public context in which James lived—has to do with his sexuality, a topic discussed by David Bergeron in his essay in this volume and in his book on homoerotic desire in James's extensive correspondence with his favorites: Esmé Stuart, Robert Carr, and George Villiers. Gendering James in contemporary critical terms is no easy task, given the complexities of giving a "name" to his desires, which were polymorphous and irreducible to any simple category—heterosexual, homosexual, bisexual. Nonetheless, the fact that James left a record of a certain kind of literary intimacy in his letters is, as Bergeron shows, a key that opens the portals of an "interior space" (30), however illusorily or fictively. Thus it would be an oversimplification to attribute to James's varied writing practices a concern solely with kingship and kingcraft. James's career trajectory as a writer was anything but marked by incidental accomplishments. Rather, he maintained an ongoing interest and capacity for literary expression that makes him a writer as well as a sovereign of importance and influence. That is, contrary to how even James may have thought of himself, his literary self-construction registers in the present as noteworthy in and of itself. Though it has yet to be written, it is conceivable that the next stage in making sense of James's historical legacy will be a literary biography that deals with the full circuit of his writings from the earliest juvenilia through to posthumously published works.

James's own approach to writing, as he advises his son Henry in book three of *Basilikon Doron,* bears repeating, if only because it hints at his sophisticated sense of self-construction. James calls writing "nothing else but a form of enregistrate speech" (cited in Fischlin and Fortier 165)—that is, a form of speech that gains permanency through the register of writing. James advocates, perhaps contrary to his own practice, "a plain, short, but stately style both in your proclamations and missives" (ibid.). He sanctions for Henry the writing of both verse and prose as inspiration strikes, with the important proviso that it not distract from the demands of rule. Perhaps most tellingly, James advises Henry to "Flatter not yourself in your labours, but before they be set forth, let them first be privily censured by some of the best skilled men in that craft that in these works you meddle with" (ibid.). Editorial intervention is advised because "your writs will remain as true pictures of your mind to all posterities" (ibid.). Further, James argues for writing in "your own language, for there is nothing left to be said in Greek and Latin already," a position that indicates a certain linguistic nationalism aimed at making "famous his own tongue" (ibid.). The politics of such a position are noteworthy if only because they proclaim a climate of tolerance for the vernacular that could not but encourage its vitality and dissemination.

The extent to which James's own writings follow upon all this advice remains questionable, as does the notion that writing represents "true pictures of your mind." Though James was not incapable of writerly self-criticism, one has to wonder about the extent to which such criticism, mild as it was, was merely an appropriate pose of public modesty hiding an elevated self-regard. In a letter to Robert Cecil, earl of Salisbury, dated July 1605, he speaks disparagingly of a lost theological work, *Collections,* written in 1584 in his late teens, suggesting that "it is in truth an old book whereof there is nothing new but the covering" (cited in Akrigg 259). But James goes on to blame the "bad" language of the book on its transcribers, somewhat undercutting his dismissive sense of the work, a typically contradictory stratagem that is one of his most distinctive literary traits. Critical self-evaluation, the plain style, restraint in the rush to publish, editorial collaboration, the certainty of future evaluation, advocacy of the vernacular, and a certain doubleness or studied ambiguity between theory and practice: all these figure in James's aesthetics.

These qualities, and the many others that contributors to this volume address, hint at the vast and inexorable repertoire of devices by which absolute power could make itself known, felt, understood, and obeyed. When James affirmed, in his October 1604 proclamation, that Scotland's and England's "inhabitants shared 'A communitie of Language, the principall meanes of Civil societie'" (cited in Patterson 31), he was affirming language as a necessary precondition to the formation of community and nation. One could not exist without the other—

nor could the sovereign preside over a nation that was not reinforced by the "communitie of Language." Thus James's own extensive appropriation of written discourse as a means of self-legitimation was profoundly tied to his notion of civil society as a function of linguistic community.

As "Britain's most scholarly king" (Sommerville, "James I" 58), James had significant influence both in his immediate political environment and in the larger political context of continental Europe. Sommerville has observed that "James was extremely sensitive about his continental reputation, both as an author and as a truly orthodox monarch" (ibid. 59). Patterson has reinforced this point, noting that

> James had spoken up for the sovereignty and autonomy of the national state at a time when the political theories of the Counter-Reformation were still at the height of their influence. How seriously his ideas were taken can be seen in the attention given to political theory in the books which poured from European presses following the publication of the *Premonition* [1609]. As a result, the discussion of fundamental political issues reached every corner of Europe. The king may fairly be said to have been one of the prophets of the new age of sovereign, independent states. (121)

Patterson's citation of Johannes Kepler's dedication of his 1619 *Harmonices mundi* to James, along with Kepler's hope that his book, "which dealt with the harmony of the heavenly bodies, would appeal to one who sought 'harmony and unity in the ecclesiastical and political spheres'" (126), gives some sense of the estimation in which James was held. Further indications of the extent to which James's writings were widely disseminated and influential are summarized by Sommerville:

> James VI and I was one of the most influential British political writers of the early modern period. His *Basilicon Doron* was a best-seller in England and circulated widely on the Continent. . . . It was translated into Latin, French, Dutch, German, Swedish and other languages. . . . The book was frequently quoted by political writers. So, too, were James' other works, and especially his speech to parliament of 21 March 1610. John Locke quoted this speech at length and approvingly. . . . Thomas Hobbes likewise praised "our most wise" King James (*Leviathan* chapter 19, final paragraph). (*King James VI and I* xv)

Similarly, Patterson cites laudatory prefatory comments to James's 1616 *Workes* by James Montague relating to "the reception given to King James's literary works by his theological opponents" (97): "'they looke upon his Maiesties Bookes, as men looke upon Blasing-Starres, with amazement, fearing they portend some strange thing, and bring with them a certain influence to worke great change and alteration in the world'" (ibid.). If anything, the hyperbole of the comments speaks as much to James's apparent reception by Counter-Reformation forces as to his own sense of literary proportion in the world. Ultimately, as Curtis Perry has argued, the "widespread dissemination of the king's works—and of the king as author—changed the way English writers of verse, scholarship, and religious controversy constructed their own authorship" (24). Not only did James's writings display a sophisticated, self-reflexive recognition of the power of the word. The actual reception and dissemination of his texts confirmed his intellectual influence and power.

For James, "enregistrate speech" is a crucial outward sign of the divine relation between the king and God, and thus it is a sign of the inner being of the king. This stratagem, so reliant on literary coding and interpretation, lies at the heart of both James's metaphysics of kingship and his writing practice, just as a profoundly literary or allegorical "fiction" (23), to use Ernst Kantorowicz's term, lies at the heart of the mystical and legal notion of the king's two bodies. As Kevin Sharpe has noted in his seminal essay on James's writings: "Poetry for James VI and I, like his devotional works, was a meditation with himself and God and a representation to his subjects of himself and God—his purest crystal" ("Private Conscience" 98). The essays gathered in this volume detail both the literariness of power and the power of literariness that distinguish James's contributions not only to history and politics but also to religious, legal, and literary culture.

II

As many of the essays in this collection demonstrate, James's interests were both wide-ranging and intertwined. From witchcraft to tobacco, law, poetics, kingship, religion, and biblical exegesis—James's writings cover an impressive range of concerns. Importantly, and not unexpectedly, these concerns overlap in their regard for the God-given rights of the king and his obligation to good government. As James notes in the second book of *Basilikon Doron,* "all arts and sciences are linked every one with [the] other, their greatest principles agreeing in one" (cited in Fischlin and Fortier 146). Nonetheless, for the sake of order and clarity, we have divided the essays here into three general areas: poetry, politics and society, and religion. In compiling this collection, we have been less concerned about providing comprehensive coverage of all James's works and more interested in offering interventions that allow a wide range of approaches to a broad sampling of works, especially those that are less known. Thus *Basilikon Doron,* perhaps James's most famous work and on which we have written elsewhere, is not treated in detail here, though many of the contributors engage with pertinent extracts from it that relate to other texts.

Essays gathered in the first section of the book address important lacunae in scholarship on James, particularly the extent to which his supposedly nonpolitical poetic writings are linked to his sovereign person. James produced and published two volumes of poetry while still the Scottish king—*Essayes of a Prentise in the Divine Art of Poesie* (1584) and *Poeticall Exercises at Vacant Houres* (1591). These works show the range of James's poetic inclinations: from translations of the great French Huguenot poet Du Bartas, through to translations of the Psalms, several sonnets, a paraphrase (of Lucan), a mini-epic, and a treatise on poetics. In addition, occasional poems are collected in MS. Bodley 165 (nine poems) and in Add. ms. 24195 (twenty-two poems); moreover, another dozen or so poems are to be found in "a number of widely scattered and not always accessible sources" (Craigie, *Poems* xii). These further demonstrate the breadth of James's scholarly and occasional interests: from poems on Du Bartas, Tycho Brahe, and Montgomerie to further translations of the Psalms, poems for Queen Anne, and a host of occasional verses dealing with topical matters, such as the death of John Shaw, the king's Master Stabler, killed in 1591 in James's service. Craigie notes that beyond this body of work is an "unfinished MS. version of the Psalms of David in metre" and that in "actual quantity, therefore, King James's verse is quite substantial" (ibid.).

Our decision to foreground James's poetry in this volume is in part a response to the fact that James's prose, and especially his political prose, has received a disproportionate amount of critical attention over the years. In many ways, such a response is entirely predictable, since James's political theories most naturally align with his position as monarch. Since most (but not all) of his poetic output occurred fairly early in his life and in a Scottish context (as Craigie states, "James's poetic career was largely over by the time he became king of Great Britain" [ibid. xiii]), the tendency to downplay it is perhaps understandable. Nonetheless, the essays gathered in this section contest such a position, with its implication that the Scottish phase of James's career is less important than the English, or that verse is less important than prose and aesthetics less significant than political theory. James's early work as a poet is no less interesting than his later prose work, especially if we accept Craigie's notion that "As a poet King James belonged wholly to the Renaissance, and it was he . . . who was the first truly Renaissance poet in Scotland" (ibid.). Moreover, significant insights can be gained from close attention to texts that use poetic strategies to address a range of matters, both public and personal, that helped form the public persona associated with *Jacobus Rex.* The focus of this section is on the instrumental relation of James's poetry to his sense of kingship, that is, how poetry and kingship are intertwined and mutually enabling strategies of self-fashioning.

Peter C. Herman's essay places James's poetry in relation to other early modern poetic writings by monarchs, especially Elizabeth I. Herman argues that

James's poetry cannot be simplistically separated from his sovereign position. Using James's mini-epic *Lepanto* as the basis of his analysis, Herman examines how James's manipulation of tropes from a monarchic perspective not only inverts conventional expectations of politicized Petrarchan discourse but is entirely conventional in its own way. For Herman, James's poetry, in its immediate historical context, functions as a form of diplomacy. In a larger historical context, Herman argues that the publication history associated with James's work plays a significant and undiscussed role in the history of authorship. Herman's essay also places James's poetic work in relation to other key Renaissance authors, including Sir Philip Sidney (upon whom James wrote an epitaph) and Edmund Spenser. Ultimately, for Herman, pleasure and political advantage come together in James's poetic oeuvre, as do monarchic display and diplomatic advantage, a function of James's basic writing position, in which "no discourse exists separate from sovereignty."

Also exploring notions of authorship as mediated by monarchic presence, Carolyn Ives and David J. Parkinson examine particular tropes used by James to signify the monstrous hybrid of king and author. For Ives and Parkinson, the young poet-king addresses issues relating to authorship and authority via topoi of origins as both source and conduit of the divine power said to inhabit the sovereign's mystic body. Ives and Parkinson argue for the complexity of James's place in the history of Scottish cultural relations. Turning their attention to the way in which gender figures in discourses of power, Ives and Parkinson suggest that James simultaneously feminized so-called "dangerous" tendencies in Scottish culture while monumentalizing the degree to which the feminine was embedded in his notions of power and eloquence. The crucial trope of the "fountain" became the means by which James articulated paradoxical constructions of kingship and writerly self-fashioning—constructions in which male and female, ruler and ruled, king and poet all contribute to the sophistication of James's self-construction as a mysterious embodiment of discursive, divine, and material power.

Traditions endure about the decline of literature and language in late sixteenth-century Scotland. Prominent among these traditions is the gendering of relationships between literature and national character and the treatment of signs of openness in Scottish culture as symptoms of decay. The early writings of James VI (especially the verse translations in *The Essayes of a Prentise*) can be read as formative documents in the development of such traditions. Poems such as *Uranie* (from Du Bartas's *Uranie*) offer significant junctures in Scottish writers' articulations of both authority and deference. Fluency—represented through water, flow, floods, and fountains—embodies two aspects of identity, the influential and the influenced. James grounds his sense of literary purpose on a dual identity for the kingly writer: vessel of a higher authority and fixed authority figure of the nation. This lingering, productive duality can be traced through James's representation in these texts of his corporeal identity. Ultimately, Ives and

Parkinson's essay argues that James's bodily representation in a variety of early texts is conflicted and ineffective because it denies him secular power in favor of divine power, thus reducing his authority. It is especially inappropriate since he must be an open, and therefore at least symbolically, feminine system if his body is to be a mystical vessel of the divine logos that receives God's word in order to disperse it.

Morna R. Fleming, in an essay studying the *Amatoria* in relation to James's statement of poetic principle, the *Reulis and Cautelis,* posits James's wish to impose a new vision of poetry on a tradition that had become stale. Through a comparative study of the principles articulated in the *Reulis and Cautelis* and demonstrated in the *Amatoria*—a collection of poems dealing with James's relation to his wife, Queen Anne of Denmark—Fleming fleshes out the crucial dimensions of James's poetics in relation to the humanist tradition to which he was responding. Placing James in a tradition that extends back to Horace's *Ars Poetica,* Joachim Du Bellay's *La deffence et illustration de la langue françoyse,* and George Gascoigne's *Certayne Notes of Instruction,* Fleming examines how James turned away from Petrarchan conventions such as the love sonnet in favor of more varied "native" styles of versification dominated by stanzaic lyrics and particular classical referents. Despite this, the pressures to conform to Petrarchan norms are evident in James's *Amatoria,* with their restricted and conflicted sense of passion overtaken, in Fleming's analysis, by James's penchant for meditative and philosophical thought.

Sarah Dunnigan's discussion of the *Amatoria* further problematizes gender and desire in relation to sovereign position, asking whether the construction of the sovereign as icon is in some way threatened by the "voicing of desire" in secular love poetry. For Dunnigan, the *Amatoria* presents a strange contradiction in which the orthodoxies of love poetry are countered by a misogynist and decidedly unamorous tone. Taking James's pronouncement "I am the Husband and the whole Isle is my Wife" as her point of departure, Dunnigan explores the erotics of James's literary self-presentation in relation to the intersection of poetic culture and the gendered identities imagined by that culture. Literary sovereignty involves the recoding, reinflection, and transgression of generic amatory expression. The Scottish Jacobean court sanctioned poetic games of desire that arguably provide a more fruitful interpretative context than do the prevailing biographical readings of James's poetry. That this coterie culture was also strongly marked by homosociality, which legitimized male power in a poetry that was explicitly misogynist, suggests a further revision of the conventions of Petrarchan abjection. Dunnigan's essay, taken in concert with Fleming's, articulates an emergent sense of the way in which James's poetics were reliant on his distinctive Scottish context, on conflicts in his writing practice between European conventions and the desire to free himself of these, and on personal conflicts having to do with how he framed complex and evasive desires relating to his own gendered position as a male monarch at the head of a homosocial court culture. In tandem, these chapters represent the first extended and diverse critical readings of James's secular love lyrics.

Simon Wortham's essay expands the context for understanding James's poetry by rethinking the king's reputation for profligate spending and giving as part of a general symbolic economy whereby James's gifts always functioned to increase his own power, prestige, and authority. Wortham sees this symbolic economy at work not only in James's gift-giving but also in his selling of titles, his coining, and, importantly, his writing. Wortham looks at the structure of giving in the prefaces to James's political works as well as, centrally, in his poetry, most notably in his tragic poem the *Phoenix,* written as a response to the death of one of James's favorites, Esmé Stuart, duke of Lennox. Wortham's essay examines the shift in the concept and practices of royal patronage at the turn of the seventeenth century and, in particular, the literary strategies adopted by James to preserve images of the bountiful monarch, even as he short-circuited or—in some cases—reversed traditional patterns of giving. In his discussion of prefatory comments to various of James's writings, Wortham notes the general pattern of the "king giving words that give back to the king possessive authority and inscrutable power." For Wortham the relation between giving and non-giving is "a non-oppositional yet continually ongoing and therefore ultimately unresolved relation" that enhances strategies of favor-giving and thus of governance. In the final section of the essay, an extended meditation on James's verse, Wortham focuses on the *Phoenix* as an exemplary model of a form of giving that is not: the poem simultaneously gives and avoids the "risk of the gift's expense." This reading adds to the understanding of the rhetorical economy of self-authorization that many of the essayists in this volume see as a crucial strategy in James's writing practices.

Curtis Perry, in the concluding essay of this section, takes this latter point a step further in his examination of late manuscript poems attributed to James in relation to the culture of libel. James Craigie's standard edition of James's poetry includes seven poems attributed to the king and circulated in manuscript during the final years of his life. These poems are public and political in nature, and there is good reason to believe they were purposefully entered into manuscript circulation, thereby using scribal publication as a way to disseminate the crown's voice. Such an intent would be in keeping, as Perry argues, with James's well-documented tendency to rely on publication as a means of government. Like his published political treatises, these poems generally attempt to present an absolutist image of royalty. Each of these poems tries to assert the familiar claim of Jacobean absolutism: political truth comes from the "knowing king." But since James's literate public persona so frequently found expression in prestige publications (folio publication of "works," official documents, the Bible translation), these late poems seem like an aberration: they circulate in miscellanies among documents that are often scurrilous, treasonous, and ephemeral. The indecorum is made all the more striking, as Perry argues, by the crown's simultaneous attempts to silence and restrict the culture of manuscript news and libel within which the poems are transmitted. For example, proclamations of 1620 and 1621 prohibited unwarranted political gossip of precisely this kind, and Jonson's masque *Newes from the New World* . . . (1620) makes a point of juxtaposing the truths of the "knowing king" with an anti-masque satirizing the kinds of unauthorized political speech fostered by newsmongers and a news-hungry populace. James's late poems grapple with a central irony. On the one hand, they all dismiss or admonish the culture of unwarranted political gossip facilitated by manuscript circulation. On the other, they themselves are forced to rely on manuscript circulation to promulgate their authoritative message. By participating in the ungovernable culture of manuscript libels, they acknowledge and, in a sense, authorize the political importance of such ungovernable material. Perry's essay looks closely at these poems and attempts to recover the complexities of response necessitated by their awkward rhetorical position. Such analysis casts light on the uneasy ways in which absolutism is maintained in the midst of what can perhaps best be described as a crisis of discursive authority.

In the second book of *Basilikon Doron,* James advises his heir, "above all vertues, study to know well your own craft, which is to rule your people," "that your principal end be to make you able thereby to use your office" (cited in Fischlin and Fortier 146). However, to study kingship is to study all crafts: "for except ye know every one, how can ye control every one, which is your proper office?" (ibid.). And so the study of the royal craft, as revealed in James's political and social writings, is hardly narrow in its focus. The essays in the second section of this book reveal in part the wide range of subject matter with which James engaged as ruler and writer.

Beginning with Louis A. Knafla's "Britain's Solomon: King James and the Law," the second section of the book deals with the monarch's writings on politics, society, and social issues. Through a compendious tour of James's works—from his political theorizing and his speeches to his subsequently recorded "Table Talk"—Knafla argues, contrary to those who depict James's thinking as slipshod and amateurish, that James held a systematic and consistent view of all aspects of the law: the nature of law itself; the law of God; the law of nations; the English legal system, including Parliament, equitable and other prerogative courts, common law, and common law courts; criminal law; and lawyers and judges. James emerges from this survey as an unwavering and decisive thinker, informed, ab initio, by a religious sense of the divine right of a king to govern.

Following on Knafla's general discussion of James and the law, the second essay in this section, Mark Fortier's "Equity and Ideas: Coke, Ellesmere, and James VI and I," focuses on the king's thought and its effect on a specific area of contention in English legal history: the struggle between common law and equity, which culminated in 1616 in the triumph of equity and the dismissal of the chief justice Edward Coke from the Court of King's Bench. Common law was regarded as both "black letter law," applied without exceptions, and as an authority that bound even the king. Equity, as dispensed in prerogative courts such as Chancery, kept an eye to setting aside the common law judgment in exceptional circumstances in the name of the king's conscience, which stood above the law. This development, which has had lasting effects on Anglo-American jurisprudence, Fortier sees as in large measure a battle of systematic ideas about law, political authority, and the distribution of power. James's consistent notion of his divinely sanctioned office, evident as early as *The True Law of Free Monarchies* and as late in the controversy as James's speech to Star Chamber in 1616, is seen to play a central role in the support given to equity in Chancery and other prerogative courts.

In "King James VI and I and John Selden: Two Voices on History and the Constitution," Johann P. Sommerville continues an ongoing debate over James's position vis-à-vis absolute or limited kingly power. This debate, alluded to in the essays by Knafla and Fortier, pits Sommerville against the historians Glenn Burgess and Paul Christianson, who argue that James's views never were or came not to be absolutist but were more in keeping with a general consensus at the time that authority was shared among king, Parliament, and the common law. Sommerville argues against the ideas that James ever changed from his early absolutist position in *The True Law of Free Monarchies* or that the political theorist John Selden and James were ever in agreement—conscious or otherwise—in their views on "mixed monarchy" and "the ancient constitution." As such, Sommerville's essay is a strong contribution to a controversy that is, no doubt, far from over.

Sandra J. Bell's "'Precious Stinke': James I's *A Counterblaste to Tobacco*" shows how James's political concerns brought him to reflect upon topics not narrowly political. The *Counterblaste* of 1604 was James's first prose work, other than political speeches, directed to his English subjects. Here he takes a harsh (and somewhat contemporary sounding) view against the evils of tobacco, especially—as Bell argues—against its corrupting influence on the English nation and its "insidious mimicking of sovereign power." Bell positions this somewhat idiosyncratic piece as partaking of the same kingly concerns and theory that inform James's more overtly and directly political pronouncements. She argues: "Like his *Basilikon Doron* and *True Law of Free Monarchies*, the *Counterblaste* is another example—if through a more indirect route and on a minor scale—of the king's desire to assert his control and authority in his new kingdom." In this way Bell demonstrates the connections between James's occasional concerns and his larger political project.

Finally in this section, David M. Bergeron's "Writing King James's Sexuality" takes us into the private sphere and the politics of the personal through an examination of James's affective life. Bergeron begins by tracing James's relations with the three young men, his male favorites, who so captured his affections over the course of his life. Bergeron then takes to task the anti-homosexual prejudice evident in dismissive evaluations over the centuries of James as man and monarch. Finally, through a reading of poems and letters to these three men, Bergeron reveals the "complicated, confusing, and even contradictory relationships that James had" with his favorites. He concludes that these writings speak of "an important and reciprocal love" that we must accept and take seriously. Bergeron's essay paints a very different portrait, of a man with very different concerns, than is revealed in many of the other essays in this book.

As Knafla's essay on the law demonstrates, James's theory of the place of kingship in the world was informed by his religious belief in divinely ordained monarchy. Religion lies at the basis of James's thinking and self-fashioning. The essays in the final section of the book explore James's writing on religious themes, all of which have ramifications for his secular career as monarch, poet, and political theorist.

The first essay in section three of this book, on writing and religion, demonstrates the connection between James's religious and political concerns. Malcolm Smuts's "The Making of *Rex Pacificus:* James VI and I and the Problem of Peace in an Age of Religious War" is at once an essay on James's sense of his role in international Christianity and on his foreign policy. Smuts desires to move past the anecdotal sense of James as a coward in his personal and political life, which purportedly resulted in the sorry attempts to appease Spain through the Spanish match in the 1620s, to discover "some sort of strategic vision"—albeit a supple and shifting one—in the king's somewhat contradictory embrace of both pacifism and militant Protestantism. From early poems, biblical exegesis, and political tracts through pronouncements and polemics following on the Gunpowder Plot, Smuts traces James's unwavering opposition to the papacy and its support of interference in Scottish and English politics. James's anti-Catholic position, however, was always tempered by his dislike of hawkish Puritans, who provided another, internal threat to his authority. Similarly, his fear of foreign powers was balanced by his distrust of his own Parliament. Smuts sees in James's role as king of peace "a story that . . . unfolded in a constantly changing international environment" yet was guided by a set of fundamental principles whose meaning and strategies changed for James over the course of his lifetime.

In "'To Eate the Flesh of Kings': James VI and I, Apocalypse, Nation, and Sovereignty," Daniel Fischlin examines the two early exegeses of the Book of Revelations that open James's collected *Workes* (1616). Here James uses biblical exegesis to construct and comment on signifying structures such as "state, nation, and monarchic dynasty." Apocalypse has a useful function in this context, since "apocalyptic end-time confirms the sacral nature of that by which it is preceded." By beginning his literary self-portrait with the end and last things, Fischlin argues, "James was reformulating a theological notion of history in which the sovereign, the nation, and the apocalyptic came together as mutually enabling concepts." Fischlin contends, however, that apocalyptic writing is fraught with "forces of contradiction and textual indeterminacy," and thus even as James articulates his vision of sacred authority, "the same vision was working to expose the anxieties circulating round the exercise of absolute power": "the end of time and thus the apocalyptic limits beyond which secular absolutism could have no further meaning."

The final three essays in this collection deal not only with James's religious pronouncements but also with the context in which they were read and received. John N. King's "James I and King David: Jacobean Iconography and Its Legacy" traces the identification of the English monarch with David, the model biblical ruler, beginning with James's predecessor Elizabeth through to his grandson Charles II. Arguing that James's identification with David is more important than his frequent association with Solomon, King traces this identification in writings such as *Basilikon Doron* and James's translations of the Psalms in particular and also in the iconographic images on the frontispieces of the publications he discusses. After James's death, King maintains, his son Charles I took up this iconography, most strikingly in *Eikon Basilike,* attributed at its publication to the recently executed king. At this point the identification of the monarch with David became a point of conflict between royalists and republicans, and King traces the latter's position in John Milton's *Eikonoclastes.* After the Restoration, King sees the battle continue, most notably in Milton's epic poems, which debunk the identification, and in John Dryden's *Absalom and Achitophel,* which reaffirms it.

James Doelman's essay tells the story of "The Reception of King James' Psalter." For a great part of his life (a translation of Psalm 104 appeared in 1584), James harbored the idea of translating King David's Psalms. As Doelman notes, his accession to the throne of England "presented the possibility of a broader scope for his Psalter: it could be a unifying element in all the British churches, or in what James hoped would ultimately be a single British church." Moreover, "[l]ike his sponsorship of a new translation of the Bible, James's work on the Psalms confirmed his role as leader of his churches." Of course, the project also furthered the identification between James and David discussed at length in King's essay here. Over the course of many years James made a certain amount of headway with this project, but it was incomplete at his death. Charles I, however, took it upon himself to have the project completed, commissioning the Scottish poet William Alexander to finish his father's work. Charles tried to have James's Psalter adopted for official use, first in Scotland, but he met with continuing resistance, which forced him to abandon his attempts. Doelman traces this resistance and argues that James's Psalter is more significant in the resistance it aroused than in its intended accomplishments.

Finally, Joseph Marshall examines James's writings at the time of the Spanish crisis of 1622 and their reception in "Reading and Misreading King James 1622–42: Responses to the *Letter and Directions Touching Preaching and Preachers.*" James's *Letter and Directions,* one of his last substantial works, was an effort to regulate anti-Catholic and anti-Spanish preaching while he was attempting to arrange peace and avoid war with Spain—partly through the Spanish marriage, which would have allied his family with Catholic royalty. James's courting of Spain ran counter to his longstanding pronouncements on the papacy and marriage with Catholics, and his attempt to control preaching on these issues met with widespread resistance. Angered by the opposition, James wrote the satirical poem "The Wiper of the Peoples Teares," which Marshall discusses briefly. James's Spanish policy failed, and he backed away from his regulation of preaching. Marshall observes: "The *Letter and Directions* remained . . . as a testimony to the fact that the king had written a work he abandoned under pressure from his readers"; moreover, "[i]t was used as a precedent by opponents of the repressive policies of King Charles I wishing to make the case that the king's word could be disregarded when he was obviously misled." Finally, when republican historians began to write revisionist histories of King James in the 1650s, the *Letter and Directions* featured prominently in their accounts of oppression and imperfection. In these last essays, therefore, we see a monarch whose sovereign texts veer inevitably out of his control and into the history of their reception—into the hands, as often as not, of those who turned James's words against the notions of sovereignty that he spent his lifetime fashioning through those very words.

Ultimately, the essays gathered in this book cannot hope to cover all of James's voluminous output as a writer. As is apparent from our overview of these essays, however, almost all of James's better known texts and many of his lesser known ones are covered here. Moreover, the analyses proceed in a number of registers, from close readings to comparative studies and studies of contexts and reception. These various approaches, together with the range of texts discussed and the detailed bibliographies appended to each essay, provide, we hope, a rich and multisided introduction for those interested in the study of the writings of James VI and I.

Notes

1. For further information on the early modern Scottish cultural context, see, among others, Brown; Burns; Edington; Goodare; Mason; Wormald (*Court, Kirk and Community*); Caie, Lyall, and Simpson; Dwyer, Mason, and Murdoch; Goodare and Lynch; and Mapstone and Wood. The introduction and annotations to David Parkinson's recently released edition of Montgomerie's poetry also contain invaluable information on Scottish court culture.
2. Following convention we use the 1616 date for the *Workes,* as was indicated on the title page by the king's printers, Robert Barker and

John Bill. Two of our contributors, Johann Sommerville and Joseph Marshall, use a 1617 dating for reasons they explain in the notes to their essays. The issue of dating the *Workes* revolves around the fact that the year 1616 ran until what we would now call 24 March 1617 (with the New Year then beginning on 25 March).

Works Cited

Akrigg, G. P. V., ed. *Letters of King James VI & I.* Berkeley: U of California P, 1984.

Ashton, Robert, ed. *James I By His Contemporaries.* London: Hutchinson, 1969.

Bergeron, David M. *King James and Letters of Homoerotic Desire.* Iowa City: U of Iowa P, 1999.

Brown, Keith M. *Bloodfeud in Scotland: Violence, Justice and Politics in Early Modern Society.* Edinburgh: J. Donald, 1986.

Burns, Jimmy H. *The True Law of Kingship: Concepts of Monarchy in Early-Modern Scotland.* Oxford: Clarendon P, 1996.

Caie, Graham, Rod Lyall, and Kenneth Simpson, eds. *The European Sun: Proceedings of the Seventh International Conference on Medieval and Renaissance Scottish Language and Literature.* East Linton, East Lothian, Scotland: Tuckwell P, forthcoming.

Craigie, James, ed. *Minor Prose Works of King James VI and I.* Edinburgh: Scottish Text Society, 1982.

———, ed. *The Poems of James VI of Scotland.* Vol. 1. Edinburgh: William Blackwood, 1955.

Disraeli, Isaac. *Literary Character of Men of Genius.* London: Frederick Warner, n.d.

Dwyer, John, Roger A. Mason, and Alexander Murdoch, eds. *New Perspectives on the Politics and Culture of Early Modern Scotland.* Edinburgh: J. Donald, 1982.

Edington, Carol. *Court and Culture in Renaissance Culture: Sir David Lindsay of the Mount.* Amherst: U of Massachusetts P, 1995.

Fischlin, Daniel, and Mark Fortier, eds. *James I:* The True Law of Free Monarchies *and* Basilikon Doron. Toronto: Centre for Reformation and Renaissance Studies, 1996.

Goldberg, Jonathan. *James I and the Politics of Literature.* Stanford: Stanford UP, 1989.

Goodare, Julian. *State and Society in Early Modern Scotland.* Oxford: Clarendon P, 1999.

Goodare, Julian, and Michael Lynch, eds. *The Reign of James VI.* East Linton, East Lothian, Scotland: Tuckwell P, 2000.

James I. *Flores Regii. Or, Proverbes and Aphorismes, Divine and Morall.* London, 1627.

———. *The Peace-maker: or, Great Brittaines Blessing.* London: Thomas Purfoot, 1618.

———. *The Workes.* London, Robert Barker, 1616. Rpt. Hildesheim: Georg Olms Verlag, 1971.

Kantorowicz, Ernst H. *The King's Two Bodies: A Study in Medieval Political Theology.* Princeton: Princeton UP, 1957.

Lee, Maurice, Jr. *Great Britain's Solomon: James VI and I in His Three Kingdoms.* Urbana: U of Illinois P, 1990.

Lockyer, Roger. *James VI & I.* London: Longman, 1998.

Mapstone, Sally, and Juliette Wood, eds. *The Rose and the Thistle: Essays on the Culture of Late Medieval and Renaissance Scotland.* East Linton, East Lothian, Scotland: Tuckwell P, 1998.

Mason, Roger A., ed. *Scots and Britons: Scottish Political Thought and the Union of 1603.* Cambridge: Cambridge UP, 1994.

Montgomerie, Alexander. *Collected Poems.* 2 vols. Ed. David J. Parkinson. Scottish Text Society, 5th series, vols. 28, 29. Edinburgh: Scottish Text Society, 2000.

Patterson, W. B. *King James VI and I and the Reunion of Christendom.* Cambridge: Cambridge UP, 1997.

Peck, Linda Levy. "The Mental World of the Jacobean Court: An Introduction." *The Mental World of the Jacobean Court.* Ed. Linda Levy Peck. Cambridge: Cambridge UP, 1991. 1–17.

Perry, Curtis. *The Making of Jacobean Culture: James I and the Renegotiation of Elizabethan Literary Practice.* Cambridge: Cambridge UP, 1997.

Sharpe, Kevin. "The King's Writ: Royal Authors and Royal Authority in Early Modern England." *Culture and Politics in Early Modern England.* Ed. Kevin Sharpe and Peter Lake. Stanford: Stanford UP, 1993. 117–38.

———. "Private Conscience and Public Duty in the Writings of James VI and I." *Public Duty and Private Conscience in Seventeenth-Century England: Essays Presented to G. E. Aylmer.* Ed. John Morrill, Paul Slack, and Daniel Woolf. Oxford: Clarendon P, 1993. 77–100.

Sommerville, J. P. "James I and the Divine Right of Kings: English Politics and Continental Theory." *The Mental World of the Jacobean Court.* Ed. Linda Levy Peck. Cambridge: Cambridge UP, 1991. 55–70.

———, ed. *King James VI and I: Political Writings.* Cambridge: Cambridge UP, 1994.

Warner, George F., ed. "The Library of James VI. 1573–1583." *Miscellany of the Scottish History Society.* Vol. 1. Publications of the Scottish History Society. Vol. 15. Edinburgh: Edinburgh UP, 1893. xi–lxxv.

Willson, David Harris. *King James VI and I.* London: Jonathan Cape, 1962.

———, ed. *A Royal Request for Trade: A Letter of King James I to the Emperor of Japan Placed in Its Historical Setting.* St. Paul, Minn.: James F. Bell Book Trust, n.d.

Wormald, Jenny. *Court, Kirk and Community: Scotland 1470–1625.* Edinburgh: Edinburgh UP, 1991.

———. "James VI and I, *Basilikon Doron* and *The Trew Law of Free Monarchies:* The Scottish Context and the English Translation." *The Mental World of the Jacobean Court.* Ed. Linda Levy Peck. Cambridge: Cambridge UP, 1991. 36–54.

Young, Michael B. *King James and the History of Homosexuality.* New York: New York UP, 1999.

I

Poetics and Kingship

1

"Best of Poets, Best of Kings": King James VI and I and the Scene of Monarchic Verse

Peter C. Herman

The poetry of King James VI and I has remained practically unexamined despite the copious attention given to his prose works and the reinvigoration of historicism in literary studies over the last twenty years or so.[1] The marginalization of James's verse, however, also points toward a larger gap concerning the verse produced by Tudor and Stuart monarchs: while one finds many investigations into how politics broadly informs the verse produced by various courtly-makers and prince-pleasers of early modern England, there has been almost nothing on the verses produced by the princes themselves. If, as Louis A. Montrose observes, "The otiose love-talk of the shepherd masks the busy negotiations of the courtier; the shepherd is a courtly poet prosecuting his courtship in pastoral forms,"[2] what happens when the otiose love-talk is articulated not by a courtier but by the king himself—in this case, James? The lack of answer to this question seems especially strange in James's case. He published two books of poetry while king of Scotland, reprinted his *Lepanto* upon his accession to the English throne and sponsored its translation into French and Latin, and his poetic accomplishments were widely recognized and celebrated (perhaps over-celebrated) during his life.

In this essay, I will show how James's position as monarch governed both the writing and the reception of his verse. James's previously ignored sonnet to Elizabeth—enclosed in a letter to her and, seemingly, intended for her eyes alone; his elegy for Sir Philip Sidney—printed in a commemorative volume; and the mini-epic *Lepanto* all reveal that James always writes *as a monarch* and never as a mere poet. The first two poems demonstrate how James used (or, more accurately in the case of the Elizabeth sonnet, *tried* to use) verse as an instrument of diplomacy. Moreover, the parallels between *Lepanto*'s (literal) ambivalence and James's foreign/religious diplomacy, together with the resonances of James's decision to republish the work as a separate piece in 1603, are instructive. The publication history of the *Lepanto* contributes to the history of authorship and shows how James took advantage of the growing authority of print authorship.

I

The sonnet James penned for Elizabeth sometime in 1586 especially demonstrates how a monarch could try to use verse as an instrument of diplomacy. Throughout much of that year James and Elizabeth haggled over the terms of the Anglo-Scots treaty, the primary sticking points being the size of James's pension and whether Elizabeth would sign an "instrument" guaranteeing that he would be her heir. In March, with firm but gentle irony, the queen rejected James's request that she sign this document:

> Tochinge an "instrument," as your secretarye terme it, that you desiar to haue me signe, I assure you, thogh I can play of some, and haue bine broght up to know musike, yet this disscord wold be so grose as wer not fit for so wel tuned musike. Must so great dout be made of fre good wyl, and gift be so mistrusted, that our signe Emanuel must assure? No, my deere brother. Teache your new rawe counselars bettar manner than to aduis you such a paringe of ample meninge. Who shuld doute performance of kinges offer? What dishonor may that be demed? Folowe next your owne nature, for this neuer came out of your shoppe. But, for your ful satisfaction, and to plucke from the wicked the weapon the wold use to brede your doubt of meanings, thes the be. First, I wil, as longe as you with iuel desart alter not your course, take care for your safety, help your nide, and shun al actes that may damnifie you in any sort, ether in present or future time; and for the portion of relife, I minde neuer to lessen, though, as I see cause, I wil rather augment. And this I hope may stand you in as muche assuranse as my name in parchement, and no les for bothe our honors.[3]

James, however, was not assured. He wanted something in formal writing, not merely a vague promise of future "performance." He tactfully responded that he did not want a signed document for himself but for others:

> And as for the instrument, quhairunto I desyre youre seale to be affixit, think not, I pray you, that I desire it for any mistrust, for I

> protest before God that youre simple promeis uolde be more then sufficient to me, if it uaire not that uoulde haue the quole worlde to understand hou it pleacith you to honoure me aboue my demeritis, quhich fauore and innumerable otheris, if my euill happ will not permitt [me] by action to acquye, yett shall I contend by goode meaning to conteruayle the same at her handis, quhome, committing to the Almichties protection, I pray euer to esteeme me.[4]

James reportedly had a fit when he read Elizabeth's reply (now lost). Observers described him as turning various shades of red and swearing "By God" that had he known "what little account the queen would make of him, she should have waited long enough before he had signed any league, or disobliged his nobles, to reap nothing but disappointment and contempt."[5] Apparently James told Elizabeth so in a letter (sadly, also lost), but the queen replied in a more temperate fashion, wondering "how possiblie my wel-ment letter, prociding from so fauteles a hart, could be ether misliked or misconstred" and reassuring James of her esteem and constant care for him. Yet despite the sweet words, she refused to raise the offered pension, and she declined to sign the instrument because such a document "fitted not our two frindeships."[6] James realized that he had gotten as much as Elizabeth would give him, and so he "digested all," signing the treaty in July.

According to G. P. V. Akrigg, sometime during 1586 James wrote a letter to Elizabeth that included a sonnet. Because both are very important and as yet have passed without notice, I quote them in full.[7]

> Madame and dearest sister,
>
> Notwithstanding of my instant writing one letter unto you yet could I not satisfy my unrestful and longing spirit except by writing of these few lines, which, albeit they do not satisfy it, yet they do stay the unrest thereof while the answer is returning of this present.
>
> Madame, I did send you before some verse. Since then Dame Cynthia has oft renewed her horns and innumerable times supped with her sister Thetis. And the bearer thereof returned, and yet void of answer. I doubt not ye have read how Cupid's dart is fiery called because of the sudden ensnaring and restless burning; thereafter what I can else judge but that either ye had not received it, except the bearer returned with the contrary to report; or else that ye judge it not to be of me because it is incerto authore. For which cause I have insert[ed] my name to the end of this sonnet here enclosed. Yet one way I am glad of the answer's keeping up, because I hope now for one more full after the reading also of these presents and hearing this bearer dilate this purpose more at large

according to my secret thoughts. For ye know dead letters cannot answer no questions; therefore I must pray you, how unapparent soever the purpose be, to trust him in it as well as if I myself spake it unto you face by face (which I would wish I might) since it is specially and in a manner only for that purpose that I have sent him. Thus, not doubting of your courtesy in this far, I commit you, madame, and dearest sister, to God's holy protection, the day and dates as in the other letter.

Your more loving and affectionate
brother and cousin than (I fear)
yet ye believe.
James R.

[Sonnet enclosed with letter][8]

Full many a time the archer slacks his bow
That afterhend* it may the stronger be. *afterward
Full many a time in Vulcan'[s] burning stow
The smith does water cast with careful ee * *eye
Full oft contentions great arise, we see,
Betwixt the husband and his loving wife
That sine* they may the firmlyer agree *since
When ended is that sudden choler strife.
Yea, brethren, loving others as their life,
Will have debates at certain times and hours.
The winged boy dissentions hot and rife
Twixt his lets fall like sudden summer showers.
Even so this coldness did betwixt us fall
To kindle our love as sure I hope it shall.

Finis J.R.

Given the correspondence between them at the time he composed this sonnet, it seems probable that the poem originated in James's desire to get beyond his anger at Elizabeth for refusing to sign the "instrument" and ameliorate her annoyance at his persistence; the references to "dissentions" and "contentions" apparently echo the queen's reference to musical "disscord" in her letter of March 1586. As such, James's sonnet represents more than an interesting diversion (when he first arrived in Scotland, Randolph reported that "the King still follows his hunting, riding and writing in metre"[9]). The poem argues that occasional strife only strengthens a relationship, and therefore he and Elizabeth are better allies for having had this argument. The sonnet demonstrates James's use of the medium of poetry to achieve a diplomatic goal—in this case, helping to smooth the relationship between Elizabeth and himself after their quarrels over money and the "instrument."

Yet the poem fascinates for a number of additional reasons. First, the imagery in this sonnet and the rhetoric of the accompanying letter demonstrate James's awareness of and desire to appropriate for his own benefit the politicization of erotic discourse permeating Elizabeth's court. The letter also demonstrates James's sensitivity to the importance of authorship: he makes absolutely sure that Elizabeth knows the sonnet comes from *his* pen, not "*incerto authore*"; moreover, James ensures that Elizabeth *knows* that he has signed this copy with his initials. Finally, while I recognize the danger of basing an argument on a lack of response, Elizabeth's refusal to acknowledge James's effort, let alone write a verse reply—even though she engages in a mock-debate in verse with Sir Walter Ralegh at precisely this time, remains among the most intriguing aspects of this poem.

The fact that James wrote Elizabeth a Petrarchan love sonnet is in itself important, for as a host of critics have shown, from the 1570s onward the rhetoric of love in the Elizabethan court became deeply entwined with the rhetoric of politics. Not only love lyrics but indeed the language of love itself, as Arthur F. Marotti writes, "could express figuratively the realities of suit, service, and recompense with which ambitious men were insistently concerned as well as the frustrations and disappointments experienced in socially competitive environments."[10] Thus, for example, Sir Christopher Hatton would write to his queen, "Madame, I find the greatest lack that ever poor wretch sustained. No death, no hell no fear of death shall ever win of me my consent so far to wrong myself again as to be absent from you one day. . . . I can write no more. Love me; for I love you. . . ."[11] Similarly, *Astrophel and Stella* simultaneously expresses Sir Philip Sidney's political and erotic frustrations, just as his *The Lady of May* and *The Triumph of the Fortress of Perfect Beauty* refigure "the queen's relationship to her courtiers as well as with her relationship to Alençon."[12]

James clearly knew about these developments, and in order to ingratiate himself further with Elizabeth, whose political and financial favor he depended on as much as any of Elizabeth's courtiers, he evidently decided to try to write using the tropes of political Petrarchism in both his poetry and his prose, with unique results. In no other letter, either before or after, does James use allegory ("Dame Cynthia has oft renewed her horns and innumerable times supped with her sister Thetis," meaning "it has been a long time since I sent the poem to you"[13]) or invoke "Cupid's dart" (which we will return to below). Additionally, this letter nuances Foucault's deconstruction of the author. The speaker's identity matters intensely to James, since Elizabeth's silence may be explained by her ignorance of the poem's source (unlikely, to be sure). As James writes, she might "judge it not to be of me because it is *incerto authore* [meaning James had not signed the original manuscript]. For which cause I have insert[ed] my name to the end of this sonnet." Yet remarkably, James's attempt to speak the erotic language of the Elizabethan court *fails*. Elizabeth ignored the poem the first time James sent it, and so far as we can tell she ignored it the second time as well. I want to offer two possible explanations for Elizabeth's declining to play along.

First, as both Marotti and Montrose point out, courtiers assimilated Petrarchan language so easily because the relationship between the lover and the beloved closely mirrored the relationship between the courtier seeking favor from a distant, withholding sovereign. The gender relationship between the lover and his beloved also reflected (at least rhetorically) the relationship between the courtier and the queen, the male being in the subservient position of *asking* for favor, which the woman (i.e., Elizabeth) can give or withhold. However, when a courtier speaks the rhetorical situation is totally different, and there is some evidence to suggest that there were specific conventions or audience expectations for monarchic verse. In a letter dated 1609 and addressed to King James I's eldest son, Prince Henry, Sir John Harington reproduces:

> A special of King Henry the Eight, when he conceived love for Anna Bulleign. And hereof I entertain no doubt of the Author, for, if I had no better reason than the rhyme, it were sufficient to think that no other than such a King could write such a sonnet; but of this my father oft gave me good assurance, who was in his household. This sonnet was sunge to the Lady Anne at his commaundment, and here followeth:
>
> THE eagle's force subdues eache byrd that flyes;
> What metal can resyst the flaminge fyre?
> Doth not the sunne dazzle the cleareste eyes,
> And melt the ice, and make the froste retyre?
> The hardest stones are peircede thro wyth tools;
> The wysest are, with Princes, made but fools. (Harington 2.248)

While in all likelihood Henry VIII did not in fact write these lines, Harington clearly thought these were the kinds of metaphors (an eagle, fire, the sun, the highly phallic piercing tool) a prince *ought* to use when composing verse because they are all associated with authority (Henry is the eagle, the sun, the hardest stone, the wisest, and of course, the prince). Therefore, Harington assures the young prince, even if he had no other basis than the words themselves, that *only* "A King could write such a sonnet." Furthermore, Harington's sense of generic propriety, his notion that when monarchs write, they write as monarchs and create metaphors reflecting their monarchic status, has much to support it in the poetic output of James's royal forebears, Henry VIII and Mary Stuart.[14]

Henry VIII penned his most famous lyric, "Pastime with Good Company," sometime in the first years of his reign, a time when an atmosphere of allegory, chivalry, and general festivity permeated the court. The chronicler Edward Hall, for example, records that at the start of the second year of his reign: "[The king exercised] hym self daily in shotyng, singing[,] dau[n]syng, wrastelyng, casting of the barre, plaiying at the recorders, flute, virginal, and in setting of songes, [and] makyng of balettes,"[15] and in all probability "Pastime" was among the "balettes" Henry composed as part of his recreations. Certainly this lyric sounds for all the world like nothing more than an early modern drinking song:[16]

> Pastime with good company
> I love and shall unto I die;
> Grudge so will, but none deny.

Yet innocuous as these lines appear, the fourth line of the first stanza—"So God be pleased, this life will I"—transforms this lyric into a vehicle by which Henry established his independence, for the words "this life will I" served to remind his audience that these desires were the desires of the king. However ludic the original circumstances of production, the line nonetheless functions as a claim to power and independence. Further, it would be hard for any courtier or lady mindful of the very few practical limitations on royal power to miss the overtone of threat vibrating in the last line of the burden:

> For my pastaunce
> Hunt, sing, and dance;
> My heart is set
> All goodly sport
> To my comfort:
> Who shall me *let*? (my emphasis)

To paraphrase, the last line demands, "Who will dare stop me from doing what I want to do?" "Pastime with Good Company" shows the way lines and phrases—no matter how conventional they may be when articulated by either a courtier (i.e., someone seeking power or favor) or someone outside the court altogether—take on an entirely different meaning when articulated by the monarch.

Furthermore, at the time when Henry penned and performed this song, he was engaged in more than chivalric playacting. He was also very much involved in the process of separating himself from his father's domestic policies through extravagant spending, lavish entertaining, and seeming indifference to the minutiae of government. As for foreign affairs, Henry instigated a belligerent foreign policy diametrically opposed to Henry VII's pacific aims. Neither shift, however, went unchallenged; indeed, Henry faced significant opposition from some members of the nobility and from such humanists as John Colet and Sir Thomas More.[17] Considered in this context, this seemingly inconsequential drinking song becomes a form of monarchic *defense*, an assertion of the king's power and independence through the putatively recreational medium of a parlor song. To paraphrase the old E. F. Hutton advertisement, when the king sings, everyone listens.

Given that Henry's poem circulated widely in both popular and courtly circles in England, Scotland, and the continent, it is very likely that James had some acquaintance with it and, hence, with monarchic verse.[18] We can be absolutely certain, however, that James knew the verses produced by his mother, Mary Stuart, since her poetry played an instrumental role in her destruction. While Mary's circumstances are in many ways the polar opposite of Henry's (he at the beginning of his ascent, she about to plunge from power), her poems, like Henry's, reflect and make use of her position as queen.

Ironically, Mary's most famous poems—the sonnet sequence to James Hepburn, the earl of Bothwell—rested among the infamous "Casket Letters," published by James's "pedagogue" George Buchanan, to prove her involvement in Darnley's murder. In these sonnets, Mary, much like Henry, speaks from a position of power, even if her intended audience (so far as we can tell) does not extend beyond the person of her lover. At several points in the sequence she invokes a cliché of Petrarchan discourse: the avowal of service and obedience to the beloved. In particular, "De vous je dis"[19]:

> Of you I say onely upholder of my life,
> I onely seke to be asseurit,
> Ye and dare presume so much of my selfe,
> To win you in spite of all envy:
> For that is the onely desire of your deir love;
> To serve and love you truely,
> And to esteme all wan hap lesse then nathyng,
> And to follow your wyll wyth myne,
> You shall knaw wyth obedience,

Not forgetting the knawlege of my leal deuty,
The quhilke I shall study to the fine that may ever please you.
Lovyng nothyng but you, in the subjectioun
Of quhome I will without any fictioun,
Live and die, and this I consent.

De vous je dis seul soustien de ma vie
Tant seulement je cerche m'asseurer,
Et si ose de moy tant presumer
De vous gaigner maugré toute l'envie.
Car c'est le seul desir de vostre chere amie,
De vous servir & loyaument aymer,
Et tous malheurs moins que riens estimer,
Et vostre volunté de la mien suivre.
Vous cognoistrez avecques obeyssance
De mon loyal devoir n'omettant lascience
A quoy j'estudiray pour toujiours vous complaire
San aymer rien que vous, soubz la sujection,
De qui je veux sens nulle fiction
Vivre & mourir & à ce j'obtempere.

As with Henry's "Pastime," Mary's language would be perfectly conventional if she occupied the conventional subject position of the Petrarchan sonneteer. However, the force of her poem lies in the extreme tension between her royal position and her Petrarchan rhetoric, for her adoption of the seemingly unexceptional pose of a lover swearing obedience to her beloved implicitly entails Mary's abandonment of her monarchic supremacy. Furthermore, she renders this contradiction explicit by concluding her poem with the verb *obtemperer*, which Cotgrave defines as to "obey" and "to be at the commaund of."[20] Monarchs are not supposed to "be at the commaund of" anybody (except of God), especially French monarchs, who were more absolutist in their political theory than their English or Scots counterparts.[21] Queens should command, not be commanded, to be obeyed, not obey the orders of others.

At other times in her sequence, Mary employs the opposite strategy: explicitly using monarchic power to entice her lover:

In his handis and in his full power,
I put my sonne, my honour, and my lyif,
My contry, my subjects, my soule al subdewit,
To him. . . .

Entre ses mains & en son plein pouvoir
Je metz mon filz, mon honneur, & ma vie,
Mon pais, mes subjectz, mon ame assubjectie
Est tout à luy. . . .

This extreme rhetoric also has extreme political consequences. Her son is, of course, the future James VI and I, and the country she offers to place in Bothwell's hands is not an abstraction, as in "My mind to me a little kingdom is." By devolving everything to "him," Mary not only declares Bothwell king of Scotland, she in effect abdicates her throne by giving him her "subjects." Truly, she makes an offer Bothwell cannot refuse, an offer only a queen can make. It is no wonder, then, that when the "Casket Letters" were made public in Buchanan's *Ane Detectioun of the Duinges of Marie Quene of Scottes* (1571), La Mothe Fénelon, the French ambassador to England, wrote that "Rhymes in French had been added which are worse than all the rest," even though they never allude to Darnley or his murder.[22]

Monarchic verse thus constituted a recognized subgenre in the early modern period. Royal authors not only wrote from an entirely different subject-position than their courtiers (i.e., a position of power), but they were *expected* to write verse that reflected their monarchic status and to comport themselves in their verse in a manner appropriate to their position. By this standard, Mary's giving away her kingdom to Bothwell is unacceptable, while Henry's use of verse to defend his royal pastimes is appropriate. This subgenre also illustrates the limitations of Michel Foucault's famous rhetorical question: "What matter who's speaking?"[23] In this case, nothing matters more than who is speaking, for the speaker *defines,* to paraphrase Foucault, "the modes of existence of this discourse" and "where . . . it comes from; how it is circulated; [and] who controls it."[24] The meaning of the verse *derives* from the speaker's identity, and in both expectation and practice, early modern monarchs wrote from a superior position.

In his sonnet to Elizabeth, however, James's monarchic status conflicts with his attempt to write a conventional piece of Petrarchan verse that for several reasons would entertain Elizabeth (hence making her more pliable to his political desires).[25] When his mother used this language, she offended by putting herself in a subservient position not compatible with her position at the top of the social hierarchy. James, though, had the opposite problem. As monarchs, Elizabeth and James were, in theory, on the same exalted plane; both considered themselves God's anointed on earth.[26] Yet nearly all the examples in James's sonnet to her are not only explicitly hierarchical but gendered as well. There is no mutuality between the "archer" or the "smith" (conventionally male) and their instruments. The early modern division of power between "the husband and his loving wife" needs no rehearsing, and the same gender relations obtain between lovers under the influence of "the winged boy." To use mathematical symbols, archer:bow=husband:wife, and smith:furnace=male lover:female beloved. When, therefore, James writes, "Even so this coldness did betwixt us fall," he does more than compare their political disagreements to a lovers' spat; rather, he implicitly compares his relationship with Elizabeth to a series of *un*equal relationships, with *himself* as the dominant partner. Given the poverty of James and his court as well as his status as a petitioner for the English throne—and English gold— Elizabeth might very well have decided not to respond because the poem implicitly figures her as an *inferior*, the bow to James's archer, the water to James's smith, the subservient wife to James's husband. The poem inverts the actual power relations between the two as well as serving to remind Elizabeth of the cognitive dissonance surrounding a powerful female monarch ruling "a stratified society in which authority is everywhere invested in men—everywhere, that is, except at the top."[27] James made a tactless blunder.

In addition, whatever his intentions, the erotic rhetoric in the letter and the sonnet invokes connotations that probably resonated very badly for Elizabeth. In both texts, James adopts the persona of the amorous lover. In the letter, he compares his apprehension at the lack of response to not hearing from one's lover: "I doubt not ye have read how Cupid's dart is fiery called because of the sudden ensnaring and restless burning." The poem culminates in a similar image:

> The winged boy [Cupid] dissentions hot and rife
>
> Twixt his lets fall like sudden summer showers.
>
> Even so this coldness did betwixt us fall
>
> To kindle our love as sure I hope it shall.[28]

In virtually all their previous (and following) correspondence, however, James and Elizabeth consistently invoke close family relationships to describe each other. In number XVI, for example, James begins by calling Elizabeth "madame and deirest sister," and he concludes by calling himself "Your trewest and assured brother and cousin."[29] Elizabeth in turn replies by addressing him as "right deare brother" and "my deerest brother and cousin the king of Scots."[30] In an earlier letter, James even calls Elizabeth "Madame and mother," signing himself as "your most loving and devoted brother and son, James R."[31]

The letter that accompanied the sonnet begins as most of the others do—"Madame and dearest sister"—but then James does something very unusual. He veers into erotic allegory and concludes with a more passionate ending than usual: "your more lovinge and affectionate brother and cousin than (I fear) yet ye believe." (Compare this with "your most louing and deuoted brother and sonn" [no. XIV] or "Youre most louing and affectionat brother and cousin" [no. XXXII]). He also (re)encloses a sonnet figuring Elizabeth and himself as lovers. While James doubtless intended Elizabeth to read this unprecedented use of erotic language as a witty invocation of common tropes and a demonstration of his ability to "talk the talk" of the Elizabethan court, the concatenation of amorous and familial terms may well have sounded suspiciously like something that haunted Elizabeth from her earliest days: incest.

Elizabeth owed her existence to the putatively incestuous relationship between her father, Henry VIII, and Catherine of Aragon. Without that "scruple," Henry VIII would not have married Elizabeth's mother, Anne Boleyn. But then Anne herself fell, and Henry charged her with incest with her own brother, Lord Rochford (some even said that Anne was Henry's illegitimate daughter, making Elizabeth's mother guilty of double incest). Thomas Cranmer, archbishop of Canterbury, argued for Elizabeth's illegitimacy on the grounds of Henry's affair with Anne's sister Mary Carey, since the definition of incest also included marriage to a former mistress's sister.[32] While Elizabeth regularly "portrayed herself in multiple kinship roles" when dealing with other monarchs,[33] James actually *was* related to Elizabeth by blood.[34] In other words, the references to "brother," "sister," and "cousin" are not purely rhetorical. Consequently, when James shifts gears and suddenly begins to compare himself and Elizabeth to lovers, he raises an issue that Elizabeth would have found most unwelcome, for it constituted one of the prime grounds for challenges to her legitimacy.

Furthermore, Marc Shell argues that "it is at the level of incest both spiritualized and secularized that Elizabeth as monarch later established herself as the national virgin queen who was at once the mother and the wife of the English people."[35] Therefore, when James writes "The winged boy dissentions hot and rife / Twixt his lets fall like sudden summer showers" or describes his agony at waiting for a response to "the sudden ensnaring and restless burning" of Cupid's fiery dart, he implicitly (and probably unwittingly) despiritualizes incest. It would be one thing for a courtier such as Hatton to use these terms when writing to Elizabeth, for he was not actually related to her. But when James uses them he sets in motion an entirely different set of connotations. Elizabeth evidently believed that the best response to such rhetoric was to pretend it didn't happen, and James got the message. He never used such language with Elizabeth again.

II

Sir Philip Sidney died on 21 September 1586, and about five months after that, in February 1587, Alexander Neville published *Academiae Cantabrigiensis Lachrymae Tumulo Noblilissimi Equitis, D. Philippi Sidneii Sacratae*, a volume of Latin verse commemorating Sidney.[36] Neville's edition gave James another opportunity to use verse as an instrument of royal diplomacy (although more successfully, and certainly more appropriately). The volume includes English and Latin versions of James's epitaph for Sidney as well as contributions from Lord Patrick Gray, Sir John Maitland, Colonel James Halkerston, Lord Alexander Seton, and the earl of Angus, none of whom are known today as poets but all of whom were deeply involved with James's highly slippery diplomacy toward England. Significantly, James's mother lost her head on February 8th, two or three weeks before Neville's volume appeared, and I propose that her death constituted the precipitating factor in James's decision to deliver contributions from himself and his courtiers. The printer, John Windet, clearly added the Scots contributions after the compositor set the volume in type: unlike the rest of the volume, the pages with the Scots elegies are not numbered, the signatures for their poems start at "K" even though the final pages of Neville's preceding letter are signatures H3r–v (thus missing "I" and "J"), and the first poem after the Scots elegies, by G. H. (Gabriel Harvey?), is on—using the actual pagination—page 1, signature A1v. Also, Windet or the compositor put the volume's title and an ornamental design on top of G. H.'s poem,[37] and the page before, signature A1r, repeats the title page. Taken together, these details of book production suggest that the Scottish elegies arrived *after* Windet had completed the volume, which in turn suggests that the Scots wrote and published their poems less out of concern for the late Sir Philip and much more in reaction to Mary's recent execution.[38]

James's contribution, it must be admitted, is neither particularly distinguished nor deep:

> Thou mighty Mars the Lord of souldiers brave,
>
> And thou Minerve, that dois in wit excell,
>
> And thou Apollo, that dois knowledge have,
>
> Of every art that from Parnassus fell
>
> With all you Sisters that thaireon do dwell,
>
> Lament for him, who duelie serv'd you all
>
> Whome in you widely all your arts did mell,

Bewaile (I say) his inexpected fall,

I neede not in remembrance for to call

His race, his youth, the hope had of him ay

Since that in him doth cruell death appall

Both manhood, wit and learning every way,

But yet he doth in bed of honour rest,

And evermore of him shall live the best.

But again, like the Elizabeth sonnet, the fact of its royal author eclipses all aesthetic considerations. We have already seen James's concern for rendering explicit his authorship, and the typography suggests that James (or one of his ambassadors) and the printer collaborated on making sure the reader knew that this sonnet constituted a monarchic performance. The poem comes first (thus indicating the social and political preeminence of its creator) and appears in English (all the other elegies are in Latin or Greek); Windet further highlights it by using italic type and slightly larger font here than for the rest of the volume. Furthermore, Windet gives the following title:

IN *PHILIPPI SIDNAEI*

interitum, Illustrisimi Scotorum

Regis carmen

Whereas Windet ascribes all the other poems to a person (either through initials or full names), this one originates from an institution, less by "James Stuart" and more by the "Illustrisimi Scotorum / Regis," the most illustrious king of the Scots. As such, the poem seems nothing more than a royal tribute to Sir Philip Sidney. The political and diplomatic resonances are, however, more complex.

Dominic Baker-Smith suggests that James's elegy for Sidney can be explained partly by their common interest in a "specifically Christian poetics."[39] Yet I know of no extant evidence suggesting that Sidney and James ever discussed poetry (despite their common interest in Du Bartas), nor do I know of any evidence proving that they ever met in person. Furthermore, Baker-Smith does not take into account the ideological gulf separating James and Sir Philip, in particular their different views concerning the role of the monarch. By at least 1580, James thought that a king should be absolute, ruling by divine right, and he expressed these views to Walsingham at their first meeting in 1583 (for which Walsingham roundly rebuked him).[40] By contrast, Sidney sided more with Buchanan and the French resistance theorists. Nor was James, as we shall see, as hot a Protestant as Sidney might have liked. The mystery of why James would go to the trouble to write an elegy and commission elegies for someone with whom he had deep ideological differences diminishes when we remember the dictum that nations have interests, not friends. Along these lines, it is worth noting that James's opinion of Sidney's poetic accomplishments shifted considerably after his accession. In 1618–19, well after James had any need to praise Sidney for diplomatic advantage, he told Ben Jonson that "Sir P. Sidney was no poet."[41]

Therefore, Baker-Smith rightly senses that however much James actually mourned Sidney, the poem also serves the Scots king's desire to "commend his own name to those, in England and abroad, who looked for a fit successor to Elizabeth, one equipped to serve the Protestant interest."[42] Granted, James uses the occasion of Sidney's death to strengthen his claim to the English throne, yet the matter is murkier than Baker-Smith allows. If this poem shows James trying to ingratiate himself with Sidney's father-in-law or, more importantly, Walsingham, Elizabeth's trusted privy councilor, while implicitly advertising himself as Elizabeth's heir, he was also exploring his options with England's Catholic enemies. In sum, this poem should not be taken as a simple declaration of principle or ambition, as Baker-Smith suggests, but as one more example of the slipperiness of James's diplomatic maneuvering and his penchant for using verse to further his political goals.

While Sidney and James may well have liked each other, the fact remains that their relations were more diplomatic than personal. Sidney's involvement with James began in 1585, when, as Roger Howell puts it, his name starts to "figure prominently in Scots affairs."[43] He was deeply involved with Walsingham's negotiations over the amount of Elizabeth's pension for James. For Sidney, his activities on James's behalf formed part of his Protestant activism since a large grant "would not only strengthen the Protestant cause north of the border but it would also help to thwart the machinations of the continental powers."[44] And although neither Howell nor Baker-Smith mention it, Sidney knew enough about James's interests to send him a gift of bloodhounds (not poems), for which James instructed his English ambassador to be sure to thank him.[45] While negotiations for an Anglo-Scots alliance were ultimately successful (although James did not get as large a pension as he would have liked nor, more importantly, an unequivocal statement about the succession), we need to remember that Elizabeth consistently resisted those who were unqualifiedly in favor of James.

The reason for this resistance is not hard to find, for if James appeared to Sidney as pro-English and (no doubt) pro-Protestant, the king was also treating with the Catholic powers. In 1585 (the same year Sidney sent James the dogs), the king not only refused to keep the Catholic earl of Arran in prison and out of favor but—as Walsingham writes with considerable disgust—the Jesuits and the duke of Guise were in Scotland with their own offers for James's "loyalty":

> For myself I give over all hope of Scotland otherwise than by force. I see no reason to think that Bellenden and Maitland's credit (now that Arran and Gray are reconciled) shall be able to prevail to keep the King in good terms with her Majesty. There are lately arrived in that realm one Hay, general of the Jesuits of the Scottish nation and one Durye that hath written against the ministers in Scotland. . . . They are sent from the Duke of Guise with very large offers unto the King . . . . I see so great treachery in that nation as I have no desire at all to have any extraordinary dealing with them.[46]

In another letter, Walsingham concludes that "The best is to deal warily with them all, for they are all born under one climate." Elizabeth evidently agreed with her counselor, for, Walsingham reports, "I can by no means persuade her Majesty to write to Gray, neither will she, in respect of the jealousy had of the King's cunning and unsound dealing, yield unto him the pension promised."[47] We therefore cannot regard James's elegy as unequivocal evidence of his devotion to Protestant humanism or of his undying devotion to the Leicester-Walsingham-Sidney faction's hostility toward Spain, as Baker-Smith argues,[48] since James clearly adhered to one principle alone: his self-interest (we will return to James's dealings with Catholic powers below).

Of course, the "letting slip" of the Protestant, pro-English Ruthven lords (who had initially fled to England for protection in the wake of James's attack on the Kirk's power) completely changed matters, and on 5 July 1586, he finally signed the Anglo-Scots alliance that Sidney and Walsingham, among others, labored to bring about. But then Walsingham brought to light the Babington plot, which would lead to the execution of Mary, Queen of Scots, and James once more consistently played a double game.

While reports famously vary as to James's reaction to his mother's death,[49] he clearly tried to keep all his options open, not knowing "whether Protestant or Roman Catholic" would eventually win.[50] As Baker-Smith argues, James may very well have intended his elegy for Sidney as an implicit endorsement of the Anglo-Scots treaty, a reassurance that both he and his chief advisers remained committed to England. This interpretation accords with James's secret understanding with Leicester that he would not break the alliance if his mother were executed, since that would mean losing the throne of England.[51] Furthermore, James continued his friendship with Henry of Navarre and delighted in the company of his favorite poet, the very Protestant Du Bartas. Yet at virtually the same time, James refused to receive Elizabeth's ambassador for several months, and he sent letters to Henry III, Catherine de Medici, and the Guises asking for support.[52] James's chancellor, Maitland, who also wrote in memory of Sidney, several months later spoke in Parliament, vowing "vengeance for Mary's blood."[53] In consequence, while the Sidney elegy contributes to the making of the Sidney legend, it figures as much as another front in James's duplicitous diplomacy, an attempt to reassure—through the medium of verse—his English allies while he secretly negotiated with their enemies.

III

The fact that James did not include either the epitaph on Sir Philip Sidney or the sonnet to Elizabeth in his published works suggests that he considered them topical ephemera rather than serious bids for poetic immortality. The *Lepanto*, however, is an entirely different story. James wrote this poem in 1585, and he not only included it in his 1591 volume, *His Majesties Poeticall Exercises,* but he appended a translation into French by Du Bartas. James then republished the *Lepanto* in 1603 and sponsored a Latin translation that appeared in 1604. Clearly, he considered this poem his masterpiece, yet the high estimation he accorded it only partly accounts for its frequent reprinting. While the 1603 and 1604 appearances are both aspects of his monarchic self-presentation to his new kingdom, since they coincided with his accession to the English throne, there is even more. The *Lepanto* partakes of three distinct (if overlapping) sets of contexts, and, as we will see, this text performs very different political work in 1585, 1591, and 1603. Furthermore, James alters his authorial self-presentation each time, in accord with these different contexts.[54]

According to the hierarchy of genres popular in the early modern period, the epic—or "Heroicall song," as James terms it—ranks the highest. As Sir Philip Sidney puts it in the *Apology,* "all concurreth to the maintaining the heroical, which is not only a kind, but the best and most accomplished kind of poetry."[55] Consequently, writing an epic is a perfectly appropriate task for a poet-king (indeed, it might be the only genre worthy of a king). Yet in 1585, when James turned to this subject, there was nothing obvious about why he would find attractive either the subject matter or the prospect of writing martial, heroic poetry.

To be sure, the story of the Battle of Lepanto (1571) seems ideally suited for epic treatment. Leading a fleet of 208 galleys sailing under the flag of a "Holy League" organized by Pope Pius V, the Spanish monarchy, and the Venetian republic, Don John destroyed the Turkish fleet in one day of fighting, and the victory of the Christian forces over the Islamic "Other" was very quickly transformed into the subject of chronicles in Spanish, Italian, and Latin.[56] Yet this triumph did not mean very much strategically, for within one year the Turks had rebuilt their navy and were making "new incursions on the Spanish protectorate of Tunis, overtaking the town for good in 1574."[57] While, as Ferdinand Braudel writes, "This victory seemed to open the door to the wildest hopes,"[58] and while seventeenth-century writers would depict this contest as a heroic event, people closer to the battle itself recognized that those hopes led nowhere.[59] Furthermore, given James's lifelong aversion to both figurative and literal military exploits (his son, Prince Henry, distinguished himself from his father by adopting an explicitly chivalric and bellicose persona[60]), the king's decisions to write the poem in the first place and then republish it require more explanation than ascribing it to a desire to write an exciting story or demonstrate expertise in a variety of genres.

The ideological work behind James's composition of the *Lepanto* becomes clearer in light of his very tenuous grasp on political power in 1585. The year before, James had the Scottish Parliament pass bills asserting "the royal authority in the state, both in theory and in practice"—no mean feat given the resistance, both in theory and in practice, of both the aristocracy and the clergy.[61] The clergy were furious at James for ending the Presbyterian system in Scotland, and a number of them fled to England. The return of the banished Ruthven lords, along with an army of 10,000 men, added to James's troubles, and we have already noted the young king's tense relations with Elizabeth and Walsingham. "Estranged from Elizabeth, menaced by the exiled lords and ministers, and aware of discontent in Scotland,"[62] James chose this moment to write an epic. As Daniel Fischlin argues, the *Lepanto* could be construed as "an empowering literary response to the contingencies of sovereign rule by a monarch struggling to achieve a modicum of internal political stability."[63] In other words, James composed and distributed the *Lepanto* as part of his (at times desperate) project of asserting monarchic authority within and without Scotland by representing himself through the highest, most "noble" genre. It would be absurd to assert that James actually believed by writing epic poetry he would become Elizabeth's heir and subdue his recalcitrant clergy and aristocracy, yet he likely intended that by interjecting himself "into the literary pantheon that contributes to [monarchic and poetic] authority" he would strengthen his prestige.[64]

In addition to demonstrating James's attempt to add some luster to his crown by appropriating the cultural authority of the epic poet, the *Lepanto* also exemplifies James's sometimes clumsy, sometimes adept strategy throughout his Scottish reign of balancing Catholic interests against those of the Protestants. First, James calls Don John (in the poem, "Don Joan") a "Generall great" (207), depicting him as an ideal leader who knows "the names of speciall men" and who, somewhat like a nautical Henry V, rows about his troops, urging them on. James also highlights Don John's nationality, consistently referring to him as "the Spanish Prince" (481, 798) and once using orthography to emphasize the point: "The SPANIOL Prince" (497). Given the presence of Spain in Scots affairs at this point, it would be hard not to read these references as a deliberate compliment, just as the Sidney elegy could be construed as a declaration of loyalty to the Protestant side. Complimenting the Spanish potentially alienates the Protestants, but James takes them into consideration as well.

The poem itself divides neatly down the middle in its valuation of the anti-Turkish forces' religion. On the one hand, in the main body of the epic, James pointedly refuses to condemn either Don John's religion or his nationality. In the Job-like scene at the start of the poem, Christ says to Satan:[65]

I know thou from that City comes,
CONSTANTINOPLE great,
Where thou hast by the malice made
The faithless Turkes to freat [fret].
Thou hast inflamde their maddest mindes
With raging fire of wraith [wrath],
Against them all that doe professe
My name with fervent fayth. (49–56; my emphasis)

Christ seems to care only about the profession of his name; none of the doctrinal quarrels dividing Christianity matter very much to him. Similarly, James consistently calls the anti-Turkish forces and the inhabitants of Venice Christians rather than Catholics, once more submerging or erasing doctrinal and theological differences in favor of a larger unity. Even God, while not endorsing all forms of observance, nonetheless declines to dwell on these distinctions in his answer to Christ:

All christians serves [*sic*] my Sonne though not
Aright in everie thing.
No more shall now these *Christians* be
With Infidels opprest. (79–82; my emphasis)

The Turkish conquest of Cyprus "moo'ved each Christian King / To make their Churches pray for their / Relief in everie thing" (150–52); urged on by Gabriel's rumor campaign, the town's population and the Venetian senate implore aid from "The Christian Princes" (190) in the conflict "twixt the Turkes / and Christians" (195–96); and the entire fleet, made up of Spanish and Italian ships, aids a "Christian Navy" (292).

Yet the angelic chorus at the poem's end displays no such ecumenicism. Its odd argument (rather, James's odd argument) is that if God gives victory to such *deficient* Christians—indeed, to people who barely deserve the title at all—imagine what he could do for Protestants:

But praise him more if more can be,
That so he loves his name,
As he doth mercie shew to all
That doe professe the same:
And not alanerlie [only] to them
Professing it aright,
But even to them that mixe therewith
Their own inventions slight:
As specially this samin time
Most plainly may appeare,
In giving them such victory
That not aright him feare:
For since he shewes such grace to them
That thinks [sic] themselves are just,
What will he more to them that in
His mercies onelie trust? (957–72)

One could dismiss these shifts in emphasis as further examples of James's lack of rhetorical skill, but they are entirely consistent with his refusal to choose unequivocally between Catholicism and Protestantism, or—perhaps more to the point—between the Catholic powers of Spain and France and the Protestant power of England.

In 1580–81, Esmé Stuart, the duke of Lennox, dominated James's thinking and affections, and while the king may have remained ignorant of the details concerning Lennox's intrigues with the Catholic powers, he nonetheless absorbed their lessons well. As David Harris Willson puts it, "he stood on the periphery of them, understanding their general drift, and was introduced to the subtle courses of a double diplomacy."[66] James soon acquired a nasty reputation for two-facedness. Elizabeth, for instance, exclaimed with no end of annoyance. "That false Scotch urchin! What can be expected from the double dealing of such an urchin as this?"[67] Beginning in 1584, James's strategy of playing Catholics off Protestants and vice versa intensified, and it continued through 1585, exactly the period during which he composed the *Lepanto*. Opportunely, in 1584 James received a letter from the Catholic duke of Guise offering friendship and protection. James regarded this letter as a means of shoring up his crumbling authority, and he responded so positively that the Spanish king, Philip, noted: "He is quite ready to confess them himself." Philip thought, in other words, that James would convert to Catholicism, a concept that James encouraged by writing to the pope: "I trust to be able to satisfy your Holiness on all other points, especially if I am aided in my great need by your Holiness."[68] At the same time, James was negotiating with Elizabeth over the fate of his mother, and in May 1585, just before he started the *Lepanto,* Elizabeth opened negotiations for a league with Scotland.

Ultimately, James realized that his interests lay with England and Protestantism, not with Spain, but he also understood that he could gain even more by keeping both in play. Consequently, as Willson writes, "Even while he sought aid from Catholic powers he strove tenaciously to improve his relations with England."[69] Or one can reframe this strategy from the opposite perspective, i.e., that he strove tenaciously to improve his relations with the Catholic powers while seeking a treaty with England. The matter is more evenly balanced than Willson's rhetoric allows, for as Willson himself points out, James's negotiations with foreign Catholic powers, together with his refusal to curb his domestic Catholic lords, enhanced "his bargaining power with Elizabeth, formed a counterpoise to the Kirk, and offered hope of survival in case of Spanish victory."[70] At the time of its composition, therefore, the *Lepanto* intervenes in James's domestic and foreign diplomacy by exemplifying his attempts to keep all his cards in play. The main body of the text assures the Catholic powers of his esteem for both their military heroes and their religion, and the angelic chorus assures the Kirk—and the English Protestants who happen to read the poem—that the king is really on *their* side. With this poem, in other words, James does not so attempt to forge a via media between the two opposing poles of Christianity as invent a strategy for maintaining maximum diplomatic advantage while avoiding a firm commitment to either side.

By 1591, however, when James published the *Lepanto* as part of his *Poeticall Exercises,* both the domestic and foreign contexts had shifted considerably. James had signed the treaty with England, the crisis over his mother's execution had passed, and he now clearly favored England and Protestantism. The formation of a moderate party within the Kirk made accommodation possible,[71] and James continued to advertise his preference for Protestantism through his disputation with the Jesuit James Gordon, his marriage to the Protestant Anne of Denmark, and his eventual containment of the Catholic northern earls with Huntly's defeat in 1589. Although James continued to infuriate with his refusal to repress completely the Catholic lords or to sever unequivocally his ties with Spain,[72] he recognized that his interests lay with Protestantism and England, not Spain and Catholicism, and he acted accordingly.

But the shift in contexts created a problem. As we have seen, the *Lepanto* carefully endorses both sides because this strategy made diplomatic sense at the time of the poem's composition. In a preface to the 1591 version, James asserts, as so many authors in this period do, that the poem has circulated in manuscript without his knowledge: "For although till now, it have not bene imprinted, yet being set out the publick view of many, by a great sort of stoln Copies, purchast (in truth) without my knowledge or consent" (198).[73] Even so, James concerns himself less with unauthorized transmission and more with unauthorized *interpretation:* "It falles out often, that the effects of mens actions comes [sic] cleane contrarie to the intent of the Author. . . . [I]t hath for lack of a Praeface, bene in somethings misconstrued by sundry" (198). In all likelihood, sundry *have* read the poem correctly, but now—in 1591—the original, evenly balanced content no longer serves James's interest, and so the "Author" adds a preface in an attempt to "guide" the reader to a more politically correct interpretation. Don John, whom the text unambiguously declares a Christian hero, James now calls "a forraine Papist bastard," and he announces that "I name not DON-JOAN neither literally nor any waies by description" (198), even though James most certainly does name him both literally and by way of description. Furthermore, James explicitly denigrates Don John's military accomplishments and Catholicism—"Next followes my invocation to the true God only, and not to all the He and She Saints, for whose vaine honors, DON-JOAN fought in all his wars" (200). The preface, in other words, accommodates the change in political and diplomatic circumstances by trying to tip the poem's careful balance toward Protestantism, even if this means contradicting what the poem actually says.

We have already seen, in his 1586 letter to Elizabeth, James's sensitivity to the question of ascription, and he adopts a similar strategy in this text by highlighting his position as monarch. The (putative) misconstruction of the poem bothers him, but the offence against his royal dignity really annoys him:

> And for that I knowe, the special thing misliked in it, is, that I should seeme, *far contrary to my degree* and Religion, like a Mercenary Poët, to penne a worke, *ex professo,* in praise of a forraine Papist bastard. . . . *For as it becomes not the honour of my estate,* like an hireling, to pen the praise of any man: *becomes it far lesse the highness of my rancke and calling,* to spare for the feare of favor of whomsoever living, to speake or write the trueth of anie. (198–200; my emphasis)

In a manner analogous to Henry VIII's warbled question, "Who shall me let?," and to Mary's "Entre ses mains," James invokes his degree, his estate, the highness, as he says, of his rank and calling to impose his interpretation on his poem. The references to the author's eminence unmistakably mark the speaking "I" of the preface as a *royal* "I," and James offers his interpretation/corrections not just as evidence of authorial intention (i.e., I—the king!—wrote the poem, so I know what it means better than you), but of the absolute monarch's will. As Goldberg suggests, in the preface "the powers of poet and king are parallel. . . . They exercise the discourse of power and the power of discourse."[74] The position James adopts, in other words, is that of king, not simply author, speaking to the reader, with the implication that the reader had better pay attention.

Yet ironically, in doing so, James draws not just on royal authority but on the growing authority of poetic authorship itself, and we can trace this development through an examination of the title pages, organization, and page layout of his books. During this period, as J. W. Saunders noted, gentlemen simply did not publish poetry.[75] Manuscript transmission was perfectly acceptable, even a mark of aristocratic identity. But because of the associations of print publication with the marketplace[76]—and because of the omnipresence of what I call anti-poetic sentiment and Steven W. May terms "the stigma of verse"—publishing a book of one's poems "could damage rather than enhance social status."[77] As John Selden marvelously puts it: "'Tis ridiculous for a Lord to print Verses; 'tis well enough to make them to please himself, but to make them public, is foolish. If a Man in a private Chamber twirls his Band-strings, or plays with a Rush to please himself, 'tis well enough; but if he should go into *Fleet-street,* and sit upon a Stall, and twirl a Band-string, or play with a Rush, then all the Boys in the Street would laugh at him."[78]

The real issue is not the supposed "stigma of print." As May has shown, many Tudor and Stuart aristocrats had no problem with publishing volumes on topics as various as religious commentaries and the importance of mothers breastfeeding their own children.[79] Moreover, monarchs had published books before (Henry VIII in particular),[80] and they clearly wrote poetry from time to time. But no monarch before James had their verses printed in a book for circulation as a commodity in the marketplace. The anonymity of the title page of his first published book, *The Essayes of a Prentise* (1584) (fig. 1), demonstrates the tentativeness with which James approached this precedent-breaking move. Even though the book of poems has a royal author, the printer presents it as an anonymous publication. The first page gives us the title—*The Essayes of a Prentise in the Divine Art of Poesie*; not insignificantly, the type gets progressively smaller and smaller, "Poesie" being nearly unnoticeable, and certainly subordinate to the more respectable term, "Essayes,"[81] as if the genre were an embarrassing admission. We are told that Vaultrollier printed the book "cum privilegio Regali," but nowhere does the title page reveal that the regal one had also made (fecit) the book.[82] The introductory sonnets reveal that key fact slowly and enigmatically, and even then the book's authorship is not apparent until the third sonnet (by "M. W."), which concludes with this couplet: "O Phoebus then rejoyce with glauncing glore, / Since that a King doth all thy court decore" (sig. *iii).

THE ESSAYES OF A PRENTISE, IN THE DIVINE ART OF POESIE.

Imprinted at Edinbrugh, by Thomas Vautroullier.
1584.

CVM PRIVILEGIO REGALI.

FIG. 1.
Reproduced by permission of the Huntington Library, San Marino, California.

With the publication, however, of *His Majesties Poeticall Exercises* in 1591, James more readily announces his responsibility for his poetic text. The title page boldly declares that "His Majesty" wrote this book, with "Majesties" published in larger type than anything else and in boldface (fig. 2). Even so, the title page of the *Lepanto* marks something of a retreat, since it privileges (like so many of the title pages of playbooks do)[83] the work over the author. Reversing the layout of the initial title page, here the first two syllables of *Lepanto* are printed in large, boldface letters (fig. 3). The reader now knows the name and rank of the text's author ("James the sixt, King of Scotland"), but the work takes precedence over the royal author. What accounts for this change from James's first book?

On the one hand, it could be argued that the shift in the layout of these title pages proves Goldberg's thesis, i.e., that here is an absolute monarch asserting his authority in the domain of authorship, thereby legitimizing authorship and removing, through the fact of his august presence, the "stigma of verse." But by 1591 the category of "poet-author" had already started to accrue considerable authority on its own as a middle-class, commercial entity. Marotti suggests that the publication of Sir Philip Sidney's literary works in the early 1590s "fundamentally changed the culture's attitudes toward the printing of the secular lyrics of individual writers, lessening the social disapproval of such texts and helping to incorporate what had essentially been regarded as literary ephemera into the body of durable canonical texts."[84] Yet Marotti also provides evidence that this shift began earlier. He points out that in the first edition of George Gascoigne's *A Hundred Sundrie Flowers* (1573), the title page (like that of James's *The Essayes of a Prentise*) omits the author's name. But in the second edition (1575), the printer gives this work an architectural frontispiece and retitles the work as *The Posies of George Gascoigne.*[85] In light of other changes between these editions, it is clear that Gascoigne was involved with the production of this second edition. And the change in the title page strongly suggests that both Gascoigne and the printer considered it commercially and culturally advantageous to make the work's authorship explicit and give it a privileged position. The buying public had started to become as interested in who wrote the work as in the work itself, and authors wanted to start accruing for themselves some of the prestige of authorship. These developments, however, emanate from the marketplace, not the aristocracy, where the notion that it is "ridiculous for a Lord to print Verses" would continue for some time yet. When, therefore, James allowed his Scots printer Robert Waldegrave to advertise the book's royal authorship, he was not so much legitimizing authorship with his royal presence as seeking to appropriate poetic authorship's growing, nonaristocratic prestige for himself. In other words, the king does not confer authority on authorship; rather, authorship confers authority on the king.

Edmund Spenser's construction of himself in the 1590 and 1596 editions of *The Faerie Queene* especially highlights this shift. As Montrose points

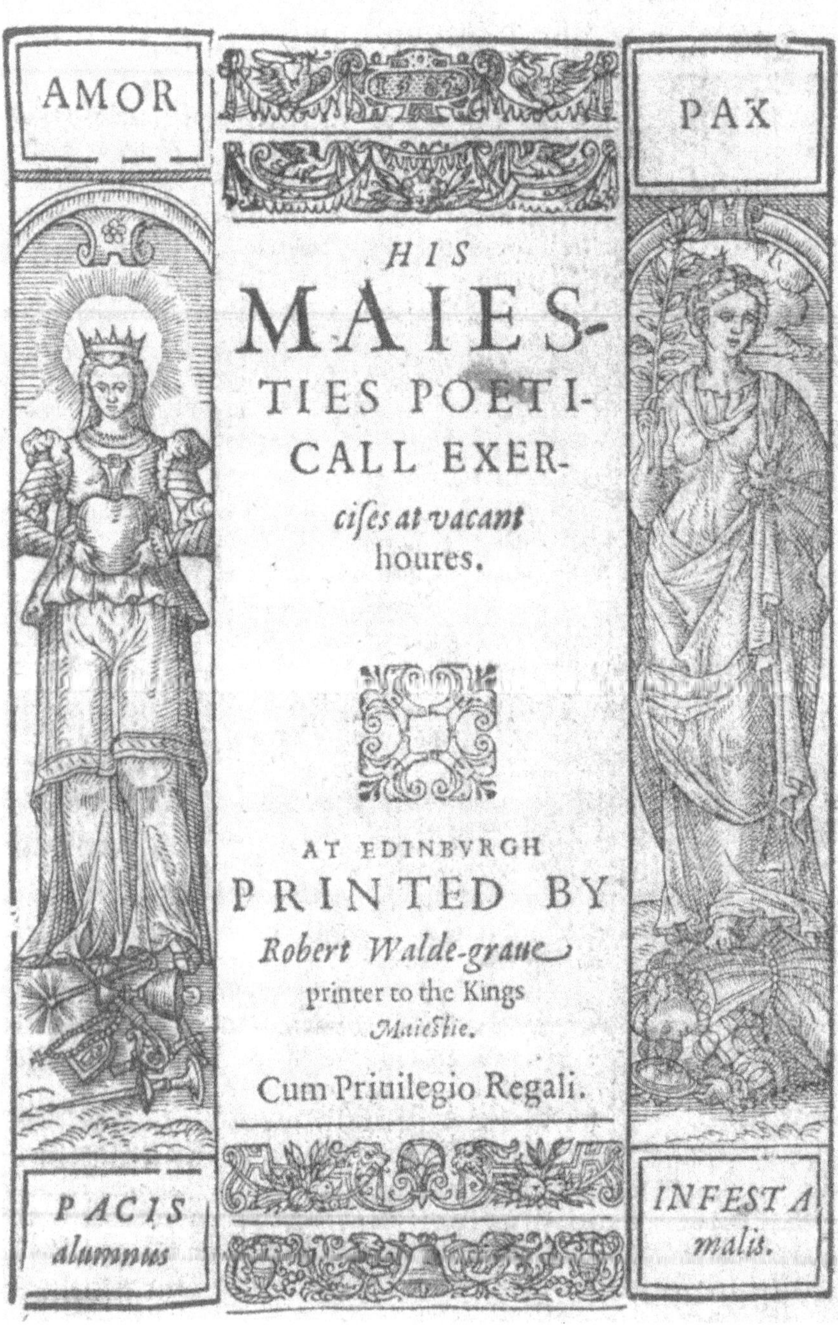

AMOR

PAX

HIS
MAIES-
TIES POETI-
CALL EXER-
cises at vacant
houres.

AT EDINBVRGH
PRINTED BY
Robert Walde-graue
printer to the Kings
Maiestie.

Cum Priuilegio Regali.

PACIS
alumnus

INFESTA
malis.

Fig. 2.
Reproduced by permission of the Huntington Library, San Marino, California.

Fig. 3.
Reproduced by permission of the Huntington Library, San Marino, California.

out, in the first edition's dedication page "the relations between ruler and subject are graphically manifested," the queen's name in boldface, capital letters while Spenser's appears "in the lower right-hand corner of the page, in much smaller and italicized type, with only the initial letters capitalized and his given name abbreviated to 'Ed.'"[86] In the 1596 edition, the printer no longer distinguished between the ruling subject and the ruled author, using the same size and type of font for both and thus signaling the rise in poetic authorship's cultural capital. "For Spenser," Montrose writes, "the material process of reproducing and distributing his poetry in printed books was culturally empowering."[87]

James clearly agreed, and I suggest that he wanted to arrogate for himself some of poetic authorship's cultural empowerment upon his ascension to the English throne in 1603. Consequently, in addition to other displays intended to underscore his new strategy, he reprinted the *Lepanto,* this time using the London printers Simon Stafford and Henry Hooke (a Latin edition appeared one year later); several small changes in book layout from the poem's original publication demonstrate that the king and the printers wanted the reader to interpret the 1603 *Lepanto* as a monarchic performance.[88] First, as the title page shows (fig. 4), Stafford and Hook print "Majesties" in larger type than anything else, and, unlike the title page of the 1591 edition, not even a syllable break draws attention away from the poem's royal authorship. Second, whereas "The Lepanto" appears as the running head on the verso pages of the 1591 edition (fig. 5), in 1603 the printer changed this phrase to "The *Kings* Lepanto" (fig. 6; my emphasis). The running head of the recto pages, "Or, Heroicall Song," is unchanged.

The question remains as to why James would take the trouble to reprint this poem as part of his accession celebrations. One reason might be that he considered this accession a propitious time to appropriate for himself once more the cultural capital of poetic authorship—epic poetic authorship in particular—so as further to legitimate himself in a country not known for its high estimation of Scotland's cultural heritage.[89] James's reputation as a royal poet, as Curtis Perry notes, had achieved wide circulation by at least 1600, and reprinting the *Lepanto* can be seen as an attempt to strengthen this image (the irony being that English poets used James to bolster poetry's sagging reputation in England).[90] In addition, he might have wanted to present something that would further reassure England of his Protestant bona fides, so he republished the 1591 preface, which asserts the author's allegiance to Protestantism and his revulsion of Catholicism. Perhaps both explanations are likely, and both demonstrate, once more, a monarch using poetry as a vehicle for politics. Yet in 1603 England already had its epic poet, Edmund Spenser. I would speculate that in addition to the reasons stated above, James may have also specifically intended the 1603 *Lepanto* to dislodge Spenser from that position.[91]

HIS

MAIESTIES

LEPANTO,

Or,

HEROICALL SONG,

being part of his Poeticall exerciſes *at vacant houres.*

Imprinted at London by Simon Stafford, and Henry Hooke.

1603.

FIG. 4.

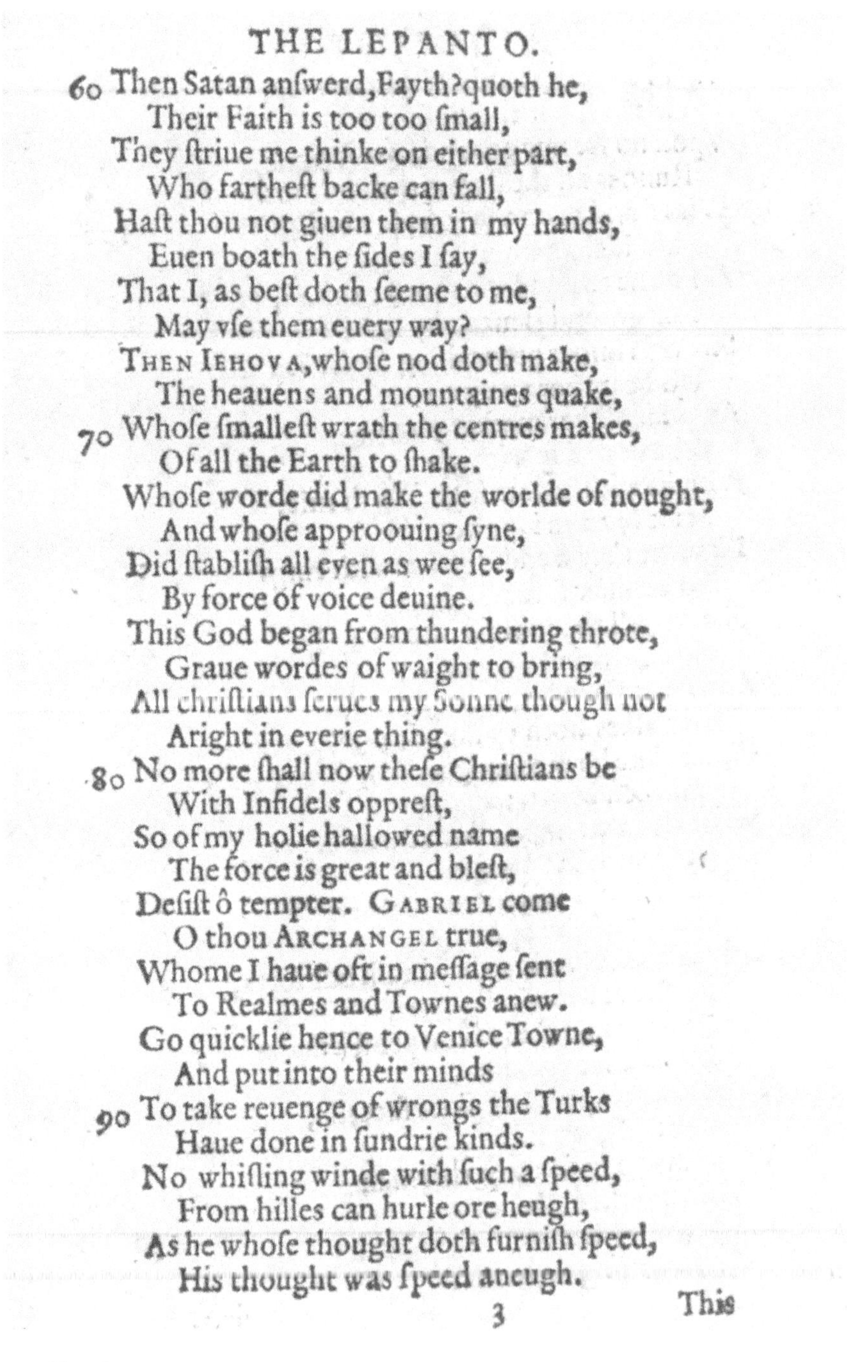

Then Satan anſwerd,Fayth?quoth he,
Their Faith is too too ſmall,
They ſtriue me thinke on either part,
Who fartheſt backe can fall,
Haſt thou not giuen them in my hands,
Euen boath the ſides I ſay,
That I, as beſt doth ſeeme to me,
May vſe them euery way?
THEN IEHOVA,whoſe nod doth make,
The heauens and mountaines quake,
Whoſe ſmalleſt wrath the centres makes,
Of all the Earth to ſhake.
Whoſe worde did make the worlde of nought,
And whoſe approouing ſyne,
Did ſtabliſh all even as wee ſee,
By force of voice deuine.
This God began from thundering throte,
Graue wordes of waight to bring,
All chriſtians ſerues my Sonne though not
Aright in everie thing.
No more ſhall now theſe Chriſtians be
With Infidels oppreſt,
So of my holie hallowed name
The force is great and bleſt,
Deſiſt ô tempter. GABRIEL come
O thou ARCHANGEL true,
Whome I haue oft in meſſage ſent
To Realmes and Townes anew.
Go quicklie hence to Venice Towne,
And put into their minds
To take reuenge of wrongs the Turks
Haue done in ſundrie kinds.
No whiſling winde with ſuch a ſpeed,
From hilles can hurle ore heugh,
As he whoſe thought doth furniſh ſpeed,
His thought was ſpeed aneugh.

FIG. 5.
Reproduced by permission of the Huntington Library, San Marino, California.

The Kings Lepanto,

Yet did the wiſdomes of the Chiefes,
  And of the generall moſt,
Compound all quarrels and debates
  That were, into that Hoſt,
Preferring wiſely as they ought,
  The honour of the Lord,
Vnto their owne, the publike cauſe,
  To priuate mens diſcord.
The feathered fame of wondrous ſpeed,
  That doth delight to flee
On tops of houſes pratling all
  That ſhe can heare or ſee,
Part true, part falſe: this monſter ſtrang
  Among the Turkes did tell,
That diuers Chriſtian Princes ioynd,
  Reſolu'd with them to mel.
Then ſpyes were ſent abroad, who told
  The matter as it ſtood,
Except in Arythmetique (as

Fig. 6.
Reproduced by permission of the Huntington Library, San Marino, California.

Certainly, James had reason for wanting to eclipse Spenser. In November 1596, books IV, V, and VI of the *Faerie Queene* appeared, and Robert Bowes informed Burghley that James wanted action taken against the poet:

> The K[ing] hath conceaved great offence against Edward [sic] Spencer publishing in prynte in the second book p[art] of the Fairy Queene and ixth chapter some dishonorable effects (as the k. demeth therof) against himself and his mother deceassed. He alledged that this booke was passed with prviledge of her mats [majesty's] Commission[er]s for the veiwe and allowance of all wrytinges to be receaved into Printe. But therein I have (I think) satisfyed him that it is not given with such p[ri]viledge: yet he still desyreth that Edward Spencer for faulte, may be dewly tryed & punished.[92]

To be sure, James's motivation here arose from something more (or less) than filial piety. Impugning his mother meant impugning his lineage. James, ever sensitive to anything that might jeopardize his chance to succeed Elizabeth, clearly considered Spenser's poem sufficiently authoritative to be a threat, and so he wanted Spenser punished. Elizabeth never responded to James's request (although perhaps she did when she and her privy council urged Spenser's appointment as sheriff of Cork), and so Spenser remained officially unsanctioned, widely read, and celebrated as England's epic poet. By publishing his own epic in 1603, James gave notice that England's king was also an epic poet. Just as the monarch sits at the head of the English church, so should the poet-king stand at the head of English poetry. In other words, the royal epic poet should occupy the place in the canon now occupied by the late (and untitled) Edmund Spenser.

While James's *Lepanto* obviously does not approach Spenser's epic in terms of sheer size, the two publications share certain formal qualities. First, each includes a letter to the reader explaining the poem's meaning and complaining of previous misinterpretations. Spenser's letter attempts to explain the allegory because the author finds himself misunderstood ("Sir knowing how doubtfully all Allegories may be construed, and this booke of mine, which I have entituled the Faery Queene, being a continued Allegory, or darke conceite, I have thought aswell for avoyding gealous opinions and misconstructions, as also for your better light in reading therof . . . to discover unto you the general intention & meaning [of this text]");[93] James also writes his preface because he has (ostensibly) been "misconstrued by sundry" (198). Second, Spenser's epic begins with a series of commendatory sonnets that are often ascribed to initials rather than full names. In the 1591 version of the *Lepanto,* James included his own commendatory sonnet at the poem's end, signing it "I. R. S." (for *Jacobus Rex Scotorum*). But for the 1603 edition, he moved the sonnet from its original place and set it immediately before the poem, signing it "I. R." (sig. A3), not "I. R. S." Doubtless, dropping the "S" signals that he rules more than just Scotland, but it also has the effect of echoing the two letter initials that Spenser used to sign his commendatory sonnets "E. S."

Though James's preface predates Spenser's by five years, that fact might not have been immediately obvious to English readers: the *Poeticall Exercises* was published in Edinburgh, making it unlikely that more than a handful of people in London had read it. With regard to the London book-buying audience, therefore, it is at least possible that a reader familiar with both texts considered James's preface an imitation of Spenser's, and because of James's position as king, it would perforce supercede Spenser's. Also, while I am not going to claim that the presence of commendatory sonnets with just two identifying initials is so unique as to prove the connection, I would point out that in 1603 there was only one epic around that had such sonnets and a defensive letter to the reader—Spenser's *Faerie Queene.* Taken together, these facts make it conceivable that James hoped his readers would be aware of the connection between the *Lepanto* and Spenser's poem. The point, however, would not be homage, since James considered the *Faerie Queene* a threat (perhaps it is lucky that Spenser died in 1599). Rather, I suggest that at some level James wanted to replace the *Faerie Queene,* which glorifies his predecessor and casts his mother as a whore, with the *Lepanto,* the king's own Protestant epic. The 1603 Lepanto, in sum, announces to his new kingdom that James, not Spenser, deserves the title of England's Protestant Virgil.

Like Henry VIII, Mary, and Elizabeth, and like many of their courtiers during this period, King James VI and I wrote poetry for both pleasure and political advantage. Yet while courtly verse is written from below, monarchic verse is written from above. That is to say, James, like his royal predecessors and fellow monarch Elizabeth, always writes *as a monarch,* never simply as a poet. Thus he reminds Elizabeth of his sonnet's royal authorship, knowing that the poem's meaning derives from the speaker's status, and thus he turns both his elegy for Sidney and the various manuscript and print versions of the *Lepanto* into vehicles for monarchic diplomacy and display. For James, no discourse existed separate from sovereignty. Ironically though, once he established himself on the English throne, his interest in book publication seemed to vanish, though he continued occasionally to write and distribute politically charged poems. So while the title page of his 1616 collected works constitutes the most elaborate construction to date of James as royal author (the full title is *The Workes of the Most High and Mighty Prince, James*),[94] he conspicuously omitted poetry from this text.[95] But even though James published no verse after 1603, his sovereign discourse nonetheless initially depended upon his manipulation of verse. As Antonio reminds both the good Gonzalo and his courtly audience in *The Tempest*[96]—a play James may have seen twice—the end should not forget its beginning.[97]

Notes

1. On James's prose, see, for example, Wormald and Sommerville. In addition, while there are several recent editions of James's political writings, the only edition of James's poetry remains *The Poems of James VI. of Scotland,* ed. Craigie. As for James's verse, as Kevin Sharpe notes, it "has received no historical and little critical evaluation" ("The King's Writ" 127). Other studies include Goldberg 17–28; Sharpe, "Private Conscience and Public Duty"; and Perry 15–24. This critical neglect, however, will soon be ameliorated by this volume and by forthcoming work from Daniel Fischlin, Sandra Bell, and Robert Appelbaum.
2. Montrose, "'Eliza, Queene of Sheapheardes'" 154.
3. *Letters of Queen Elizabeth and King James VI. of Scotland,* vol. 46, no. XIX, 30–31.
4. *Letters* no. XX, 32.
5. *Letters,* headnote to no. XXI, 33.
6. *Letters* no. XI, 34. Even so, Elizabeth adds that she "haue sent you a lettar that I am sure containes all you desired in spetiall wordes, I trust it shal content you" (34). To my knowledge, this letter has been lost, although David Harris Willson assumes that it contained "a revised statement concerning the succession" (72).
7. *Letters of King James VI & I* 71–72.
8. The annotations of obscure words are my own.
9. Qtd. in Willson 72.
10. Marotti, "Love is not Love" 398. See also May 224–27 and passim as well as Montrose, "'Eliza, Queene of Sheapheardes.'"
11. Qtd. in Marotti, "Love is not Love" 399.
12. Montrose, "Celebration and Insinuation" 26.
13. I am grateful to Anne Lake Prescott for her help with this reference.
14. On Elizabeth as a monarchic poet, see Jennifer Summit's article, "'The Arte of a Ladies Penne': Elizabeth I and the Poetics of Queenship" *ELR* 26 (1996): 395–422.
15. Hall 515.
16. All references to Henry's poetry are to Ray Siemens's selection of Henry's verse forthcoming in *Reading Monarchs Writing: The Poetry of Henry VIII, Mary Stuart, Elizabeth I and James VI/I* (MRTS).
17. Hall, for example, reports that "the ancient fathers much doubted [the prudence of Henry's jousting], considering the tender youth of the king, and divers chances of horses and armour: in so much that it was openly spoken, that steel was not so strong, but it might be broken,

nor no horse could be so sure of foot, but he may fall" (520). For resistance in the council to Henry's declaration of war on France, see Baker-Smith 131–32.

18. Richard Pace, in a letter to Wolsey, noted that the royal almoner incorporated this lyric into a sermon preached in the King's hall in March of 1521 (*L&P Henry VIII* III [i]: 447, #1188). In Scotland, the music of Henry's "Pastyme with good companye" appears, without lyrics, in the commonplace book of Robert Edward (1616–96) and, prior to that, in the commonplace book of his father, Alexander of Dundee (Edinburgh, National Library of Scotland, Panmure ms. 9,450), and it is mentioned as the first of the shepherd's songs in *The Complaynt of Scotland* (1549; London: Early English Text Society, 1872, 64). The song also achieved international circulation: Melchiore de Barberiis's tenth lutebook (Venice, 1549) contains a version headed "Pas de mi bon compagni." I am grateful to Ray Siemens for supplying me with these citations, which are taken from his forthcoming edition of Henry's complete lyrics (Early English Text Society).
19. Mary's sonnets were first published in George Buchanan, *Ane Detectioun of the Duinges of Marie Quene of Scottes* (1572), and I have used this edition for both the French and the Anglo-Scots translation. The headnote to the sonnets does not state who did the translation, although it is possible that it was Buchanan.
20. Cotgrave sig. Kkk iiiiiv.
21. On England as a mixed monarchy, see Fink; Guy 13–46, esp. 17–19; Hanson 240–52; and Eccleshall.
22. Qtd. in R. H. Mahon, *The Indictment of Mary Queen of Scots* (Cambridge: Cambridge UP, 1923), 25.
23. Foucault 138.
24. Ibid.
25. See Perry's analysis of the tensions between James's status as monarch and Petrarchan poetics in James's early love poems (21–23).
26. In no. XVII, Elizabeth explicitly endorses James's theory of absolute kingship: "Since God hathe made kinges, let them not unmake ther authorite, and let brokes and smal rivers acknowledge ther springes, and flowe no furdar than ther bankes. I praise God that you uphold euer a regal rule" (*Letters* 27).
27. Montrose, "'Shaping Fantasies'" 31.
28. Akrigg avers that lines 11 and 12 "are intelligible as they stand. Apparently the King, when copying his poem, carelessly left out some word such as 'joys' after 'his'" (*Letters of King James* 72). Craigie, however, using a later copy of the poem (he dates it from 1604) from a different source (Hatfield mss., *Historical MSS. Commission, Part*

XVI [1933], 393), gives exactly the same reading (*Poems of James VI* 2: 171), suggesting that "his" means "the lovers belong to Cupid" rather than referring to Cupid's "joys" or whatever.

29. *Letters,* no. XVI, 24–25.
30. *Letters,* no. XVII, 27, 28.
31. Akrigg, *Letters of King James,* Letter 15 (3 August? 1585), 64.
32. Shell, *The End of Kinship* 109–10.
33. Shell, *Elizabeth's Glass* 69.
34. Henry VII's daughter Margaret was James's grandmother.
35. Shell, *The End of Kinship* 113. Shell expands this argument in the introduction to *Elizabeth's Glass,* 3–73.
36. All citations will be to the facsimile reproduction of this text in *Elegies for Sir Philip Sidney* (1587).
37. There are in fact two sets of "K" signatures, which caused me no end of confusion when I went to find James's poem.
38. Baker-Smith 94.
39. See also Campbell 45–49.
40. Read II: 212–13. According to Willson, Walsingham "told James that his power was insignificant, that he was too young to judge affairs of State, that he should rejoice in such a friend as Elizabeth, and [most interestingly] that young kings who sought to be absolute were apt to lose their thrones" (51).
41. Qtd. in Craigie, *Poems of James VI* 2: 234.
42. Baker-Smith 93, 94.
43. Howell 106.
44. Ibid.
45. Letter to Lewis Bellenden, dated 12 April 1585, in *Letters of King James.*
46. Qtd. in Read II: 246.
47. Qtd. in Read II: 248.
48. Cf. Baker-Smith 95.
49. See the summary of the various reports of James's reactions—which range from his being entirely unmoved to swearing revenge for his mother's death—in Stafford 17.
50. Ibid.
51. Stafford 13, who relies on Sir Robert S. Rait and Annie I. Cameron, *King James's Secret* (London, 1927).
52. Stafford 18.
53. Stafford 21.
54. My approach to the thematic significances of book production is deeply indebted to David Scott Kastan and Leah Marcus.

55. Sidney 49.
56. Craigie, "Introduction," *Poems of James VI* 1: lix–lx; Appelbaum 9.
57. Appelbaum 22; *New Cambridge Modern History, vol. II: The Counter-Reformation and Price Revolution,* ed. R. Wernham (Cambridge: Cambridge UP, 1979), 252–53 and 353–54.
58. Braudel 2: 1103; Appelbaum 23.
59. Michel de Montaigne, for instance, uses this battle as an example of why we should not interpret earthly events as indicators of divine will: "It was a notable Sea-battle, which was lately gained against the Turkes, under the conduct of Don John of Austria. But it hath pleased God to make us at other times both see and feele other such, to our no small losse and detriment" (*Essayes of Montaigne* 172). Donald Frame translates these lines as: "It was a fine naval battle that was won these past months against the Turks, under the leadership of Don John of Austria; but it has certainly pleased God at other times to let us see others like it, at our expense" (*Complete Essays of Montaigne* 160).
60. See Strong 115; also Herman, "'Is this Winning?'" 2.
61. Lee 64.
62. Willson 51.
63. Fischlin 5.
64. Fischlin 8.
65. All references to the *Lepanto* are to *Poems of James VI,* ed. Craigie 1: 198–258; I have silently adopted the modern usage of u/v and i/j.
66. Willson 39.
67. Qtd. in Willson 39, who also cites these other examples of English exasperation to James's "diplomacy": "'The King's fair speeches and promises,' wrote an English noble, 'will fall out to be plain dissimulation, wherein he is in his tender years better practised than others forty years older than he is.' He 'is holden among the Scots for the greatest dissembler that ever was heard of for his years'" (39). Indeed, reading over their correspondence and Walsingham's various reports of his negotiations with James, it is hard not to have the sense that during the early years of James's reign Elizabeth considered him an intensely annoying little twerp who exasperated her beyond measure. Even so, James did get what he wanted, perhaps using apparent weakness to his advantage.
68. Both quotes are cited in Willson 51.
69. Willson 52.
70. Willson 81.
71. Willson 71.
72. Even though James threw the Spanish agent, Colonel Semple, in prison after the defeat of the Armada ("with great Protestant zeal," as Willson says), he nonetheless allowed him to escape (Willson 84).

73. Even though some of James's poetry made its way into two English miscellanies—*Englands Parnassus* and John Bodenham's *Bel-Vedére, Or the Garden of the Muses* (1600) (Perry 24; May, "Tudor Aristocrats" 16–17)—there is no evidence that the *Lepanto* underwent unauthorized manuscript transmission, which suggests that James is making up this scenario of uncontrolled transmission. Furthermore, James's poetry rarely appears in contemporary miscellanies, and an entry in Stephen Powle's commonplace book suggests that the king rather tightly controlled the copying of his lyric verses. Concerning "In Sunny Beames the Skye Doth Shewe Her Sweete," Powle writes that the poem was "Geaven me by Master Britton who had been (as he sayed) in Scotland with the Kinges Majesty: But I rather thinke they weare made by him in the person of the Kinge" (qtd. in Marotti, *Manuscript,* 14).
74. Goldberg 18.
75. Saunders. On the Protestant roots of anti-poetic sentiment and how the attacks on poetry constitute a shaping presence in early modern poetic production, see my *Squitter-wits and Muse-haters;* also May 17. See also Richard Helgerson, *Self-Crowned Laureates: Spenser, Jonson, Milton and the Literary System* (Berkeley: U of California P, 1983).
76. On book publishing's movement from an elite to a mass market, resulting in the industry's losing "its glamour" and becoming "an almost humdrum affair," see Lisa Jardine, "The Triumph of the Book" (*Worldly Goods: A New History of the Book* [New York: Norton, 1996], 135–80). While Jardine's point is to examine how "the staggering escalation in book production in the course of the sixteenth century was consistently driven by commercial pressures" (179–80), she also implicitly helps explain why aristocrats, who define themselves by their lack of involvement in commercial affairs, would shy away from publishing much themselves.
77. Wall 26. Wall does not dispute the existence of Saunders's "stigma," but she brilliantly elucidates the gender issues involved with "being a man in print."
78. Qtd. in Marotti, *Manuscript* 228.
79. May, "Tudor Aristocrats" 15, 17.
80. However, the title page of Henry's book attacking Luther hardly privileges its royal authorship. The first two words of the title, *Libello Huic,* are printed in bold letters, and they are twice as big as the rest: *Regio Haec Insunt.* Underneath we have a table of contents, but Henry is not mentioned until the fifth item, "Libellus regius adversis Martinum" (the title page is reproduced in Neville Williams, *Henry*

VIII and His Court [London: Weidenfield & Nicolson, 1971], 86). In this case, the matter supercedes authorship in importance.

81. One wonders if James intended a reference to Montaigne's *Essais*, first published in 1580–81.
82. Cf. May's analysis, "Tudor Aristocrats" 16.
83. See Kastan 216–18.
84. Marotti, *Manuscript* 229–30.
85. Ibid., 223–25.
86. Montrose, "Spenser's Domestic Domain" 87.
87. Ibid.
88. Even so, the reception of the 1603 *Lepanto* pales in comparison to the huge success of the 1603 *Basilikon Doron*, which went through eight editions in 1603 alone (Wormald 51).
89. In England, according to the earl of Northumberland, "the name of Scots is harsh in the ears of the vulgar," and the more sophisticated "feared 'swarms of tawny Scots' who, locust-like, would devour office and wealth." The degree of contempt was so great that "the decapitated skull of a Scottish king was used as a flowerpot in the English royal conservatory" (Kishlansky 78).
90. Perry 23.
91. As fantastically hubristic as this suggestion may sound, James never exhibited a lack of self-esteem, and the celebrations surrounding his ascension may have further encouraged his inflated sense of poetic accomplishment.
92. Qtd. in Goldberg 1.
93. Spenser 15.
94. Interestingly, the printer uses the same size font for "Workes" and "James," thereby privileging neither one, as is the case in James's previous publications.
95. Craigie notes, however, that a manuscript in the British Museum (ms. add. 24195), entitled *All the kings short poesis that ar not printed,* may represent "the intention, never carried out," to publish a companion volume to the 1616 collected prose of James's poetry ("Introduction," *Poems of James VI* 2: xxiii). On the other hand, given that the manuscript was revised by Prince Charles and Thomas Carey, James's Groom of the Chamber, and corrected by the king himself, it is equally plausible that they wanted this collection to remain private.
96. According to Frank Kermode's introduction to *The Tempest* in the Riverside edition, Shakespeare's company performed the play at court in 1611 and in 1612–13 (1606).
97. I am very grateful to San Diego State University's College of Arts and Letters for awarding me a Faculty Development Program, half-time

leave grant that allowed me to research this essay as well as a CAL Micro-Grant which paid for the illustrations. I also want to thank Daniel Fischlin for commissioning this essay and for his help along the way.

Works Cited

Appelbaum, Robert. "War and Peace in James VI/I's *Lepanto.*" *Reading Monarchs Writing.* Ed. Peter C. Herman. Also *Modern Philology.* (Both forthcoming.)

Baker-Smith, Dominic. "'Great Expectations: Sidney's Death and the Poets." *Sir Philip Sidney: 1586 and the Creation of a Legend.* Ed. Jan Van Dorsten et al. Leiden: Brill, 1996. 129–44.

———. "'Inglorious glory': 1513 and the Humanist Attack on Chivalry." *Chivalry in the Renaissance.* Ed. Sydney Anglo. Woodbridge, England: Boydell, 1990. 83–103.

Bell, Sandra. "Kingcraft and Poetry: James VI's Cultural Policy." *Reading Monarchs Writing.* Ed. Peter C. Herman. (Forthcoming.)

Braudel, Ferdinand. *The Mediterranean and the Mediterranean World in the Age of Philip II.* 2 vols. Trans. Sian Reynolds. New York: Harper and Row, 1972.

Campbell, Lily B. "The Christian Muse." *Huntington Library Quarterly* 8 (1939): 29–70.

Cotgrave, Randle. *A Dictionarie of the French and English Tongues.* London, 1611.

Eccleshall, Robert. *Order and Reason in Politics: Theories of Absolute and Limited Monarchy in Early Modern England.* Oxford: Oxford UP, 1978.

Elegies for Sir Philip Sidney (1587). Ed. A. J. Colaianne and W. L. Godshalk. Delmar, N.Y.: Scholars' Facsimiles and Reprints, 1980.

Fink, Zera. *The Classical Republicans: An Essay on the Recovery of a Pattern of Thought in Seventeenth-Century England.* Evanston: U of Illinois P, 1945.

Fischlin, Daniel. "'Like a Mercenary Poët': The Politics and Poetics of James VI's *Lepanto.*" *Essays on Older Scots Literature.* Vol. 3. Ed. Sally Mapstone. East Linton: Tuckwell P. Forthcoming.

Foucault, Michel. "What is an Author?" *Language, Counter-Memory, Practice: Selected Essays and Interviews.* Ed. Donald F. Bouchard. Ithaca: Cornell UP, 1977. 113–38.

Goldberg, Jonathan. *James I and the Politics of Literature: Jonson, Shakespeare, Donne and Their Contemporaries.* Rpt. Stanford: Stanford UP, 1989.

Guy, John. "The Henrician Age." *The Varieties of British Political Thought, 1500–1800.* Ed. Quentin Skinner. Cambridge: Cambridge UP, 1993. 13–46.

Hall, Edward. *Hall's Chronicle Containing the History of England during the Reign of Henry the Fourth and the Succeeding Monarchs to the End of the Reign of Henry the Eighth* [original title: *The Union of the Two Noble and Illustre Famelies of Lancastre & Yorke*]. Ed. Sir Henry Ellis. London: J. Johnson et al., 1809.

Hanson, Donald W. *From Kingdom to Commonwealth: The Development of Civic Consciousness in English Political Thought.* Cambridge, Mass.: Harvard UP, 1970.

Harington, Sir John. *Nugœ Antiquœ: Being a Miscellaneous Collection of Original Papers in Prose and Verse.* Ed. Henry Harington. 2 vols. London: W. Frederick, 1775.

Herman, Peter C. "'Is this Winning?': Prince Henry's Death and the Problem of Chivalry in *The Two Noble Kinsmen.*" *South Atlantic Review* 62.1 (1997): 1–31.

———. "'Mes subjectz, mon ame assubjectie': The Problematic (of) Subjectivity in Mary Stuart's Sonnets." *Reading Monarchs Writing.* Ed. Herman. Forthcoming.

———. *Squitter-wits and Muse-haters: Sidney, Spenser, Milton and Renaissance Anti-poetic Sentiment.* Detroit: Wayne State UP, 1996.

———, ed. *Reading Monarchs Writing: The Poetry of Henry VIII, Mary Stuart, Elizabeth I, and James VI/I.* Medieval and Renaissance Text Society. Forthcoming.

Herman, Peter C., and Ray Siemens. "Henry VIII and the Poetry of Politics." *Reading Monarchs Writing.* Ed. Herman. Forthcoming.

Howell, Roger. *Sir Philip Sidney: The Shepheard Knight.* Boston: Little, Brown, 1968.

James VI and I. *Letters of King James VI & I.* Ed. G. P. V. Akrigg. Berkeley: U of California P, 1984.

———. *The Poems of James VI. of Scotland.* 2 vols. Ed. James Craigie. Edinburgh: Scottish Text Society, 1955.

Kastan, David Scott. "Shakespeare After Theory." *Opening the Borders: Inclusivity and Early Modern Studies, Essays in Honor of James V. Mirollo.* Ed. Peter C. Herman. Newark, Del.: U of Delaware P, 1999. 206–24.

Kishlansky, Mark. *A Monarchy Transformed: Britain 1603–1714.* London: Penguin, 1996.

Lee, Maurice. *Great Britain's Solomon: James VI and I in His Three Kingdoms.* Urbana: U of Illinois P, 1990.

Letters of Queen Elizabeth and King James VI. of Scotland. Ed. John Bruce. Camden Society; Old Series, vol. 46.

Marcus, Leah S. *Unediting the Renaissance: Shakespeare, Marlowe, Milton.* New York: Routledge, 1996.

Marotti, Arthur F. "Love is not Love: Elizabethan Sonnet Sequences and the Social Order." *ELH* 49 (1982): 396–428.

———. *Manuscript, Print, and the English Renaissance Lyric.* Ithaca: Cornell UP, 1995.

May, Steven W. *The Elizabethan Courtier Poets.* Columbia: U of Missouri P, 1991.

———. "Tudor Aristocrats and the Mythical 'Stigma of Print.'" *Renaissance Papers* (1980): 11–18.

Montaigne, Michel de. *The Complete Essays of Montaigne.* Ed. and trans. Donald Frame. Stanford: Stanford UP, 1965.

———. *The Essayes of Montaigne: John Florio's Translation.* New York: Modern Library, n.d.

Montrose, Louis A. "Celebration and Insinuation: Sir Philip Sidney and the Motives of Elizabethan Courtship." *Renaissance Drama* n.s. 8 (1977): 3–35.

———. "'Eliza, Queene of Shepheardes,' and the Pastoral of Power." *English Literary Renaissance* 10 (1980): 153–82.

———. "'Shaping Fantasies': Figurations of Gender and Power in Elizabethan Culture." *Representing the English Renaissance.* Ed. Stephen Greenblatt. Berkeley: U of California P, 1988. 31–64.

———. "Spenser's Domestic Domain: Poetry, Property, and the Early Modern Subject." *Subject and Object in Renaissance Culture.* Ed. Margreta de Grazia, Maureen Quilligan, and Peter Stallybrass. Cambridge: Cambridge UP, 1996. 83–132.

Perry, Curtis. *The Making of Jacobean Culture: James I and the Renegotiation of Elizabethan Literary Practice.* Cambridge: Cambridge UP, 1997.

Read, Conyers. *Mr. Secretary Walsingham and the Policy of Queen Elizabeth.* 2 vols. Oxford: Oxford UP, 1925.

Saunders, J. W. "The Stigma of Print: A Note on the Social Bases of Tudor Poetry." *Essays in Criticism* 1.2 (1951): 139–64.

Sharpe, Kevin. "The King's Writ: Royal Authors and Royal Authority in Early Modern England." *Culture and Politics in Early Stuart England.* Stanford: Stanford UP, 1993. 117–38.

———. "Private Conscience and Public Duty in the Writings of King James VI and I." *Public Duty and Private Conscience in Seventeenth Century England.* Ed. J. Morrill, Peter Slack, and Daniel Woolf. London: Macmillan, 1994. 77–100.

Shell, Marc. *Elizabeth's Glass.* Lincoln: U of Nebraska P, 1993.

———. *The End of Kinship: "Measure for Measure," Incest, and the Ideal of Universal Siblinghood.* Stanford: Stanford University Press, 1988.

Sidney, Sir Philip. *An Apology for Poetry.* Ed. Forrest G. Robinson. Indianapolis: Bobbs-Merrill, 1970.

Sommerville, J. P. "James I and the Divine Right of Kings: English Politics and Continental Theory." *The Mental World of the Jacobean Court.* Ed. Linda Levy Peck. Cambridge: Cambridge UP, 1991. 55–70.

Spenser, Edmund. *The Faerie Queene.* Ed. Thomas P. Roche. New Haven: Yale UP, 1978.

Stafford, Helen G. *James VI of Scotland and the Throne of England.* New York: Appleton, 1940.

Stevens, John. *Music and Poetry in the Early Tudor Court.* Lincoln: U of Nebraska P, 1961.

Strong, Roy. *Henry, Prince of Wales and England's Lost Renaissance.* London: Thames and Hudson, 1986.

Stuart, Mary (Mary, Queen of Scots). *Sonnets.* George Buchanan, *Ane Detectioun of the Duinges of Marie Quene of Scottes.* London, 1572.

Wall, Wendy. *The Imprint of Gender: Authorship and Publication in the English Renaissance.* Ithaca: Cornell UP, 1993.

Willson, David Harris. *King James VI and I.* London: Jonathan Cape, 1956.

Wormald, Jenny. "James VI and I, *Basilikon Doron* and *The Trew Law of Free Monarchies:* The Scottish Context and the English Translation." *The Mental World of the Jacobean Court.* Ed. Linda Levy Peck. Cambridge: Cambridge UP, 1991. 36–54.

2

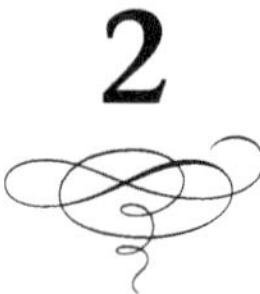

"The Fountain and Very Being of Truth": James VI, Poetic Invention, and National Identity

Carolyn Ives and David J. Parkinson

James VI formulated his notions regarding the connection between kingship and authorship during his adolescence. In the span from commencement of personal rule (1579) to abduction in the Ruthven Raid (1582), the young Scottish king discovered what would be for both his reigns the defining themes connecting monarch and author. He figured the energies of each in terms of copious, inexhaustible flow—fluency—in many senses. For the young James, his self-fashioning as monarch and author can best be synthesized in the topic of origins. Both types of authority take as their emblem the fountain, traditionally likened to the heart, a source unaugmentable by any tributary, but also a conduit of divine power. *The Essayes of a Prentise in the Divine Art of Poesie*—the volume of essays, translations, and original verse James published in 1585, shortly after his escape from his Ruthven captors—works insistently upon this theme.

The more attentive among the writers at James's court were alert to this insistence. Among them was Alexander Montgomerie, who wrote an occasional piece, "The Navigatioun," which refers to flow as both dangerous and reassuring:

> We shaip to saill neir the Septentrion
>
> Touards the North and helthsome regione
>
> Nou callit Scotland, as we haif hard report
>
> Of wandring fame vhilk fleeth ay athort

Quhair presently beginneth for to ring
So sapient a ying and godly King,
A Salomon for richt and judgment.
In eviry langage he is Eloquent.
All Lands about do beir of him record.
He is the chosen vessell of the Lord. (ll. 73–82)

By the early 1580s, James already exhibits the doubleness as source and "vessell" that would mark his reign. He uses images of water to emphasize the fluidity of his position as both king (source of power and vehicle for God's will) and poet (source of poetry and vehicle for the muses' power). Furthermore, his bodily representations—of both his physical body and his body of work—also rely on the gender distinctions that arise out of such dualities: as source, he is fixed, masculine; as vessel or vehicle, he is unstable, feminine. He becomes a hybrid of both self and other, a paradox that, rather than reconcile or diminish, he uses to his advantage.

With his self-awareness, even self-construction, James is a more complex figure in the history of cultural relations in Scotland than the clichés about his reign admit. To a great extent, he is the author of this complexity: to a degree unprecedented for a Scottish monarch (even given the literary reputations of James I, IV, and V, as well as Mary), James had a literary identity, as both apprentice practitioner and also lawgiver of Scottish poetry; he was both authoritative and deferential.[1] Fluency embodies both aspects of identity, the influential and the influenced, throughout *The Essayes.* In that collection of verse and criticism, James's images of floods and fountains reveal what Benedict Anderson has called "the older imagining, where states were defined by centres, borders were porous and indistinct, and sovereignties faded imperceptibly into one another."[2] For James, a certain indistinctness (irony, allusiveness, indirection) may have served political ends, with reference both to the neighboring kingdom of England and the aggressively anti-monarchic Kirk at home. What was at least as necessary was a clear presentation of his own double authority as king and poet, and in drawing attention to this at junctures in his writings, James was heir above all to James I, first prisoner and then lawgiver, as well as one of the earliest named Scottish poets, bearing the name of *auctor* through the sixteenth century.

Introducing a recent collection of essays on modern Scottish literature, Christopher Whyte envisions the productive influence that thinking about gender as a system containing diversity can have on thinking about nation. Identifying an oppressively exclusionary nationalism of self-absorbed, grand old men, marked by aggressiveness, xenophobia, and boozy nostalgia, he seeks instead "a range of possible ways of being Scottish."[3] Drawing on the works of Judith Butler and Eve Kosofsky Sedgwick, Whyte makes the case that "Precisely because in small, minority, emergent cultures, national identity can never be taken as given, these are privileged sites for the study of gender and its interaction with other factors in the formation of identity."[4]

This claim has large implications for the growing debate about the intersections of culture and politics in early modern Scotland, in particular from the Union of the Crowns in 1603 to the Union of the Parliaments in 1707. Even today, Scottish culture and literature tends to be represented as having passed through a brief golden age, preceded by barrenness and followed by nostalgia. In particular, literary historians often fix on the reign of James IV, 1489–1513, as Scotland's golden moment.[5] However, the still-influential emphasis on triumphant Scottishness in the literary production of Henryson, Dunbar, or Douglas is highly ironic, especially given the intense engagement of Scottish readers and writers with English poetry during the reign of James, an engagement fueled by the hugely stepped-up importation and circulation of that poetry in printed form.

A prominent example will serve to uncover this irony. Into the sixteenth century, Scottish writers recognized Chaucer's body of work as an integral part of their poetic tradition: for all their awareness of conflicted historical traditions, they often declared that they were writing in "Inglis." Chaucer was exemplary mainly because he had already achieved the status of "auctour." With Scottish manuscripts and prints of Chauceriana circulating during the reign of James IV, this auctorial status took an assured, permanent hold on Scottish readers and writers just as they began to envision their own national literary tradition. Chaucer offered them the pattern of authorship, and from the ascription of the *Kingis Quair* to James I onward, they based their conceptions and practices of authorship on this pattern. Given what might be represented as the apparent indebtedness of a junior national literature to a senior, there is a risk of thinking about this literary culture as if it predicted its own demise: Flodden, or the Reformation, or royal capitulation/departure of one sort or another, were just at hand; and the confident bond between eloquent literature and devoted reader seemed no sooner made than broken.

Nostalgia reigned in its place: "There was a Glory."[6] "Ultimately the Union was responsible for making nostalgia the most characteristic emotion in the Scottish national psyche."[7] Seeing the passage from medieval to modern as the defining Scottish pattern of irreparable loss, Edwin Muir expressed a view in 1936 that reveals, and still exerts, influence: "The disintegration of Scottish poetry was accompanied by a disintegration of the Scots language, and both calamities, again, were brought about in part by political causes. Once the language was broken up, the old fusion between thought and feeling was lost, and a far-reaching dissociation set in, one of the most characteristic expressions of which was fantasy, which was an abortive and never quite serious attempt to achieve a synthesis between thought and feeling."[8] Thus emphasis on linguistic death emerged much earlier, in fact: at the beginning of the eighteenth century when Allan Ramsay rediscovered the Bannatyne Manuscript (the principal source of late medieval Scottish verse; dated 1568 by the scribe, with erasures of earlier dates), he professed having difficulties with its language, even though only a century-and-a-half had passed since its composition. Ramsay's struggle to comprehend is significant because of contemporary associations of fluency with power: at the time of the Act of Union of the Parliaments of England and Scotland (1707), Scottish writers opposing the act represented loss of fluency in one's own native language as loss of "national integrity."[9]

Whether in the eighteenth century or the sixteenth, politics reasserted itself in characteristic, predictable ways (internecine rivalry, treasonously opportunistic deals with the English), and broke up culture, which for many settled gradually into wishful retrospection. After zenith and collapse, the logical next phase in this history was attempted recuperation, with attention to accounts of salvage operations through which the riches of the past were recollected and enshrined. The protagonists of recuperation were represented as antiquarians and folklorists; their monuments were volumes such as the Bannatyne Manuscript and Ramsay's *Ever Green* (1724)—even Robert Burns's contributions to *The Scots Musical Museum* or Sir Walter Scott's *Minstrelsy of the Scottish Border.* What such a history emphasizes is the filial piety, prodigious memory, zealous energy, and, often, the coterie coziness of the rescuer, who in this role was praised less for being one who recreated and revised because of immediate personal and political circumstances than for being a devoted servant to the past. That is, a past when Scotland was more a nation than it was in the sixteenth or seventeenth century. The literature of that past was estimable because it made or reflected national character—taken as virile, masculine, energetic, and independent. It was a patrilinear literary tradition, with a father (Chaucer) whose strong sons (Henryson, Douglas, Dunbar) could draw upon and yet preclude him. Signs of openness, especially to less completely naturalized English models than that of Father Chaucer, were taken as signs of decay. If there must be a debt, let it be to one's own recognized ancestors, just as for Scottish kings, presumed descendants of the Irish Fergus, the myth of inviolability endured.[10] In their revisioning and finishing of Chaucerian texts, sixteenth-century Scottish poems were represented by their eighteenth-century editors as closed systems, much as Scotland itself was presented (*Nemo me impune lacessit*).

As Whyte suggests, these myths about the fall and partial rescue of Scottish literature are ripe for revaluation. Nowhere riper than in the case of James VI. Bluntly, James is a villain of traditional Scottish cultural history. He sold out and headed south. Starved and centerless, language, literature, music, art, and architecture fragmented and expired. This crude summary has been vigorously contested,[11] but James himself continues to languish under disapproval. It may be relevant that James does not cut a conventionally impressive figure in cultural memory: Sir Anthony Weldon's damningly memorable portrait of the waddling, slurping, twiddling king; Henri IV's gibe about the wisest fool in Christendom; the perennial gossip about drinking, hunting, and intimate male friends—these hardly produce a traditional image of masculine assertiveness and confidence.[12] In what is traditionally regarded as feminine behavior, James lied, sobbed, wheedled, stormed, was or appeared to have been influenced and prevailed upon, and leaked away to an English throne. Even, or especially, in his efforts to assert and extend authority—his pursuit of the English crown, but meanwhile also his assertion of episcopacy against the outspoken Presbyterianism of the Kirk, and his fascinated involvement in the Scottish witch-craze—James is taken to have been acting out, reiteratively, the need to demonize the perceived opponent as "the locus of a particular kind of gendered and imaginary power seen as threatening," an imaginary power that "was a necessary construction of the very hierarchies that sought to eradicate it."[13] Ironically, therefore, both James and his opponents explicitly used the same gender distinctions, attacking what they perceived to be feminine or untrustworthy. As thus constructed, James's own demonologies interestingly prefigure those of traditionally nationalist histories of Scotland.

Poets and monarch participated in the fabrication of a gendered hierarchy of cultural and political value, in which what must be protected is depicted as most masculine, and what threatens, the "monstrous double," most feminine. In doing so, they had recourse to well-established medical discourse on gender. Galen's was not the only model for sexual difference, but it predominated until the eighteenth century. According to Thomas Laqueur, Galen "demonstrated at length that women were essentially men in whom a lack of vital heat—of perfection—had resulted in the retention, inside, of structures that in the male are visible without."[14] Although some degree of equality is implied by Galen's belief in the ability of both men and women to produce sperm (suggesting that both parties play equally important roles in the reproductive process), the idea that women are inferior men underlies this belief.[15] It is easy to impose a hierarchy upon things that are similar enough to be comparable: women as a separate sex, as Other, are not as easily disregarded or shoved into the lower end of the hierarchy as women who are perceived to be flawed men, even if both depictions of women are perceived as threatening.[16] In the one-sex model, gender distinctions become more fluid, more easily detached from their respectively associated sexes.

The concepts of sex and gender, therefore, presented less rigid borders in the sixteenth century than they did in the eighteenth century, when the idea was rejected that "nuanced differences between organs, fluids, and physiological processes mirrored a transcendental order of perfection."[17] Upon belief in the fluidity of gender distinctions James founded his theory of invention as enabling principle of authorship and kingship. The gendered hierarchializing his belief entailed cannot escape the blurring of categories and the discovery of doubles. As Daniel Fischlin says about James's *Daemonologie*,

> Just as Satan is God's monstrous double, so is the absolute monarch a monstrous double to Satan, if only for the fact that both use forms of counterfeit to produce the illusory nature of their power. This anxious formulation is at the core of the rhetorical and ideological structures evident in *Daemonology*, however sublimated such structures may be. The consistent emphasis evident in these passages on counterfeiting—and the mimetic relationship implicit among God, Satan and James—betrays an intense anxiety about any form of power founded upon such a counterfeit.[18]

James's feminizing of dangerous tendencies in Scottish culture, and his demonstration of the inescapability of the feminine in his concepts of power and eloquence, are hence of deep significance for the development of Scottish cultural identity.

Clearly, the concept of Scotland as feminized is not entirely new. Nor is it exhausted: in his introduction to *Gendering the Nation*, Whyte examines the similarities between "the politics of nation and the politics of gender." He borrows a passage from Butler's *Gender Trouble*, but substitutes "Scottish" for "feminist," "nationality" for "gender," and "pre-Union" for "precultural." The result is the following:

> The postulation of the "before" within Scottish theory becomes politically problematic when it constrains the future to materialize an idealized notion of the past when it supports, even inadvertently, the reification of a pre-Union sphere of the authentic Scottish. This recourse to an original or genuine Scottishness is a nostalgic and parochial idea that refuses the contemporary demand to formulate an account of nationality as a complex cultural construction. This ideal tends not only to serve culturally conservative aims, but to constitute an exclusionary practice within Scottish theory, precipitating precisely the kind of fragmentation that the ideal purports to overcome.[19]

Whyte describes Butler's original passage as a "warning against the dangers of imagining an Edenic state of society before patriarchy," but he appropriates the theory to warn against the idealization of the Scottish past. Such idealization leads only to the unstable essentialization that becomes evident in James's poetry.

Envisioning a national literary culture as both masculinely intact and femininely derivative produces inconsistencies, traces of which can be located in sixteenth-century Scotland; after all, a crucially problematic originary figure for this culture is none other than the father of English poetry, Geoffrey Chaucer. In her early article "The Scottish Chaucer," Louise Fradenburg claims that "For fifteenth- and sixteenth-century Scottish poets, Chaucer is neither a poet to be slavishly imitated, nor simply a text to be plundered and ignored at will; instead, through a richly complicated process of historical revisionism, Chaucer's text authorizes, and helps to articulate, the dream of a sophisticated vernacular poetry in 'Scottis.'"[20] We would like to reflect for a moment on this assertion: Chaucer is more than a poet to be imitated, yet his body of work is recognized by Scottish poets as integral to their poetic tradition. They must do more than simply imitate Chaucer: they may rewrite, revise, refinish, but never simply imitate or emulate.

The sixteenth century saw the increased circulation of Scottish texts with authorship—texts that were signed, claimed by poets who wanted their works to be recognizable and recognized. As Fradenburg points out, Henryson "finished" the Chaucerian *Troilus and Criseyde* with his *Testament of Cresseid*, and in doing so he presented his text as more than an imitation: it is a revisionary, judgmental conclusion to a Chaucerian text.[21] Chaucer's *Troilus*, although it participates in the revisioning of the Troy story, is not the final word: it leaves an ambiguity at the end that allows for future rewriting. Henryson's *Testament*, on the other hand, participates in a long history, a tradition of literature, yet as a conclusion it leaves no room for future revisioning. Like Henryson's *Testament*, the *Kingis Quair* (ascribed in its unique witness, Bodleian ms. Arch. Selden B. 24 to James I) is also related to *Troilus and Criseyde*.[22] The *Quair* is also a revisioning of this text (and also, again like the *Testament*, related to the *Knight's Tale*), but of form rather than plot; James I (or whoever wrote the text—the Scots seemed quite willing and happy to believe it was written by James) revised Chaucer's courtly lyric strategy. The narrator of *The Kingis Quair* revisioned the lyric at the end of Book III of *Troilus*—the lyric inset within a narrative—from that of a lover "narwe masked and yknet" (III.1734) to that of a liberated lover, one who may offer the final word on love—from the outside, as it were—in a satisfied closure. Again, what Chaucer seemed to have left unfinished receives closure in the work of his strong Scottish poetic sons.[23]

Reception and remaking of Chaucer provided a model, and perhaps a motive or even a provocation, for the Scottish pursuit and accommodation of French literary authority. Alain Chartier, Clément Marot, and later Salluste Du Bartas and Pierre de Ronsard offered Scottish writers stylistically, but also politically, valuable counterweights to an acclimatized but necessarily discrete English canon. From the outset of his literary activity in 1584—in *The Essayes of a Prentise in the Divine Art of Poesie*—James VI was preeminent at such balancing acts. In the *Essayes* as well as his treatise on poetics, A *Short Treatise*

Containing Reulis and Cautelis to Be Observed and Eschewed in Scottis Poesie, he draws repeatedly on Du Bellay and Ronsard (*La deffence et illustration de la langue françoyse*, 1549, and *L'Abrégé de l'Art Poétique*, 1565) as well as George Gascoigne (*Certayne Notes of Instruction*, 1575).

Negotiating between French and English cultural orbits, James may have been following the advice of his late mentor, Esmé Stuart, sieur d'Aubigny.[24] In *Reulis and Cautelis*, ironically, he is at least as close to the spirit of his "detested preceptor," the preeminent Scottish humanist George Buchanan,[25] only to repudiate that spirit by reserving its power for the crown: the king is the only poet with the scope to comment on policy, and this scope derives from his kingship, not his authorship.

Interestingly, one place in the *Essayes* where bodies of water represent original versus derived political power is James's verse amplification (in five octave stanzas) of a simile in book five of the epic *Pharsalia* by the Latin poet Lucan, would-be assassin of Nero. James's choice of text is significant because of Lucan's potential to "become a focus for republican loyalties."[26] The simile, however, opposes rebellion: were "all the floods" to "stay their course from running in the see" (ll. 1–2), they would not diminish the ocean, any more than by continuing to flow would they augment it. Continually advancing the cycle of evaporation and precipitation, the substance of the ocean is the source of the rivers, not contrariwise (ll. 9–16):

So even siclike: Though subjects do coniure
For to rebell against their Prince and King:
By leaving him, although they hope to smure
That grace, wherewith God maks him for to ring,
Though by his gifts he shaw him selfe bening,
To help their need, and make them thereby gaine,
Yet lack of them no harme to him doth bring,
When they to rewe their folie shalbe faine. (ll. 25–32)

As a depiction of sovereign power, the ocean dominates as much by generosity of circulation as by sheer overwhelming scale. This is an image of dynamic distribution of "gifts" as benevolence, to be opposed to which is sheer folly. Nature affirms monarchy.

Likewise, nature, the second divine revelation, witnesses divine power as generosity. It is relevant that another translation in the *Essayes* is of Psalm 104, a biblical text "persistently identified" as a Protestant model for two kinds of meditation on "the creatures": "emblematically, as a rich source of moral lessons and exempla which the meditator should derive and apply to his own life; and symbolically, as sacramental objects invested by God with significances which may reveal something about God to the meditator."[27] As in the version of Lucan's simile, the sea is both generous and vast here, but it is also a restless, unknowable container of hierarchialized plenitude, a figure of royal eloquence, and not of eloquence bound merely (as Jonathan Goldberg sees James's "linkage of discourse to power") to regularity and decorum:[28]

> How large and mightie are thy workis, O Lord!
> . . . Heirof the Seas (which dyuers skaile
> Of fish contenis) dois witnes beare: Ilk saile
> Of dyvers ships upon the swolling wawes
> Dois testifie, as dois the monstrous whaile,
> Who frayis all fishes with his ravening Iawes. (ll. 65, 68–72)

In the same stanza as the Lucan translation, and immediately following the treatise on prosody that the Lucan immediately precedes, this version of Psalm 104 (incipit "O Lord inspyre my spreit and pen to praise / Thy Name, whose greatnes farr surpassis all") establishes the final authorization for James's sovereignty. The "monstrous whaile" threatens the lesser sea creatures "with his ravening Iawes," and God has in fact punished humanity with deluge (ll. 17–24).

Speaking through nature, his signifying words prior to the things they signify, God authorizes the poet-king, who "with his possession of, and power over, language, can guide all its other users in social action and natural knowledge."[29] In James's translation of the *Uranie* of Salluste Du Bartas, is not the largest "feild" of poetic endeavor

> his praise, who brydles heauens most cleare,
> Maks mountaines tremble, and howest hells to feare?
> That is a horne of plenty well repleat:
> That is a storehouse riche, a learning seat,
> An Ocean hudge, both lacking shore and ground,
> Of heavenly eloquence a spring profound. (ll. 225–30)

Here, as elsewhere in the *Essayes* and throughout James's later writings, the mental work of his writing continues to be, as Kevin Sharpe argues, contestive and appropriative:

> Like Elizabeth's, James's writings, through representation and self-presentation, attempt to reaffirm and reauthorise paradigms that

> sustained his divine right; and to control the arena of interpretation and discourse. Just as the Authorised King James Bible and his exegeses of Scripture claimed contested texts for the crown, so royal poetry, with its echoes of Virgil and Horace, Cicero and Sidney, appropriated an ambiguous classical tradition, which some deployed to defend republics, for the monarchy.[30]

James claimed texts by translating—indeed, revisioning—them, and thereby he asserted control over their ideologies. A feature of these claims is James's elevation of his own language, Scots, at the expense of Latin and Greek. Thus the king countered Buchanan's fidelity to the classics. James elevated Scots by emphasizing "the power of poetic invention rather than the imitation of past models: the renovation of Scots poetry would flow from the present, from court and king, rather than from submission to the example of the past"—submission inculcated by none other than George Buchanan, leading proponent of the theory that kings are subject to law and the community, and antagonist to any "comparison between the king's power to make the law and that of artists to set the rules for their own art."[31] In the *Essayes*, then, James was already grappling as a sovereign author with the problem of how to "legitimize—or relegitimize—his kingship."[32]

Watery themes reemerge purposively in James's political writing of the late 1590s. Jenny Wormald argues that this writing "should be viewed, initially at least, as the product of a mind at work rather than a closed and fixed one having already determined on the theme he had decided to lay before the world."[33] What may impress instead is the coherence of James's purpose from the *Essayes* to *Basilikon Doron*, and the consistency of his figuration. In the preface to *Basilikon Doron*, for instance, James addresses the reader thus:

> Charitable Reader, it is one of the golden Sentences, which Christ our Saviour vttered to his Apostles, that there is nothing so couered, that shal not be reuealed, neither so hidde, that shall not be knowen; and whatsoeuer they haue spoken in darkenesse, should be heard in the light: and that which they had spoken in the eare in secret place, should be publikely preached on the tops of the houses: and since he hath said it, most trew must it be, since the authour thereof is the fountaine and very being of trewth.[34]

When James placed his own writing in this context, he assigned to himself a double authority, as both king and poet, in both modes a figure of Christ. Presumably the figure of the fountain is meant to portray James as a powerful, life-giving force. Representation of courts as fountains ("wherby the people by the cleannes therof be longe preserued in honestie, or by the impurenes therof, are with sundry vyces corrupted"[35]) is widely distributed, but the fountain seems in some ways an odd metaphor for a king "seeking to reduce both state and people / To a fix'd order":[36] the body of water issuing from its source is an open and, therefore, feminine system, a susceptible entity. In *Basilikon Doron*, James puts it thus: "Neither can any thing in his government succeed well with him (devise and labour as he list) as comming from a filthie spring, if his person be unsanctified."[37] The body of the king, however, must be presented as a strong, powerfully closed, and masculine system, not a vulnerable body, especially if he is to be the manifestation of the sovereignty of his realm.[38] Powerful closure involves excision. James argues that as head of the state, the king "will be forced to cut off some rotten member . . . to keep the rest of the body in integrity."[39] Again, James grounds his authority upon "his natural identity with the father of the family and the head of the body."[40]

Looking at James's poems as well as his political writings, Goldberg concludes that interest in freedom is sustained and characteristic throughout both kinds: "A 'free' monarch was how he styled himself in his first treatise on kingship, and it was the freedom of the mind that he addressed in his supposed first poem."[41] Still, freedom is hardly an active principle here: James often represented himself as a passive vessel to be filled with divine truth, from Christ and from the Muses; like his kingdom, his physical body must be open to true inspiration, and yet closed against pollution.[42] This is, even for a king, a physically impossible task. James represented himself as the very Other that during his reign he tried sporadically to suppress. Just as the female mystic was feared by late medieval church authorities because she was "too open" and could therefore receive bad as well as good, so James feared those accused of witchcraft, "twentie women given to that craft, where ther is one man . . . for as that sexe is frailer then man is, so is it easier to be intrapped in these grosse snares of the Devill, as was over well proved to be true, by the Serpents deceiving of Eva at the beginning, which makes him the homelier with that sexe sensine."[43] There would appear to be a "large gap between the 'truth' proferred as self-evident by James, and the 'truth' that emerges from a close reading of the ambiguities and discontinuities in James's texts."[44] Such ambiguities and discontinuities can be traced back to James's earliest published writing, in the *Essayes*. Here already (as later in *Basilikon Doron*, where "the chiefe commendation of a Poeme is, that when the verse shall bee shaken sundrie in prose, it shall bee found so rich in quicke inuentions, and poeticke flowers, and in faire and pertinent comparisons; as it shall retaine the lustre of a Poeme, although in prose"[45]), nature, poetic invention, and the workings of kingly intention intersect at notions of fluency.

Right away in the preface to his *Reulis*, James explains why invention is crucial to the making of poetry in Scots during his reign: "as the tyme is changeit sensyne, sa is the ordour of poesie changeit," the key feature of change in this order being the observance of what James calls "flowing."[46] Briefly, he encapsulates many features of prosodic tact in this term: the implications for pace and rhyme of primary and secondary stress in multisyllabic words; the need to maintain at least the potential for regularity of meter and caesura; the "indifference" of stress of monosyllables and certain disyllables; apocope and syncope; and feminine rhymes (chapter 2). Song lays bare the prosodic strengths and weakness of verse:[47] James concludes that "youre eare man be the onely judge, as of all the uther parts of flowing, the verie tuichestane quhairof is musique," one allusion among several in the treatise to the innateness of poetic skill, for "gif Nature be nocht the chief worker in this airt, Reulis wilbe bot a band to Nature."[48]

Following Du Bartas, James continued to associate fluency and power. As a whole, the *Uranie* might well have been translated to articulate this relationship, but nowhere more than in the passage following, in which the language of poetry becomes influential through its intrinsic fluidity:

> The harmony of nomber tone, and song
> That makes the verse so fair, it is so strong
> Over us, as hardest Catos it will move,
> With spreits aflought, and sweete transported love.
> For as into the wax the seal's imprent
> Is lyke a seale, right so the Poet gent,
> Doeth grave so vive in vs his passions strange,
> As maks the reader, halfe in author change.
> For verse's force is sic, that softly slydes
> Throw secret poris, and in our sences bydes,
> As makes them have both good and euill imprented,
> Which by the learned works is represented.[49]

Dangerously detached from moral imperatives—as apt to imprint "ill" as "good"—the harmonious insinuations of poetry must be governed. Accordingly, James limits the play of invention, even while he emphasizes its indispensability:

> Bot sen invention is ane of the chief vertewis in a poete, it is best that ye invent your awin subject your self and not to compose of sene subjectis. Especially, translating any thing out of uther language, quhilk doing, ye not onely assay not your awin engyne of inventioun, bot be the same meanes ye are bound as to a staik to follow that buikis phrasis quhilk ye translate.

> Ye man also be war of wryting anything of materis of commoun weill or uther sic grave sene subjectis (except metaphorically, of manifest treuth opinly knawin, yit nochtwithstanding using it very seidil) because nocht onely ye essay nocht your awin inventioun, as I spak before, bot lykewayis they are to grave materis for a poet to mell in.[50]

Seeking an identity of inimitable (artistic, but also political) ingenuity, James looks forward to autonomy. He perceives the opposition between "acquired rules and natural, spontaneous imitation of Nature . . . and, most important of all, between imitation of other writers and the poet's own independent work" and aspires to become "the first to tread a particular path, . . . all credit and honour . . . due to him for that primacy."[51] However, he recognizes the dangers of an unbound invention generally available, and he reserves political discourse—too grave for a mere poet to trouble with (and to make trouble with)—by implication, to the poet-king, himself. James may assimilate political "invention," to "imagining" and "creation" instead of "fabrication" and "falsity," but then he insists on the strict limits within which this function may operate.[52]

The discourse of eloquence and influence in the *Essayes* provides an especially illuminating context for the modulations of body and gender in James's political theory. After all, at eighteen, James already knew about the "painful ambiguity which adhered to the Scottish crown."[53] For him, sovereignty was abysmally contingent. Seized by the aristocratic junta known as the Ruthven Raiders (1582), James learned anew how vulnerable he was, politically and physically, to powerful adversaries among the aristocracy and in the Kirk. His personal inclinations subjected him to his opponents: the Ruthven Raiders had taken control in order to expel the royal favorites Esmé Stuart, newly created duke of Lennox, and Captain James Stewart, the newly inserted earl of Arran. Escaping in 1583, James watched his former captors scurry for cover, then published his *Essayes*. Political and literary pursuits run together. In the *Essayes*, James refers to the losses of the raid—above all, in the *Phoenix*, to the death of Esmé Stuart, expelled to France.[54] He situates various anxieties, about the vulnerability of kingship as well as poetics in Scotland at the end of the sixteenth century, and begins to develop an iconography of invention and eloquence that situates and addresses vulnerability in both kinds.

The focus of James's anxieties is the body of the king, that decisive manifestation of what Michael Camille sees as the body's metaphorical capacity to represent "any bounded system," but also "the site of intense visual scrutiny and surveillance . . . subject to the bonds of feudal lordship and . . . at the same time caught in a cosmic network that controlled both its internal and external movements." We witness individual bodies bound by other, larger systems: the microcosm at the mercy of the macrocosm. Camille compares the human body to "an insect trapped in a spider's web of fate," perhaps illustrating just how insignificant man and his body were (we use the masculine purposefully here). Few owned their own bodies; only those privileged enough to own seals—"public visual signs represented through pre-eminent body types"—possessed their own bodily representations.[55] In the passage from *Uranie* quoted above, James shows his appreciation of the equivalence between such self-possession ("as into the wax the seal's imprent / Is lyke a seale") and the power of the poet (who "right so . . . Doeth grave so vive in us his passions strange").

James's representation of his physical body places him in an odd position: first, as divinely appointed monarch, he becomes spiritual authority mediating between God and his own kingdom; yet because he is merely a vehicle (for the Muses as poet and for God as king), he is also presented as one who has little inherent power or authority. Perhaps this is appropriate, for James, as a vassal to God, his feudal lord, and as a subordinate to his poetic inspiration, the Muses, supposedly speaks their messages, not his own. However, his self-representation as a mere vehicle for the divine logos is not consistent with his desire to also present himself as a fixed and whole authority figure of the nation or as one who holds complete control over his own body, a body he implicitly attempts to define as a closed and masculine system.

As king and author, James represented his body of work as well as his own physical body as a closed system. Closing his sovereign body to the excesses and pleasures of life, James attempted to appear completely "perfect" and masculine; this attempt is embodied by the extended, complex discussion, in *Basilikon Doron*, of mediating practices (in which kings are not unlike actors).[56] This representation of his physical body (and body of work) is flawed precisely because of its guise of perfection. First of all, no body (or text) is capable of being completely closed: even while he manifested sovereignty, James required food and drink to survive, even though (following precepts in manuals of kingship, the "Institutions of Princes") he might have chosen carefully exactly what entered his body, just as he selected matter to read; unable to control his bodily functions, he, too, needed to rid his body of toxins and his kingdom of seditious, corruptive discourse (again, both according to instituted practices); finally, he did not possess the ability to remain free of disease or of other bodily afflictions, nor would he have always been able to control what he felt (James's emotional excesses being the subject of comment throughout his reign) or even how he (let alone his kingdom) responded to the texts he (or it) consumed. To some extent, he was able to rule his acts and utterances, but pain, love, or fear might have arisen, far out of his control; no body is ever closed. Entirely characteristic of his age, James's focus (in the *Essayes* and also in *Basilikon Doron*) on externals such as dress and speech affected only the outside of the body; even if he believed that the external can influence the internal, he thus demonstrated that the body is not closed.[57] James's vision of a royally cool, controlled body does not occur naturally as a God-given gift. It is unnatural, and therefore impossible to maintain. Similarly, no text can ever remain completely closed: it is open to ingestion, interpretation, digestion, and purgation—as well as revision, misinterpretation, and destruction. No matter how authoritative James wished his body of work or his sovereign to appear, both ultimately remained open and vulnerable when released into the world.

James's bodily self-representation is ineffective because it denies himself earthly power in favor of divine power, thus reducing his authority. It is inappropriate, especially if his body is to be a mystical vessel of the divine logos, for he must be an open, and therefore at least partially feminine, system in order to receive God's word and disperse it. As king, he must exercise control over the bodies of others. As Camille points out, women "were associated with the dangers of excess, with speaking too much and too loosely, and with the artifices of representation—their fashionable clothes and cosmetics."[58] In translating *Uranie*, James is only too aware of this danger when he characterizes mercenary poetic excesses as harlotry. And in *Basilikon Doron*, he genders artifice in significantly familiar terms when he warns that "it is not the principall part of a Poeme to rime right, and flowe well with manie pretie wordes."[59]

James is a paradox of bizarre and ironic inversions in many ways, from such trivial contrasts as that between his advice to Prince Henry in *Basilikon Doron* about polite eating and Sir Anthony Weldon's anecdotes about his own foibles at table, to larger issues of authority and power, including but not limited to God and the muses. Ironically, however, James seems to be the author of his own self-representation as a "monstrous hybrid": there are political advantages to being both open and closed, fluid and contained, ruler and subservient, masculine and feminine, for these are contradictory constructions at whose intersection the figure of Christ is usually found. The feminine body is problematic not only because it is "open" but also because it is Other: it occupies the realm of the mysterious, a position that threatens preestablished authority and power.

Camille describes the medieval image of a corpse of a young woman whose body is unabashedly displayed: "For medieval viewers the body that is revealed beneath her shroud in all its sensuality was not a sign of promise, but of decay, not of the beauty but the fatal fallen nature of the female body."[60] The female body, presumably the most open of bodies due to the nature of sexual intercourse, remains open even in death, yet the openness of her soul to receive eternal life does not appear to be an issue in this case. What is prominent instead is the definitiveness of decay. Even if consistent as an open system, the body of woman lacks consistency within the binaries of spirit and flesh.[61] In fact, woman appears to occupy the unstable boundary between these two polar opposites, a position usually reserved for Christ—and a position that James apparently wanted to appropriate. The most complete of bodies, the most glorified—Christ's body—was also the most fragmented and mysterious, "a workaday body, in its regular accessibility, in the pain of its suffering; and yet it was quite different—it was glorious, eternal."[62]

We must wonder about the relationship between the open, feminine body, often compared to that of Christ (the most open and nourishing of bodies), and the whole, closed, masculine bodily system that King James apparently required. The slipperiness with which the gender system functions within Galen's one-sex model mirrors the fluidity within both James's writings and his kingship. James represented himself as king and poet, ruler and ruled, masculine and feminine—contradictions that never quite receive reconciliation. Indeed, he celebrated these contradictions with his endless water references and metaphors: water as an open system is necessarily vulnerable, yet it is also capable of preserving or destroying life. Perhaps for James this paradox was both appropriate and necessary. Perhaps he desired the freedoms that being this hybrid allows.

Notes

1. Jack 125; Bushnell, "George Buchanan" 108.
2. Anderson 26.
3. xiv.
4. xvi. See also Butler 8; and Sedgwick 148.
5. Lewis 66; Fradenburg 153–71; and Bawcutt 78–81.
6. Whyte xv.
7. Gordon Brown 34.
8. Edwin Muir, *Scott and Scotland: The Predicament of the Scottish Writer* (London: Routledge, 1936), 114–15.
9. Gordon Brown 44.
10. Mason, *Scots and Britons* 10
11. Jack 126; Jack and Rozendaal xxix.
12. Ashton 10–16.
13. Fischlin 8.
14. Laqueur 4.
15. Guilia Sissa, "Subtle Bodies," *Fragments for a History of the Human Body: Part Three*, Michel Feher, Ramona Naddaff, and Nadia Tazi, eds. Zone 5 (1989), 141.
16. Dollimore 251–52.
17. Laqueur 149.
18. Fischlin 15.
19. Whyte xiii, xii.
20. Fradenburg, "Scottish Chaucer" 175.
21. Fradenburg, "Scottish Chaucer" 168–69.
22. Fradenburg, "Scottish Chaucer" 174–75.
23. Spearing 107–9, 164, 201.
24. Jack and Rozendaal 471–73.

25. Bushnell 104; Pocock 298.
26. Norbrook 46.
27. Lewalski 162.
28. Goldberg 19.
29. Reiss 230.
30. Sharpe 131.
31. Bushnell 110, 108 n.74.
32. Mason 120.
33. Wormald 49.
34. James VI and I, *Political Writings* 3.
35. Elyot 246. On the later sixteenth-century circulation of this topic, see Malcolm Smuts, "Court-Centred Politics and the Uses of Roman Historians, c. 1590–1630," in Sharpe and Lake.
36. Webster, *The Duchess of Malfi* 1.1.5–15.
37. James VI and I, *Political Writings* 12.
38. Kantorowicz 271, 302–13; Jonathan Sawday, *The Body Emblazoned: Dissection and the Human Body in Renaissance Culture* (London: Routledge, 1995), 106, 189.
39. Fischlin and Fortier 75.
40. Bushnell, *Tragedies of Tyrants* 75.
41. Goldberg 22.
42. Williamson 59.
43. James VI and I, *Daemonology* 1:5, *Minor Prose Works* 30.
44. Fischlin and Fortier 40.
45. *Political Writings* 55.
46. Cf. Bernhart 453.
47. Shire 158–63.
48. James VI and I, *Essayes of a Prentise* sig. Lii^{v}, Kii^{v}.
49. James, *Essayes* sig. Eii.
50. James, *Essayes* sig. Mii^{v}.
51. Castor 82, 115.
52. Anderson 15.
53. Williamson 46.
54. Bergeron 33–34.
55. Camille 62, 68, 72.
56. James VI and I, *Political Writings* 49.
57. Elias 63.
58. Camille, *Image on the Edge* 53.
59. James VI and I, *Political Writings* 55.
60. Camille, "Image and the Self" 78.
61. Beckwith 35.
62. Rubin 111.

Works Cited

Anderson, Benedict. *Imagined Communities: Reflections on the Origin and Spread of Nationalism.* London: Verso, 1983.

Ashton, Robert. *James I by His Contemporaries.* London: Hutchinson, 1969.

Bawcutt, Priscilla. *Dunbar the Makar.* Oxford: Clarendon P, 1992.

Beckwith, Sarah. "A Very Material Mysticism: The Medieval Mysticism of Margery Kempe." *Medieval Literature: Criticism, Ideology and History.* Ed. David Aers. Brighton: Harvester P, 1986. 34–57.

Bergeron, David. *Royal Family, Royal Lovers: King James of England and Scotland.* Columbia: U of Missouri P, 1991.

Bernhart, A. Walter. "Castalian Poetics and the 'Verie Twichestane Musique.'" *Scottish Language and Literature, Medieval and Renaissance: Fourth International Conference 1984 Proceedings.* Ed. Dietrich Strauss and Horst Drescher. Frankfurt: Peter Lang, 1986. 451–58.

Bushnell, Rebecca W. "George Buchanan, James VI and Neo-classicism." *Scots and Britons.* Ed. Mason. 91–111.

———. *Tragedies of Tyrants: Political Thought and Theater in the English Renaissance.* Ithaca: Cornell UP, 1990.

Butler, Judith. *Bodies That Matter: On the Discursive Limits of "Sex."* New York: Routledge, 1993.

Camille, Michael. "The Image and the Self: Unwriting Late Medieval Bodies." *Framing Medieval Bodies.* Ed. Sarah Kay and Miri Rubin. Manchester: Manchester UP, 1994. 62–99.

———. *Image on the Edge: The Margins of Medieval Art.* Cambridge, Mass.: Harvard UP, 1992.

Castor, Grahame. *Pléiade Poetics: A Study in Sixteenth-century Thought and Terminology.* Cambridge: Cambridge UP, 1964.

Chaucer, Geoffrey. *The Riverside Chaucer.* 3rd ed. Ed. Larry D. Benson et al. Boston: Houghton Mifflin, 1987.

Dollimore, Jonathan. *Sexual Dissidence: Augustine to Wilde, Freud to Foucault.* Oxford: Clarendon P, 1991.

Elias, Norbert. *The Court Society.* Trans. Edmund Jephcott. New York: Pantheon, 1983.

Elyot, Thomas. "The Image of Governance (1541)." *Four Political Treatises.* Intro. Lillian Gottesman. Gainesville: Scholars' Facsimiles, 1967. 203–426.

Fischlin, Daniel. "'Counterfeiting God': James VI (I) and the Politics of *Daemonology.*" *Journal of Narrative Technique* 26 (1996): 1–29.

Fischlin, Daniel, and Mark Fortier, eds. *James I.* True Law of Free Monarchies *and* Basilikon Doron. Toronto: Centre for Reformation and Renaissance Studies, 1995.

Fradenburg, Louise Olga. *City, Marriage, Tournament: Arts of Rule in Late Medieval Scotland.* Madison: U of Wisconsin P, 1991.

———. "The Scottish Chaucer." *Proceedings of the Third International Conference of Scottish Language and Literature (Medieval and Renaissance).* Ed. Felicity Riddy and Roderick J. Lyall. Glasgow: Glasgow UP for the University of Stirling, 1984. Rpt. *Writing After Chaucer: Essential Readings in Chaucer and the Fifteenth Century.* Ed. Daniel J. Pinti. New York: Garland, 1998. 167–76.

Goldberg, Jonathan. *James I and the Politics of Literature.* Baltimore: Johns Hopkins UP, 1983.

Gordon Brown, Ian. "Modern Rome and Ancient Caledonia: The Union and the Politics of Scottish Culture." *The History of Scottish Literature II: 1660–1800.* Ed. Andrew Hook. Gen. Ed. Cairns Craig. Aberdeen: Aberdeen UP, 1987. 33–49.

Jack, R. D. S. "Poetry Under James VI." *The History of Scottish Literature I: Origins to 1660.* Ed. R. D. S. Jack. Gen. Ed. Cairns Craig. Aberdeen: Aberdeen UP, 1988. 125–39.

Jack, R. D. S., and P. A. T. Rozendaal, eds. *The Mercat Anthology of Early Scottish Literature 1375–1707.* Edinburgh: Mercat, 1997.

James VI and I. *The Essayes of a Prentise, In the Divine Art of Poesie.* Edinburgh: Vautrollier, 1584. Rpt. Amsterdam: Theatrum Orbis Terrarum, 1969.

———. *Minor Prose Works of King James VI and I.* Ed. James Craigie. Scottish Text Society. Edinburgh: Blackwood, 1982.

———. *The Poems of King James VI of Scotland.* 2 vols. Ed. James Craigie. Scottish Text Society. Edinburgh: Blackwood, 1947–55.

———. *Political Writings.* Ed. Johann P. Sommerville. Cambridge: Cambridge UP, 1994.

Kantorowicz, Ernst. *The King's Two Bodies.* Princeton: Princeton UP, 1957.

Laqueur, Thomas. *Making Sex: Body and Gender from the Greeks to Freud.* Cambridge, Mass.: Harvard UP, 1990.

Lewalski, Barbara K. *Protestant Poetics and the Seventeenth-Century Religious Lyric.* Princeton: Princeton UP, 1979.

Lewis, C. S. *English Literature in the Sixteenth Century Excluding Drama.* Oxford History of English Literature, vol. 3. Oxford: Clarendon P, 1954.

Mason, Roger A. "George Buchanan, James VI and the Presbyterians." *Scots and Britons.* Ed. Mason. 112–37.

———, ed. *Scots and Britons: Scottish Political Thought and the Union of 1603.* Cambridge: Cambridge UP, 1994.

Montgomerie, Alexander. *Collected Poems.* Ed. David J. Parkinson. Edinburgh: Scottish Text Society, 2000.

Norbrook, David. "Lucan, Thomas May, and the Creation of a Republican Literary Culture." *Culture and Politics in Early Stuart England.* Ed. Sharpe and Lake. 45–66.

Pocock, J. G. A. "Two Kingdoms and Three Histories? Political Thought In British Contexts." *Scots and Britons.* Ed. Mason. 293–312.

Reiss, Timothy J. "Poetry, Power, and Resemblance of Nature." *Mimesis: From Mirror to Method.* Ed. John D. Lyons and Stephen G. Nichols. Hanover N.H.: UP of New England for Dartmouth College, 1982. 215–347.

Rubin, Miri. "The Person in the Forum: Medieval Challenges to Bodily 'Order.'" *Framing Medieval Bodies.* Ed. Sarah Kay and Miri Rubin. Manchester: Manchester UP, 1994. 100–22.

Sedgwick, Eve Kosofsky. *Tendencies.* Durham: Duke UP, 1993.

Sharpe, Kevin. "The King's Writ: Royal Authors and Royal Authority in Early Modern England." *Culture and Politics in Early Stuart England.* Ed. Sharpe and Lake. 117–38.

Sharpe, Kevin, and Peter Lake, eds. *Culture and Politics in Early Stuart England.* Stanford: Stanford UP, 1993.

Shire, Helena Mennie. *Song, Dance, and Poetry of the Court of Scotland Under King James VI.* Cambridge: Cambridge UP, 1969.

Spearing, A. C. *Medieval to Renaissance in English Poetry.* Cambridge: Cambridge UP, 1985.

Webster, John. *The Duchess of Malfi.* Ed. John Russell Brown. London: Methuen, 1964.

Whyte, Christopher. "Introduction." *Gendering the Nation: Studies in Modern Scottish Literature.* Ed. Christopher Whyte. Edinburgh: Edinburgh UP, 1995. ix–xx.

Williamson, Arthur H. *Scottish National Consciousness in the Age of James VI.* Edinburgh: John Donald, 1979.

Wormald, Jenny. "James VI and I, *Basilikon Doron* and *The Trew Law of Free Monarchies.*" *The Mental World of the Jacobean Court.* Ed. Linda Levy Peck. Cambridge: Cambridge UP, 1991. 36–54.

3

THE *AMATORIA* OF JAMES VI: LOVING BY THE *REULIS*

Morna R. Fleming

James VI is not noted as a love poet. Indeed, in many scholarly minds he is not noted as a poet at all, but such judgments ignore a substantial body of interesting work. James was unique among European monarchs in that he published his own works in addition to offering the conventional royal patronage to Alexander Montgomerie, John Stewart of Baldynneis, Alexander Hume, William Fowler, Thomas and Robert Hudson, and others who have been described as the Castalian Band, but who will be referred to in this paper as the Jacobean court poets.[1] The close-knit, self-referencing and self-perpetuating coterie culture that developed among the group, with evidence of internal circulation of ideas, images, and rhetorical poses, was clearly congenial to James, and it can be seen as a literary predecessor to the political Bedchamber band that was formed in London in 1603.

A number of reasons could have moved James to involve himself actively in poetry in the early 1580s. He had formed a close relationship with his cousin Esmé Stuart, sieur d'Aubigny, later duke of Lennox, who was probably the first to expose him to contemporary French culture and who introduced the young king to the works of the Pléiade group inspired by Pierre de Ronsard. The other most influential member of the group was Joachim Du Bellay, whose *La défense et illustration de la langue française* (hereafter *Défense*) set out the aesthetic, literary, and nationalistic principles on which the group worked.[2] James perhaps saw a mirror image in his own situation: the young king as the theoretician, and the older Alexander Montgomerie as the established court poet.

Aubigny's recreation of the French-influenced courtly milieu represented for James a dramatic contrast to the dour atmosphere of the schoolroom under his tutor George Buchanan. Released from Buchanan's tutelage and the enforced rigor of Latin and Greek studies, James was free to explore this new literary world, supplied in addition by his mother's library, to which the more liberal Peter Young had already introduced him.[3] The library included collections of French and Italian poetry, romances and pastorals. As was common in European Renaissance courts, Scottish courtiers read and wrote poetry as a gentlemanly pastime, the poetry of contemporary France long seen in Scotland as providing the ideal models to read, translate, and imitate. Alexander Montgomerie, the ablest practitioner in the group, was an admirer of the French laureate Pierre de Ronsard, of whose poems he made a number of direct translations and imitations in Scots.

The banishment of the duke of Lennox was the impetus for James's long allegorical poem *Phoenix*, which is the first evidence of his attempts to use poetry to represent the emotional and political control he frequently felt impotent to exercise in reality. It is very probable that John Stewart of Baldynneis, one of the older members of the coterie, wrote uplifting poetic epistles to James during the time he was imprisoned by the Ruthven Raiders in 1582–83—another illustration of poetry performing either as consolation for injuries or as substitute for political intervention.[4]

Perhaps the most persuasive reason for James's involving himself actively in poetry was that he had seen its power used as a weapon against his mother Mary, Queen of Scots, and he was determined to ensure that the poetry produced during his reign was to his own design. Sandra Bell has argued most persuasively that James's *Short Treatise Containing Reulis and Cautelis to Be Observed and Eschewed in Scottis Poesie* (hereafter *Reulis and Cautelis*)[5] was written as a political as well as a poetical statement, to make clear to his subjects that poetry should not be used—as it had been by poets like Sir David Lindsay and Robert Sempill—for satirical attacks on the church or the monarchy.[6] It will be remembered also that James took issue with Edmund Spenser's character of Duessa in Book 1 of *The Faerie Queene*, demanding that Queen Elizabeth punish the poet for traducing Mary, Queen of Scots in this manner. In the same way that he would make his ideas of kingship clear in *Basilikon Doron* in 1599, James's first articulation of a theory of poetics informed literate Scots of his aesthetic, literary, and political views.[7]

James had obviously read Joachim Du Bellay's *Défense*, the first essay dedicated to the French language in terms of its potential as a literary language. Although Du Bellay is a primary source, there is, as was conventional for the time in any kind of formal treatise, considerable evidence of influence from other near-contemporary European and English treatises on poetry as well as from Horace's *Ars Poetica*.

Despite his familiarity, through the court coterie, with the Scottish poetry of the previous ages, James clearly did not wish to be seen to continue or develop the old forms and styles but rather to start afresh with a completely new poetic principle, hence his *Essayes of a Prentise in the Divine Art of Poesie* of 1584—the first publication of the new Scots authorized verse—a collection of sonnets written by him, augmented and embellished by dedications by various members of the coterie.[8] James's own poems are partnered by the *Reulis and Cautelis*, heavily based on French precept and example. The *Reulis and Cautelis* specifically mentions Du Bellay's *Défense* in the preface, and James is clearly following the Frenchman in both his nationalism and his specific rules for the writing of poetry. James's reason for writing is not quite the same as Du Bellay's, however. As the French title makes clear, Du Bellay was very conscious that the French vernacular was not regarded in some quarters as "proper" for poetic expression, not at all the equal of Latin or Greek. He intended to show that if the French language were developed appropriately by poets, it could be used in every situation, and that the very production of French verse and prose should be seen as a political act to the glory of the country. Although James adopted some of the nationalistic rhetoric, he was confident that the Scots language was already rich enough to cover every need. It appears he was more concerned with outlining his own ideas of what Scots poetry should be and, more importantly, what it should not be. James clearly wanted to distance himself from his mother's own poetry, which had been written in French; this is a link between the *Reulis and Cautelis* and *Basilikon Doron*, where he advises Prince Henry: "I would also aduise you to write in your own langage: for there is no thing left to be said in Greeke & Latine already, & ynow of poore scholers would match you in these languages: & besides that, it best becommeth a King to purifie & make famous his owne language, wherein he may go before all his subjectes; as it setteth him well to doe in all honeste and lawfull thinges."[9] James reinforces the link with the Scottish past by quoting as illustrations in the *Reulis and Cautelis* poems by Alexander Montgomerie, who combined a love of and interest in contemporary French poetry with a very strong foregrounding of Scots lyric, especially from the mid-century work of Alexander Scott.

It is important to mention at this stage that James did not acknowledge the source of these quotations; indeed it is possible to read them as ad hoc examples created by the writer to illustrate his current points. The notion of authority in the coterie group is slippery, since work was produced only in manuscript and circulated among the group. It is impossible to know what the original form of any poem was, what interpolations were suggested by which member of the coterie, or who was the originator of repeated and borrowed phrases and images, for such manuscript productions are "inherently malleable," and it is frequently very difficult to establish precise authorship.[10] It is significant, therefore, that James submitted his poems to the press so they would be produced in a form that was fixed and unchangeable, although even here he was at the mercy of the anglicizing tendencies of the printer.

As James sought to establish a new Scots poetic, similarly the French manifesto describes the means by which aspiring writers can use the vernacular in new ways, ignoring the works of already established French poets like Marot, Héroët, Mellin de Saint-Gelais, and Scève: "on pourra trouver en notre langue . . . une forme de poésie beaucoup plus exquise, laquelle il faudrait chercher en ces vieux Grecs et Latins, non point es auteurs français" (ch. 2, p. 82) (one could produce in our language . . . a much more exquisite type of poetry, the models for which would have to be sought in Greek and Latin writings, not in poetry already written in French).[11] Clearly Du Bellay felt, as James did, that the poets of the immediately preceding age had written superficially and unsubstantially, for entertainment rather than with any serious purpose in mind. James may also, as mentioned above, have had the writers of the immediately preceding reign in mind in his desire to move forward. Perhaps he was sending a clear signal to all aspiring poets how to write if they wished to please their king.

James's treatise is a manual of versifying for apprentice poets, described as "docile bairns of Knawledge," writing in Scots. That Scots is worthy of such attention is never an issue; it is taken as given, the language being a natural part of a man's intellectual development. James takes pride in Scots as a different language, not a version of English "quhilk is lykest to our language, zit we differ from thame in sindrie reulis of poesie" (67). This may be read as a veiled reference to his other source text, George Gascoigne's *Certayne Notes of Instruction Concerning the Making of Verse or Ryme in English* (hereafter *Certayne Notes*), published in 1575.[12] The churlish reviewer could accuse James of plagiarism, in that he does not reveal this very important second source, but in the early modern period it was perfectly permissible to use one text as the basis of a reply that takes the argument forward. In saying that Scots poets need a different instruction from that given to English poets, James may well be covertly alluding to Gascoigne, trusting that his readers will pick up the hint. In any case, he disagrees with Gascoigne on a number of points of principle, which then become essential differences between the poetics of the two languages.

A further impetus is that "lyke as the tyme is changeit sensyne, sa is the ordour of Poesie changeit. . . . [Q]uhat I speik of Poesie now, I speik of it as being come to mannis age and perfection, quhair as then it was bot in the infancie and chyldheid" (67). There is a sense of timeliness about both James's reign and the need for a new poetic to celebrate it, but where Du Bellay appeals to the Greek and Latin classics, James's appeal is to the great Christian writer Paul. The sense that he is the first Protestant king of Scotland shows in the much more serious tone he brings to his dealings with poetry, as he alludes to St. Paul's first letter to the Corinthians: "When I was a child, I spake as a child, I understood as a child, I thought as a child: but when I became a man, I put away childish things" (1 Corinthians 13: 1). As religion has now come of age, so has poetry. Clearly, the topic is a branch of literature that deserves close study and has important things to say. James is particularly concerned with the technicalities of the writing in order to ensure that Scots poets should say these things properly, in a fit manner.

In his strictures on technique, James takes the classical line also advocated by Gascoigne in his *Certayne Notes*, arguing for "Inventioun" and against slavish imitation, advocating a reliance on imagination to produce the best writing: "For gif Nature be nocht the chief worker in this airt, Reulis wilbe bot a band to Nature, and will mak yow within short space weary of the haill art: quhair as, gif Nature be chief, and bent to it, reulis will be ane help and staff to Nature" (68).

What James describes as Nature seems to be the same faculty as Du Bellay's divine power: "Cette divinité d'invention qu'ils ont plus que les autres, de cette grandeur de style, magnificence des mots, gravité des sentences, audace et variété des figures, et mille autres lumières de poésie: bref cette énergie et ne sais quel esprit qui est en leurs écrits, que les Latins appelaient *genius*" (59) (That divine power of inventiveness that they display above all others, elevated style, magnificent diction, roundness of expression, boldness and variety of metaphor, and a thousand other poetic gifts: in short that energy and indefinable spirit found in their writing, which the Latin writers called *genius*). This is exactly the instruction James gives his "docile bairns."

Similarly, the poet who uses the ideas of others is not using his "rype ingyne . . . and walkned witt," as James put it in his "Sonnet Decifring the Perfyte Poete"; he is merely copying others: "translating any thing out of vther language, quhilk doing ye not onely essay not your awin ingyne of *Inuentioun*, bot be the same meanes ye are bound, as to a staik, to follow that buikis phrasis quhilk ye translate" (78). Du Bellay also thought that those who confined themselves to translations were betraying the original writers and, if they were using translation as a means of enriching French literature, betraying the language itself. These *traducteurs* are better called *traditeurs*, echoing the Italian saying *traduttore traditore* (traitor translator). James does not take as strong a line as Du Bellay, who describes those who slavishly imitate (or, as he says, "transcribe") Virgil and Cicero into the vernacular as "ces reblanchisseurs de murailles qui . . . se rompent la tête" (75) (these whitewashers . . . who cudgel their brains). Imitation of the styles and tropes of the classics rather than slavish translation is what the Latin writers did, which is a more fruitful way of developing an underdeveloped literature: "Imitant les meilleurs auteurs Grecs, se transformant en eux, les dévorant" (60) (Imitating the best Greek writers, transforming themselves into Greeks, devouring their works). Although he does not use the same imagery of digestion, which is such a vivid aspect of Du Bellay's description, it is clear from the *Reulis and Cautelis* and from his own practice that James considers a thoroughgoing knowledge of the classics of Greek and Latin literature to be essential to a competent poet. His description of "the perfyte poete" makes this abundantly clear in its references to "walkned witt," "skilfulness, where learning may be spyit," and especially "with memorie to keip quhat he dois reid." Originality is not divorced from imitation and borrowing; rather it is seen to best effect in the skill with which the ideas, figures, and tropes of predecessors and contemporaries are incorporated into a new work.

In addition to the classical reading that had been so much a part of James's literary development, the influence of court music on the poetry of the period is also evident in his remarks on what he calls *"Flovving,"* by which he means rhythm, and on line length and rhyme. Throughout the *Reulis and Cautelis*, James confuses "foot" and "syllable," although the meaning is always clear. He advocates an iambic meter (although Gascoigne rather disparaged lack of variety in meter) and specifically approves fourteen- and twelve-syllable lines, with "*Sectioun*" (his own coining from a French rhetorical term) or caesura carefully marked after a long syllable "for the Musique, because that quhen zour lyne is ather of xiiij or xij fete, it wilbe drawin sa lang in the singing, as ze man rest in the middes of it, quhilk is the *Sectioun*" (72). He is clearly conscious of the sound of the language and the way the position of a word in a line can affect pronunciation and thus the "flow" of the line, and he argues strongly for meaning over artifice. There may be an anti-medieval or anti-formula-writing stance in his injunction that poets "put in na wordis ather *metri causa* or zit for filling furth the nomber of the fete" but that every word must have its due weight "in cace ze wer speiking the same purpose in prose" (75). This is advice he later reiterated to Prince Henry, when, in the third book of *Basilikon Doron*, he wrote: "if ye write in vers, remember that it is not the principal part of a poëme to rime right, and flow wel with manie prettie wordes; but the chiefe commendation of a poëme, is, that when the verse shall bee shaken sundrie in prose, it shalbe found so rich in quick inuentions & poëtick floures, as it shal reteine the lustre of a poëme although in prose"(186). This brings him logically to the question of rhyme and rhythm, and again the French and Scots treatise writers share one opinion. The serious poet should eschew the use of polysyllabic rhymes purely for effect or to show cleverness. James selects for special castigation the practice of "ryming in termes," where the same sound is repeated in rhyme words with little regard for the sense.

Du Bellay gives specific advice on verse form and the use of the caesura, and he aims to point aspiring poets in the right direction by giving precise and clear directions on what method to follow and what to avoid. Everything, ultimately, is governed by the "jugement de l'oreille" (the judgment of the ear), and anything that offends, however traditional, is to be plucked out. Following the Frenchman very closely, James insists that the ear must tell the writer what is correct. It is the poet himself who makes the judgment, not any outside authority: "zour eare man be the onely iudge as of all the vther parts of *Flovving,* the verie twichestane quhairof is Musique" (74). It is significant that James should make specific mention of music, for so many of the songs and lyrics written at the Scottish court were indeed set to music—some by the English Hudson brothers, both accomplished musicians—either through the practice of recycling old tunes by writing new words to them, in the manner of the *Gude and Godlie Ballatis,* or by setting old poems to new tunes. This of course is one way in which texts circulated throughout the coterie, and they would become subtly different as they were set to music.

James follows the medieval and classical categorization of texts in requiring that diction and style must correspond to the matter of the poem. As all literatures have high, middle, and low styles, James advocates different types of diction, rhetorical devices, line length, stanza form, and rhyme schemes for the various types of verse that could be written. In most cases he gives examples, some from his own work, others from that of his "maister-poete" Montgomerie, although most of the terminology comes straight from Du Bellay's *Défense* rather than from Gascoigne's *Certayne Notes.* He singles out for special mention and commendation typically Scottish forms, such as flyting and alliterative diction, which is one important distinction of Scottish poetry from English, for Gascoigne does not approve of alliterative verse in English, and is also a departure from DuBellay, who is contemptuous of traditional French kinds. James's term "literall" is directly derived from the French *"lettrisé."*

Decorum is very important to James in all aspects of poetry. Related to classical decorum derived from Horace's *Ars Poetica* in terms of subject matter and diction is his advice on the use of metaphor, called *"Comparisoun:"* "let sic a mutuall correspondence and similitude be betwixt them as it may appeare to be a meit Comparisoun for sic a subiect" (77). This is in agreement with Du Bellay's view that antonomasia is preferred to simple naming of persons and that epithets have to be newly made to add real meaning to their nouns. Circumlocution in epithets is preferred to *vocables composez,* as the latter means "making a corruptit worde, composit of twa dyuers simple wordis, as 'Apollo gyde-Sunne'" (77). This is one area where James disagrees with another Frenchman whose work he found particularly congenial, Salluste Du Bartas: the Frenchman had a predilection for this type of locution, of which James was very sparing when translating the *Uranie.*[13]

Specific stanza forms are also indicated for particular types of poem, the names sometimes quite deliberately taking the French name for a form that already existed, as in his naming of Ballat Royal, derived from the French *chant royal*, or *ballade* stanza, for "any heich and graue subiectis, specially drawin out of learnit authouris" (80), which had been used consistently by Scottish poets since the medieval period. Similarly, what James calls Troilus verse, to be used for "tragicall materis, complaintis, or testamentis" (81), is rhyme royal, so named because of James I's use of it in the *Kingis Quair,* but by this appellation it becomes patently linked with Chaucer's verse. As James makes clear in his introductory remarks, he sees Scots and English (both the languages and the peoples) as inevitably drawing ever closer, as "English . . . is lykest to our language" (67), and thus they should draw on the same shared cultural heritage. It seems evident that James is making a conscious break from his Scottish predecessors, however illustrious, in favor of an adherence to European (including English) styles. The stanza for love poetry, the six line Common verse, is simply Ronsard's *vers commun,* which Gascoigne calls the Ballade. The sonnet is defined as fourteen decasyllabic lines with an interlaced rhyme scheme, following the pattern of those quoted in the *Reulis and Cautelis,* used for "compendious praysing of any bukes, or the authouris thairof, or ony argumentis of vther historeis, quhair sindrie sentences and change of purposis are requyrit" (81)—not, one notices, for love poetry. And there is no mention, as there is in Du Bellay, of Petrarch as the model to follow in the sonnet form.

Although this is almost a decade ahead of the great vogue for sonnet writing in England—stimulated by the pirate print of Sidney's *Astrophel and Stella* and Samuel Daniel's *Delia* in 1591—James, despite an inevitable awareness of the French Pléiade's Petrarchan developments in the sonnets of Ronsard, Du Bellay, Baïf, Jodelle, Saint-Gelais, and later Desportes, sees no place for the love lyric in sonnet form. The numerous examples of love poems and sonnets—both original works and imitations produced by Montgomerie, the "ballates of luve" that Alexander Hume wrote at this period in his career, the rather strange and wistful poems on love and friendship written by John Stewart, and the major Italian-inspired sonnet sequence, *The Tarantula of Love,* which William Fowler must have been working on at the same time, and all of which were circulating around the court—did not create in James any real desire to imitate. He saw poetry as more fitted for elevating works as a branch of courtly education, or indeed a metapoetic: poetry used as a means of praising poetry itself, as is seen in the first published works *The Essayes of a Prentise.*

Given the difficulties of attribution within the coterie, it is dangerous to be dogmatic about James's personal sensibilities in the matter of poetry, but it seems clear that he was not really interested in Petrarchan lyrics. His extant work shows a preference for varied styles of versification, for stanzaic lyric rather than sonnets.[14] Where they are found, love lyrics appear to have been composed more or less to order, one or two pieces actually subtitled "at her Majesty's desire," and hence apparently composed after the king's marriage in 1590. James Craigie's edition of *The Poems of King James VI of Scotland* includes two different tables of contents for *Amatoria,* both in Prince Charles's handwriting. The first table appears on fol. 2v of Add. ms. 24195, while the second is on fol. 82v. The poems are printed in the order in which they appear in the very anglicized Add. ms. 24195, which is generally in groupings of twos, with one longer sequence of six. The numbers in brackets correspond to the editorial numbers given by Craigie. Common to the two tables are a double sonnet entitled "A complaint against the contrary Wyndes that hindered the Queene to com to Scotland from Denmarke" (1); two individual sonnets, "To the Queene" (2) and "To the Queene, Anonimos" (3); a pair of sonnets specially composed to show the difference in styles (4); a sequence of six sonnets (5); "Constant Loue in All Conditions," in Ballat Royal stanzas (6); "A Dier at Her M:ties Desyer" (a dier or dyer being a type of complaint) (7); "A complaint of his mistressis absence from Court" (8); and "A Dreame on His Mistris My Ladie Glammis" (9). To this heterogeneous collection, presumably from the 1580s and early 1590s, the later table adds two songs, "What Mortall Man" (11) and "When as the Skilfull" (12), as well as a double sonnet, "Not Orientall Indus" and "Faire Famous Isle" (32). Craigie does not include this last pair in *Amatoria* because they appear much later in the manuscript.[15] Although there are elements of Petrarchism in these love lyrics, this is no more marked than it would be in any European poetry, where the tropes and conceits of Petrarch had become commonplace. Far more noticeable is the native tradition of versification and the classical coloring.

What is interesting about the two tables of contents is the different perceived narrative that organization imposes on the poems. The table appearing on fol. 2v appears to be intended to create a Petrarchan sequence, beginning with formal stanzaic poems of complaint about the mistress's absence, the dream vision, and the protestation of constant love, modulating thereafter into songs that hint at the arrival of the true love. The sonnet sequence itself is similarly controlled, beginning with two complaints against the winds and Cupid for keeping the lovers separate, then two poems of elaborate although conventional praise, to a somewhat cynical pair of sonnets showing how easy it is to manipulate the Petrarchan rhetoric; these are followed by a further eight sonnets which show in their rhetoric exactly the kind of intertextuality that was inevitable in the coterie culture.

The second scheme on fol. 82v reorganizes the poems to bring the songs to the fore, almost as if the mythical characters were prophesying the marriage of Anne and James. The attestation of constant love, the complaints of absence, and the dream vision then become part of the poet-lover's tormented thoughts of the lady before he meets her in life. In this scheme, the specially constructed pair of sonnets to show the difference in styles is placed at the end, as if either to dampen their cynicism, or thoroughly to undercut everything that has gone before.

Before looking at the poems in detail, the question of attribution must be addressed. Curtis Perry's research has raised major difficulties for literary critics who have until now viewed James's poems as a means of exploring the king's literary sensibilities. Where James's name is associated with a literary text—particularly where that text has been corrected, amended, or attributed in the king's own hand, which is the case of Add. ms. 24195—the literary critic has to assume that the king assumed authorship and thus was engaged in textually constructed authority. The collaborative nature of coterie poetry-making renders it impossible to decide whose was the major part of the undertaking.[16] Given that through his own or his son's editorial hand, James claimed authorship of these poems, they will be examined as at least collaborations, if not wholly self-authored pieces. According to Add. ms. 22601, the poems of questionable attribution are the second stanza of (1), both sonnets of (4), most of (5), (6), (7), (8) and (9).

The two songs, which the fol. 82v contents page places first in *Amatoria*, are composed in traditional stanzaic form, both in eight-line stanzas of four tetrameter lines rhymed *a b a b* followed by three trimeters and a dimeter, in the first song rhymed *c c c b* and in the second *c d c d*. The similarity of the structures, and the underwritten classical parallel of the myth of Hero and Leander, which is specifically evoked in the second song, seem to suggest that this is a pair of related poems, referring to the betrothal of James to Anne of Denmark—neatly conflating historical reality with mythological antecedent.

Neither of these songs has any indication of addressee, and thus they give the impression of being poetical recreations or exercises, the kind of writing expected by a fiancée, particularly a royal fiancée. Given the similarity between the situations of the two pairs of lovers, it is possible that the later editorial hand decided the poems were so apposite that they should be attributed to the historical situation. On the other hand, the first song—appearing also in ms. Bodley 165 in a very much denser and earlier Scots than the Add. ms. 24195 version—uses the "common language" advocated in the *Reulis and Cautelis;* it does not include any high flown comparisons, suggesting that it may just be a sincere expression of feeling to the future queen, although the critic must always be wary of such romantic notions. That the addressee could be described as "my halfe in all" (49) suggests an unusual (for James) measure of equality conferred on the lady. The second song, in this reading, is a more sophisticated rendering of the natural separation into a mythological equivalence, elevating the subjects from the ordinary "mortall man" and his love not only to one archetype of separated lovers but to two: first Hero and Leander separated by a sea, as Scotland is from Denmark; then Pyramus and Thisbe "[d]euyded onlie by a wall" (19).

Whatever the status of these two songs, a very different impression is given in the poem "Constant Loue in all Conditions," which creates a traditional Scottish winter scene reminiscent of medieval Scots texts:

> Now doeth disdainfull Saturne sadd and olde
>
> With ycie bearde enioye his frosen raigne
>
> His hoarie haires and snowie mantle colde
>
> Ou'rcouers hills and euerie pleasant plaine (1–4)

Perhaps this could be seen as a very Scottish version of Petrarch's "Ponmi ove 'l sole occide I fiori e l'erba" (Put me where the sun burns flowers and grass) (*Rime* CLXV), but the native tradition appears much stronger, specifically deriving from the wintry scene at the beginning of Robert Henryson's *The Testament of Cresseid,* some of Dunbar's descriptions of the Scottish winter, and indeed James's own Sonnet 6 from the beginning of the *Essayes.*[17] There is also the Pléiade precedent of the naturalistic description of the world rather than the highly stylized, enameled medieval lapidary descriptions. Love is exiled from this icy landscape, as "no Cupide with his golden bate / Darr make there harts his harbour where he hants" (11–12), and the "kindlie courage," the sexual drive and potency of birds and beasts, is frustrated and imprisoned by the all-pervasive cold. Only the persona, not being a beast, does not forget his love despite the cold. Rather than a Petrarchan fire and ice opposition, this is a more intellectual affirmation that man's reason, his sense of the rightness of loving, enables him to maintain the "inward flame" (21) despite "winters frost [or] sommers heate" (23). Where the Petrarchan would oppose the heat of love to the cold of the lady's disdain, James's persona contends with the very literal cold of winter, displaying the rational view so central to his vision.

Although this poem is written in the Ballat Royal stanza of eight pentameter lines rhymed *a b a b, b c b c*—described in the *Reulis and Cautelis* as for "heich and graue subiectis"—the language is very plain and unadorned, as befits the description of the weather. There is only light classical reference: to wintry Saturn ruling the earth and to exiling longed-for Flora of the springtime in the first stanza; to Cupid chased away from the deadened hearts of birds and beasts until "mounting Phoebus make[s] them to reuert" (16) to their accustomed "kindlie courage" (15) in the second. There is no god in the final stanza: man appears to be standing against both gods and nature. Despite its physical form, the poem is constructed almost like a sonnet. The first stanza sets the scene, as would be expected in the first quatrain of a sonnet; the second depicts the animals and how they are affected by the prevailing cold; and the final stanza, like the sestet of a sonnet, sets the persona in opposition to these animals, opposing reason to the senses and love to naked sexuality. As will be seen later, James did not always show the same facility in handling the tighter sonnet structure; this is one of the more successful poems in the collection, for it allows his natural inclination to copiousness fuller rein.

Even more Ciceronian *copia* is noted in "A Dreame on His Mistris My Ladie Glammis," apparently a medieval dream vision, but with classical imagery and an amalgam of Virgil, dream theory, the theory of the humors, and Delphic as well as Sibyllic oracles and emblems. Although this is one of the poems of questionable attribution, its form and structure as well as its content make it very likely that James was the prime mover in its composition. What is always noticeable about James's writing is the humanist classical background that appears to come so naturally to him and that depends on a like-minded reader for full appreciation. Here he uses his own learning to create something new, exactly as he advocated in the *Reulis and Cautelis.*

The dreamer refers to Virgil's *Aeneid* in the "ports of horne" (11), which introduces the notion of the twin Gates of Sleep. One of these is said to be of horn, allowing an easy exit for shadows that are true. The other is of ivory, perfectly made, but the spirits send visions that are false in the light of day (*Aeneid* vi: 893–96). The shape-changing god Morpheus grants the dreamer a vision of his lady who "bow[s] her doune / And ioyn[s] the rubies sine . . . vnto mine" (37–40) and presents him with "a tablet and an Amethyst" (43), which when he awakes he finds are still there, proving that the dream was no vision but a true experience. An analysis of the origin of the dream shows that dream theory is still potent in James's intellectualizing.[18]

James again follows his own instructions, using antonomasia in "the statelie forcked hill" for Parnassus, "the christall siluer spring / Of flying horse and riding foule" for the Hippocrene, and "Lycian Lord that Deïtie / Whome Delphos did adore . . . the sacred Sisters Monarch greate" for Apollo. He sets the scene for the dream vision in exactly the same way his predecessors had done, calling to the god of poetry to inspire his endeavors and help him interpret the dream.

The amethyst is interesting, as it is "in forme of hart" (109), evoking reminiscences of a number of "heart" poems from the earlier sixteenth century that were derived from the Scottish practice of sending heart-shaped jewels to the beloved.[19] Similarly, the long disquisition on the magical powers of the gem situates the poem and its theme soundly in the humanist-rational mindset, but with echoes of the irrational medieval beliefs in such powers. The amethyst, a symbol of love and its pains, is valued for its power to protect its owner against drunkenness and poison, and to give courage and strength in battle. The rational, local development of this poem is in direct contrast to the amorous Petrarchism coming from Europe, but it shows that James was deeply conscious of the current conventions and sought to subvert them by proposing a very manly alternative to the conventional love-wracked poet:

In spite of all the poysoned lookes
    Of Dames I shall not swerue . . .
For suire he can not worthie be
    To be accompted deare
By anie Dame that in his brest
    A womans hart dois beare. (135, 141–44)

The pun in the last line adds the note of dry humor noted in many of the coterie poems, in which the Scots appear to be mocking the effete Europeans swooning over their loves. This refusal to be enslaved to love and to a woman appears almost a national trait; it is seen in many of the Jacobean poets and derived from the rather misogynist view that had been present in Scottish writing for more than a century. The Scotsman is genetically armed against female wiles. Only Cupid can shoot through his defenses, because he is a worthy adversary—perhaps because the last property of the amethyst is:

A hunter for to aide,
In end to catch his pray, the fruict
Of all his travell made. (158–60)

The detailed description of the hunting scene that follows this explanation strongly suggests that here James is using some of his own experience of a much-loved occupation; this is further hinted at by his persona's description of himself as "prentise past / Into that Princelie game" (161).

The tablet, however, is rather different, being a tiny gold-leaf book, whose pages depict various emblems, each described and with an explanatory motto. The book itself represents the lady in her chastity and purity, while the engravings are "[t]he diuers passions . . . / That walters in her thought" (179–80). The first emblem depicts a naked man roasted by the sun's heat, and stung by flies, but charmed by music into not feeling the pain. This represents the woman's "Siren" voice, charming the hearers. The second emblem is an open hand holding the lady's heart ready to be shot by Cupid's arrow, signifying willingness to love. The emblem depicting the lady is a conventional image of the lady as sun outshining all others through her beauty and virtue:

The other on the vtter side
The Sunne hath shining bright
Into the midst, with stars about
Bot darckned by his light
And as that dittie sayes, As Sunne
Amongst the stars does shine,
So she her sexe surpasseth far
In vertues most diuine. (201–8)

Exactly as prescribed in the *Reulis and Cautelis,* there is no portrait of the lady: "Ye sall rather prayse hir uther qualiteis nor hir fairnes nor hir shaip; or ellis ye sall speik sum lytill thing of it and syne say that zour witts ar sa smal and zour utterance sa barren, that ze can not discryue any part of hiur worthelie" (77). In the poem "the art of sume Apelles fine" (233) is asked to do the portrait justice. The emblem was a novelty from Europe—the linking of text with image literalizing the metaphors, predominantly of Petrarchism, that had become so pervasive. In this respect, the ambivalence in straddling the old and new literary worlds is seen in James's stanzaic poetry, showing an awareness, if not a predilection, for the native style of versifying married to a determination to be part of the new poetry.

The final stanza is intriguingly ambivalent. Coming immediately after the lines suggesting that the whole interpretation has been a dream within the dream, the reference to "Titan mine" could be the lady as sun or Apollo as god of poetry:

Now may you see ô Titan mine,
No distance far of place,
Nor other thought can out of me
The thought of yow deface,
In absence are ye present still
And euer so in sight,
No wonder is, what Monarch may
Resist a womans might. (261–68)

"Titan mine" is finally the lady, elevated far above him, like the ladies of the courtly love convention, and thus ever present, not subject to the vicissitudes of nature, and a protective force for the exercise of rationality against the dangers of emotional attack from other mere women who would try to win him. The poet has made an intellectual voyage of discovery through his dream, for poetry in James's view is an intellectual undertaking. Love is simply not a suitable "sentence" for this kind of exercise of learning and knowledge.

As he refused to capitulate to the otherwise almost universal vogue for love poetry, James appears always to be trying to remake the conventions in a new way. The "Complaint of His Mistressis Absence from Court," which may refer to the same "Ladie Glammis," is written in what is conventionally called rhyme royal but which James renamed Troilus verse. This poem appears to show the collaborative principle strongly at work. The Scottish tradition of alliteration as commended in the *Reulis and Cautelis* is used effectively in the opening lines:

Whill as a statelie fleeting castle faire

On smoothe and glassie salt does softlie slide

With snowie sheets all flaffing here and thaire. . . . (1–3)

The /s/ sound does create a gentle, zephyr-like breeze mirroring the calm conditions at the start of the voyage, while the /f/ alliteration links semantically with the following references to fortune and the fate that will befall the travelers, the "foolish pilgrims of the seas / Inflamd with following fortunes fickle baite" (8–9).

At first this late sixteenth-century poem looks back to medieval allegory in its depiction of the lover basking in the sunlight of his lady's presence, thinking himself secure as a ship on a calm sea, but then the absence of the lady is seen as the disappearance of the sun and the rising of a storm. Where a Petrarchan would have developed the metaphor of the storm-tossed mariner mirroring the lover's distraught condition, what differentiates this poem both from its medieval precedents and from the contemporary convention is the rather more baroque development of the imagery:[20]

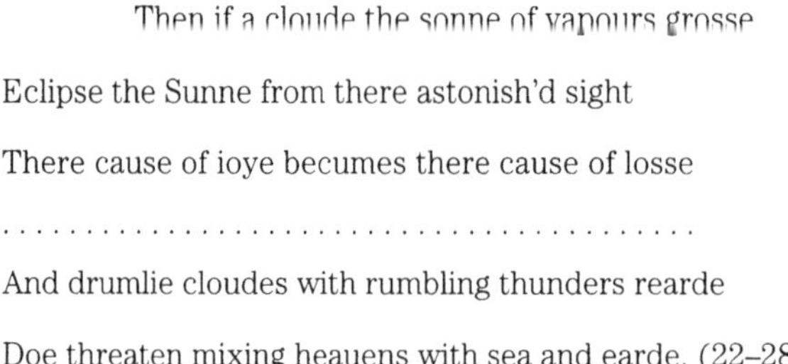

Then if a cloude the sonne of vapours grosse

Eclipse the Sunne from there astonish'd sight

There cause of ioye becumes there cause of losse

. . . .

And drumlie cloudes with rumbling thunders rearde

Doe threaten mixing heauens with sea and earde. (22–28)

The meteorological fact of the development of clouds is given a human explanation: the "vapours grosse" drawn up by the heat of the sun become a cloud "born" of the sun, covering the face of its father or eclipsing him through jealousy. The punning "sonne" and "Sunne" reinforces the novelty of the figure. The figurative mode is very much more important than the superficial use of Petrarchan commonplaces such as the lady as sun, and the rational intellectualizing of the phenomenon denies the amorous content. In the same way as is seen in "Constant Loue in All Conditions," the description of the natural world is much more important than the reference to the lady. The reader is given six stanzas of naturalistic description of a sea voyage made hellish by an advancing storm before the lady's absence from court is mentioned and equated with Apollo's withdrawal of the sun from the sky. The *vers rapporté* of the penultimate stanza is an amalgam of old

Scots practice found in the *Kingis Quair* and French conventions taken from the *Grands Rhétoriqueurs,* seen also in the poetry of Ronsard:

> The Court as garland lackes the cheefest floure
>
> The Court a chatton toome that lackes her stone
>
> The Court is like a volier at this houre
>
> Wherout of is her sweetest Sirene gone.
>
> Then shall we lacke our cheefest onlie one?
>
> No, pull not from ws cruell cloude I praye
>
> Our light, our rose, our gemme, our bird awaye. (50–56)

The ambivalence and the tension between worlds are evident in the very native diction, in the verse form and particularly in the correlative structure, where all the images in the first four lines are collected together in the final line. Interestingly, Ronsard used the same imagery in his elegy to Mary when she left France, and it is conceivable that this trope, the gaping void at the center, was grafted on to what was previously a straightforward description of a sea voyage that turned into a disaster, showing James's ability to incorporate the newer developments from continental literature into the existing tradition.[21]

The final stanza reminds us of Montgomerie's lyric "Lyk as the Dum Solsequium," the natural comparison of the lover's attraction to the lady:

> Bot what my Muse, how pertlie thus thou sings
>
> Who rather ought Solsequium like attend
>
> With luckned leaues will wearie night take end. (59–61)

Clearly, this is a lover-like pose, as the Muse is far too facile (the force of "pertlie"). The reference to Montgomerie's and Ronsard's images points to the ludic intertextuality of the poem and shows a much more sophisticated consciousness than James is often credited with, perhaps of course because these parts of the poem are Montgomerie's in a larger scale collaboration. It also draws attention to the artificiality of the trope by comparison with the hell of a real storm at sea, where the passengers are described as "Diuells in Plutoes court . . . ranged" (42). This is reminiscent of the imagery Montgomerie used for the Lords of Session in his Sonnet XXI. "A complaint of his mistressis absence from Court" is a poem that patently illustrates the effects of the coterie on composition, and whether James actually borrowed lines written by others of the group or reformulated their images into his own words, the result is an effective and successful poem.

Although he stipulated a quite different purpose for the sonnet in his *Reulis and Cautelis*, James was on occasion prepared to turn his hand to the amatory sonnet, perhaps having been encouraged by his queen. The fourteen sonnets in *Amatoria* are more Petrarchan in imagery than the longer lyrics, with the same classical coloring, and mainly constructed in the Scottish interlaced rhyme scheme that James recommended. Although most of these are now, after Perry, of questionable attribution, there appears to be a strong flavor of Jacobean sensibility and style in many of them. Perhaps most illuminative of this attitude to the composition of love poetry are "Two Sonnets to her M:tie to Show the Difference of Stiles," the two styles being honesty and artificiality. These were composed in the 1590s, long after the writing of the *Reulis and Cautelis,* and they demonstrate a greater ease with the rhetoric than the earlier sonnets do. Perhaps to Anne's dismay, they clearly show how the conventions of the Petrarchan sonnet could be used for a totally invented statement of emotion. In order to heighten the effect of artificiality in the second sonnet, the one professing honesty is put first. Pleading to be excused from writing, the poet explains:

> Long since forsooth my Muse begunne to tire
>
> Through daylie fascherie of my own affaires
>
> Which quench'd in me that heauenly furious fire. (5–7)

This is not the Petrarchan fire of love, but the Horatian divine fury that animates poets and stimulates their imaginations, but here it is quenched by the day-to-day business of running the kingdom. James is admitting that he was never a poet first and foremost, but a monarch, the only rank he believed could be inspired by any type of divinity, and now very much a king oppressed by the petty quarrels continually arising in court. He is also denying the Petrarchan commonplace that life to the poet-lover revolves entirely around the lady, every aspect of everyday living significant only inasmuch as it relates to her. Throughout his life, James used poetry in an attempt to control events that were beyond his political powers—as can be seen from the passion in the Bothwell sonnets—but he does not seem to have felt any need to discuss amorous emotions in this way.[22] In an apparent farewell to poetry, although really only to any pretense at love poetry, he concludes: "Now ar Castalias floods dried up in me / Like suddain shoures this time of yeere ye see" (13–14). Comparing "Castalias floods" to "suddain shoures" relegates the production of verse to a seasonal occupation, or an activity appropriate for only one period in a man's life. The writing of love poetry is seen as a kind of poetic puberty, a stage which must be gone through in order to reach literary adulthood.

The second sonnet now reveals its artificiality. The Muse is still sleeping and the verse is "barren," but the name of the queen and her "inchaunting fame" (19) will arouse her and allow the poet to write. Interestingly, the queen is clearly not the poet's Muse. The poem appears to recall the journey to Denmark, when James was taken from his native land:

> And Eagle like on Theatis back to flee
>
> Wher she commaunded Neptune for to be
>
> My Princely guard and Triton to attend
>
> On artificial flying tours of tree. (22–25)

Again the imagery is classical, and James is very conscious of his own social position, protected by Neptune. He is willing to write only for someone who is of the same social rank: "Then since your fame hath made me flie before / Well may your name my verses nou decore" (27–28). As is required by the *Reulis and Cautelis,* her name relates decorously to his verses. The poem does not praise Anne for herself; rather her name adds a decoration to James's achievement.

While clearly a "poeticall exercise," and demonstrating the artificiality of the tropes, the pair of sonnets is also rather playful in conception and reminds the reader of the intertextuality found in a great deal of the poetry of the period, where poets would reply to each other's verses either out of pure enjoyment in the exercise or in a spirit of competition.[23] These poems do work as poems, and they are constructed neatly as parallels. As is conventional in this kind of lyric, the poem is all about the writer rather than about the queen who is the ostensible subject and addressee—a trait seen in most of the other sonnets, some of which were clearly written before James and Anne actually met.

One of the more successful of these earlier sonnets is "O Cruell Cupide," printed as the second stanza of the complaint against the winds, which vividly employs the gothic imagery that many of the Jacobeans delighted in and which is seen frequently in the *Tarantula* sonnets of William Fowler. Using heavy alliteration, James describes his love as a literal sickness, boiling him alive:

> I frie in flammes of that envenomed darte
>
> Which shotte me sicker in at ather eye
>
> Then fastned fast into my hoalit harte. (20–22)

The imagery of sickness is literalized in a particularly horrific way, indeed in a forensic description:

> My bones are dried there marrowe melts awaye
>
> My sinnowes feebles through my smoaking smarte
>
> And all my blood as in a pann doeth playe. (24–26)

This is a particularly Scottish development of the Petrarchan image, similar in style to the stylistic innovations in fifteenth-century Italy by poets like Serafino and Thebaldeo, who literalized Petrarch's images without taking account of the underlying structure of the Florentine's sequence. It is yet another strand of European influence, perhaps introduced by William Fowler, the only member of the court group to concentrate on Italian poetry for his imitations. It could also perhaps be described as a peculiarly Scottish form of the emblem, which was another method of concretizing the metaphor.

Another successful poem that takes a more conventional stance is "To the Queene, Anonimos," which draws a transparent veil over the identity of the writer. The poem opens with an echo of Petrarch in "That blessed houre when first was broght to light" (1), but more so with an echo of the classical Judgment of Paris, where three goddesses vie for the chance to protect Anne. Although the queen is the apparent subject of the poem, James shows the usual egotism of the sonneteer, compounded by his own royal position: by naming his queen "Our earthlie Juno" (2), he automatically becomes Jove. Before naming the three goddesses he proclaims himself king of the gods and "happie Monarch sprung of Ferguse race" (9), tracing his lineage back to its origins. Only in the sestet are the queen's attributes mentioned, making this sonnet as Italianate in structure as it is in rhyme scheme (*a b b a a c c a, d e e d f f*). She is "wise Minerue when pleaseth the" (10), "chaste Diana" (12) when occupied in sporting pursuits, and finally: "Then when to bed thou gladlie does repaire / Clasps in thine armes thy Cytherea faire" (13–14). This is a successful closure, the use of "Cytherea" rather than, say, "lovely Venus" creating an effectively scanning line, but the sole focus of the poem is James and what he makes of his queen. His choice of activities brings out the particular quality required. That she is named for the goddesses serves to heighten his own sense of status rather than to praise his consort.

A group of six sonnets, printed as a six-stanza poem in the manuscript, shows the same mixture of traditional native and Petrarchan tropes. The first of these sonnets is a very neatly localized version of "Voyant ces montz" by Mellin de Saint-Gelais[24]—the only obvious translation in the set, and probably appealing because of the natural landscape description in the original. Here the persona compares himself with the Cheviot hills, starting neatly with natural and human comparisons:

> There foote is fast, my faithe a stedfast stone
>
> From them discends the christall fontains cleare
>
> And from mine eyes butt fained force and mone
>
> Hoppes trickling teares with sadd and murnefull cheare. (5–8)

The alliteration here reinforces the patterning of the comparisons, which are unforced and generally successful, and the poetic diction is lightly handled, but the sestet, rather than following Mellin's straightforward if unusual comparison, divides lines and ideas at the caesura, creating a rather odd impression. The original sestet began:

> Mille troppeaux s'y promenent et paissent
>
> Autant d'amours se couvent et renaissent
>
> Dedans mon coeur que seul est ma pasture. (9–11)
>
> (A thousand flocks ramble and feed there, and as many loves breed and are reborn in my heart, which is my only pasture.)

Since James had added detail to his octave, when he came to the sestet he found he had too many images to fit into the six lines, as in:

> From them great windes doe hurle with hiddeous beir
>
> From me deepe sighs, greate flocks of sheepe they feede
>
> I[n] flockes of love, no fruicts on them appeare. (9–11)

This is a common failing in James's writing, although it is not as noticeable in more copious stanzaic verse. The attempt to cram in more comparisons than the sonnet will really bear is a sign of James's discomfort with the straitjacket of the short lyric form generally, and it is a sign of his insight that he knows his own limitations as a poet.

James preferred very visual, natural similes, such as the topographical comparison in "the Cheuiott hills" and the image of the lizard feeding on the human face, which is a traditional Scottish image for loving looks, used frequently by Montgomerie in poems to James and probably derived from Pliny: "Since Lezardlike I feede vpon her face / And suckes my satisfaction from her sight" (35–36). Similarly conventional to Scottish verse and to Montgomerie in particular is the image of the marigold, the flower that always follows the sun and cannot live without its rays: "No more may I, then marigolde by night / Beare blossomes when no sighte of Sunne I haue" (37–38). The comparisons work well, playing on the duality of the lady as beloved face (the lizard) and life-giving sun (the flower), and once again showing James's proclivity for natural imagery rather than the rarefied Petrarchan. Such preference for, and competence in, depicting aspects of the real Scottish landscape add a dimension of natural realism that could be said to lead on ultimately to the work of William Drummond of Hawthornden.

This is also evident in the fifth sonnet, which conflates classical and natural images very effectively. "[T]hat crooked crawling Vulcan" becomes synonymous with the fire he uses in his forge, buried under ashes "whill by his heate he drie / The greene and fizzing faggots made of tree" (59–60). Although this looks at first sight to be a gothic version of the traditional Petrarchan fires of love that produce tears in the lover, it is more effectively a natural image of sap-filled wood burning, the onomatopeoic "fizzing" suggesting the spitting of the drying sap. Native diction and idiom give this poem its effectiveness, as when the spark of love is described as "that litle sponke and flaming eye" (61), which, once given oxygen, will "bleaze brauelie forth and sparkling all abreed" (62), despite being "smor'd vnder coales of shame" (66). This is clearly a remembered sight of the reviving of the fire that has been damped down (or "smor'd") under peats or coals during the night. In addition to the native diction, the pronunciation by a Scot would add assonance, particularly in the first quatrain: "*A*n-vnder *a*shes c*o*lde as *o*ft we s*ee* / *A*s senseles d*ea*de whill by his h*ea*te he dr*ie*" (58–59, emphases added). The Scottish ownership of the Petrarchan commonplace could hardly be more strongly marked, showing the writer to be a highly competent innovator in his own terms.

These poems illustrate that James had to have good reason for writing amatory lyrics and did not readily turn his hand to the form. He spends very little time discussing love poetry in the *Reulis and Cautelis,* and where he mentions it, he advises poets to use "commoun language" and "wilfull reasonis, proceeding rather from passioun nor reasoun" (76). As has been seen, James does in large measure obey his own rules, and where his philosophical and meditative inclinations or love of the Scottish landscape are concerned he can produce successful poems. Once he has a suitable comparison, a situation or an image, he can write extremely vividly and effectively, especially in the extended lyric form, but in sonnets he imitates the fashionable Petrarchism seen in his French reading and in the works of Montgomerie or William Fowler in his Italianate mode. The images found in these sonnets are either conventionally classical, or Petrarchan metaphors derived from his own reading and from the works of the other poets at or visiting court, or very peculiarly Scottish images, like those of the heart sent as a gift, or—from the natural world—the lizard and the marigold. A generalized Petrarchan rhetoric appears in sonnets and stanzaic poems that are more often specifically localized than situated in a mythological or medieval landscape. This, however, should not be surprising, as amatory lyrics were not of any real interest to the leader and patron of the court poets; moral and philosophical works coming from Europe carried much more weight. His preferred poet in French was, after all, the Huguenot Salluste Du Bartas, whose work he translated, and he deeply disapproved of Montgomerie's attraction to Ronsard's lyrics. James evidently felt at one time, or perhaps intermittently, that it was the done thing to write love lyrics, perhaps to please the queen: the subtitles often make clear that this was Anne's taste more than his own.

James was a competent versifier in extended lyric modes and in the sonnet form when he was using it as suggested in the *Reulis and Cautelis.* He has been described above as a precursor of William Drummond of Hawthornden. While this should not be taken as a judgment based on poetic accomplishment, there are similarities in terms of adherence to traditional forms that have largely been superseded elsewhere in the literary world, a thorough knowledge of current European trends—whether fashionable in English poetry or not—and a deep and abiding love of the natural world that pervades his most successful poetry.

Notes

1. Although the terms "Castalian" and "Castalian Band" are widely used by literary scholars and are convenient shorthand terms to define the court coterie poets and the period of their flourishing, they have no authority from the poets or the literary texts of the period. Priscilla Bawcutt has recently argued most persuasively—in a paper given at the 9th International Conference on Medieval and Renaissance Scottish Language and Literature held at St. Andrews University in June 1999—that the term post-dates the 1580s, when most of the poetry was produced, and is probably derived from James's epitaph on Montgomerie, where he appeals to "Ye sacred brethren of Castalian band" to commemorate Montgomerie's poetic genius. This was then picked up by Helena Mennie Shire and popularized through her writings on the period.
2. Wendel-Bellenger.
3. The contents of James's library, including the volumes he received from Queen Mary, are listed in Warner.

4. Poems like "Ane Prayer and Thankisgiwing," "To His Rycht Intierlie Belowit Friend," and "To His Maiestie in Fascherie," in addition to a number of poems addressed to ladies or in female voice, which could equally be veiled expressions of succor to the king. Stewart's poems are found in Crockett, *Poems.*
5. Craigie, *Poems* 1: 65–83.
6. This idea was expressed in a paper given at the 9th International Conference in St. Andrews in June 1999.
7. Jack, in his introduction to the *Reulis and Cautelis* in *The Mercat Anthology*, sets the treatise firmly alongside *Basilikon Doron* as evidence of James's stamping of his impression on the new Jacobean age.
8. Craigie, *Poems* 1: 1–96.
9. Craigie, *Basilikon Doron* 1: 186. The version quoted is the anglicized printed Waldegrave edition of 1599.
10. The phrase is Marotti's, in *Manuscript* 135.
11. All translations from French are my own.
12. Smith 1: 46–57.
13. For instance, Du Bartas's "Dieu lance-foudre" (32) is translated as "The *Thundrer*" and "Sur le ciel porte-feux à son gré le promeine" (120) as "Vpon the fyrie heauen to walk at list." In both these instances, the Scots is simpler, perhaps more conventional, but more poetically effective.
14. Perry has recently raised this issue. Perry has uncovered the "lost" manuscript that was the basis of J. O. Halliwell's *Poetical Miscellanies from a Manuscript Collection of the Time of James I* (London: Percy Club, 1845). This is BL Add. ms. 22601, where poems in folios 24 to 36v are attributed to "Sr Thomas Areskine of Gogar." Many of these poems also figure in BL Add. ms. 24195, where they are attributed to James under the editorial title "Amatoria." James Craigie, in his canonical edition of James's works, commented on the alternative attribution, but he decided that this was evidence of a collaboration between the lifelong friends rather than a theft by James of another's work. Perry's article vividly illustrates the difficulties of attribution inherent in poems of this period.
15. Craigie, *Poems* 2: 68–89, 94–98, and 118.
16. The same problem of attribution is found in the series of seven poems printed in Gullans's edition of *English and Latin Poems of Sir Robert Ayton,* where there has clearly been collaboration among Ayton, William Alexander, and Alexander Craig while they were students together. Gullans discusses the issue at 16–17.
17. In the early sonnet, James also describes winter by reference to Saturn:

Or let them think, they see god Saturne olde,

Whose hoarie haire owercouering earth maks flie

The lytle birds in flock, fra tyme they see

The earth and all with stormes of snow owercled. (7–10)

18. This is clearly a *somnium* or allegorical dream according to the description given of the three truthful kinds of dreams in Macrobius's commentary on Cicero's *Dream of Scipio*. Such a dream is God-given as opposed to being internally induced.
19. Mary, Queen of Scots sent a gift of a heart-shaped diamond ring to Elizabeth of England accompanied by a poem in French representing the diamond's own voice. Although the original has been lost, the poem survives in two Latin translations "Adamas loquitur," and Robin Bell has reconstructed it in English as "The Diamond Speaks," 21.
20. By "baroque" I mean the tendency to look for exotic comparisons, which in slightly later English poetry could be described as "metaphysical."
21. These lines were later filched by Alexander Craig in "Scotlands Teares," written to lament the departure of James to the throne of England in 1603, published in *The Poeticall Essayes of Alexander Craige Scotobritane* (London, 1604), 18–20, and collected in *The Poetical Works of Alexander Craig of Rose-Craig 1604–1631* (Glasgow: Hunterian Club, 1837).
22. James wrote three very vividly worded sonnets after the earl of Bothwell broke into his chamber and threatened him in 1591. They are printed in Craigie, *Poems* 1: 110–11.
23. Henry Constable, an English poet who was in Scotland at the time of the king's marriage, replied wittily and teasingly to his complaint of contrary winds. See Grundy, *Poems of Henry Constable* 142. In addition, an English version of Montgomerie's "Thyne ee the glass vhare I beheld my [hairt]" is found in his *Diana,* 117.
24. In Stone 1: 181–82.

Works Cited

Bell, Robin, ed. *Bittersweet within my Heart: The Love Poems of Mary, Queen of Scots.* San Francisco: Chronicle Books, 1992.

Craigie, James, ed. *The Basilikon Doron of King James VI.* 2 vols. Edinburgh: Scottish Text Society, 1944.

———, ed. *The Poems of King James VI of Scotland.* 2 vols. Edinburgh: Scottish Text Society, 1955–58.

Crockett, Thomas, ed. *The Poems of John Stewart of Baldynneis.* 2 vols. Edinburgh: Scottish Text Society, 1913.

Grundy, Joan, ed. *The Poems of Henry Constable.* Liverpool: Liverpool UP, 1960.

Gullans, Charles, ed. *The English and Latin Poems of Sir Robert Ayton.* Edinburgh: Scottish Text Society, 1963.

Jack, R. D. S., and P. A. T. Rozendaal, eds. *The Mercat Anthology of Scottish Literature.* Edinburgh: Mercat P, 1997.

Laing, David, ed. *The Poetical Works of Alexander Craig of Rose-Craig 1604–1631.* Glasgow: Hunterian Club, 1837.

Marotti, Arthur. *Manuscript, Print and the English Renaissance Lyric.* Ithaca: Cornell UP, 1995.

Perry, Curtis. "Royal Authorship and Problems of Manuscript Attribution in the Poems of James VI and I." *Notes and Queries* 46:2 (June 1999): 243–46.

Smith, G. Gregory, ed. *Elizabethan Critical Essays.* 2 vols. Oxford: Clarendon P, 1904.

Stahl, William Harris [trans. with intro. and notes]. *Commentary on the Dream of Scipio/Macrobius.* New York: Columbia UP, 1952.

Stone, Donald Jr., ed. *Oeuvre poétique française Mellin de Saint-Gelais.* 2 vols. Paris: Société des Textes Françaises Modernes, 1993.

Warner, Sir George, ed. *The Library of James VI., 1573–1583.* Edinburgh: Scottish History Society, 1893, *Miscellany,* vol. 1.

Wendel-Bellenger, Yvonne, ed. *La défense et illustration de la langue française.* Paris: Larousse, 1972.

4

Discovering Desire in the *Amatoria* of James VI

Sarah M. Dunnigan

love is *represented*, entrusted to an aesthetic of appearances
(it is Apollo, *ultimately*, who writes every love story)

Roland Barthes, *A Lover's Discourse*

truly thou wast borne before in our hearts; but thou wishest also to be
thumbed in our hands; and laying aside thy majesty,
thou dost offer thyself to be gazed upon on paper,
that thou mayest be more intimately conversant among us.

George Herbert's comment of 1620 lays bare the paradox of how to read the body of secular love poetry attributed to James VI and I.[1] The predominant biographical reading of these lyrics, which remain relatively obscure within the tentative Jamesian poetic canon, assigns them an identifiable object of desire. In "gazing upon" the twenty lyrics of the *Amatoria*, then, are we "intimately conversant" with the difficult ways in which James loved Anne and with contrastingly erotic devotion to certain courtly gentlewomen? Or should James's amatory voice be interpreted as the rhetorically flexible construct attributed to other Renaissance love lyricists, the playful exploration of erotic *personae*, that mirrors the enduring Jamesian fascination with royal and literary authorities? Is the creation of the distant, disembodied sovereign icon as theorized by Louise Fradenburg imperilled by the mere voicing of desire?[2] James's secular love poetry has failed to find substantial critical attention.[3] Despite some textual complications, its apparent insignificance in the context of the king's literary canon might well be attributed to the poetic and generic preferences that James expounded in his early literary career. Yet the sheer diversity of the *Amatoria* miscellany has conventionally proved perplexing to interpreters, its frequently rebarbative tone and misogynistic *pointe* held up as contradiction of amatory orthodoxies: as "love poems, they are exceptionally antifeminine" and "singularly unamorous."[4]

The inscription above the first *Amatoria* sonnet might suggest that James offered these lyrics as a nuptial gift to his future bride and sovereign, Anne of Denmark. Ironically, the insidious disenchantments of the sonnet sequence (if indeed it can be conceived as such) may confirm the received historical portrait of James—at least the contemporary English public fashioning of the king, which does not suggest an auspicious love poet. Weldon remarked that he "was not very uxorious," and Anne herself was allegedly "grieved at the little esteem she thought he had for her, though, one would think, she could not but be sensible it was not personal to her, but to the whole Sex, (whom he was taxed with looking on, as necessary Evils). . . . She grew to despise him for his Want of Spirit, and took . . . little care to conceal her mean Opinion of him."[5] Famously, such "little esteem" is publicly manifest through the fiercely antifeminist rhetoric of the *Daemonologie* and by the *Basilikon Doron*, which proclaims in deference to conventional ideology the spiritual and political subordination of woman to man, wife to husband. The Jamesian doctrine of political absolutism is crystallized by a marital analogue: "I am the Husband and the whole Isle is my Wife."[6]

The conjectural body of James's amatory poetry offers provocations and complexities that can be fruitfully explored through cultural contextualization (the literary soil of the Scottish Jacobean court) as well as sensitivity to the subtleties of gender and sexual identity that stem from the poetic culture James himself helped create. In discovering desire(s) in these neglected texts, this essay proposes that the poetry is a complex emblem of literary sovereignty at a culturally neglected period of the king's career. It seeks to shed light on both the rhetorical and conceptual aspects of James's erotic philosophy and poetics.

The heterogeneous collection of lyrics known as the *Amatoria* never formed part of the official canon of James's poetry if judged by editions of the king's work published within his lifetime. It is principally contained in two manuscripts, BL Add. 24195 ("All the kings short poesis / that ar nor printed") and Bodley 165, both of which display a degree of editorial revision clearly independent of James himself.[7] In Add. 24195, both the main title ("All the kings . . . ") and the majority of the prefatory titles are considered later additions, chiefly by Charles I (which, in a sense, confers a degree of royal "authenticity").[8] The recent research of Curtis Perry, however, has brought to light a further manuscript, BL Add. 22601, which contains copies (sometimes structurally reorganized) of the major *Amatoria* texts and an attribution to Sir Thomas Erskine ("Sr Thomas Areskine of Gogar").[9] This discovery further complicates the existing degree of textual interference in the previous two manuscripts, already implying that their extant texts are to a degree imperfect and corrupt.

Perry persuasively proposes that the discovery of Add. 22601 most convincingly suggests a collaborative venture between James and Erskine (lifelong friends, as Perry notes), rather than wholly negating the king's authorship of these texts. Consequently, the title of one sonnet, "To the Queene Anonimos," may perhaps be construed as a playful acknowledgment of collaboration, a willful evasion of kingly identity (though the corroborated title of Add. 24195 still implies some desire to lay sovereign authorial claim to the corpus). Perry's contention also substantiates with greater clarity the nature of the courtly literary culture that emerged during the period of James's early reign: in the 1580s and 90s, the Scottish court provided an intimate, self-sufficient (and self-perpetuating) locus of literary production. Its cloistered intimacy, far greater than in its Elizabethan courtly counterpart, fostered the creation of an elite poetic milieu that reflects the characteristics of a coterie culture as defined in studies by Arthur Marotti and others.[10] None of the secular amatory works by this court's principal lyricists (for example, Alexander Montgomerie, William Fowler, and John Stewart) was published.[11] Existing solely in manuscript form (often in "presentation" volumes to the king, such as Stewart's *Rapsodies of the Authors Youthfull Braine,* belonging to the mid 1580s), this body of poetry was, by implication, circulated within the court's inner literary milieu. Subject to endless recreation through oral (or musical) performance, such texts are of necessity more fragile, less stable entities than publicly sanctioned, printed poetry. James himself clearly participated in the coterie culture of poetic exchange and "game," which permitted him to indulge in playful poetic identities: "kingly" self-representation is frequently eschewed in favor of inventive self-fashionings, richly illustrated by the creation of poetic names and different personae within the inner, so-called "Castalian" or Jacobean circle grouped around the king.[12] Accordingly, the collaborative nature of the amatory texts attributed to James can coherently be conceived as a natural product of this literary environment of exchange and intertextual allusion. It is therefore probable that the *Amatoria* texts found various circles of reception: within the immediate "Castalian" coterie (which, significantly, appears to have licensed more playful or ambiguous representations of the royal self; Montgomerie's poetry is an apt exemplar of such royal incarnations) and within more extended royal and courtly circles (the first sonnet of the *Amatoria,* for example, occasioned a "reply" from Henry Constable).[13]

This persuasive poetic milieu for the composition of these *Amatoria* lyrics should be contextualized with the historical specificity implied by the apparently social and occasional nature of the early sonnets (for example, in the inscription "A complaint against the contrary Wyndes that hindered the Queene to com to Scotland from Denmarke"). This has led to the delineation of a clear chronology for the Anne "sequence":

> This double sonnet [the first two] *must* have been written in 1589 in the five weeks between 15th September—the day when James learned that the fleet bringing Anne of Denmark to Scotland had been scattered by a storm, that her ship had taken refuge at Oslo and that she would not come to her husband's kingdom till the next year. . . .
>
> The opening lines of this sonnet [the third] *make it certain* that it was composed after James had arrived in Norway towards the end of October 1589, its closing ones suggest that it was actually written after he had met Anne of Denmark for the first time about the middle of the next month (my italics).[14]

Though the occasion of the opening sonnets—the impending royal marriage and the voyage to Norway delayed by "contrary wyndes"—is attested by contemporary accounts such as James Melville's,[15] the assumption of such apparent topicality and systematic correlations should be treated with some skepticism (especially since the titles were a later addition and even, perhaps, expediently inferred). The critical desire to "authenticate" these texts—to unearth the "sincerity" of the lyrics and detect the validating presence of a royal authority—is reductive, insensitive to the rhetorical complexity of the Renaissance love lyric per se, which frequently offers not the transparent reflection of an inner life (sovereign or not) but an imaginatively invented amatory self. The literally biographical reading is uneasy with the apparently nuptial Anne "sequence" which ultimately portrays a love ending in disillusion and dissolution, and with the lyrics of erotic persuasion to conjectural mistresses. The inference that James—and possible collaborators such as Erskine—engaged in poetic games of desire (therefore perpetuating the literary culture which at that moment he was instrumental in creating) might be more persuasive than the suggestion that such lyrics offer evidence of adultery. (The latter is the terminus ad quem of the biographical argument and a veiled concern of Allan Westcott's guarded conjectures, offering an interesting parallel to the profound crises surrounding the publication of love poems ascribed to James's mother Mary, Queen of Scots. In that sense, the anxieties of royal authorship were inherited).[16]

In 1584 James first exercised royal literary authority by the publication of the self-consciously titled *The Essayes of a Prentise in the Divine Art of Poesie,* which contained his poetic manifesto *A Short Treatise Containing Reulis and Cautelis to Be Observed and Eschewed in Scottis Poesie.* Although in many ways an immature work, this prose treatise has been undervalued in terms of British Renaissance poetics. It is clearly pertinent in relation to the *Amatoria* poetry it most probably predates. The *Reulis* has been established as a work of predominantly rhetorical theorizing, indebted to the ascendancy of the vernacular in European literary thought and which (although derivative in part, reflecting the technically prescriptive *grand rhétoriqueur* treatises) clearly and consciously articulates Scottish linguistic and literary difference from English, as opposed to European, writing.[17] Yet what role and significance is the secular love lyric assigned in this royally sanctioned renaissance, which, as R. D. S. Jack has demonstrated, instead favored the creation and translation of religious and philosophical works? Within the Scottish Jacobean coterie, writers frequently allude to James's translation of Du Bartas's *L'Uranie ou Muse Celeste* (published in 1584) which castigates works of secular love as immature, duplicitous, and blasphemous;[18] elsewhere James pledges devotion to Uranie, or the "heavenly muse" in the promulgation of a Protestant poetics. Nevertheless, this early prose treatise offers some suggestive strictures for a renaissance in love poetry.

In the *Reulis and Cautelis* James advocates the use of "commoun language with some passionate wordis":[19] "commoun" may be intended in a linguistic or stylistic sense (to be distinguished from "heich, pithie, and learned wordis" or "corruptit and vplandis wordis" as a kind of golden mean), or it may simply denote the use of familiar or well-known terms (the *Amatoria* certainly shuns the linguistic mannerism and esoterism of James's coterie). Yet amatory language should be expressive and emotive: to convey "wilfull reasonis, proceeding rather from passioun, nor reason."[20] That the poetic lover should argue from emotion rather than reason may merely reinstate the ancient antagonism between love and the rational faculty, but it significantly exempts amatory poetry from the analytic and logical qualities—"witt" and "reasons fitt"—that James prescribes elsewhere for a Scottish poetics.[21] Ironically, the corollary is that the ideal Jacobean love poem should possess a kind of emotional integrity or sincerity. The sheer power of feeling or passion must compel the faithful royal poet to write "viuelie" of desire.[22] The criterion of "authenticity" in the creation of love poems should prevail over any carefully orchestrated self-presentation—an ironic prescription (perhaps deliberately so), given the probable collaborative nature of production as Perry infers. Yet one ironic envoi by James himself confirms Sidney's skepticism that amatory lyricists seldom "feel those passions which easily . . . may be betrayed by that same forcibleness or *energeia* (as the Greeks call it) of the writer":[23]

My Muse hath made a willful lye I grante,
I sung of sorrows neuer felt by me;
I haue as great occasion for to wante,
My loue begunne my blessing for to be.
How can I then excuse so lowd a lye?

Emotional license or inventiveness (indeed mendacity) is here permitted. This apologetic coda on feigning ends a poem ostensibly addressed to (or commissioned by) Anne—"A Dier at her M:ties desyer"—where the lover's sacrifice is prevented by the sudden realization that he martyrs himself for a wholly worthless beloved:

> yett if the endles smarte & sorrowe I sustaine
>
> Were suffered for sume worthie wight, I happie wolde remaine
>
> I wolde me happie thinke if thus I martyred ware
>
> For sume sweete Sainct in sacrifice that both were good and faire
>
> But ô allace my paine and restles griefe it growes.[24]

The very sovereign precept of authenticity seems to require subversion in the context of the king's own apparent poetic practice, which, in the context of Perry's research, acquires further linguistic and circumstantial ironies.

If the *Amatoria* is an exercise in poetic and amatory "dissembling," the *Basilikon Doron* was resolutely offered as a mirror of James's "very minde." Here James declares that the king should serve as an emblem of truth: "artificial" courtly fashions should be shunned, as also a language "fairdit with artifice" (Craigie, *Basilikon Doron* 1:178, 170). Much of James's instruction to Henry is concerned with the cultivation of an image or illusion suggestive of integrity. The disavowal of "all affectate formis," the fascination with "inwarde" and "outwarde" forms of representation, and the ironic advocacy of a self-revelation that requires the subject to be "trustie and secreate": each strategy of self-representation (or rather the evasion of it) is mirrored in the representational evasiveness of the *Amatoria*.[25] If the courtier as lover/lover as courtier figure may be aligned to Puttenham's portrait of courtly dissembling, then the figure of the lover/king might bear comparison to Machiavelli's prince (William Fowler translated *Il principe* in the 1580s, an apposite addition to the Jamesian manifesto of vernacular translation). "To play thy self with thy awin consait / and lat nane knaw quhat thow dois mene":[26] duplicity and guile, the expedient sustaining of illusion, are political "virtues" mirrored in the language of the love lyric written at court. In one sense, the *Amatoria* (especially as a collaborative enterprise) might be regarded as a kind of eroticized politics.

Such playful ironies, however, are not only characteristic of the intimate coterie culture but perhaps stem from the innovative potential that James invested in the amatory genre. The sixth chapter of the *Reulis and Cautelis* expresses the fear or anxiety of literary repetition and argues generally for invention at the expense of imitation. In the creation of a distinctively national literature, love poetry, perceived as inherently derivative in its identity, must strive toward innovation: "Ze man also be warre with composing ony thing in the same maner, as hes bene ower oft vsit of before. *As in speciall,* gif ye speik of loue, be warre ze descryue zour *Loues* makdome, or fairnes. . . . [F]or thir thingis are sa oft and dyuerslie writtin vpon be Poëtis already, that gif ze do the lyke, it will appeare, ze bot imitate, and that it cummis not of zour awin *Inuentioun,* quhilk is ane of the chief properteis of ane Poete" (my italics).[27] The beauty of the female beloved (*descriptio pulchritudinis*) is singled out as a topic where invention should be solicited: "ze sall rather prayse her vther qualiteis, nor hir fairnes, nor hir shaip: or ellis ze sall speik some lytill thing of it, and syne say, that zour wittis ar sa smal, and zour vtterance so barren, that ze can not discryue any part of hir worthelie: remitting alwayis to the Reider, to iudge of hir, in respect sho matches, or excellis *Venus,* or any woman, quhome to it sall please yow to compaire her."[28] It may be in deference to this early prerequisite that the *Amatoria* seldom conceives the figure of the beloved in conventionally physical terms (at least through the iconographical language of the blazon). Paradoxically, the love poetry associated with James delineates the physicality of desire while rarely evoking the sensuality of its object.

The title of the collection (whether authorial or not) is appositely all-embracing for this heterogeneous assembly of "amatory" lyrics; such multiplicity, of course, may itself attest the collaborative nature of the *Amatoria* enterprise. The most immediate resonance of the term "amatoria" is Ovidian: the irony (not least the misogyny) of Ovid's *Ars Amatoria* is certainly present, though James's poetic "I" seldom assumes the didactic, preceptorial posture of its narrator. Although the term does not seem to appear as a defined genre in any of the most likely texts of Renaissance poetics (for example, in Scaliger's *Poetices libri septem* of 1581), at least in a purely verbal sense "amatoria" can simply be glossed to mean "the amorous, the erotic."

In the arrangement of Add. 24195, the collection opens with a series of twelve sonnets.[29] If unity is intended by the editorial numbering and the *Amatoria* was conceived as a sequence offering a coherent narrative of desire, the first three sonnets are in essence lyrics of courtship: the lover sues for reciprocal desire, persuading an indifferent other of his "paine" and "Melancholie." Anticipation of their union, the joy and anxieties of that eventual union as endured by the lover, then remorse for the diminution of that love (a "like sorrow" shared by both) constitute the trajectory of desire until the final sonnet, in which the female beloved is accused of infidelity and the lyricist's own desire extinguished *sans regrette.* Though Anne is posited as the recipient in only the first six sonnets (significantly, those which precede the disenchantment), is this, in its conjectural totality, an ironic sequence for the queen who is made to assume the role of a flawed beloved? Why should the fairly graceful nuptial sonnets, protesting "paine" but certain of the beloved's "louing" response, end in disenchantment (the contradiction for the logic of the biographical reading)? The original design of these sonnets is irrecoverable (if indeed a coherent structure existed for poems that were most likely conceived independently and collaboratively), and the issue of whether Anne's name was intended to "decore" each sonnet (especially the later ones) irresolvable. The first six sonnets, grouped under titles, may have been presented to Anne as a poetic gift, a commemoration of her arrival in Scotland and her accession to the throne, though there is no record of their presentation to her; by contrast, they may have been produced for the sovereign literary coterie at the court.

If we divest these sonnets of the potential politicking between the sovereign and his bride, the abstract figure of the beloved can be defined as an absent presence who has a tenuous physical and spiritual form. Even when solicited, it is only as she impinges on the lover himself; she is scarcely a Laura or Beatrice who ceaselessly (and innocently) compels her poet to proclaim her moral and physical beauties. The paired sonnets illustrative of two different rhetorical "stiles" are presented as responses to the beloved's "request" (l. 2). The first confesses to creative failure; and although the second proclaims the inspiration of her "enchanting fame," the first melancholy response is sufficient to render the beloved an imperfect and limited Muse. Creative power is fallible—"Now ar Castalias floods dried up in me / Like suddain shoures this time of yeere ye see" (ll. 13–14)—as is implicitly (in accordance with the frequent associative bind between poetry and the female beloved) the lover-poet's sexual power. In either sense, this sonnet serves to qualify the power of the beloved's allegedly "enchaunted fame" that bears the poet "alofte" in the opening sonnet and the sixth: "Frome natiue soile to follow on your name / And Eagle like on Theatis back to flie / Wher she commaunded Neptune for to be" (ll. 7–9). Here the image of the "Eagle like" lover seems to communicate an imperialistic sense of sexual power (even acquisitiveness), evoking Jupiter's possession of Ganymede. In the contemporary context of James's poetic assertions, the confession of creative aridity might seem a surprising, even if jesting, circumscription placed on royal literary supremacy. Authority, however mercurial, is embodied in the figure of woman, who here possesses greater sexual and rhetorical power.

The gendered imbalance of sexual power is the kernel of Jonathan Goldberg's interpretative paradigm for James's love poetry, which argues for a typology of power in these sonnets: "He invokes the ideal of political suppression for conquest in the realm of love."[30] Goldberg's Foucauldian power arguments (the etymological and literal authority of the sovereign *auctor*) are persuasive for many aspects of Jacobean cultural relations, but that the *Amatoria* should dissect the alliance between female beloved and male lover in terms of sexual and emotional power is scarcely remarkable within the context of the Renaissance love lyric, a genre devoted to mourning and celebrating the intrinsic instabilities of "power" and abjection. Further, Goldberg presents James (the "voice" of these texts is unambiguously assigned a sovereign authorial identity) in sole possession of sexual authority where that authority is arguably subject to delicate oscillations. In one sonnet, sexual desire, nurtured "secrete and unseen," is portrayed as a dangerously latent force. Desire has the capacity to delude the lover into believing it "sensles deade":

> Although that crooked crawling Vulcan lie
>
> An-vnder ashes colde as oft we see
>
> As senseles dead whill by his heate he drie
>
> The greene and fizzing faggots made of tree
>
> Then will that litle sponke and flaming eye
>
> Bleaze brauelie forth and sparkling all abreed
>
> With wandling wp [up] a wondrous sight to see
>
> Kithe clearlie then and on the faggots feede
>
> So I am forc'd for to confesse indeed
>
> My sponke of loue smor'd under coales of shame
>
> By beauties force the fosterer of that seede
>
> Now budds and bursts in an appearing flame.[31]

The intensity of such repressed, almost self-consuming desire makes the lover guilty ("smor'd" is peculiarly apt); the revelation or imagined consummation of desire is almost unwilled. The sonnet pivots around the idea of false appearance and beguiling illusion (the topos of representation informs James's writing throughout and recurs significantly in works produced by the Jacobean coterie[32]) as a startlingly tactile, aurally rich language that replicates the moment of the orgasmic blossom.

In James's love poetry, the distribution of power is uneven. In the act of desiring, the lover of necessity renounces autonomy. The tyrannical little love-god Cupid is invoked in the second sonnet to claim the sovereignty of his nominally sovereign subject (in conventional Renaissance love discourse, love-god and mortal are analogous to sovereign and unruly subject). The self-autonomy which Cupid here denies the lover is reasserted or contradicted by the subsequent sonnet. Here, the lover intensifies the consolations offered by the beloved through the quiet yet firm parenthesis confirming a sovereign identity: "Then happie Monarch sprung of Ferguse race" ("To the Queene, Anonimos," l. 9). This self-legitimizing reference to the fabled genealogy of Scottish sovereignty (which James frequently invoked in other contexts, hence associating himself with the source and origin of kingship) contrasts with the mythological lineage assigned to the beloved, who here seems persuasively to be Anne. As Minerva, Diana, and Venus incarnate (the sonnet opens with her creation), she symbolizes wisdom, chastity, and love (perhaps the sensual rather than the heavenly Venus, given the embrace of line 14). In these mythical guises, the beloved serves or obliges her "Monarch":

> That talkes with wise Minerue when pleaseth the
>
> And when thou list sume Princelie sporte to see
>
> Thy chaste Diana rides with the in chase
>
> Then when to bed thou gladlie does repaire
>
> Clasps in thine armes thy Cytherea faire. (ll. 10–14)

Each occasion presents James's desire as foremost; each virtue exists as if purely to oblige the lover's whims ("when pleaseth *the* / when *thou* list / when . . . *thou* gladlie"). The notoriously intrusive comment of line 6, "And as of female sexe like stiffe in will" (in reference to the goddesses' indecision, perhaps an oblique allusion to the Judgment of Paris) epitomizes the typically insidious quality of James's amatory misogyny, here offered as a "witty" parenthesis; such fabled feminine recalcitrance is, in the final sonnet, rhetorically manipulated. Not just the three deities but all women are indicted by this generalizing assertion (the characteristic grammar of misogyny). By implication "our earthlie Juno . . . our gratious Queene" (l. 2, where the pronoun implies a collective sense of queenly possession, an appropriately honorific gesture) is not exempt from feminine frailty. Since Minerva, Diana, and Venus cannot agree "who protect her shoulde by right" (by reason of their equal claims to authority as "Goddesses of equall might"), a greater authority is invoked to quell the dispute: "It was agreed by sacred Phoebus skill / To ioyne there powers to blesse that blessed wight"(ll. 7–8). As Goldberg notes, "sacred Phoebus" is identified with Apollo, and Apollo, as the god of poetry and prophecy in particular, remained James's favored mythological persona.[33] The king appears as the ultimate agent of resolution, restorer of "political" and poetic order, by the final couplet. Even if the Phoebus/Apollo allusion is refuted as another instance of Jamesian self-legitimizing, the sonnet still establishes a sexual hierarchy of authority that submits female to male: god rules goddess as, by implication, the king his queen. The opening sonnets, if imagined as a gift to Anne, are a paradoxical, almost self-negating commemoration of her nuptial promise. Their contexts of social and textual production are therefore intriguing.

Aspects of the latter poem suggest that it constructs an ideal vision of compliant or ordered desire, a perfect kingdom of sexual authority. The creation of unity and order is also evinced in purely rhetorical terms. Ideas of analogy and correspondence structure many of these sonnets: lover and beloved, for example, are conceived as the marigold and the sun (a hallmark trope of Scottish Jacobean poetry) bound in a relationship of fruition and nurture. In the first sonnet, parallels obtain between divine and earthly, inner and external states, macrocosm and microcosm. The fifth (in structural rather than chronological numbering), in the mode of Petrarchan pantheism, constructs a physical topography of love, founded on the resemblance between lover and landscape (Scottish rather than Italianate, in a gesture that might endorse the *Reulis'* nationalistic self-consciousness): "the Cheuiott hills doe with my state agree."[34] The ordered, sequential structure by which the analogies are declared recalls (in another moment of royal legitimizing) James's own "perfect" precept of "summaire raisons suddinlie applied / For euerie purpose vsing reasons fitt":[35]

> For as there toppes in cloudes are mounted hie
> So all my thoughts in skies be higher gone
> There foote is fast, my faithe a stedfast stone
> From them discends the christall fontains cleare
> And from mine eyes butt fained force and mone
> Hoppes trickling teares with sadd and murnefull cheare
> From them great windes doe hurle with hiddeous beir
> From me deepe sighs greate flockes of sheepe they feede
> I flockes of loue, no fruicts on them appeare
> My houpe to me no grace can bring or breede.[36]

The lover's body is anatomized by the degree to which it mirrors the land's physical features and effects. That tears should reflect streams, or sighs the winds, are resolutely conventional, but more unusual or defamiliarizing abstract comparisons are drawn. Contemplation of the beloved is an abstruse pursuit: "thoughts" of her are likened to the Cheviot "toppes" obscured by cloud, delicately suggesting (in a rare moment of Neoplatonic suggestiveness) that so rarefying the beloved obscures or veils her true form, and that she herself is similarly elusive or illusory. The tone is more reverential toward love than before: the lover's passion is rooted as deeply as the hills are to the earth's foundation; the assertion of "faithe"(ful) desire as "a stedfast stone" has a quasi-religious tenor. But the analogies are not always "fitt" or felicitous: "flockes of sheepe . . . / flockes of loue" is a faintly comic, scarcely persuasive correspondence. In the couplet—"In these alike, in this we disagree / That snowe on them and flammes remaines in me"—the obviously desired sense of *concordia discors* is slight.

Analogy is executed more successfully in the following sonnet when fused with the idea of metamorphosis (itself a conventional trope of the Petrarchistic Renaissance love lyric). As "man, a man am I composed all" (the lack of a kingly or divine identity is here marked), the lover is a microcosm of the four elements; but qua lover he uniquely "of mankinde . . . / . . . posseseth onlie one" (ll. 4–5).

My flames of loue to firie heauen be past
My aire in sighs euanish'd is and gone
My moysture into teares distilling fast
Now onelie earthe remaines with me at last (ll. 6–9)

The conceit is rich in implication. In retaining the "earthly" part—which is, according to Elyot, "of substance grosse and ponderous, . . . set of all elementes most lowest"[37]—the lover portrays desire as an incorruptible element of his being. It is accordingly rooted in the body but deprived of any Neoplatonic conception of physical matter as sensually degrading or corrupt. Yet the primacy of "earthe" also suggests the lover's mortality, especially when allied to the ultimate metamorphosis of line 13. In death, the body's earth is united with the earth of its grave: "Send als my earth, with earth for to remaine." This almost liturgical refrain suggests a kind of reciprocity unforthcoming from the beloved herself. The final plea, "restore me to my selfe again," though a familiar request for the beloved's grace (sexual consent or compliance), will rescue the lover from such imminent death. The particular phrase "my selfe" sustains the sonnet's intensely physical sense of self, confirming the lover's being as neither unitary nor stable.

If these sonnets can be said to articulate a coherent philosophy of desire, then it is a resolutely sensual or sexual vision. Desire is inflamed by the "wonder" of the beloved's "beautie" and not, as in the orthodox Petrarchistic text, by her superlative moral wisdom as well. The ultimate consummation is therefore not spiritual: the reductive, vaguely threatening last line of one sonnet, "I houpe Madame it shall not be for nought,"[38] clearly implies that "nought" is the beloved's refusal to be sexually compliant. The putative sequence of the *Amatoria* does not therefore culminate in an overarching moral or philosophical resolution (in that sense, James fails to achieve the intellectual ambition with which contemporaries such as Montgomerie or Fowler, for example, anatomize desire). Unsurprisingly, the figure of woman does not reveal a Petrarchan capacity for salvation but rather a peculiarly feminine (and entirely proverbial) moral flaw:

O womans witt that wauers with the winde
When none so well may warie now as I

As weathercocke thy stablenes I finde
And as the sea that still can neuer lie.[39]

As the "sequence," or at least the first of the identifiably Anne sonnets, began with frustrated efforts to breach the literal absence that separated lover and beloved (or bride and groom), so the final poem of this putative sequence implies the beloved's abstract "absence" through her lack of faith and constancy. *His* loyalty is proclaimed: "I fail'd not to fullfill / All sort of seruice to a Mistres dewe" (ll. 9–10: masculine virtue, feminine weakness is asserted in a Cixousian binarism). Yet this apparent lapse on the beloved's part makes the lover not disconsolate but almost cheerfully resigned: "What shall I saye, I neuer thoght to see / That out of sight shoulde out of languor be" (ll. 13–14). He will not languish for a fallen ideal.

Desire is finally exiled from a series of sonnets from which arguably the beloved was always absent; it is a consummately self-obsessed sequence and, in that respect, ironically a collaborative venture in pursuit of a coherent sovereign identity. Yet in lyrics outside the sonnet series, absence is made to address the perilous survival of love through separation. In the two, stanzaically varied lyrics, "What mortall man may liue but hart" and "When as the Skilfull Archer False," the lovers' separation by seas again prompts James's biographers to ally both to the occasion of James's delayed voyage to Anne.[40] Yet in the first lyric the lovers have been united before separation: "& syne hou ue sa soone uar shedd / & lost oure lang desirit ioy" (ll. 17–18). Their separation contrasts with the spurious or feigned reasons for absence invented by inferior lovers, who "abuse[s] / thaim venus boy" (ll. 23–24) and thus the nature of true earthly love. Different kinds of absence are contested in the second lyric, but it presents the relationship as itself imperfect. The opening Hero and Leander analogy (oddly interpreted as a direct analogue of Anne and James) offers the triumph of love over adversity to which the lovers, who are the poem's subject, are expressly contrasted. The analogue of Pyramus and Thisbe—"Deuydid onlie by a wall"—dramatizes love's failure as its inability to become articulate:

The verrie like did ws befall
As them of whome I shewe before
We distant are by such a wall
And often spacke by such a bore
Whill enuie called a naile
There through so strate

As made our moyen faile
To speake of late. (ll. 25–32)

Another absence is portrayed in the lyric entitled "A complaint of his mistressis absence from Court." This text elegizes the loss of a female subject to the court, conceived as the deprivation of an exquisite ornament or artifact that had once embellished "Plutos court" (as opposed, by implication, to its former incarnation as Venus's):

The Court as garland lacks the cheefest floure
The Court a chatton toome that lackes her stone
The Court is like a volier at this hour
Wherout of is her sweetest Sirene gone.
Then shall we lacke our cheefest onlie one?
No, pull us not from ws [us] cruell cloude I praye
Our light, our rose, our gemme, our bird awaye. [41]

This privation is felt collectively—"*Our* Princelie Court" (l. 45)—which might further strengthen the case for collaborative authorship or the status of the *Amatoria* as an exemplar of coterie poetry; this is not a love poem per se but a panegyric or praise of a courtly female subject. Significantly, the poem deploys "Troilus verse," which the *Reulis and Cautelis* advocated to express "Tragicall materis" (at one moment, death appears as an implicit reason for her absence: "pull us not from ws cruell cloude I praye"). "Haste golden Titan thy so long'd returne / To cleare the skies where now we darckned mourne" (ll. 62–64): the lyric concludes in anticipation of her return. The figure of Apollo/Phoebus—that familiar mythographic emblem of Jamesian self-representation—is invoked several times but not solely, as Goldberg argues, for the purpose of self-representation.[42] The Apollo symbolism of this particular lyric has a wider compass: it embraces the idea of the literal-metaphoric storm that enfolds the court conceived as a ship, evanescently "Neptunes bride" (l. 4); the figurative radiance of the mistress, who is ultimately herself conceived as the sun whose loss darkens the court; and even the poetic response to the latter: "Bot what my Muse, how pertlie thus thou sings / Who rather ought Solsequium-like attend / With luckned leaues till wearie night take end" (ll. 59–61). The implication is sexual: despite the absence of the mistress/Apollo (by which figuratively the flower seals its petals), he thrives at the mere recollection of her "alluring grace" (l. 48). Hence the Apollo symbolism has seemingly a dual purpose, fusing the image of the restorative beloved and, implicitly, that of the king himself, in league with Aeolus, the wind-god, in causing the chaos which only his return can dispel.[43]

The erotic philosophy these lyrics articulate in fairly coherent fashion seems to occlude any possibility for the expression of mutual love. Does the idea of mutuality (in a sense, the democratization of desire) preclude the exercise of Jamesian authority? In the *Amatoria* collection, sexual or erotic absolutism does not always prevail. In the lyric "What mortall man may liue but hart," reciprocal love is hymned. Each lover is the other's "half in all"; their parity is "consolation":

bot be the contraire i reiose
quhen i persaue ue marrois be
in trouble sorrou & in uoise
that is ane thinge quhilk confortis me
  the prouerbe makis relation
  that lykis in tribulation
  is uratchis consolation
    so nou ar ue. (ll. 41–48)

This evokes a mutual love unqualified by irony,[44] endowed with a piety or frame of religious reference absent from the other *Amatoria* love lyrics:

i pray the lorde abone
to send it til us soone
fairueill quhill that be done
  & after ay. (ll. 53–56)

Although simply an appeal that the lovers be reunited, the supplication nevertheless lends a quiet intensity to this slight but compelling lyric.

Such lyrics gesture toward a parity of desire which Goldberg's claim for a pervasively one-sided discourse of power underestimates. Those texts expressive of a less aggressive or imperial(ist) desire are arguably the most intellectually and thematically provocative. The longest, most narratological and conceptually ambitious of the *Amatoria* lyrics, "A dreame on his Mistris My Ladie Glammis,"[45] offers a recondite portrait of desire but one that also intimates the possibilities of redemptive eros. The account and attempted exposition of a dream in which a *donna angelicata* presents the poet-dreamer with the tokens of "A tablet and an Amethyst" (l. 43), the "dreame" is linked generically to the Petrarchan dream vision, its *petrarchisti* variants, and arguably to the contemporary vogue for allegorical narrative within the Jacobean coterie. The dreamer's desire to expound the apparent arcana of the dream (and how to classify the dream itself with implicit allusion to Macrobius's categories) is held in tension with the lover's impulse to construe the dream vision as the assurance of reciprocal love. "A dreame" has been praised for its "originality"[46]; certainly, its carefully orchestrated symbolism and the intimation of a quasi-mystical love are distinctive, at least within the extant Jamesian oeuvre.

Given the characteristic misogynistic impulse of the *Amatoria,* the poem also offers a more redeemed version of woman (at least the iconography of the secularized Virgin rather than the Whore). The beloved mistress is conceived as an "Idée," suffused with the term's Neoplatonic resonances of rarity and spiritual virtue, who acts (contra the beloved of the Anne sonnets) as an unequivocal muse:

> Loe here she is who makes thee trade
>
> The statelie forcked hill,
>
> Whose pleasant grasse beginnes to fade
>
> So trampled by thee still,
>
> Lo here she is who makes thee drinke
>
> The christall siluer spring
>
> Of flying horse and riding foule
>
> As ancient Poëts sing. (ll. 25–32)

Not only does she inspire the lover to create (here specifically portrayed through the poetic iconography of the Scottish Jacobean coterie) but she herself, and by implication secular love, is appositely the sole subject of such aspiringly rarefied poetry; this contradicts, of course, the literary ideals James espoused in his "officially" sanctioned or published poetry:

> Loe here the subiect and the wings
>
> Of thy high flying verse
>
> That mountes aboue the flammie vaults
>
> And to the heauen does pearse. (ll. 33–36)

Her beauty is emblematically portrayed by the visual tableau of the "Sunne . . . shining bright / Into the midst, with stars about / Bot darckned by his light" (ll. 202–4). This recalls the conventional Petrarchistic conceit of the beloved as the sun (also a favorite "Castalian" or Jacobean poetic trope) mirrored in the apostrophe to the literal sun in whom he seeks her "shaddowe." The image is further glossed by the "dittie," as if to recall the inscription attached to the image in an emblem book: "As sunne / Amongst the stars does shine, / So she her sexe surpasseth far / In vertues most diuine" (ll. 205–8). She kisses the dreamer, an act objectified by the imagistic mode of the blazon which reifies female beauty—here, the lips and teeth—into a precious object: "With this me thought she bowed her doune / and ioyned the rubies sine, / (That hides her iuorie rankes and smells / Of Nectar) vnto mine" (ll. 37–40).

This partial "conversion" of the beloved into a precious stone reflects the emblematic status of the stone and tablet. The attempt to attach "mottos" (or "ditties") to each presents the most elaborately conceitful writing of the *Amatoria;* it also echoes the propensity for emblematic imagery and structure in the poetry of Montgomerie and Fowler. The stone's fusion of "purple" and "gray" tones mirrors the dreamer's bodily humors (his being composed of "flames" and "earthe," as in the sixth sonnet of the "sequence"). The stone's proverbial "secret vertue[s]" as a "remeade" against inebriety are applied to the province of desire: "So shall my harte be still preserued / By vertue from aboue, / From staggering like a drunken man / Or wauering into loue" (ll. 129–32). Drink's "poisonous" allure is likened to the "poysoned lookes / of Dames I shall not swerue" (ll. 135–36; the concept of woman throughout is defined by extremes of virtue and vice). Other women are antagonists—threatening the integrity of his love—whom he can subjugate with the aid of the amethyst: "That with my conquering hand I may / Enforce my foes to flie" (ll. 139–40; the Jamesian lover, characteristically self-obsessed, perceives himself as an object of desire).

The third and last interpretation of the stone rests on its "force / A hunter for to aide / In ende to catche his pray, the fruict / Of all his trauell made" (ll. 157–60). The assertion, "So am I an prentise past / Into that Princelie game" (ll. 161–62), is persuasively a kingly self-reference (James in his role as "the hunting king" and as the author of *The Essayes of a Prentise*). Yet it also connotes the game of amatory pursuit. As lover he desires to seek and possess his "pray / That prayes on me, and is of all / My passion'd thoughts the stay" (ll. 166–68). The Ovidian myth of Diana and Actaon implicit in this confession has been inverted according to gender: the victim is now female, the hunter male.

The tablet's visual characteristic of pure distilled gold represents the mistress's "chastnes." Its visual and symbolic import is intensely detailed, evoking the oddly visceral detail of the sonnet "sequence": "The crawling scores of ameling blacke / That on the golde are wrought, / The diuers passions represents / That walters in her thought" (ll. 177–80). Her "Syren voice diuine" is abstrusely imaged as "A nacked man . . . / Whome Phoebus rosts with hote reflexe / And stinging flees doe teare, / Yett sitting in the forrest greene" (ll. 182–85). This figure might be identified as Orpheus, another of James's mythological personae.[47] Again the parallel between literal and abstract senses is strained. How is she to be compared to this suffering Orpheus? Is she oblivious to her apparent pain by "Esteeming so" the "ioye" of those whom she enchants by her voice?

Quizzical interpretiveness prevails: the dreamer is reluctant to perceive yet another emblem—the beloved's heart held by "ane hand . . . / Whill Cupide with his bended bowe / And golden arrow aime, / To shoote his firie subtle shaft / For pearcing of the same" (ll. 219–24)—as signifying her unwilling submission to the Ovidian golden arrow; rather he reads (or manipulates) the image as the offering of her heart to "Be shotte into for me"(l. 228). The final exegesis rests on the union of tablet and amethyst (lover and mistress) "both knitt together be / Euen by a string" (ll. 244–45). Literal and metaphorical senses delicately interweave: the "threed" which binds the emblems to one another symbolizes the "threed" which only fate or death in the guise of Atropos can sever.

The dreamer sanctions the felicity of their love in a way that blends caution and authority. Apollo (in his prophetic role) has guided him, yet the possibility remains that "verrie truth" is not revealed. In allusion to the discourse on the reliability of dreams which opened the poem, the dreamer concedes that such consolation may be illusory. Yet even the duplicity of a false vision is embraced as a "gladd deceate": "so my guesse / In gladnes doth me keepe" (ll. 259–60). Distance is transformed into intimacy, absence into presence by the efficacy of desire.

The "Dreame" is untypical of the *Amatoria* collection in assenting to the idea of love as the source of erotic and spiritual bliss (the naïf lover confesses to being "glad" three times). While wedded to the generic mode of the Petrarchan visionary allegory, it renders the divine consolation of that mode (the beloved who returns as an incarnation of divine *caritas* to redeem the lover) in a secular sense. The beloved's visitation serves almost to license or endorse the dreamer's desire. But the nature of that desire is in itself recondite or arcane: the process of emblematic (or allegorical) interpretation by which the lyric is structured lends that love a kind of intellectual credence. This in turn may reflect that logical and analytic aspect of poetry extolled by James's treatise and cultivated within the Jacobean poetic culture at large. Further, the beauty of James's beloved is not represented in simple descriptive terms. Rather her physical and abstract forms are displaced into recondite symbolic images. The "Dreame" mistress is desired not for what she herself is (her essence) but for the symbolic weight she is made to bear: a riddling interpretation impinging on the lover as desire returns to its source in the self.[48] The other "leafe" of the tablet is bare, but the dreamer conjectures that it is "ordain'd to containe" the image of the beloved herself. The absence of inscription is therefore apt: the supreme representation of the beloved, and the desire she inspires, are by necessity unrealizable and so unwritten. Though the other emblems signify "Her qualities most rare" (l. 238), "So shoulde her selfe, though viuelie no / Yett best it can be there" (ll. 239–40): the most "viuelie" represented incarnation of the beloved would be, by implication, her actual living presence.

euen so all uemen are of nature uaine
& can not keip no secreit unreueild
& quhair as once thay do conceaue disdaine
thay are unable to be reconceild
fulfillid uith talk & clatteris but respect
& oftentymes of small or none effect.[49]

The seventeenth-century copyist or editor of BM 24195 entitled the text, from which the above stanza is extracted, "A Satire against Woemen." The *Amatoria* as a collection, as already suggested, is studded with misogynistic points. Yet the mere insertion of this "Satire" between two ostensibly (or conventionally) amatory lyrics (whether authorially sanctioned or not) raises questions about the acceptability, or more aptly the "invisibility," of misogyny within an amatory context. Is the "Satire" meant to endorse in an extended way the predominantly "antifeminine" quality of the collection? How does its inclusion impinge upon or refine our understanding of the coterie culture from which it stemmed?

The poem is founded on a single premise: that woman's "essential" nature (manifest in her social, moral, and sexual conduct) is predetermined by nature itself. She acts "uithout regard or schame" as instinctively as "skoles of herring flees the quhaile for feir." Seven stanzas provide illustration of the analogy (with only two expatiating on female flaws), and endorse the view that sixteenth-century literary antifeminism was as much an exercise in rhetorical virtuosity as in quasi-philosophical argument.[50]

as falconis are by nature faire of flicht
of kynde as sparhalkis far excells in speid
as marlzonis haif in springing greatest micht
as gooshalkis are of nature geuin to greid
as mauuses of kynde are geuin to sing
and laiurokkis after candlemess to spring. (ll. 1–6)

The rhetorical catalogue seeks to communicate a rich natural diversity: the first two stanzas list a variety of birds (the "falcons . . . sparhalkis . . . pyettis, gleddis" implicitly portray woman as predator); the third wild or more exotic creatures ("tigris," "lyons," "beiris"); the fourth smaller "woodland" animals; the fourth and fifth various aquatic creatures (including the mermaid, commonly the symbol of a prostitute).

Both the rhetorical "listing" structure and the types of creatures recall the genre of medieval bestiary.

Conceptually, the lyric's "argument" is neither innovative nor ingenious but derivative and citational in the characteristic antifeminist mode. James's conceitful wit can be deconstructed into a series of orthodox essentialist points. The vices assigned "all wemen"—successively vanity, indiscretion, animosity, garrulity, ambition, material avarice, deceitfulness, and artifice—constitute the familiar indictment, in Bloch's terms, of woman's "overdetermination" or "excess," her lack of "mesure" (l. 50).[51] Not (as man) made in the image of God, woman is associated with sensual, not least bestial, characteristics. The basis for this tacit assumption of James's satire originates in Aristotelian creational biology, which conceives the female species as imperfectly derived from the male (*mal occasionatum*).[52] The Renaissance debate whether woman could be considered fully human might be argued to be the terminus ad quem of James's lyric: that female nature is predetermined to the same degree that "greate olde pyckes will eate the young and small" bears comparison to the patristic association of women with "other monsters of Nature."[53]

The *Amatoria* clearly stems from James's Scottish reign. This essay has drawn attention to distinct and recognizable literary "imprints" upon its poems that characterize the Scottish Jacobean (or "Castalian") coterie culture. The inclusion of such a starkly antifeminist piece as the "Satire" within a context that largely conceives the female subject as an orthodox beloved has, in the context of Scottish medieval and Renaissance traditions of literary antifeminism, particular precedent. The "Satire" may not be a conscious imitation, but its fusion of the amatory and non-amatory recalls the Bannatyne Manuscript, compiled by George Bannatyne, an Edinburgh merchant, during the reign of Mary, Queen of Scots. Gathered under the general prefatory heading of "ballattis of luve" are the formal retractions and recantations of the traditional *querelle des femmes* controversy.[54] Their inclusion within Bannatyne's all-encompassing generic title suggests that the entrenched paradigm of female duality—the Virgin/Eve paradox, with its theological and philosophical roots—is peculiarly enacted by this variant of the Renaissance amatory lyric. The archetypal sonnet-mistress, fickle, cruel, and uncharitable, can incur the displeasure and revulsion of her lover (witness the Anne sonnets) or prove a source of moral corruption. Giordano Bruno's canonical treatise on spiritual love even seeks to justify why the object of Petrarch's remarkable adoration should have been a woman. The "Satire"'s apparent "amatory antifeminism" should not therefore be regarded as an unusual aberration but rather as exemplary of a culturally acceptable facet of coterie literary production.

The "Satire" is most striking for the subtle defensive maneuver of the envoi. In this "Exposition" (or what the other manuscript copy more aptly terms an "excuise"), the speaker atones to "ye damis of uorthie fame":

> since for your honouris I employed my caire
> for uemen bad heirby are lesse to blame
> for that they follou nature eueryquhayre
> and ye most uorthie prayse [and] quhose reason dantis
> that nature quhilk into youre sexe so hantis. (ll. 56–60)

The castigator becomes the apologist. This is a complete volte-face: even "uemen bad" are "redeemed" for being helpless to act other than instinctually; and "uorthie" women are granted a characteristically male rationality. That the text's significance depends on its poem's interpreter or recipient prompts interesting speculation on its original context. If a recitation or performance by James himself, the "exposition" may have deferred to female courtiers or gentlewomen in attendance; if an exclusively male audience or readership—the homosocial environment in Eve Kosofsky Sedgwick's definition—then the obsequious eulogy seems a more ironic jest. The "Satire" succeeds in exposing the discursive paradox at the heart of courtly, and especially amatory, lyric: who addresses whom? The poem demonstrates how the sexual politics of the courtly environment could be manipulated by the lyricist (and perhaps most adroitly by the sovereign?), and how the standard tropes of antifeminism can be construed as if playful mimicry. (The potentially collaborative nature of the text also admits the possibility for the sovereign's deft self-exoneration.)

How ultimately should constructions of the feminine in the *Amatoria* be construed? Goldberg asserts that "James's attacks on women explore the strategies of discursive power, the negations and disclaimers and the annihilative erasures that ensure the monarch's freedom and truth."[55] That may justly be claimed of the political and ideological strictures in place at the Jacobean courts. The *Amatoria* lyrics—dually conceiving woman as a redeeming, quasi-Petrarchan beloved and as the faithless corrupter of male purity—remain within the orthodox conceptual limits of what might be termed the love lyric's "screen of representation" (Luce Irigaray's phrase), the symbolic veil drawn across the figure of woman. Goldberg asserts that James consistently "imposes his power" on the beloved, which may implicitly in certain instances be Anne. Yet this imposition is imaginatively replicated in many varieties of (male-authored) Renaissance love lyric. The female subject, or rather object, of desire is "controlled" or subjugated by the poet-lover's positioning of her within the established symbolic system of representation. This imaginative reification can be partly conceived as a reactionary response to the emotional and sexual power wielded by the female beloved. As Linda Woodbridge notes, "the sonnet mistress at her best is as potent a symbol of feminine dominance and power as the

Renaissance ever provided."[56] Notionally, she is therefore in possession of the sovereignty which the king literally embodies; one symbolic authority theoretically challenges another.

The lyric mistress is also a male invention. "A Dreame" works to fragment precisely this creative act by portraying the ideal beloved as the construct of symbolic "parts."[57] Goldberg proposes that James's amatory antifeminism reflects the larger ideological authority of his writings (which constitute the "instrument of royal power"). In contrast, the readings of the *Amatoria* here suggest that the oscillations of sexual power are "written into" or implicit per se within texts of desire. The lyrics exemplify the sheerly rhetorical construct of woman in the amatory poem: converted into an aesthetic artifact in "A Dreame" and "A complaint," and a topic of rhetorical *inventio* and conceptual "wit" in "A Satire." In "A Complaint," the speaker suggestively encloses his antifeminism within an expiatory fictive framework. A homosocial context for these particular lyrics (which substantiates the collaborative argument) is implied by the persistent positioning of woman as an object of discursive exchange, a "structure" mirrored at large in Scottish Jacobean literary culture; even the final sonnets of the alleged Anne sequence subjugate her presence to the lover's imperial dominion. Only the beloved of "A Dreame" eludes the lover's intellectual grasp. And, in the end, James's angelic or demonic women (merely) reflect the enduring feminine types of an early modern imagination.

This essay has been an exploration of desire in the *Amatoria*, the corpus of love poetry conventionally assigned to James. But desire is more subtly inflected in James's other early poetry, and it may also be imposed upon, or concentrated around, the figure of the king. These two ramifications of Jamesian desire serve as closure to this essay. In relation to the Elizabethan courtly context, it has become a critical truism that the amatory idiom was put to political service. Classically, Louis Montrose's readings argued that "desires for wealth, status, and power might be intentionally disguised or unconsciously displaced in metaphors of erotic or spiritual desire."[58] Elizabeth, the willfully symbolic incarnation of chastity, was conceived as another Laura. The female gender of the monarch is assumed as the precondition for such political Petrarchism (Leonard Forster's term). Marotti declares its end on James's 1603 succession: "Instead of a Queen who recognised the reality of ambition, manipulated it, and allowed it to be expressed in the language of love, there was a king on the English throne, a man whose earlier sonnets to his wife were perfunctory performances and who misread the ambitious designs of many of his courtiers as love and affection for his person."[59] This assertion wholly ignores the literary environment of the Scottish Jacobean court, in which poems exploiting the verbal and conceptual affinities between courtly and sexual petition were addressed to a male monarch. James's elect poetic coterie can largely be defined as a masculine elite (though there is evidence to suggest possible persuasive exceptions). The poetry of the Jamesian "brotherhood" displays an intense literary rivalry, a competitive culture in which the sovereign's poetic and political approval is anxiously courted. James, in essence, was an object of desire. Alexander Montgomerie was particularly fêted (at least until the complications of his Catholic sympathies) by his royal patron. His lyric, "Befoir the Grekis Dois Enterpryse," presented in the *Reulis and Cautelis* as the paradigm of the Jacobean amatory poem, compares the predicament of a lover awaiting the beloved's judgment to the Greek invocation of Apollo to proclaim the end of the Trojan war. Yet what if Apollo in his prophetic role signifies the king himself as the instrument of oracular truth? The lyric may easily be divested of the amatory reading (significantly, that publicly sanctioned by James) and conceived as a veiled appeal on Montgomerie's part for political or courtly advancement. But the amatory and political readings are not mutually exclusive; each is implicit within the other. This equivocalness is part of the poetic texture, not least another instance of Puttenham's courtly *allegoria* or dissembling. In another lyric by Montgomerie, Apollo's presence "me restores from lyfe to death," and a series of sonnets addressed to James after political disfavor occasionally phrase the physical and emotional exile as if from a beloved (evoking Fradenburg's phrase that the art of sovereign love depends on "the careful management of . . . desire").[60] The sensual resonance of complete surrender and fulfillment in the Greek Apollo lyric should not be obscured. Although detailed analysis of these and other similar Scottish Jacobean lyrics lies outside the scope of this present reading, it is interesting to note these ambiguously erotic incarnations of James and to question whether they reflect, in Sedgwick's terms, a network of social structures in which the homosocial cannot be distinguished from the homosexual.[61]

This is the cultural and literary context from which James's own "tragedie," the *Phoenix,* springs, written in commemoration of the death of Esmé Stewart (1542–83), James's French cousin who arrived in Scotland to assert his right to the Lennox title. The young sovereign who entered into "great familiarity and quyet purposes" with the older French courtier (the embodiment of alterity) lavished gifts and appointments on him. Lennox at once created political and clerical disquiet; his fate was the eventual exile and death that James's "tragedie" allegorizes. This text mirrors the erotic duplicity of Jacobean coterie poetry. David Bergeron has interpreted James's self-professed "Metaphoricall Invention" as the poetic embodiment of the king's love for his cousin, proposing that the femininity of the "Phoenix rare" that symbolizes Lennox reflects James's "sexual confusion."[62] But the conviction with which Bergeron perceives homosexual desire is not transparently sanctioned by the poem itself. The poem seeks consolation as well as the expression of loss. As an emblem of resurrection, the conventionally female phoenix permits, in the language of the poem's medieval tragic convention, a "comike end"; that this mythical bird should serve to incarnate Lennox ensures at least the symbolic perpetuity of the sovereign's desire. Bergeron is right to perceive the fluidity of gender: the beauty of the bird's "body whole" is described rhetorically in a way analogous to the female blazon. The familiar Jamesian iconography is clearly present (suggesting a symbolism loosely disguised or coded): the king himself can therefore be construed in the allusions to "Phoebus bricht" and to Apollo, "who brunt with thy reflex / Thine onely fowle, / through loue that thou her bure" (ll. 260–61). Lennox is thus imaginatively resurrected—possessed of "a longer lyfe"—by James's desire, but the metaphor of the immolated bird, the dead Lennox, surely evokes the destructive quality of desire too.[63] There are echoes here of the guilt and shame that intruded into the *Amatoria* sonnets' discourse of desire. Bergeron's unambiguously celebratory and assertive reading might be qualified: this is also a valediction. Though the poem profoundly registers its grief (in Bergeron's phrase, "the wonderful love he has known"), and represents the most overt expression of homoerotic love in the Jamesian canon, some politically cogent and controversial points are also made (the "shelter" offered to the Catholic Lennox by the lover-king in defiance of his political mentors).

Given the queer king of the English court, it is perhaps ironic that the pre-1603 poetry does not succeed, at least explicitly, in subverting the gender of the conventional beloved. That the politicized erotics of the *Phoenix* should have been published in the 1584 *Essayes* perhaps suggests the greater freedom or risk taken in the fashioning of the pre-1603 royal image. The English accession arguably repressed, in literary terms, the Jamesian fictionalizing of the intimate. The *Phoenix* elegy resolutely flouts James's own precepts, published in the same volume, of the poetic censorship of politics. Such a proscription, perhaps fostered by the awareness that the discourse of desire, with its delicate folds of meaning, has unstable boundaries, is swiftly transgressed.

The preconceptions imposed on James's love poetry, at least the body of love poetry assigned to his name, are to an extent those imposed by James himself in his articulation of a sovereign poetics. The perceived critical failure of James to create (orthodox) love poetry mirrors the treatise's sense of the failure of (orthodox) love poetry. The *Amatoria* as a whole does not achieve the innovative originality James prescribed for the "Castalian" love literature that would thread into the Scottish Jacobean Renaissance. If compared to the love poetry of his practitioners, it fails to achieve their arch mannerist conceitfulness; nor does it engage in rhetorical or philosophical terms with the Petrarchan or Neoplatonic paradigms then in vogue (as such, then, it is unorthodox). Its misogyny is less startling once recontextualized in a pervasive tradition. But there *are* moments of erotic intensity. The peculiar distortions of its amatory language can yield arresting conceits, and the analytic construction of meaning (love allegorized, then deconstructed) in "A Dreame" is playful. The teasingly interpretative glosses James provides for the

"Satire" and the "Dier" disclose a keen alertness to how the expectations of genre—and so the responses of (a female) audience or readership—can be manipulated. These are poems where the restrictions of preconceived limitations that James assigned to the love lyric seem to be transgressed, whether consciously or not. The *Phoenix* elegy, and the poetry conventionally assumed to address Anne, are in a sense "public" love poems, where the language of desire passes the edge of proscribed meaning into regions of uncertainty and ambiguity. Such ambiguity may well be an inevitable product and device of the ultimately playful, collaborative coterie culture, and perhaps politically the reason why James "publicly" devalued the genre. James is a writer of contradiction and paradox.

Ultimately, the *Amatoria* is a text of provocation rather than a coherent *ars amatoria.* Coexisting with the self-authenticating myth of Apollo/Phoebus and the implicit legitimizing of male power or superiority in the explicitly antifeminist poetry are more subtle and changeful invocations of power: a language of abjection and subjugation to desire's tyranny ("coales of shame") and intellectual mystification. The articulation of a coherent royal subject is never fully achieved, the notion of sovereignty remaining fluid and mercurial when enclosed in these poems about desire. The *Amatoria* suggests the creation of an enigma in pre-1603 Jacobean culture: a mercurial literary confidence and playfulness which, if contextualized within the Scottish homosocial coterie culture, intimates that royal authority was shared and sovereign desire dispersed in poems offered to the literary court public of the first Jacobean period. "To play thy self with thy awin consait and lat nane knaw quhat thow dois mene": the *Amatoria* is arguably the most evasive representational text of Jamesian writing, at once enriched and circumscribed by its own artful resonances.

Notes

Throughout the essay, "Jamesian" is used to refer to the writings associated with James; "Jacobean" designates the wider cultural and literary context of James's court(s) and supplements the conventional designation "Castalian."

1. Doelman (7) cites this in translation from Grosart's edition as an "oration" to James. It is, however, published as an epistle of 18 May 1620, by Hutchinson: "Sane, gestabaris antea in cordibus nostris; sed Tu vis etiam manibus teri, semotaque Maiestate, charta conspiciendum Te praebes, quo familiarius inter nos verseris"; Hutchinson, *The Works of George Herbert* 458.
2. Fradenburg 71.

3. Discussion of the *Amatoria* can be found, briefly, in the editorial comments of Westcott and in Craigie *Poems;* in Wilson 89; Markland 139; Fraser 52; Jack, "Poetry under King James VI" 128, 130; Goldberg, *James I* 22–25; and McClure 106–7.
4. Goldberg, *James I* 24; Jack, "Scottish Poetry" 128.
5. Weldon 2: 5; an anonymous and possibly spurious memoir cited in Lewalski 17.
6. *Political Works* 272; discussed by Goldberg, *James I* 143.
7. The poetic texts cited in this essay are based on either of the two manuscript sources, Bodley ms. 165 and BL Add. 24195. For convenience, reference will also be made where appropriate to the editions by Westcott and Craigie. Each ms. is described respectively in Westcott xi–xvi, and Craigie, *Poems* 1: lxxi–vii. Bodley 165 contains only two of the BL *Amatoria* texts, "As Falcounis Ar" (ff. 43r–44v), and "If Mourning Micht Amende," later titled "A Dier at her M:ties Desyr" (ff. 46r–v). There are interesting linguistic differences between the texts which show the later anglified revisions of original Scots orthography, suggesting a clear pre-1603 dating and the cultural sensitivity of post-Union linguistic affiliations.
8. For further details see Westcott xiv–xv, and Craigie, *Poems* 2: 206–10.
9. See Perry 243–46. I am most grateful to Professor Perry for letting me consult his article in advance of its publication.
10. See Marotti, *John Donne* and *Manuscript;* Pebworth; Woudhuysen.
11. The exception is William Alexander's *Aurora,* published in 1604 but generally considered to have been written in the late 1590s. On the popularity of manuscript circulation and the alleged "vulgarity" of print, see Woudhuysen 14–15.
12. The "Castalian" epithet alludes to the stream on Mount Parnassus, named after the nymph Castalia; the poetic allusion is frequently cited in poetry by James, and it forms a common poetic trope in the writings of the court coterie.
13. Craigie, *Poems* 2: 225. See also Grundy, "Introduction" 28–31, and Constable's other two sonnets to James (140–41), one of which proclaims James's poetic separation from "others hooded with blind loue" (implying that profane love is an unfit sovereign subject). Marotti (*Manuscript* 14) also cites a likely imitation of the first *Amatoria* sonnet by Nicholas Breton in Stephen Powle's commonplace book: "A passionate Sonnet made by the Kinge of Scots uppon difficulties ariseing to crosse his proceedinge in love & marriage with his most worthie to be esteemed Queene."
14. Craigie, *Poems* 2: 225, and endorsed by Westcott 69–74, Wilson 89, and Bingham 16ff.

15. Melville 369–73.
16. Westcott (78–79, later endorsed by Craigie, *Poems* 2: 228) identifies the poetic subject of "Ane dreame on his Mistris the Lady Glammis" as "Anne, a daughter of Sir John Murray, later first earl of Tullibardine, a companion of the King's childhood and later master of his household," citing the evidence of two documents alluding to her marriage to Patrick Lyon, Lord Glamis, in 1595. Westcott conjectures that for the implicit reason of moral decorum, the "Dreame" must have been written "before her marriage in 1595, though not long before, since even at that date she was scarcely more than a child." He assumes that the prefatory title, denoting Anne Murray's married title, was a later addition. Yet given the sexual etiquette of the court—its apparent tolerance of kingly favorites or mistresses, which need not have implied a sexually adulterous liaison—there seems no reason to assume that the lyric was *not* composed after the marriage of either Anne Murray or James himself. Lyrics expressive of seemingly intense desire could be exchanged at the Scottish Jacobean court between female and male courtiers as tokens of social complement and poetic cultivation.
17. See Jack, "James VI," and Clewett; and see the essay by Morna Fleming in the present volume for further discussion. Although the treatise stems from a period of conscious literary "separatism" from English poetry (and consequent intensification of French influence), James still contributed an elegy to the 1587 Cambridge collection of panegyrics on the death of Sidney.
18. On James's translations of Du Bartas see in particular Prescott 176–78. The prefatory sonnets to *The Essayes of a Prentise* (1584) (sig. Aiijv–Cr; Craigie, *Poems* 1: 9–14) reveal James's Virgilian ambition; they also imply the generic superiority both of epic and imperialistic, martial and heroic subjects. (James implicitly perpetuates the Renaissance association of gender and genre: the ornamental, secular lyric is feminized compared to the masculine rhetorical "body" of epic.) It is perhaps significant that James praises Petrarch—in his sonnet "On Mr W. Fullers Translation of Petrarchs Triumphe of Loue" [William Fowler's *Triumphs*]—for loyalty to his vernacular and the "triumphe" of "chastnes, deathe, and fame" over earthly love.
19. *Essayes* sig. Liiijv; Craigie, *Poems* 1: 76.
20. *Essayes* sig. Liiijv; Craigie, *Poems* 1: 76.
21. *Essayes* sig. Kiiijr, "Sonnet Decifring the Perfyte Poete" ll. 1, 3; Craigie, *Poems* 1: 69.
22. *Essayes* sig. Kiiijr; Craigie, 1: 76.
23. *An Apology for Poetry,* ed. Shepherd 138. James's own precept of *energeia* appears in the sonnets prefacing the treatise.

24. There are two copies of this poem: one in Bodley 165 in Scots orthography (clearly the original), the other in BL 24195, an anglified version which is the text given here. This coda to "A Dier at ['on' is crossed out] Her M:ties Desyr" appears only in Add. 24195, f. 13r, prefaced by "the sonnett lakkis heere quhiche interprettis all the matter"; Craigie, *Poems* 1: 78. The "sonnett" inscription is in a different hand from the two already evident in the main text, and the sonnet itself is inscribed on a separate sheaf.
25. Craigie, *Basilikon Doron* 1: 170. Goldberg, (*James I* 148) comments that in the *Basilikon Doron*, James "offered and withdrew himself at once." But note the lover's desire in the "Dier": "I only craue a spectacle to be" (l. 53); Goldberg does not comment upon this interesting poetic remark.
26. "Sen Thocht Is Frie," Craigie, *Poems* 1: 133, based on the Scots inscription in the Maitland quarto ms. f. 105v; a version in English, entitled "Song. The First Verses That Euer the King Made," is found in Add. ms. 24195, ff. 51r–v.
27. *Essayes* sig. Mijr; Craigie, *Poems* 1: 78.
28. *Essayes* sig. Mijr; Craigie, *Poems* 1: 78.
29. The *Amatoria* contents are listed on f. 2r, where the poem "From Sacred Throne" is listed as the first "Sonet." The sonnets, found on ff. 4r–9r, are numerically divided into five sections, as reproduced in Craigie, *Poems* 1: 68–73. There are minor revisions in the later hand.
30. *James I* 29.
31. Penultimate sonnet, f. 9r, ll. 1–12.
32. The fourth sonnet of the series in the *Essayes* on literary ideals proclaims that poetry, in its art of verisimilitude, should "deceaue" the senses; artistic "truthfulness" or fidelity is achieved at the expense of duplicity, an interesting parallel to the amatory poems.
33. A dedicatory sonnet to James in the *Essayes* proclaims Apollo "The Mightie Father of the Muses Nyne," which places the king at the paternal(istic) source and origin.
34. As Westcott and Craigie point out, this is modeled on a sonnet by Mellin de Saint-Gelais but it exemplifies the fairly inventive quality of "Castalian" translation, not least by the nationalistic attentiveness to landscape.
35. "Sonnet Deciphring the Perfect Poet," ll. 2–3.
36. f. 6r; Craigie, *Poems* 1: 70, ll. 2–12.
37. *The Boke named The Gouernour*, ed. H. H. S. Croft (2 vols.; London, 1883) 1: 4.
38. "Although that crooked crawling Vulcan lie," l. 14.

39. f. 9v; Craigie, *Poems* 1: 72, ll. 1–4.
40. The text for the first lyric is based on the Scots orthography of Bodley 165, f. 52v; Craigie, *Poems* 95–97; "When as the Skilful Archer False" is found only in Add. 24195, f. 29v; Craigie, *Poems* 1: 98.
41. Add. 24195, ff. 14r–16r; Craigie, Poems 1: 81, ll. 50–56. There are minor corrections in the later hand.
42. *James I* 24–25.
43. One might even suggest that the supplication to Apollo here is a (playful) veiled appeal to the king, hence the lyric is not collaborative but written by a literary courtier; these are fluid, open-ended texts.
44. "Constant Loue in All Conditions" (f. 10r; Craigie, *Poems* 1:73) declares fidelity only on the part of the lover.
45. ff. 16v–24v; Craigie, *Poems* 1: 82–9.
46. Jack, "Poetry under King James" 130.
47. Also a common emblematic figure: see Henkel and Schoene (1610) for a variety of Orpheus emblems to which James might be alluding.
48. The coupling of invention with the physical description of the beloved in the treatise might here be consciously realized by James. The rhetorical invention of the beloved in the "Dreame" is likened to the portrait of "sume Apelles fine": in both instances, a male creation.
49. The copy in Bodley 165, ff. 43r–44r (Craigie, *Poems* 1: 91–93) given here is in Scots, again suggesting a date of composition securely in the 1580s or early 90s; it is placed between the *Phoenix* elegy on Esmé Stewart and the lyric "If mourning micht amende." In Add. 24195, ff. 25r–27r, the anglified text is placed between the "Dreame" and "What Mortall Man"; it is a relatively fair copy.
50. On the antifeminist or *querelle des femmes* poem as purely a rhetorical exercise see Woodbridge 17, and Jardine 162. McClure (107) asserts that the "Satire" is "the most extreme instance in all James's work of a poem written purely to display his knowledge in witty form," but such "knowledge" seems to be purely of an established literary genre and ideological mode.
51. Bloch 47.
52. See Maclean 42.
53. Maclean 12.
54. Bannatyne's division into "four pairtis" is thus constructed: "The first / Ar songis of luve The secund ar / Contemptis of luve And evill wemen / The thrid ar contempis of evill / fals vicious men [and the defense of women] And the fourt / Ar ballattis detesting of luve / And lichery": NLS ms. 1.1.6, f. 211r; Ritchie 3: 240.
55. *James I* 25.

56. Woodbridge 189. The negotiation of sovereignty against the intrinsically imperialist discourse of desire (the Cupid metaphor) is perhaps also influenced by gender: in Mary, Queen of Scots's love lyrics, arguably sovereignty is abnegated, the queenly body sexualised; in the Jamesian poetry of desire, sovereignty is symbolically asserted.
57. This process of interpretation serves as the "substantial and real gift" offered to the reader according to Goldberg, *James I* 21–22.
58. "Celebration and Insinuation" 26; see also his "'Eliza, Queene of shepheardes'" and "Of Gentlemen and Shepheards."
59. Marotti, "'Love is not Love.'" See also Javitch.
60. Fradenburg 73.
61. See Sedgwick, esp. "Introduction" 1–15, and "Swan in Love: The Example of Shakespeare's Sonnets" 28–48. For fuller discussion of poetic homoeroticism between Montgomerie and James, see Sarah M. Dunnigan, "Erotic Politics and Poetic Practice at the Courts of Mary Queen of Scots and James VI," *Terranglian Territories: Proceedings of the Seventh International Conference on the Literature of Region and Nation* (Frankfurt am Main: Peter Lang, 2000), 361–77.
62. Bergeron, *Royal Family* 26–34 (33). *King James and Letters of Homoerotic Desire* represents Bergeron's most recent exploration of the relationship in the context of James's other epistolary writing. On the subject of Renaissance homosexuality see, for example, among a number of publications, Bray, and the collection of essays, *Queering the Renaissance,* ed. Goldberg.
63. The phoenix also symbolizes the female beloved in an amatory context: for example, in Petrarch's *Rime* 185; and Thomas Watson, *Hekatompathia or Passionate Centurie of Love* (1582), sonnets XI and XXXIX. The phoenix conceit also occurs in James's "A Sonnet on Du Bartas": "His pen in Phoenix . . . shall change" (l. 28, Craigie, *Poems* 102). Guss (162) discusses Petrarch's use of the phoenix, where the mythical bird is portrayed as an analogue of his desire (in "Qual piu diversa e nova") in the endless dissolution and recreation of itself.

Works Cited

Bodley ms. 165

BL Add. 24195

NLS ms. 1.1.6

Barthes, Roland. *A Lover's Discourse: Fragments.* Trans. Richard Howard. (*Fragments d'un discours amoureux,* 1977). London: Penguin, 1990.

Bergeron, David. *King James and Letters of Homoerotic Desire.* Iowa City: U of Iowa P, 1999.

———. *Royal Family, Royal Lovers: King James of England and Scotland.* Columbia: U of Missouri P, 1991.

Bingham, Caroline. *James VI of Scotland.* London: Weidenfeld and Nicolson, 1979.

Bloch, Howard R. *Medieval Misogyny and the Invention of Western Romantic Love.* Chicago: U of Chicago P, 1991.

Bray, Alan. *Homosexuality in Renaissance England.* London: Gay Men's Press, 1982.

Clewett, Richard M. "James VI of Scotland and his Literary Circle." *Aevum* 47.5–6 (1988–89): 445–46.

Craigie, James, ed. *The Basilikon Doron of King James VI.* 2 vols. Edinburgh: William Blackwood & Sons, 1955; 1958.

———, ed. *The Poems of James VI of Scotland.* 2 vols. Edinburgh: Blackwood, 1958.

Doelman, James. "'A King of thine own heart': The English Reception of King James VI and I's *Basilikon Doron.*" *Seventeenth Century* 9 (1994): 1–9.

Fradenburg, Louise Olga. *City, Marriage, Tournament: Arts of Rule in Late Medieval Scotland.* Madison: U of Wisconsin P, 1991.

Fraser, Antonia. *James VI of Scotland and I of England.* London: Weidenfeld and Nicolson, 1974; 1994.

Goldberg, Jonathan. *James I and the Politics of Literature: Jonson, Shakespeare, Donne and their Contemporaries.* Stanford: Stanford UP, 1989.

———, ed. *Queering the Renaissance.* Durham: Duke UP, 1994.

Grundy, Joan, ed. *The Poems of Henry Constable.* Liverpool: Liverpool University Press, 1960.

Guss, Donald L. *John Donne Petrarchist: Italianate Conceits and Love Theory in the Songs and Sonnets.* Detroit: Wayne State UP, 1966.

Henkel, Arthur, and Albrecht Schoene, eds. *Emblemata: Handbuch zur Sinnbildkunst des XVI und XVII Jahrhunderts.* Stuttgart: J.B. Metzler, 1967.

Hutchinson, F. E., ed. *The Works of George Herbert.* Oxford: Clarendon P, 1941.

Jack, R. D. S. "James VI and Renaissance Poetic Theory." *English* XVI (1967): 208–11.

———. "Poetry under King James VI." *The History of Scottish Literature.* 4 vols. General ed. Cairns Craig. Vol. 1 ed. R. D. S. Jack. Aberdeen: Aberdeen UP, 1988. 125–39.

James VI and I. *The Political Works of James I.* Cambridge, Mass: Harvard UP, 1918.

Jardine, Lisa. *Still Harping on Daughters: Women and Drama in the Age of Shakespeare.* Brighton: Harvester P, 1983.

Javitch, Daniel. "The Impure Motives of Elizabethan Poetry." *Genre* 15 (1982): 225–38.

Lewalski, Barbara Kiefer. *Writing Women in Jacobean England.* Cambridge, Mass.: Harvard UP, 1993.

Maclean, Ian. *The Renaissance Notion of Woman: A Study in the Fortunes of Scholasticism and Medical Science in European Intellectual Life.* Cambridge: Cambridge UP, 1980.

Markland, Murray F. "A Note on Spenser and the Scottish Sonneteers." *Studies in Scottish Literature* 1 (1966–67): 136–40

Marotti, Arthur F. "'Love is not Love': Elizabethan Sonnet Sequences and the Social Order." *ELH* 49 (1982): 396–428.

———. *John Donne, Coterie Poet.* Madison: U of Wisconsin P, 1986.

———. *Manuscript, Print and the English Renaissance Lyric.* Ithaca: Cornell UP, 1995.

McClure, J. Derrick. "'O Phoenix Escossais': James VI as Poet." *A Day Estivall.* Ed. Alisoun Gardner-Medwin and Janet Hadley Williams. Aberdeen: Aberdeen UP, 1990. 96–111.

McIlwain, Charles H., ed. *The Political Works of James I.* New York: Russell and Russell, 1965.

Melville, Sir James. *Memoirs of His Own Life.* Edinburgh, 1827.

Montrose, Louis. "Celebration and Insinuation: Sir Philip Sidney and the Motives of Elizabethan Courtship." *Renaissance Drama* 8 (1977): 3–35.

———. "'Eliza, Queene of shepheardes,' and the Pastoral of Power." *ELR* 10.2 (1980): 153–82.

———. "Of Gentlemen and Shepheards." *ELH* 50 (1983): 415–59.

Pebworth, Ted Larry. "John Donne: Coterie Poetry and the Text as Performance." *Studies in English Literature* 29 (1989): 61–75.

Perry, Curtis. "Royal Authorship and Problems of Manuscript Attribution in the Poems of King James VI & I." *Notes and Queries* 46.2 (1999): 243–46.

Prescott, Anne Lake. *French Poets and the English Renaissance: Studies in Fame and Transformation.* New Haven: Yale UP, 1978.

Ritchie, W. Tod, ed. *The Bannatyne Manuscript.* 4 vols. Edinburgh: Blackwood, 1928–34.

Sedgwick, Eve Kosofsky. *Between Men: English Literature and Male Homosocial Desire.* New York: Columbia UP, 1985.

Shepherd, Geoffrey, ed. *An Apology for Poetry or The Defence of Poesy.* Manchester: Manchester UP, 1980.

Weldon, Anthony. "Character of King James." *Secret History of the Court of King James the First.* 2 vols. Ed. Walter Scott. Edinburgh, 1811.

Westcott, Allan F., ed. *New Poems by James I of England.* New York: Columbia UP, 1911.

Wilson, D. H. *King James VI and I.* London: Jonathan Cape, 1956.

Woodbridge, Linda. *Women and the English Renaissance: Literature and the Nature of Womankind 1540–1620.* Brighton: Wheatsheaf, 1984.

Woudhuysen, H. R. *Sir Philip Sidney and the Circulation of Manuscripts 1558–1640.* Oxford: Clarendon P, 1996.

5

"Pairt of My Taill Is Yet Untolde": James VI and I, the *Phoenix*, and The Royal Gift

Simon Wortham

"The Fountaine of Liberalitie"?: James and the Gift Economy of Renaissance Power

Historical accounts of the life and court of James VI and I frequently place a great deal of emphasis on the king's reckless extravagance. S. J. Houston refers to the spiraling expenditure recorded in the Exchequer accounts once James had acceded to the English throne. In 1603, "divers causes and rewards" amounted to £11,741; by 1605, these costs had risen to £35,239. "Fees and annuities" paid to courtiers accounted for £27,270 in 1603; two years later, the annual expenditure had gone up to £47,783. "Festivities were numerous and opulent," writes Houston. "When in 1613 the Treasury was empty, James managed to raise £93,000 to spend on the marriage of his daughter."[1] Maurice Lee, Jr., similarly traces a pattern of "persistent prodigality" more seriously damaging to the royal finances than the "occasional extravagances," noting that "gambling and feasting and lavish weddings became the commonplaces of court life."[2] Such descriptions of the king's taste for luxury and expense are too numerous to mention, forming part of a traditional picture of James as idle, foolish, cowardly, and slovenly; they are sketched most vividly in Anthony Weldon's rancorous *The Court and Character of King James.*

Moreover, evidence supporting James's reputation as a prodigal king is discovered long before his accession to the English throne. Jenny Wormald shows how Exchequer officials in Scotland, replying in 1591 to the king's demand for details concerning the financial management of his royal parks and other possessions, were barely able to restrain their frustration and anger at James's unwillingness to admit responsibility for unbridled expenditure and waste, writing testily that the king must "begyne to prove als carefull of your own necessitie as your majesty hes done and daylie dois of utheris."[3] Notwithstanding such warnings, "the spendthrift before 1603 was the spendthrift thereafter, on a greater scale," declares Wormald, not least since the king of England "had much more to give."[4] Indeed, the literature written to celebrate James's arrival in London and the commencement of his duties as English monarch indicates that the king's reputation went before him. Ben Jonson, in a poem composed in honor of James's first attendance at high session of Parliament, tellingly suggests that the successful monarch would be one who, "with the power of the King, / The temp'rance of a private man did bring."[5] In slightly different vein, Henry Petowe in *England's Caesar* rather optimistically imagines James as a source of light and wealth, addressing him as "blessed Sunne of our Felicitie" and urging him to "let thy bright beams gild our posteritie."[6] The entertainments given to the acceding monarch in 1604 were funded in no small measure by monies from the capital's financial circles and societies, and the tone taken by writers such as Petowe aimed to scotch damaging rumors of the king's wastefulness and thereby counter a widespread feeling that James might become a liability and a drain on the capital's finances.

While critics often present James's squandering of money as evidence of personal failing—sometimes constructed through an image of sexual abnormality, whereby James gave abundantly as the result of dangerously unstable, uncontrollable homosexual passions—others have drawn attention to the strong pressure placed on the royal patron to uphold his "traditional role as guarantor of justice and giver of favour."[7] Linda Levy Peck describes a well-developed, complexly stratified, and highly ritualized system of court patronage in early Stuart England. This system had its own political and cultural customs, conventions, and linguistic codes, in which the monarch dispensed bounty as a specific form of general exchange underlining and promoting intricately balanced relations of favor, allegiance, obligation, service, and honor. In the world of the Renaissance court, Peck tells us, patronage furthermore functioned as a form of performance, providing an excellent way to theatricalize power. In early modern Europe, as in archaic societies, the spectacle of expenditure orchestrated during ritualized events of seemingly exorbitant giving established a particularly vivid means of demonstrating wealth, status, and prestige.[8] In the context of this more detailed account of Renaissance court patronage, subject indeed to significant expansion in England with the "monarchy of the Tudors,"[9] Peck presents a picture of James as a king beset by manifold claims for bounty (in his first speech to the English Parliament, James bemoans "the multitude and importunitie of Sutors," "indisceete in craving," who have been quick to prey on his "infirmitie"[10]). These claims needed careful consideration if the balance of political relations was to be upheld amid constantly changing circumstances of courtly service, preferment, and intrigue. On the other hand there were the binding demands of precedent, reputation, and princely duty (which admittedly James himself had helped establish and extend, through overgenerous practice but also, in *Basilikon Doron,* for example, through written support given to the idea that a king should "use true liberality in rewarding the good and bestowing frankly for . . . honour and weal"[11]).

In this light, James's attitude to the demands of royal patronage can be seen as far more ambiguous than the traditional picture of the unheeding wastrel suggests. Peck shows that the king was well aware of the difficulty he experienced in dispensing favor appropriately. As early as 1592 he had Parliament in Scotland pass a law to protect him from suitors. In his initial address to the English Parliament, the new monarch apologized "that I could not satisfie the particular humours of every person, that looked for some advancement or reward at my hand since my entrie into this Kingdome." James went on, "if I had bestowed Lands and rewards upon every man, the fountaine of my liberalitie would be so exhausted and dried, as I would lacke meanes to be liberall to any man." In fact he begged the pardon of the assembly "that I have been so bountifull: for if the meanes of the Crowne bee wasted, I behoved then to have recourse to you my Subjects, and bee burdensome to you, which I would bee lothest to bee of any King alive."[12] Here, James cleverly played on the fears caused by the reputation that went before him to set limits to clients' expectations of royal benevolence.

Accordingly, during the first decade of his reign in England, the lord treasurer Robert Cecil set about drawing up a set of instructions to govern and restrict the dispensation of patronage, published in 1610 as the *Book of Bounty*. This forced potential suitors to submit their claims to an official body standing between royal patron and client, to ensure that overhasty or excessive giving be avoided. The nascent bureaucratization of a system of court patronage hitherto sharing a strong affinity with archaic types of exchange ritual found in premodern forms of social organization and symbolic economy may well have brought about the beginning of a gradual erosion of Renaissance court patronage in its specific form of a process of general exchange and performance demonstrating and legitimizing kingly wealth, power, and prestige through highly conspicuous expenditure. However, what may have been lost in terms of archaic forms of establishing repute seemed to be made up for in actual profit during James's reign. Alongside the creation of official monitoring procedures, the use of a favorite to broker the patron-client relationship contributed, according to Peck, to the development of a patronage system founded on financial transactions primarily organized around the exchange of material (rather than symbolic) resources, showing itself less concerned with the values of honor and duty associated with the gift economy of the sixteenth-century Renaissance court than with the immediate concerns of the royal balance sheet. Peck singles out in particular the buying and selling of titles and offices by the crown, which provided funds when Parliament voted inadequate subsidies or when income from crown revenue was insufficient to meet the king's needs; this created a situation in which, uncharacteristically, money flowed to the patron rather than the client. Peck argues that this policy, pursued much more strictly on an investment-return basis, "also served as a way to screen too many worthy suitors; that is, those who could pay were given grants."[13]

However, this emphasis on straightforward financial calculation and exchange may entail a simplification of what the sale of titles policy actually achieved. In *English Politics and The Concept of Honour 1485–1642,* Mervyn James shows how through the sale of titles James was able not only to amass much-needed capital but also to expand and ideologically redefine the aristocracy by conferring noble rank on "the 'new men'": lawyers, officials, merchants, and a middle class generally influenced by the rise of Tudor humanism and providentialist belief, who subscribed to a concept of honor based on a moralization of politics and the growth of a civil society served by diplomacy, beneficence, and social virtue.[14] Their inclusion in spheres of power and influence through the sale of titles effectively diluted the ranks of the feudal aristocracy, whose honor code emphasized, on the contrary, competitive self-assertion, family loyalty and the right of self-authentication, often demonstrated through forms of bravado and violent combat which had made them a source of political conflict, instability and dissidence that historically the crown had found extremely difficult to quell. Indeed, during the sixteenth century a feuding nobility had especially troubled the Stuart monarchy in Scotland.[15] Thus the sale of titles policy did not simply replace received patterns of general or symbolic exchange encompassing notions of allegiance, obligation, service, and honor with harder marketplace transactions based solely on the transfer of material resources, as Peck claims. More precisely, it eroded the archaic and ritualized spectacle of expenditure that had been a key aspect of Renaissance court patronage, shoring up in its place a different sort of symbolic economy in which the value of honor was reoriented toward a concept of polity. Here the king not only profited financially through the sale of titles. What he received in return, in the form of a redefined aristocratic class with a refashioned understanding of the bonds of loyalty and duty, helped (in the short term period of James's reign at least) to bolster Stuart power and authority politically and ideologically. What was so clever about the sale of titles was that it provided a way for James to salvage and reshape, within a general economy of power structures and forms of symbolic exchange partaking of values that were not simply reducible to the level of marketplace transaction or the logic of monetary worth—a logic that, through the development of an organized, capitalistic money economy in the period, had been perceived as a threat to the essentialist and absolutist principles of Stuart rule (not least, challenging James's emphasis on, as Jonathan Goldberg puts it, "Roman law in which the power of rule derives from ownership of the ruled,"[16] and by extension ownership of the sum of their material resources and dealings).

James was able therefore to uphold such principles against the anti-absolutist logic of money without actually necessitating costly recourse to archaic forms of ritualized expenditure (limitless giving as an expression of total ownership) on which Renaissance court patronage as a specific form of general exchange had hitherto been predicated. Introduced into a long-standing system of monarchic giving, such niggardliness—understood as a different kind of assertion of symbolic value and possessive authority over and above the material than found in the more familiar forms of expense characterizing the gift economy of early modern power—is reflected in James's monetary policy after 1604, whereby the king tried to attract an "immovable and perpetual stocke" of gold through enhancing its value at the Mint.[17] The policy of stockpiling gold led to the unremitting drainage from the domestic economy of the now comparatively devalued silver coinage, frequently debased and artificially inflated in value by the Tudors, that served as "effective" currency in the period. This apparent expenditure of money made from the less precious metal constituted an assault on the developing capitalist money economy as well as the relativistic concept of worth and logic of exchange-value embodied within it (thus expending only expense itself in the form of that which was felt by the crown to jeopardize the integrity of the king's money). At the same time, the storing up of the nation's gold reserves in place of silver (however unsuccessful the attempt) aimed to return to and preserve a form of value that, alongside its image of solid and stable worth, could not practicably be spent in cash terms—gold coins being simply too valuable for use in everyday transactions.

"Giving Others Words": James's "Style of Majesty"

Returning to Peck's idea of giving as a form of performance indispensable to the general economy of political and ideological relations in the early seventeenth century, Goldberg in *James I and the Politics of Literature* sketches in similar vein the closely orchestrated style of royal display adopted by the new king, whereby throughout his coronation pageant "James's pose was that he gave but could not receive."[18] The entertainments presented to James depicted an amplitude of light, symbolizing a coming era of justice, prosperity, and stability, and emanating from the eye of the sun-king in order to dispel the "shadows," "clouds," and "foggy mists" that were felt to have gathered since Elizabeth's death in 1603.[19] While giving much joy to the amassed spectators, James—in contrast to Elizabeth, who performed the role of central actor in her coronation pageant—"played at being apart, separate." He "passes through untouched and unchanged" Goldberg tells us, reluctant to receive the gaze of the city's populace, restricting visibility of the source of the gift of light by reclining with mannered complacency in his carriage.[20] Indeed, through the seemingly limitless expenditure of his solar powers, James is imagined by Petowe to radiate beams "as dazleth all spectator's eyes,"[21] cleverly forestalling the critical possibilities of reciprocated looking that caused such anxiety to surround the theatricalization of Renaissance kingship—perhaps most famously in the pages of *Basilikon Doron,* where kings, "set upon a public stage in the sight of all people," risk scrutiny by an onlooking population who "pry in the least circumstance of their secretest drifts."[22]

However, while royal power manifested itself by giving (and in a sense not giving) light, enabling the subject's paradoxically blinded gaze into being not least by ensuring that the perception of subjects be thought of as inescapably a condition of the king's dazzling solar presence, for Goldberg it also imparted itself in other ways. "Royal power expresses itself by giving others words,"[23] he asserts. Thus James, by teaching Latin to his favorite Robert Carr, caused some controversy concerning the Scots' perceived disregard of the English language at court, an anxiety interestingly allied—within an interplay of money and words as given objects under a patronage system operating as both a form of general exchange and performance—to growing disquiet at the extent to which Scots recipients of royal bounty outnumbered the English.

James also favored his son and heir Prince Henry with words in the form of the king's gift: *Basilikon Doron,* of course. Yet here again the royal gift was not simply or straightforwardly given. Goldberg understands this written exercise of "fatherly authoritie" in terms of his assertion that "James depends upon Roman law in which the power of rule derives from ownership of the ruled": even as gift, *Basilikon Doron* remained the possession of the king, to be viewed and read "according to the integritie of the author," while the prince to whom James gave his words also fell under an assertion of ownership through an analogy in which the text itself is described by James as "this birth of mine."[24] Thus, unsurprisingly, *Basilikon Doron* has as its "constant theme" Henry's "indebtedness to his father"[25]: the royal gift squarely places its recipient in debt.

James's style of majesty is that he plentifully gave light and expressed royal power through giving others words, yet in both these examples the gift was neither wholly expended within a spectacle of limitless extravagance nor, more complexly, was it actually invested or conferred in expectation of eventual return. Rather, the gift produced "indebtedness"—the dependence of the subject's eye and perceptive being upon the solar force of the king, the prince's obligations to his father—without really being given at all. James always already owned the king's gift to his son—in fact, bestowing it as an expression of his ownership of both the work and the prince. The luminosity of James's coronation pageant created indebtedness (in Michael Drayton's *A Paean Triumphall,* for example, the king's "reflection" instills a feeling of "joy" and a sense of "duties" in the hearts of subjects[26]), although the king was "hardly seen, and when seen, hardly offer[ed] himself to his viewers,"[27] his resplendent solar energies dazzling the spectator's eye so that the royal image as the source of light and seeing actually remained ungiven in the visible. Here, within the figurative imaginary of Jacobean power, we can trace a similarity with James's style of patronage evinced by the sale of titles policy. Without resorting to the bare logic of an investment-return transaction, dangerously allied in the political sphere to the contractual theories of government espoused by Buchanan and Knox, a kind of symbolic economy can be seen to be upheld (that is, one organizing itself upon the affirmation of a form of value imagined to transcend the material) that actually managed to shun recourse to ritualized spectacles of expenditure on which the bestowal of royal favor as a form of general exchange had previously rested.

The circumstances surrounding the failure of the Great Contract of 1610 can be interpreted along similar lines. The famous "bargain" James offered Parliament turned out to be no bargain at all, the king in the final analysis proving unwilling to forego certain royal prerogatives, refusing to exchange them as saleable items for funds he felt in any case were rightfully his. Yet even as the unprecedented and ultimately doomed cash deal between monarch and Parliament was being thrashed out, James, in order to distance himself from the logic of monetary exchange, portrayed the Great Contract in terms redolent of the double-edged gift economy of Jacobean rule. In absolutist style the king declared the "bargain" to be "without example." On the surface of things, James presented the forfeiture of particular privileges as an unparalleled sacrifice akin to the archaic custom of potlatch, which provided a means of restoring and enhancing prestige through unrivaled expense. However, as contract was replaced by gift in the king's rhetoric, this depiction of matchless expenditure was reversed at the self-same moment James described the deal using the double-speak of early seventeenth-century court patronage. Like applicants for royal favor, "dutiful subjects" were to "present" a case to the sovereign, who in turn would "give . . . an answer" as it would "become" him: of course, such images of kingly bounty ran entirely contrary to the direction of the flow of money James was anticipating.[28] Here, while buttressing the language and symbolic economy of the gift to resist the anti-absolutist logic of contract or money, James's giving intended giving nothing, giving nothing away.

Or, at least, if his giving gave nothing away, James didn't quite give nothing at all. Rather, gifts of favor, coins, light, or words gave back to the king what might otherwise be imagined as under threat—subject to potential loss, fragmentation, or dispersal within the conditions of power and rulership of the late sixteenth and early seventeenth centuries. The sale of titles restored and reshaped the symbolic value and ideological currency of aristocratic allegiance, duty, and service (and contained the potentially dissenting energies of an emergent middle class) within an overhauled patronage system that maintained the royal coffers. The manufacture of predominantly gold coins at the expense of silver money served the creation of "an immovable and perpetual stocke" of, effectively, non-money stamped with the possessive mark of the king's image. The dazzling solar imagery of Jacobean rule redeemed monarchy's profound secrecy precisely through power's display. James's gift of words reclaimed and preserved the king's possessive authority in the very act of giving. Thus, insofar as he gave at all, James gave to himself. This is the style of the (self-styled) "free" monarch, who can "pleas thy selfe with thy concaite / And lett none knowe what thou does mean,"[29] whose freedom and power, as Goldberg puts it, "consists in his ability to please himself,"[30] to give himself freedom and pleasure without recourse to a circuit of meaning or contractual exchange going beyond "the style of majesty, that knows / No rival but itself."[31] Even the theory of divine right so important to James in *The True Law of Free Monarchies* serves less to enforce monarchy's obligations to another, higher authority outside itself than to uphold a formal symmetry between the earthly and the heavenly sovereign through which the king's legitimacy and power originates in his own self-begetting and self-regenerative energies: nowhere are these more apparent than in the circularly validating logic and rhetorical strategy of *The True Law* itself.[32] James's "self-referential and absolute style"[33] is just as evident in his relations with his predecessor on the English throne. When, in return for a gift of horses in 1585, James promised Elizabeth anything she desired, even pledging himself through an assertion of fraternal obligation (an interchange Goldberg makes much of), in reality the Scots king can be seen through such protestations to assert the primacy of family ties over the exclusion of aliens from succession, as dictated by Henry VIII's will, thereby giving *himself* legitimacy as the rightful heir to the English crown.[34]

This idea of the king giving words that give back to the king possessive authority and inscrutable power can be developed in relation to the various prefaces James wrote for his published works. These follow a clear pattern: the king bemoans the unlicenced and prematurely widespread dissemination of his text, often seeing this as the cause of various misinterpretations of his work. He thus justifies the insertion of some prefatory material in order to counter misreading and ensure that his meaning and intention is followed accurately. For instance, in the preface to his poem *Lepanto,* included in the *Poeticall Exercises* of 1591, James complains that "although till now, it have not bene imprinted, yet being set out to the publicke view of many, by a great sort of stoln Copies, purchast (in truth) without my knowledge or consent, it hath for lack of a Preface, bene in some things misconstrued." The king therefore wrote a brief introduction in order to "resolve the ignorant of their error, & mak the other sort inexcusable of their captiousnes."[35] With similar reserve, James had only seven copies of *Basilikon Doron* printed in its first edition of 1599, "the printer being first sworne to secrecie."[36] This indicates that the king aimed at a limited audience of family and nobility (alongside Henry to whom James's fatherly advice was directed), although as Daniel Fischlin and Mark Fortier point out, the fact that "the royal holograph was in Scots, but the first limited edition was in English, may suggest that James had bigger plans for his book, especially in terms of demonstrating his competence as a ruler to a suspicious English public."[37] Thus the king's indignity at his exposure to a wider readership may have been more than a little feigned, James presenting himself as writing primarily for an intelligent and sophisticated audience formed within the manuscript culture of a courtly elite in order to distance himself from the more demeaning image of the man in print who was thought to act, in his preface's own terms, as "mercenary" or "hireling." "But since, contrary to my intention and expectation," wrote James in an appended note to the reader, "this Booke is now vented, and set foorth to the publicke view of the world, and consequently subject to every man's censure." Faced with such unlicensed dissemination of his work, the king declared himself "now forced . . . to publish and spread true copies thereof, for defacing of the false copies that are alreadie spread, as I am enformed," cleverly enabling him to widely circulate his work without appearing to actively seek publication in vulgar print. Moreover, James's preface once again served to "cleare such parts thereof, as in respect of the concised shortnesse of my Style, may be misinterpreted therein": while in other sections of *Basilikon Doron* James warns his son that excessively elaborate speech, ornate and overly expressive writing, or lavish display increase the chance of misperception, here concision is taken as the cause of error or captiousness on the reader's part.[38] As a comparable example, the day before the English edition of *An Apologie for the Oath of Allegiance* was published in 1609, a royal proclamation was issued calling in copies of the first edition. (Editions in French and Latin were also published in London in 1609, while a Latin edition appeared in Amsterdam and a Dutch edition appeared in Leyden in the same year.) Subsequently, a revised version was produced, including a long introduction, "A Premonition to All Most Mightie Monarches, Kings, Free Princes and States of Christendome," given in part to remedy apparent misunderstandings of James's meaning in the briefer, original work.

In simple terms James's prefaces seem to offer additional material written subsequent to the primary part of the text, appended to rectify initial oversights, to elaborate on or generally augment the original version. From a practical point of view, however, this supplementary writing would have been received by a wider readership as an integral part of the published book, appearing prior to the main body of text although it was composed afterwards and delimiting from the outset an appropriate reading of the book's contents. This reversal and representation of chronological order—whereby what was written after appears before what came first—enables James's prefaces to inhabit and order the interpretative space normally occupied by the reader in the construction of textual meaning. James's prefaces, while seeming to furnish the recipient with an "extra" (James giving not merely words but the interpretation of those words), therefore provide once more a means to exercise possessive authority over both the readership and the authored gift. By restoring to the king's book a sense of wholeness, integrity, and unequivocality of meaning, the prefaces demonstrate the extent to which originality and ownership are underscored by and dependent on the supplementarity of James's writing.

This supplementarity is the very means to the end of James's "self-referential and absolute style" of kingship and kingly writing "that knows / No rival but itself": while seeming to offer more, James only gives back to himself, since giving is the expression of property rights and the reader a function of the author's possessive force. Thus while semiotic extravagance and linguistic concision, liberality and restraint in respect of language, are both, vexingly, a cause for similar kinds of concern in *Basilikon Doron*, the very interchangeability of these terms can in fact be taken by the king to provide a solution to the seemingly inextricable problem it presents: James can give more in order to give less, for both amount to the same thing. (Writing in praise of moderation, somewhat ironically given the very different patterns of fluctuation between generosity and retentiveness we've traced so far in the king's "style of majesty," James in *Basilikon Doron* explicitly asserts this similarity of seeming opposites, asking, "what differeth extreame prodigalitie, by wasting all to possesse nothing; from extreame niggardnesse, by hoarding up all to enjoy nothing?"[39]) Furthermore, an ingeniously sustained interchange between parsimony and unsparingness enables James to reconfigure through his own textual activity the relations of literary production and reception linked to manuscript circulation in the early modern period. Wendy Wall argues that here a close relationship was imagined between the free circulation of manuscripts, unfettered by legal rights and the restrictive values of ownership, among a courtly elite and the "ostentatious expenditure, lavish liberality, and conspicuous consumption" that members of the aristocracy identified themselves with in order to "set themselves apart from the growing merchant class" they associated with thrift, purchase, rate. However, this imagined connection within courtly circles between the aristocratic "free of purse" and the free circulation of texts does not, for Wall, entail "a democratic interplay of language," "radical indeterminacy" of meaning, or "liberatory flux" in readerly terms. Rather, such forms and images of generosity operating within and underscored by the manuscript culture of the period served to "consolidate the restrictive social boundaries that protected an empowered social group."[40] Like James, the participants in manuscript circulation gave freely in order to retain their ideological power, to preserve their hierarchicized identity, to delimit their "high" status. James gave (and in a sense withheld) his work in print in such a way that it could be repositioned within the characteristic relations and values of this privileged textual and social pattern of exchange.

The complicated connection between giving and not giving—a non-oppositional yet continually ongoing and therefore ultimately unresolved relation—surrounding the bestowal of royal favor, the policy relating to the sale of titles and the production of sovereign coins, the unrivaled "style" and solar imagery of Jacobean power, and in particular the imparting of James's words, is one that for the remainder of the essay I would like to explore in closer detail by looking at James's verse. Here, among a literature that has barely received any kind of critical attention let alone modern analysis utilizing the kinds of perspectives developed in recent forms of historical and theoretical criticism, it is possible to trace the complex processes of textual construction underlying and energizing the (enabling) problematic of power's symbolic economy we've so far located in relation to the more familiar topics of royal patronage, Renaissance spectacle, and kingly prose.

"Reviving Her by That Which Made Her Die": James's Phoenix

James was most productive as a poet during the 1580s. *The Essayes of a Prentise in the Divine Art of Poesie*—including a twelve-sonnet sequence *Invocations to the Gods,* the poetic tragedy *Phoenix,* and his translation of the *Uranie* from Du Bartas—were published in Edinburgh in 1585, and *His Majesties Poeticall Exercises at Vacant Houres*—including *Lepanto* and a translation of Du Bartas's *The Furies*—appeared in 1591. Aside from coterie writing, James seems to have shelved his more literary aspirations upon his accession to the English throne, although, as Kevin Sharpe notes, revision of earlier material suggests he may have envisaged a collection of poetical works after his prose works of 1616. There is also evidence to show a renewed interest in poetry in the latter years of his reign. According to Sharpe, while the king's writings generally were "penned as acts of government," his poems, "though often personal and meditative in tone, are permeated with the language and experience of power, difference and contest." Thus James's translation of *The Furies,* which concerns the fall of man and the corruption of natural order, allows the king to associate "royal authority with divine order and the subject's constitutional health," thereby complementing *The True Law* in objecting to contractual theories of government of the kind proposed by Knox and Buchanan. *Lepanto,* likewise, "did not only celebrate a battle"—the victory of Don Juan of Austria over the Turks in 1571—but, through picturing Christian forces united in a holy league against the infidel, "gestures to an ecumenical hope for a reunified *republica Christiana,*" reflecting James's concern with reconciling religious tensions and diffusing their unsettling political effects and implications at home. For Sharpe, James's verse mediates "God's divine order and reason," setting the seal of authority on royal poetry. He demonstrates how the king's verse often becomes charged with political language and imagery that "associates poetry with government" and suggests that James's *Reulis and Cautelis* implies a close connection between the proper observance of the formal rules of poetry and the responsibilities of government facing the king.[41] To support this, Sharpe points to the fact that in *Basilikon Doron* we find James telling

Henry, "let your own life be a law book," and in the epistle dedicatory to his work on Scottish poetry, the king proclaims that "Caesar's workes shall justly Caesar crowne."[42] Of course, James negotiated his relationship with Elizabeth and strove to secure his succession in part through gifts of poems to the queen, while his sonnets written to woo Anne of Denmark are similarly shot through with motifs of power. James's expressions of love often draw upon the idioms and parlance of political diplomacy.

In the twelve-sonnet sequence *Invocations to the Gods* included in *The Essayes of a Prentise,* James once more asserts a relationship between kingly verse and monarchic power, reiterating the idea that a prince is justly crowned by means of his works.[43] The verses dedicate themselves to and crave inspiration from the classical deities. In the first sonnet, Jove is entreated to kindle James's poetry in order that it acquire verisimilitude, impressing on "all that it reid" a sense that the events being portrayed are visible "in verie deid" (ll. 6–8). Similarly, in the second sonnet Apollo is begged to assist James in conveying "the glasse and picture true" (l. 12) of his subject matter. It is the veracity of the king's poetry that is here imagined to confer authority upon him, albeit dependent upon the "pen" and "Ingyne" of the poet (sonnet 11, l. 4) that conjures a feeling of the tangibly "real"—which in the fourth verse paradoxically leaves the reader's duped senses "so bereaved" and their "eyes and earis . . . deceaved" (ll. 13–14). In fact this paradox resolves itself to the extent that the rendering achieved by James's "unrivalled" poetry is imagined to coalesce with and restore fullness, plenitude, and presence to its object, as we shall see in regard to his tragedy *Phoenix,* where the "taill" wrought in verse by James wholly renews the mythical bird. Artfulness, skilled artifice, establishes the true monarch and the truth manifested by the king, just as in *Basilikon Doron* the prince is always and everywhere associated with acting, appearing, dressing, speaking, and writing, despite James's warnings concerning excessive contrivance and display. In the sixth sonnet, James therefore beseeches Apollo to bestow the crown according to the triumphs of royal poetry, imploring "graunt the forsaid suitis of myne / All syve I say, that thou may crowne me syne" (ll. 13–14).

On one hand, then, it is true depiction (howsoever conditional upon royal art), on the other the stimulation received from the gods that establish the power and validity of these verses. Interestingly, just as verisimilitude and poetic rendering overcome their otherwise antagonistic coupling under the guise and through the form of kingly verse, so any inconsistency or friction between the faithfully represented "object" and the deified "subject" or source of poetic imagination is also overcome in the sonnets as the difference and distance between the two is collapsed within the self-reflexive focus of the poems themselves. The classical gods that supply the king with the impetus for writing also substantially constitute the subject matter of these verses, James fundamentally concentrating his descriptions of the seasons upon their divine power so that the poems become a circular matter of praising the deities who inspire them. Thus the sonnets present themselves as evidence once more of James's "self-referential and absolute style." While the monarch overtly heaps copious praise on the "Immortal Gods" above, the self-reflexivity and reversibility of faithfully portrayed content and kingly poetic art mean that James, when honoring divinity as the substance of his poems, ultimately lavishes admiration and acclaim on himself. "My subjects all shalbe of heavenly thing" he declares in the last sonnet (l. 11). By turning the source and stimulus of poetic art into its subject matter, James can invert the hierarchical relations suggested at the surface level of the sonnet sequence, transforming gods into subjects of his absolutist "style" of power and authority. All this is done, of course, within a totalized and self-reproducing internal economy of language and representation whose circuit of meaning operates continuously without recourse to an "other" or "outside" referent (the divinity of the gods being symmetrical with and indeed identical to James's royal "ingyne") that might threaten potential loss or damage to the full presence and unrelenting plenitude of absolutism. Indeed, in a way that resembles the paradoxically unifying turn to supplementarity in James's prefaces, it is precisely through concourse with forms of divinity reflecting royal power that such uninterrupted wholeness is achieved, James entreating the gods, "I pray you let my verses have no lack" (sonnet 11, l. 14). By juxtaposing images of plenty that permeate the surface level of his verse with the more stealthy exercise of non proliferate reserve happening at the level of poetic structure and form, the poetics of exchange found in the twelve-sonnet sequence yet again indicates the complexly interwoven relations of retentiveness and abundance that configure the imaginary, and underpin the exercise, of kingly rule.

Yet perhaps the ultimate emblem of this "self-referential and absolute style" is James's *Phoenix,* written in praise of Esmé Stuart. Esmé arrived in Scotland from France in 1579 and quickly became an important influence on the thirteen-year-old monarch. Although the year before Esmé's arrival James Douglas, earl of Morton, had resigned his regency into the hands of James, he remained the most powerful Scottish peer. By 1581, however, Esmé had brought about the execution of Morton for the crime of having contrived the murder of James's father Darnley in 1567, thus installing himself as unrivaled favorite. Apparently glad to be rid of the overbearing ex-regent, the young king created his father's cousin duke of Lennox in 1582, but Esmé's meteoric rise met with considerable hostility, particularly from the extreme Presbyterian faction at court. It was suspected that Lennox was an agent of the Guises and the pope, and that his conversion to Protestantism was feigned. James soon learned, as Lee puts it, "how fiercely and implacably hostile Andrew Melville and his friends in the kirk could be toward anyone who was suspected, as Esmé was, of unsoundness in religion."[44] In the same year a group of Scottish nobles, led by the earl of Gowrie and seizing on the opportunity provided by a brief period of separation between Lennox and

James, kidnaped the king in the famous Ruthven Raid and held him captive for ten months. The source of Esmé's power—his custody of the young monarch—vanished at a stroke, for he was without sufficient friends or influence in courtly and noble circles. Esmé was forced to leave Scotland, and he died in Paris within a year. Although correspondence from Robert Bowes, English ambassador in Scotland in 1582, to Sir Francis Walsingham suggests that during his detention James underwent "great change and alteration in his conceit and favor towards the duke"[45]—being persuaded by his captors of Lennox's disobedience to the crown—nevertheless after Esmé's death the king was careful for the rest of his life to protect and advance his four remaining children. Perhaps self-preservation drove James to renounce Lennox or, more likely, Bowes's letter distorts the true picture of his feelings during the Ruthven incident to convince England of returning harmony between the Scots king and nobility. The publication in 1585 of his poetical tragedy *Phoenix* honoring Esmé's memory clearly indicates the endurance of James's affection.

During his brief career at the Scottish court, one of Esmé Stuart's principal achievements was that, building on the love of poetry inspired in James by Buchanan, he set in motion the organization of a circle of poets by his patronage of Alexander Montgomerie. The duke of Lennox brought to the Stuart king the ideas and style of the Valois court. If, as Craigie asserts,[46] it was from France that the Renaissance came to Scotland and from there that James took his poetic models and doctrine—the king's library shelves being stacked with predominantly original works in French or French translations of the classics—then Esmé was of some importance in strengthening this influence. (Of course, alongside *Phoenix* in *The Essayes of a Prentise* we find James's own translation of the Uranie by the immensely erudite and highly serious, deeply religious French Huguenot poet Du Bartas.) Esmé's tutorship tended to overlook the teaching of the principles of governance and policy; instead, through an emphasis on the value of a scholarly and literary education, it catalyzed James's poetic ambitions. In Lee's terms, it "gave him a task for poetry and argument and flattery, and encouraged him to believe he was more gifted than other men."[47] This phrasing is peculiarly apt. In line with the self-reflexive patterns of exchange characterizing James's rulership, what Esmé gave the king was a sense of his royal gift, his kingly power to render through poetry. James in turn transformed the source of inspiration for his *Phoenix* into the poem's subject matter, as in the sonnet sequence turning the enlivening spirit into the subject of his words and regal style, reversing the direction in which the gift is imparted, and so in extolling Lennox giving praise only to himself. Therefore, as much as he was imagined to influence the youthful sovereign, Lennox—by way of an exchange taking place through poetry—happened to mirror the manner of James's absolutism. Through his metaphorical portrayal as a mythical creature, the only one of its kind, able by self-immolation wholly to consume and expend itself and then find renewal among its own ashes, Esmé in poetic form as the Phoenix comes to reflect, embody, and epitomize "the style of majesty, That knows / No rival but itself."

The poem begins, however, with an account of possible losses. James asserts that fortune, friendship, health, or reputation, though temporarily lost, may ultimately be regained (ll. 8–21). The "death of frends," for example, although terrible, is not beyond remedy, since "although the same cannot return, yet men / are not so rare, but you may get the like." Here, ordinary "men" are presented as both expendable and redeemable because subject to a relativistic, anti-absolutist logic of exchange that matches "like" for "like" or that happily takes similar for the same. This kind of exchange shares an affinity with the relational and extrinsic concept of value on which the early modern money economy developed apace. In contrast, the Phoenix, akin to gold, has its value and meaning rooted essentially and absolutely in its own vehicle and form. The Phoenix has no "like," since it is a creature whose "kynde, whose kin, whose offspring, they all be / In her alone" (ll. 32–33). Eternally unique, always self-same, one might say the Phoenix establishes a concept of presence, but furthermore she is unable (as money is able) to proliferate her "kynde," reflecting the inextricable interplay between abundance and restriction in the economy of value and power underpinning James's rule. Pondering her demise, James implicitly associates the Phoenix's self-reproductive energies with the restorative force of his poetry, remarking that "only one at onis did live . . . though I her praise revive" (ll. 34–35). Here James both praises the Phoenix for its wondrous powers of renewal and presents his praiseful verse as effectively the source of such rebirth, once again evincing the "self-referential and absolute style" by exchanging reflexively, taking as the same and not merely similar, origin and issue (this being the very motif of the Phoenix).

To the extent that the Phoenix exemplifies the royal gift that Lee suggests Esmé "gave" the young monarch through instilling in him a "task for poetry," in James's poem it meets with both "love" and "reverence" but also "proud *Invy*" and "ill intent" (ll. 106–40), the same duplicitous combination of publicly sworn allegiance and insidious greed that so vexed the disbursement of kingly bounty in the context of Renaissance court patronage. Indeed, overwhelmed by jealousy, the "ravening fowls" (l. 141)—presumably the nobles hostile to the duke of Lennox and the favor shown him—cruelly pursue the Phoenix with a mind to possess and destroy her utterly. James tells us this voracious band "spaird her not a haire, and that she "laked help in any sort" (ll. 169 and 175). Esmé's political isolation after the Ruthven Raid is here represented in terms of an image of the absolute destruction and expense of the Phoenix as exemplar of the royal gift (one that, unlike money, cannot be bargained with) but also according to an image of reserve, since in more fundamental terms the Phoenix's eternal uniqueness entirely precludes interference or contact from others "in any sort." The total lack of help shown her preserves the hermetically bounded and self-identical presence of the royal gift at the very moment of utter abandonment and ruination. Indeed, the "ingrates" that cause her "undeserved fall" have "clene miskend her" (ll. 140–61)—their inability to recognize or acknowledge the royal gift paradoxically salvaging it to the extent that the Phoenix and, indeed, the *Phoenix* thereby elude reduction to the non-self-referential and anti-absolutist exchange-value of an account. Since she "lake[s] help in any sort" from those motivated by want (we are told that Esmé's detractors envy others "in better cace," [l. 130]), the Phoenix is characterized by the lack of a "lack," which in psychoanalytic terms divests femininity of a stake, placing it outside the phallocentric forms and patterns of conflict and exchange that threaten castration, severance of a part. Esmé's feminization as the self-renewing mythical bird does away, then, with the masculine part, so that even as she is sacrificed the Phoenix as embodiment of the royal gift attains self-regenerating presence without entering into risk of loss.

Exiled from Scotland, the Phoenix "returnde againe / Where she was bred," a reference to Lennox's banishment to France (ll. 184–85). Here the Phoenix experiences "such desire to burn herself" (l. 219)—Esmé dying within a year of leaving Scottish shores. Derrida suggests that to remain gift, the gift cannot be conferred and recognized, since this immediately spurs feelings and forms of gratitude and obligation that annihilate the gift's very idea (although we've seen how James, through gifts of light and words, for example, was able to create indebtedness while preserving the gift as ungiven).[48] For Derrida, then, the gift cannot ever truly be bestowed, cannot journey from self to other, cannot travel. Thus the gift has nowhere to go but itself, and furthermore to itself as non-gift, since it cannot realize itself, cannot fulfil its nature and purpose through being given. Ultimately, then, the gift resorts to itself only as non-gift within an eternally self-canceling gesture. The gift always returns to itself and always destroys itself within a simultaneous movement (of non-movement). This is what happens when the Phoenix, after an excursion that leaves her unacknowledged and so unspent even though she is "spaird not a hair," revisits her origins and there finds annihilation. Yet the "countray" to which the Phoenix returns is not characterized by relentless devastation and disarray. Rather it is one of idyllic, perpetual possibility, "where storms dois never blow, / Nor bitter blasts, nor winter snows, nor raine, / But sommer still" (ll. 185–87). Since the Phoenix's self-destruction upon her own originating ground demonstrates that the royal gift remains absolutely ungiven, its very idea is felicitously renewed (rather like sovereign gold coins, too valuable for use in everyday circulation, that return to James's "immovable and perpetual stocke," their positive absolute value renewed through the negation of a negation turning them into non-money).

Once the Phoenix has departed "homeward," the king sends after her a messenger "to know the yssew and event" (ll. 183–89). James—somewhat impossibly, for Derrida—seems to desire a reckoning of the gift, apparently wishes to bring the gift to account. Yet how can the Phoenix as gift, as present and presence, be illuminated through language, which itself recognizes the severance of the "object," which predicates itself upon the object's loss? How can the Phoenix be subjected to a textual exchange premised on the idea of the gift's enumeration? Interestingly, the "yssew and event," origin and issue, are here once more presented as inextricable (precisely the theme of the Phoenix's wondrous power), so that, as in the twelve-sonnet sequence, verisimilitude and poetic rendering complement rather than contradict one another. James's messenger shows "like diligence" in his "returne" as "in his going there," (ll. 190–96), suggesting a symmetrical relationship between the "event" of the Phoenix's resolute return to its origins and the faithful return of the "yssew," in the form of a narration, mediated poetically by the king, to the king himself.

The messenger tells the king of the Phoenix's demise, leaving James teetering precariously on the verge of despair, but then, having "made us both a while to holde our peace," he breaks the silence and suspense by declaring the creature's fabulous rebirth, thus:

> Pairt of my taill
> is yet untolde, Lo here one of her race,
> Ane worm bred of her ashe: Though she, alace
> (Said he) be brunt, this lacks but plumes and breath
> To be lyke her, new gendred by her death. (ll. 253–57)

The "untolde pairt" of the messenger's "taill" functions rather like James's prefaces. While seeming to furnish an "extra" or supplement, the "pairt" in fact restores wholeness and presence to both the "yssew and event," the Phoenix and the poetically rendered story alike. This previously withheld "pairt" is not simply a severed portion of the whole, since it is itself "untolde," conveying a sense of limitlessness, of an unrestricted fullness that could withstand, exceed and exhaust endless recounting. In its "untolde" relation the "pairt" thus exemplifies and accommodates the whole, the unbroken "everything" that is brought together in the "yssew and event." And since, as well as imparting an idea of inexhaustible plenitude, it is also "untolde" in the sense of being unspent, the "pairt" is not subject to the sacrificial loss and divisive violence supposedly imposed on the "object" by language. James charges the messenger to "tell me out the rest" in "no ways for to spair" (ll. 211–12). Overcoming the fragmenting effect of recounting, the unsparing "taill," through reconfiguring expense as reserve, wholly remedies the utter destructiveness of those that "spaird her not a haire." Moreover, the "pairt" of the "taill" that here renews the unspent royal gift, the Phoenix, within the unlacking space of poetic language, in fact compensates for the absence of "plumes" characterizing the worm that rises from the creature's ashes. Earlier in the poem, James alone recognizes the Phoenix's uniqueness by the "hewe" and "shape" of the bird (l. 88). The reflexive and symmetrical relation of these unrivaled beings (and of their self-begetting energies) returns at the moment the "taill" rendered in James's poem is punned with, and thus takes the same place as, the bird's "plumes." In similar fashion, the want of "breath" that stalls the Phoenix's rebirth is supplied by the "breath" of language, the messenger's tale styled as poetry by the king. Interestingly, the creature that rises from its own ashes is "new gendered." As Esmé is figuratively feminized through his transformation into an eternally self-regenerating source of inspiration—and the Phoenix thereby divested of a masculine part—the "taill" (now suggesting woman's pudenda) of the royal gift is placed beyond the realm of castrating phallocentric exchange and the threat of loss attendant upon recounting. By such means does James offer a poetic reckoning of the Phoenix as exemplar of the royal gift, in a way that brilliantly avoids the risk of the gift's expense. As with his prefaces, James's poetic "taill" gives nothing away. Instead it gives back to itself from the outset what might otherwise be "stoln" or taken from it by readers and subjects through its seeming offer of an account and, as an unwanted implication, the suggestion of kingship's accountability. In fact, in its economic meaning, the "taill" taxes the reader, demands a duty, orders the payment of dues (in this poem, both to Esmé and James). The tail in law refers to "a fee or freehold estate. . . . Limited and regulated as to its tenure and inheritance by conditions fixed by the donor" (*OED*). Like the king's gift of words to his heir, it establishes and expresses the donor's property rights, his possessive authority and power.

Cecil's assertion that "for a King not to be bountifull were a fault,"[49] however well grounded in Renaissance theories of kingship, was clearly made in the face of a growing feeling at the time that the king was bountiful *to* a fault. Despite more balanced work of the kind done in recent years by Wormald and Peck, this image of James has endured to the present day. Yet on closer inspection, the king's bounty, the royal gift, can be seen as caught up in ingenious patterns of symbolic exchange within an elaborate general economy that aims, by resisting the logic of contract and money, to reserve without expense absolutist power and worth, and that forestalls the relativistic exchange-value and critical possibility of an account in the very form of the king's gift of words. Through a complex interplay between the inexhaustible and the unspent, Stuart rule felt itself revived by that which ultimately brought about its own demise. Indeed, to go further, we might say that James, by vesting and celebrating death in an unrivaled creature who lacks a head to cut off (the Phoenix's eternal renewal embodied in an uncastratable "taill"), and long before the sacrificial loss of 1649, may well have reserved even death as the apogee of Stuart kingship.

Notes

1. Houston 24–25.
2. Lee 133–34, 149.
3. Qtd. in Wormald 198.
4. Ibid. 198–99.
5. Jonson 420–23.
6. Petowe 240.
7. Peck 31.
8. It may be helpful to sketch very briefly some of the main lines of development of notions of the gift, general economy, and symbolic exchange in the twentieth century, in order to locate the theoretical coordinates of my discussion. Marcel Mauss's groundbreaking inquiry into the question of the gift within the field of anthropology, to which Peck refers in her article, attempts to show that exchange rituals in archaic societies, rather than operating simply at the level of individual activity, established well-organized, collective relations within a general economy—that is, a system that transcended the restricted economy of financial or material transactions. In contrast, Georges Bataille's reading of Mauss's *The Gift,* locatable in a quite different, radical tradition of social-scientific thought, calls into question the more or less stable and functional patterns of bestowal and reciprocity within this general economy, emphasizing and celebrating instead the symbolic centrality of expenditure without reserve, of destructive wastage, manifested in the archaic ritual of potlatch. Later theorists such as Jean Baudrillard and Jacques Derrida have drawn attention to the fact that the elaborate and extravagant squandering of wealth characterizing the potlatch nevertheless produced a significant return in the form of universal respect, approbation, and social status, ruling out the possibility of an entirely one-sided and therefore wholly expended gift. However, Bataille's rethinking of the significance of the gift marks an important theoretical shift in relation to Mauss, inasmuch as Bataille locates excessive usage to the point of violence and destruction—manifested in the sacrilized events of exorbitance found in the potlatch—as the central principle upon which premodern forms of social organization and economy were predicated, suggesting an important idea of the practical realization and fulfillment of use-value only in and by means of its expense. For Baudrillard, working partly on the basis of an engagement with Bataille's work, the productivist and utilitarian imperatives of modern capitalism have sought to exclude archaic, symbolic rituals of loss of the kind manifested in the potlatch, but they have nevertheless produced new forms of excess through the

spiraling velocity of "sign value" within the semiotic and simulational orders extending from the early modern period to the present. Thus the notions of excess, destruction and loss, as they relate to gift exchange, are complicated by Baudrillard's analysis of the formations of contemporary capitalism, since excess cannot be seen as existing in a straightforward conceptual or historical opposition to utility. Complementing this idea that through a non-oppositional relationship, excess continues to permeate the utilitarianism of modernity, my analysis of James's "style" of giving seeks to demonstrate that, in the early modern period, expense such as that described by Bataille in the context of archaic rites of sacrifice did not necessarily exclude reserve. Nor as gift did it always, as Derrida might be taken to suggest, inevitably give itself, invest itself, circulate itself, in anticipation of return. Rather, through a reading of James's *Phoenix* I argue that giving, expenditure, expense, even death, can be viewed *as from the outset* an unsharing expression of Stuart ownership, possessive force, retention, renewal, reserve, establishing itself *without recourse to* the acknowledgment offered by the donee.

9. Peck 31.
10. James VI and I, *Speach* 496.
11. James VI and I, *Basilikon Doron* 52.
12. James VI and I, *Speach* 495.
13. Peck 41.
14. See James passim.
15. The rebelliousness of the Scots aristocracy, many of whom could boast the equivalent of a standing army where James VI could not, led the king to draw increasingly on support from the rising middle classes, the lairds and burgesses of Scottish towns, to create a via media counterbalancing the disruptive force of the nobility. This policy can be viewed as the forerunner to the sale of titles by James I in England, offering further evidence that this was done not simply for immediate financial gain. See Fraser 65.
16. Goldberg 117.
17. Larkin and Hughes 336–38. For a more detailed account of my argument in this section, see Wortham 334–59.
18. Goldberg 134.
19. These images recur in a number of poems written to celebrate James's accession to the English throne. See, for example, Petowe, Daniel, and Dekker.
20. Goldberg 31.
21. Petowe 242.
22. James VI and I, *Basilikon Doron* 5. See also Goldberg xii–xiv.

23. Goldberg 19.
24. James I and VI, *Basilikon Doron* 11. Qtd. in Goldberg 135.
25. Goldberg 119.
26. Drayton 404.
27. Goldberg 32.
28. Qtd. in Fraser 127.
29. From James's supposed first poem, "Since Thought Is Free, Thinke What Thou Will." Qtd. in Goldberg 22.
30. Goldberg 23.
31. From Jonson's *Prince Henry Barriers.* Qtd. in Goldberg 40.
32. In *Basilikon Doron,* of course, the "style of majesty" is simultaneously "the style of Gods," the symmetry between the heavenly sovereign and earthly kings being such that "even by God himself are they called Gods." See Fraser 69.
33. Goldberg 40.
34. Ibid. 15–16.
35. James VI and I, "Author's Preface" passim.
36. James VI and I, *Basilikon Doron* 5.
37. Fischlin and Fortier 27–28.
38. James VI and I, *Basilikon Doron* 5.
39. Ibid. 38.
40. Wall 52–53.
41. Sharpe 124–31.
42. Qtd. in Sharpe 131.
43. James VI and I, *Essayes* passim.
44. Lee 45–46.
45. Letter from Robert Bowes, English Ambassador in Scotland to Sir Francis Walsingham, 14 December 1582. Qtd. in Ashton 115–17.
46. See Craigie's introduction to the first volume of his two-volume edition of James's poems.
47. Lee 46–47.
48. See Derrida passim.
49. *Proceedings in Parliament, 1610.* 2 vols. Ed. Elizabeth Read Foster. New Haven: Yale UP, 1966. 1: 6. Qtd. in Peck 36.

Works Cited

Ashton, Robert. *James I by his Contemporaries.* London: Hutchinson, 1969.

Bataille, Georges. *The Accursed Share.* Vol. 1. New York: Zone Books, 1991.

———. *Literature and Evil.* New York: Marion Boyars, 1985.

———. *Visions of Excess: Selected Writings 1927–1939.* Minneapolis: U of Minnesota P, 1985.

Baudrillard, Jean. *For a Critique of the Political Economy of the Sign.* New York: Telos Press, 1981.

———. *Symbolic Exchange and Death.* London: Sage, 1993.

———. *The Transparency of Evil: Essays on Extreme Phenomena.* London: Routledge, 1993.

Daniel, Samuel. *Panegyric Congratulatory. The Progresses, Processions and Magnificent Festivities of King James I.* Vol. 1. Ed. John Nichols. New York: Burt Franklin, 1966. 125–26.

Dekker, Thomas. *The Magnificent Entertainment Given to King James. The Dramatic Works of Thomas Dekker.* Ed. Fredson Bowers. Cambridge: Cambridge UP, 1955. 252–98.

Derrida, Jacques. *Given Time: 1. Counterfeit Money.* Chicago: U of Chicago P, 1992.

Drayton, Michael. *A Paean Triumphall:* In *The Progresses, Prolessions and Magnificent Entertainments of King James I.* Ed. John Nicholls. Vol. 1. New York: AMS Press, 1966. 402–7.

Fischlin, Daniel, and Fortier, Mark. "James VI and I and the Literature of Kingship." The True Law of Free Monarchies *and* Basilikon Doron. Ed. Daniel Fischlin and Mark Fortier. Toronto: Centre for Reformation and Renaissance Studies, 1996. 13–33.

Fraser, Antonia. *James I.* London: Book Club Associates, 1984.

Goldberg, Jonathan. *James I and the Politics of Literature: Jonson, Shakespeare, Donne, and Their Contemporaries.* California: Stanford UP, 1989.

Houston, S. J. *James I.* London: Longman, 1973.

James I. "The Author's Preface to the Reader." *The Lepanto. His Majesties Poeticall Exercises at Vacant Houres.* Edinburgh: Robert Waldegrave, 1591. 198–201.

———. *Basilikon Doron. The Political Works of James I.* Ed. C. H. McIlwain. New York: Russell and Russell, 1966. 3–52.

———. *The Essayes of a Prentise, in the Divine Art of Poesie. Edinburgh, 1585. A Counterblaste to Tobacco. London, 1604.* London: Edward Arber, 1869.

———. *The Poems of James VI of Scotland.* Ed. James Craigie. Vols. 1 and 2. Edinburgh: William Blackwood and Sons, 1955, 1958.

———. *A Speach, As it was Delivered in the Upper House of the Parliament to the Lords Spirtiuall and Temporall . . . on Munday the XIX Day of March 1603. Being the First day of the First Parliament. The Workes of the most high and mightie Prince, James.* London: Printed by Robert Barker and John Bill, 1616.

James, Mervyn. *English Politics and The Concept of Honour 1485–1642.* Kendal: Past and Present Society, 1978.

Jonson, Ben. *Panegyre on the Happie Entrance of James our Soveraine to His First High Session of Parliament. The Progresses, Processions and Magnificent Festivities of King James I.* Ed. John Nichols. Vol. 1. New York: Burt Franklin, 1966. 420–23.

Larkin, James F., and Paul L. Hughes, eds. *Stuart Royal Proclamations: Volume I Royal Proclamations of King James I 1603–1625.* Oxford: Clarendon P, 1973.

Lee, Maurice, Jr. *Great Britain's Solomon: James VI and I and His Three Kingdoms.* Urbana: Illinois UP, 1990.

Mauss, Marcel. *The Gift: The Form and Reason For Exchange in Archaic Societies.* London: Routledge, 1990.

Peck, Linda Levy. "'For a King not to be bountiful were a fault': Perspectives on Court Patronage in Early Stuart England." *Journal of British Studies* 25.1 (1986): 31–61.

Petowe, Henry. *England's Caesar. The Progresses, Processions and Magnificent Festivities of King James I.* Ed. John Nichols. Vol.1. New York: Burt Franklin, 1966. 235–44.

Sharpe, Kevin. "The King's Writ: Royal Authors and Royal Authority in Early Modern England." *Culture and Politics in Early Stuart England.* Ed. Kevin Sharpe and Peter Lake. London: Macmillan, 1994. 117–38.

Wall, Wendy. *The Imprint of Gender: Authorship and Publication in the English Renaissance.* Ithaca: Cornell UP, 1993.

Wormald, Jenny. "James VI and I: Two Kings or One?" *History* 68 (1983): 187–209.

Wortham, Simon. "Sovereign Counterfeits: The Trial of the Pyx." *Renaissance Quarterly* 49.2 (1996): 334–59.

6

"If Proclamations Will Not Serve": The Late Manuscript Poetry of James I and the Culture of Libel

Curtis Perry

For better or worse, King James VI and I is widely known as "the greatest man of letters among English monarchs."[1] To his many detractors, this has contributed to the image of James as the wisest fool in Christendom, a pedant out of touch with the realities of government. More recently, however, critics and historians have attempted to recover ways in which the king's writings can be understood in terms of those realities, as variously successful interventions in the political and ideological culture of Scotland, England, and Europe.[2] As a result, many of James's public writings have come to be seen as governmental in intent: specifically, as attempts to assert interpretive power over potentially dissenting voices and thus to limit, in various ways, the discursive and interpretive freedoms of his subjects.[3] More than any other monarch, James forged a connection between absolutism and the authority of the printed word.

If this is self-evidently the case in some of James's overtly political writings, the same governmental intent is detectable in James's early literary works. Thus, for example, James's first book of poems, *The Essayes of a Prentise* (1584), contains a "Paraphrasticall Translation" of a passage from one of Caesar's speeches in book 5 of Lucan's *Pharsalia* comparing the ruler's subjects to tributary streams and reminding them that the ocean (the king) would not be diminished if they ceased to flow. James's paraphrase ends with an "ennvoy" recommending conservatism to subjects: "Then Floods runne on your wounted course of olde, / Which God by Nature dewly hes provyded."[4] This is followed in the volume by a treatise on poetry in which the king warns poets against "wryting any thing of materis of commoun weill" since they are "to grave materis for a Poet to mell in [interfere with]" (1: 79).[5]

James's two volumes of poetry were published early in his career, while he was still only King James VI of Scotland, but there is manuscript evidence to suggest that he may have been planning another collection of poems to appear after the 1616 folio publication of his prose works.[6] Though this volume never materialized, James continued both to write poems and to think of his poetry as public until very late in life. James Craigie's edition of James's poems includes seven attributed to the king, written between 1618 and 1623, and circulated widely in the manuscript miscellanies of the period.[7] Since manuscript culture flourished alongside print culture during this time, such circulation—especially in the many miscellanies of the 1620s and 30s—can amount to a kind of publication.[8] Indeed, these late poems are overtly public in conception, and several are admittedly prompted by important political events (the admiralty of Buckingham, for example, or Prince Charles's marriage negotiations). It is possible to see them, consequently, as an extension of James's characteristic reliance on authoritative publication.

At the same time, since James's literate public persona so frequently found expression in prestige publications (folio publication of "works," official documents, the Bible translation), these late poems seem like an aberration: they circulated in miscellanies among documents that are often scurrilous, treasonous, and ephemeral. To give but one example of this, consider the surroundings of James's poem "Off Jacke and Tom" in one fairly typical verse miscellany (Rawlinson Poet 26, f. 21v).[9] The same volume contains a few poems attacking "these rascall Scotts" (f. 1), the wildly popular poem "The Parliament Fart" (ff. 7–8), several poems capitalizing on the lurid details of the murder of Sir Thomas Overbury (ff. 17v–18v), a poem criticizing the duke of Buckingham (f. 14), and a copy of a poem sometimes called "The King's Five Senses," which—in the guise of praying that the king might avoid lovely and captivating favorites—suggests that he is in fact vulnerable to them (ff. 72–73).[10] The volume, which may have been compiled over a considerable period of time, also contains royalist verse, such as a copy of Richard Corbett's early Caroline poem attacking Parliament for its opposition to the duke of Buckingham (f. 8v).[11] As in many such miscellanies, heterogeneity is the rule: this volume contains pieces written out in a variety of hands and reflecting numerous political agendas. Nor is it uncommon for such miscellanies to contain bits of court news, letters, and polemical political writing in addition to such poems.

The public circulation of poems attributed to James in such collections is a far cry from the kind of publication we tend to associate with the king. Some sense of its indecorum may be gained by comparison with the attitude toward the ungoverned circulation of political gossip expressed in Ben Jonson's masque *Newes from the New World Discovr'd in the Moone* (1620). This masque celebrates James as "the truth" and "the knowing king," and juxtaposes these attributes with an anti-masque parodying the irresponsible circulation of political gossip and news.[12] As the entertainment opens, three Heralds offer "newes" begotten of "Phant'sie" to a trio of interested parties: a Chronicler, a Printer, and a Factor (513). The Chronicler merely wants any and all information in order to fill up his "great booke, which must bee three Reame of paper at least" (514). The Printer, who is eager to turn a profit on news, seeks to purchase "good Copie . . . , be't true or false" (514). The Factor needs news too, for he is in the business of scribal newsletters: "I doe write my thousand Letters a weeke ordinary, sometime twelve hundred, and maintaine the businesse at some charge, both to hold up my reputation with mine own ministers in Towne, and my friends of correspondence in the Countrey; I have friends of all rancks, and of all Religions, for which I keepe an answering Catalogue of dispatch; wherein I have my Puritan newes, my Protestant newes, and my Pontificall newes" (514). As Jonson's parody suggests, such newsletters were an important vehicle for the circulation of political gossip (including poems) beyond London, and it is quite common to find material of this kind recopied into the commonplace miscellanies of the period. Consequently, Jonson's Factor can be seen as standing for this more general culture of manuscript production and circulation: we might imagine that his "cataloque of dispatch" includes poems of various kinds, unpublishable political polemic, anecdotal political news, comic squibs, and so on.

In the most general formulation, Jonson's anti-masque satirizes erroneous ideas of textual authority in the handling of affairs of state. The Chronicler's "great booke" parodies the idea—characteristic in Jacobean England of antiquarians, topographical and chorographical writers, and chroniclers of recent events—that scrupulous exactitude with minutiae might serve "to give light to posteritie in the truth of things" (514).[13] But since he lacks discrimination and judgment, the Chronicler's handling of the "matter of State" is limited to the most trivial factual record: "I ha' beene here ever since seven a clocke i'the morning to get matter for one page, and I thinke I have it compleate; for I have both noted the number, and the capacity of degrees here; and told twice over how many candles there are i'the roome lighted" (514). The Printer cares nothing for such accuracy. He thrives instead on customers for whom printing is itself authenticating: "It is the Printing of 'hem makes 'hem news to a great many, who will indeed beleeve nothing but what is in Print" (515). The Factor, finally, caters to an audience eager for secrets and inside information, and therefore willing to accept the authority of anything circulated by hand: "I would have no newes printed; for when they are printed they leave to be newes; while they are written, though they be false, they remaine newes still" (515).

Since such newsmongers are incapable of rendering the truth of state, the Heralds offer them a fanciful, poetic description of the inhabitants of the moon: the anti-masque implies that this is the sort of lunatic nonsense promulgated as news in these falsely authorized reports. By contrast, the final portion of the entertainment celebrates James as the inspiration to a wise race, elevated above such fancy, who recognize and accept the royal truth. To signal the beginning of the masque's second portion, a Herald addresses the king directly:

> We have all this while . . . adventured to tell your Majestie no newes; for hitherto we have mov'd rather to your delight, than your beliefe. But now be pleased to expect a more noble discovery worthie of your eare, as the object will be of your eye; a race of your owne, form'd, animated, lightened, and heightened by you, who rapt above the Moone far in speculation of your vertues, have remain'd there intranc'd certaine houres, with wonder of the pietie, wisedome, Majesty reflected by you.(522)

The members of this race, inspired by contemplation of James (and "that excellent likeness of your selfe, the truth" [522–23]), descend and perform a series of songs culminating in the following chorus:

> Joyne then to tell his name,
>
> And say but JAMES is he:
>
> All eares will take the voyce,
>
> And in the tune rejoyce,
>
> Or truth hath left to breath, and fame hath left to be. (525)

This song puts forward an ideal of social harmony in which subjects, instead of circulating unreliable political report, would merely join in the choir repeating the hallowed truth of the monarch. Of course, that is what Jonson too is doing. James had been reiterating this same idea for decades. His comment on political poetry in *Essayes of a Prentise* might be taken as a gloss on *Newes from the New World:* "be war of wryting any thing of materis of commoun weil . . . they are to grave materis for a poet to mell in."

Jonson's masque draws an absolute distinction between the king's truth and the unauthorized treatment of "matter of State" in texts produced by sublunary subjects. Attentive and loyal subjects, too, are imagined as being "above the Moone far in speculation." It is the centrality of such ideas to the ideology of James's court that makes his political, manuscript poetry seem at first glance so odd: even by the time of Jonson's entertainment some of James's late poems were circulating in the manifestly sublunary world parodied in the person of the Factor. Nor does this seem accidental. At least one of them—a poem criticizing speculation about a comet seen in the sky during the winter of 1618 and which was taken by some as an omen of political upheaval[14]—explicitly attempts to intervene in the Factor's milieu. This poem ("King James on the Blazeing Starr") advises subjects to keep political speculation to themselves:

> I wish the curious man to Keepe
> His rash imaginations till hee sleepe:
> Then let him dreame of famine, plague, and warre,
> And thinke the match with Spayne hath rays'de this starre:
> And let him thinke that I theyre Prince, and Mynion
> Will shortly change; or which is worse religion. (2: 173)

The kinds of imaginations here enumerated are indeed typical of the libels and news pieces in miscellanies. And James's verse, like Jonson's masque, dismisses such speculation as the stuff of dream and fancy.

By contributing his own poetry to the culture of manuscript "newes," however, James tacitly acknowledges its real importance in the making of political opinion. In fact, James's poem itself demonstrates his ambivalence about the culture of political gossip. On the one hand, it dismisses speculation about the comet's portent as trivial. In a magnanimous tone, the king allows subjects freedom to generate such fantasies: "These Jealousies I would not have bee treason / For him whose fancy over-rules his reason" (2: 173). But on the other hand he acknowledges that such inventions can have an unwarranted influence upon the minds of credulous subjects:

> But to bee sure hee did no hurte, t'were fitt,
> Hee should bee bold to pray for no more witt,
> But onely to conceale his dreame: for there
> Are they that would believe all hee dares feare. (2: 173)

To put this into Jonson's terms, the king needs to meddle with sublunary fantasies—in themselves not worth bothering with—out of concern for unenlightened subjects. But this of course tacitly acknowledges limits to the social harmony celebrated at the end of Jonson's masque. For all his insistence to the contrary, this poem records James's recognition that "the knowing king" cannot remain safely above sublunary circulation.

Attention to the micro-political context of Jonson's masque reinforces this same point: unauthorized political gossip had in fact become a challenge to what Jonathan Goldberg calls the king's power of "discursive imposition."[15] For, as recent commentators have pointed out, Jonson's masque responds (like James's poem) to a rash of unauthorized political speculation. In 1619, James's son-in-law Frederick, the Elector Palatine, was offered the crown of Bohemia by nobles who had deposed their Catholic king the year before. Accepting the crown in these circumstances meant precipitating conflict with Spain and the Catholic powers in Europe, and when Frederick did so toward the end of the year he was counting on his father-in-law's support. England seemed pulled toward a more active role in support of Protestant interests in Europe. These developments were the subject of enormous interest and enthusiasm in England, where James's policy of peaceful negotiation with Spain had never been popular. And interest in the diplomatic negotiations precipitated by these events was fed by a burgeoning news culture. Jonson's masque, composed during the final months of 1619 when these events were at a boiling point, criticizes the excessive circulation of unauthorized political opinion and exhorts the court to follow James's lead regarding the crisis in Europe.[16]

More broadly, as is suggested both by James's poem and Jonson's masque, the unauthorized expression of "rash imaginations" was increasingly a matter of official concern during the last half of James's reign. For though such political gossip was not a new phenomenon, there seems to have been a marked growth in the culture of manuscript libel and "newes." Widespread interest in the scandal surrounding the marriage of Robert Carr and Frances Howard and the murder of Sir Thomas Overbury may have provided the catalyst for this development in 1615–16.[17] And animosity toward Buckingham, coupled with anxiety about relations with Spain and the proposed Spanish match, ensured a continuing interest in the kinds of political gossip dispersed throughout the realm in newsletters, scribally produced pamphlets, manuscript poems, and the like. In December of 1620, James issued a proclamation "against excesse of Lavish and Licentious Speech of matters of State." In July of 1621, he felt compelled to issue a second proclamation to the same effect, ordering "loving subjects, from the highest to the lowest, to take heed how they did intermedle by pen or speech with causes of state, and secrets of government, either at home or abroad."[18] Moreover, James's concern was well-founded: recent historians who have begun to assess this material have agreed with James about its importance to the political climate of late Jacobean England.[19]

Laws and proclamations, as Thomas Cogswell has suggested, could deal fairly effectively with the Printer's excesses.[20] The Factor's, by contrast, were impossible to regulate, though handwritten material does occasionally display formal signs of fear of prosecution such as disclaimers or omitted names.[21] The most interesting of the king's late manuscript poems attempt (like "On the Blazeing Starr") to correct the ideological excesses of manuscript culture itself, thereby trying to extend the king's powers of "discursive imposition" beyond the immediate reach of the law. The remainder of this essay will look closely at two such poems from 1622–23, with an eye toward uncovering what their rhetorical and representational strategies can tell us about the king's constructions of his own authorship amidst this crisis of unauthorized and ungovernable political discourse. The first of these poems, entitled "The Wiper of the Peoples Teares / The Dryer upp of Doubts & Feares" was apparently written in early 1622 as a response to an anonymous libel "lett fall in Court" (2: 182). Though we do not have a copy of this libel (entitled "The Comon's Teares" [2: 183]), its title, together with James's response, makes it clear that it must have had to do with the undue prominence of the duke of Buckingham and with his perceived opposition to anti-Spanish interests in the House of Commons.[22] The second is the eight-stanza pastoral poem entitled "Off Jacke and Tom," in which the king advises his subjects not to worry about Prince Charles's marriage negotiations with the Infanta nor about the risks involved in his trip to Spain in 1623.

Each of these poems attempts to answer the unprecedented volume of unauthorized political commentary generated in response to diplomatic relations with Spain. Each, consequently, is designed to address a specific set of micro-political concerns. But each of them also demonstrates the degree to which manuscript culture itself was perceived as a threat to the style of discursive authority so central to the Jacobean idea of monarchy. "The Wiper," which defends Buckingham and the king's prerogative, recognizes the political importance of manuscript libel and acknowledges the crown's failure to contain it. Though the poem threatens the purveyors of manuscript libel with destruction, it becomes clear that such threats merely mask the crown's powerlessness in such matters: the poem is itself all that James can do to rein in the culture of manuscript libel. "Off Jacke and Tom" attempts to mollify outraged response to Prince Charles's trip, but it also participates in an ongoing ideological contest over the nature of royal authority and the centrality or otherwise of the king's speech. This is one of the reasons for its use of pastoral conceits: it responds to decentralized depictions of the state caged in pastoral by writers like William Browne. Part of the urgency of this counterattack stems from the threat posed to royal centrality by the decentralized nature of manuscript discourse. Each poem, in other words, participates in ideological debates about the nature of royal authority that extend beyond the immediate diplomatic crisis in Europe. These poems—which defend and construct the authority of "the knowing king" in the ephemeral medium of "rash imaginations"—try to grapple with the decentralization of discursive authority implicit in the very medium they simultaneously use and denounce.

Since I am treating these poems as attempts to recuperate the king's discursive authority, it is worth noting that they are subject to the kinds of collaborations which routinely contributed to the crown's self-construction. For though James himself was unquestionably interested in writing, it is inaccurate to see all of the public texts that bear his name as the product of a single consciousness. James's speeches and proclamations were sometimes written collaboratively or by others, usually (though not always) to fit the crown's agendas.[23] The savvy John Chamberlain implied that the same sorts of collaboration may be involved in the production of the king's political poetry. He seems to be describing "Off Jacke and Tom" in the following remark from a letter to Sir Dudley Carleton: "For want of better matter I send you here certain verses made upon Jacke and Toms journey (for the Prince and Lord Marques went through Kent under the names of Jacke and Tom Smith). They were fathered at first upon the king, but I learne since that they were only corrected and amended by him."[24] Since critics tend instinctively to privilege poetry as authentic self-expression, hints of this sort have generally been disregarded. But as I have described elsewhere, there is ample evidence to think that many of the manuscript poems attributed to James may have more complicated origins than has hitherto been assumed.[25]

The public persona of a monarch is produced collaboratively. Accordingly, as his sponsorship of the authorized Bible translation suggests, James probably understood his authorial function more broadly than have subsequent critics. Though the poems under discussion here are attributed to James and clearly speak from the authorized position of the crown, I imagine a range of possible scenarios behind their composition: James may have penned them; they may have been (as Chamberlain suggests in the case of "Off Jacke and Tom") written by others, vetted by the king, and then fathered upon him; or they may have been written for, and authorized by, the king. My guess is that there are examples of each kind of production among the poems attributed to James and collected by Craigie in the standard edition of the king's poetry. The remainder of this essay will not be concerned with questions of attribution. But it is worth noting at the outset that while I will refer to the poems in question as James's, I understand royal authorship in this broader sense. I am treating these poems as public, political documents intended for manuscript circulation: they speak for the crown, but they may or may not have been literally produced by the hand and heart of the king.

"The Wiper of the Peoples Teares" (2: 182–91) is an angry response to a specific verse libel. As such, it contains James's fullest and most explicit commentary on the whole culture of libel parodied in the person of Jonson's Factor and belittled in James's own poem "On the Blazeing Starr." Given the gentle, paternal quality of its title, James's poem threatens libelers with a remarkable vehemence:

Kings doe make Lawes to bridle yow

Which they may pardon, or embrue

Their hands in the best blood you have

And send the greatest to the grave. (188: 115–18)[26]

The genial and forgiving attitude toward the political imaginings of subjects expressed in 1618 is here replaced by stern admonition and anger. By 1622 James had seen the culture of unwarranted political gossip and libel grow rapidly, despite his proclamations. Where he had previously dismissed such political expression as the fantastic delusions of a few troubled subjects, this passage acknowledges the circulation of treasonous material by and among the courtly elite ("the best blood"). Imagining the purveyors of libel in these terms recasts such treasonous discourse as politically important, making it the cause of conflict between the king and his "greatest" nobles.

In defending royal authority, the poem also offers an anthology of the seditious opinions so offensively bandied about in "railing rymes and vaunting verse" (182: 23). Several of these, predictably, have to do with the ongoing crisis surrounding England's relations with Spain and the marriage negotiations of Prince Charles. Indeed, the connection is made explicit when the king warns subjects not to become involved in "our princely match" (186: 85). Elsewhere, James chides his subjects for wondering if he has secretly supported Catholicism: "Why doe you push me downe to hell / By making me an Infidell" (188: 133–34). And many of the poem's most urgent passages refer to fallout from the failure of the Parliament of 1621. James had called that Parliament because he needed a war subsidy. In the diplomatic crisis provoked by Frederick, parliamentary support was needed to strengthen James's hand and make the threat of English power more formidable to Spain. But after a promising beginning, he dissolved it when the zealous patriotism of Commons—in the form of a petition demanding war with Spain and that Charles be married to a Protestant—encroached on royal prerogative. James's poem rails at the presumption of Parliament, insists that kings should not be forced to beg for aid, and claims that kings know best how much the state can afford to pay in subsidies:

Was ever king call'd to Account
Or ever mynd soe high durst mount
As for to knowe the cause and reason
As to appoint the meanes and season
When kings should aske their subjects ayd
Kings cannot soe be made afraid
Kings will Comand and beare the sway
Kings will inquire and find the way
How all of yow may easiely pay. (186: 66–74)

For good measure, James also attacks the antiquarian basis for parliamentary opposition. Where supporters of the liberty of the House of Commons looked back to Magna Carta as its guarantee, James argues that "the Charter which yow great doe call / Came first from Kings to stay your fall" (188: 119–20). Though there may be something of this attack on antiquarian speculation in Jonson's parody of the Chronicler, one feels here that the ideological conflicts surrounding James's style of absolutism have been clarified and polarized by recent political events. The poem also explicitly defends the duke of Buckingham. And since Buckingham's commitment to Protestantism was doubted by many in the House of Commons, this can be seen as part of the same cluster of immediate topical concerns.[27]

Beyond this, the poem is everywhere concerned to emphasize prerogative and *arcana imperii,* twin staples of the Jacobean orthodoxy. Thus, in language familiar to any student of King James, the poem asserts over and over that "God and Kings doe pace together, / But vulgars wander light as feather" (183: 9–10). In this regard, the poem's defense of Buckingham is of particular interest for the way it yokes together a very specific claim about royal favorites and a much more general statement about the autonomous and absolute authority of kings:

> Content your selfe with such as I
> Shall take neere, and place on highe
> The men you nam'd serv'd in their tyme
> And soe may myne as cleere of cryme
> And Seasons have their proper intents
> And bring forth severall events
> Whereof the choyse doe rest in kings
> Who punish, and reward them brings
> O what A calling weere A King
> If Hee might give, or take no thing
> But such as yow should to him bring
> Such were A king but in A play
> If hee might beare no better sway. (184: 33–45)

The poem's powerful association of favoritism and prerogative here pinpoints one of the larger issues at stake in the many attacks on Buckingham: by the time "The Wiper of the Peoples Teares" was written, potentially treasonous attitudes about favoritism and prerogative had been rehearsed in innumerable libels. In addition to attacks on Buckingham himself, manuscript material dealing with James's previous favorite, Robert Carr, earl of Somerset, and his involvement in the scandal surrounding his marriage to Frances Howard and the murder of Sir Thomas Overbury, continued to circulate in the manuscript miscellanies of the 1620s.[28] Indeed, as Alastair Bellany argues, residual interest in the Overbury affair helped shape perceptions of Buckingham throughout his political career.[29] The resulting tendency to see favoritism and corruption as recurring Jacobean problems shifts the blame to James and thus raises questions about the viability of his brand of absolutism. As a result, discourse on favoritism became an important vehicle for the expression of deeper concerns about court corruption and royal prerogative in the 1620s and beyond.

One sign of this is the remarkable popularity, in the political miscellanies of the 1620s and 30s, of comparative discussions of royal favorites. One of the more popular examples of this fascination with favorites, for example, recounts a particularly scandalous version of the fall of Somerset and the rise of Buckingham; it notes of the former that "we cannot read of any that ever was soe great a favorite as Somerset, neither the Spensers with Edward 2. nor the Earl of Warwick with Henry the 6 nor the Duke of Suffolk with Henry the 8th as this man was with the Kinge."[30] Another example of this kind of writing—in circulation by the early 1630s—is Sir Henry Wotton's comparison between Buckingham and Elizabeth's favorite the earl of Essex "in the time of there estates of favour." After Sir Henry Yelverton compared Buckingham to Hugh Spencer—favorite of Edward II—in the Parliament of 1621, this comparison too became the subject of manuscript polemic.[31] More generally, many political miscellanies from this period intersperse Buckingham material with poems and newsletter excerpts dealing with past favorites like Somerset, Essex, and even Ralegh.[32] Since James's poem seeks to defend Buckingham from unfavorable comparison with previous servants of the crown ("The men you nam'd serv'd in their tyme / And soe may myne as cleere of cryme"), I presume that the libel James is responding to participates in this development as well. Such comparative interrogations of favoritism—like parliamentary invocations of Magna Carta—attempt to erode the absolutism of the present by facing it with the alternative authority of precedent. This is one reason for the vehemence of James's defense of his favorite: beyond annoyance with the specific allegations of "The Comons Teares" lies the recognition that attacks on Buckingham involved treasonous speculation into the nature and limits of kingship.

In other libels, the connection between favoritism and prerogative is still more explicit. One of the popular political poems of the day, for example, imagines the duke as a pivotal player in a contest between king and subject, court and city:

Wee are a game at cardes, the Councell deale
The lawyers shuffle, & the clergye cutts
The king doth win his subjects Common weale,
The Duke keeps stakes, & therfore ever putts
The stake farre from the cittie: thus they jumpe
Wee fare the worse, because the Duke is trumpe.

In another version of the same poem, the last half-line reads "prerogative is trump."[33] Both endings appear frequently in verse miscellanies, and their interchangeability may be an index of the degree to which complaints about royal favoritism implied criticism of the king's prerogative in the minds of James's subjects. James's treatment of favoritism in "The Wiper of the Peoples Teares" responds to this kind of association: defending Buckingham against the kind of unflattering historical comparison apparently contained in "The Comons Teares" necessarily means defending absolutism and prerogative. That is to say, the vehemence of the poem's defense of Buckingham stems from a deeper concern with the kinds of anti-monarchic ideologies whose articulation is made possible by the culture of manuscript libel. The poem is concerned simultaneously to defend absolutist ideologies and to attack the culture of libel because, for James, the circulation of political gossip and the threat to royal absolutism are necessarily interrelated phenomena.

However, if the poem shows us how seriously James took libel, it also demonstrates his inability to stop it. Indeed, the poem is written in acknowledgment of the failure of royal proclamations against libel. Here are the poem's last lines:

Then hold your pratling spare your penn
Bee honest and obedient men
Urge not my Justice I am sloe
To give yow your deserved woe.
If proclamations will not serve
I must do more, Peace to preserve
To keep all in obedience
And drive such busie bodies hence. (190: 171–78)

By 1622 it had become clear to James that proclamations would not serve to curb libel. Some other solution was needed. To address this problem, the poem indulges in a series of impractical threats based on ideological fantasies of omnipotent kingship: the king can pluck up disobedient subjects like "stinkinge weeds" (185: 28), kill the proudest with a glance of his "sharpe aspect" (185: 52), and bring ruin with merely an "angrie browe" (190: 167). The "censures" of government contained in libels are merely "vapours" (185: 56–57) that the king has not hitherto deigned worthy of notice. James tells his subjects that "Hee doth disdaine to cast an eye / Of Anger on you least you die" (190: 149–50).

But for all that, the poem is itself the king's attempt to "do more." It represents an effort to extend the reach of the crown's strictures, putting James's authoritative message into the very medium he hoped to bridle. Seen in this way, the poem undermines its own depiction of monarchy's all powerful "angrie browe," demonstrating instead the limits of the king's power. Instead of imposing his will upon the culture of unauthorized news and libel, the king must finally rely on it in a last-ditch effort to reestablish his own authority. Remarkably, then, this poem embodies the paradoxical and self-contradictory nature of the king's late manuscript poetry: in order to assert its own powers of discursive imposition, the crown is forced to embrace the very medium that has challenged it. Thus, as a unique document in the late Jacobean struggle over libel, "The Wiper of the Peoples Teares" casts light simultaneously on the kinds of political importance ascribed by James to this culture of political gossip and on the impossible challenge it posed to the idea of discursive authority so central to the ideology of "the knowing king."

In February of 1623, Charles and the duke of Buckingham attempted to speed up marriage negotiations with the Spanish Infanta by traveling to Madrid. Since the journey was clearly going to be controversial, their departure was taken in secret: while in England they traveled under the assumed names Thomas and John Smith. Predictably, as news of the excursion leaked out, it provoked a great deal of criticism. The idea of the Spanish match was itself unpopular, and it seemed foolhardy to many to place the prince in the hands of the enemy. Charles's safe return, in October of 1623, was the occasion of enormous celebrations among the relieved populace.[34] Not surprisingly, anxieties about the prince's trip and animosity toward the idea of the Spanish match added further fuel to the culture of unwarranted political discourse the king had criticized a year earlier in "The Wiper of the Peoples Teares."

The manuscript poem "Off Jacke and Tom" responds to the widespread criticism of the prince's journey by recasting Charles's courtship in a pastoral idiom: the shepherds Jack and Tom have left Arcadia on a journey of love that promises to "bring to Greece / The Beauteous prize, the Golden ffleece" (29–30). The use of pastoral conceits here is presumably motivated in part by the mode's heavily politicized recent history, which featured both the anti-courtly poems produced by the Spenserian poets and the royalist pastoral of Jonson's masque Pan's Anniversary (1621).[35] Pastoral—always a traditional mode for political complaint—had become by 1623 a crucial vehicle both for James's vision of England and for a strand of nostalgic Elizabethan nationalism openly opposed to the king's delicate handling of Spain. "Off Jacke and Tom," in other words, attempts to intervene simultaneously in the culture of manuscript libel and in the ideological contests figured in the pastoral poetry of late Jacobean England. This at any rate is how a contemporary audience would have understood its project.

Some sense of the interrelatedness of these two contexts may be gained by looking at a pastoral poem written toward the end of 1623: Robert Herrick's "A New-yeares Gift Sent to Sir Simeon Steward." In it, Herrick praises the wholesome mirth of rural Christmas festivities by contrasting them with the anxious political climate engendered by unwarranted political gossip:

> No newes of Navies burnt at Seas;
> No noise of late spawn'd *Tittyries:*
> No closset plot, or open vent,
> That frights men with a Parliament:
> No new devise, or late found trick,
> To read by th'Starrs, the Kingdoms sick:
> No ginne to catch the State, or wring
> The free-born Nosthrills of the King,
> We send to you; but here a jolly
> Verse crown'd with *Yvie* and with *Holly.*[36]

As several critics have noted, the jolliness of such mirth tends to be deeply conservative, resonating with the royalist attitudes of *The Book of Sports* (1618) and imagining a timeless social harmony that overrides political opposition.[37] Herrick here makes this unusually explicit, imagining festive unanimity and pastoral retreat as the antidotes to a culture of irresponsible "newes" associated with parliamentarian opposition to the "free-born" king.

The poem's reference to "late spawn'd *Tittyries*" is suggestive as well: it alludes to a secret brotherhood of gentlemen—popular in "taverns and other debauched places" in London toward the end of 1623—who took their name from the first words of Virgil's first eclogue, calling themselves "Tytere tues."[38] Members of this group were investigated by the Privy Council and seen as enemies of the state, but their specific purposes remain unknown. Nevertheless their use of Virgil's famous opening line would seem to invoke the oppositional ideology associated with some kinds of pastoral during the second half of James's reign.[39] Annabel Patterson argues, for example, that the name alludes to the circumstances of Virgil's eclogue—in which Tityrus lounges under a shade tree while others are exiled—and that it was intended to comment on England's selfish unwillingness to defend Protestant interests in Europe.[40] The phrase also presumably alludes more generally to Virgil's special laureate status as the poet of empire, since in *The Fortunate Isles* (1625), Jonson has Iohphiel describe John Skelton as "*Poet* Laureate to *K. Harry,* / And *Tytere tues* of those times" (7: 717–18). My guess therefore is that the Tityre Tues in London fancied themselves representatives of a brand of aggressive, imperial-minded patriotism opposed to the Jacobean policy of negotiated peace.

The choice of Virgil's eclogues in particular also suggests as much. In the hands of the Spenserian poets, pastoral had come to be associated with nostalgia for an ideal of Elizabethan Protestant imperialism and antipathy to James's diplomacy. The laureate trajectory of Spenser's career—moving from pastoral toward epic in imitation of Virgil—associated his memory with the imperial ambitions of Protestant England, and the willfully archaic nativism of *The Shepheardes Calender* made Spenserian pastoral a privileged mode for the celebration of nostalgic nationalism.[41] As Joan Grundy argues, the opening of the first book of Browne's *Britannia's Pastorals* (1613) alludes to the *Aeneid, The Shepheardes Calender,* and *The Faerie Queene,* announcing itself as a pastoral poem with epic, and therefore imperial, implications.[42] The Spenserians, in short, gave pastoral a nationalist charge. It seems likely, therefore, that by associating themselves with Virgil's eclogues, the Tityre Tues were claiming affiliation with this brand of imperial-minded nostalgia associated with pastoralism by Browne and others.

Indeed, *Britannia's Pastorals* offers the richest articulation of this pastoral attitude, combining nostalgia for Elizabeth and thinly veiled criticisms of James with chorographic celebrations of British localities in the mode of Drayton's *Poly-Olbion* (part one, 1612).[43] Thetis, a goddess whose combination of female virtue and oceanic power hearkens back to Queen Elizabeth, presides over Browne's Britannia, and in the poem's second book (published in 1616) her careful government of the sea is explicitly compared with depictions of court corruption designed to allude to James.[44] In Book 2, Song 1, to offer just one pointed example, Thetis surveys her oceanic realm to make sure that her mighty subjects are not oppressing others. This provides the occasion for a long diatribe on the evils perpetrated by great favorites and the tendency of kings to let such oppression go unchecked.[45] The implied criticism of James's favoritism, especially in the wake of the scandals surrounding Robert Carr's involvement with the poisoning of Sir Thomas Overbury, could hardly be clearer:[46]

> if a King behold such favourites
> (Whose being great, was being Parasites,)
> With th'eyes of favour; all their actions are

To him appearing plaine and regular:
But let him lay his sight of grace aside,
And see what men hee hath so dignifiede,
They all would vanish, and not dare appeare,
Who *Atom-like,* when their *Sun* shined cleare,
Dance'd in his beame. (2: 23–31)

Beyond such explicit criticism, the poem's celebration of the landscape and localities of "deare BRITANNIA" (1: 2) tacitly attempts to construct a form of patriotic nationalism totally unconnected to king and court. This, as Leah Marcus describes, is part of the ideological project of Spenserian pastoral in Jacobean England: "In these poems, which may usefully be considered under the rubric of pastoral, royal authority is conspicuous by its absence: the landscape, through its decentralized configuration, subtly undermines the Stuart vision of an England repastoralized from the court through the promulgation of Stuart policies toward the countryside."[47] The seemingly incongruous mixture of epic and pastoral in Browne's poem offers a generic solution to dissatisfaction with James and the court by locating England's imperial greatness in the countless localities of its countryside.

Along with their decentralized landscapes, these poems also rely on a decentralized idea of discursive authority. Browne, for example, lavishes considerable attention on a festival in which England's true poets (contemporaries mentioned are Chapman, Drayton, Jonson, Daniel, Brooke, Davies, and Wither) sing to entertain Thetis (2: 29–38). This stands, in Browne's fiction, as a pastoral alternative to corrupted courtliness, implicitly asserting that true poetry is made in service of the nation, not the king. This may also allow us to recognize how, from the crown's perspective, Browne's brand of pastoralism might be lumped together with the culture of manuscript news and gossip: both discourses challenge the central power of the king's word, relying—implicitly or explicitly—on a more dispersed and decentralized idea of authoritative speech.

Thus, in response both to unwarranted criticism of Charles's journey and to the oppositional tenor of recent pastoral poetry, "Off Jacke and Tom" is concerned to assert national unanimity and the overriding authority of "Royall Pan." The poem's final stanza seems representative in this regard of the attitudes of the crown:

Kinde Sheapperdes, that have lov'd them longe
bee not soe rashe, in Censuring wronge
Correct your ffeares, leave off to murne

the Heavens will favour there returne,

Remitt the Care, to Royall Pan

Of Jacke his Sonne, and Tom, his Man. (43–48)

By asserting that public censures are well-intended and unnecessary, the poem attempts simultaneously to check libelous political opinion and promulgate an image of the realm as united under the careful stewardship of its godlike king. Patterson discusses this stanza as characteristic of not only James's political attitudes in general, but also a strain of royalist pastoral used to express them and oppose the pastoralized ideology of Browne and the Spenserians.[48]

Its politics, for example, are very like those of Jonson's *Pan's Anniversary,* an entertainment that also imagines England as an Arcadia united under royal Pan. After two anti-masques (provided by ridiculous, foreign Boeotians), the Arcadian masque celebrates the harmony of the realm under Pan:

come you prime Arcadians forth, that taught

By PAN the rites of true societie,

From his loud Musicke, all your manners wraught,

And make your Common-wealth a harmonie. (534)

The centrality afforded royal Pan in each of these texts offers a king-centered idea of nationalism to oppose the nativist and anti-courtly patriotism of the Spenserians. As with "Off Jacke and Tom," the masque's emphasis on national harmony was designed to counteract the increasingly noisy dissent spurred by the crisis in European politics.[49] For the Jacobean court, as for its opponents, pastoral seems to have had a definite ideological purpose. And—as Jonson's masque, James's poem, and the "Tytere tues" all suggest—these ideologies became increasingly polarized in the wake of the Bohemian crisis.

Beyond the forceful reiteration of this Jacobean pastoral ideology in its last stanza, however, "Off Jacke and Tom" is strikingly inconsistent in its conceits. For where the last stanza responds to the real political situation of 1623 by acknowledging the censures of subjects and asserting the political centrality of royal Pan, the bulk of the poem seeks to render Jack's departure in purely amatory terms. Most of the poem uses conventional pastoral tone and setting in order to depict the prince's journey as apolitical in nature: it is not national politics but love—"which prences stoute / to pages turnes" (25–26)—that has drawn Jack and Tom from Arcadia. In fact the poem explicitly depoliticizes the differences between one nation and the next, transforming political opposition into a purely mental landscape whose differences are used merely to allegorize the varying emotions of the lover:

Love is a world of manye Spaynes
where Coldest Hilles, and hottest playnes
With Barren Rockes, and ffertyle ffeildes,
by turne dispayre, and Comffort yeildes.
  Butt whoe can doubte of prosperous lucke
  where Love, and ffortune, doth conducte. (31–36)

As with this gesture toward "Spayne," the poem alludes throughout to the real contours of its subject. The opening lines, for example, insinuate that Jack's safety and the "glory" of the state are real concerns:

Whatt: suddayne Chance hath darkt of late
the glorye of th'Arcadian State
the ffleecye fflocke, refuse to feede
the Lambes to playe the Ewes to breede.
  The Altars smoak the Offringes Burne
  that Jacke and Tom, may safe Returne.

The Springe neglects his Course to keepe
the Ayre contynuall stormes doth weepe
The prettye Byrdes, disdayne to singe
the Meades to smyle, the Woodes to springe
  The Mountaynes droppe the ffountaynes mourne
  tyll Jacke and Tom, doe safe Returne. (1–12)

At the same time, however, these lines refigure the intense anxiety occasioned by Charles's journey as no more than the ambient distress of Arcadian nature at the unease and departure of its beloved shepherd Jack. This use of the pathetic fallacy is common in Renaissance pastoral, but here it allows the poem to assert that instead of opposing Jack's journey, Arcadia shares in and reflects his emotional unrest.[50]

This is inconsistent with the overt political assertions of the poem's final stanza, and in fact it makes sense to think of the poem as having two distinct sections. The first section of the poem treats "prencely Jacke" (16) as a special shepherd but deems political categories like rank and national affiliation irrelevant. Love is a universal force greater than political rank. It turns princes to pages and contains within it "manye Spaynes." This is of course the crux of the poem's depoliticized revision of the prince's journey, for it allows the poem to imagine the Spanish match in purely personal terms.

The poem's penultimate stanza reverses this:

> Thie grandsire greate, thie father to
> were thine examples, this to doe
> Whose brave attempts, in heate of Love,
> both ffraunce and denmarke, did approve.
> Soe Jacke and Tom doe nothing newe
> when Love and ffortune they pursue.

Instead of being universal, Jack's love is here refigured as a specially dashing emulation of father and grandfather. Moreover, the specific references to France and Denmark here (so unlike the depoliticized reference to love as "a world of manye Spaynes") dispense with the fiction of Arcadia that is maintained for most of the poem. Where the bulk of the poem distances Jack from real political reference, this stanza compares Charles's journey to Spain to James's trip to Denmark, justifying the former with reference to precedent and implying that kings and princes are unlike their subjects. This change of register leads into the forceful and more explicit political assertions quoted above from the poem's final stanza. The ambient mourning of Arcadian nature is transformed into the "rashe" censure of shepherds. Arcadia is metamorphosed from a world of love to a nation of royal authority.

Each of the poem's two sections is designed to use the generic resources of pastoral to respond to criticism of the prince's journey. The final stanzas, as we have seen, invoke a recognizable Jacobean pastoral vision in which England is united under the monarch and subjects are enjoined not to meddle in affairs of state. By contrast, the amatory conceits that structure the first section of the poem allow the authoritative voice of the king to make use of conventions traditionally used to veil the political complaints of the disempowered: songs and poems describing Arcadian discontentment or the unrequited love of shepherds bring with them the generic expectation that they may stand for real political dissatisfaction.[51] As employed by the king, however, this long-standing conventional use of pastoral is neatly reversed: instead of using the distancing fictions of amatory pastoral to enable otherwise dangerous discourse, "Off Jacke and Tom" uses them to promulgate a less overtly political version of events that were already discussed and written about too openly for the king's taste. In this way, the depoliticizing fiction of the poem is in keeping with James's familiar emphasis on *arcana imperii.* It offers the king's subjects a noncontroversial way to think about Charles's journey while simultaneously imagining the state as happily unified. If pastoral is traditionally used as a vehicle for political speech, the first section of this poem offers pastoral fictions as a way to avoid it.

The inconsistencies in the poem's fictions signal an important ambivalence of purpose. The first section, which presents an apolitical version of the prince's journey, seems designed merely to deflect and soften criticism. The poem's conclusion, which dispenses with the depoliticizing fictions of love, responds more directly to the problem of unauthorized speech. Instead of attempting to justify the prince's journey, the last stanza of the poem shifts its focus to a more direct attack on the kinds of "rashe" censures it provoked. If we imagine this poem (like "The Wiper of the Peoples Teares") to be a publication in the crown's voice intended to intervene in the culture of manuscript news, the poem's inconsistencies bespeak the self-contradictory nature of its project. Where much of the poem seems designed merely to inject an uncritical version of events into the manuscript culture, the end of the poem explicitly criticizes that culture itself. In other words, the poem's self-divisions demonstrate the crown's contradictory attitudes toward the culture of manuscript libel: the poem evinces both a desire to make use of manuscript culture for public relations purposes and a need to denounce it for its decentralization of political discourse and for meddling with the *arcana imperii.* The very abruptness of the change may also indicate the urgency of the problem, as if the writer—despite his more immediate concern with perceptions of Charles's journey—felt the need finally to assert command over unwarranted discourse even at the cost of violating the poem's conceits. In short, the inconsistencies of "Off Jacke and Tom" are the formal manifestation of the ambivalence built into these late manuscript poems, which simultaneously acknowledge, make use of, downplay, and denounce the unauthorized circulation of political material in scribal publications of the 1620s.

In some regards, attention to these late manuscript poems reinforces the most familiar ideas about the governmental style of King James I. They are evidence, for example, of his concern with writing, of his insistence upon *arcana imperii,* and of the centrality of "discursive imposition" to his idea of authority. Indeed, since James's brand of absolutism has tended to seem heavy-handed to subsequent critics and historians, it is tempting to see these poems as little more than a series of clumsy responses to the public relations crisis stemming from the Bohemian situation and ongoing diplomatic relations with Spain. But they were also intended to respond to another kind of public relations problem: the development of a flourishing culture of political gossip and news that offered readily available alternatives to the crown's perspective to readers all over the country.

Seen in this light, the poems are more than just single-minded reiterations of the same old Jacobean orthodoxy. Instead, they are attempts to grapple with an urgent new challenge to established absolutist ideals. And while they continually attempt to rearticulate the ideologies of the "knowing king"—emphasizing, like the masques of the same period, the king's monopoly over political wisdom and speech—these poems also acknowledge in various ways the degree to which a king's authority must compete with other voices. They attempt to cow these voices with threats, placate them with images of cultural unanimity, or merely dismiss them. But by participating in the ungovernable culture of manuscript libel, they nevertheless acknowledge and in a sense authorize the real political importance of such ungovernable material. As we have seen, the poems themselves attempt uneasily to finesse this tension.

In its broadest outlines, James's dilemma resembles what Kevin Sharpe has described as a central problem of Renaissance authority: "the very developments that led to the predominance of the word in the exercise of political authority also sowed the seeds of challenge to a monopoly or control of discourse, hence to power."[52] Yet James's descent into manuscript publication suggests, I think, that he perceived the threat posed to the crown's discursive authority during the second half of his reign as extraordinary in nature. And since historians have recently been suggesting that the libels and tracts circulated in manuscript may have had an important role to play in "the ideological origins" of the Civil War, there is now every reason to think this assessment accurate.[53] Though James's late manuscript poems attempt to salvage the centrality of the crown's voice, the paradoxes inherent in this project instead underscore the degree to which the growth of networks for the circulation of unauthorized writing had by the 1620s rendered his absolutist model of political discourse obsolete.

Notes

1. Sisson 48. See also Akrigg.
2. For example: Clark, Goldberg, and Sharpe ("The King's Writ").
3. Sharpe ("The King's Writ"), for example, describes the impetus for the Bible project as follows: "an official translation proscribed the Geneva Bible and sought to define the parameters of hermeneutic freedom opened by the translation of the scriptures" (118).
4. James 1: 63. Subsequent citations will be given parenthetically. In all quotations I silently modernize i/j and u/v. Norbrook ("Lucan") offers a nuanced account of politicized appropriations of Lucan's poem in Renaissance England. Since Caesar comes off badly in Lucan's poem, James's choice is an odd one. Norbrook writes that "while it was common for extracts from classical texts to be invoked without regard for

context, some of James's subjects must have felt uneasy about his apparent admiration for the enemy of Rome's liberties" (57).

5. The bracketed gloss is based on the glossary in vol. 2 of James.
6. Add. ms. 24195 is a carefully prepared collection of James's poems corrected by James himself. Craigie (James 2: xxii–xxiii) notes that "its title-page and the nature of its contents suggests that its preparation was not unconnected with the publication in 1616 of the folio volume containing all the prose works which the king had composed up to that date." The suggestion is echoed by Sharpe ("King's Writ"), 127.
7. The poems are reproduced in James 2: 172–93. Craigie's notes in each case list several manuscript versions of these poems (2: 256–67).
8. For recent studies that challenge the anachronistic assumption that only printed texts are published, see Love and Marotti. On the boom in verse miscellanies during the 1620s and 30s, see Marotti 68–69.
9. I discuss James's poem in detail below.
10. On the popularity of "The Parliament Fart," see Marotti 113–15. The curious can find one version of the poem printed in Whitlock 289–92. "The Five Senses" is reprinted in Drummond 296–99, though there is little reason to think the poem was written by him. See Bellany, "Poisoning" 470–75. The treasonous nature of the piece may be suggested by the fact that John Rous transcribes only about half the poem into his commonplace book, as if expurgating the riskier sections (Add. mss. 22959 and 28640 [bound together and consecutively foliated], f. 105).
11. This poem—"The Wisest King"—is reprinted in Corbett 82–83.
12. Jonson 7: 523, 524. Subsequent citations for all the masques will be given parenthetically.
13. The Chronicler seems also to be an antiquary. At one point he says to the Heralds, "Sir, nothing against Antiquitie I pray you, I must not heare ill of Antiquitie" (517). As Sharpe (*Sir Robert Cotton* 37–47) has explained, early Stuart antiquarianism often went hand in hand with the chronicling of contemporary events and even with topographical and chorographical projects. Jonson here does not seem to be parodying any one in particular, but James was generally suspicious of such studies. Plans to revive the Society of Antiquaries in 1614 were halted by James's displeasure; the antiquary Henry Spelman reports that James opposed the society since he had not been assured that they would "decline all matters of state" (qtd. in Evans 14).
14. Here is a poem from Rawlinson ms. D. 1048, f. 50v. "A starr of late appeared in Virgoes traine / Which from the North unto the South did post amaine / If England be North, and South be Spayne / Then Charles sitt fast and looke unto thy waine."

15. Goldberg 20.
16. See Sellin, and also Butler ("Jonson's Newes").
17. I am indebted here to Bellany ("Poisoning"), who offers the fullest extant account of the early Stuart manuscript libel.
18. Larkin and Hughes 496–97, 519–20.
19. See the following: Bellany, "Rayling Rymes" and "Poisoning"; Cogswell 20–53; Cust; Fox.
20. Cogswell describes James's control of the press as "the envy of many continental rulers" (21).
21. Harley ms. 791, for example, contains transcriptions of several poems attacking the duke of Buckingham in which the names have been replaced by empty parentheses.
22. See Lockyer 89–115.
23. For a discussion of the collaborative nature of one of James's most important speeches, and of the outside interests it seems to have served, see Munden. Though James claimed responsibility for dictating his proclamations, there is evidence that at least some were drafted by others: see Larkin and Hughes v–vi, 495–96.
24. Chamberlain 2: 484.
25. Perry "Royal Authorship."
26. Craigie reproduces two slightly different versions of the poem on facing pages. Since the variants seem to me accidental and sloppy rather than programmatic, I quote from them indiscriminately, in each case selecting the more felicitous reading. Parenthetical citations refer to James, vol. 2, and include both page and line numbers.
27. Lockyer 114–15.
28. Farmer makes available a typical collection containing poems on both Carr and Villiers. Beyond that, such combinations are too common to require further enumeration.
29. Bellany, "Poisoning" 440–54.
30. Harley ms. 4302, f. 44v. I have expanded abbreviations in this quotation. This account of Carr appears in several manuscripts from the 1620s and 30s, either as "The Five Years of King James" or as "A Discourse of Passages Between the Earls of Essex, Northampton, and Somerset, the Countess of Somerset, Sir Thomas Overbury, and others." It was later published under the former title (London, 1643). One beautifully produced manuscript volume dedicated to the enumeration of lord high stewards and the more notorious trials they presided over (Harley ms. 2194) excerpts parts of "The Five Years" without attribution and intermingles them with more official accounts of the trial of Somerset. In this text, the same catalog of favorites is reprinted, though Pierce Gaveston is added (f. 77).

31. Wotton's piece exists in manuscript form in Harley ms. 4287. See also Smith 2: 413–14. For the Buckingham and Spencer comparison see Egerton ms. 2026, ff. 48v–49v.
32. For example, Sloane ms. 826—one of the most important sources for the anti-Buckingham material collected in Fairholt—contains a transcription of a letter from Essex to Thomas Egerton (ff. 3–4) sandwiched between a list of Buckingham's grievances and a collection of anti-Buckingham poems. The commonplace book of John Rous follows a series of poems on Buckingham and the political crises of the 1620s with a lurid report of the treason of the carl of Somerset that has the following header: "This was newes in 1615 when Somerset & his countes were in question about Sr Tho. Overbury's death" (Add. mss. 22959 and 28640, f. 153v).
33. Add. mss. 22118, f. 5v, and 29492, f. 56, respectively.
34. See Lockyer 135–65, and Cogswell 6–53.
35. The Spenserian poets are described in detail in Grundy. Norbrook (*Poetry and Politics* 207–34) offers the best account of their opposition to James's policies. Butler ("Ben Jonson's *Pan's Anniversary*") has described Jonson's masque as an example of the ideological polarization of late Jacobean England. I am here accepting Butler's argument for the dating of Jonson's masque.
36. Herrick 126.
37. See Marcus (*Politics of Mirth* and "Politics and Pastoral"), and Stallybrass.
38. The name—a misspelling of Virgil's "Tityre tu"—and description are supplied in Yonge 70.
39. I have discussed early Jacobean pastoral at some length (Perry, *Making of Jacobean Culture* 50–80). Norbrook (*Poetry and Politics* 207–13) describes the political contexts surrounding the revival of pastoral poetry in the Spenserian mode after the death of Prince Henry.
40. Patterson 144–45.
41. On Spenser's relation to the Virgilian career, see Helgerson, *Self-Crowned Laureates* 21–100.
42. Grundy 74–75.
43. For a useful account of Drayton's chorographic project, see Brink 81–90. On the Jacobean politics of chorography see Helgerson, *Forms* 107–47.
44. In Samuel Daniel's *Vision of the Twelve Goddesses* (1604), Thetis represents "power by Sea" (Daniel 3: 188).
45. Browne bk. 2: 22–24. Subsequent citations will be given parenthetically.

46. As part of this same long catalog of overlooked corruption, the following seems to refer directly to the murder of Overbury and to speculation that Prince Henry may have been poisoned as well: "The divelish *Polititian* all convinces, / In murdring Statesmen and in poisoning Princes" (2: 23).
47. Marcus, "Politics and Pastoral" 142. See also Helgerson, *Forms* 128–31.
48. Patterson 145–47. See also Perry, *Making of Jacobean Culture* 50–59.
49. The case is made by Butler ("Ben Jonson's *Pan's Anniversary*").
50. In the January eclogue of Spenser's *Shepheardes Calender,* for example, Colin's sheep are pale and wan, as if in reflection of their master's emotions ("All as the sheepe, such was the shepheards looke": Spenser 421).
51. See, for example, Patterson.
52. Sharpe, "King's Writ" 118.
53. Bellany, "'Rayling Rymes'" 310, and Cogswell, 51–53.

Works Cited

Add. mss. British Library. London.

Akrigg, G. P. V. "The Literary Achievement of King James I." *University of Toronto Quarterly* 44 (1975): 115–29.

Bellany, Alastair. "The Poisoning of Legitimacy? Court Scandal, News Culture and Politics in England, 1603–1660." Diss. Princeton U, 1995.

———. "'Rayling Rymes and Vaunting Verse': Libellous Politics in Early Stuart England, 1603–1628." *Culture and Politics.* Ed. Sharpe and Lake. 1993. 285–310.

Brink, Jean R. *Michael Drayton Revisited.* Boston: Twayne, 1990.

Browne, William. *Britannia's Pastorals.* Menston, Yorkshire: Scolar Press, 1969.

Butler, Martin. "Ben Jonson's *Pan's Anniversary* and the Politics of Early Stuart Pastoral." *English Literary Renaissance* 22 (1992): 369–404.

———. "Jonson's *Newes from the New World,* the 'Running Masque,' and the Season of 1619–20." *Medieval & Renaissance Drama in England* 6 (1993): 153–78.

Chamberlain, John. *Letters of John Chamberlain.* 2 vols. Ed. Norman Egbert McClure. Philadelphia: American Philosophical Society, 1939.

Clark, Stuart. "King James's *Daemonologie:* Witchcraft and Kingship." *The Damned Art: Essays in the Literature of Witchcraft.* Ed. Sydney Anglo. London: Routledge, 1977. 156–81.

Cogswell, Thomas. *The Blessed Revolution: English Politics and the Coming of War, 1621–1624.* Cambridge: Cambridge UP, 1989.

Corbett, Richard. *The Poems of Richard Corbett.* Ed. J. A. W. Bennett and H. R. Trevor-Roper. Oxford: Clarendon P, 1955.

Cust, Richard. "News and Politics in Early Seventeenth-Century England." *Past and Present* 112 (1986): 60–90.

Daniel, Samuel. *The Complete Works in Verse and Prose of Samuel Daniel.* Ed. Alexander B. Grosart. 5 vols. London, 1885–96.

Drummond, William. *The Poetical Works of William Drummond of Hawthornden.* Ed. L. E Kestner. Vol. 2. Manchester: University Press, 1913.

Egerton mss. British Library. London.

Evans, Joan. *A History of the Society of Antiquaries.* Oxford: Society of Antiquaries, 1956.

Fairholt, Frederick W., ed. *Poems and Songs Relating to George Villiers, Duke of Buckingham.* London, 1850.

Farmer, Norman. "Poems from a Seventeenth-Century Manuscript with the Hand of Robert Herrick." *Texas Quarterly* 16.4 (1973): special supplement.

Fox, Adam. "Ballads, Libels and Popular Ridicule in Jacobean England." *Past and Present* 145 (1994): 47–83.

Goldberg, Jonathan. *James I and the Politics of Literature: Jonson, Shakespeare, Donne, and Their Contemporaries.* Baltimore: Johns Hopkins UP, 1983.

Grundy, Joan. *The Spenserian Poets: A Study in Elizabethan and Jacobean Poetry.* London: Edward Arnold, 1969.

Harley mss. British Library. London.

Helgerson, Richard. *Forms of Nationhood: The Elizabethan Writing of England.* Chicago: U of Chicago P, 1992.

———. *Self-Crowned Laureates: Spenser, Jonson, Milton and the Literary System.* Berkeley: U of California P, 1983.

Herrick, Robert. *The Poetical Works of Robert Herrick.* Ed. L. C. Martin. Oxford: Clarendon P, 1956.

James VI and I. *The Poems of James VI of Scotland.* Ed. James Craigie. 2 vols. Edinburgh: Scottish Text Society, 1955–58.

Jonson, Ben. *Ben Jonson: The Man and His Work.* Ed. C. H. Herford, and Percy and Evelyn Simpson. 11 vols. Oxford: Clarendon P, 1925–52.

Larkin, James F., and Paul L. Hughes, eds. *Stuart Royal Proclamations.* Vol. 1. Oxford: Clarendon Press, 1973.

Lockyer, Roger. *Buckingham: The Life and Political Carrer of George Villiers, First Duke of Buckingham.* London: Longman, 1981.

Love, Harold. *Scribal Publication in Seventeenth-century England.* Oxford: Clarendon P, 1993.

Marcus, Leah. "Politics and Pastoral: Writing the Court on the Countryside." *Culture and Politics.* Ed. Sharpe and Lake. 139–59.

———. *The Politics of Mirth: Jonson, Herrick, Milton, Marvell, and the Defense of Old Holiday Pastimes.* Chicago: U of Chicago P, 1986.

Marotti, Arthur F. *Manuscript, Print, and the English Renaissance Lyric.* Ithaca: Cornell UP, 1995

Munden, R. C. "James I and 'the growth of mutual distrust': King, Commons, and Reform, 1603–1604." *Faction and Parliament: Essays on Early Stuart History.* Ed. Kevin Sharpe. Oxford: Clarendon P, 1978. 43–72.

Norbrook, David. "Lucan, Thomas May, and the Creation of a Republican Literary Culture." *Culture and Politics.* Ed. Sharpe and Lake. 45–66.

———. *Poetry and Politics in the English Renaissance.* London: Routledge & Kegan Paul, 1984.

Patterson, Annabel. *Pastoral and Ideology: Virgil to Valéry.* Berkeley: U of California P, 1987.

Perry, Curtis. *The Making of Jacobean Culture: James I and the Renegotiation of Elizabethan Literary Practice.* Cambridge: Cambridge UP, 1997.

———. "Royal Authorship and Problems of Manuscript Attribution in the Poems of King James VI & I." *Notes and Queries* 46 n.s. (1999): 243–46.

Rawlinson mss. Bodleian Library, Oxford University. Oxford.

Sellin, Paul R. "The Politics of Jonson's *Newes from the New World Discover'd In the Moone.*" *Viator: Medieval and Renaissance Studies* 17 (1986): 321–37.

Sharpe, Kevin. "The King's Writ: Royal Authors and Royal Authority in Early Modern England." *Culture and Politics.* Ed. Sharpe and Lake. 117–38.

———. *Sir Robert Cotton, 1586–1631: History and Politics in Early Modern England.* Oxford: Oxford UP, 1979.

Sharpe, Kevin, and Peter Lake, eds. *Culture and Politics in Early Stuart England.* Stanford: Stanford University Press, 1993.

Sisson, C. J. "King James the First of England as Poet and Political Writer." *Seventeenth Century Studies Presented to Sir Herbert Grierson.* Oxford: Clarendon P, 1938. 47–63.

Sloane mss. British Library. London.

Smith, Logan Pearsall. *The Life and Letters of Sir Henry Wotton.* 2 vols. Oxford: Clarendon Press, 1907.

Spenser, Edmund. *Poetical Works.* Ed. J. C. Smith and E. de Selincourt. 1912. Rpt. Oxford: Oxford UP, 1970.

Stallybrass, Peter. "'Wee feaste in our defense': Patrician Carnival in Early Modern England and Robert Herrick's 'Hesperides.'" *Renaissance Historicism.*

Ed. Arthur F. Kinney and Dan S. Collins. Amherst: U of Massachusetts P, 1987. 348–66.

Whitlock, Baird W. *John Hoskins, Serjeant-At-Law.* Washington, D.C.: University Press of America, 1982.

Yonge, Walter. *Diary of Walter Yonge.* Ed. George Roberts. London, 1848.

II

Prose, Politics, and Society

7

Britain's Solomon: King James and the Law

Louis A. Knafla

James VI and I, as king of Scotland and of England, was a keen student of the law. Educated in the Roman civil and canon law tradition, he wrote and spoke both formally and informally on the law and legal matters from the beginning to the end of his public career. He was also involved in numerous legal controversies that occurred in the church, the royal court, Parliament, and the courts of law. According to Archbishop Williams, who gave the address at James's funeral in Westminster Abbey on 7 May 1625, of the four major accomplishments of his reign, the first was care of religion and the second was administration of justice (Williams 46–60). Thus law should receive a prominent place in any reconsideration of the history of James's writings and his reign.[1]

Britain's "Solomon" was unique in his legal views among most of his English contemporaries. Schooled in the civil law tradition on the continent as well as in Scotland and England, he had unusually clear ideas on the structure of the law as well as on questions concerning lawmaking and law-giving. James was, above all, a European. His five major works of political thought were written within European political traditions, and many of his works were written for a European audience, with several translated into French, Dutch, and Latin. James read more continental works than he did English ones, hired European research assistants, and imported European scholars. As Johann Sommerville has concluded, there is no evidence that James owed any intellectual debt to English writers.[2]

It is surprising, then, that scholars of early modern Europe have not examined the relatively complete legal system that James envisioned. Nor have many scholars of early modern England acknowledged the significance of law in his treatises and speeches, let alone his knowledge of common law. The evidence suggests that he was happy to discuss God's natural, civil, or municipal law, and that he did not hesitate to become involved in legal disputes whether they occurred in Europe or the British Isles. He acquired a working knowledge of English common and civil law and showed critical insight in discussing the English legal system. What made James unique was his vision of the relationships between various English legal institutions and the *jus gentium* (law of peoples or nations).

Little has been written about James I and the law since the age of Charles McIlwain, when scholars sought the legal origins of the American republic and modern democracy in the ideas of seventeenth-century legal writers.[3] Since then his views on law have been examined in relationship to Parliament, ecclesiastical, prerogative, and common law courts, as well as in relation to some of the major cases coincident with his reign. These include *Calvin's Case* (Ex Ch. 1608), *Bonham's Case* (CP. 1610–11), the *Earl of Oxford's Case* (Chanc. 1615), the *Glanvill* and *Allen* cases (KB. 1614–15, SC. 1616), and the case of *Commendams* (PC. 1616).[4] Generally though, in law as in literature, the conceptual whole of James's thinking has escaped us (Collier 1993). More recently, with the rise of revisionist scholarship, there has been a debate on the question of whether James's views and actions on the law were those of an absolute or a constitutional monarch.[5]

The purpose of this essay is to explore, from the original record, the particular views that James expressed on law from the beginning to the end of his reigns. This exploration will rely not only on his most popular legal works such as the *True Law,* (1598), *Basilikon Doron* (1599), *Apology* (1607), and the *Remonstrance* (1615)—works which underwent multiple editions—but also on all his writings and speeches in which he addressed any aspect of law. While James's writings are the central focus of my analysis, I will also examine the Scottish and English contexts and changes in his views over time in the following sequence: law in general, the law of God as revealed in the Scriptures, the law of nations, English law and legal system, Parliament, equity and prerogative courts, the common law and its courts, criminal law, and lawyers and judges.

Law

James did not hesitate to write on the law as king, even though many contemporaries believed that kings should rule and not write. His view on kings as legal authors was decisive: "Let him write like a King, every Line a Law, every Word a Precept, every Letter a Mandate" (*Workes* [1616] sig. 2v). Relying on Solomon, "the greatest king," and Samuel, "the greatest judge," James related that Samuel wrote not only two books for the king, but also his own on the law of the king, where Samuel tried to keep the king from declining into tyranny and the people from running into liberty. According to James, Solomon also wrote, on his own accord, some 3,000 parables and 5,000 songs (ibid. sig. 4r–v). James then explored the ancient kings who did not write—from the Assyrians, Persians, Greeks, and Syrians—to the English kings from Alfred onward who did write, comprising "a cloud of witnesses" (ibid. sig. 4v–12v). Summarizing what he had done for England in religion and law by 1616, James concluded that "God hath given us a Solomon" (ibid. sig. 13r–14v).

James held that there were three kinds of law, and he named them in hierarchical order with reference to the duties between a free and absolute monarch and his people. The first was the law of God, or of the Scriptures. The second was the fundamental law of the kingdom, or the law established by king, Parliament, and the courts. The third was the law of nature (True Law [1598] 192–93). James's belief that the customary laws of the land were superior to the law of nature (Proverbs #194) was strong evidence, in his mind, of the relationship between God's and a nation's law. Eschewing the view of Roman law that power came from a grant of the people, James promulgated a notion that kings were covenanted by God before they were anointed, and once anointed their power on earth was free of laws subject to royal policy.[6]

The evidence unquestionably supports the thesis that James VI and I had a consistent view of the law throughout his speeches, letters, and tracts. Within those works, he consistently used the term "Pattern" when discussing the law, suggesting that he himself had a pattern of knowledge on the subject that was rooted deeply in conscious thought.[7] The key to that pattern was God. James spoke and wrote as a man of God, and as a theologian. He viewed law as the subject of "God's Law," and his perception of natural law, international law, and English law stemmed from God. He easily inherited the "sword and the book" as the symbols of English monarchy in the iconography of the Elizabethan age.

God's Law

One cannot emphasize sufficiently the importance of religion and the Scriptures in the world of early modern Protestants. Scripture became the ultimate source of authority, and representations of Scripture were read literally (Weimann). Spiritual meanings became more important than institutional orders. Physical representations of the "great chain of being" and feudal class structure were now infused with a theocratic order where divine imagination was being replicated on earth. Striving for salvation, men on earth had the spiritual obligation to put the Scriptures into play. The worship of God led to the worship of king, governors, officials, and parents.[8] James's writing on the law of God demonstrates consistency, from his first discussion of the subject in the *True Law* and *Basilikon Doron* in 1598–99 to his parliamentary speeches of the 1620s. The law was God's law. Father of the King James Bible, James saw his moral imperative as acting on earth as God directed him from heaven.

James's sense of the particular relations between theology and the law was based on the following sequence of beliefs: God created Adam, giving him the choice of life or death, and he chose death. And so God gave man a church and rulers who confirmed his faith. He then gave man the law, which he wrote, and raised up godly rulers to administer it. After man's corruption, God sent his son Jesus to instruct man in his faith, followed by the Twelve Apostles, who were teachers of the old and the new law. For James, then, rulers must place law at the forefront of their obligations to God and the people whom they rule (Paraphrase [1588] 7–12).[9]

In his first written work on this subject, at age twenty-two, James described God's throne in heaven and his kingdom. From the throne came thunder and lightning, representing the severity and horror of his judgments against the wicked by the old law, and seven burning lamps, representing the Holy Spirit and the "new Law of the Gospel of Christ." In the middle of the throne were four beasts, or "cherubims," to execute his commandments (Paraphrase 14). On earth, God placed four angels on its four corners to execute his judgments in every part of the world and to make seals on the foreheads of the elect (ibid. 21). People were placed on trees to serve as civil and ecclesiastical magistrates (ibid. 25–26). Following the six plagues caused by the blowing of angels' horns, the seventh trumpet blast from the seventh angel marked Judgment Day. The kingdoms left standing, those of the Sancta Sanctorum, would make up the kingdoms of Christ—the people who were judged and saved (ibid. 35–36).

The pope's heretical monarchy, erected by the devil in the form of a dragon, was allowed to increase in worldly power, tyranny, and usurpation until it was destroyed by the fourth, fifth, and sixth trumpets. Once the tyranny of the pope (called the "Great Whore," whose mother was Babylon) was destroyed, the faithful would be saved. God had to destroy the pope's followers because they would never repent, not even with corporal punishment. Only with the destruction of the pope and his followers would God's true monarchy shine in perpetuity (ibid. 39–59). James envisioned magisterial seats, and the persons sitting on them had the "judgment or power of judging" given to them by God (ibid. 63). He considered these to be kings or their delegates. He also saw the souls of those who were beheaded and put to death. All the unbelieving, the murderers, fornicators, sorcerers, idolators and liars could be seen in the lake, burning with fire and brimstone (ibid. 67).

"Kings are in the word of God itself called Gods, as being his Lieutenants and Vice-gerents on earth, and so adorned and furnished with some sparkles of the Divinity" (Speech [1605] 500). Since the people asked God for a king, he gave them one, and thus they could never renounce the monarchy. Since he was elected by God, the people owed him obedience, and he owed them good religion, laws, justice, and equity. This was confirmed by the king's coronation oath, which laid out the respective duties and obligations as summarized by Samuel and implemented by Solomon (True Law [1598] 194–99). The king, as their overlord, originally owned everything. Scottish and English law provided ample evidence of this condition: hoards found under the earth, things washed up on the shores, property owned by bastards at their deaths and by inheritors without heirs, all reverted to the king. But a king, like Jesus, had thorns on his crown to show how much he cared for his people (Meditation [1620] 612–14).

Monarchy was, in this view, the supreme state on earth. Kings were called gods by God, and thus embodied divine power on earth. They could make and unmake subjects, and exercise the power of life and death. "Settled kings," however, ruled by settled law made with their people. Kings were bound by oath to observe the "fundamental laws" of the country; they faced the wrath of God if they failed to do so. James added that no king was more bound to rule with his people than himself (Speech [March 1610] 529–31). Moreover, kings should be kings of peace, both at home and abroad. At home they should see that wrongs were punished, or forgiven with mercy, when circumstances permitted (Meditation [1619] 590–92; Proverbs #199).

The chief law of a king, however, was the health of his commonwealth. He could interpret, mitigate, and suspend laws, but in doing so he was accountable to God (True Law [1598] 203–4). If wicked, he might have been sent by God as a plague for the people's sins. Only God could cast him down. As with magistrates, the higher the bench one sat on, the harder the fall for incurring God's displeasure (True Law 206–10).[10] James espoused good magistrates. Even Moses, who followed God's directions daily, relied on secular magistrates for customary law (Proverbs #133).

The devolution of monarchy in England, however, differed from that in Israel. Since in their inception the British Isles were scarcely inhabited, their first king was Fergus, king of Ireland. He brought the Irish to Scotland, whereupon he and his successors established laws throughout the isle. James's mission to reunite England and Scotland was conceived in his vision of an originally united people under one king. Both the "fundamental" and the "civil" law established that there were kings before courts and parliaments, and in Scotland (and England) this was evidenced in the Chancery rolls (True Law [1598] 201–2). Since the laws of both countries were species of the same fundamental law, there was an opportunity here to bring them together.[11]

James distinguished himself from the medieval view that the king was under both God and the law, a view penned in England by Bracton in his famous thirteenth-century treatise and continued into the sixteenth century by writers such as Sir Thomas Smith (Loades 1–6). While Elizabeth was queen by act of Parliament, in Scotland the succession was determined by hereditary right. For James, the English Succession Act of 1543 that barred his mother Mary from the

English throne was unconstitutional because the law that governed succession was the law of God, not of Parliament. This view was supported by Sir Thomas Craig, the Scottish lawyer who was the prime promoter of Anglo-Scots union (Craig 1603). Under Calvinist thought, statutes must be consistent with the law of God, where it was specifically stated: "Observe the Statutes of your heavenly King, And from his Law, make all your Laws to spring" (*Basilikon Doron* 137).

The king, in the secular world, was subject only to those civil and common laws and customs that were agreeable to the divine law of God (Merbury [1581]). Kings should fear God and subjects should obey them. Godly kings were to read and meditate on the law of God; Scripture contained commands and prohibitions, and kings were to obey both (*Basilikon Doron* 149). James recommended Proverbs and Ecclesiastes, which he ascribed to Solomon, as the best guides for following the law of God (ibid. 150). In the end, the law of the state could not diminish divine or natural law, and the prerogatives of the king were still beyond those of Parliament and the courts.[12] Even prerogatives, however, were defined by usage. Should any king stretch them, "it would cause his people to bleed" (Commons Proceeds. [1614] 17).

James's model for kingship was Solomon, "Yahweh's beloved." The son of David, Solomon was perhaps Israel's wisest and most notorious monarch. Cosmopolitan, he consolidated the country politically, created new administrative districts, increased international trade, and built cities and an elaborate palace and temple in Jerusalem. He asked God for wisdom, and his wisdom was seen to exceed that of Egypt and the Middle East.[13] In Samuel, the famous judge, we have the story of how David began, and Solomon completed, the creation of a monarchy out of the loose federation that preceded it. David's creation was another model for James. God gave his judgments to the two kings so they could imitate him (Speech [1616] 549). Thus the institution of monarchy was God's device to consolidate the kingdom.[14]

This view of Solomon, however, was only one side of the story. Solomon also caused political and religious opposition, stretched his finances by overspending, and raised taxes significantly. The resulting unrest led to a great schism after his death. Ten centuries later, Matthew, an ancestor of Jesus, recalled the death and destruction that followed in the wake of Solomon's rule. James, however, saw a positive parallel between what Solomon and he had done for religion and the law in their respective countries.

The connection between James and his version of Solomon was made decisively by Archbishop John Williams in his funeral oration. Each was the only son of his mother, white with ruddy complexion. Both were infant kings who had a rough minority rule. Each was twice crowned and the most learned king of his era. Each was a prose and verse writer, possessed of eloquent words and elocution. Both were close to God and the greatest benefactors of their churches. Each had hostile enemies in their last days and left their world in a chaotic state (Williams).

Perhaps the first conscious attempt to draft the king's view of where he stood between God and people in England was the sermon preached at his coronation in 1603 by Thomas Bilson, bishop of Winchester. It would be difficult to argue that Bilson made this speech on his own without discussing it fully with James. The public occasion was simply too important for the bishop's random thoughts. Comprising fourteen pages, the speech is unusually clear and direct. Kings are gods by their office, charged with the duties of "ruling, judging, and punishing in God's stead" (Winchester sig. A6r). They exercise God's power over the goods, lands, bodies, and lives of their subjects. They are "keepers and supporters of the whole law" (ibid. sig. B4r). Their purpose is to repress the unbridled lusts of man's corruption: adultery, incest, rape, robbery, perjury, conspiracy, murder, rebellion, and treason (ibid. sig. C5r). Wherever Jesus is described as a king in the Scriptures, he wears the contemporary ornaments of that office. Thus kings are allowed sword, crown, scepter, and throne to exercise their rule in God's name (ibid. sig. A7r–v).

James came to his new throne with expectations of peace. Presaging his foreign policy, which would end the wars in Ireland and the war with Spain, James saw himself in Solomon's footsteps, bringing peace, grace, and song to city and countryside.[15] Unlike Don Juan, he would not stir up religious persecution, invoking God's name for vain honors. Instead he would rule in peace until he heard the song of angels (Lepanto [1603] sig. A3r–v). James had no difficulty placing the seat of his several thrones in London. Addressing the mayor, aldermen, and commoners of London at his accession, he told them that he saw himself seated in "the chamber of our imperial crown."[16] Hence he saw London not only as the seat of the king of England but also as the seat of the other kingdoms he ruled.

No longer simply king of Scotland, James perceived his newly acquired kingdoms as an increase in his divinely given powers. But he did so within a clearly prescribed context of law. He acknowledged the local municipal laws and saved to himself those laws he saw as God's gift to his person. As Bruce Galloway has argued, James was flexible and pragmatic in dealing with the institutions of his kingdoms. While he wished to achieve integration in the long term, he was quite willing to allow each kingdom its own Parliament, council, and courts of law. It was, after all, the Scottish Parliament that had given him perpetual authority over spiritual and temporal matters in 1584, which he began to practice in Scotland and England from 1603 (Wormald, "James VI and I" 42–45).

James also had no difficulty asserting himself as God's anointed ruler. Writing on oaths of allegiance in 1607, he quoted the Scriptures widely, holding that monarchs were the ministers of God ordained to govern both the ecclesiastical and secular state. Neither pope nor people could depose a monarch because the king, as supreme magistrate, was the minister of God (Apology [1607] 250–56, 270–71, 284–86).[17] He attributed the current concept of sedition as one put forward by the papacy against all Christian kings, free princes, and states

(Premonition [1609] 332–36). Responding to Roman Catholic writers who supported papal excommunication of kings, he had their most notorious works burned in the churchyard of St. Paul's Cathedral (Declaration [1612] 366).

Law of Nations

James believed that in England, unlike Scotland, the law of nations (Roman civil and canon law) was too neglected. This neglect, which he discovered after his accession to the English throne, led him to discuss the subject. Common lawyers, he said, discouraged non-lawyers from its study, and the common law at times encroached upon its principles. This was unfortunate for James because the law of nations was based on customs older than English municipal law. Thus he pledged himself to try and keep both legal systems, and keep them free of corruption (Speech [1616] 555). This was a major reason why he failed to stand by his lord chancellor, Sir Francis Bacon—a champion of civil law education—when he was accused of taking bribes. James, partial to Roman civil law, thought it was significant for inclusion in any legal system because of its highly intellectual jurisprudence, its general principles germane to all peoples (the *jus gentium*), and its applicability to foreign diplomacy and treaties.[18]

The one "nation" that James hoped to create was the union of England and Scotland, and the failure of the union was perhaps the greatest of his reign. He wished for a union of laws and of persons, a marriage as he called it.[19] The zeal he devoted to this cause was unique. Putting an English edition of his *Basilikon Doron* to press in London at 2–3 a.m. the morning following Elizabeth's death was a precocious act. With its publication he sought to convey not only his vision of secular and spiritual powers under one monarch, but also the dream of a public union (Fischlin and Fortier 26–33).

James's only success in this area was the decision of the English judges to accept the post-nati—those born in Scotland after the accession of James I of England—as English citizens (Knafla, *Law and Politics* 71–73, 184–86). Examining the nations comparatively, he believed that a union of the countries' "general laws" would be tenable, since some of Scotland's real and personal property law was derived from English equity, and some of its statute law was similar. He believed that a union of their laws would assist the process of law reform and raise the clarity and effectiveness of England's legal system (Speech [1607] 511–13, 520–25).

The union was James's greatest project for England and the British Isles. He used his kingship of England and Scotland as a platform to reconcile Christians of all denominations in Europe (Patterson 75–132). He saw himself as a European in the sense that he was conversant with Roman civil, canon, and local customary or vernacular laws. He enjoyed the intellectual company of prominent classicists and civilian jurists such as Isaac Casaubon, Pierre Du Moulin, Marc'Antonio de

Dominis, Alberico Gentili, and Hadrian Saravia (Sommerville, "James I" 60–64). He used them to fight papal claims of secular authority and to create an undivided monarchial secular power throughout Europe (Patterson 120–23).

James's goal was a Europe where all monarchs were absolute in their spheres, where states ceased to be in conflict with one another, and where Christianity, once unified, would flourish (Patterson ix). The legal system that would bind these states together would be the law of nations. Had he been a lawyer or a theologian instead of a king, he would have been a precursor to Hugo Grotius, the father of modern international law. Instead, his legal knowledge was developed only so far, and he spent his years in England locked in combat with common law lawyers and judges.

English Law and Legal System

James traced the origin of English law to three hundred years before the birth of Christ. It was the fundamental law of kings (the *jus regis*) descended in a free monarchy (Speech [1607] 520). The common law grew out of it as the local customs of the people. James was an adherent of what he called the "old laws." In this sense, he can be seen as a conservative reformer who wished to see as much of the law of the land preserved as was appropriate (Speech [1624]). Legal change should come gradually, prompted only by new circumstances. Thus he believed that law was timely for the occasion: "the present occasion is the reason of the law" (Table-Talk #74; Proverbs #14). In the end, he expressed confidence in the English system of juries determining the facts, judges meting out sentences, and kings exercising mercy (Apophthegms #10).

Among the considerable writing on James I and English law, a polarization has developed: authors have come to distinguish between the "common law" and the "civil law" minds of the early-seventeenth century as exemplified in the works of Sir Edward Coke and Dr. John Cowell. This distinction has been significantly overdrawn. Simply speaking, the hallmark of "custom" was not in the sole possession of the common law mind. Civil lawyers also believed in the force of custom, particularly in France, Spain, and Scotland.[20] Both "camps" believed that customary law was the highest form of man-made law, and that law was grounded on "reason" (Knafla, "Influence of Continental Humanists").

There is no a priori reason for separating the legal thought of James from his common law contemporaries on this basic premise. James's major debate with common lawyers was over the "artificial reason" of the common law expounded by Coke, but not by other common law spokesmen such as Sir John Davies (Knafla, "Common Law" 176–81). From 1610 to 1624, James arranged conferences between judges to resolve problems of jurisdiction and thorny issues such as the use of prohibitions. He had few controversies with judges after the crisis of 1616. He preferred to work with judges, not against them. His problems with Coke were not unique. Chief Judge Baron Altham, and Judges Thomas Walmsley, Peter Warburton, and Sir David Williams had their own difficulties working with the chief justice.[21]

James's view of the English legal system was colored by biblical and civilian traditions. Outlined in his Scottish work (*Basilikon Doron*), it was reinforced in his later English writings. James considered that the primary duty of a king was to discharge his office with justice and equity. Since people, like apes, followed by example, a "lawful king" made and executed good laws for his people as their natural father and master, then died in peace. A "usurping tyrant" did not keep good laws, fell by "unlawful rebellions," and died leaving "infamous memories" and unpunished rebels (*Basilikon Doron* 155–56). Moreover, kings should use their powers carefully. They should not "stretch" their royal prerogatives but use them sparingly, as an art in the science of government (Meditation [1621] 621).

For James, the key to good laws was their immediate execution. The king should "do justice" for the love of justice, not for his own passions, as "God ever looketh to your inward intention in all your actions." Thus the monarch should "mix Justice with Mercy, punishing or sparing, as ye shall find the crime to have been wilfully or rashly committed, and according to the by-past behaviour of the committer" (*Basilikon Doron* 1599: 157). When administering the law, a monarch should not be gracious in order to win the obedience of his people. As Moses said, "justice should be friendless" (ibid. 159; Apophthegms #47).

James advised that the monarch, in order to keep the law, should visit each principal part of the country every year and hear complaints. He should choose councilors wisely and impartially from all quarters; he should also see that they have the right qualities for the office, are men of known wisdom, honesty, and good conscience, and are well practiced in their craft. He should watch them daily to see that they obey the laws precisely. Their offenses should be punished more severely than those of others. No one should be allowed to oppress the king's subjects. In the end, people should be judged by their actions: "Let your life be a lawbook and mirror to your people" (*Basilikon Doron* 167–70). When confronted in 1621–24 with the corruption of ministers and judges, he would follow these tenets.

James had a strict view of the boundaries of the courts. Befuddled initially by the plethora of courts civil and common, secular and ecclesiastical, local and central, he praised the legal system of Denmark, where there was one court system and one law-book: "Happy Kingdom!" Accepting the English hybrid system, he ordered that each court remain within its boundaries and not encroach upon the jurisdiction of others (Speech [1616] 556–58, quote at 556). Addressing Parliament, he used the analogy of keeping "every river within his own banks and channels" (Speech [1609] 534–35). Addressing the judges of England, he told them to regard one another as brothers and their courts as sisters. Judges should have reverence for one another, and bind themselves to their courts and within their law. "You are Law-givers, and not Law-tellers" (Speech [1616] 560). If laws were not enforced, responsibility lay at the feet of clergy and judges (Speech [March 1610] 537–38). He told them, when giving judgment, to do good and do it well: "Laws have not their eyes in their necks, but in their foreheads" (Speech [1621] sig. B4r–Cv, quote at Cr–v).

He also had strong words for litigants. He exhorted them to sue only in the court that had the most appropriate process for their complaints, to accept the procedures, and to acquiesce in the judgments. He would rather have upheld an unjust decision than have questioned one of his judges. Complaints against judges were only acknowledged in cases of bribery and corruption. He also encouraged them to eschew novelties, citing recent innovations to which Edmund Plowden had objected in his Reports (Speech [1616] 560–61). Thus James never spoke of an "ancient constitution." Instead, he believed that all ancient customs existed by the grace of monarchy and comprised the fundamental laws of the realm. To sort out, clarify, and condense them into a more meaningful body of law was the job of Parliament.

Parliament

In his first speech to the English Parliament in 1603, James held that God had provided him with parliaments as his birthright. God had sent him to be their king and governor: "I am the husband, and all the whole Isle is my lawful Wife; I am the Head, and it is my Body; I am the Shepherd, and it is my flock" (Speech [1603] 485–88, quote at 488). They were the high court of Parliament, the king's great council, assembled by him to abrogate old laws and make new ones. He was their head, and they were there as his body to give him their best advice. They were to "deliberate on your conscience to determine how far those things agree with me and the weal."[22] They were not there to meddle with his office or his government (Speech [March 1610] 357; Speech [1624]). As the eyes of the people, they could discover inconveniences and injustices and raise grievances. But only he could provide correction (Parliamentary Proceeds. [1610] I: 101–3). He and they would rule for the public good and not for private ends.

Parliament was not a subject that James discussed in his formal writings. The king's view of Parliament was revealed largely through his published and unpublished speeches. As he had written earlier of the Scottish Parliament, it was the "King's head court." Comprising the king and the three estates (lay lords, ecclesiastics, and commoners), all four bodies had to give their assent, but only the king's scepter gave a statute or ordinance the force of law (True Law [1598] 202). These statutes could not be made by the common multitude but only by a few reasonable men knowledgeable in the law (Table-Talk #113). He would not, however, introduce a new custom without their consent (Table-Talk #139).

The king preferred to make laws with "the whole Common-wealth." But since there were more laws than could be enforced effectively in both Scotland (Burns 14–17) and England, what the countries needed was not more laws but fewer ones, for the most grievous problems, "well put in execution."[23] There were already too many penal statutes, for example, which, if enforced, would bring injustice (Parliamentary Proceeds. [1610] I: 103). Statutes against papists were equally too numerous, couched with obscurities and intricacies (ibid. 14–15). It was more important to execute a few good laws with good judges and magistrates than to have a raft of them on the books (Speech [1603] 494).

James would not allow "rash and hair-brained fellows" to invent their own laws nor introduce novelties (Speech [1605] 506). Where the law was unclear, the king was judge (ibid. 519). He would not put up with others interfering in the legal process (Speech [1621] sig. Cv) or with hastily drafted bills (Speech [1624]). No law was better than defective law. "Dead law is no law but a corpse" (Commons Proceeds. [1614] 15). Both houses of Parliament had privileges by right in statute law, to which they were parties. But these privileges had been given to them by the grace of kings. They could maintain them only by keeping within their limits (Commons Debates [1621] 528–30).

Reminding members of Parliament that he was answerable to God alone, James warned them to "remember that the Thrones that you sit on are God's, and neither yours nor mine" (Speech [1600] 490–44, quote at 494). Parliament was there at his will, and members should not sit there for long periods of time debating endless questions. Their primary duty was to support the king's state and his necessities, present the grievances of the people, and propose legislation to resolve them (Speech [March 1610] 528–29). Members were certainly not there to dispute or meddle with his prerogatives. They could complain of grievances, but they could not call into question his powers to correct the grievances that were under his jurisdiction. For example, in the case of impositions, the Commons raised the problem, and he took care of it (Speech [May 1610] 101–3). With regard to the problem of monopolies, the Commons made their complaints, he investigated and punished the ones he discovered, and left judgment of the others to them (Speech [1621] sig. A3r–Br).

The monarch's conflict with Parliament over patents of monopoly was the first item James addressed in his speech to the country following his coronation. He said that while Elizabeth had proposed to revoke all grants of monopoly, circumstances precluded her from doing that. He took the position that all monopolies would be examined in the Privy Council by due course of law. In the meantime, he suspended the execution of any grant of monopoly, except those given to corporations or companies, until it was examined and approved. His position was that no one could sue in a court of law for either protection or exemption from such a grant, for that would be "contrary or repugnant to the laws of this realm" (Speech to Country [1603] 1). Thus his position was that matters pertaining to the prerogative fell under that part of English law which was the king's law, above the law of Parliament or the courts.

While Parliament could not make or unmake patents of monopoly, the judicial powers of the House of Lords enabled the judges who sat there to determine if a patent, or any of its clauses, had deficiencies. The Lords had this power by the grace of the king. Thus the ordinary course of the law (due process) in these matters was sanctioned by the king (*Workes* 1616: 13r–14v). As in handling abuses in the management of monopolies, proof would be determined by hard evidence and judicial precedent.

James held that laws were best made in Parliament and that his job was to see that they were tough laws (Premonition [1609] 240–42). He preferred that they made either tough law or no law. Otherwise, the law would become a mockery of the people (Table-Talk #12). There were some areas that required new laws, such as the reform and codification of penal laws (Speech [May 1610] 103) and the regulation of alehouses and informers (Speech [1621] B2v–B3v). He urged Parliament to get on with the job. He held that when he saw that people were vexed by patents and other instruments which troubled and exhausted their purses, "it makes my hair stand upright" (Speech [1621] sig. B4r). However, if Parliament did not do its job, then he might intervene. Thus in 1624 he claimed the right to alter statutes (in this case a preamble he had not seen), but he did not exercise it (Foster 198). He did, however, reserve the right to comment on bills as he signed them in the closing session before both houses (Speech [1624]).

James's attitude toward Parliament changed as a result of the failed negotiations over the Great Contract of 1610. As he reflected in his speech of October 31 that year, no king had spoken so much to his Parliament with so little result. He should rule with a Parliament, but he questioned if it was lawful for his subjects to rebut him as much as they had done. His people were not required to love him, but they were required to obey him. James concluded that he had the patience of Solomon, but his subjects must fulfill their duty (Speech [March 1610] 537–38). Subsequently he reiterated the separation of powers as he saw it. The king would not accept Parliament's attacks on government officials nor on his royal proclamations, which, he claimed, still had the force of law (Speech [1624]). Policy, however, suggested that the best use of proclamations was not to make law, but to encourage Parliament to do so (Parliament Proceeds. [1614] 18, 476). While his relations with them became strained through the Parliaments of 1614, 1621, and 1624, he still worked with them through his last days. It was good for the commonwealth, he said, to hear from, speak to, and confer with them (ibid. 19). No king could have better counsel than 470 MPs (ibid. 139–42).

Contributing to his cooling view of the utility of the English Parliament was the problem of Henry IV of France and the Estates General. When the Third

Estate declared that popes could depose kings and that killing a king could be a meritorious act, James began to see "popular" bodies in a more negative light (Remonstrance [1615] 381–91). Adhering to the doctrine of Henrician sovereignty that denied rights to those who had "their head out of the kingdom," James held "that obedience is due to Kings by the Law of God, and not dispensable by any Spiritual or Temporal authority" (ibid. 427, 431). Henry VIII, through Parliament, had saved the country from such outside influences, and Edward III had provided the ultimate defense of free monarchy by enacting treason laws against "whosoever shall imagine or machinate the King's death" (ibid. 452–68, quote at 462). Citing the courage of Kings Henry II and John in their day, James saw "sovereign kings" as the best leaders of Parliament and the only alternative to a papal usurpation of England (ibid. 481–84).

By the end of his reign, however, James had contributed to the House of Lords becoming the highest court in the land. Through the development of its specialized committee structure, it developed procedures for the trials of major officials and privy councilors in the Parliaments of 1621 and 1624. In 1621 James's deflection of attacks against monopolies to his legal counsel led to the Lords trial of Attorney-General Sir Henry Yelverton (Commons Debates 5: 118–19; Zaller 116–24). This led to the trial of Sir Giles Mompesson for the mismanagement of patents of monopoly (Foster 153–55). Once the doors of investigating corruption had been unlocked, the trial and impeachment of Lord Chancellor Sir Francis Bacon followed (Zaller 75–90).

The view of James throughout these proceedings was that while he appointed the best law officers and judges, he would not spare them if they acted unjustly. Instead they would be left to the course of the law (Commons Debates [1621] II: 2–13). If the Lords, as a court of record, had jurisdiction but lacked a process to handle such injustices, then by his grace they would have to develop one (Lords Debates [1621] 12–16). They would have to prosecute those who were accused of crimes against their king and his subjects (Commons Debates [1621] IV: 203–9). The growth of the Lords as a high court, however, had its negative consequences. It split the king's Privy Council and emboldened MPs who saw their privileges as a birthright. Once James had Coke arrested for their "Protestation" and thrown into the Tower of London, he had to dissolve Parliament. For the first time in his reign, he charged the Commons with usurping his royal authority (Zaller 188–90).

By the end of 1624, the role of the Lords as a judicature had increased significantly. The House was now hearing cases of privilege, appeals from numerous local, equitable, and ecclesiastical courts, and hundreds of cases on writ of error from the King's Bench. The impeachment of Lionel Cranfield, earl of Middlesex, for bribery and oppression in 1624 was brought on behalf of the king (Ruigh 303–44), as was that of John Digby, earl of Bristol (ibid. 345–81). These trials led to the drafting of standing orders that established the House as a formal court of law

(Horstman; Foster, 137–39, 149–63). From James's perspective, his use of the royal prerogative contributed to the judicial development of Parliament.

Equity and Prerogative Courts

James held that his royal prerogative stemmed from his godly duty to provide justice and equity. It was part of the "pattern" established by the law of God that kings had walked in the past (True Law [1598] sig. 1). He also considered courts of equity to be closest to his prerogative, and thus the Chancery the highest court of equity, if not the highest court in the realm, after Parliament. His preference for Chancery was because of its civil-law-like procedure and its historical development of exercising the king's conscience. Relying on the establishment of the court's bill procedures and law by precedent under Chancellor Ellesmere, he declared its independence from other courts without appeal. Since the Chancery sought no other jurisdiction than its own, he praised it as a model court (Speech [1616] 558). The exercise of the royal conscience was necessarily "arbitrary," he said, to countermand the barren rules of formal law (Proverbs #79). Therefore the royal conscience had to be placed in the best hands.

The king's view of equitable jurisdictions and prerogative courts would not have been expressed had not the clash between common law and equity developed in the years of 1604 to 1616 (Fortier). These expressions enable us to understand why he became so embittered toward Sir Edward Coke. James claimed that Coke's speeches against the Chancery and chancellor in the King's Bench were "odious and inept." If the chancellor acted for the king, then only the king could issue a *praemunire* against him. If any court overflowed its banks, as did Coke's attack on Chancery injunctions from the King's Bench, it would be deleterious to the state (Speech [1616] 559).

James saved his most severe censure of legal matters to writs of prohibition, which were issued by common law courts against matters pending or concluded by ecclesiastical and equity courts. In 1609 he attempted to state the obvious by wishing that every central court had a declared jurisdiction that was clearly set down in rules. Whenever a court varied from that jurisdiction, the King's Bench or Chancery could issue a prohibition to stay the suit at hand and resolve the question of which court had jurisdiction over the matter. The problem, as he saw it, was that every court was "striving to bring in most 'moulture' to their own mill," giving rise to a multitude of suits, which impoverished the people and brought disrepute to authority (Speech [March 1610] 534–35). Reform was required, but that was Parliament's responsibility (ibid. 537–38). When Parliament abandoned it, and disputes between the courts continued to arise, James said in homiletic despair: "My sheep hear my voice" (Speech [1616] 552).

The other major prerogative court was the Star Chamber. While James did not discuss what historians would call "prerogative courts" explicitly, he held that all conciliar courts with equitable jurisdiction were prerogative courts because they emanated from the king, his conscience, and Privy Council more closely than the common law courts. They also used English bill procedure. James clearly preferred judicial procedures by English bill over Latin writs and forms of action. "Prerogative" courts were conciliar using equitable law. James held the Star Chamber in high regard. He also praised both its composition of lords, bishops, and judges and its jurisdiction, where both actions and attempted actions were punishable. He further praised its use, because there the lowest could sue the highest for the greatest sums. Moreover, it was the court where dishonoring the king's prerogative could be sued and punished (Speech [1616] 559–60).

Common Law and Courts

James's opinions of English common law fluctuated throughout his reign, shaped by the issues of the day. When he was attempting to persuade Parliament to pass the Act of Union, he declared that English common law was the best municipal law of any country in the world. But he also said, in the next breath, that the common law had obscurities, questions and uncertainties that required parliamentary legislation to amend and polish. Putting it in layman's terms, he said that the common law needed to have the "rust" swept off (Speech [1607] 527–28).

James had a number of criticisms of the common law. First, it needed to be purged of its imperfections, and that would have to be done by the king in Parliament, England's absolute authority in making law. Second, it should be rendered into the English language instead of barbaric legal French and medieval Latin, so that it could be read and understood by all. James noted that Jesus had his title written in vernacular Hebrew, not Greek or Latin (Meditation [1620] 615–17). Third, it would be better to have a settled text, like Roman civil law, rather than a mixture of old customs, cases, and statutes (Speech [March 1610] 532–34). Taking a page out of Sir Francis Bacon's writings on law reform, James stood for the law's wholesale reform (Bacon 5: 84–87, 6: 57–71).

Neither common lawyers nor judges should meddle with those of other common law courts, nor with the king's prerogative. They should keep to their own rooms in Westminster Hall (Speech [1616] 558). But common law, as the "positive law" of the country, was not autonomous. For James, common law was good law because it extended the royal prerogative by precedents. Kings reserved the right to clarify the law when it was unclear (Speech [1607] 519). Upholding the jurisdiction of the ancient courts, James was also critical of their lax enforcement of what he termed "good laws." These included the licensing of too many alehouses, the erection of too many cottages on commons, the encroachment of London's environs on the surrounding countryside, the failure to enforce the vagrancy laws, and the lack of regulatory laws for the maintenance of highways and bridges (Speech [1616] 566–68). He also heard of many officials who had extorted the public in those matters by taking excessive fees. James cautioned people not to assemble in multitudes to protest such activities but to petition his Privy Council, who would examine the complaints and deal with them by law. He considered the correction of officials, and his protection of them, as belonging to his royal prerogative, to maintain "those ancient duties and privileges, which have descended upon us with the succession of our kingdoms" (Speech to Country [1603] 2).

James's view of the common law was framed in ecclesiastical terms. His earliest writings on secular law were concerned with the crime of witchcraft. The existence of witches, he held, had been proved by Scripture (Demonology [1597] 95–96). The whole art of magic was unlawful, ranging from astrology to charms, circles, conjuring, and witching. All of these were evil customs created by papists, and thus the detestable work of the devil (ibid. 118–19). The diseases caused by witchcraft could only be cured by prayer, and the perpetrators by examination, judgment, and punishment: "To be put to death according to the Law of God, the civil and imperial Law, and municipal Law of all Christian nations" (ibid. 134). For James, God and law were one. The magistrate who would not act accordingly was both sinful and unlawful. Judges were safe from all harm in dispensing the power of their office because the devil could not intervene where God "strike[s] by his lawful Lieutenants" (ibid. 120). Thus when there was evidence of criminal behavior, justices of the peace (JPs) must gather the evidence and Assize judges interpret it, not shirking to render the ultimate punishment (ibid. 131). God would protect those lawful lieutenants who followed the proof as legal process required. James then cited Solomon, who said that it was a great crime to condemn the innocent and let the guilty go free (ibid. 136).

When addressing the judges in the Star Chamber, the Stuart king praised the system of circuit courts represented by the Assizes, which he called an ancient and laudable custom. He saw the institution as one of both law and government, punishing the major offenders and supervising and giving instructions to county governors. He placed importance on the justices' advice given to the county JPs, who then reported the legal state of affairs in the county to the chancellor (which reports James said he read). He also noted that the judges preferred to sit on commissions of *nisi prius* rather than on gaol delivery because the former was profitable and the latter was not. He advised senior members of the bench that delivering the gaols was more important to the country than hearing private suitors (Speech [1616] 562–63). In all these matters, James anticipated the problems in the relationship of Assizes to the central government and the localities that modern legal historians have studied.[24]

Criminal Law

The "crime wave" of the late sixteenth and early seventeenth centuries was a key challenge to the English legal system and its practitioners. James became aware of this after the Gunpowder Plot of 1605, when he examined the criminal justice system and became informed of the burgeoning gaol calendars. His writings and speeches on crime and the criminal law demonstrate a broad continuity between his earliest and latest years in England. They also reveal a keen understanding of English criminal law and the criminal justice system.

The worst crimes, according to James, were witchcraft, premeditated murder, incest, sodomy, poisoning, and false coinage.[25] For offences against the monarch, the choice to punish or pardon was his (Table-Talk #61, 104). He would let the heart, the circumstances, and quality of the offender dictate the result. He praised the actions of Kings Henry II, John, and Henry VIII in establishing the legal independence of England from Rome, and the *Treason Acts* of Edward III and Henry VIII (Remonstrance [1615] 466–67). Crimes of oppression, which were pardonable, he would censure sharply, especially when "overcommonly" committed by those of the greatest rank against the poor and oppressed. He cited the title given his grandfather, "the poor man's King" (*Basilikon Doron* [1599] 157–59). James was not, however, in favor of too much capital punishment, noting that Henry VIII was "ill-natured" to have killed so many subjects.[26] He believed that crime was a condition of man (sin), and that punishment was inflicted to fulfill God's law, not to deter evil (Proverbs #12, 22).

The Gunpowder Plot, discovered and aborted on 5 November 1605, led to James's eloquent speech to Parliament on 9 November, where he thanked God for saving his family and members of Parliament from destruction at the hands of the pope's agents.[27] His published discourse on the event centered on Thomas Winter's confession, which he reprinted verbatim (Powder Treason [1606] 234–40). He also gave thanks to local law officials, and especially the justices of the peace, for the arrests and careful gathering of information that led to the conviction and execution of the principal culprits (ibid. 241–46). Citing Old Testament writings, he used the occasion to reiterate his position that all secular magistrates were ministers of God and that their powers were delegated by the king through the prerogatives God had bestowed on his office (Apology [1607] 284–86). He also used the plot to defend England's harsh laws against "papists" who would not abide by the laws of the land (Premonition [1609] 290–92, 299–300). The laws on this subject, he said, were fine, and lacked only better enforcement (Speech [March 1610] 544).

Later he attributed the failed plot to the pope's belief that he could depose kings.[28] James considered the pope to be the anti-Christ of the Apocalypse, the plague of locusts in the Roman church who made the eighth form of government (Premonition 309–28). James spent considerable ink on continental defenders of the papacy. He considered it his Christian duty to respond to their writings, and he hired men to keep him up to date on their works. When Conrad Vorstius, a scholar at the University of Leiden, wrote that popes had the lawful authority to excommunicate kings and that papal doctrines were agreeable to the Church of England, James had his works burned in St. Paul's churchyard as well as at Cambridge and Oxford universities (Declaration [1612] 369–80). James also intervened in the problems between the French monarchy, the Third Estate, and the pope. He charged the French clergy and Third Estate with "parricide" for arguing that it was a crime for a Frenchman to defend his king against papal authority (Remonstrance [1615] 381–95). Reiterating the law of God, he held that a subject's obedience to his king was "not dispensable by any Spiritual or Temporal authority."[29]

James was keenly interested in the application of the laws concerning religious practices. Taking a line of policy from Elizabeth I, he said he had no difficulty with those who pursued their souls in peace. He honored all those who expressed their opinions in the "old controversy" (between Catholic and Protestant). Likening Roman Catholics as his mother church to Jews as their forefathers, James wished to show compassion by lessening the onerous legal burdens on papists and Puritans (Speech [1603] 490–93). He would not, however, tolerate Puritans who demonstrated their contempt of civil magistrates, or papists who practiced papal supremacy. He had always asked only that people "may content themselves soberly and quietly with their own opinions, not resisting to the authority, nor breaking the law of the Country" (*Basilikon Doron* [1599] 143–44).

The Scottish king used strong words in writing about crimes committed by the nobility in that country, which he considered to be a natural sickness brought about by the arrogant conceit of their greatness and power. They thrived on oppression, maintained servants and dependants against the laws, and would "bang about" against neighbors. They needed to be taught to keep the laws "as precisely as the meanest." As he wrote to Prince Henry, "Rest not until ye root out these barbarous fiends." He urged his son to execute laws against guns and "traitorous Pistolets," honor those who are obedient, have them in his court, and "beat into their ears" that the chief point of service is their power to procure due obedience to the law. Henry should not spare those "great men who wrack the whole country," he wrote, and should use all the punishments against them that the law will permit (*Basilikon Doron* 161–63).

Neither did the Scottish king spare the "burghers," the merchants and craftsmen. Merchants believed that the commonwealth existed for their lawful gain and trade, and they enriched themselves at the expense of the rest of the people. They transported things of necessity out of the country, brought in things unnecessary, and sometimes imported nothing. They bought the worst wares and sold them at the best prices. Their law was always to raise prices, never drop them. James's solution was to expand the numbers of informers, searchers, and honest treasurers to account for them, and to codify and enforce rigorously the regulatory offenses against such practices. Jurors, he wrote, must be encouraged to convict, and magistrates to sentence (*Basilikon Doron* 164).

James had a more tolerant view of crimes committed by the peasantry in both Scotland and England. He attributed some of that to what we would today call socioeconomic crime. He suggested that the poor needed more relief—a problem that contributed to theft. To punish thieves was God's law; how to punish was the law of each state (Table-Talk #114). Aware not only of the crime wave of the period, he was also aware of some of its causes.[30] The expansion of the London suburbs, with residences built by the gentry and nobility, and increased traffic from country to city, encouraged highway robberies (Speech [1616] 568–69).

Looking at the economy as a whole, James believed that the country lacked legislation to preserve its industries and environment. Laws were needed to preserve shipping, timber, hunting, and wild game. Sports should be preserved, but hunters should not be allowed to use nets and guns (Speech [March 1610] 546–47). Above all, courts existed to do justice swiftly. He cited the example of his Court of Marshalsea, where he gave speedy justice to all complaints of wrongdoing against anyone in his royal court while traveling in the country (Table-Talk #57).

Lawyers and Judges

James took to the grave a jaundiced view of lawyers. Expressed in the later years of his life, this view may have stemmed from his struggles with common lawyers and judges down to 1616 and then to 1624. Lamenting the "new cockerell lawiers that begin to crow as soon as they are set downe in the pit" and courtroom scenes "many times more like a cockpit then a grave counsaile," James had relations with common law lawyers and judges that were often tempestuous, and his views on common law process were highly critical.[31] At common law, a lawyer who had a good case would have to beware of his opposing counsel using bribery or trickery to win the day (Apophthegms #27). James may have been seen as an "enemy" of common lawyers, but this view must be placed within the context of his larger views on litigation in the era, which have been documented by modern scholars (Brooks 9–25).

In all "settled" monarchies, where law had been established (since the time of Moses), kings deferred their legal judgments to their magistrates (Speech [1616] 550). Once chosen by their king, judges and JPs were his delegates, enjoying his full power and unchallenged authority. People must obey them as they would their monarch and never speak evil or disrespectfully of them (True Law [1598] 199–200). James saw Samuel as the greatest judge because he favored religious reform[32] and presided over the emergence of Israel from a loose federation to a monarchy—from a tribal society to a nation state under King David.[33]

James attributed the successful implementation of the law to "subaltern" magistrates—local JPs whose duty was to search out perpetrators with care, conduct trials with due diligence, and punish severely as an example to other persons disposed to evil (Speech [1605] 504–5). He seemed to have a firm understanding of the role of the magistrate (judges and JPs) in the legal system.[34] Acknowledging that JPs were a mixed bag in quality, some being "Slowbellies" and others "busy-bodies," he tried to appeal to their sense of being "worthy" of their office (Speech [1616] 564). They should teach as well as judge in their courts, and they should set an example of impartiality in their communities (Proverbs #112).

James had difficulties with judges of the central courts because he expected more of them than of JPs. Because of their extensive education and profession, he expected them to have the qualities of kings. Thus he charged them to do justice "uprightly" and indifferently between subject and subject for God and their king (Speech [1616] 555). He had his reservations, however, concerning law made by judges, who were "law-givers" and not "law-tellers"—parliamentarians being the latter (ibid. 560). Declare the law where it is clear, he said, and interpret it where it is obscure by common sense, reason, and logic. Do not make it (ibid. 556). When judges "made" law with precedents in their courts, James expected them to consult together, as the MPs and lords did in Parliament (ibid. 551). While he never expressed an opinion on the Court of Exchequer Chamber—that loose affiliation of senior judges who met on occasion to decide how they should rule in major cases—he would have preferred it to become a formal court ranking over the other common law courts (like preemptory courts of appeal who hear "reference" cases in modern times). In essence, this was also his problem with Sir Edward Coke and the dispute over the exercise of the Chancery's injunction for parties in common law litigation. James, who dreamed of a Samuel, had a Coke.

Conclusion

While there were some Cold War era historians who viewed James favorably, they were few and far between. The image of the evil king, James VI and I, of the David Harris Willson tradition has been replaced in the 1990s with the image of an enlightened, renaissance king, warts and all. Legal historians are often in the far reaches of general historical interpretation, and much of the legal historical writing on the early Stuart era contains the biases of the former historiographical tradition. Many of them have seen the role of James in the legal system as a thorn in the side of the hallowed common law tradition. They have also seen James as a pro-civilian advocate of absolutist rule who perceived the common law and its traditions as an alien system. Few legal historians, however, have read the works of James; most of them have drawn their view of him from others.

Several conclusions emerge from this study of James's writings in relation to the law. First, the administration of justice was a major concern of his monarchy. Second, he attempted to rule as a Solomon—a king who was willing to write about law, make law, and enforce it decisively. Third, his cosmopolitan view of law and legal systems enabled him to accept the English hybrid of courts and jurisdictions and credit their roles in the country's legal life. Fourth, his thoughts remain surprisingly well developed and credible in an age when many English contemporaries could not understand their own confusing, multilayered legal system or the principles on which it was based.

James suffered no fools. Assured in his belief in an absolute, divine right monarch, he had the luxury of saying what he thought. In many instances he railed at English law, lawyers, and judges with hyperbole that lacked a balanced understanding of the issues. He gave those whom he considered to be against him sufficient ammunition to attack him for his lack of knowledge of the English constitution and legal system. The real story, however, is perhaps on the side of James VI and I. Given his lack of training and experience in English law, where did he learn what he knew? In 1614 he said that he learned English law from the privy councilors and judges of Elizabeth I, to whom he listened intently, and he was proud to have so many of them still with him (Commons Proceeds. [1614] 141–42). He might not have made the same statement so positively after 1621. While James wished to see the law operate without conflict and discordant notes, perhaps he did not rule in peace until he heard the angels sing.

Notes

1. The author wishes to thank Alan Cromartie, Mark Fortier, Henry Horwitz, and Johann Sommerville for their criticisms and suggestions.
2. Sommerville ("James I"), the conclusion at p. 62. It is important to note Sommerville's study of James's citations. Of some 200 writers referred to in his *Workes,* hardly any were English. When he met John Selden in 1618, James had never met or heard of him, nor of Sir John Fortescue. I conclude from this evidence that James obtained much of his knowledge of English laws and customs from reading records and works he felt no compunction to note or cite, and from talking with the people around him.
3. See in particular McIlwain, *High Court* xxxvi–xliii; and, more generally, Gooch.
4. The most recent assessment of these cases in their broader context is by Fortier. I wish to thank Dr. Fortier for a prepublication copy of his article.
5. John Kenyon was one of the first scholars to see a quite different James—one who separated theory from practice, operated within the framework of the common law, and was more constitutional than

Elizabeth I (Kenyon 8). The debate is analyzed cogently by Johann Sommerville in this volume. The view of James as a constitutional monarch has been enlarged by Glenn Burgess (*Politics* and *Absolute Monarchy*), with the main rebuttal to these positions coming from Sommerville, who argues that James VI and I was, from beginning to end, an absolute, divine right monarch ("James VI" and "English and European Political Ideas"); see more generally Sommerville's *Royalists and Patriots*, esp. the 1999 edition).

6. Burns (284–87) makes an important discovery in finding that James changed his published version of the *Basilikon Doron* to read that ancient policy of the kingdom, rather than ancient and fundamental laws of the country, upheld free monarchy.
7. His first use of it in his writings was in the *True Law* (1598), where he wrote of good kings following in the pattern framed by God and nature: the dedication to Prince Henry, sig. 1. James dedicated his *Workes* (1616) to his son Charles, as the *Basilikon Doron* was to his now deceased brother Prince Henry. He was doing this out of duty, he said, for preservation, "as a pattern," for Charles to see his own prerogative. Good kings "walked in the ways of their Fathers," as "the pattern of God and Nature have framed."
8. For example, Sir John Hayward's *Answer*, published on James's accession.
9. All short titles of works noted in the text in parentheses, without authors, are works of James. The year of publication or writing follows the short title so that the reader may ascertain chronology without referring to the bibliography. Citations of his works are found in the bibliography under James, in alphabetical order by short title.
10. For recent analyses of the *True Law*, see Wormald "James VI and I"; Fischlin and Fortier 24–26; Burns 231–42; Sommerville *King James VI and I*, 17–20; and Craigie, *True Law*.
11. The influence of Sir Thomas Craig and his work on *jus* (law of nature and of nations) and *lex* (the laws of individual states) is assessed by Burns (257–67).
12. For recent analyses of the *Basilikon Doron*, see Wormald "James VI and I"; Fischlin and Fortier 26–33; Burns 242–54; Sommerville *King James VI and I*, 10–16; and Craigie *Basilikon Doron*.
13. The standard version of the story is by Gifford, who argues for its inclusion on the grounds of being divinely inspired (7–17).
14. Weems 5: 361–75, for the most modern text and commentary on Solomon; and Birch 2: 947–68, for the same on Samuel. Current scholarship, however, casts doubt on whether this was part of the original Old Testament.

15. *Englands Wedding Garment, Or A preparation to King Iames his Royall Coronation* (London: Thomas Pavier, 1603), sigs. A3v and B2r–v. The authorship is unknown.
16. His Letter (1603) 2. See also his Speech (1605) 524–25, and Speech (1624).
17. For an analysis of the Apology, see Sommerville *King James VI and I*, 20–22.
18. Speech (March 1610) 532–33. For the continental background to James's political and legal thought, see Salmon.
19. Speech (1603) 488, Speech (1605) 506, Speech (1607) 511–13. The best discussion of the Union project, and of its history in this period, is Levack.
20. The history of the "ancient constitution" debate, and the thesis stated above, is best summarized by Sommerville "The Ancient Constitution Reassessed."
21. Dawson 68–73. Williams reported that he and others "did once very roundly let the Lord Coke know their minds, that he was not such a master of the law as he did take on him, to deliver what he list for law and to despise all other" (J. P. Collier 446–48).
22. Speech (1605) 506–7, the quote at 507. He spoke similarly in his Speech to Parliament in March 1610 (535)
23. *Basilikon Doron* 156, Speech (1603) 494, and Speech (March 1610) 535. An assessment of James's interest in particular laws is in Foster 189–90.
24. Most of these problems have been studied by James Cockburn in his *Calendar of Assizes* and his later articles, summarized in his "Introduction" to the Assize records. James also held that the role of the chancellor in this business had slackened in the previous period and that he stood for restoring it. This suggests that James also agreed with Chancellor Ellesmere on Chancery reform—Knafla, *Law and Politics* 105–22.
25. He considered incest one of the most odious crimes of the era (Table-Talk #125).
26. Table-Talk #40; Proverbs #39, 49. James argued in Proverbs that it was fear that brought kings to put so many people to death, not crime.
27. Rptd. in McIlwain, *Political Works* 281–89.
28. Apology 250–56, 270–71; see also Premonition: 296–99, 332–33.
29. Remonstrance: 427. He then defended this position with a history of the ancient and medieval church.
30. Perhaps the most detailed examination of the crime problem in the late sixteenth century is that of McIntosh.
31. For numerous quotations from James on lawyers, see Prest 260–61.

32. 1 Samuel 7.
33. 1 Samuel 8–12, esp. 1 Samuel 10: 17–27 and 11: 12–15. See in general, Birch 2: 947–68.
34. The classic study is Langbein, 5–125, on the Marian statutes.

Works Cited

The writings of King James used in this chapter are drawn from *The Workes of the Most High and Mightie Prince, Iames By the Grace of God, King of Great Britaine, France and Ireland, Defendor of the Faith, &c. Published by James, Bishop of Winton, Dean of the King's Royal Chapel* (London: Robert Barker and John Bill, royal printers, 1616). A 1620 reprint containing his meditation on St. Mathew is Huntington Library copy HEH 61826. Bishop Montague prepared a Latin edition that was published in 1619: *Serenissimi Principis Jacobi opera.* This was reprinted with the later Meditations in Frankfurt, 1689.

The individual writings are cited below under James. Several modern editions of some of these works exist, which readers should consult. See especially those of McIlwain, Sommerville, and Fischlin and Fortier.

Akrigg, G. P. V., ed. *Letters of King James VI & I.* Berkeley: U of California P, 1984.

Ashton, Robert, ed. *James I by his Contemporaries.* London: Hutchinson, 1969.

Bacon, Francis. *The Letters and Life of Francis Bacon Including All the Occasional Works.* Ed. James Spedding et al. 7 vols. London, 1857–59.

Baker, J. H. *The Legal Profession and the Common Law: Historical Essays.* London: Hambledon, 1986.

Birch, Bruce C., ed. *The New Interpreter's Bible.* Vol. 1. Nashville: Abingdon Press, 1998.

Brooks, Christopher W. *Lawyers, Litigation and English Society Since 1450.* London: Hambledon, 1998.

Burgess, Glenn. *Absolute Monarchy and the Stuart Constitution.* New Haven: Yale UP, 1996.

______. *The Politics of the Ancient Constitution: An Introduction to English Political Thought 1603–1642.* University Park: Pennsylvania State UP, 1992.

Burns, J. H. *The True Law of Kingship: Concepts of Monarchy in Early-Modern Scotland.* Oxford: Clarendon P, 1996.

Christianson, Paul. *Discourse on History, Law, and Governance in the Public Career of John Selden, 1610–1635.* Toronto: U of Toronto P, 1996.

______. "Royal and Parliamentary Voices on the Ancient Constitution." Peck, *Mental World.* 71–95.

Cobbett, William, ed. *The Parliamentary History of England. 1806–20.* Rpt. New York: AMS Press, 1966.

Cockburn, J. S. *Calendar of Assize Records: Home Circuit Indictments Elizabeth I and James I: Introduction.* London: Her Majesty's Stationery Office, 1985.

______. *A History of English Assizes 1558–1714.* Cambridge: Cambridge UP, 1972.

Collier, J. P. *The Egerton Papers.* London: Camden Society, 1840.

Collier, Susanne. "Recent Studies in James VI and I." *English Literary Renaissance* 23:3 (1993): 509–19.

Commons Debates 1621. Wallace Notestein, Frances Relf, and Hartley Simpson, eds. *Commons Debates 1621.* New Haven: Yale UP, 1935.

Commons Proceeds. 1614. Maija Jansson, ed. *Proceedings in Parliament 1614* (House of Commons). Philadelphia: American Philosophical Society, 1988.

Craig, Thomas. "Concerning the Right of Succession" (1603). Published as *The Right Succession to the Kingdom of England.* London: Daniel Brown, 1703.

Craigie, James, ed. *Basilikon Doron.* Edinburgh: Scottish Text Society, 1944, 1950. Series 3, vols. 16, 18.

______, ed. *The Poems of James VI of Scotland.* Edinburgh: Scottish Text Society, 1958. Series 3, vol. 26.

______, ed. *Trew Law of Free Monarchies.* Edinburgh: Scottish Text Society, 1982. Series 4, vol. 14.

Dawson, John P. *The Oracles of the Law.* Ann Arbor: U of Michigan P, 1968.

Doelman, James. "'A King of Thine Own Heart': The English Reception of King James VI and I's Basilikon Doron." *Seventeenth Century* 9:1 (Spring 1994): 1–9.

Fischlin, Daniel, and Mark Fortier, eds. The True Law of Free Monarchies *and* Basilikon Doron. Toronto: Centre for Reformation Studies, 1996.

Fortier, Mark. "Equity and Ideas: Coke, Ellesmere, and James I." *Renaissance Quarterly* 51.4 (1998): 1255–81.

Foster, Elizabeth Read. *The House of Lords, 1603–1649.* Chapel Hill: U of North Carolina P, 1983.

Galloway, Bruce. *The Union of England and Scotland 1603–1608.* Edinburgh: John Donald, 1986.

Gifford, Andrew. *A Dissertation on the Song of Solomon: With the Original Text, Divided According to the Metre, and a Poetical Version.* London: A. Millar, 1751.

Gooch, George Peabody. *The History of English Democratic Ideas in the Seventeenth Century.* Cambridge, 1898; New York, 1912; Toronto, 1927.

Hayward, Sir John. *An Answer to the First Part of a Certain Conference.* London: Eliot's Court Press, 1603.

Horstman, Allen. "A New Curia Regis: The Judicature of the House of Lords in the 1620s." *Historical Journal* 25:2 (1982): 411–22.

James VI and I. Apology 1607: "Triplici nodo, triplex cuneus. Or an Apologie for the Oath of Allegiance. Against the Two Breves of Pope Pavlvs Qvintvs, and the late Letter of Cardinall Bellarmine to G. Blackwell the Arch-priest" [1607]; in *Workes,* 247–86. See also the facsimile reproduction of the B.L. copy of the second edition (1609), *De Triplici Nodo. The Corrected Copy for the Second Edition.* Alburgh: Archival Facsimiles, 1987.

———. Apophthegms: *Witty Apophthegms Delivered at Several Times, and upon Several Occasions, By King James.* London: Matthew Smelt, 1662.

———. *Basilikon Doron* 1599: *ΒΑΣΙΛΙΚΟΝ ΔΩΡΟΝ. Or His Maiesties Instrvctions to his Dearest Sonne, Henry The Prince* [1599]; in *Workes* 137–89.

———. Declaration 1612: "A Declaration Concerning the Proceedings with the State Generall, of the United Provinces of the Low Countreys, in the cause of D. Conradus Vorstius" [1612]; in *Workes* 347–80.

———. Demonology 1597: "Daemonologie, In Forme of a Dialogve, Diuided into three Bookes" [1597]; in *Workes* 91–136.

———. Lepanto 1603: *His Maiesties Lepanto, Or, Heroicall Song, being part of his Poeticall exercises at vacant houres.* London: Simon Stafford and Henry Hooke, 1603.

———. Letter to London 1603: "The Copie of the K. Maiesties letter to the L. Maior of the Citie of London, and to the Aldermen and Commons"; in *Englands welcome to Iames.* London: E. W. and C. K., 1603.

———. Meditation 1619: "A Meditation Vpon the Lords Prayer: Written by the Kings Maiestie, For the benefit of all his subiects, especially of such as follow the Court"; in *Workes* 571–99.

———. Meditation 1620: "A Meditation Vpon the 27. 28. 29. Verses of the XXVII. Chapter of Saint Matthew. Or a Paterne for a Kings Inavgvration." *Workes,* 601–22.

———. Paraphrase 1588: Paraphrase on St. John: "A Paraphrase Vpon the Revelation of the Apostle S. Iohn" [1588]; in *Workes* 7–72.

———. Powder Treason 1606: "A Discovrse of the Maner of the Discoverie of the Powder-Treason, Joined with the Examination of some of the Prisoners" [1606]; in *Workes* 223–46.

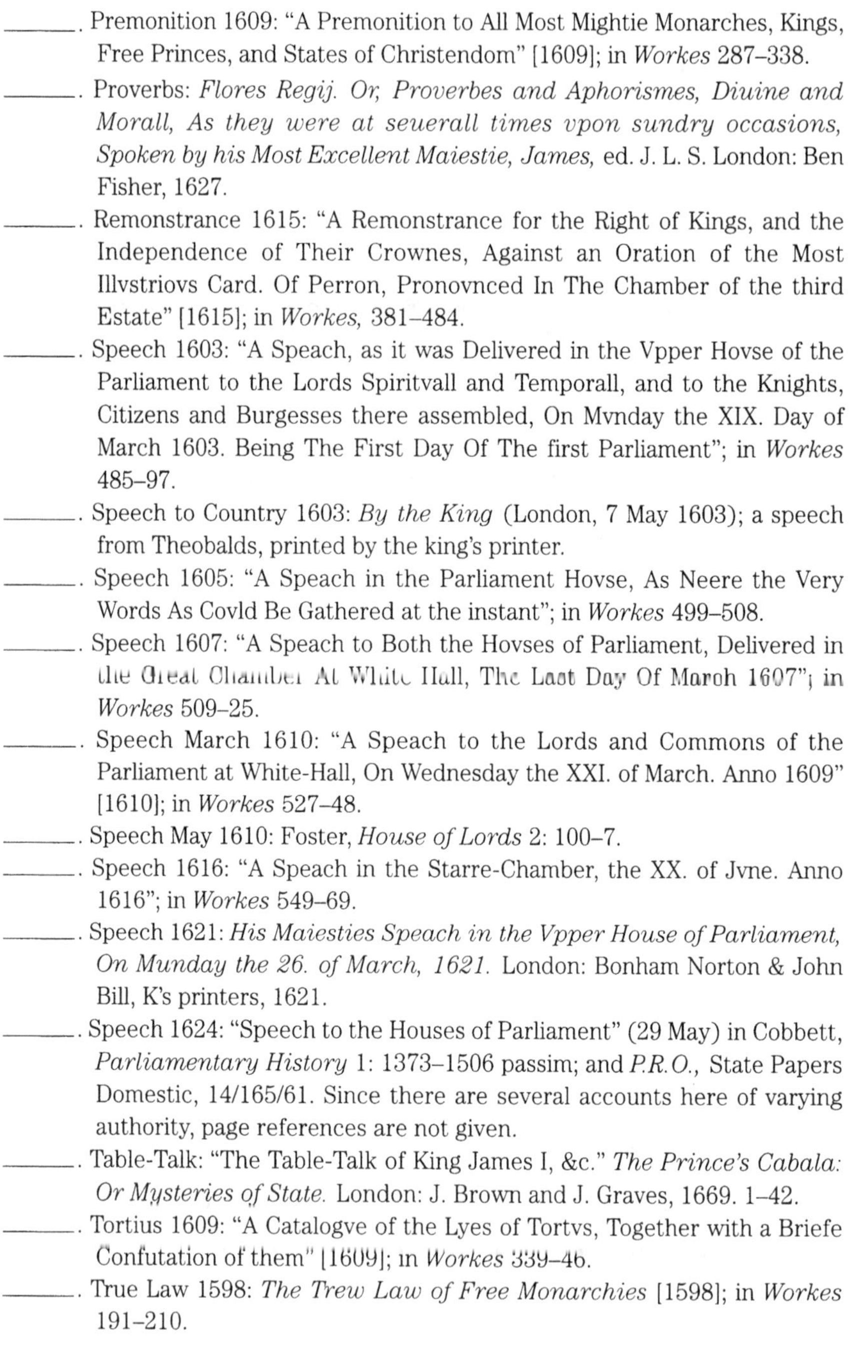

———. Premonition 1609: "A Premonition to All Most Mightie Monarches, Kings, Free Princes, and States of Christendom" [1609]; in *Workes* 287–338.

———. Proverbs: *Flores Regij. Or, Proverbes and Aphorismes, Diuine and Morall, As they were at seuerall times vpon sundry occasions, Spoken by his Most Excellent Maiestie, James,* ed. J. L. S. London: Ben Fisher, 1627.

———. Remonstrance 1615: "A Remonstrance for the Right of Kings, and the Independence of Their Crownes, Against an Oration of the Most Illvstriovs Card. Of Perron, Pronovnced In The Chamber of the third Estate" [1615]; in *Workes,* 381–484.

———. Speech 1603: "A Speach, as it was Delivered in the Vpper Hovse of the Parliament to the Lords Spiritvall and Temporall, and to the Knights, Citizens and Burgesses there assembled, On Mvnday the XIX. Day of March 1603. Being The First Day Of The first Parliament"; in *Workes* 485–97.

———. Speech to Country 1603: *By the King* (London, 7 May 1603); a speech from Theobalds, printed by the king's printer.

———. Speech 1605: "A Speach in the Parliament Hovse, As Neere the Very Words As Covld Be Gathered at the instant"; in *Workes* 499–508.

———. Speech 1607: "A Speach to Both the Hovses of Parliament, Delivered in the Great Chamber At White Hall, The Last Day Of March 1607"; in *Workes* 509–25.

———. Speech March 1610: "A Speach to the Lords and Commons of the Parliament at White-Hall, On Wednesday the XXI. of March. Anno 1609" [1610]; in *Workes* 527–48.

———. Speech May 1610: Foster, *House of Lords* 2: 100–7.

———. Speech 1616: "A Speach in the Starre-Chamber, the XX. of Jvne. Anno 1616"; in *Workes* 549–69.

———. Speech 1621: *His Maiesties Speach in the Vpper House of Parliament, On Munday the 26. of March, 1621.* London: Bonham Norton & John Bill, K's printers, 1621.

———. Speech 1624: "Speech to the Houses of Parliament" (29 May) in Cobbett, *Parliamentary History* 1: 1373–1506 passim; and *P.R.O.,* State Papers Domestic, 14/165/61. Since there are several accounts here of varying authority, page references are not given.

———. Table-Talk: "The Table-Talk of King James I, &c." *The Prince's Cabala: Or Mysteries of State.* London: J. Brown and J. Graves, 1669. 1–42.

———. Tortius 1609: "A Catalogve of the Lyes of Tortvs, Together with a Briefe Confutation of them" [1609]; in *Workes* 339–46.

———. True Law 1598: *The Trew Law of Free Monarchies* [1598]; in *Workes* 191–210.

______. *The Workes of the Most High and Mighty Prince, Iames . . .* London: Robert Barker and John Bill, 1616–1620.

Jones, W. J. *Politics and the Bench: The Judges and the Origins of the English Civil War.* London: George Allen & Unwin, 1971.

Kenyon, J. P. *The Stuart Constitution.* Cambridge: Cambridge UP, 1966.

King, John N. "The Royal Image, 1535–1603." *Tudor Political Culture.* Ed. Dale Hoak. Cambridge: Cambridge UP, 1995. 104–32.

Knafla, Louis A. "Common Law and Custom in Tudor England: or, 'The Best State of a Commonwealth." *Law, Literature, and the Settlement of Regimes.* Ed. Gordon J. Schochet. Washington, D.C.: Folger Shakespeare Library, 1990. 171–84.

______. "The Influence of Continental Humanists and Jurists on English Common Law in the Renaissance." *Acta Conventus Neo-Latini Bononiensis.* Ed. R. J. Schoeck. Binghamton, N.Y.: Medieval & Renaissance Texts and Studies, 1985. 60–71.

______. *Law and Politics in Jacobean England.* Cambridge: Cambridge UP, 1977.

Langbein, John H. *Prosecuting Crime in the Renaissance.* Cambridge, Mass.: Harvard UP, 1974.

Levack, Brian P. *The Formation of the British State: England, Scotland, and the Union, 1603–1707.* Oxford: Clarendon P, 1987.

Loades, David. *Tudor Government: Structures of Authority in the Sixteenth Century.* Oxford: Blackwell, 1997.

Lords Debates 1621. *Notes of Debates in the House of Lords . . . 1621, 1625, 1626.* Ed. Frances Helen Relf. London: Royal Historical Society, 1929. Camden Society, 3rd series, vol. 42.

McIlwain, Charles Howard. *The High Court of Parliament and Its Supremacy.* New Haven: Yale UP, 1910.

______, ed. *The Political Works of James I.* Cambridge: Harvard UP, 1918.

______. McIntosh, Marjorie Keniston. *Controlling Misbehavior in England, 1370–1600.* Cambridge: Cambridge UP, 1998.

Merbury, Charles. *A Briefe Discourse of Royall Monarchie.* London: Vautrollier, 1581 [Charles English edition, Pollard & Redgrave #17823.5].

Parl. Proceeds. 1610. *Proceedings in Parliament 1610.* Ed. Elizabeth Read Foster. 2 vols. New Haven: Yale UP, 1966.

Patterson, W. B. *King James VI and I and the Reunion of Christendom.* Cambridge: Cambridge UP, 1997.

Peck, Linda Levy, ed. *The Mental World of the Jacobean Court.* Cambridge: Cambridge UP, 1991.

Prest, Wilfrid R. *The Rise of the Barristers: A Social History of the English Bar 1590–1640.* Oxford: Clarendon P, 1986.

Ruigh, Robert E. *The Parliament of 1624: Politics and Foreign Policy.* Cambridge, Mass.: Harvard UP, 1971.

Salmon, J. H. "Catholic Resistance Theory, Ultramontanism, and the Royalist Response, 1580–1620." *The Cambridge History of Political Thought 1450–1700.* Ed. J. H. Burns. Cambridge: Cambridge UP, 1991. 219–53.

Sommerville, Johann P. "The Ancient Constitution Reassessed: The Common Law, the Court and the Language of Politics in Early Modern England." *The Stuart Court and Europe.* Ed. R. Malcolm Smuts. Cambridge: Cambridge UP, 1996. 39–64.

———. "English and European Political Ideas in the Early-Seventeenth Century: Revisionism and the Case of Absolutism." *Journal of British Studies* 35 (1996): 168–94.

———. "James I and the Divine Right of Kings: English Politics and Continental Theory," in Peck, *Mental World,* 55–70.

———. *Royalists and Patriots: Politics and Ideology in England 1603–1640.* London: Longman, 1999.

———, ed. *King James VI and I: Political Writings.* Cambridge: Cambridge UP, 1994.

Tanner, J. R. *Constitutional Documents of the Reign of James I* A.D. *1603–1625 with an Historical Commentary.* Cambridge: Cambridge UP, 1952.

Weems, Renita J., et al., eds. *The New Interpreter's Bible.* Nashville: Abingdon P, 1997.

Weimann, Robert. *Authority and Representation in Early Modern Discourse.* Baltimore: Johns Hopkins UP, 1996.

Williams, Bishop John. *Great Britains Salomon. A Sermon preached at the funerall of the king, James.* London: J. Bill, 1625.

Winchester, Bishop of. *A Sermon preached at Westminster before the King and Queeenes Maiesties, at their Coronations on Saint Iames his day, being the 28. of Iuly. 1603.* London: Clement Knight, 1603.

Wootton, David, ed. *Divine Right and Democracy: An Anthology of Political Writing in Stuart England.* Harmondsworth: Penguin, 1986.

Wormald, Jenny. "James VI and I, *Basilikon Doron* and *The Trew Law of Free Monarchies:* The Scottish Context and the English translation" in Peck, *Mental World,* 36–54.

———. *Lords and Men in Scotland: Bonds of Manrent, 1442–1603.* Edinburgh: University of Edinburgh Press, 1985.

Zaller, Robert. *The Parliament of 1621: A Study in Constitutional Conflict.* Berkeley: U of California P, 1971.

8

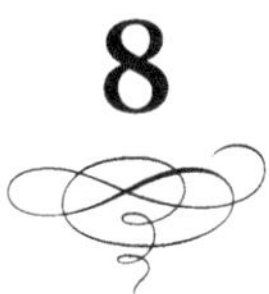

Equity and Ideas: Coke, Ellesmere, and James VI and I

Mark Fortier

The legal strife in England in 1616, whereby Edward Coke, the chief justice, was dismissed from the King's Bench and the prerogatives of king and equity triumphed over common law (the former until 1642, the latter into our own time), has been understood in various ways in historical and legal scholarship. One longstanding and continuing scholarly tradition looks at the characters of the principal personages involved. In this mode of analysis, historical and legal events are the product of the characters of prominent people. To Coke, for instance, has been ascribed a "personal ruggedness of character," a "crabbed and uncouth personality," an arrogance of bearing, and a narrowness of intellect—an anonymous letter to Coke after his dismissal called him a greedy "legal Tyrant" who "delight[ed] to speake much, but not to heare other men."[1] Lord Ellesmere, the chancellor, had the "timidity of a man of his age," was "obstinate and difficult," or was a tough-minded politician with "an ability to grasp problems and get the job done."[2] James I has been called variously "the wisest fool in Christendom" and "Great Britain's Solomon"—he, of course, invariably perceived himself as the latter. Most recently in a long line, Glenn Burgess has argued that "[Coke's] fall in 1616 had as much to do with an intransigent personality as with any differences between Coke, Bacon, Ellesmere and James I on fundamental principles."[3] The stubbornness, strength, irascibility, and folly of these men become the great forces molding early modern history.

Such an approach does seem particularly relevant in accounting for certain moments in the events of 1616—for instance, when James was able to call before him the common law judges, intimidating and coercing them into agreeing to consult him personally before rendering judgment in any case involving his prerogative. As S. R. Gardiner has written: "The sovereign was the dispenser of favours, and was capable of making his ill-will felt in many ways. When that sovereign was voluble and opinionative, it was hard for the judges, unless they were men of more than ordinary firmness, to hold their own in his presence."[4] Even Coke fell to his knees, but, alone of all the judges, he refused to acquiesce before the king's wrath.[5] Coke was eventually dismissed from office; his strength of personal resolve—or his obstinacy and inflexibility—in large measure brought about his downfall. In moments like this, character and personality appear as important, even decisive, factors in the outcome of major historical events.

Some years ago, early modern history began to stress the importance of human personality in a new, less grandiose way in the work of historians who found "the motor of political change in the day-to-day rivalries, the personal plots and factional intrigues that surrounded the person of the monarch."[6] Clannishness replaced great men. In this light, as one historian put it, a new picture was "slowly being built out of minute details," which indicated that the major legal and political issues of 1616 were the product of "a rift among those who opposed the powerful Howard faction."[7]

In its emphasis on actors driven by the forces of everyday life—if in little else—this brand of historiography bears some similarity to the work of the Marxist historian Christopher Hill. Hill shows great respect for the revolutionary thought and character of those like Gerard Winstanley and John Milton. Concerning those closer to the center of monarchy or capital, however, Hill tells another story. For Hill, the early seventeenth century was a time of newfound wealth and influence for common lawyers and of a Chancery engaged in protecting the interests of landlords and big merchants. Thus, "The conflict of courts in the sixteenth and early seventeenth centuries, of which we hear so much, was in part a struggle of rival groups of lawyers for the profitable business that was going on."[8] Legal theorists and practitioners within the status quo, if not revolutionary thinkers, become, in Marx's phrase, "personifications of economic relations."[9]

What is underemphasized, or radically circumscribed, in such approaches are ideas and high principle, and recent historians have been accused of "stripping ideology and ideas from our view of early seventeenth-century politics."[10] They have argued, for instance, that king, Parliament, and law courts were more or less in agreement on constitutional issues, and there was little on the level of principle for them to quarrel about.[11] Besides, from this point of view, principles and ideas are not what motivate historical and political behavior anyway.

Various attempts have been made to restore ideas as a basis for understanding early modern history. Kevin Sharpe, moving away from the belief that self-contained ideas have a direct impact on historical events, nonetheless finds ideas at work woven through the textual and linguistic life of the culture broadly conceived; he writes, "a better understanding of the seventeenth century requires a fuller study of the relationship of ideas, values and styles to politics and the exercise of power."[12] Such a study entails a movement away from "key texts" and major works in intellectual history toward an interest in the metaphors and analogies of the period in the texts of everyday life. J. P. Sommerville, however, taking a very different approach, argues that not only did Englishmen indeed have radically different overall outlooks in the early seventeenth century,[13] but, for instance, James's political philosophy "explains much about his actions. . . . [A]nd his practice was not sealed from his thoughts."[14]

History is made by many different kinds of forces, which come into play with different effects in different situations. Personalities, institutions, social and economic conjunctions, and ideas are set in motion by events and move to the fore as circumstances allow or induce them. The struggles of 1616 were not simple events. Firstly, they were moments in any number of ongoing struggles (between men, courts, clans, institutions, ideas, from Tudor England to the Civil War), and they are moments in a history that continues (through the merger of the courts of common law and equity in the nineteenth century and the furthering and development of equitable principles in the twentieth) into our own day. Secondly, the struggles of 1616 were of different sorts, some specifically between King's Bench and king concerning the royal prerogative, some between King's Bench and Chancery concerning the jurisdiction of courts. Moreover, these contentions were fought out in different ways, sometimes by physical intimidation, sometimes by words and argument. If we narrow our focus to the struggle between King's Bench and Chancery over common law and equitable principles, we are dealing with an area in which ideas and argument were explicitly a ground of struggle. It would be curious if it were otherwise: where if not here—in the struggle between views of law at the highest level and law's relation to divinity, justice, and the basic political structures of the nation, a struggle between highly developed and powerful legal and political thinkers—would we expect ideas, specifically systematic intellectual principles capable of practical application, to come into play? It may be rare that ideas affect history, but it is less rare when they are the ideas of powerful people with powerful intellectual capacities.

My argument, then, is that in the triumph of equity over the common law (so that equitable principles and remedies continue today to be used to correct unjust results at common law, even if a separate court of equity has itself been dissolved) ideas mattered and that much of the battle was a struggle between the systematic thought of prominent men. The point is not that ideas, especially the ideas of prominent thinkers, are always uppermost, but rather that such ideas are part of the system of historical causality and play a greater part at some moments than at others.

There were at least two systems of thought at work in the struggle between common law and equity in 1616. First there were the legal debates between Coke on the one hand and Ellesmere and the "chancery men" on the other. The first part of this essay examines the debates between these two camps, especially in the central case reports of the struggle—*The Magdalen College Case, The Earl of Oxford's Case,* and *The King and Doctor Gouge*—and in the account of the decree by which Chancery was vindicated. However, it would be too narrow to think such arguments were the whole story. The legal debates took place in conjunction with the political vision of James I, which was articulated on this particular issue in his speech to the Star Chamber. James argued from quite a different set of principles, and yet they were the same principles that governed his thought from as far back as his time in Scotland. The second part of this paper, therefore, examines James's writings to see how the relation between equity and common law fits into a different and yet consistent and powerful pattern of thought.

I

Views vary widely on the legal arguments of 1616. Although Gardiner was able to write, "On the question of the jurisdiction of [Chancery] it has been universally admitted that Coke was wrong,"[15] John P. Dawson argues that the "common lawyers of the seventeenth century were wholly justified in rejecting" the arguments put forward on behalf of Chancery.[16] While for Louis A. Knafla, "Ellesmere wrote the modern definition of the equitable jurisdiction of the Chancery into the pages of the later law books,"[17] for Dawson the events of 1616 were an immense setback to the working partnership of common law and equity,[18] and J. H. Baker suggests that the fusion of common law and equity in the Judicature Act of 1873 was a final—if much belated—victory for Coke.[19] We might wonder about a victory that was over 250 years in the making—and which then involved integrating equity only by letting it continue to prevail; we might also ask if the earl of Oxford would have walked away from our contemporary courts of legal and equitable jurisdiction without some remedy.

Seen from a present legal perspective, the issues involved in this situation are, as one lawyer I consulted put it, "a nightmare." (It must have appeared similarly so at the time.) The complexities of res judicata and estoppel that would result for the college and Oxford, since neither was a party to the initial action, as well as the college's "dirty hands" in any attempt to benefit from an illegal contract, render very tricky any attempt to predict what common law results might follow in today's law from the decision in *The Magdalen College Case.* Moreover, modern equity provides a number of grounds on which Oxford might have relied: unjust enrichment, constructive trust, proprietary estoppel. Oxford might also today have relied upon restitutionary principles. To an observer open to the merits of the positions of both sides, the dispute unfolds as a balance of complex and sophisticated arguments. The historian W. J. Jones writes that in 1616 "The modern attitude towards case law can hardly be said to have existed, and Coke has been described as wandering at random over the cases in question."[20] One with a less sanguine view of twentieth-century judicial reasoning, however, may find in the seventeenth-century cases recognizable and consistent legal reasoning not so different in quality from our own.

The Magdalen College Case was a decision in King's Bench on a moot question between John Warren and John Smith over tenancy of a house in London's Covent Garden. The house was on land sold many years before by Magdalen College to Queen Elizabeth. The purpose of the sale was to avoid the prohibition in the statute of 13 Eliz. 1, c.10, whereby, inter alia, sales and long leases of land by masters and fellows of colleges were rendered void and of no effect. Since sales to the monarch were not expressly forbidden by the statute, the sale to Elizabeth allowed the college to transfer the land indirectly to a Genoan merchant, Benedict Spinola, to whom the college was in debt. Elizabeth transferred the land to Spinola, as the college directed her, and Spinola in turn, in 1580, sold the land—seven acres—to Edward de Vere, earl of Oxford, who built 130 houses upon it. The lease of one of these houses devolved through a number of intermediaries to John Warren. On his death, Oxford was succeeded by his son Henry de Vere, a notorious drinker and womanizer, who was later imprisoned for his opposition to the Spanish marriage. Meanwhile, before 1616, the new master of Magdalen College, Barnaby Gooche, or Gouge, had succeeded in installing John Smith in the same house. Warren brought an action of ejectment against Smith, but Warren's lease expired before the case could be heard. Warren, however, asked the court to decide the question of right to tenancy anyway.

The case turned upon ownership of the land. If the earl of Oxford's title was good, then so was Warren's lease; if the college retained title, then Smith's lease was good. For the court, the central question was the interpretation of the statute voiding the sale of college land. Coke rejected the claim that sales to the queen were not prohibited by the statute. The statute, designed to maintain religion and advance good learning, protected spiritual livings and institutions against the impoverishment, decays, and dilapidations that follow upon long leases and sales. For Coke the intent of the statute would be utterly circumvented if sales to the monarch were not prohibited: a "by-way" would be left open "by which the said great and dangerous mischiefs should remain, and the necessary and profitable remedy depressed."[21] In the preface to part XI of his *Reports,* Coke's brief summary casts the case in this light, as dealing with the public interest: "And iustly doth the Case of Magdalen Colledge in Cambridge challenge the next place: which tendeth to the maintenance of Gods true Religion, the aduancement of liberall Arts and Sciences, the supportation of the Ecclesiastical state, the preseruation and prosperity of those two famous Sisters, the Vniversities of Cambridge and Oxford, and of all the Colledges within the Realme, and the establishment of Hospitals, and provisions for the poore."[22] With regard to the royal prerogative, Coke argued that since religion and learning were "the main Pillars which support the Kings Crown," the king of all others should not be exempt from the act.[23]

Moreover, the king is "the Fountain of Justice and common Right" and as God's lieutenant cannot do a wrong,[24] and to exempt the king and allow him to be a conduit for illegal transfers would be to make of him "the Instrument of fraud and covin."[25] Warren's lease, deriving from the sale of the land to the queen and then to Spinola and to the earl of Oxford, was therefore not good in law; since the sale to the queen was void, the title of the college was still good, as was Smith's lease from the college.

Although the case turned upon a moot question between Warren and Smith, its effect was to render vulnerable the earl of Oxford's title to land and houses worth £20,000 in leases. Neither the earl nor the college had been parties to the case, so the interests of neither were specifically considered by Coke. However, Coke's later terse response to Oxford's plight—"Caveat emptor"[26]—indicates that there was little hope for sympathy or remedy at common law. Oxford, therefore, turned to equity and Chancery for protection.

Chancery relied on no specific equitable doctrines nor on any of the standard maxims to decide in favor of Oxford. Jones has argued that the Elizabethan court of Chancery did not have a highly developed theory of equity or conscience.[27] Indeed Ellesmere reasoned by drawing connections between equity and the law of God: "And Equity speaks as the Law of God speaks."[28] For the law of God, Ellesmere draws upon Deuteronomy: "He that builds a House ought to dwell in it; and he that plants a Vineyard ought to gather the Grapes thereof."[29] Ellesmere continues: "And yet here in this Case, such is the Conscience of the Doctor [Gouge], the Defendant, That he would have the Houses, Gardens and Orchards, which he neither built nor planted: But the Chancellors have always corrected such corrupt Consciences, and caused them to render quid pro quo."[30]

In addition to stressing God and conscience, Ellesmere also invokes "proportionable Satisfaction" and the reciprocity of benefit and recompense, in the latter instance employing an example from trust law: "as if *Cestui que use,* sell the Land to one that hath no Notice of the Use, and dieth; by Reason that he had the Benefit of the Sale, his Executors were ordered to answer the Value of the Land out of his Estate." Later the decision draws again upon scripture for the rule "*To do as one would be done unto.*"[31] Ellesmere's notion of equity, therefore, is a somewhat large, vague, and eclectic mix of ideas of fairness—what amounts to a sense of *ex aequo et bono:* "The Cause why there is a *Chancery* is, for that Mens Actions are so divers and infinite, That it is impossible to make any general Law which may aptly meet with every particular Act, and not fail in some Circumstances."[32] Similarly, John Cowell, in his ill-fated book *The Interpreter,* had said that the chancellor "subiecteth himselfe onely to the lawe of nature, ordering all things *iuxta aequum & bonum.*"[33]

The remedy sought by Oxford was not to overturn the decision in King's Bench as to title to the land, which would be beyond equitable jurisdiction, but to give him compensation for his loss, "the true Value of the New Building and

Planting since the Conveyance, and convenient Allowance for the Purchase."[34] This remedy, asserted Ellesmere, was neither an examination of, nor in opposition to, the judgment at common law. However, a problem arose: the defendant Gouge refused to answer Oxford's suit, arguing that a judgment at common law could not be questioned in Chancery. Although, as we have seen, for Ellesmere there was in this case no examination of the common law judgment per se, the chancellor asserted his prerogative: "The Chancellor must give Account to none but only to the King and Parliament."[35] But had Parliament spoken?

The statute of 7 Edw. 3, c.1 set out a *praemunire*, or summons, and harsh sanctions for anyone who, inter alia, would "sue in any other court, to defeat or impeach the judgements given in the King's court." Moreover, the statute of 4 Hen. 4, c.23 asserted, "after judgment given in the courts of our lord the King, the parties and their heirs shall be thereof in peace, until the judgment be undone by attaint or by error." In 1598, late in the reign of Elizabeth, in the case of *Finch* v. *Throckmorton*, the question had arisen as to whether these statutes prohibited recourse to Chancery after common law judgments. The question had been put to all the common law judges of England, who interpreted the statutes as prohibiting recourse to Chancery for any cause that had been determined at common law.[36] For Coke, this decision reenforced his view of the primacy of the common law in England: just as the king had given away his judicial power to the judges and was bound by presumptions that he could not act in conflict with the intentions of law and statute, Chancery and equity too were to submit to the power of the common law.[37] In the third and fourth parts of his *Institutes*, Coke continued to invoke these statutes and assert that Chancery and equity could not interfere after judgment at common law unless in a particular case equitable power of relief was granted by Parliament.[38]

Such a position left very little scope for equitable jurisdiction. Equity could deal with cases in which the common law had no competence—trusts, for instance—or perhaps in cases where there were potential suits in both common law and equity and where there had been no preceding case at common law. In such a case, however, this interpretation of the statutes might not rule out a subsequent action in King's Bench. At any rate, this interpretation prohibited recourse to equity in those situations, such as Oxford's, in which the injustice in the eyes of equity arose only as a consequence of a judgment at law.

In the years subsequent to *Finch* v. *Throckmorton*, Ellesmere continued to examine parties after judgment at common law, and his *Breviate* of 1615 reexamined the statute of 4 Hen. 4 from the perspective of Chancery.[39] Part of Ellesmere's reasoning appears in *The Earl of Oxford's Case*, where he enumerates cases in which equitable relief only possible after an unjust result at common law had been given; he concludes: "when a Judgment is obtained by Oppression, Wrong and a hard Conscience, the Chancellor will frustrate and set it aside, not for any error or Defect in the Judgment, but for the hard Conscience of the Party . . . these are not within the Statute, 4 *H.* 4, *c.* 23."[40] Moreover, "the Statute of 4 *H.* 4, *Chap.* 23, was never made nor intended to restrain the Power of the *Chancery* in Matters of Equity, but to restrain the Chancellor and the Judges of the Common Law, only in matters meerly determinable by Law, in legal Proceedings, and not in Equitable, and that they should be constant and certain in their own Judgments, and not play Fast and Loose."[41]

Between Coke and Ellesmere there were two very different views of equitable jurisdiction. In the case at hand, Coke's view would leave Oxford with nothing but the admonition to let the buyer beware; the common law had decided on title, and no hardship to the earl or discreditable motive on the part of Gouge was to be considered. On the other hand, although Ellesmere was narrowly correct to distinguish between equitable relief and overturning the common law judgment, the effect of equity's intervention was to take from the college free title to property worth £20,000 pounds and substitute in effect a very likely undesirable or unmanageable purchase of £20,000 worth of land and houses.

Gouge refused to answer Oxford's suit, so Ellesmere had him imprisoned in the Fleet for contempt. Gouge then brought an action of habeas corpus before the King's Bench: this is the case of *The King and Doctor Gouge.* The case ended inconclusively. Coke took the common law position: "Consider the Statutes of 27 E. 3. cap.1. & 4 H. 4 cap.13. It would tend to the downfal of the Common Law, if Judgments here given, should be suffered to be called in question in Courts of Equity."[42] There was some question, however, whether Gouge had been imprisoned on matters relating to the common law judgment or on other matters. Part of the confusion was because the parties in *The Magdalen College Case* were different from those in *The Earl of Oxford's Case.* Coke decided there was not enough evidence to decide the question and therefore Gouge could not be helped. The bill in Chancery was then sent for, and it appeared to deal with the same land as in the common law case. The matter was adjourned until further clarification could be had from Chancery.

The conflict between King's Bench and Chancery, however, was to be decided in a different forum. The question of the interpretation of 27 Edw. 3, c.1 and 4 Hen. 4, c.23, in response to the growing tension between Coke and Ellesmere over common law and equity and Coke and the King over royal prerogative, was this time, unlike in 1598, put before a new panel of so-called "chancery-men." This label is somewhat misleading. As Jones points out, common law judges often sat on Chancery courts,[43] and the members of the panel had complex relations to the common law. Randell Crew was a judge who had earlier worked with Coke; Henry Yelverton was a judge and solicitor-general who was to become attorney-general; Henry Montague would replace Coke as chief justice. Moreover, Montague had argued for the plaintiff in *The Magdalen College Case,* Yelverton and Crewe for the defendant.[44] Most important was Francis Bacon, the attorney-general soon to replace Ellesmere as lord chancellor. Bacon's presence was most likely decisive. He had a number of grounds for opposing Coke. Lucy Aikin noted the importance of personal animosity between Bacon and Coke in Coke's downfall; this animosity is evident in Bacon's account to the king of his exchanges with Coke: "I was a little plain with my lord Coke in these matters; and when his answer was, that he knew all these things,—I said, he could never profit too much in knowing himself and his duty."[45] Bacon was also concerned with his own possibilities of advancement. Finally, he worked from a set of developed legal positions, which could in turn be related to his political theory and ultimately to his grandest philosophical schemes. Bacon favored strong royal authority and a flexible, somewhat equitable, notion that "salus populi lex suprema," which was in keeping with the inductive method of his natural philosophy and also ran counter to Coke's sense of the rigidity of common law.[46] This new panel decided that neither statute barred recourse to Chancery after a judgment at law.

As to the statute of Edward III, the panel made a number of arguments. First, since the statute attempted to curb acts "*in prejudice and disherison of our lord the King,*" this could not apply to Chancery, since the king cannot be disinherited of jurisdiction by his own prerogative court. Secondly, the statute allowed recourse to Chancery for remedy, and "it is opposite in it selfe, that the Chancery should give both the offence and the remedy." Thirdly, the penalties provided were too severe except if they were directed only against recourse to foreign jurisdictions; this, the panel argued, was the object of the statute: to prevent recourse to foreign courts. The statute had nothing to do with suits in Chancery.[47]

The statute of Henry IV, they argued, made no mention of Chancery. This omission was telling in light of the petitions that led to the enacting of the statute. The original petition, among its complaints, referred to recourse to Chancery after judgments at law. This petition was denied by the king. It was only a different petition, which did not refer to Chancery, that received the king's approval. Finally, like Ellesmere, the panel argued in the alternative that if the statute barred suits in Chancery, it barred only the questioning of the common law judgments themselves, not the pursuit of equitable questions that follow upon those judgments without putting them at issue.[48]

The statutory interpretation involved here is sophisticated and not unpersuasive. Indeed the legal reasoning in these cases—given the separation of the courts of common law and equity and Coke's necessary confinement to common law principles—is generally careful and compelling. One wonders if there was any more blunder and politics in these decisions than in some recent decisions of, say, the United States Supreme Court. These early modern cases are instances of a genuine struggle of ideas and reasoning. One cannot help but believe, however, that the statutory interpretation would have been different if the questions had been put back into the hands of Coke and the common law judges. As decisive as the reasoning of the panel was the king's decision to put the question in their hands. That James put the question to Chancery was the result of a number of factors, including most likely the king's political bias toward Chancery and his personal and political hostility toward Coke. James's actions were also informed, however, by his political theory, which brought him to favor Chancery and equity over King's Bench and common law. Since the decision to arbitrate and declare was in his hands, James's views were as important as any factor in the triumph of equity. The final section of this paper, therefore, explores James's political philosophy as an important if not solely decisive element in this central moment in English legal history.

II

James VI and I was, as monarchs go, a prolific and systematic theorist of his own authority. His defense of absolute royal prerogative began in Scotland in 1598 with *The True Law of Free Monarchies.* Opinions of *The True Law* as a work of political philosophy have varied widely. Early in the twentieth century, John Neville Figgis and J. W. Allen took opposed positions: for Figgis it contains "the doctrine of Divine Right complete in every detail";[49] Allen found it impossible to extract from James's work any distinct theory of kingship or the state.[50] Charles McIlwain described it as "the most comprehensive of all [James's] political writings,"[51] while Wilfrid Harrison doubted "to what extent a significant doctrine of the divine right of kings is to be found in King James's not too coherent book."[52] However coherent *The True Law* may or may not be, if it is seen in the context of James's later political writings and of his various political struggles, what does emerge is great theoretical consistency. What follows is, therefore, a tracing of James's basic political ideas from his time in Scotland through his encounters with the English parliament and finally to his pronouncements on common law and equity.

The True Law arose in the context of James's struggles with the Scottish Kirk, or reformed church, and to a lesser extent with the Scottish nobility. While unruly nobles plagued James's early life, by the time of his adulthood it was the leadership of the church that provided him with his most troubling opposition. Most notable among this leadership was Andrew Melville, who once took the king by the sleeve and called him "God's sillie vassall," and who attacked James's handbook of kingly advice, *Basilikon Doron,* for its "Anglo-pisco-papisticall Conclusiones."[53] These struggles were played out against a philosophical background dominated by George Buchanan, James's childhood tutor and, in *The Powers of the Crown in Scotland,* one of the most incisive critics of absolute monarchy.

The True Law is a justification of James's absolute authority in the face of this opposition. It begins by grounding kingly power in the Bible. "Kings are called Gods by the propheticall King *David,* because they sit upon God his Throne in the earth, and have the count of their administration to give unto him," James writes.[54] Here he refers to Psalm 82:6, a passage James drew upon on many subsequent occasions: the sonnet beginning *Basilikon Doron*, for instance, opens "God giues not Kings the stile of Gods in vaine, / For on his Throne his Scepter doe they swey."[55] Here in a nutshell is James's argument. The authority of kings over their subjects is given them by God, and in consequence they need answer to no one but God. This authority was given by God to kings in the time of Samuel and Saul, and in James's interpretation, 1 Samuel 8:9–20 confers absolute and limitless authority on the monarch over his subjects. In this passage, Samuel warns the Israelites, who have asked for a king, that kings will take whatever they want from the people, who will have no redress. In James's reading, God is here making clear to the people what they are asking for, so that in future they will be bound by their agreement in full knowledge of this arrangement:

> As he would say; When ye shall finde these things in proofe that now I fore-warne you of, although you shall grudge and murmure, yet it shal not be lawful to you to cast it off, in respect it is not only the ordinance of God, but also your selues haue chosen him vnto you, thereby renouncing for euer all priuiledges, by your willing consent out of your hands, whereby in any time hereafter ye would claime, and call back vnto your selues again that power, which God shall not permit you to doe.[56]

In essence, the Israelites have willingly and clear-sightedly handed over to the king all legal right to object to his future treatment of them.

For James, as a Christian king, the institution of monarchy in the Bible is the only just pattern for kingly authority over the people:

> Now then, since the erection of this Kingdome and Monarchie among the Iewes, and the law thereof may, and ought to bee a paterne to all Christian and well founded Monarchies, as beeing founded by God himselfe, who by his Oracle, and out of his owne mouth gaue the law thereof: what liberty can broiling spirits, and rebellious minds claime iustly to against any Christian Monarchie; since they can claime to no greater libertie on their part, nor the people of God might have done. . . ?[57]

James asserts that he has absolute authority over his people just as the kings of the Israelites had absolute authority over theirs. Along with authority over his people, however, a king has a duty to God to reign as a just, caring, and protecting ruler. James is always mindful of this duty; in fact, *The True Law* begins not with a defense of royal authority but an assertion of royal duty: "as the Fathers chiefe ioy ought to be in procuring his childrens welfare, reioycing at their weale, sorrowing and pitying at their euill, to hazard for their safetie, travell for their rest, wake for their sleepe; and in a word, to thinke that his earthly felicitie and life standeth and liueth more in them, nor in himselfe; so ought a good Prince thinke of his people."[58] A good king will, therefore, "maintain all the lowable and good Lawes made by [his] predecessours" and "maintain the whole countrey, and every state therein, in all their ancient Priuiledges and Liberties,"[59] since stability and order are essential to the well-being of a people. What James asserts, nonetheless, is that a king is only answerable to God in this regard, not to his subjects: "a good king will frame all his actions to be according to the Law; yet hee is not bound thereto but of his good will, and for good example-giving to his subjects."[60]

This argument takes up only the first half of *The True Law,* yet it is the foundation of James's subsequent political thought. The rest of the book reaffirms the same position on different grounds. James argues next from history: Scotland is historically a free, or absolute, monarchy. This means both that the Scots, like the Israelites, submitted to the absolute authority of the king—unlike other nations in which the king's authority might have traditionally accepted limitations—and that the orderly and stable running of the country demands that this tradition of absolute authority not be disrupted in any way. Next James argues from two analogies to show the logical and moral superiority of absolute monarchy and the absurdity of any system that allows the people to rise against royal authority. The king is to the people as a father is to his children and as a head is to the body. For James the conclusions are inescapable: "for the fathers part . . . consider, I pray you what duetie his children owe to him, & whether vpon any pretext whatsoeuer, it wil not be thought monstrous and vnnaturall to his sons, to rise vp against him, to control him at their appetite, and when they thinke good to sley him, or cut him off, and adopt to themselues any other they please in his roome."[61] In the same way, "for the similitude of the head and the body, it may very well fall out that the head will be forced to garre cut off some rotten member . . . to keepe the rest of the body in integritie: but what state the body can be in, if the head, for any infirmitie that can fall to it, be cut off, I leaue to the readers iudgement."[62]

The final part of *The True Law* is a practical consideration of tyranny and rebellion. Is there any good to be gained from rebelling against a bad king? James, of course, argues that there is not. Not only is such rebellion never justified, but rarely if ever will a king rule so badly that a country will be better off with the chaos and disorder that necessarily follow upon his overthrow.

From a secular, post-Enlightenment, democratic point of view *The True Law* is highly unconvincing. It is important, however, to understand how securely it is rooted in early modern habits of thought. Sharpe, for instance, points to the central importance of analogical reasoning, the commonplaces of father of the family and head of the body as analogies for kingship, the importance of systems of balance in duties and rights, and the importance of biblical endorsement in the discourses of early modern England.[63]

Most specifically relevant for an understanding of the legal events of 1616 are James's brief reflections in *The True Law* on law and equity.[64] He draws upon the equitable maxim that *summum ius,* the strictest right, can become *summa iniuria,* the greatest wrong, unless checked by royal discretion. He then places the dictum within his general theory of royal authority:

> For albeit it be trew that I haue at length prooued, that the King is aboue the law, as both author and giuer of strength thereto; yet a good king will not onely delight to rule his subiects by the lawe, but euen will conforme himselfe in his owne actions thervnto, alwaies keeping that ground, that the health of the common-wealth be his chiefe law: And where he sees the lawe doubtsome or rigorous, he may interpret or mitigate the same, lest otherwise Summum ius bee summa iniuria: And therefore generall lawes, made publickely in Parliament, may vpon knowen respects to the King by his authoritie bee mitigated, and suspended vpon causes onely knowen to him.[65]

The king will, in most circumstances, bind himself by the law, but since his first duty from God is the health of the commonwealth, he will mitigate the law when it is "doubtsome or rigorous" and when its strict enforcement would spawn injustice.

In *Basilikon Doron,* James's second major political text of this period, he gives a sense of equity as the second degree of "service of God by man." The first degree is "by prayer in faith towards God"; the second is "by workes flowing therefra before the world," or "the exercise . . . of equitie towards your neighbour."[66] Equity, as defining relations toward others, is, therefore, a religious duty. James also expands on the particulars of the king's equitable discretion:

> Vse Iustice, but with such moderation, as it turne not in Tyrannie: otherwaies *summum Ius,* is *summa iniuria.* As for example: if a man of a knowen honest life, be inuaded by brigands or theeues for his purse, and in his owne defence slay one of them, they beeing both moe in number, and also knowen to be deboshed and insolent liuers; where by the contrarie, hee was single alone, beeing a man of sound reputation: yet because they were not at the horne, or there was no eye-witnesse present that could verifie their first inuading of him, shall he therefore lose his head? And likewise, by the law-burrowes in our lawes, men are prohibited vnder great pecuniall paines, from any wayes inuading or molesting their neighbours person or bounds: if then his horse breake the halter, and pastour in his neighbours medow, shall he pay two or three thousand pounds for the wantonnesse of his horse, or the weaknesse of

> his halter? Surely no: for lawes are ordained as rules of vertuous and sociall liuing, and not to be snares to trap your good subiects: and therefore the lawe must be interpreted according to the meening, and not to the literall sense thereof: *Nam ratio est anima legis.*[67]

The king's discretion is to be used in such situations where the strict letter of the law creates an obvious injustice. The correction of injustice, however, should not lead to an intrusive redistribution of deserts: "Learne also wisely to discerne betwixt Iustice and equitie; and for pitie of the poore, rob not the rich, because he may better spare it, but giue the little man the larger coat if it be his; eschewing the errour of young *Cyrus* therein: For Iustice, by the Law, giueth euery man his owne; and equitie in things arbitrall, giueth euery one that which is meetest for him."[68] The error of young Cyrus, who thought a larger boy was justified in taking a large coat from a small boy and giving him his own smaller coat in return, was to go beyond the bounds of correcting injustice, ignoring just ownership at law in the name of a higher idea of equity—but one so high as to overturn justice and public security.

James, then, positions royal prerogative as bound by God to a sense of justice above the strictures of the law, but only to the degree that the law leads to injustice, and not to the extent of giving those without what doesn't by right belong to them. James was not interested in promoting an equity that would overturn traditional property and class relations, of which he was, ultimately, the greatest beneficiary. *The Earl of Oxford's Case,* after all, involved protecting the property rights of a very wealthy man.

The True Law and *Basilikon Doron* are texts from James's Scottish period, and their immediate context was his struggle with the Kirk and the Scottish nobility—a contest in which James emerged as victor, so that by the time of his accession to the English throne, he ruled in Scotland with little opposition from nobles or churchmen. James brought to his relations with the English Parliament the same ideas at work in *The True Law.* James addressed Parliament in a series of speeches, in 1604, 1605, 1607, and 1610. As J. H. M. Salmon writes, "These pronouncements were compatible with *True Law* but they extended and modified the theory by placing it in the context of English practice."[69]

Such a view runs counter to the assertions of Paul Christianson and Glenn Burgess that James's discourse and perhaps his theoretical position changed in 1610.[70] Sommerville has effectively rebutted this position,[71] but what is most important is that James's pronouncements in England are understandable as applications of his Scottish ideas to a different context. James had always stressed the traditions of a settled kingdom as a moral and practical check on the actions of a monarch, although his allusion to William the Conqueror (and not to Magna Carta) in *The True Law*[72] implies that for James England too was a free monarchy, and any traditional checks on his power could and should be overridden if he saw fit to do so (although circumstances would be rare and dire indeed when any monarch but a tyrant would override such traditions). James was also, as in his pronouncements on the common law, prone to interpret English traditions as more favorable to his prerogatives than they actually were or than others saw them as being.

In the speech of 1604, James draws upon the analogy of head and body.[73] He also distinguishes between a lawful king and a tyrant: a lawful king makes laws for the common weal, not for private ends; he rules the kingdom not for the satisfaction of his desires, but to advance the wealth and prosperity of his people.[74] In the speech of 1605, James writes, "Kings are in the word of GOD it selfe called Gods, as being his Lieutenant and Vice-gerents on earth."[75] He also resorts once again to the analogy of head and body: this time James is the head and Parliament is the body, which has no head of its own but is "nothing else but the Kings great Councell."[76] In his speech of 1610 James reworks the same ideas: "For Kings are not only GODS Lieutenants vpon earth, and sit vpon GODS throne, but euen by GOD himselfe they are called Gods." Moreover, "Kings are also compared to Fathers of families: for a King is trewly Parens patriae, the politique father of his people. And lastly, Kings are compared to the head of this Microcosme of the body of man."[77] James also makes the point that in a settled kingdom, such as England, a good king is bound to observe the fundamental laws of the land, since otherwise uncertainty and instability would arise: "a King gouerning in a setled Kingdome, leaues to be a King, and degenerates into a Tyrant, assoone as he leaues off to rule according to his Lawes."[78]

James was much more successful dealing with the Scottish Kirk than he was with the English Parliament. His troubled relations with Parliament at best resulted in debilitating stalemate: Parliament, at least late in the reign, unconvened for years at a time (in 1615 to 1616, however, Parliament was unusually active), leaving James's court economically enfeebled.[79] Why James was less successful with his ideas in England than he had been in Scotland has been explained in various ways. McIlwain, for instance, writes, "James I himself was a true Scot, and to the end of a fairly long life and an English reign of over twenty years could never appreciate or even understand the English constitution."[80] Alan Smith outlines early modern English constitutional theory as follows: "In Jacobean England then the dominant constitutional theory, accepted by king, Parliament and common lawyers alike, was of a balanced constitution which was founded on certain inalienable rights possessed by both Crown and subjects and safeguarded by common law, with the law itself based on principles which could not properly be challenged by men: principles enshrined in the laws of God, nature and reason, however these might be defined."[81]

Put in these terms, English constitutional theory was broad enough to encompass James's beliefs. Conrad Russell has argued that the king's divine right was only one of many recognized divine rights—those of fathers, Parliament, nobility, and so forth—and these rights had to be articulated together.[82] Such an account runs the risk, however, of appearing disingenuous and being misleading and unhelpful: certainly James thought of the king's divine right as of a different order and magnitude than other men's rights. Sommerville, on the other hand, sees much less unanimity in English political thinking: "there was no unity on the questions of the nature and limitations of royal authority, the relationship between the law and the king, and the role of Parliament in church affairs."[83] He insists that James and those of his party were "absolutist" in their political beliefs.[84] Such a label needs qualifying if it is to have any accuracy in pinpointing James's position: although James believed that no subjects had the right to oppose his actions and that the power given him by God over his subjects was in some sense absolute, his theory also asserts over and over that only a tyrant would exercise his authority counter to the laws and traditions of the nation, except in extreme and unusual circumstances. In this regard, Christianson is right to "challenge . . . the assumption that, for the early Stuarts, divine right meant absolutism, which in turn meant arbitrary rule by the Crown."[85] Even if there was a political consensus, as broadly defined, the range of possible views on the proper hierarchy and weight of royal and parliamentary authority was obviously wide enough, as Burgess admits,[86] to give rise to disagreement and struggle. In this context, James's speeches to Parliament did little to smooth over relations.

James most likely understood the English constitution more than he sympathized with it. However, despite his failures with Parliament, he was able, under the right circumstances, to shape English traditions to his advantage. Moreover, he was still sometimes capable of bringing his political ideas successfully to bear on this task. All three of these propositions are supported by an examination of James's engagement with English common law.

The law marks a third area, in addition to his dealings with church and Parliament, in which James employed the same ideas in a struggle between his authority and those who would oppose it. The events of 1616 were preceded by a long history of interest by James in systems of law. He was raised in the civil law tradition of Scotland, and in *The True Law* he finds that the civil system fits well with his views on royal authority. As McIlwain writes, "Such a theory leaves no place for the law of the land or the authority of the estates of the Realm when they conflict with the king's will," and he notes the connection between James's view of royal prerogative and the absolutist principles of Roman civil law.[87]

Moving to England, James developed a complex relation to the common law. In large measure he never lost his theoretical preference for the civil law. This preference, however, needed to be abandoned, modified, or at least disguised in the English context. For instance, when John Cowell published his law dictionary of 1607, *The Interpreter*—which extoled civil law over common law—James, who was most likely in secret sympathy with Cowell, was forced to censure the book in the face of parliamentary disapproval and take the conciliatory position of his speech of 1610.[88] In that speech, James argues that, as a king ruling in a settled kingdom, he must follow the traditional and established laws insofar as they do not conflict with the fundamental nature of his prerogative. Moreover, although James claims great esteem for civil law, "the profession thereof seruing more for generall learning, and being most necessary for matters of Treatie with all forreine Nations,"[89] he writes: "as a King I haue least cause of any man to dislike the Common Law: For no Law can bee more fauourable and aduantagious for a King, and extendeth further his Prerogative, then it doeth."[90] On the first point, that a king in a settled kingdom should uphold the laws of that kingdom, Sommerville points out that this idea is rooted in *The True Law;* he argues that "There is no reason to suppose that James changed his mind on any fundamental question of political theory after his accession to the throne of England."[91] On the second point, that James greatly esteemed civil law systems, there is no reason for doubt. The last point, however, that common law extends royal prerogative further than any other system, seems grounded in disingenuousness, wishful thinking, or willful blindness. At best, James is taking, as he did in the *commendams* case,[92] an extremely favorable view of common law traditions in their upholding of royal prerogative. James ends his discussion of common law by suggesting grounds for improvement (clearer language, settled texts, consistent reports and precedents) and discussing jurisdictional prohibitions—the source of the conflicts of 1616.

James wished that jurisdictions were clearly limited, so that in any case in which a court overstepped its jurisdiction there would be clear grounds for a prohibition from the court of King's Bench, or even more appropriately from Chancery (here he signaled the preference so important in his decision of 1616). He was not against prohibitions in this context, since their purpose was "to keepe euery Riuer within his owne banks and channels."[93] On the other hand, the "swelling and ouerflowing" of prohibitions, as courts attempted to bring more and more within their own jurisdictions is not a good thing. James's office was "to make euery Court conteine himselfe within his own limits."[94] Courts other than common law courts should keep within their jurisdictions, while courts of common law should be less prodigal in multiplying prohibitions—issuing them only in lawful form and "vpon a iust and reasonable cause."[95] Here we see James's longstanding preference for order at almost any cost and his sense of his own role as a controlling force above the fray.

His culminating statement on the law is his speech to the Star Chamber in 1616. Theodore Plucknett makes a number of points concerning the significance of the Star Chamber as the venue for this speech. Like Chancery, Star Chamber was a prerogative court separate from the common law. It was also the court it which James could sit personally in judgment—a practice opposed by Coke, since the king lacked training in the artificial reasoning of the law and had given away his personal right to sit in judgment of his judges. In Star Chamber James, in a "triumph of the principle of personal monarchy," sat as "judge over all his judges." As Plucknett further points out, decisions in Star Chamber were more arbitrary than the equitable decisions in Chancery, which might explain why the abolition of Star Chamber during the Civil War did not lead to the abolition of Chancery, which was recognized as serving a useful and necessary role in areas such as trust and fraud.[96]

Here James speaks once again from a broad sense of first principles. As usual, he begins, as he says, "*A Ioue principium*"—with God.[97] There is the requisite invocation of Psalm 82: "for Kings sit in the Throne of GOD, and they themselues are called Gods."[98] In the context of the law, therefore, a hierarchy of authority is established: kings owe obedience only to God; judges, whose authority is given them by kings (who receive it from God), owe obedience to both God and kings. For James, a basic principle of such an arrangement was that just as it is atheism and blasphemy to question what God has the right to do, it is wrong for judges to question the king's prerogative: "That which concernes the mysterie of the Kings power, is not lawfull to be disputed; for that is to wade into the weaknesse of Princes, and to take away the mysticall reuerence, that belongs vnto them that sit in the Throne of God."[99] James hereby condemns Coke's attempts to submit aspects of the royal prerogative to common law judgments.

James also invokes his oft-repeated model of a settled kingdom. In such a kingdom, kings have delegated their right of judgment to subordinate magistrates, but kings do not thereby give away their own power to judge. Moreover, there are two kinds of law: God's law and the law of the king. Kings are subject to God's law and must establish and follow the will of God. Judges, on the other hand, are subject to the law of the king, which they are to interpret and not alter. The settled law of the land, such as the common law in England, must be governed by God's law, which is free and supreme. Unless the law of the land is dependent upon God's law, it is unjust and unlawful. In addition, the law of a settled kingdom means not only that there is an onus on the king to rule by that law—and here James renewed his coronation oath to maintain the law of the land—but also that there is an onus on the various courts of that law to resist innovation and alteration and to stay within their limits and bounds, not encroaching on the traditional prerogatives of other courts.

What, in this context, is the appropriate relation between the common law courts and Chancery? As a court of equity, Chancery is "the dispenser of the Kings Conscience."[100] It works not by altering the law, "not making that blacke which other Courts made white," but by mixing mercy with justice, tempering the strict rules of law, where the rigor of the law might undo a subject. James professes a special obligation to the Chancery, which is independent of all other courts and from which there is no appeal but to the king himself: "as I am bound in my Conscience to maintaine euery Courts Iurisdiction, so especially this, and not suffer it to sustaine wrong yet so to maintaine it, as to keepe it within the owne limits, and free from corruption."[101] In this last regard, Chancery must work according to precedents "warranted by Law in the time of the best gouerning Kings, and most learned Chancellours."

James then launches into a relatively direct attack on Coke:

> It is the duetie of Iudges to punish those that seeke to depraue the proceedings of any the Kings Courts, and not to encourage them any way: And I must confesse I thought it an odious and inept speach, and it grieued me very much, that it should be said in *Westminster* Hall, that a *Premunire* lay against the Court of Chancery and Officers there: How can the King grant a *Premunire* against himselfe?
>
> It was a foolish, inept, and presumptuous attempt, and fitter for the time of some vnworthy King.[102]

James concludes: "And therefore sitting heere in a seat of Iudgement, I declare and command, that no man hereafter presume to sue a *Premunire* against the Chancery."

The triumph of equity, therefore, fit in with James's long-standing views on the nature of royal authority in a settled kingdom. In England, the common law is the law of the land. But the law of the land also embraces a separate court of equity, and equity, as the law of the king's conscience, the exercise of his prerogative for mercy and fairness, is closer to the king and closer to God's law. The king's conscience and the court of the king's conscience are subject to no one but God and the king himself. In a settled kingdom, courts must be kept within their traditional limits, but since English tradition includes an equitable court of final appeal, both tradition and the principles of Christian monarchy support the priority of Chancery. Moreover, the priority of Chancery is in keeping not only with English tradition as James sees it, but with his enduring and consistent views on the relations between God and king, king and subjects, and, consequently, king and law.

Therefore, among the forces at work in 1616, we should not underestimate the political philosophy of the monarch, which must have influenced his decision to hand over a highly sophisticated dispute on legal principles to a panel made up of those favoring Chancery in a way that coincided with his own systematic conclusions, and which thoroughly informed his own final pronouncement on the dispute. In examining James's writings, we see an ongoing political theory that leads to the justification of the triumph of equity over the common law. In the context of this theory and justification—along with whatever political and personal forces were also at work—James put the question of jurisdiction to the "chancery men." As we have seen, in more strictly legal forums, the relation of equity and common law was being debated in very different terms. The king's decree in 1616 and its effect on subsequent Anglo-American legal history is in large part the result of an interplay between James's theory and the legal arguments of Coke and Ellesmere. The triumph of equity should be understood as the kind of historical event in which the ideas of powerful men were in large measure determinative and, in the case of James's ideas, quite possibly decisive. Indeed, James's success in imposing his theoretical position on the relation between common law and equity has been his most lasting influence on Anglo-American society. It has survived, mutatis mutandis, long after the demise of the divine right of kings.

Notes

1. Gardiner 1, 6, 17; "Coppie of an advertisment" 1–2.
2. Baker, *Common Lawyers* 373; Knafla 61, 64.
3. Burgess, *Absolute Monarchy* 207.
4. Gardiner 24.
5. Ibid. 13–19.
6. Sharpe, *Culture and Politics* 2.
7. Jones, *Politics and the Bench* 27; idem, "The Crown and the Courts" 179, 191.
8. Hill 150–51.
9. Marx 179.
10. Sharpe, *Culture and Politics* 2.
11. Smith 164.
12. Sharpe, *Politics and Ideas* xi.
13. Sommerville, *Politics and Ideology* 3.
14. Idem, "James I" 58.
15. Gardiner 24.
16. Dawson 132.
17. Knafla 162.
18. Dawson 152.
19. Baker, "Common Lawyers" 392.
20. Jones, "Crown and the Courts" 194.
21. Coke, "Case of the Master" 1099.
22. Coke, "La Vnzme Part" n.p.
23. Coke, "Case of the Master" 1098.
24. Ibid. 1100.
25. Ibid. 1103.
26. *The King and Doctor Gouge* 116.
27. Jones, *Elizabethan Court* 420.
28. *The Earl of Oxford's Case* 6.
29. Ibid. 5.

30. Ibid.
31. Ibid. 8.
32. Ibid. 6.
33. Cowell n.p.
34. *The Earl of Oxford's Case* 6.
35. Ibid.
36. Knafla 159.
37. Ibid. 160; Baker, *Introduction* 112.
38. Coke, *Third Part* 120, 123; Idem, *Fourth Part* 86.
39. Knafla 163, 167.
40. *The Earl of Oxford's Case* 10–11.
41. Ibid. 15.
42. *The King and Doctor Gouge* 115.
43. Jones, *Elizabethan Court* 21.
44. Coke, "Case of the Master" 1095.
45. Aikin 31–34; *Collectanea Juridica* 3.
46. For Bacon's political theory and its relation to his natural philosophy, see Wormald and Martin as well as Burgess, *Absolute Monarchy* 86–90. Also, as early as 1612 in his essay "Of Judicature," Bacon had advised the kind of consultation between sovereign and judges which Coke so objected to in the *commendams* case of 1616.
47. *The King's Order and Decree in Chancery* 127–28.
48. Ibid. 130–32.
49. Figgis 138.
50. Allen 252.
51. McIlwain xxxvii.
52. Harrison 31.
53. Lee 85.
54. James VI and I 64.
55. Ibid. 1.
56. Ibid. 69.
57. Ibid. 70.
58. Ibid. 65–66.
59. Ibid. 65.
60. Ibid. 75.
61. Ibid. 77.
62. Ibid. 78.
63. Sharpe, *Politics and Ideas* 7, 14–16, 32.
64. James's thinking about equity developed in a Scottish context somewhat different from the English. As he wrote in 1616: "There is no Kingdome but hath a Court of Equitie, either by it selfe, as is heere in *England,* or else mixed, and incorporate in their Office that are Iudges

in the Law, as it is in *Scotland*" (James VI and I, 216). However, as he recognized in 1607, "All the Lawe of Scotland for Tenures, Wards and Liueries, Seigniories and Lands, are drawen out of the Chauncerie of England, and for matters of equitie and in many things else, differs from [England] but in certaine termes" (ibid. 173). Equity had an influence in Scotland through both canon and civil law (see Macfarlane 33–34). On the other hand, George Buchanan, James's anti-absolutist tutor, argued against any royal prerogative to bend the law or assert the monarch's personal sense of justice against it (65–75).

65. James VI and I 75.
66. Ibid. 13.
67. Ibid. 43.
68. Ibid. 45.
69. Salmon 249.
70. Christianson 72–95; Burgess, *Politics* 154.
71. Sommerville, "English and European Political Ideas" 171–72.
72. James VI and I 74.
73. Ibid. 136, 143.
74. Ibid. 143.
75. Ibid. 147.
76. Ibid. 155.
77. Ibid. 181.
78. Ibid. 183.
79. Hirst 96–125.
80. McIlwain xxxvi.
81. Smith 164.
82. Russell 106.
83. Sommerville, *Politics and Ideology* 4.
84. Idem, "English and European Political Ideas" 168.
85. Christianson 72.
86. Burgess, *Absolute Monarchy* 209.
87. McIlwain xxxix, xli.
88. Ibid. lxxxvii–lxxxix.
89. James VI and I 185.
90. Ibid. 184.
91. Sommerville, *Politics and Ideology* 64.
92. *Collectanea Juridica* 19.
93. James VI and I 187.
94. Ibid. 188.
95. Ibid.
96. Plucknett 192–95.
97. James VI and I 206.

98. Ibid. 204.
99. Ibid. 213.
100. Ibid. 214.
101. Ibid.
102. Ibid. 215.

Works Cited

Aiken, Lucy. *Memoirs of the Court of King James The First.* Vol. 2. 2nd ed. London: Longman, Hurst, Rees, Orme & Browne, 1822.

Allen, J. W. *A History of Political Thought in the Sixteenth Century.* London: Methuen, 1957.

Baker, J. H. "The Common Lawyers and the Chancery." *Irish Jurist* 4 (1969): 368–92.

———. *An Introduction to English Legal History.* 3rd ed. London: Butterworth, 1990.

Buchanan, George. *The Powers of the Crown in Scotland.* Trans. C. F. Arrowood. Austin: U of Texas P, 1949.

Burgess, Glenn. *The Politics of the Ancient Constitution: An Introduction to English Political Thought, 1603–1642.* London: Macmillan, 1992.

———. *Absolute Monarchy and the Stuart Constitution.* New Haven: Yale UP, 1996.

Chamberlain, John. *The Chamberlain Letters: A Selection of the Letters of John Chamberlain Concerning Life in England From 1597 to 1626.* Ed. Elizabeth McClure Thomson. New York: Putnam, 1965.

Christianson, Paul. "Royal and Parliamentary Voices on the Ancient Constitution c. 1604–1621." *The Mental World of the Jacobean Court.* Ed. Linda Levy Peck. Cambridge: Cambridge UP, 1991. 71–95.

Coke, Edward. *La Vnzme Part des Reports de Sr. Edw. Coke.* London, 1619.

———. *The Third Part of the Institutes of the Laws of England.* London, 1644.

———. *The Fourth Part of the Institutes of the Laws of England Concerning the Jurisdiction of Courts.* London, 1644.

———. "The Case of the Master and Fellows of Magdalen Colledge of Cambridge." *The Reports of Sir Edward Coke.* Part XI. London, 1658. 1094–1109.

Collectanea Juridica: Consisting of Tracts Relative to the Law and Constitution of England. Vol. 1. London, 1791.

"A Coppie of an advertisment to Sir Ed. Cooke, Anno 1617." British Library Add. ms. 40838. 1–5.

Cowell, John. *The Interpreter.* [1607]. Rpt. Amsterdam: DaCapo Press, 1970.

Dawson, John P. "Coke and Ellesmere Disinterred: The Attack on Chancery in 1616." *Illinois Law Review* 36 (1941): 127–52.

The Earl of Oxford's Case. The Third Part of Reports of Cases Taken and Adjudged in the Court of Chancery. London, 1716. 1–16.

Ellesmere, Thomas, Lord. *The Priviledges and Prerogatives of the High Court of Chancery.* London, 1641.

Figgis, John Neville. *The Divine Right of Kings.* 1914. Rpt. New York: Harper and Row, 1965.

Gardiner, Samuel R. *History of England from the Accession of James I to the Outbreak of the Civil War 1603–1642.* 1887–91. Rpt. Vol. 3. New York: AMS, 1965.

Harrison, Wilfrid. *Conflict and Compromise: History of British Political Thought 1593–1900.* New York: Free Press, 1965.

Hill, Christopher. *Change and Continuity in Seventeenth-Century England.* Rev. ed. New Haven: Yale UP, 1991.

Hirst, Derek. *Authority and Conflict: England, 1603–1658.* Cambridge, Mass.: Edward Arnold, 1986.

James VI and I. *Political Writings.* Ed. Johann P. Sommerville. Cambridge: Cambridge UP, 1994.

Jones, W. J. *The Elizabethan Court of Chancery.* Oxford: Clarendon P, 1967.

———. *Politics and the Bench: The Judges and the Origins of the English Civil War.* London: Allen and Unwin, 1971.

"The Crown and the Courts in England 1603–1625," *The Reign of James VI and I.* Ed. Alan G. R. Smith. New York: Macmillan, 1973. 177–94.

The King and Doctor Gouge. The Reports of Edward Bulstrode. Vol. 3. London, 1688. 115–16.

The King's Order and Decree in Chancery. Reports or Causes in Chancery. Ed. George Cary. London, 1650. 115–36.

Knafla, Louis A. *Law and Politics in Jacobean England: The Tracts of Lord Chancellor Ellesmere.* Cambridge: Cambridge UP, 1977.

Lee, Maurice, Jr. *Great Britain's Solomon: James VI and I in His Three Kingdoms.* Urbana: U of Illinois P, 1990.

Macfarlane, L. J. *William Elphinstone and The Kingdom of Scotland 1431–1514.* Aberdeen: Aberdeen UP, 1985.

Martin, Julian. *Francis Bacon, the State, and the Reform of Natural Philosophy.* Cambridge: Cambridge UP, 1992.

Marx, Karl. *Capital.* Vol. 1. New York: Vintage, 1977.

McIlwain, Charles, ed. *The Political Works of James I.* 1918. Rpt. New York: Russell and Russell, 1965.

Peck, Linda Levy, ed. *The Mental World of the Jacobean Court.* Cambridge: Cambridge UP, 1991.

Plucknett, Theodore F. T. *A Concise History of the Common Law.* 5th ed. London: Butterworth, 1956.

Russell, Conrad. "Divine Rights in the Early Seventeenth Century." *Public Duty and Private Conscience in Seventeenth-Century England.* Ed. John Morrill. Oxford: Clarendon P, 1993. 101–20.

Salmon, J. H. M. "Catholic Resistance Theory, Ultramontanism, and the Royalist Response, 1580–1620." *Cambridge History of Political Thought 1450–1700.* Ed. J. H. Burns. Cambridge: Cambridge UP, 1991. 219–53.

Sharpe, Kevin. *Politics and Ideas in Early Stuart England: Essays and Studies.* London: Pinter, 1989.

———, ed. *Culture and Politics in Early Stuart England.* Houndmills, Basingstoke, Hampshire: Macmillan, 1994.

Smith, Alan G. R. "Constitutional Ideas and Parliamentary Developments in England 1603–1605." *The Reign of James VI and I.* Ed. Alan G. R. Smith. New York: Macmillan, 1973. 160–76.

Sommerville, J. P. *Politics and Ideology in England, 1603–1640.* London: Longman, 1986.

———. "James I and the Divine Right of Kings: English Politics and Continental Theory." *The Mental World of the Jacobean Court.* Ed. Peck. 55–70.

———. "English and European Political Ideas in the Early Seventeenth Century: Revisionism and the Case of Absolutism." *Journal of British Studies* 35 (1996): 168–94.

Wormald, B. H. G. *Francis Bacon: History, Politics and Science, 1561–1626.* Cambridge: Cambridge UP, 1993.

9

King James VI and I and John Selden: Two Voices on History and the Constitution

Johann P. Sommerville

This essay is about the political ideas of James VI and I. In the last couple of decades, "revisionist" historians have argued that there was little political disagreement among people in early Stuart England. In particular, they have contended that there were few if any absolutists and little fear of absolutism. Indeed, James VI and I was himself no absolutist, they argue. "Revisionist" ideas have become extremely influential, though they have not won universal assent. Among the foremost of the revisionists is Paul Christianson, who has put forward a set of detailed and powerful arguments in favor of the thesis that ideological harmony characterized early seventeenth-century England. At the center of his account is the thinking of James VI and I. Nowadays, then, the king's political ideas are of fundamental importance to a major historiographical debate.

James VI and I was not only a writer but also the ruler of three kingdoms, and as a monarch he exercised considerable power. The links between political power and literature have received much scholarly attention of late. Students of literature sometimes see Jacobean England as an absolute monarchy, in which the authority of the king and his court exercised a dominant influence on cultural life.[1] Historians, however, are less certain that James's power *was* absolute, or that he wanted it to be. Traditionally, the king has been regarded as a firm advocate of royal absolutism. But more recently "revisionist" historians have argued that he was really a constitutionalist who supported limited kingship. To grasp the links between literature and the exercise of political power in the Jacobean age, we need to understand the nature of James's regime. No texts cast more light on that subject than the king's own political writings.

So this essay is about the political works of King James VI and I. But it is also about his younger contemporary, the eminent English lawyer and philologist John Selden. At first glance, it may seem odd to compare the king's ideas with Selden's. Not so long ago, James had a secure place in the history of political thought as a proponent of absolute monarchy by divine right.[2] Selden also had an established scholarly reputation, but certainly not as an advocate of divine right kingship. Though Selden is arguably better known as a historian of English law and Jewish antiquities than as a political thinker, he did, indeed, write on matters of political theory.[3] But his ideas have generally been seen as very different from those of James I. James's works, it used to be agreed, belong to a tradition of divine right theorizing that stretches from medieval defenses of imperial power against papal encroachment to justifications of Louis XIV's rule by French absolutists like Jacques-Bénigne Bossuet. Selden's thinking, by contrast, has been regarded as an example of modern natural law theorizing—a form of intellectual endeavor often said to have begun only around the opening decades of the seventeenth century. Later in that century, the highly influential German natural law thinker Samuel Pufendorf looked back on his precursors in the field, naming Grotius as its pioneer, and Hobbes and Selden as leading successors of Grotius.[4] In 1706 Jean Barbeyrac traced much the same pedigree, again listing Selden as one of the major modern writers on natural law.[5] More recently, Richard Tuck has taken a similar line, viewing Selden as an important proponent of modern theories of natural rights or natural law.[6] James VI and I's ideas of divine right monarchy emphasized the God-given powers of kings and the biblical basis of the subject's duty of nonresistance. Modern natural law theorists, on the other hand, derived political conclusions from secular reasoning about human nature and needs; they granted the people power to resist their ruler if he broke his contract with them or did things likely to destroy them. James argued in favor of strong royal rights. Selden, on the other hand, was a vocal critic of royal policies in the Parliaments of the 1620s, and sided with Parliament in the Civil War.

So why compare James and Selden? The answer is that recent scholarship has questioned the notion that the two men had very different ideas, claiming instead that they both subscribed to the doctrine of the ancient constitution, albeit with slightly different emphases. The theory of the ancient constitution, we are told, was quite distinct from both divine right absolutism and natural law thinking. Supporters of the idea of the ancient constitution appealed to English history and the common law in order to answer questions about the rights and duties of kings and subjects. By contrast, natural law theorists and divine right absolutists based their claims not on history or custom but on abstract reasoning and texts of Scripture. The notion that Selden and James shared the same basic political outlook sits well with the more general claim that English political thinking in the

Jacobean age was a matter of consensus, not conflict. This view has been widely voiced of late by so-called "revisionist" historians. Prominent among them is Christianson, who has argued forcefully for it in a series of influential articles and in a prize-winning book.

A while back, John Pocock asserted that there was a single dominant ideology in early Stuart England: the theory of the ancient constitution. Christianson takes the same basic stance, placing ancient constitutionalism at the center of his account of the Jacobean consensus. In James's reign, he says, people agreed on political matters, since pretty well everyone endorsed some version of the doctrine of the ancient constitution. Christianson argues that James I and Selden were representatives of mainstream constitutionalist thinking and that James was no absolutist—or at least that he came to abandon absolutism. In what follows, we shall survey his ideas on James and Selden. We shall see that the two writers did *not* hold the same or similar political views. James was, and remained, a divine right absolutist. Selden was not and had never been. The first section of this essay discusses the claims of Christianson. The second analyzes the political thinking of James. The third is about Selden. And the fourth briefly recapitulates the argument of the whole.[7]

I

According to Christianson, many commentators have mistakenly supposed that "the early Stuart kings of England" espoused "absolutist divine right monarchy."[8] They have, he informs us, wrongly assumed "that, for the early Stuarts, divine right meant absolutism, which in turn meant arbitrary rule by the crown."[9] Christianson contends that in Scotland James VI did indeed adopt absolutist theory, especially in the *True Law of Free Monarchies,* which was first published in 1598.[10] He confesses, too, that after James became king of England, "a similar theory of absolute monarchy continued to resonate through the arguments" he used "against the claims of Catholic divines." However, Christianson asserts, the theory "found little or no articulation in his public speeches."[11] Admittedly, during his early years in England, James was probably still influenced by his experiences with the Scottish Parliament, where laws were made by the king and "'but craved by his subjects,'"[12] and as late as 1607 the king "had not yet learned to speak in common law discourse." But three years later this "changed dramatically," for on 21 March 1610, James treated Parliament to "a creative speech" in which he broke decisively with absolutist ideas, abandoning his earlier support for absolute or even arbitrary rule and fashioning a case for "constitutional monarchy created by kings."[13] The speech of 1610 is fundamental to Christianson's interpretation of James, and to his claim that the king abandoned his old absolutism for new constitutionalist ideas that aligned him with thinkers like Selden. In a well-known essay, Jenny Wormald addressed the question of whether James VI and I was really "two kings or one."[14] Christianson contends that in matters of political theory the answer is two, and that the moment when the first metamorphosed into the second is 21 March 1610.

When James addressed parliament on 21 March, he intended to distance himself from the political views of John Cowell, Regius Professor of Civil Law at Cambridge, and Samuel Harsnett, bishop of Chichester, against whom the House of Commons had recently complained. Both men had expressed high views of royal authority, annoying people in Parliament. Cowell, for example, had claimed (as Christianson observes) that the king of England was "'above the Law by his absolute power'" and that "'simply to binde the prince to or by these laws [the laws of England], were repugnant to the nature of an absolute monarchy.'" Such views, says Christianson, crudely spelled out ideas the king had expressed more mutedly in the *True Law.*[15] So whatever affection James may have harbored for arbitrary or absolute rule had evaporated by March 1610, when he dramatically signaled his conversion to constitutionalism. True, it was a form of constitutionalism in which the monarch retained "a creative initiative."[16] But it was constitutionalism none the less, and it aligned James with "the medieval common law legacy," one branch of which had "stressed the creative initiatives of kings."[17]

Christianson does not spend much space on explaining exactly *why* James so dramatically changed his political views in 1610. He tells us that the king intended to "distance himself from Cowell,"[18] but he does not delve into the questions of why James wanted to do this or whether there were any other features of the political context of March 1610 that might have led James to revise his earlier pronouncements on politics. In Christianson's account, the revolution in James's thinking was the result of a genuine conversion to "the discourse of the common law," resulting from his increasing familiarity with the English legal system—and perhaps from a reading of medieval common lawyers, whose tradition he echoed.[19] Earlier, James had supported "natural law absolutism" and displayed a "universalist mentality" on issues of political theory. But from 1610 onward he based his claims on common law constitutionalism. In a speech of 1616, indeed, he "extended the theory of 'constitutional monarchy created by kings' to cover all English magistrates"; though he made a few comments on the divine origins of kingship that "echoed some of the discourse of James VI," his purpose was "to support an argument for 'constitutional monarchy created by kings,' not absolute monarchy."[20] In 1610 James VI, the advocate of absolute or arbitrary rule, gave way to James I, the constitutionalist, who reigned from then until 1625. Or perhaps only until 1621. In that year, says Christianson, the king suggested to the Commons that English monarchs were empowered to alter ancient constitutional arrangements concerning parliamentary privilege, though he declared that he himself would preserve them. A king who can alter the constitution is a dubious sort of constitutional monarch, and Christianson admits that James's claim can easily be read "as an absolutist argument."[21] James I took over from James VI in

1610, but he seemingly abdicated in favor of his former self in 1621—or perhaps he passed on the crown to a third James.

What, according to Christianson, was so new about the position the king adopted in the speech of 21 March 1610? He does not go into any great detail on exactly which powers an absolute or arbitrary monarch possesses, nor on what it means for a king to have a "creative initiative"—and we might wonder whether the gap between absolute kings and ones with really large initiatives is all that great. But he does map out what he takes to be some important general differences between the speech and James's earlier ideas. In the *True Law,* the king had advocated "natural law absolutism." In other words, James had claimed that rulers are absolute monarchs who are bound only by the laws of God and nature—universal moral absolutes—and who can flout the law of the land arbitrarily. The James of the 1610 speech, however, maintained that "Kings ruled by arbitrary will only at the start of societies"; in later times monarchs had set up laws and institutions (like Parliament and the courts) through which they had undertaken to rule. They and their successors were bound to govern by these laws, and they confirmed their obligation in a coronation oath. The oath was a binding contract, which held just as strongly as God's agreement with Noah that "Summer and Winter, and Day and Night shall not cease, so long as the earth remaines." This argument, suggests Christianson, was "a direct contradiction of Cowell's contentions."[22] Though the substance of James's theory was quite different from what it had been in the *True Law,* his references to God provided a veneer of continuity.[23] But they were now employed not in favor of arbitrary or absolute rule but to show that kings were limited monarchs who, like God Himself, "could not go back on their word."[24]

In other respects too, claims Christianson, the new theory expressed in the speech broke decisively with the king's old ideas, despite some superficial resemblances which might confuse the unwary. In the *True Law,* James had indeed "stressed the duty of kings to obey their coronation oaths," and he did the same thing in the speech of 21 March 1610. So at first glance it might seem that his position was unchanged. But in fact, suggests Christianson, the *True Law* "had attacked any attempt to see the oath as a contract between king and people which both parties could judge." The teaching of the speech was very different, and there the oath was portrayed as a fully binding contract. In other words, the *True Law* made the king and not his subjects the sole judge of whether he had broken his oath, while the speech permitted both to decide and act accordingly. Again, says Christianson, James attacked tyranny in his early works and also in the speech of 1610, but his definition of tyranny had changed crucially by the time of the speech. In *Basilikon Doron* (1599), the king had argued that a tyrant is a monarch who governs "according to his passions," while in the speech he "redefined a tyrant not as a ruler who ruled for his own pleasures, but as one who did not rule 'according to his Lawes.'" This was, remarks Christianson, "a more than subtle shift," and he uses it to support his fundamental contention that James abandoned his support for absolute or arbitrary rule and came to see himself as a constitutional monarch.[25] Absolutists, his case goes, thought that the king had no obligation to govern "'according to his Lawes.'" The fact that James came to acknowledge such an obligation therefore indicates that he had stopped being an absolutist. In the 1610 speech, James spoke in praise of the common law, stressing how favorable it was to royal power.[26] The king's "emphasis upon the firm support for monarchy provided by the common law," Christianson tells us, "proclaimed that James had abandoned both the natural law absolutism and much of the universalist mentality displayed in his earlier works."[27] James VI based his political views on abstract universal principles, but James I came to stress the importance of history and common law in assessing the rights and duties of the English. So too did other mainstream Jacobean theorists, including John Selden.

According to Christianson, James's 1610 speech soon elicited a response from the common lawyer Thomas Hedley, who mapped out an alternative account of the ancient constitution in an oration to the House of Commons, delivered on 28 June. Hedley and James agreed (so Christianson's case goes) in seeing England as a constitutional and not an absolute monarchy. But while James argued that English constitutional arrangements had been instituted by his predecessors, Hedley claimed they were rooted in the common law, which he saw as superior to both king and subject. James championed "constitutional monarchy created by kings," but Hedley opted for "'constitutional monarchy governed by the common law,' in which the common law stood above kings and parliaments and distributed both royal prerogatives and the liberties of the subjects."[28]

A third version of ancient constitutionalism, says Christianson, was soon articulated by John Selden. This was a theory of English government as a "mixed monarchy." "In response to the 'constitutional monarchy created by kings' voiced by King James," and to Hedley's idea of government by the common law, Selden's *Jani Anglorum Facies Altera* of 1610 "detailed an extensive history of the laws and constitution of England as a 'mixed monarchy.'" In this book, and again in *Titles of Honor* (1614) and *The Historie of Tithes* (1618), Selden used humanist philology and English and European evidence "to establish and refine a historical interpretation of the English constitution as a mixed monarchy in which the king, nobles, clergy, and freemen had shared sovereignty from the very beginning."[29] The publication of *Jani Anglorum* in 1610, Christianson informs us, was "a major event in the representation of England's ancient constitution as a 'mixed monarchy.'" Selden's theory was set firmly within the ancient constitutionalist tradition, but "openly competed with" the rival interpretations of James and Hedley. According to Selden, "a mixed aristocracy" held sovereignty under the ancient Britons, and a "mixed monarchy" under the Anglo-Saxons and Normans. The "crowning glory of Selden's attempt to establish his interpretation of the English constitution as a mixed monarchy through historical scholarship" was the second edition of *Titles of Honor,* published in 1631. But in the 1630s and later Selden became increasingly interested in natural law, and he abandoned his concern with English and European history. During the last twenty-three years of his life—from 1631 to 1654—he "published no more treatises which drew their evidence from English and European history"; instead he devoted his attention "to natural law and universalist political theory."[30]

To sum up, Christianson argues that just as there were two King Jameses, with markedly different political theories, so there were two Seldens, though in the latter case the first transmogrified into the second around 1631–35 rather than 1610. The second James and the first Selden were connected, since both were ancient constitutionalists who spoke the language of the common law. They were also more closely linked, for Selden's theory of mixed monarchy, which lay at the center of his thinking, was intended as a direct reply to the views expressed in James's speech of 21 March 1610. The theories of the two men openly competed for public support in the years after 1610, when ancient constitutionalism, not absolutism or natural law thinking, was the main mode of political speculation in England. All these claims are examined in what follows. We shall see that there was just one King James, that he never became a convert from absolutism to constitutionalism, and that he never learned to speak the language of the common law. There was also only a single John Selden, who wrote on a wide range of historical topics, both before and after the 1630s, but who never said much about mixed monarchy and did not reply to King James.

II

Though Christianson has constructed a forceful case for claiming that the absolutist James VI became a constitutionalist in 1610, the balance of the evidence indicates that the king's ideas did not change significantly in that year—nor did they shift back again in 1621. James VI and I were one and the same person. True, the king toned down some of his opinions for Parliament's consumption in March 1610. But the views he then expressed were not significantly different from his earlier ideas, and the moderation of his tone is easily explained by historical circumstance: that year the king was in the middle of delicate negotiations with the Commons over the Great Contract—a scheme by which he would give up certain traditional rights in return for a settled parliamentary revenue and thus at last solve his perennial financial problems.[31] If the Commons believed the king could not be trusted to keep his promises, they were unlikely to endorse the contract. So the king had a large financial incentive for stressing that his word was his bond. This does not show that he had been converted to constitutionalism.

According to Christianson, James became a constitutionalist in 1610, though his conversion was not apparently permanent, and by 1621 he was sliding back into his old absolutist ways. Other scholars have failed to notice the king's changes of mind. The same goes for James's own contemporaries, none of whom commented on the revolution in his majesty's thinking. James himself made no remark on it. Christianson tells us that the king had abandoned the absolutist teachings of the *True Law* by the time that he gave the speech of March 1610. The *True Law* was published anonymously, and for many years the king did not publicly admit writing it. In 1617 his collected works were printed. If James had really renounced the ideas of the *True Law,* he could quietly have excluded it from his *Workes.* But now, for the first time, he openly acknowledged his authorship of it by printing it alongside his other writings. When James brought out a new edition of *Basilikon Doron* in 1603, he added a new, long preface, updating his views and explaining his meaning to his English audience. Similarly, he appended a note to the Latin version of his *Premonition,* intended to prevent misunderstandings by continental readers.[32] But the *True Law* and the speech of 1610 were reprinted in the *Workes* without any addenda explaining that the two texts were incompatible and that the king now wholly rejected his old absolutist ideas. In 1619 they came out in Latin translation, in the king's *Opera.* Again there was nothing whatever to indicate that the king endorsed only the speech and not the *True Law.* Christianson contends that James continued to use absolutist arguments against Catholics after he had abandoned them in secular contexts. Catholic publicists were highly sensitive to such inconsistencies on the part of Protestants, and many of them attacked the king's political ideas in the course of the controversy over the oath of allegiance. None, however, seems to have noticed that in the domestic arena James had given up claims he was still using against Catholics, though they could have made polemical hay of this point—if it had been true. But perhaps Catholics, and other contemporaries, were simply obtuse on James's theories. To determine whether the king became a constitutionalist, we need to turn to what he said.

In the speech of 21 March 1610, James held that the first kings had ruled arbitrarily but that later monarchs governed through laws and through established institutional mechanisms. He himself undertook to abide by the settled arrangements that existed in England. In "the first originall of Kings," he declared, "their wills at that time serued for Law; Yet how soone Kingdomes began to be setled in ciuilitie and policie, then did Kings set downe their minds by Lawes." Once laws had been established, rulers were under an obligation to maintain them, "So as euery iust King in a setled Kingdome is bound to obserue that paction made to his people by his Lawes, in framing his gouernment agreeable thereunto." A "King gouerning in a setled Kingdome," he added, "leaues to be a King, and degenerates into a Tyrant, assoone as he leaues off to rule according to his Lawes." If the ruler did govern tyrannically, he could not indeed be actively resisted by his subjects, but he would certainly be called to account by God: "And though no Christian man ought to allow any rebellion of people against their Prince, yet doeth God neuer leaue Kings vnpunished when they transgresse these limits." "Therefore," he concluded, "all Kings that are not tyrants, or periured, will be glad to bound themselues within the limits of their Lawes."[33] In short, James held that good kings ought to rule according to the laws. Does this make him a constitutionalist? And does it show that he had abandoned the absolutism of his earlier writings? The answer to both questions is emphatically no.

Virtually every political thinker in early modern Europe claimed that kings ought to rule in a law-abiding fashion, governing by established laws. Absolutists—writers like Jean Bodin, Adam Blackwood, William Barclay, and Jacques-Bénigne Bossuet—emphatically did *not* license kings to rule arbitrarily. Christianson tells us that the standard assumption has been that for the early Stuarts absolutism "meant arbitrary rule by the crown."[34] But it seems that no early modern absolutist equated absolute with arbitrary monarchy, nor has any modern historian of absolutism done so either. In the words of J. H. Burns, "It would have been inconceivable, in the classical, medieval, and humanist traditions of European society that a political community could be ruled otherwise than by means of law."[35] Bossuet, the most famous French absolutist of the reign of Louis XIV, drew a very strong distinction between absolute and arbitrary power. Under an arbitrary monarch, he held, "there is no law but his will," whereas absolute kings governed by settled laws and protected their subjects' rights of property and personal freedom. He praised the latter type of government but scorned the former as "barbarous and odious."[36] Bossuet thought that kings ought to obey the laws, though they could not be coerced into doing so. William Barclay similarly argued that kings should allow themselves to be directed by the law, though no one could use force to make them keep it. Kings, he claimed, should set their subjects a good example by obeying their own laws.[37] The German absolutist Henning Arnisaeus said the same thing, observing that subjects will abide by the law more willingly if they see their king doing so as well.[38]

James adopted an identical stance in the *True Law,* asserting that "a good king will frame all his actions to be according to the Law; yet is hee not bound thereto but of his good will, and for good example-giuing to his subiects."[39] In 1606 he told Parliament that "wee under God havinge power to be the maker of the lawe would be example to other of keepinge the lawe."[40] In 1616 he was still keeping the law in order to set an example: "I haue as willingly submitted my interest to the Lawe, as any my Subiects could doe; and it becomes mee so to doe, to giue example to others."[41] Writers like Arnisaeus and the rest thought that kings cannot be compelled to observe the law because they themselves make it. In the *True Law* James also spelled out that the king is the lawmaker: "the lawes are but craued by his subiects, and onely made by him at their rogation, and with their aduice."[42] This was not a doctrine on which he had changed his mind much by 1610, for in the March speech he declared that laws in Parliament "are properly made by the King onely; but at the rogation of the people, the Kings grant being obteined thereunto."[43] Christianson argues that James's speech of 1610 broke with absolutism when it said that a ruler "leaues to be a King, and degenerates into a Tyrant, assoone as he leaues off to rule according to his Lawes." As we saw, he claims that this was "a more than subtle shift" from James's earlier absolutism.[44] But in the *True Law,* James asserted that "a good king will frame all his actions to be according to the Law." It is difficult to see how this differs much from what he said in the speech. In any case, there was nothing in the least novel in the idea that tyrants flout the law. In his extremely influential *Six livres de la République* of 1576, Bodin—the most famous of French absolutists—argued that a tyrant did not regulate his actions "according vnto his lawes," while a good king did so.[45] James denied that rulers may blithely ignore the law, but so too did all absolutists. It does not follow that he—or they—were constitutionalists.

Constitutionalists thought that royal authority was circumscribed by a constitution, whether written or customary. If the king issued orders unauthorized by the constitution (or by fundamental laws, to use a commoner contemporary term), people had no obligation to obey him. Again, if some dispute arose about the distribution of power between the king and Parliament or between various courts of law, it was the constitution, not the king, that should resolve it. The essence of constitutionalism is the idea that the rights and duties of public officials and private citizens are specified by a constitution superior to and independent of the king's will. The courts will enforce constitutional law regardless of what the king commands. It does not make much sense to describe as constitutionalist—rather than absolutist—the view that the king can override the constitution when he deems it necessary, or that its provisions are unenforceable, or that it grants the king not limited but absolute power.

In 1628, the absolutist cleric Roger Maynwaring was impeached by Parliament for the political views he had expressed in sermons delivered before the king. Speaking against him, John Pym (a leading member of the House of Commons and an outspoken critic of royal absolutism) admitted that he seemed to place some limitations on the king's power. For instance, Maynwaring said the king had to respect the substance of established laws, though he did not need narrowly to abide by their letter. Pym observed, however, that Maynwaring left it entirely up to the king to judge what the substance of the law was. In effect, therefore, the monarch's arbitrary judgment decided what was to be done in England, and subjects had no remedy against him if the king in fact infringed their legal rights. The so-called limitations that Maynwaring placed on royal power, said Pym, "leave the judgment arbitrary and the subject remediless; so they are limitations in show, not in substance." Maynwaring might mouth empty words about limitations, but he was an absolutist and deserved to be punished.[46] Absolutists like Maynwaring and Bodin and Bossuet held that kings ought to govern in a law-abiding way, but they also held that subjects were bound to obey them however they governed—provided only that they did not decree things directly contrary to God's orders (such as the Ten Commandments, which were commonly seen as a summary of natural law). It would be nice if kings ruled constitutionally, but no one could make them do so.

When James spoke of limits on royal power in the 1610 speech, did he have in mind enforceable limitations or was he thinking rather of "limitations in show, not in substance"? At the time of the speech he had a sizable incentive to make a show of limiting his power, since if the Commons believed that he would abide by the concessions he granted them—dropping old feudal rights—they might vote him large sums. As it turned out, they ultimately decided against the Great Contract. It is doubtful that he succeeded in convincing them that he really thought his power *was* limited in substance. Nevertheless, Christianson argues that this was indeed his position in 1610, and at least for a while thereafter. As we saw, he points out that in the *True Law* James had attacked "any attempt" to see the coronation oath "as a contract between king and people which both parties could judge," and he suggests that by 1610 the king had abandoned this absolutist attitude—the attitude of Maynwaring and the rest, which allowed the king alone to determine the extent of the power.[47] From 1610 then (goes Christianson's case), James permitted his subjects as well as himself to judge whether he had breached his oath and exceeded his powers. Presumably, once the people had judged that his majesty had indeed gone beyond the bounds of his authority, it was open to them to take appropriate action by disobeying his unconstitutional commands—perhaps even by disciplining him to ensure that he mended his ways in the future. If they were empowered to judge but take no action, the restrictions on his authority would be mere "limitations in show, not in substance." Christianson does not tell us just who—in the king's new constitutional theory of 1610—was to judge royal power on the people's behalf, but two possibilities suggest themselves: Parliament and the law courts. The difficulty is that after March 1610 James clearly *denied* that either could judge his powers (or prerogatives, as they were called). Indeed, he said that subjects should not debate his prerogative. Nor did he admit that anyone could disobey him if he acted unconstitutionally. It looks very much as if he did *not* permit the people to judge what powers he had limited himself to in his coronation oath and that the restrictions he had then accepted were "limitations in show, not in substance."

In the *True Law,* James made plain just when subjects ought to obey or disobey their king: "their obedience, I say, ought to be to him, as to Gods Lieutenant in earth, obeying his commands in all things, except directly against God, as the commands of Gods Minister."[48] God's commands—set out in Scripture and in the moral absolutes that constituted the law of nature—concerned religious and ethical duties, but they were silent on the English constitution. So people were bound to obey James even if he gave them orders that flouted established constitutional custom. Subjects could never resist tyrannical kings; they must be obeyed unless their orders contradicted God's. There is little evidence to suggest that James had changed his mind on this vital issue by 1610. According to

Christianson, though, James had abandoned absolutism and been converted to constitutionalism by March of that year. He had come to accept that both the people and himself were entitled to judge the limits of his authority. But in fact, even after March 1610 James made it abundantly clear that his subjects had no right to judge his royal powers.

One bone of contention that divided James from the people as represented in the House of Commons was impositions, extra-parliamentary levies on exports and imports. Many people in Parliament believed they were unconstitutional and illegal because they infringed the principle that taxation requires the consent of the taxed. As the Commons' petition of temporal grievances put it in 1610, "The policy and constitution of this your Majesty's kingdom" guarantees to subjects "such a propriety [or property], as may not without their consent be altered and charged." The Commons passed a bill condemning impositions as illegal: "be it declared and enacted" that impositions "without assent of parliament . . . are and shall be adjudged in the law void and to none effect."[49] A constitutional monarch, we might expect, would have welcomed discussion of his powers by his subjects' elected representatives in the Commons. He might have disagreed with their judgment, but he would surely have supported their right to express it, and he would have been happy to work with them in reaching some mutually acceptable accommodation. In fact, James took a very different line. Even in the conciliatory speech of 21 March, the king had told Parliament that "I wil not be content that my power be disputed vpon."[50] After the Commons discussed impositions, he vigorously returned to the same theme in a trenchantly worded oration delivered on 21 May 1610. "I would not have you judge in general of my prerogative," he told Parliament, and he went on to inform them that they "ought not to question what the king may do." They were simply not to discuss his right to levy impositions, though if they found some or all of them inconvenient, they could notify him and he might do something about it—for a sufficient consideration. James did not see himself and Parliament as equal partners in the business of delimiting his prerogative: "good kings are helped by parliament not for power but for convenience that the work may seem more glorious."[51]

So Parliament had no authority to pronounce on the limits of the king's power. But perhaps James recognized such authority in the judges of the common law courts. Certainly, Sir Edward Coke—who served James as chief justice of the Common Pleas and then of the King's Bench—granted them extensive power in constitutional matters. So too did that pugnacious lawyer Nicholas Fuller. James did not agree. He called Fuller a "villain" and sacked Coke from his post in 1616.[52] Coke's dismissal underlined the dependence of the judiciary on the crown, making it clear to the other judges that it was not a good idea to disagree too strongly with his majesty's opinions. Given that they were appointed and could be removed by the king, they were likely to accept his interpretation of the nature and limits of royal power. Even if James *had* admitted that the judges were authorized to determine the limits of his prerogative, this would arguably have been to accept only a shadowy and insubstantial limitation, for the king judged the judges. In fact, however, James granted no such right to anyone, including the judges. In 1616 he set out his ideas on their powers and duties in a speech in Star Chamber. "Incroach not vpon the Prerogatiue of the Crowne," he commanded the judges, ordering them not to deal with any matters concerning the prerogative until they had taken instructions from the king or his council. "As for the absolute Prerogatiue of the Crowne," he declared, "that is no Subiect for the tongue of a Lawyer, nor is lawfull to be disputed." Just as it was "Atheisme and blasphemie to dispute what God can doe," so it was "presumption and high contempt in a Subiect, to dispute what a King can doe." The task of judges was to enforce the laws, which expressed the king's will, not to debate royal power.[53] Again, lawyers in their pleadings in court were to "presume not to meddle with things against the Kings Prerogatiue, or Honour." If they erred on this point, "the Iudges will punish you; and if they suffer it, I must punish both them and you."[54]

Coke held that it was the common law, as interpreted by judges and Parliament, which should decide on the extent of the king's prerogative and, more broadly, on the constitution as a whole. For example, the common law defined the nature and limits of inferior jurisdictions, such as those of Chancery and the church courts. James vigorously disagreed. Disputes between courts over jurisdiction were to be decided by the king, he said, not by the common law: it "is a thing Regall, and proper to a King, to keepe euery Court within his owne bounds.[55] When some of Coke's allies tried to assert the inferiority of Chancery to the common law courts by bringing charges of *praemunire* against it, alleging that it had exceeded its power, James countered by insisting that he alone could pronounce on the limits of jurisdiction of the various courts. Henceforth he would resolve such disputes, and no one was again to charge Chancery with *praemunire:* "I declare and command, that no man hereafter presume to sue a *Premunire* against the Chancery."[56] In the placatory speech of 21 March 1610, the king had already made it perfectly plain that only he was to determine the jurisdictional boundaries of his courts: "So is it my office to make euery Court conteine himselfe within his own limits."[57] He also made it abundantly clear that he could alter the ancient nature and composition of the courts if he saw reason. For instance, the court of High Commission—the most powerful of the church courts—had formerly been "common amongst a great part of the Bishops in England," but James told Parliament that he had "thought good to restraine it onely to the two Archbishops," informing them that he intended to stick to this resolution "except I see other great cause."[58]

Constitutional monarchs rule within limits defined by a constitution. If they try to evade the limits, people simply disobey them, as they are legally and morally obliged to do. As long as citizens act according to the constitution, it is very difficult for the ruler to become a tyrant. Preventing tyranny is a cardinal purpose of constitutional monarchy. Two months after the conciliatory speech of March 1610, James addressed Parliament again, and once more he touched on the question of tyranny. Some members of the Commons had argued that kings ought not to have the power of levying impositions, since they could abuse it to the public detriment. They believed there should be—and were—fundamental constitutional laws which limited the king's power in order to protect subjects against possible abuses. A constitutionalist king could hardly have avoided agreeing with this general principle, though he might have quibbled about applying it to impositions. He would surely have applauded the Commons' efforts to set out the crown's constitutional limits and so forestall tyranny. This was not how James reacted. Because a king might abuse his authority, he asked Parliament,

> should we have power to set him limits? Pray beware of such arguments. You must not set such laws as make the shadows of kings and dukes of Venice; no Christians but papists and puritans were ever of that opinion. If you have a good king you are to thank God, if an ill king he is a curse to the people but preces et lachrimae [prayers and tears] were ever their arms. But may you therefore bridle him? . . . You cannot so clip the wing of greatness. If a king be resolute to be a tyrant, all you can do will not hinder him. You may pray to God that he may be good and thank God if he be.[59]

According to James, his subjects had no choice but to trust him to rule well. "Kings," he declared, "must be trusted."[60] But the whole point of constitutional government is that individuals, including kings, cannot be trusted and ought therefore to be bridled in order that they cannot become tyrants, however resolute they are.

In his speeches of 1610, as in the *True Law,* James gave the people no right whatever to judge the limits of his power or the meaning of his coronation oath. He accepted restrictions on his authority but they were insubstantial, for if he ignored them his subjects would still be bound to obey him. Yet though they were unenforceable, they did mark out moral if not legal constraints on his authority. What, then, did the king commit himself to when he took his coronation oath in 1603? The answer is not wholly clear, since surviving texts differ. James certainly undertook to keep and confirm the laws that his predecessors on the English throne had granted to the people. But he may well have added a clause affirming that this applied only to laws "agreeing . . . to the prerogatives of the Kinges" of England. Half the extant texts have this addition. If James swore the oath with this clause, then what he committed himself to was upholding his own power and those laws that were compatible with it. Doubtless this was something the king really could have been trusted to do.[61]

Perhaps James swore to keep only those laws that accorded with his prerogative. In any case, he made it perfectly patent—in and after 1610, as well as before—that he alone (with the aid of his appointees on the Privy Council) was to judge the nature and limits of that prerogative. He alone, too, could determine the boundaries between the jurisdictions of his courts, and he could alter the established composition of such a court as High Commission if he found it convenient. In 1610 members of the Commons had discussed royal powers, arguing that some of them could be abused and so should be limited. James retorted that he could as easily claim that they had misused their privileges and ought therefore to be deprived of them.[62] In 1621 he reverted to this theme when the Commons employed its privilege of free speech to discuss foreign policy and the king's project to marry his son Charles to a Spanish princess. James thought they had no business talking about such matters, which were the exclusive preserve of the royal prerogative. So he warned them "to beware to trench vpon the Prerogatiue of the Crowne, which would enforce Vs, or any iust King to retrench them of their priuiledges, that would pare his Prerogatiue and flowers of the Crowne."[63] The ancient constitution gave them certain privileges, but the king could take these away if he found cause. Christianson has suggested that the king here departed from the constitutionalism he had so dramatically adopted in 1610. In fact, he never had been a constitutionalist—except, perhaps, in show. Throughout, James held that free monarchs like himself possess absolute power, though good kings (again like himself) could be trusted to exercise it in accordance with their subjects' welfare and established laws. In the conciliatory speech of March 1610 he noted that people had been worried about whether he intended to maintain existing laws and institutions or "alter the same when I thought conuenient, by the absolute power of a King."[64] James denied that he had any intention to subvert the common law. He did not deny that he had "the absolute power of a King."

In substance, the *True Law* and James's later writings have much in common, though his emphasis varied from work to work. Nor is it easy to detect any revolutionary shift from a natural law language in the early writings to "common law discourse" in 1610 and later. Common lawyers did, indeed, have an extensive technical vocabulary, but James made very little use of it. Tort and seisin, heriots and hundreds, deodands and demurrers, oyer and terminer, scire facias and stare decisis, are all conspicuous by their absence in his writings. Common lawyers regularly appealed to historical precedent in order to justify their views on the constitution. James also sometimes appealed to history. Does this mean that he was, after all, an ancient constitutionalist and a speaker of the language of the common law? Decidedly not. Four linked points are in order here.

Firstly, people of every kind of ideological complexion—including absolutists—appealed to history. In James's lifetime the vast majority of political writers of all varieties held that innovation was almost always bad, that things had been better at some remote—and, we might add, mythical—point in the past. This was not an attitude confined to common lawyers. There is very little evidence that James read any common law treatises.[65] On the other hand, Jean Bodin's classic absolutist *Six livres de la République* was in his library from an early date, and when the Scottish (and French) civil lawyer Adam Blackwood came to England to congratulate James on his succession to the throne, the king took him into his library, where Blackwood's reply to George Buchanan's theories of limited monarchy was proudly displayed.[66] James's own writings agreed with those of Blackwood and Bodin on many points, and like them he used history to confirm his views.[67] Bodin's vast tome is stuffed full with historical examples, though he was an absolutist and no speaker of common law discourse. He and Blackwood responded to theorists of legitimate resistance who argued that the European past showed that monarchs got their powers from the people, to whom they were accountable. They employed history to prove the opposite.

This leads on to the second point, namely that ancient constitutionalism consists of using history to show that by immemorial custom kings are subject to limitations they cannot break. Like Bodin and Blackwood, James used history to undermine, not support, this thesis. Ancient constitutionalists viewed Magna Carta—the cornerstone of English liberties—as a compendium of immemorial rights. James, on the other hand, held that it had been granted by the crown to restore stability in a political crisis—"The Charter which yow great doe call / Came first from Kings to stay your fall"—and that the crisis had arisen as a result of the actions of rebels and enemies of monarchy—"ffrom an vniust Rebellion moued / By such as Kingdomes little Loued."[68] Coke and like-minded common lawyers were happy to use precedents from weak kings' reigns to confirm their view that royal power was limited. James, by contrast, thought the right precedents were ones drawn from the times of strong monarchs.[69]

Thirdly, the notion that there is some kind of theoretical incompatibility between an absolutist discourse of divine right or natural law on the one hand and talk about precedents and history on the other is a modern invention with little to recommend it. Absolutists like Bodin and Blackwood regularly employed historical examples, and there was no tension at all between this and their theoretical convictions about royal power. Absolutists believed that kings should ordinarily abide by the settled laws they or their ancestors had introduced. Laws made in the past were still valid if some more recent sovereign had not abrogated them. To find out what these laws were, it was necessary to investigate the past. Many seventeenth-century French writers regarded their king as an absolute monarch, yet they debated questions of the ordinary jurisdictional structure of the courts in largely historical terms. They held that the king could override settled arrangements in a case of necessity or for reason of state, but that he ought otherwise to maintain them, and thus history and precedent were usually of the utmost importance in answering constitutional questions.[70] James similarly advised his son Charles against "stretching his royall Prerogatiue but where necessitie shall require it."[71]

Fourthly, James did not in fact drop talk about divine right, or about reason and nature, after 1610. Discussing the king's speech in Star Chamber of 1616, Christianson quotes him as saying that the common law ought not to derogate from the law of God. James declared that there is one "Law, of all Lawes free and supreame, which is GODS LAW: And by this all Common and municipall Lawes must be gouerned: And except they haue dependance vpon this Law, they are vniust and vnlawfull." He also told the judges they should use precedents from the times of the best kings in deciding cases. Christianson concludes that though there might have been disagreement on who the best kings were, James appealed in this speech "to English legal experience, not to an abstract theory of divine right," thereby signaling his continued adherence to the constitutionalism he had so dramatically adopted in 1610.[72] But this is exceedingly difficult to sustain, for as we have just seen the king was here at pains to point out that the common law was subordinate to divine right. A little later in the speech he insisted, too, that the common law had to be compatible with his own natural reason and common sense. Ancient constitutionalists like Coke said that the law should be interpreted by the "artificial reason" of the judges and other legal experts. James disagreed, declaring that the judges' "interpretations must be alwayes subiect to common sense and reason" and informing them that "I will neuer trust any Interpretation, that agreeth not with my common sense and reason, and trew Logicke."[73] The king held that natural reason and divine law trumped ancient custom.

In his speeches to Parliament James was often concerned with concrete proposals to change old laws, so it is scarcely surprising that he sometimes touched upon past legislation. Rather, it is striking how rarely he made any concrete mention of case-law precedents or statutes. The *True Law* was not, of course, a speech to Parliament, but an abstract treatise. If we want to sustain the thesis that there was a dramatic change in how James talked about politics, it makes sense to compare the *True Law* or *Basilikon Doron* not with speeches given to Parliament—often for narrow and immediate political or legislative purposes—but with a treatise the king penned late in life—*A Meditation upon the 27. 28. 29. Verses of the XXVII. Chapter of Saint Matthew* (1619). This work on kingcraft drew a lengthy parallel between the crowning of Christ with thorns before the crucifixion and "the cares and crosses, that a King must prepare himselfe to indure in the due administration of his office."[74] Its language throughout was that of Scripture and divine right, not history and the common law. In style as well as substance it was singularly unlike the writings of John Selden, which were historical to the core.

III

According to Christianson, John Selden responded to King James's speech of 21 March 1610, by formulating a theory of mixed monarchy. This theory, Christianson tells us, was central to Selden's outlook from 1610 until the 1630s, when he shifted from ancient constitutionalism to a universalist approach to politics, based on natural law. In his early writings, so the case runs, Selden strongly advanced the claim that the English constitution was and had long been a mixed monarchy. After 1610, this theory openly competed for public support with James's ideas, and Selden continued to refine it well into the reign of Charles I. The 1631 edition of *Titles of Honor* was "the crowning glory of Selden's attempt to establish his interpretation of the English constitution as a mixed monarchy through historical scholarship."[75] None of this is easy to sustain.

Selden was a prolific writer of works of linguistic and historical scholarship. He was also a common lawyer, and some of what he wrote was concerned with English legal history. In 1616 he published an edition of Sir John Fortescue's *De Laudibus Legum Angliae,* along with a couple of other treatises on legal history. He retained his interest in such writings long afterward, and in 1647 published the medieval law-book known as *Fleta* as well as an elaborate dissertation on it.[76] The dissertation is a detailed survey of the influence of Roman Law in England and elsewhere, and it continues the discussion of themes that Selden had already addressed in *Jani Anglorum* and *Titles of Honor.* In 1652, just two years before his death, he penned a scholarly introduction to Roger Twysden's massive edition of texts by ten medieval historians (*De Decem Scriptoribus*), again reverting to topics he had dealt with in his early writings.[77] From an early date, he also concerned himself with the literature and antiquities of the eastern Mediterranean. In 1617 he published *De Dis Syris,* a study of the gods of the ancient Syrians and neighboring peoples. It was this book which won Selden a truly international scholarly reputation. His *Historie of Tithes* (1618) brought him notoriety in England and first called him to the attention of James I. Using a very wide range of sources in Hebrew, Latin, Anglo-Saxon, and many other languages, Selden argued in *The Historie of Tithes* that ancient and modern peoples had arranged the details of ecclesiastical finance to suit the convenience of the state. His account of tithes strongly suggested that they were not due to the clergy by divine right—or at least that their *jure divino* status had gone largely unrecognized. Since many English clerics believed that tithes *were* by divine right, there was an outcry against Selden's book, and he was made to keep silent while assaults on it were published by Richard Montagu and other defenders of the church's rights. Much later, Selden returned to attacking clerical pretensions in his *De Synedriis* of 1650–55, a massive work that surveyed church-state relations among the ancient Jews and also had much to say about more recent European and English history. While *The Historie of Tithes* had questioned the divine right foundations of tithes, in *De Synedriis* it was the clergy's claims to the power of excommunication that were at issue. The continuity between the two works was obvious and was spelled out in the latter.[78]

The idea that Selden abandoned his interest in English and European history after the early 1630s has little to commend it. He continued to write on these themes much later—in the dissertation on *Fleta* and the *De Decem Scriptoribus*, and in many passages of his works on Jewish antiquities, including *De Synedriis* and *De Jure Naturali & Gentium, iuxta Disciplinam Ebraeorum* (1640). These last two books are thoroughly historical in approach, and betray little sign that Selden had been converted "to natural law and universalist political theory," as Christianson suggests.[79] Indeed, Pufendorf later commented that the chief shortcoming of *De Jure Naturali & Gentium* was precisely that it confined itself to analyzing "the decisions of a single nation"—the ancient Jews—on natural law, and that this was insufficient to establish "a law that would obligate all nations."[80] Selden believed that the early Christians had been steeped in Jewish attitudes. He held that to understand ancient Christian views on, say, excommunication (a central subject in *De Synedriis*), it was necessary to examine Jewish practices. *De Synedriis* therefore mounted an extremely detailed survey of Jewish judicial institutions, especially the great Sanhedrin (which many clerical authors depicted as an ecclesiastical body, but which Selden portrayed as a secular parliament).

In *De Synedriis,* Selden deployed an essentially historical argument in order to contribute vitally to current political and ecclesiastical debate, asserting that Presbyterians and other clericalists were mistaken to suppose that there were Jewish precedents for the clergy's claims to jurisdiction over the laity. In other works by Selden, the immediate practical applications of the historical argument are also obvious. *The Historie of Tithes* is a case in point. But in a number of his writings, the practical message (if any) is far from clear. One of his first works was a discussion of ancient British history entitled *Analecton Anglo-Britannicon,* which was published in 1615 but written about ten years earlier.[81] He returned to the same theme in the *Jani Anglorum Facies Altera* of 1610. Christianson has detected a defense of mixed monarchy in the latter work, and he also says that it "openly competed" with James I's political views as expressed in his speech of 21 March. But it is extremely difficult to find much about mixed monarchy in it, and there seems to be no evidence that it was intended as a response to the king.

James was extremely interested in replies to his writings, but he seems never to have suspected that Selden had written one. Until Selden was summoned before the king in 1618 for publishing *The Historie of Tithes,* James had never heard of the lawyer. At their meeting, neither Selden nor James betrayed the slightest awareness that the former had already responded to the latter.[82] If Selden had really replied to the king, as Christianson tells us, and if he had offered a political theory that "openly competed" with James's thinking, then it is odd that neither of them noticed. Nor does anyone else appear to have spotted that Selden was attacking the king or that he was defending mixed monarchy. As we saw, Christianson informs us that the 1631 edition of *Titles of Honor* was the crowning glory of Selden's career as a theorist of mixed monarchy. He also observes, however, that "Few either then or since have grasped the firm support for the common law and for English mixed monarchy embedded in the overwhelming detail of its pages."[83] In fact, he names no one at all who recognized that the book was a defense of mixed monarchy, and it is likely that no one at all did so. One of the work's more acute readers was Thomas Hobbes, who refers to it approvingly in *Leviathan,* where he styles it a "most excellent Treatise" on "the originall of Titles of Honour."[84] Hobbes strongly disliked ideas of mixed monarchy, but he was unaware they were being defended in *Titles of Honor,* which he took to be about titles of honor—as its title indeed suggests. After 1640 a number of English writers, including Philip Hunton, gave expression to theories of mixed monarchy, but few of them drew significantly on *Titles of Honor.* Replying to Hunton and others, Sir Robert Filmer castigated their hypotheses, but he passed over Selden in silence. Yet he was well aware of the 1631 edition of Selden's book: in other works he cited it repeatedly to confirm his own absolutist reading of the English constitution.[85]

In England before 1640, many members of the Commons argued that the king could not tax or legislate except with the consent of the two Houses of Parliament. This position could be and commonly was supported by references to Fortescue's *De Laudibus Legum Angliae,* which Selden edited in 1616. Few English writers went much beyond Fortescue's claims in the decades before the Civil War. In *Jani Anglorum Facies Altera* and *Titles of Honor* Selden made a number of comments about ancient and medieval history, but he did not commit himself to Fortescue's account of the constitution, and certainly he added nothing whatever to Fortescue's theory. In 1642 Charles I's "Answer to the Nineteen Propositions" put forward the notion that sovereignty in England was held by king, lords, and Commons in coordination. The "Answer" fueled a fertile debate on mixed government, and writers like Hunton and George Lawson refined the discussion in the 1640s and 50s. Lawson was well-informed about German as well as English debates on mixed states; in fact, in the opening decades of the seventeenth century it was German rather than English thinkers who provided the most subtle and compelling accounts of mixed government. We tend to think of the Holy Roman Empire in around 1600 as an amalgam of sovereign states of various sizes, but Germans commonly regarded it as a monarchy, though admitting that the emperor shared power with territorial princes, free cities, and others. Bodin, they knew, had claimed that sovereignty is absolute and indivisible, but they contended that his theory needed refining, and that mixed constitutions, in which sovereignty was divided, were perfectly feasible. Christoph Besold was an especially prolific and influential theorist of mixed monarchy; in Julian Franklin's words, he provided "a theoretically decisive account of the divisibility of sovereignty in a mixed constitution."[86] Selden seems to have known little of the German debates or of Besold. Besold, on the other hand, was familiar with Selden's *Jani Anglorum* but wholly unaware that it defended mixed monarchy, instead citing it on the drastic changes that William the Conqueror had introduced in England.[87]

So Hobbes, Besold, and all other readers of *Titles of Honor* and *Jani Anglorum* apparently failed to notice that they were defenses of mixed monarchy. How the point came to elude them becomes evident if we turn to the books themselves. *Jani Anglorum* surveys various aspects of ancient and medieval history—for instance, discussing the reliability of Geoffrey of Monmouth (and concluding that he was not reliable), attacking Salic Law and defending the notion that women are capable of governing, and noting that William the Conqueror ended allodial tenures and altered many of the laws of the Anglo-Saxons.[88] The book reads largely like a straightforward account of important aspects of early English history, in which Selden has done his best to come to terms with primary source materials on his subject, giving the reader a balanced and judicious summary of some of the main changes that occurred up to the time of Henry II. While Sir Edward Coke argued that English law had remained largely unaltered since the earliest times, Selden showed that this was not so. Whether and how far it ought to be changed again in the future he did not determine. Selden nowhere referred to works by James, and he said nothing at all to suggest that he had the king's 1610 speech in mind when he wrote. Most of the book is not about constitutional theory. Only toward the end of the volume did Selden say anything that could be interpreted as defending mixed monarchy. There he asserted that laws require lawmakers and also guardians of the law, perhaps aiming a barb at the ancient constitutionalist idea (of Coke and others) that the English common law, being customary, needed no lawmaker—a notion that had recently been attacked by the Jesuit Robert Parsons.[89] Who, asked Selden, had been the lawmaker in times past? He claimed that among the ancient Britons government in each region had been in the hands of an aristocracy, while under the Anglo-Saxons legislation occurred in an assembly of the estates or parliament. Lawmaking, he affirmed, still took place in Parliament, where the three estates met together in harmony to provide for the public weal. Before the Anglo-Saxon period, the guardians of the law were the lawmakers themselves, but afterward they were the king, the high constable, the chancellor, and some other notables. Under the Normans, earls also had some power of lawmaking in their own localities.[90]

Christianson informs us that Selden described government "under the ancient Britons," as "a mixed aristocracy"[91]. Yet according to Richard Tuck, Selden specifically "repudiated" the idea that the ancient British constitution had been a "mixed government" and instead portrayed it as pure aristocracy.[92] Certainly, Selden did not refer to the ancient British government, nor, indeed, to the governments of the Anglo-Saxons and Normans, as mixed. Besold used terms like "mixed state" and "mixed species of commonwealth" frequently, and he asserted that "the first kingdoms that were in the world, were not monarchies, but rather mixed states."[93] Selden does not employ such terminology at all. Of course, it is possible to defend mixed government without referring to it by that name. But Selden combined saying nothing about the name with saying precious little about the thing. True, he argued that laws had been and still were made in Parliament. But nowhere in *Jani Anglorum* did he commit himself to the claim that kings in England *have* to make law in Parliament or that they share sovereignty with the two houses. Moreover, his book made it plain that constitutional arrangements could change in the course of time. Earls under the Normans had possessed some legislative power in their localities, but they did not do so now. Some but not all laws and institutions had been altered after the Norman Conquest. The past record was manifestly not a definitive guide to present practice. The very composition of Parliament had been changed by kings, and Selden related that Henry III had drastically reduced the number entitled to sit there.[94] It is an odd sort of mixed monarchy in which the king's changeable will determines just who is to share power with him. In any case, there is little in *Jani Anglorum* to suggest that Selden thought kings *did* share sovereign power with Parliament. Absolutists like Bodin and Blackwood recommended that the king seek the advice of parliaments and use their deliberations as the basis for lawmaking. Selden says hardly anything to imply that the two houses had more than a deliberative or advisory role in medieval times. If he had a theory of mixed monarchy in 1610, he did not see fit to share it with the readers of *Jani Anglorum.*

In 1614 Selden published the first edition of his *Titles of Honor,* a book about the origins and later history of titles like "duke," "earl," "knight," and so on. While James I and other theorists of divine right monarchy argued that kingship was the first and best form of government, Selden claimed that the primeval form was "a popular State or Democracie," and that it was from democracy that monarchy originated.[95] This notion was certainly compatible with ideas of mixed and limited kingship, and even of legitimate resistance. If democracy was the first form of government, presumably the people had initially been sovereign. Royal power could then easily be construed as derived from the people and granted according to conditions set out in an original contract or fundamental laws, which limited the ruler's power and gave his subjects rights of resistance against him. Selden may have had such views in mind when he described democracy as the original form of government, but he did not spell them out. In 1631 he published a new and greatly revised edition of *Titles of Honor.* During the later 1620s Selden had been an outspoken critic of royal policy, and his activities in connection with the parliamentary session of 1629 led to a spell of imprisonment. Though he was released on bail after a couple of years, it was not until 1635 that the king finally commanded that he be "wholly discharged and set free."[96] So in 1631 he had good reasons for toning down passages in *Titles of Honor* that Charles I or the court were likely to find offensive. The book had in fact been in the press as early as 1621, but it was "staied"—perhaps for political reasons—and clearly he revised it before it was finally published.[97] Yet Christianson tells us that the 1631 edition of the book was the crowning glory of Selden's long quest to provide a complete historical defense of mixed monarchy. This is a striking claim, but not one that is easy to substantiate.

While the first edition of the book asserted that democracies preceded monarchies, the second stressed the antiquity of kingship, countenancing the view that Adam himself had been "the first King and Governour" and affirming that "divers good Autors have without question supposed the Monarchique government, both to have been presently upon the first times, and also that, in the frame of Nature it selfe, Man as a civill Creature was directed to this forme of subiection."[98] So Selden had quietly dropped the idea that kings derive power from the people, instead arguing for a theory of natural and original monarchy reminiscent of his contemporary Sir Robert Filmer. In other respects, too, the second edition of *Titles of Honor* was compatible with Filmer's ideas, and (as we saw) Filmer repeatedly cited it. Christianson tells us that the book talked about "the mixed monarchy of the Anglo-Saxons" and claims that "Selden stressed the centrality of assemblies for judgment and advice, the Micel Synods or Witenagemots of the Anglo-Saxons, the *consilia* or parliaments of the Normans and their successors."[99] But Selden did not portray Anglo-Saxon and later England as a mixed monarchy, in which the king shared sovereignty with the two Houses of Parliament. At one point—many hundreds of pages into the book—he did, indeed, discuss "the *Iurisdiction* that belonged to the dignities of the *Saxon Ealdormen* or *Earles*, and *Thanes*," declaring that when they met in "the greatest Court or Councell"—known as the witenagemote—they had "either . . . a *deliberative power* which concerned their assenting to new Lawes" or a judicial power to try cases in the court. Selden also mentioned that around 711 King Ine of Wessex "made his Lawes" with the consent of the bishops and others.[100] So kings in past times had legislated in public assemblies, allowing their nobles to deliberate on important matters and try lawsuits. This looks like an unsurprising statement of plain historical fact, which absolutists such as Filmer and James I would have been happy to endorse. Filmer had no qualms at all about admitting that kings sought the advice of parliaments from the remotest times: "Against the antiquity of parliaments we need not dispute, since the more ancient they be, the more they make for the honour of monarchy."[101]

Perhaps, though, Selden was saying something rather more contentious than that kings in times past had commonly consulted their subjects on important matters. Perhaps he was arguing for the joint sovereignty of the crown and the two Houses of Parliament. He may well have believed that the king was or should be a mixed and limited monarch. In his parliamentary speeches of the 1620s, he strongly opposed attempts to stretch the royal prerogative, and in the Civil War he sided with Parliament. But in the *Titles of Honor* of 1631 he had little to say about the idea that sovereignty in England was shared by the king and the two houses. In 1629 Charles had dissolved Parliament and imprisoned Selden and other obstreperous members of the Commons. It was far from clear that he would summon Parliament again. The courtier Sir Francis Kynaston argued that the king was fully empowered to govern without Parliament, and that even if he chose to summon it there was no need for him to include the Commons.[102] Sir Robert Filmer held that English subjects had no ancient right to elect representatives to sit in Parliament. He cited Selden's book to confirm his claim.[103] As Christianson himself shows, in *Titles of Honor* Selden says nothing to suggest that kings were bound to summon the people's representatives to meet in the Commons, or that the Commons had anciently been a part of Parliament.[104] What he said is perfectly compatible with the ideas that the king may exclude the Commons if he pleases and that Parliament's powers in legislation are in any case only deliberative or advisory. If this was a theory of mixed monarchy, it was so vague that it was quite acceptable to Charles I and his courtiers. In the later 1630s Selden got on increasingly well with the royal court, befriending the king's leading minister William Laud. In 1637 his book was used by the Irish judges to support an extension of royal rights. Selden's "defence of mixed monarchy," says Christianson, "thereby became a means for extending the power of the Crown in Ireland, the opposite purpose for its creation, thereby turning it into a sort of Frankenstein's monster of learning." But perhaps the judges can be forgiven for failing to notice that the book was a defense of mixed monarchy, since so few other people noticed either. *Titles of Honor* was, as Daniel Woolf says, "a gargantuan piece of work, blazing a trail for later writers such as Burke and Debrett."[105] Like Burke and Debrett it was a useful reference tome, in which England's nobles and gentry might find much material about titles of honor—a subject of great interest to them. And like Burke and Debrett it was a somewhat dull work, more easily dipped into than read whole. Frankenstein's monster makes good popular cinema. *Titles of Honor* would not.

IV

So the thesis that there were two Jameses and two Seldens is unconvincing. A single James ruled in both England and Scotland, and his basic political ideas did not alter much between 1598—when he published the *True Law*—and the end of his reign. After 1603 he did indeed sometimes change the tone of what he said, as he learned to work with and through English institutions. Moreover, whatever he may have hoped, he was not all-powerful, and relied financially on the good will of his subjects. To encourage their generosity, he was quite capable of stressing the kinder and gentler face of royal absolutism, and of emphasizing just how seriously he took his obligation to rule in a law-abiding manner. Yet he never deviated from the fundamental conviction that he alone held sovereignty in England, and if the Commons trenched too far upon his powers, he was liable to assert his sovereignty vigorously, as he did in 1621. Nor did he become a convert from divine right thinking to historical theorizing or "common law discourse." Like most of his contemporaries who wrote on politics, he drew on several kinds of argument, basing claims on scriptural authority, the classics, history, and reason. The rigid distinction between theories grounded on history or the ancient constitution and others centered on abstract universal principles or divine and natural rights is a thoroughly modern, not early modern, one. It dates from the French Revolution, and from British efforts to drive a wedge between such French abstractions as the rights of man and their own conservative and empirical approach to politics. Both history and divine right feature in varying doses in James's writings. Throughout, however, he held that municipal laws were subordinate to divine law, and that God gave free monarchs absolute power to rule their realms.

James never ceased to be a proponent of the divine right of kings. Selden never became one. From his earliest to his latest writings, his approach to scholarship was historical. He described past practices and institutions, attempting to place them in their historical context. In the earlier part of his career he wrote much on English history, while in the later his main concern was with Jewish customs. But it does not do to exaggerate the differences between the early and the late John Selden (perhaps somewhat unfortunately for scholars, since it means they have no good excuse for not reading the massive Latin tomes he produced in his last two decades). In his last major work, *De Synedriis,* he had a good deal to say not just about Judaism but also about early Christianity, the history of church-state relations in France, Spain, and England, and Erastianism in Europe as a whole.[106] In the early *Historie of Tithes* he already displayed interest in Jewish matters. That book used history to cast doubt on divine right claims for tithes, and *De Synedriis* questioned the *jure divino* notions that Presbyterians used to support their ideas on excommunication. In his writings on English secular history, Selden ignored rather than assaulted divine right arguments. He did not attack James's ideas, nor did he assert any very clear theory of mixed monarchy. If we like, we can read doubts about *jure divino* kingship into what he said, but these are expressed only briefly in the 1614 edition of *Titles of Honor* and scarcely mentioned later. In *Table Talk,* published long after his death, Selden trenchantly remarked that "A King is a thing men have made for their owne sakes for quietness sake," and declared that "To know what obedience is due to the prince you must looke into ye contract betwixt him & his people."[107] There is nothing so forthright in his historical writings, nor, indeed, in his works on Judaism. The suppression of *The Historie of Tithes,* and spells of political imprisonment in 1621 and 1629–31, taught Selden the merits of caution. As he put it in *Table Talk,* "The wisest way for men in these times is to say nothing."[108]

Notes

I am very grateful to the Huntington Library, and to the Graduate School of the University of Wisconsin, Madison, for funding that made possible the writing of this essay.

1. E.g. Goldberg 22–3, 24, 117, 265–66.
2. McIlwain, *Political Works* xl; McIlwain, *High Court* 348; Greenleaf 66. Other examples are in Sommerville, *Royalists and Patriots* 227–28 .
3. A fine discussion of Selden's work as a historian is Woolf 200–42.
4. Pufendorf, *De Jure Naturae* v–vi (preface).
5. Barbeyrac's preface to his edition of Pufendorf, *Le Droit de la Nature* 1: lxxviii–ix.
6. Tuck, *Natural Rights* 205–21, and "The 'Modern School of Natural Law.'"
7. Views which are broadly similar to those of Christianson (though they differ in some important respects) are set out in Burgess, *Absolute Monarchy* and *Politics of the Ancient Constitution.* Some criticisms are in Sommerville, "Revisionism Revisited: A Retrospect," in *Royalists and Patriots* 224–65. The main difference between the ideas of Burgess and Christianson on James I is that the former claims that "Neither James VI nor James I ever merited the label 'absolutist'" (Burgess, *Absolute Monarchy* 42), while Christianson, as we shall see, draws a sharp distinction between the absolutist James VI of the *True Law of Free Monarchies* and the constitutionalist James I of 1610 and later.
8. Christianson, "Royal and Parliamentary Voices" 71.
9. Ibid. 72.
10. Ibid. 72–74.
11. Ibid. 74.
12. Ibid. 291 n.16, quoting *True Law.* The relevant passage is in James VI and I, *Political Writings* 74.
13. Christianson, "Royal and Parliamentary Voices" 76, and "Ancient Constitutions" 92.
14. Wormald.
15. Christianson, "Royal and Parliamentary Voices" 76. The quotations from John Cowell are from Cowell sig. 2Q1a, 3A3b.
16. Christianson, "Royal and Parliamentary Voices" 77.
17. Ibid. 76.
18. Ibid. 77.
19. Ibid. passim, esp. 76–77, 94.
20. Ibid. 77, 85.
21. Ibid. 92–3.
22. Ibid. 77. The quotation from James is from the speech of 21 March 1610, in *Political Writings* 183. The biblical text is Genesis 8:22.
23. Christianson, "Royal and Parliamentary Voices" 76.
24. Ibid. 77.

25. Ibid. 292 n.28, 77. James discussed tyranny in *Basilikon Doron,* in *Political Writings* 20–22. The quotation about tyranny from the speech of 21 March 1610 is in *Political Writings* 183.
26. James VI and I, speech of 21 March 1610, in *Political Writings* 184–85.
27. Christianson, "Royal and Parliamentary Voices" 77.
28. Ibid. 72.
29. Christianson, *Discourse on History* 7.
30. Ibid. 9, 11, 17, 30, 285.
31. The context of the king's speech is discussed in Gardiner 2: 63–69.
32. James VI and I, "Candido Lectori," in *Apologia* 4to ed. sig. V5a; 12mo edition, sig. H3a; *Opera* 349. James's *Workes* is dated 1616 on the title page, but of course the year 1616 ran until what we would call 24 March 1617 (since New Year then began on 25 March, though we conventionally date it from 1 January). The indefatigable letter writer John Chamberlain recorded the appearance of James's *Workes* in a letter to Sir Dudley Carleton, London, 8 February 1617 (*Letters of John Chamberlain,* ed. Norman Egbert McClure, 2 vols., Philadelphia: American Philosophical Society, 1939, 2: 51)
33. James VI and I, speech of 21 March 1610, in *Political Writings* 183–84.
34. Christianson, "Royal and Parliamentary Voices" 71.
35. Burns 16.
36. Bossuet 263.
37. Ibid. 83–86. Barclay 72, 370, sig. D1a
38. Arnisaeus 65.
39. James VI and I, *True Law,* in *Political Writings* 75.
40. James VI and I, Speech to Parliament of 18 November 1606, in Huntington Library, Ellesmere mss. 1746, f. 1b.
41. James VI and I, Speech in Star Chamber 1616, in *Political Writings* 209.
42. James VI and I, *True Law,* in *Political Writings* 74.
43. James VI and I, Speech of 21 March 1610, in *Political Writings* 183.
44. Christianson, "Royal and Parliamentary Voices" 292 n.28.
45. Bodin 212; bk. 2, ch. 4.
46. John Pym's speech at a conference between the House of Lords and the House of Commons, 4 June 1628, in Johnson, Keeler, et al. 4: 107.
47. Christianson, "Royal and Parliamentary Voices" 292 n.28.
48. James VI and I, *True Law,* in *Political Writings* 72.
49. Foster 2: 266, 411.
50. James VI and I, Speech of 21 March 1610, in *Political Writings* 184.
51. Foster 2: 104, 105.

52. An important recent article on the ideological and jurisdictional disputes which underlay Coke's dismissal is Fortier. James called Fuller a "villain" in a letter of 1607 to Robert Cecil, earl of Salisbury; *Letters of King James VI & I* 293–95, at 294.
53. James VI and I, Speech in Star Chamber 1616, in *Political Writings* 212, 214.
54. Ibid. 218.
55. Ibid. 213.
56. Ibid. 215.
57. James VI and I, Speech of 21 March 1610, in *Political Writings* 188.
58. Ibid. 191.
59. Foster 2: 103.
60. Ibid. 2: 104.
61. Legg 89–90, xcix–ci.
62. Foster 2: 103.
63. Declaration of 1622, in *Political Writings* 261.
64. James VI and I, Speech of 21 March 1610, in *Political Writings* 180.
65. Sommerville, "James I" 62–63.
66. Warner XV: ix–lxxv, at xlii. Gabriel Naudé, "Adami Blacvodaei Elogium," in Blackwood sig. e4a–b.
67. The similarities between the writings of James and his English supporters on the one hand, and such continental absolutists as Bodin and Blackwood on the other, are discussed in Sommerville, "English and European Political Ideas."
68. James VI and I, "King Iames his verses," in *Poems* 188.
69. James VI and I, qtd. in Jones 155.
70. This line of thinking is discussed in Church.
71. James VI and I, *A Meditation upon the 27. 28. 29. Verses of the XXVII. Chapter of Saint Matthew* (1619), in *Political Writings* 249.
72. Christianson, "Royal and Parliamentary Voices" 86; James VI and I, Speech in Star Chamber 1616, in *Political Writings* 210.
73. James VI and I, Speech in Star Chamber 1616, in *Political Writings* 211–12.
74. James VI and I, *Meditation,* in *Political Writings* 229–49, at 233.
75. Christianson, *Discourse on History,* 9.
76. Selden, "Ad Fletam Dissertatio." The standard modern edition is *Ioannis Seldeni,* ed. Ogg. Christianson, *Discourse on History* 285, misdates the book to 1653 and appears to confuse the medieval text known as *Fleta* with Selden's dissertation on it.
77. Selden, "Ad Lectorem" i–xlviii. Christianson makes no mention of this work.
78. Selden, *De synedriis* 1: 528–29.

79. Christianson, *Discourse on History* 285.
80. Pufendorf, *De Jure Naturae* vi (preface).
81. Selden, Analecton, preface, sig. 4a, is dated "Kal. Februar. Anno. MDCVII." In *De Dis Syris* sig. a6a, Selden describes the *Analecton* as "opus ante duodecem & amplius annos conscriptum": "a work written twelve and more years ago."
82. The meeting is described in Selden, *Vindiciae secundum Integritatem* 18. In ibid. 16, Selden says that James had never even heard his name before then.
83. Christianson, *Discourse on History* 282.
84. Hobbes, 69 (ch. 10, p. 46 in the edn. 1651).
85. Filmer 66, 67, 76, 77, 84.
86. Franklin 328.
87. Besold 23, 30.
88. Selden, *Jani Anglorum* 11–14, 27–30, 61–62.
89. Ibid. 123. Parsons criticized Coke's notion that the English common law was a law without a lawmaker: 12–13, 267.
90. Selden, *Jani Anglorum* 123–27, 132.
91. Christianson, *Discourse on History* 30.
92. Tuck, *Philosophy and Government* 208.
93. Besold 200 ("in mixta Reipublicae specie"), 233 ("Primo quae in Mundo fuerunt Regna, non Monarchiae, sed mixti potius fuerunt Status"), 237 ("Statum mixtum").
94. Selden, *Jani Anglorum* 125–26.
95. Selden, *Titles of Honor* (1614) 4–5.
96. Selden, *Vindiciae secundum Integritatem* 52; Berkowitz 290.
97. Christianson, *Discourse on History* 369 n.28.
98. Selden, *Titles of Honor* (1631) 5.
99. Christianson, *Discourse on History* 228, 245.
100. Selden, *Titles of Honor* (1631) 591, 632.
101. Filmer 53.
102. [Kynaston] 158b, 147b.
103. Filmer 54, 66–67. In 1608 James I had similarly argued that in early times there had been just one house of Parliament: Huntington Library, Ellesmere mss. 1763, 3.
104. Christianson, *Discourse on History* 381 n.184.
105. Woolf 238.
106. Selden, *De synedriis* at, e.g., 1: 185–86, 205, 216–18, 301–2, 352 (the early church); 360–62 (France and Spain); 363–86, 425–28 (England and elsewhere); 429–36, 528–31 (Erastianism).
107. Selden, *Table Talk* 61, 137.
108. Ibid. 92.

Works Cited

Arnisaeus, Henning. *De Jure Majestatis libri tres.* Frankfurt, 1610.

Barclay, William. *De regno et regali potestate.* Paris, 1600.

Berkowitz, David Sandler. *John Selden's Formative Years: Politics and Society in Early Seventeenth-Century England.* Washington, D.C.: Folger Shakespeare Library, 1988.

Besold, Christoph. *Discursus Politici.* Strasbourg, 1623.

Blackwood, Adam. *Opera Omnia.* Ed. Gabriel Naudé. Paris, 1644.

Bodin, Jean. *The Six Bookes of a Commonweale.* Trans. Richard Knolles (1606). Ed. Kenneth Douglas McRae., Cambridge, Mass.: Harvard UP, 1962.

Bossuet, Jacques-Bénigne. *Politics Drawn from the Very Words of Holy Scripture.* Trans. and ed. Patrick Riley., Cambridge: Cambridge UP, 1990.

Burgess, Glenn. *Absolute Monarchy and the Stuart Constitution.* New Haven: Yale UP, 1996.

______. *The Politics of the Ancient Constitution: An Introduction to English Political Thought 1603–1642.* University Park: Pennsylvania State UP, 1992.

Burns, J. H. *Absolutism: The History of an Idea.* The Creighton Trust Lecture. London: U of London P, 1986.

Burns, J. H., and Mark Goldie, eds. *The Cambridge History of Political Thought 1450–1700.* Cambridge: Cambridge UP, 1991.

Christianson, Paul. "Ancient Constitutions in the Age of Sir Edward Coke and John Selden." *The Roots of Liberty: Magna Carta, Ancient Constitution, and the Anglo-American Tradition of Rule of Law.* Ed. Ellis Sandoz. Columbia: U of Missouri P, 1993. 89–146.

______. *Discourse on History, Law, and Governance in the Public Career of John Selden, 1610–1635,* Toronto: U of Toronto P, 1996.

______. "Royal and Parliamentary Voices on the Ancient Constitution c. 1604–1621." *Mental World,* ed. Peck. 71–95.

Church, William F. *Richelieu and Reason of State.* Princeton: Princeton UP, 1972.

"Coram Dno Rege tertio die Novembris 1608." Huntington Library, Ellesmere mss. 1763. [This is a record of a Privy Council meeting in which Coke and James debated royal powers.]

Cowell, John. *The Interpreter: or Booke containing the Signification of Words.* Cambridge 1607.

Filmer, Sir Robert. *Patriarcha and Other Works.* Ed. Johann P. Sommerville. Cambridge: Cambridge UP, 1991.

Fortier, Mark. "Equity and Ideas: Coke, Ellesmere, and James I." *Renaissance Quarterly* 51 (1998): 1255–81.

Foster, Elizabeth Read, ed. *Proceedings in Parliament 1610.* 2 vols. New Haven: Yale UP, 1966.

Franklin, Julian H. "Sovereignty and the Mixed Constitution: Bodin and His Critics." *The Cambridge History of Political Thought 1450–1700.* Ed. J. H. Burns, and Mark Goldie. Cambridge: Cambridge UP, 1991. 298–328.

Gardiner, Samuel Rawson. *History of England from the Accession of James I. to the Outbreak of the Civil War 1603–1642.* 10 vols. London: Longmans, Green, 1883–84.

Goldberg, Jonathan. *James I and the Politics of Literature: Jonson, Shakespeare, Donne, and Their Contemporaries.* Baltimore: Johns Hopkins UP, 1983.

Greenleaf, W. H. *Order, Empiricism and Politics: Two Traditions of English Political Thought 1500–1700.* Oxford: Oxford UP, 1964.

Hobbes, Thomas. *Leviathan.* Ed. Richard Tuck. Cambridge: Cambridge UP, 1991.

James VI and I. *Apologia pro Iuramento Fidelitatis . . . cui praemissa est Praefatio Monitoria,* 1609.

______. "King Iames his verses made vpon à Libell lett fall in Court" (c. 1622–23) in *The Poems of James VI of Scotland,* ed. James Craigie, Scottish Text Society, third series, vols. 22 and 26. Edinburgh, 1955–58. 2:182–91.

______. *Letters of King James VI & I.* Ed. G. P. V. Akrigg. Berkeley: U of California P, 1984.

______. *Opera.* London, 1619.

______. *The Poems of James VI of Scotland.* Ed. James Craigie, Scottish Text Society, third series, vols. 22 and 26. Edinburgh, 1955–58.

______. *The Political Works of James I.* Ed. Charles Howard McIlwain. Cambridge, Mass.: Harvard UP, 1918.

______. *Political Writings.* Ed. Johann P. Sommerville. Cambridge: Cambridge UP, 1994.

______. "The Reporte of his mats. speech in Parliament the xviijth day of November 1606." Huntington Library, Ellesmere mss. 1746, ff. 1a–7a.

Johnson, R. C., M. F. Keeler, et al., eds. *Proceedings in Parliament 1628.* 6 vols. London: Yale UP, 1977–83.

Jones, W. J. *Politics and the Bench.* London: Allen and Unwin, 1971.

[Kynaston, Sir Francis]. "A True Presentation of Forepast Parliaments." B.L. Lansdowne mss. 213, ff. 146a–176b.

Legg, J. Wickham, ed. *The Coronation Order of King James I.* London: F. E. Robinson, 1902.

McIlwain, Charles Howard. *The High Court of Parliament and Its Supremacy.* New Haven: Yale UP, 1910.

______, ed. *The Political Works of James I.* Cambridge, Mass.: Harvard UP, 1918.

Pagden, Anthony, ed. *The Languages of Political Theory in Early Modern Europe.* Cambridge: Cambridge UP, 1987.

Parsons, Robert. *An Answere to the Fifth Part of Reportes lately set forth by Syr Edward Coke.* St. Omer, 1606.

Peck, Linda Levy, ed. *The Mental World of the Jacobean Court.* Cambridge: Cambridge UP, 1991.

Pufendorf, Samuel. *De Jure Naturae et Gentium Libri Octo* (1672; rev. edn. 1688). Trans. C. H. Oldfather and W. A. Oldfather. Oxford: Clarendon P, 1934.

______. *Le Droit de la Nature.* Ed. Jean Barbeyrac. 2 vols. Amsterdam, 1706.

Sandoz, Ellis, ed. *The Roots of Liberty: Magna Carta, Ancient Constitution, and the Anglo-American Tradition of Rule of Law.* Columbia: U of Missouri P, 1993.

Selden, John. "Ad Fletam Dissertatio." *Fleta seu Commentarius Juris Anglicani sic Nuncupatus . . . subjungitur etiam Joannis Seldeni Ad Fletam Dissertatio Historica.* London, 1647. 453–553.

______. "Ad Lectorem, Ioannes Seldenus, De Scriptoribus hisce nunc primum editis." [1652] *Historiae Anglicanae Scriptores X.* Ed. Twysden. i–xlviii.

______. *Analecton Anglo-Britannicon.* Frankfurt, 1615.

______. *De Dis Syris.* London, 1617.

______. *De synedriis & praefecturis iuridicis veterum Ebraeorum.* 3 vols, London, 1650–55.

______. *Ioannis Seldeni Ad Fletam Dissertatio.* Ed. David Ogg. Cambridge: Cambridge UP, 1925.

______. *Jani Anglorum Facies Altera.* London, 1610.

______. *Table Talk of John Selden.* Ed. Sir Frederick Pollock. London: Quaritch, 1927.

______. *Titles of Honor.* London, 1614.

______. *Titles of Honor.* London, 1631.

______. *Vindiciae secundum Integritatem Existimationis suae.* London, 1653.

Sommerville, Johann P. "English and European Political Ideas in the Early-seventeenth Century: Revisionism and the Case of Absolutism." *Journal of British Studies* 35(1996): 168–94.

______. "James I and the Divine Right of Kings: English Politics and Continental Theory." *Mental World,* ed. Peck. 55–70.

______. *Royalists and Patriots: Politics and Ideology in England 1603–1640.* Second ed. London: Longman, 1999.

Tuck, Richard. "The 'Modern School of Natural Law.'" *Languages of Political Theory,* ed. Pagden. Cambridge: Cambridge UP, 1987. 99–122.

______. *Natural Rights Theories: Their Origin and Development.* Cambridge: Cambridge UP, 1979.

______. *Philosophy and Government 1572–1651.* Cambridge: Cambridge UP, 1993.

Twysden, Roger, ed. *Historiae Anglicanae Scriptores X.* London, 1652.

Warner, George F. "The Library of James VI. 1573–1583. From a Manuscript in the Hand of Peter Young, his Tutor." *Miscellany of the Scottish History Society.* vol. 1. Publications of the Scottish History Society. XV: ix–lxxv.

Woolf, D. R. *The Idea of History in Early Stuart England: Erudition, Ideology, and "The Light of Truth" from the Accession of James I to the Civil War.* Toronto: U of Toronto P, 1990.

Wormald, Jenny. "James VI and I: Two Kings or One?" *History* 68 (1983): 187–209.

10

"Precious Stinke": James I's *A Counterblaste to Tobacco*

Sandra J. Bell

In the late sixteenth century, tobacco was introduced, originally for medical purposes, to a receptive English market. In the 1570s, the plant was regularly imported, but there was also some domestic cultivation in English herbal gardens, and London had already become a center of clay pipe manufacturing. Tobacco's popularity quickly increased, expanding from medicinal to social uses, and creating a burgeoning London trade. Import and export documents record the spectacular rise in consumption of the plant: in 1603, England imported approximately 25,000 pounds of tobacco; by 1628, this had risen to 370,000 pounds, and by 1700 it reached 38 million pounds.[1] These numbers do not include the tobacco regularly smuggled into the country: in *The Honestie of this Age* (1614), Barnaby Rich claimed there were "vpward of 7 000 houses" in London selling tobacco, including many that had "no other trade to liue by."[2] In 1618, Horatio Busino recorded that tobacco was "in such frequent use that not only at every hour of the day but even at night they keep the pipe and steel at their pillows and gratify their longings. . . . So much money is expended daily in this nastiness that at the present moment the trade in tobacco amounts to half a million in gold, and the duty on it alone yields the king 40 000 golden crowns yearly."[3] Despite the often prohibitive cost,[4] English consumers smoked as much tobacco as they could import, and grew increasing amounts at home. Literary references to tobacco proliferated after the 1590s, and a number of prose tracts and poems made it their primary focus. Many authors praised tobacco's medicinal and social properties, but not all were convinced of the benefits of this New World plant. In 1604, shortly after his accession to the English throne, James I entered the controversy over tobacco with a short prose tract entitled *A Counterblaste to Tobacco*.[5]

A Counterblaste to Tobacco was, outside of political speeches, the first of James's writings directed toward his English subjects. It was originally published anonymously, although the prefatory letter "To the Reader" clearly identifies its author. James develops three arguments here. He begins by reminding his readers of tobacco's association with the barbarous inhabitants of the New World and with the Spanish, who early on maintained the monopoly on the favored variety of leaf; the king argues that English civility is undermined through reverse colonization and dependence on the Spanish. Fully half of the *Counterblaste* is dedicated to refuting tobacco's alleged medicinal value. Medical arguments lead to a discussion of the "sinnes and vanities" (96) of tobacco use; the English are "raking" the "markes and notes of vanitie" (99) upon their bodies, with the result that individual bodies are weakened and unable to fulfill their duties to crown and country. James emphasizes the cumulative harm of tobacco, from diseases of the physical body to corruption of the body politic. He also argues against the common contemporary representation of tobacco as omnipotent and even divine—such representations are suitable for the monarchy, he argues, but not for a foreign plant. Each succeeding argument reinforces his portrayal of tobacco as a threat to English civilization, not least in its insidious mimicry of sovereign power.

James's desire to create a vision of himself as a strong and authoritative figure, knowledgeable about English customs, and ready to defend his new realm and his own role within it, is not uncharacteristic, especially at the beginning of his new reign. His earlier political tracts—*Basilikon Doron* and *The True Law of Free Monarchies,* republished in 1603—outline his belief in a strong, unquestioned monarchy, and his understanding of his own and his subjects' responsibilities. This vision is reaffirmed in the *Counterblaste.* His early political speeches acknowledge and attempt to calm English fears of a foreign ruler, and the *Counterblaste* is careful to present James as a supporter of English customs and civilization, and a defender of England against foreign invasion. Appearing in 1604, the *Counterblaste* participates in many of the rhetorical and political strategies characteristic of James's early reign, all of which are calculated to consolidate his position and dispel the fears of the English.

"To the Reader"

James's prefatory letter introduces the paradoxical nature of tobacco. On the one hand, the weed is among those "base and contemptible" matters "too low for the Law to looke on, and too meane for a King to interpone his authoritie, or bend his eye vpon" (85); tobacco is such a "light argument," a mere "trifle," that James feels the need to apologize for writing the pamphlet: "If any thinke it a light Argument, so is it but a toy that is bestowed vpon it. And since the Subiect is but of Smoke, I think the fume of an idle braine, may serue for a sufficient battery against so fumous and feeble an enemy" (85). This *humilitas* topos, in which an apparently self-deprecatory James claims for himself an "idle braine," might lead to the dismissal of the *Counterblaste* as itself idle or trifling. The Latin translation of James's *Opera* of 1619, which gives the author of the *Counterblaste* as *Lusus Regius,* seems to support this view.[6] However, James's pamphlet then undermines the claim of triviality by asserting that even apparently small or base corruptions can have serious consequences that might demand the attention of the perspicacious monarch:

> Our Peace hath bred wealth: And Peace and wealth hath brought foorth a generall sluggishnesse, which makes vs wallow in all sorts of idle delights, and soft delicacies, the first seedes of the subversion of all great Monarchies. . . . My onely care is that you, my dear Countrey-men, may rightly conceiue euen by this smallest trifle, of the sinceritie of my meaning in greater matters, neuer to spare any paine, that may tend to the procuring of your weale and prosperitie. (85–86)

As a powerful and responsible ruler, the king will take note of every action and object in his commonwealth, from great matters to the "smallest trifles" of daily life. Similarly, in *Basilikon Doron,* James advises Henry to "know all crafts; for except ye know every one, how can ye control every one, which is your proper office."[7] As historian Jenny Wormald stresses, the king's interest in the details of his subjects' lives was central to his mode of government in Scotland,[8] and the *Counterblaste* indicates that he will continue this method with his English subjects. However, in order to assert the negative aspects of the "fumous and feeble" enemy, the king is placed in the awkward position of admitting the strength of tobacco's threat.

The *Counterblaste* also follows James's tradition of approaching statecraft indirectly, through more peripheral subject matter. In Scotland, at a young age, the king entered politics through poetry, a pastime relegated in *Basilikon Doron* to a section entitled "Of A King's Behaviour in Indifferent Things." In 1584, the year James took personal control of his Scottish reign, he published his first collection of poetry, *The Essayes of a Prentise in the Divine Art of Poesie,* a work dedicated simultaneously to redirecting the course of Scottish poetry and to establishing the authority of the king. In both countries, James announced his sovereignty through textual means, and through seemingly "indifferent" or "trifling" subject matter.[9]

James clearly states in the preface to the *Counterblaste* that the growing popularity of tobacco is a serious concern of national importance. Peace and wealth, he declares, have led to self-indulgence, and "all sorts of people [are] more carefull for their priuat ends, then for their mother the Common-wealth" (84). The clergy, the nobility, lawyers, the common people, all have become "negligent" and "prodigal," and it is up to the monarch to reinstate order and instill a sense of the subjects' duty: "For remedie whereof, it is the Kings part (as the proper Phisician of his Politicke-body) to purge it of all those diseases, by Medicines meete for the same: as by a certaine milde, and yet iust forme of gouernment, to maintaine the Publicke quietnesse, and preuent all occasions of Commotion: by the example of his owne Person and Court, to make vs all ashamed of our sluggish delicacie, and to stirre vs vp to the practice of all honest exercises"(85). The medical metaphor permits James to examine not only the individual, physical bodies of his subjects, but also the greater concern of the health of the body politic, and the role of good government in curing these individual and collective ills. Like his *Basilikon Doron* and *The True Law of Free Monarchies,* the *Counterblaste* is another example—if through a more indirect route and on a minor scale—of the king's desire to assert control and authority in his new kingdom.

"Base Corruption and Barbarity"

James begins his tract by outlining the "foolish and groundless first entry" (88) of tobacco into England: by undermining its source and primary associations, the king hopes to weaken tobacco's hold on his subjects:

> [Tobacco] was first found out by some of the barbarous *Indians,* to be a Preseruative, or Antidot aganst the Pockes, a filthy disease, whereunto these barbarous people are (as all men know) very much subiect. . . . [S]o that as from them was first brought into Christendome, that most detestable disease, so from them likewise was brought this vse of *Tobacco,* as a stinking and vnsavourie Antidot, for so corrupted and execrable a Maladie, the stinking Suffumigation whereof they yet vse against that disease, making so one canker or venime to eate out another. (87–88)

Despite the fact that tobacco is named an antidote here, the emphasis of the association is on the barbarity of the native American Indians and the base corruption of venereal diseases. The alliance of tobacco with the pox should, James states, make people "loath to haue taken so farre the imputation of that disease vpon them as they did" (89). In an ironic comment later in the *Counterblaste,* James states that "[a]s for curing of the Pockes, it [tobacco] serues for that vse but among the pockie Indian slaues. Here in England it is refined, and will not deigne to cure heere any other then cleanly and gentlemanly diseases" (95). The connection of tobacco with venereal diseases and "pockie Indian slaues" (95) is meant to undermine tobacco's authority. James needs to deny tobacco's ability to cure such ailments in order to maintain his own role as "Phisician" of his commonwealth, both literally—as a mysterious, divine healer of diseases through the cure of the king's touch—and metaphorically—as an example of good government. Awkwardly, James must then reassert his own connections to disease—as "Phisician"—and both admit to and deny tobacco's curative powers, in order to reaffirm the plant's barbarous associations.

The demonization of native American Indians in many New World exploration pamphlets provided James with the material further to assert English civility against New World barbarity.

> Shall wee, I say, that haue bene so long ciuill and wealthy in Peace, famous and inuincible in Warre, fortunate in both, we that haue bene euer able to aide any of our neighbours (but neuer deafed any of their eares with any of our supplications for assistance) shall we, I say, without blushing, abase our selues so farre, as to imitate these beastly *Indians,* slaues to the *Spaniards,* refuse to the world, and as yet aliens from the holy Couenant of God? Why doe we not as well imitate them in walking naked as they doe? in preferring glasses, feathers, and such toyes, to golde and precious stones, as they do? yea why do we not denie God and adore the Deuill as they doe? (88)[10]

The voluntary addiction to such a "sauage custom" (88) would result, James implies, in a reverse colonization, the Americanizing—the "Indianizing"—of the English through tobacco use. Instead of the English traveling to the New World to civilize the inhabitants there, the New World, in the form of tobacco, was traveling to England to debase English customs, to undermine English self-sufficiency and, James suggests, to threaten religious faith.[11]

The king's concern is not only the Americanization of England. He is likewise concerned with England's position in relation to Spain, which had laid claim to most of the land where tobacco was produced. James declares the Spanish king is "comparable in largenes of Dominions, to the great Emperor of *Turkie*" (88).[12] Despite the increasing production of tobacco in English colonies such as Virginia, English smokers continued to favor the Spanish leaf. Rather than gaining riches through their new colonies, James argues that the English are paying gold and silver to Spain in return for so much smoke. Tobacco thus represented a threat to England from both the New World and the Old. Perhaps in 1604, the year of an Anglo-Spanish truce, it was important for James to include a denunciation of the Spanish; there were worries in England, as there had been in Scotland, that the king harbored Catholic sympathies. It is fitting, then, that James uses his tract to clarify his own position against the Spanish, while at the same time admonishing the English for their increasing reliance on Spanish imports.

James also cunningly associates tobacco's entrance into England with Sir Walter Ralegh, out of favor and imprisoned in the Tower in 1604: "It was neither brought in by King, great Conquerour, nor learned Doctor of Phisicke . . . it seemes a miracle to me, how a custome springing from so vile a ground, and brought in by a father so generally hated, should be welcomed vpon so slender a warrant" (88–89).[13] Ralegh was not the first to introduce tobacco into the country, though he was an avid smoker and tobacco was imported by those who voyaged to the New World under his patronage. Thomas Harriot, who accompanied English colonists to Roanoke Island in 1585, refers to tobacco's importation into England in his *A Brief and True Report of Newfound Land of Virginia* (1599).[14] Ralegh's treachery had little directly to do with tobacco, but James connected the two to emphasize the treasonable nature of both. As Henry Buttes states in *Dyets Dry Dinner,* "Our English Vlisses, renomed Syr Walter Rawleigh . . . hath both farre fetcht it, and deare bought it."[15]

In the *Counterblaste*'s opening salvo, then, James associates tobacco with threats to the self-sufficiency and strength of England. The English—"ciuill and wealthy in Peace, famous and inuincible in Warre," who have never "deafed" their neighbors' ears "with any of our supplications for assistance"—are becoming too reliant on this American weed, a weed used by the diseased, barbarous, godless Indians, imported by the increasingly powerful Spanish, and associated with traitors at home.

"Profitable Physicke"

When James wrote *A Counterblaste to Tobacco,* he contributed to a growing literature about this New World plant. Early allusions to tobacco began with the earliest voyages to the New World, and the practices of smoking, snuffing, and chewing tobacco had all been noted by the close of the sixteenth century.[16] For the aboriginal peoples of what would become South, Central, and North America, tobacco played an important part in many ceremonial and spiritual practices, but its medical uses assured tobacco's popularity in Europe.

Tobacco's ready acceptance in England was fostered by overwhelming praise from the European medical community, which saw tobacco as a wondrous new drug able to cure almost every affliction. While many early herbals and travel writings mention tobacco's virtues, the most popular handbook on the medical use of tobacco was Nicolas Monardes's *Secunda parte del libro* (Seville, 1571), translated into English by John Frampton in 1577 with the title *Joyfull Newes out of the Newe Founde Worlde.* This book became essential reading for English physicians and lay people; it gives descriptions of plants "brought from our Occidentall INDIAS," advice for growing tobacco, and explanations of its properties and virtues. The marginal notes to Monardes's text give some idea of the exhaustive list of ailments readily cured by tobacco: "paines of the head; any grief of the body; griefes of the Brest; griefe of the stomacke; grief of the stone; griefes of the windes; euill of the Mother; euill breath; Wormes; euil of the Ioyntes; colde swellinges; toth ache; Chilblaines; Venom & venemous woundes; old sores; rotten and cankered woundes."[17] The tobacco leaf was warmed and applied to the body; its juice was employed, either pure or as part of a syrup, internally and externally; it was mixed with other herbs; and the smoke was either wafted over the body or inhaled. As Anthony Chute states in his *Tabaco* (1595), "I thinke that there is nothing that harmes a man inwardly from his girdle vpward, but may be taken away with a moderate vse of *Tabacco.*"[18] Cures for ailments from the girdle downwards, and for all manner of external sores, were also documented. Tobacco was also considered advantageous in the treatment of diseases of the mind, especially melancholy. There seemed no end to the possibilities of this new panacea.

The apparent omnipotency of tobacco is a principal reason James needs to counter its increasing popularity. The king claims it is his prerogative, not tobacco's, to act as "Phisician" for both English bodies and the body politic. As he did in his references to the pox, James again attempts to connect tobacco to the disease rather than the remedy, leaving him the monarch's traditional role as adviser on and healer of the country's ills.

James spends a large section of the *Counterblaste* countering the medical claims of tobacco's efficacy. Tobacco had been readily accepted into European medical practice because it fit easily into the Galenic theory of the four humors or complexions.[19] Tobacco, while providing comfort and a cure for most complaints, was especially popular with such prevalent illnesses as the rheum: the hot and dry properties of tobacco provided a "contrarie application" to the rheum's excessive wetness and cold. Basing his own arguments likewise on the four humors, James decries the universal application of contraries as a means to better health, here as a cure to the rheum:

> euen as the smoakie vapours sucked vp by the Sunne, and staied in the lowest and colde Region of the ayre, are there contracted into cloudes and turned into raine and such other watery Meteors: So this stinking smoake being sucked vp by the Nose, and imprisoned in the colde and moyst braines, is by their colde and wett facultie, turned and cast foorth againe in waterie distillations, and so are you made free and purged of nothing, but that you wilfully burdened your selues: and therefore are you no wiser in taking *Tobacco* for purging you of distillations, then if for preuenting the Cholicke you would take all kinde of windie meates and drinkes,

> and for preuenting of the Stone, you would breede grauell in the Kidneyes. (91–92)

James shows his knowledge of current medical practices while mocking the universal application of such practices, and he yet again associates tobacco with the illness rather than the cure.

Tobacco's claims to omnipotency and sovereignty are a threat to similar claims made by the monarchy, and both use the rhetoric of paradox. James's self-sustaining contradictory discourse has been explored by Jonathan Goldberg, who notes that contradictions "are essential to the discourse of power."[20] The king simultaneously presented himself as both open and available, mysterious and unknowable. Yet in the *Counterblaste,* he continually attempts to undermine tobacco's tendency to ambiguity, to paradox; it is just such a paradoxical nature—or the ability to defy paradox—that James mocks in his description of tobacco's curative properties:

> such is the miraculous omnipotencie of our strong tasted Tobacco, as it cures all sorts of diseases (which neuer any drugge could do before) in all persons, and at all times. . . . It cures the Gowt in the feet, and (which is miraculous) in that very instant when the smoke thereof, as light, flies vp into the head, the vertue thereof, as heauie, runs downe to the little toe. . . . It refreshes a weary man, and yet makes a man hungry. Being taken when they goe to bed, it makes one sleepe soundly, and yet being taken when a man is sleepie and drowsie, it will, as they say, awake his braine, and quicken his vnderstanding. . . . O omnipotent power of Tobacco! (94–95)

James claims that such a paradoxical nature is logically impossible, but the king's own representation of monarchy relies on just such an ability to be all things to all people.[21]

"Sinnes and Vanities"

As tobacco became more available and familiar, the English turned from purely medicinal uses of the drug to social uses. James describes tobacco's infiltration into English customs as a debasement of civility and hospitality: "[I]s it not a great vanitie, that a man cannot heartily welcome his friend now, but straight they must bee in hand with *Tobacco*? No it is become in place of a cure, a point of good fellowship, and he that will refuse to take a pipe of *Tobacco* among his fellowes, (though by his owne election he would rather feele the sauour of a Sinke) is accounted peeuish and no good company" (98).[22] Tobacco use infiltrated traditional English customs with foreign elements, as James warns with his reminder of tobacco's uncivilized origins and connections with Spain. In 1604, however, the Spanish were not the only foreigners England feared. On his arrival in England, James had to allay apprehensions that there would be an invasion of barbarous Scots into positions of government; he assured his new subjects that he wished to uphold English customs and laws, and that any changes would be made by the Scots. In *Basilikon Doron,* James advises changing certain Scottish practices of "sheriffdoms" and "regalities" to conform with English practices—he urges his son Henry to "draw [them] to the laudable custom of England, which ye may the easilier do being king of both, as I hope in God ye shall" (126). His early speeches likewise clearly advocate English supremacy. A speech of 1607 outlines his preferences: "you here haue all the great aduantage by the Vnion. . . . Is not here the seate of Iustice, and the fountaine of Gouernment? must they not be subiected to the Lawes of England?"[23] Having reaffirmed English civility at the cost of the Scottish, James is, in the *Counterblaste,* determined to uphold English superiority, and he redirects the fear of a foreign, barbarous invasion from the Scots onto tobacco. He also counters denunciations of Scottish incivility with a number of examples that point to the coarse and debauched state of English conduct. The sin of tobacco taking even ensures the survival of other, more traditional English sins: "yet can you neither be merry at an Ordinarie, nor lasciuious in the Stewes, if you lacke Tobacco to prouoke your appetite to any of those sorts of recreation" (96). James is able simultaneously to uphold English traditions and incriminate the English in their corruption.

The changes to English customs also reached into domestic practices and structures. The English table, "a place of respect, of cleanliness, of modestie" (98), is represented as being choked by smoke, and the husband is not ashamed "to reduce thereby his delicate, wholesome, and cleane complexioned wife, to that extremitie, that either shee must also corrupt her sweete breathe therewith, or else resolue to liue in a perpetuall stinking torment" (98–99). The wife also forgets her proper offices: "the Mistresse cannot in a more manerly kinde, entertaine her seruant, then by giuing him out of her faire hand a pipe of Tobacco" (98). Tobacco's connection with the low and unlawful—being "merry at an Ordinarie" or "lasciuious in the Stewes"—also implies an element of impropriety in the mistress's "entertainment" of her servant. Tobacco's association with the overturning of decorum threatens the relationships of husband and wife and master and servant—fundamental social structures whose stability and integrity are barometers of the health of the larger body politic, whose stability James is pledged to protect.

Connecting tobacco to debauched behavior or the lower classes in order to emphasize the corruption of decorum and civility is a method James also used in a letter he wrote in 1604 to the high treasurer, Thomas, earl of Dorset, in which the king comments on the "nomber of ryotous and disordered Persons of meane and base Condition, whoe, contrarie to the use which Persons of good Callinge and Qualitye make thereof, doe spend most of there time in that idle Vanitie [tobacco smoking], to the evill example and corrupting of others, and also do consume that Wages whiche manye of them gett by theire Labour, and wherewith there Families should be relieved" (qtd. in Brooks 1: 406–7).[24] James here compares these "meane and base" individuals to "the better sort," who "have and will use the same [tobacco] with Moderation to preserve their Healthe."[25] The letter's differentiation between the "meaner" and "better" sorts is not upheld in the *Counterblaste,* where people of all classes are admonished for taking tobacco.[26] The *Counterblaste* therefore further stresses the corruptive and disruptive nature of tobacco, a substance that confuses hierarchical relationships between husbands and wives and masters and servants. It is also a threat, James argues, to the stability of the relationship between subjects and their king and country.

Though James does not use the term addiction, he does comment on the way tobacco has become not simply a fashion, to take on and put aside, but a necessity that changes the very nature of English customs and bodies. So many "haue had such a continuall vse of taking this vnsauorie smoke" that they "are not able to forbeare the same, no more than an olde drunkard can abide to be long sober, without falling into an vncurable weakenesse and euill constitution: for their continuall custome hath made to them, *habitum, alteram naturam*" (95–96).[27] Through habitual use, tobacco insinuates itself into the very nature of the English, and this addiction then requires an unending supply of tobacco. While James begins his pamphlet condemning the object of desire, tobacco, he turns in this final segment to reprimand those who desire.

In this section of the *Counterblaste,* the king is concerned to point out not just the vanities of smoking, but the very real threats of tobacco addiction to the national security of England: "[I]s it not the greatest sinne of all, that you the people of all sortes of this Kingdome, who are created and ordeined by God to bestowe both your persons and goods for the maintenance both of the honour and safetie of your King and Common-wealth, should disable your selues in both . . . having by this continuall vile custome brought your selues to this shamefull imbecilitie?" (96). Duty to the crown and country, here as in other writings, is James's central concern. The analysis of the effect of tobacco on the individual subject—whether it be his or her physical, spiritual, or moral state—is also a discussion of the subject's loyalty to the monarch and the commonwealth. Subjects must be willing to bestow their "persons" for the safety of their king and country, but James claims that an addiction to tobacco makes his subjects unfit to serve as soldiers:

> [H]e cannot be thought able for any seruice in the warres, that cannot endure oftentimes the want of meate, drinke, and sleepe, much more then must he endure the want of *Tobacco.*[28] In the times of

> the many glorious and victorious battailes fought by this Nation, there was no word of *Tobacco:* but now if it were time of warres, and that you were to make some sudden *Caualcado* vpon your enemies, if any of you should seeke leisure to stay behinde his fellowe for taking of *Tobacco,* for my part I should neuer bee sorie for any euill chance that might befall him. (97)[29]

James earlier characterizes habits such as tobacco taking as "idle delights" and "soft delicacies" (84), the "childish affectation[s] of Noueltie" (87); here he claims such "mollicies and delicacie were the wracke and ouerthrow, first of the Persian, and next of the Roman empire" (97), and that they are slowly dissipating the strength of individual bodies and the English body politic. The martial English body is weakened, even feminized and infantilized, and thus unable to fulfill its duties to the crown and commonwealth.

The second point of James's final argument is that subjects must be willing and able to donate not only their persons but also their "goods" to the national cause. Too many, however, are wasting money on tobacco: "disabled in their goods" as well as their bodies, some of the gentry "bestow[] three, some foure hundred pounds a yeere vpon this precious stinke, which I am sure might be bestowed vpon farre better vses" (97). Money meant for English coffers is given to Spain for a substance that does little good and much harm. The desire for tobacco is represented as an economic as well as a physical, moral, and spiritual drain on the country.

The *Counterblaste* is neither simply a satirical jab at fashions nor a minor foray into medicine by a pedantic king. Throughout the *Counterblaste,* James associates tobacco with the decay of English customs, civility, religion, and national pride, and with the acceptance of foreign and dangerous vanities. The result of using tobacco is a people unable and unwilling to fulfill their duties to their king and country. The high moral tone of the *Counterblaste*'s final passage rings with righteous hyperbole, revealing James's acute awareness of tobacco's temptations:

> Haue you not reason then to bee ashamed, and to forbeare this filthie noueltie, so basely grounded, so foolishly receiued and so grossely mistaken in the right vse thereof? In your abuse thereof sinning against God, harming your selues both in persons and goods, and raking[30] also thereby the markes and notes of vanitie vpon you: by the custome thereof making your selues to be wondered at by all forraine ciuill Nations, and by all strangers that come among you, to be scorned and contemned. A custome lothsome to

> the eye, hatefull to the Nose, harmefull to the braine, dangerous to the Lungs, and in the blacke stinking fume thereof, neerest resembling the horrible Stigian smoke of the pit that is bottomlesse. (99)

By "raking" the "markes and notes of vanitie" upon their bodies, the English not only harm themselves: they reveal the weaknesses in the king's authority. Sickly, unsound subjects are unable to contribute either their "persons" or their "goods" to uphold the commonwealth, and their physical condition announces their refusal of the king's command.

"The Force of Perswasion"

James ends the preface to the *Counterblaste* with a statement of hope and doubt: "If my grounds be found true, it is all I looke for: but if they cary the force of perswasion with them, it is all I can wish, and more then I can expect" (85). The king understands the addictive character of tobacco, but he also understands the influence exerted by royal authority and royal rhetoric. Certainly many of his subjects were willing to agree with James's criticisms of tobacco, not because of their truth or persuasiveness, but because he was king.[31] In August 1605, for example, when James visited Oxford University, he was entertained with a debate on tobacco and health. The respondent was Sir William Paddy, physician to the king (and a tobacco addict), and not surprisingly the decision accorded with the well-known beliefs of James.[32] The *Counterblaste* also persuaded other writers to take up the king's cause. Samuel Daniel, poet and writer of court masques, includes a passage ridiculing tobacco in *The Queenes Arcadia*, a masque performed during the royal visit to Oxford.[33] In *Faultes faults, and nothing else but faultes* (1606), Barnaby Rich echoed the content and tone of the *Counterblaste* to deride tobacco's claims to omnipotence: "O Soueraigne *Tobacco!* that art a medicine for euery malady, a salue for euery sore. . . . [T]hey say it will make a leane man fatte, and a fatte man leane. But I know it hath made many wise men to become fooles, and it hath made some fooles again to become wise men. It cannot be denied, but it makes men sociable, and he that can but take a *Pipe of Tobacco,* drink *Bottle Ale,* and play a game at *Noddie,* is a companion for a knight."[34]

James's pamphlet certainly motivated anti-tobacco literature early in his government, when many had hopes of patronage from the new king, and the *Counterblaste*'s influence continued throughout James's reign. Rich, detailing the many excesses of London in *The Honestie of This Age* (1614), belittles tobacco's preventative powers with references that echo the king's tract: "I cannot see but that those that doe take it fastest, are as much (or more) subiect to all these infirmities, (yea and to the poxe it selfe) as those that haue nothing at all to doe with it."[35] During the king's visit to Cambridge in 1614–15, students were warned that "noe Graduate, Scholler, or Student of this Universitie presume to resort to any Inn, Tavern, Alehouse, or *Tobacco-Shop* at any tyme dureing the aboade of his Maiestie here; nor doe presume *to take tobacco in St. Marie's Church* or Trinity Colledge Hall, uppon payne of finall expellinge the Universitie" (Nichols 3: 44). Ben Jonson had mocked tobacco takers in his plays even before the publication of the king's pamphlet, but as his much later masque *The Gypsies Metamorphosed* (1621) shows, writers persevered in playing to the king's dislike of tobacco.[36] The pamphlet continued to influence writers after the king's death: the anti-tobacco movement was supported by subsequent rulers—including Oliver Cromwell—who were concerned with the overwhelming popularity of tobacco, and in 1672 the *Counterblaste* was reprinted as the first piece in a collection of anti-tobacco writings entitled *King James His Counterblaste to Tobacco.*[37]

Despite James's condemnation and the support for his medical, moral, and political arguments, tobacco was still defended by many writers, and its medical and social use grew apace through the seventeenth century. During James's reign, the colonies in Virginia and Maryland supplied increasing amounts of the leaf, but England's overwhelming consumption meant that Spanish tobacco was still in demand. Faced with this burgeoning market, and the pressure from both users and growers, the king found he could not politically enforce the *Counterblaste*'s condemnation. The demand was not just unstoppable: it grew at an alarming rate. If, in the end, James could not control the demand for tobacco, he attempted to control the supply by prohibiting domestic production, and regulating and taxing imports.[38] Tobacco became essential to the establishment and growth of the new colonies, however, and brought increasing revenue to the crown.[39] The king's actions appear hypocritical, for he became more and more dependent on the money made from the very substance he condemned, but there was no way that he, or subsequent rulers, could suppress the tobacco trade completely.

Entering his new kingdom in 1603, James was eager to present himself as a concerned and dutiful monarch, and he used his writings to build and sustain this image. Newly arrived from a country so often reviled by the English as uncivilized and crude, James wished to stress his own civility. His political tracts reveal an expertise gained from thirty-six years of rule in Scotland, and his poems indicate an artistic and cultural interest and sophistication. The *Counterblaste* allowed him not only to show his knowledge of contemporary medical theory and practice, but to transfer suspicions about Scottish barbarity onto the foreign tobacco, and to show himself a strong proponent of English culture and civilization. Certainly the *Counterblaste* permitted him to praise England as a strong and peaceful nation, but here he also suggests the barbaric potential of the English, whom he characterizes as in need of the strong guidance he could provide.[40] The Scots import, however, could not compete with the New World's. If subsequent medical studies have shown James's arguments to have some truth to them, they nevertheless have not carried the "force of perswasion" with them—not in the twentieth century, and certainly not in the seventeenth.

Notes

1. See Gray and Wyckoff. These numbers are also mentioned in Knapp 134, and Goodman 59. Information on the clay pipe trade is from Goodman 64. The approximate date of 1570 is supported by Brooks, whose volumes are an extensive source for early tobacco literature. See also Dickson passim for discussion of some of the texts in Arents's collection, and 131–32 for further confirmation of the 1570 estimate.
2. *STC* 20986: 26. "There is not so base a groome, that commes into an *Alehouse* to call for his pot, but he must haue his pipe of *Tobacco,* for it is a commoditie that is nowe as vendible in euery Tauerne, Inne, and *Alehouse,* as eyther Wine, Ale, or Beare, & for *Apothocaries Shops, Grosers Shops, Chaundlers Shops,* they are (almost) neuer without company, that from morning till night are still taking of Tobacco" (25–26).
3. *Calendar of State Papers, Venice,* vol. 15 (1617–19): 101.
4. Costs fluctuated depending on quality, supply, and taxation: "in 1597, a pound cost 35 shillings; in 1599 the finest kind commanded the almost incredibly high price of £ 4/10. . . . Sixteen shillings was demanded . . . in 1600, and 33 shillings in 1603" (Brooks 1: 84).
5. *A Counterblaste to Tobacco,* in *Minor Prose Works of King James VI and I,* ed. James Craigie (Edinburgh: Scottish Text Society, 1982).
6. Craigie asserts that the Latin tag "could hardly have been done by the editor of the volume, Bishop Montague, who was also Dean of the Chapel Royal, without his royal patron's knowledge and consent" (209). Craigie's statement that "James was in deadly earnest when he penned *A Counterblaste to Tobacco* and . . . any humour that there may be in it is ironical, not real" is arguable. Many of James's works reveal a satirical wit.
7. *The True Law* 146.
8. Wormald: "As in the state, so in the church the key to royal success was personal intervention by a king who stepped down from his throne and joined in as one of the protagonists in the hurly-burly of debate" (197).
9. For a more detailed examination of the connection of James's first published collection of poetry in 1584 (which included a treatise on Scottish poetry) to his politics, see my "Kingcraft and Poetry: James

VI's Cultural Policy," in *Reading Monarchs Writing: The Poetry of Henry VIII, Mary, Queen of Scots, Elizabeth I, and James VI/I*, ed. Peter Herman (forthcoming). Helena Mennie Shire calls James's poetic treatise "the manifesto of the new poetry of Renaissance Scotland" (98). Gregory Kratzmann agrees the treatise is "written as part of a programme aimed at the establishment of a poetic Renaissance" (1: 105).

10. Knapp argues that the English do prefer "toyes" over gold and jewels, as evidenced in their willingness to pay substantial sums for insubstantial smoke (10).
11. The relationship of Indians to God becomes somewhat contradictory in this passage, as Indians are either heathen savages, not knowing God, or devil-worshipers. The relationship between the church and tobacco grew more and more complicated. In 1642, Urban VIII issued a papal interdiction against tobacco use in the church: "'Even during the mass they defile the doorways with tobacco juice'" (qtd. in Brooks 1: 79–80). Tobacco became so woven into the fabric of life in the New World colonies that its leaf was often used as a form of legal tender, and in 1639–40, the clergy were paid "'ten pounds of tobacco per poll for every titheable person'" in their parishes (qtd. in Brooks, 1: 104).
12. This echoes the anxiety about the Turks manifested in the king's poem *The Lepanto* (1591), although the threat of Roman Catholicism presented by Spain in the *Counterblaste* did not stop James from praising Don Juan of Austria, leader of the Catholic forces against the Turks at the battle of Lepanto. See my "Writing the Monarch."
13. Both Craigie and Knapp understand "the father generally hated" to mean Ralegh. Certainly Ralegh was a well-known proponent of tobacco; he apparently cured his own tobacco in the Tower (Dickson 3: 99), and smoked just before his execution to "'settle his spirits'" (Aubrey, qtd. in Brooks 1: 342). Traitors continued to be made more traitorous by their association with tobacco. In 1605, "T. W." notes that the imprisoned Gunpowder Plotters "'rather feasted with their sins, than fasted with sorrow for them; were richly appareled, fared deliciously, and took Tobacco out of measure, with a seeming carelessness of their crime'" (qtd. in Knapp 305 n.34). In a list of smoking vanities, Joshua Sylvester connects tobacco smoke to the "*smoak* of *Powder-Treason, Pistols, Knives,* / To blow-up Kingdoms, and blow-out Kings lives." *Tobacco Battered and the Pipes Shattered,* 574. *STC* 21654.
14. Harriot, a smoker himself, apparently died of nose cancer (Goodman 48). In his prose satire *Mundus alter et idem* (1605), Joseph Hall also blames Ralegh—in the person of "a well-born but worthless nobleman"—for introducing tobacco into England (Dickson 171).

15. *STC* 4207.
16. Brooks 1: 17, 19. Brooks notes that these early references are often oblique, and that the first specific reference to tobacco was in Jacques Cartier's *Breif recit, & succincte narration, de la nauigation faicte es ysles de Canada, Hochelage & Saguenay* (1545), translated by John Florio in 1580 (1: 20). See also Dickson 115.
17. Henry Buttes extends this list of curable ailments in *Dyet's Dry Dinner* (1599) and briefly notes the dangers of tobacco: it "[m]ortifieth and benummeth: causeth drowsiness: troubleth & dulleth the senses: makes (as it were) drunke: dangerous in meale time." These last two points seem especially ironic, as tobacco is here the eighth course of a "dry" meal.
18. *STC* 5262.5
19. Goodman points out that "the success with which a commodity crosses from one culture to another depends on whether this new object can be given a meaning within the host culture" (41). Tobacco, as Knapp indicates, crossed into not only medical culture, but into the English desire for more cerebral stimulants and their demand for "trifling imports" (10).
20. Goldberg, 11.
21. In the opening sonnet to *Tobacco battered*, Sylvester states the English are under

    . . . the proud *Oppression*

    Of th'*Infidel,* usurping FAITH'S Possession,

    That Indian Tyrant, onely *England's* Shame.

    Thousands of *Ours* heer hath Hee Captive taken,

    Of all Degrees, kept under slavish Yoak,

    Their *God,* their Good, *King,* Countrey, Friends forsaken,

    To follow *Folly,* and to feed on Smoak.

    Though Sylvester depicts tobacco negatively, as a tyrant, he still equates it with the role of ruler. He later claims that "Don TOBACCO hath an ampler Raign / Than Don PHILIPPO, the Great *King* of *Spain* / (In whose dominions, for the most, it grows)" and that it "Hath more *Disciples* than CHRIST hath (I fear) / More Suit, more service (Bodies, Souls, and Good)" (575).
22. In a similar vein, James comments that "divers men very sound both in iudgement and complexion, haue bene at last forced to take it

[tobacco] also without desire, partly because they were ashamed to seeme singular, (like the two Philosophers that were forced to duck themselues in that raine water, and so become fooles aswell as the rest of the people)" (98).

23. *The Political Works of James I,* ed. Charles Howard McIlwain (New York: Russell and Russell, 1965), 294. On the Scots as an illness of the body politic, "an invasion of what was perceived to be a foreign body," see Peck 210.
24. For a wonderfully excessive list of tobacco's lowly clientele, see Sylvester's *Tobacco battered:* "Theeves, Unthrifts, Ruffians, Robbers, Roarers, Drabbers, / Bibbers, Blasphemers, Shifters, Sharkers, Stabbers, / This is the *Rendez-vous,* These are the Lists, / Where doe encounter most TOBACCONISTS" (578).
25. There is an obvious difference in how the *Counterblaste* ridicules the medicinal properties of tobacco, and this letter accepts the moderate use of tobacco by certain individuals. In the *Counterblaste,* James does briefly "admit . . . then, and not [confess] that the vse thereof were healthfull for some sorts of diseases" (95).
26. In *The Herball* (1597), a publication directed generally toward gentlewomen, John Gerard differentiates between the positive and negative uses of tobacco by different classes of female healers: "I sende this iewell vnto you women of all sorts, especially to such as cure and helpe the poore and impotent of your countrie without rewarde. But vnto the beggerly rabble of witches, charmers & such like couseners, that regarde more to get money then to helpe for charitie, I wish these fewe medicines far from their vnderstanding" (qtd. in Brooks 1: 347).
27. The connection between tobacco takers and drinkers is based on their similar effects of "drunkenness," and on the common use of the word "drink" rather than "smoke" when referring to taking a pipe of tobacco.
28. This is an unfortunate argument, as tobacco supporters claim that smoking can allay hunger, thirst, and fatigue.
29. Interestingly, Richard Klein notes that cigarettes would later become "the indispensable companions of soldiers in combat, relied upon to sustain their courage and endurance in the face of intolerably stressful circumstances" (xi).
30. Craigie wonders if this should read "taking," but "raking" suits not only the extreme language of the final paragraph, but also the vision of the visibly unhealthy English body James describes earlier. It also hints at a form of self-abuse.
31. Philartes, the pseudonymous author of the anti-tobacco tract *Work for Chimny-sweepers: or a warning to Tobacconists* (1602),

claims—like James—that "to the wiser sort this treatise will seeme at the first a fruitless labour, of an idle braine," but—unlike James—he worries that he opposes the beliefs of many "[a]uthorities of expert and learned men" (*STC* 12571). Because of his position as king, James did not need to apologize for his convictions, and he did not suffer the same response as Philartes, who was answered by Roger Marbecke in a response to *Chimny-sweepers* entitled the *Defence of Tobacco* (1602): "men of great learning and iudgement, men of right good bringing vp, men of fine, and deinty diet, men of good worth, and worship, yea men, of right honorable estate, and calling; do like of the smell of Tabacco well inough. Why then should it be so mightily condemned by you, for such an horrible stinker?" (*STC* 6468).

32. Nichols 1: 534, 550–51 (noted in Brooks 1: 60). "An creber suffitus Nicotianae exotiae sif sanis salutaris? Neg." [Is frequent smoking of Nicotine good for one's health? No.] To the Second Replyer, who made an argument supporting tobacco, James said "he [the replyer] would have proved by an enumeration or induction that tobacco must need be good, because Kings, Princes, Nobles, Earles, Lords, Knights, Gentlemen of all countries and nations, reckoning a number, loved it. The King gave instance that there was one King that neither loved nor liked it, which moved great delight" (Nichols 1: 550–51). Brooks lists many other rulers who disliked tobacco, and who punished smokers not merely with taxes but with mutilation and death (1: 71–75).

33.

> For whereas heretofore, they wonted were,
> At all their meetings, and their festiualls,
> To passe the time in telling witty tales,
> In questions, riddles, and in purposes,
> Now doe they nothing else, but sit and sucke,
> And spit, and slauer, all the time they sit. . . .
> But sure the times to come when they looke backe
> On this, will wonder with themselues to think
> That men of sense could euer be so mad,
> To sucke so grosse a vapour, that consumes
> Their spirits, spends nature, dries vp memorie,
> Corrupts the blood, and is a vanitie. (3.1.1150–64)

In *Complete Works.*

34. *STC* 20983: 9. Rich also notes that "the humorous" "have beene alreadie brought to the stage, where they haue plaide their partes, *Euerie man in his humour*" (4–5).
35. *STC* 20986: 25.
36. After devouring a feast of sinners, Cock-Lorrel and the Devil partake of tobacco, "Which since in Countrey, Court, and Towne, / In the Devils Glister-pipe smoakes at the nose / Of Polcat, and Madam, of Gallant, and Clown" (1131–33).
37. Craigie notes that in this collection, the king's is the first of seventy-nine anti-smoking writings. A second edition of this collection appeared in 1672, with a different title page: *Two Broadsides against Tobacco. Collected and Published as very proper for this Age* (213).
38. In *Tobacco battered,* Sylvester hopes that James will support his "armed Pen" with

    the *Trident* of some sharp *Edict,*
    Severe enacted, executed strict,
    Clense all the Staules of This *Augean* Dung,
    Which hath so long corrupted Old and Young;
    Or, at the least, impose so deep a *Taxe*
    On all these *Ball, Leafe, Cane,* and *Pudding Packs:*
    On Seller, or on Buyer, or on Both. (579)

39. By the 1660s, tobacco duties accounted for approximately five percent of all government income (Goodman 150).
40. The *Counterblaste* was not intended for his Scottish audience; tobacco did not become fashionable there until a decade or more later. In a speech of 1617, James implies that the Scots had learned tobacco smoking from the English. A letter to Lord Keeper Bacon in June of 1617 records the king's wish that "the Scottish nation would be as docible to learn the goodness of England as they are teachable to limp after their ill . . . for they had learned of the English to drink healths, to wear coaches and gay cloaths, to take tobacco, and to speak neither Scotish nor English!" Although James notes that the Scots need to follow England's more civilized behavior, he was "pleased to enumerate" the "diseases of the times" in both nations (Nichols 3: 345).

Works Cited

Bell, Sandra. "Writing the Monarch: King James VI and *Lepanto.*" *Other Voices, Other Views: Expanding the Canon in English Renaissance Studies.* Ed. Mary Silcox, Helen Ostovich, and Graham Roebuck. Newark: U of Delaware P, 1999.

Brooks, Jerome E. *Tobacco: Its History Illustrated by the Books, Manuscripts and Engravings in the Library of George Arents, Jr.* 4 vols. New York: Rosenbach, 1937–52.

Buttes, Henry. *Dyets Dry Dinner.* (1599). *STC* 4207.

Chute, Anthony. *Tabaco.* (1595). *STC* 5262.5.

Daniel, Samuel. *The Queenes Arcadia: The Complete Works in Verse and Prose of Samuel Daniel.* Ed. Rev. Alexander B. Grosart. New York: Russell & Russell, 1963.

Dickson, Sarah. *Panacea or Precious Bane: Tobacco in Sixteenth Century Literature.* New York: New York Public Library, 1954.

Goldberg, Jonathan. *James I and the Politics of Literature.* Baltimore: Johns Hopkins UP, 1983.

Goodman, John. *Tobacco in History: The Cultures of Dependence.* London: Routledge, 1993.

Gray, S., and V. J. Wyckoff. "The International Tobacco Trade in the Seventeenth Century." *Southern Economic Journal* 1 (1940): 1–26.

James VI and I. *A Counterblaste to Tobacco. Minor Prose Works of King James VI and I.* Ed. James Craigie. Edinburgh: Scottish Text Society, 1982.

———. *James I.* The True Law of Free Monarchies *and* Basilikon Doron. Ed. Daniel Fischlin and Mark Fortier. Toronto: Centre for Reformation and Renaissance Studies, 1996.

Jonson, Ben. *The Gypsies Metamorphosed.* (1621).

Klein, Richard. *Cigarettes Are Sublime.* Durham: Duke UP, 1993.

Knapp, Jeffrey. *An Empire Nowhere: England, America, and Literature from the "Utopia" to "The Tempest."* Berkeley: U of California P, 1992.

Kratzmann, Gregory. "Sixteenth-Century Secular Poetry." *The History of Scottish Literature: Origins to 1660.* Ed. R. D. S. Jack. 4 vols. Aberdeen: Aberdeen UP, 1988. 1: 105–24.

Marbecke, Roger. *Defence of Tobacco.* (1602). *STC* 6468.

Nichols, John, ed. *The Progresses, Processions and Magnificent Festivities of King James the First.* 4 vols. London, 1823. New York: Burt Franklin, n.d.

Peck, Linda Levy. *Court Patronage and Corruption in Early Stuart England.* Boston: Unwin Hyman, 1990.

Philartes. *Work for Chimny-sweepers: or A warning to Tobacconists.* (1602). *STC* 12571.

Rich, Barnaby. *Faultes faults, and nothing else but faultes.* (1606). *STC* 20983.

———. *The Honestie of this Age.* (1614). *STC* 209826.

Shire, Helena Mennie. *Song, Dance and Poetry of the Court of Scotland under King James VI.* Cambridge: Cambridge UP, 1969.

Sylvester, Joshua. *Tobacco battered and the Pipes Shattered.* 1616–17. *STC* 21654.

Wormald, Jenny. "James VI and I: Two Kings or One?" *History* 68 (1983): 187–209.

11

Writing King James's Sexuality

David M. Bergeron

Writing James's sexuality cuts in at least two directions: how James himself wrote of desire and how others then and since have written about the king's sexual interests. For four centuries writers of various kinds have been assessing, analyzing, and most often condemning James's sexuality. This essay traces the trajectory of the reaction to James's sexuality from his contemporaries to our contemporaries, and it also looks briefly at how James himself wrote about desire. A seventeenth-century writer refers to James's "lascivious" and "scandalous" behavior; an eighteenth-century writer comments on the "ductile licentiousness" of his relationships; a nineteenth-century writer refers to the "gross indecency" of his letters to favorites; and a late twentieth-century writer observes James's "domesticated carnalities." These perspectives encapsulate the dominant view as we cross the centuries, but they should be challenged by James's own writing of desire, primarily in his letters.

But why and how do these rather harsh and often heavy-handed judgments come about? The problem can be summed up simply and accurately: James directed his greatest love to male favorites. The homosexual nature of James's love has been the stumbling block for writers. We encounter, if I may borrow Eve Sedgwick's term, the "epistemology of the closet."[1] The nervous recognition of James's preference for men has led to a variety of responses, which I sum up as four major reactions. First, historians and others respond with a negative moral judgment, finding hints of James's homoerotic desire to be repulsive. Second, other writers simply avoid the topic altogether and therefore leave it unwritten; or, they engage in coy discourse and try to change the subject. A third group tries to rationalize James's behavior and explain it away, as in the idea that men way back then seemed to value male friendship highly, and so did James. Finally, many writers implicitly or explicitly insist that we need not take matters of James's sexuality and love interest seriously; besides, whatever love he may have expressed for other men was destined to be fickle and inconsistent: it could not last. These responses open the closet door ever so slightly but only to slam it firmly shut: out of sight, out of mind.

Because I have confronted the matter at length elsewhere,[2] I will offer here a summary of James's three principal male favorites: Esmé Stuart, Robert Carr, and George Villiers. In September 1579, the thirty-seven-year-old Frenchman Esmé Stuart d'Aubigny entered for the first time into the Presence Chamber at Stirling Castle where he immediately prostrated himself before his cousin, the thirteen-year-old James, who embraced him and received him graciously. Thus began the intense relationship between the two: the love-starved adolescent king and the sophisticated French courtier. In ways probably unexpected for both, they developed an intense and ever-deepening love, documented in numerous letters and reports from nervous observers both in Scotland and England, most of whom feared that Esmé intended to lead the king and Scotland into the unwelcome embrace of Catholicism. Esmé had left behind in France a wife and children; they never joined him in Scotland, although occasional discussion hinted that his wife might arrive. James saw to it that she did not.

A major stumbling block in the relationship, Esmé's Catholicism, disappeared when Esmé converted to James's brand of Protestantism. This action I see as a sign of his love for James and another way in which he turned his back on the family in France. But even his conversion did not satisfy the band of Scottish churchmen and noblemen who felt threatened by Esmé's emerging and growing political power and his clear influence on James. Fanned by religious fears and encouraged by the English court, these forces joined to abduct James in August 1582, forcibly separating James from Esmé, whom he would never see again. A prisoner, James acquiesced to the demand that he exile Esmé, who left Scotland in December 1582 for his native France, where he died in May 1583.

Not until early in James's English reign do we encounter another male who completely captivated the king, although a number from the remainder of James's time in Scotland and in the first few years in England can lay some passing claim to the designation "favorite." But Robert Carr, a Scot who traveled with James's entourage to London in 1603, became the first serious claimant to James's mature love. He came to the king's attention as the result of a fall from his horse in the accession day tilt in 1607. James liked his handsome appearance and insisted that Carr be given appropriate medical care. James, ever the pedant, even attempted to teach Carr Latin. In any event, by the end of 1607, the letter-writer John Chamberlain can casually write that Carr reigns as the new favorite, having recently also been made a gentleman of the bedchamber, a position of increasing importance.[3] From this important political position Carr, through James's unstinting generosity, began to accumulate other titles and properties, which culminated in 1613 with his becoming earl of Somerset. Increasing political power followed in the wake of such success, to the consternation of Queen Anne, Prince Henry, and Robert Cecil.

Along the way, Carr developed an intense, if tortuous relationship with the minor writer Thomas Overbury, who became a kind of secretary to Carr, assisting him in many political chores. James clearly did not like this arrangement, and his jealousy contrived to offer Overbury an overseas appointment. When Overbury refused, James shipped him off to the Tower, from which he wrote many fascinating and revealing letters to Carr, which document a love they shared. Out of distaste and probable jealousy, Overbury himself opposed Carr's efforts to marry Frances Howard, countess of Essex. But Carr persisted, even though Frances Howard remained married. She eagerly sought an end to her marriage to the earl of Essex, whom she claimed was impotent. The summer of 1613 stayed busy with divorce proceedings that often took bizarre twists. When the council of churchmen would not grant the divorce, James simply put some bishops on the panel who would vote in favor. Frances Howard got her divorce, and on 26 December 1613, with James's full support, she and Carr were married. James always urged his favorites to marry so long as their marriage did not interfere with their obligations to the king. Unknown to practically everyone, Thomas Overbury's September 1613 death in the Tower had been planned by the countess with the likely connivance of Carr. By the fall of 1615, the whole sordid murder plot began to unravel. To James's credit he did little to protect his favorite; indeed, he created some distance from him. Carr and his wife went on trial in May 1616, where the jury found both guilty of involvement in Overbury's murder. James commuted their sentences and put them under a kind of house arrest in the Tower. Interestingly, in the trial Francis Bacon skillfully used Overbury's letters to Carr to help condemn him.

Certainly by 1615, James had become weary and wary of Carr, whose insolent behavior had begun to take its toll on their relationship. For one thing, James feared that Carr might be desperate enough to cast aspersions on the king and link him to the murder. Savvy court factions decided to make their move and speed Carr's political demise. They fastened onto George Villiers as a handsome young man destined to catch the king's attention. Villiers became part of the strategy for the downfall of Carr, and it worked. A new rising sun displaced the waning Carr.

The king and Villiers met on James's progress in 1614; by 23 April 1615, the twenty-three-year-old Villiers became a gentleman of the bedchamber, following the pattern of Carr. Many commentators in the period took cognizance of Villiers's extraordinary beauty, and a number tacitly admitted his homoerotic attractiveness, including Francis Bacon and Bishop William Laud. Small wonder that James felt similarly drawn to this dashing young man. Recent commentators have speculated that he may have satisfied James's sexual desire in an encounter at Farnham in 1615, based on the evidence of his letter about the occasion, in which he says that he shall never forget Farnham, "where the bed's head could not be found between the master and his dog" (the affectionate term for Villiers).[4] Clearly he had stolen James's heart, and the king responded by pouring out gifts. Villiers swiftly became viscount in 1616, earl of Buckingham and a member of the Privy Council in 1617, marquis in 1618, and finally duke of Buckingham in 1623. (His title Buckingham will be the name used for him throughout the remainder of this paper.)

Buckingham's marriage in May 1620 to Katherine Manners did nothing to blunt his relationship with the king; it did, however, vastly expand his wealth. He became the major patron for his kinsmen, enhancing the economic and political status of all of them. James in effect adopted Buckingham's family, exhibiting affection for the children of the extended family in ways he never demonstrated toward his own. Similarly, his concern for Katherine and their daughter remained both constant and genuine. In the relationship with Buckingham, James had found a family.

His love for Buckingham spurred James to return to writing poetry: he wrote verses about Buckingham's marriage, his being made Lord Admiral of the Navy, his house and entertainment at Burley, and the desire for a healthy child. In September 1622, the Venetian ambassador Giorlamo Lando wrote in his dispatch an astute analysis of Buckingham's position, admitting the envy of some at the court. The ambassador, who finds Buckingham modest, affable, kind, and courteous, says that James "has given him all his heart, who will not eat, sup or remain an hour without him and considers him his whole joy."[5] This writing sums up as well as any Buckingham's status and James's love for him.

In 1623 Buckingham took enormous risk: he accompanied Prince Charles on his slightly hare-brained trip to Spain with the purpose of concluding the marriage negotiations for the Infanta Maria. This "Spanish match," as many called it, fit into the puzzle that constituted James's foreign policy. Buckingham and Charles arrived in Madrid on 7 March, to the complete surprise of the Spanish. For the next seven months they negotiated, arriving at acceptable marriage arrangements but failing to win the right to bring the Infanta to England. Indeed, by the time they landed back in England in October even Charles and Buckingham opposed the Spanish match. Universal rejoicing greeted them because they had not brought the Infanta with them. The whole arrangement eventually collapsed—no Spanish marriage. Much of 1624 focused on the political repercussions of the Spanish match, as accusations flew about Buckingham's behavior in Spain. James defended him and eventually sent him to France to negotiate marriage there for Charles. In late March 1625 James died, with Buckingham at his side.

We turn now to see how others regarded the king's love for these male favorites. The seventeenth century lays the foundation for the responses to come, ranging from understatement to virulent denunciation of James. The second half of the century busily produced a number of studies of James's reign, at least seven appearing in the 1650s alone. Perhaps the first flush of the Commonwealth period inspired or liberated writers to plunge into accounts of the earlier Stuarts. Bishop Godfrey Goodman, who wrote during James's lifetime but whose work was not published until the nineteenth century, may take the prize for understatement when he offers this assessment of James's character: "I must needs blame him, that he was a man wonderfully passionate, much given to swearing, and he was not so careful of his carriage as he might be."[6] Goodman adds later about James and his queen Anne, "yet they did love as well as man and wife could do, not conversing together" (1: 168). Goodman fails to explore why James and Anne do not "converse"—a synonym, doubtless known to the bishop, for sexual relations. Little discourse of love, another sign of loving conversation, passed between James and Anne. Goodman explains the fall of Robert Carr as being attributable to the natural abating of love and affection: "therefore to have choice of dishes best pleaseth the palate: so truly I think the King was weary of an old favorite" (1: 225). Other writers will build on this analysis but add a harsher edge; where Goodman sees a natural process, others will see sinister signs of James's inconstancy.

John Oglander, knighted by James at Royston in 1615, writes in his commonplace book (first published in the twentieth century). James "was the chastest prince for women that ever was, for he would often swear that he had never known any other woman than his wife."[7] But Oglander knows that is not exactly the issue; thus he adds: James "loved young men, his favourites, better than women, loving them beyond the love of men to women. I never yet saw any fond husband make so much or so great dalliance over his beautiful spouse as I have seen King James over his favourites, especially the Duke of Buckingham" (196). Oglander's perspective seems relatively benign, devoid of the tougher judgment of his contemporaries. He heaps praise on Buckingham, for example, calling him "the greatest subject that England ever had" (41).

No such restraint governs the assessment of Francis Osborne, writing in 1658, who believes that James's favorites interfered in the king's relationships with his subjects. Osborne warms to his topic:

> Now, as no other reason appeared in favour of their choyce but handsomnesse, to the love the king shewed was as amorously convayed, as if he had mistaken their sex, and thought them ladies; which I have seene Sommerset and Buckingham labour to resemble, in the effeminatenesse of their dressings. . . . Nor was his love, or what else posterity will please to call it . . . carried on with a discretion sufficient to cover a lesse scandalous behaviour; for the kings kissing them after so lascivious a mode in publick, and upon the theatre, as it were, of the world, prompted many to imagine

> some things done in the tyring-house, that exceed my expressions no lesse then they do my experience.[8]

Here we find disapproving moral judgment at full throttle; others will imitate Osborne, but no one will surpass his assessment. Osborne hits most of the issues: scandalous behavior, suspicion of effeminacy, and confusion of appropriate sexual direction for one's affections. For good measure Osborne indulges a theatrical metaphor, calculated to raise the suspicions of many of his readers; for what has the theater been but a hotbed of sexual confusion and indulgence? Given what he has seen in public, Osborne races to contemplate what may be going on behind the stage in the tiring house. Part of him would doubtless like to know, to peer into that closed space, but moral restraint keeps Osborne from venturing farther.

Knighted at Whitehall in 1610 and having served in Parliament, Edward Peyton offers another contemporary view in his book, published in 1652: "Now King James, more addicted to love males then females, though for complement he visited Queen Anne, yet never lodged with her a night for many years."[9] After the queen's death, Peyton adds, "the king sold his affections to Sir George Villiers, whom he would tumble and kiss as a mistress" (2: 348). Continuing in this same vein, Anthony Weldon, writing in 1650, says of James's new infatuation with Villiers that "the King was more impatient, then any woman to enjoy her love."[10] Osborne, Peyton, and now Weldon—an unholy trio determined to castigate James and his court on moral grounds while offering titillating examples—explore the "effeminacy" issue, which works in two directions: the favorites look like women, and James acts like a woman in his lack of restraint. Without saying so explicitly, these early writers raise questions about the "masculine" quality of these relationships, hinting that they are "unnatural."

Weldon offers a particularly cynical account of James's leave-taking from Robert Carr as he went off to face charges of complicity in the murder of Thomas Overbury. Weldon refers to James's "seeming affection," how he hung about Carr's neck, "slabboring his cheeks," and how "he lolled about his neck" (102–3). All such expressions Weldon finds offensive as he also finds them merely examples of dissimulation on James's part. This perspective broaches the question of James's constancy in love, a point that Weldon further explores in his discussion of Buckingham (146ff.). Weldon concludes that the king had grown weary of Buckingham and that Buckingham hated the king. Therefore, one can infer that the relationship could not have been meaningful. According to Weldon, during the trip to Spain in 1623 Buckingham "made Court to the Prince, and so wrote himselfe into his affection, that *Damon* and *Pythias* were not more deare each to other" (151). What does this reveal about Buckingham's constancy, and what does it say about Charles's poor judgment? The publisher of the 1650 edition, in an address to the reader, says of Weldon's account: "here we may see what a Slave King James was to his Favourites" (sig. A3v).

Although commenting on the "lascivious appetites" of the Stuart period, Michael Sparke (1651) presents a rather measured assessment of James's involvement with favorites.[11] He documents the fall of Carr and the rise of Villiers, noting of the latter: "On this *man* the King casts a particular *affection,* holding him to bee the onely *properest,* and best *proportioned* and *deserving Gentleman* of *England,* whereupon he entertained him into favour" (65). Sparke at least offers a rationale for James's choice and love, that "particular affection" which becomes part of the king's entertaining. Arthur Wilson, writing in 1653, also focuses on the decline of Carr and rise of Buckingham, calling attention to Queen Anne's antipathy to Carr, which may have derived "from an apprehension that the Kings love and company was alienated from her, by this *Masculine conversation* and *intimacy.*"[12] Wilson has correctly defined the problem: masculine conversation and intimacy resonate with sexual overtones and exclude the queen. Writing of Buckingham's meteoric rise, Wilson says: "To speak of his Advancement by *Degrees,* were to lessen the Kings Love" (104). Showered with gifts and entertained into James's favor, Buckingham "now reigns sole *Monarch* in the Kings affection, every thing he doth is admired for the *doers* sake" (105). He runs faster, dances better, jumps higher than anyone. Wilson concludes: "the King is not well without him, his *company* is his *solace.*" If not altogether approving, Sparke and Wilson nevertheless counter the shriller accounts of their contemporaries by focusing on what same-sex relationships provided the king.

To close this brief account of late seventeenth-century writing about James's sexuality, we circle back to representations of his behavior with favorites. Bishop John Hacket notes a pattern dating to James's adolescence: "from the time he was 14 years old and no more, that is, when the Lord *Aubigny* came into *Scotland* out of *France* to visit him, even then he began, and with that Noble Personage, to clasp some one *Gratioso* in the Embraces of his great Love."[13] This account constitutes one of the rare notices of James's relationship with Esmé Stuart, lord Aubigny. At the moment at which he writes, Hacket says that "the Marques of *Buckingham* was the *Parelius*" (i.e., the mock sun). Further, "This Lord was our *English Alcibiades* for Beauty, Civility, Bounty, and for Fortitude." In Hacket's succinct phrase, he "rul'd the King's Affections." Roger Coke, grandson of Sir Edward Coke, lord chief justice under James, puts the matter similarly: "But whilst the King was wallowing in Pleasure, he wholly gave himself up to be governed by Favourites."[14] Coke disapproves, partly on social and political grounds. He brazenly recalls the example of Edward II and his love for Gaveston, "A Person of far more accomplished Parts than *Buckingham,* for *Gaveston* was bred up with Edward" (1: 97). But for James, an "old King . . . to dote upon a young Favourite, scarce of Age and to commit the whole Ship of the Commonwealth . . . to such a *Phaeton,* is a Precedent without any Example" (98). Hacket may find Buckingham to be a "Parelius" and an "Alcibiades," but Coke sees him as an unworthy "Phaeton," soaring high but destined to fall. Yet surely Coke has hit a raw nerve to liken James and Buckingham to Edward II and Gaveston, these two noted for their homosexual love.

Eighteenth-century writers do not seriously alter the portrait of James's sexuality; however, they do embellish with some details. Picking up a theme enunciated in the earlier century, James Welwood writes that James "was for the most part unhappy in his *Favourites;* being oblig'd to abandon one upon the account of *Overbury's* Murther; and coming to hate another the latter part of his life as much as he had ever lov'd him before."[15] If James remained "unhappy" in his favorites and came in fact to hate them, then we can readily dismiss the possibility of a meaningful love relationship. The implicit moral judgment says that James got what he deserved—end of any exploration of the epistemology of the closet. Edward Hyde Clarendon, writing in the seventeenth century but not published until the eighteenth, joins a long list of commentators who remark Buckingham's exceptional beauty: all who gazed on him "were quickly directed towards him, as a Man in the Delicacy and Beauty of his Colour, Decency and Grace of his Motion, the most rarely accomplished they had ever beheld."[16] Some, Clarendon adds, attempted "to discountenance his Effeminacy, till they perceived he had masked under it so terrible a Courage as would safely protect all his Sweetnesses." Recognizing that his description of Buckingham might suggest effeminacy, Clarendon moves quickly to head off that charge by noting terrible courage. Many who write of Buckingham's beauty find themselves in a bind, fearful of what this description might reveal about themselves. By knocking down the allegation of effeminacy, Clarendon ironically opens an appreciation of male beauty.

William Harris puts the onus back on James: "And from his known love of masculine beauty, his excessive favour to such as were possessed of it, and unseemly Caresses of them, one would be tempted to think, that he was not wholly free from a vice most unnatural."[17] At last someone calls the perceived problem "unnatural," which had been implied by others. Not surprisingly, Harris's "history" depends heavily on the writing of Osborne, Weldon, and Peyton. Indeed, mainly he recycles their views. Harris includes a note about his procedure and simultaneously underscores his moral superiority: "I have now given my authorities for the assertion in the text [of James's debauchery], the inference I leave to the reader, being unwilling to say more on a subject so disagreeable to the ears of the chaste and virtuous" (74). Harris cloaks himself in the mantle of historical objectivity, being a "meer relator." He concludes magnanimously: "Had I met with any thing favourable to *James* in this matter, I would have declared it with great pleasure; but I cannot allow myself to invent, in order to vindicate." Harris raises to a high but dubious art a disingenuous perspective posing as history.

Catherine Macaulay does not even pretend objectivity; she seeks to demonstrate in her history that the Stuarts tyrannically opposed liberty. She strives to make the world safe for the Hanoverian monarchs. Her "Introduction" acknowledges her bias and confronts the matter of possible censure: "The invidious censures which may ensue from striking into a path of literature rarely trodden by my sex, will not permit a selfish consideration to keep me mute in the cause of Liberty and Virtues."[18] As the pioneering first woman to write and publish British history, Macaulay might have been puzzled to learn of Horace Walpole's judgment in the *DNB* that her history had "manly virtues." Macaulay writes bluntly and imaginatively: "The unrivalled Villiers now shone forth in all the gaudy plumage of royal favour. James found in the disposition of the youth an unbounded levity, and a ductile licentiousness, which promised as glorious a harvest as vice and folly could desire" (1: 98). Vice, folly, gaudy plumage all culminate in Macaulay's pithy phrase "ductile licentiousness," as our minds strain to grasp all the implications of this memorable phrase. Moral judgment colludes with the trivial nature of James's indulgence to discredit any seriousness or genuine love in this relationship. James, ever inconstant, pursued Buckingham because, according to Macaulay, Somerset (Carr) had changed "from a trifling obscene buffoonery to a gravity tinctured with sadness." James preferred someone more ductile. Macaulay concludes that James's "friendship, not to give it the name of vice, was directed by so puerile a fancy, and so absurd a Caprice, that the objects of it were ever contemptible" (1: 265). Her rhetorical move in this sentence compels us to accept "the name of vice" to characterize James's behavior with his favorites. A man given to puerile fancies cannot be expected to have serious, loving relationships and certainly not with other men who at best display gaudy plumage.

The eighteenth century also provides the first editions of some primary documents pertinent to the topic of James's sexuality: namely, some of his letters and a few from Buckingham, carefully sanitized whenever the editor chooses. For the first time, readers can hear the king's and Buckingham's voices through their own writing. The interest in editing reflects a major scholarly concern of this century. Drawing on the resources of the Advocates Library in Edinburgh, David Dalrymple Hailes produces a number of letters. He insists in his preface that this collection is not "intended as a satyre on King James and his ministers: but it will be remembered that I only publish what others have written."[19] He does not like to record the "servile adulation of courtiers, or the petulant familiarity of an overgrown favourite." A decade later Philip Hardwicke prepared an edition of state papers, including letters from James and Buckingham; but he found himself repulsed by some of them. He writes: "It would be endless to transcribe more letters in this nauieous [*sic*] style betwixt the King and his favourite; there are several in an indecent one."[20] Clearly these editors encounter difficulty in these letters that they find morally repugnant. Hardwicke in fact contrasts such letters with those of the earl of Bristol, where we may find "a manly and clear style," opposite to what we see in those of "the insolent and capricious Favourite" (1: 473). I will let Macaulay have the last word about these letters from an eighteenth-century perspective: "All his [James's] letters to his favourite Villiers are written in a style fulsomely familiar, many of them indecent, with very unusual expressions of love and fondness" (1: 265n). Behind the designation "very unusual" lurk the more direct terms of "vice," "unnatural," "caprice," "puerile fancy," and "ductile licentiousness." Writers about James's sexuality exhibit a ductile quality also, but only with regard to rhetoric; on the issue of morality they stand steadfast, railing against James's scandalous behavior.

Speaking for many historians who would like to avoid any consideration of James's sexuality, Friedrich von Raumer writes in 1835 that although people greeted James as a "new Solomon," this illusion lasted but a few months; therefore, "the greatest honour which historians now shew this King, is to pass rapidly over his reign, in order to arrive at the more attractive period of the rebellion."[21] Raumer betrays not only an unwillingness to confront details of James's private life but also a clear historical prejudice, not unknown to earlier centuries. Writing favorably about Buckingham, Katherine Thomson, in her biography of 1860, says that despite his many virtues Buckingham "may yet have been tinged with vices that infallibly brush away much of the finest attributes of virtuous youth."[22] Thomson softens the moral impact by shifting the blame: "it must . . . be allowed, that to remain incorrupt in the reign of James, would have argued almost superhuman strength of character." This historian succeeds in passing rapidly over any troubling issues of sexual behavior.

The nineteenth century did its own version of editing, primarily by making some early texts available. For example, Sir Walter Scott in 1811 published his *Secret History of the Court of James the First,* in which he included the writing of Weldon, Peyton, and Osborne, among others. In a footnote to Peyton's discussion of James's "addiction" for males rather than females, Scott appends this observation: "Weldon and Osborne have already borne testimony to the odd familiarities which James used with his favourites, and which were, to say the least, most disgusting and unseemly."[23] Severe moral judgment remains intact as it crosses the centuries. In 1839 John Brewer edited the writings of Bishop Godfrey Goodman, where he saved his moral scorn for Anthony Weldon, as found in a footnote: "Let it be remembered, that Weldon's book was written for and dedicated to a lady; and yet this monster of impurity has never scrupled to introduce into his narrative the most licentious and indecent tales,—to enter upon their details with a minuteness which shows the filthiness and malignity of his heart."[24] From Brewer's morally superior position, one that would protect women from indecent tales, he glosses over issues of veracity and historical accuracy.

The prolific John Jesse (1815–74), starting in 1840, wrote *Memoirs of the Court of England During the Reign of the Stuarts,* which underwent some sixteen editions on into the twentieth century—vivid testimony to its popularity. Jesse readily sums up much nineteenth-century perspective on James and his favorites, ideas that he does not invent. But he does add some new wrinkles; for example, he notes James's publication of a meditation on the Lord's Prayer (1619), which James dedicated to Buckingham. Jesse finds this dedication offensive:

"More hypocritical trash than this, or, at any rate, a more conflicting line of conduct, it would be difficult to imagine."[25] Jesse warms to the topic: "what can be more incongruous than his introducing so sacred a subject to a gay and thoughtless courtier, whose complaisance, and pretended interest in his Majesty's pursuits, could surely only have originated in a desire to gratify the weak monarch by the usual arts of adulation!" (1: 91). Later, Jesse refers to Buckingham as occupying the "odious position as a favourite" (3: 54). If one studies James's dedication to Buckingham in the Lord's Prayer publication, it comes across as reasonable and measured, as it gives credit to Buckingham for having encouraged James to write on this topic. Jesse's moral judgment clouds his understanding. Having already concluded that Buckingham is a "thoughtless courtier" and one given to "profligate amours" (1:89), Jesse cannot allow the religious text to be tainted by Buckingham's "presence" in the dedication.

We notice how Jesse's rhetoric stacks the cards against James and Buckingham: their relationship cannot have been genuine, given a weak monarch and a courtier who had only "pretended interest" in James. Jesse adds: "That James's friendships, which had their birth in mere outward accomplishments, should have been extremely brief in their existence, is scarcely to be wondered at" (1: 91). The writer ignores that James remained faithful to both Esmé Stuart until forced exile drove him from Scotland and with Buckingham until death. But, Jesse writes, "to fickleness he [James] added insincerity. . . . It was in his nature to hug a favourite at one moment and to ruin him at the next." This version of history completely distorts the actual record. Jesse speculates: "Had James lived, the fall of that magnificent favourite would, in all probability, have been as rapid as his rise." Given the durability of the relationship of Buckingham with King Charles, one has no basis for such speculation. But if the writer can make some kind of case of fickleness and inconstancy, this diminishes the relationships without even invoking moral judgment. To "prove" James's fickleness, Jesse concludes the discussion by quoting Anthony Weldon's account of the final departure of James from Robert Carr—a dubious and historically misleading move.

It comes as no surprise to find that Jesse has observations to make about the correspondence between James and Buckingham. He echoes the eighteenth-century moral revulsion. The letters abound, Jesse writes, "with evidences of, to say the least, very undignified familiarity, and sometimes with gross indecency" (1: 89). Jesse cites some examples, asserting that Buckingham addresses the king with a "strange parade of familiar titles." "Familiarity" becomes the sticking point, but only if one has no sympathy for James and Buckingham's loving relationship. In another volume, Jesse shifts gears, no longer focusing on being morally outraged: "As the style of correspondence which was carried on between James and Buckingham can scarcely have failed in affording amusement, another specimen or two may not be unwelcome" (3: 80). But, we may ask, amusing to whom? Here, too, Jesse occupies a superior position, regarding the letters as mere toys, playful exercises that have no meaning. At such moments one might prefer moral outrage to this smug but harsh position that inherently denigrates the love that the letters inscribe.

"To say the least" becomes a recurring, modifying phrase for both Scott and Jesse. This they say as they appear ready to refer to the indecency or gross familiarity of James's relationships with his favorites. Why not, on the other hand, say the *most*? The writers remain content to say the least, thereby erasing the details of sexuality in history. In what became one of the standard historical works on the Stuarts of the late Victorian era, Samuel Gardiner in his ten volumes in fact has little to say about James's sexuality; in some ways, given his scope, he says the least. He refers to James's "infelicity" in the selection of his companions.[26] Gardiner asserts that James "had been attracted by the strong animal spirits and the handsome features which were common to both [Carr and Buckingham]; and habit soon forged firmly the links of the chain which bound him to the inseparable companions of his leisure hours" (3: 75). By saying so little Gardiner begs the question. What exactly constitute "strong animal spirits," and how can we know? Did Carr and Buckingham only occupy James's "leisure hours"? What does it mean to be bound to James by "links of the chain"? Gardiner also claims, taking his cue from earlier writers, that Carr looked "upon the king's company as a necessary evil, which must be endured on account of the benefits which were to be obtained" (2: 319). Such a statement leads inevitably to discrediting any possibility of mutual love. Elsewhere Gardiner refers to Carr and Buckingham as "light-hearted, giddy youth" (3: 76)—not to be taken seriously. This historian leaves largely unwritten the matter of James's sexual behavior.

If, as we cross into the twentieth century, we expect to leave behind all vestiges of moral judgment on this topic, we will be mistaken. Many of the perspectives found in the writing of historians and others will sound quite familiar, ranging from the question of effeminacy to moral revulsion to the assumption that nothing important happened. Some writers offer new versions of rationalizations to chase away implications of homosexual behavior. Charles Williams can begin the survey with the assessment that Buckingham "combined almost feminine looks with a high masculine nature."[27] This comes as the perfect solution: the writer acknowledges Buckingham's apparent effeminate appearance but combines this with his "masculine nature." Williams adds, somewhat oddly: "He was one of those rare phenomena in which there almost seems to dwell a spirit who can at will either sex assume" (242). On what Williams bases this judgment we cannot know. He later writes that Buckingham functioned "without the mature masculinity of Arran or the more vulgar violence of Somerset" (264). Williams struggles mightily to avoid the subject of possible homosexual interests by insisting that Buckingham simultaneously possessed some effeminate qualities and yet a masculine nature. Therefore, he seems to be an acceptable and appropriate object for James's attention. Buckingham, the "archetypal Favourite of dreams," captured James completely: "Even more astonishingly he conquered James

Stuart's son. He did it with no help but that of his own *spiritual nature*" (264, my emphasis). If one studies the correspondence of Buckingham with Charles and reads of their trip together to Spain in 1623, one could not conclude that only Buckingham's "spiritual nature" captured Charles, who found Buckingham physically attractive, if differently from his father. Williams quotes in full the extraordinary letter from James to Buckingham in which the king proposes that they make a new marriage at Christmas (see letter below); but Williams assumes that James wrote the letter to Charles, which produces several bizarre moments of interpretation (293). Although Williams never explains clearly what kind of relationship James and Buckingham had, he can in his discussion of Parliament produce this startling analysis: "It also had a kind of spiritual homosexuality; it was married to itself" (246). In all likelihood Parliament has seldom been so described.

Charles Cammell includes in his 1939 biography of Buckingham a whole chapter on "The Beauty of Buckingham." In a subsequent chapter he tries to define the relationship of king and subject, and he knows he treads on perilous territory. But he finds James to be innocent of homoerotic behavior: "It was his education and his religion . . . that saved James from sharing that license of the Caesars, which had recently reappeared in so notorious an instance as the French King Henri III; for James was of those that love immoderately the beauty and gracefulness of an Adonis."[28] We can breathe more easily knowing that James has been "saved" from such activity and how wonderful that his education and religion made him proof against notorious behavior. Cammell adds: "Saved by Buchanan and the Bible from sinking into the excesses of the Ancients, James centred on their Idealism." In the letters to Buckingham and in other utterances James seems guilty only of "euphuistic extravagance"—exuberant and exaggerated expressions (85). Cammell does not have to exercise moral judgment against James because he is guilty of nothing untoward, except for a little exuberance in his letters. Characterizing the letters as "euphuistic," Cammell summarily dismisses them as anything that we should take seriously, echoing Jesse and others.

In two different books, David Mathew makes another case for James's innocence: he urges James's "paternalistic" approach to Buckingham. "Again any other theory of their relationship would seem most improbable in the light of the romantic friendship which the restrained and isolated Prince [Charles] was soon to feel for the favoured courtier."[29] In a second, later book Mathew returns to the topic, insisting that "It has always seemed to me that King James's relations with his last favourite were technically innocent."[30] Mathew works through several reasons for this presumed innocence, including that Buckingham's mother could not have had "the cosy relationship which she worked up with the king if he had seduced her favourite son." But his most compelling reason circles back to the prudish Charles: "He was linked with Buckingham by the strongest friendship of his whole life. Surely this development would have been impossible if the favourite had been his father's *mignon*?" (292). I particularly like Mathew's question mark at the end of that sentence. Perhaps unintentionally it betrays uncertainty, a nervous unwillingness to explore these issues too closely.

Even the 1990s do not completely escape some of these analytical problems of trying to establish James's innocence. Maurice Lee Jr., echoing Mathew, believes that Buckingham's increasingly close relationship with Charles means that he could not have been James's lover. Also, Lee naively suggests that James's encouraging his favorites to marry rules out any homoerotic relationship. Finally, he opens a new possibility, one that no one in four centuries of analysis had raised: "James was one of those people, perhaps more numerous . . . than we suppose, who are simply not much interested in physical sex at all."[31] This argument, which cannot be proven, gets rid of the potential homosexual problem very deftly: not homosexuality but *asexuality*. We have come a long way from the mid-seventeenth-century's railing about James's lascivious behavior with his favorites but in an odd, unsatisfactory way. How can we avoid acknowledging James's homoerotic desire? We can assert that such things just did not interest James, all evidence to the contrary conveniently ignored. At this moment in 1990, historical analysis has not experienced a breakthrough; it has instead indulged in an unsubstantiated hedge or dodge.

Godfrey Davies lapses into the conventional understanding of James's behavior: "The King's extreme partiality for his favorites, and the unseemly embraces he bestowed on them in public, naturally has given rise to suspicions, or even charges, that his behavior in private was still worse."[32] If only Davies had included the theatrical metaphor, we would know that we reside in 1658 with Francis Osborne's assessment. Davies makes an interesting choice of words in "naturally," forcing us to think perhaps of things unnatural. He also cites one of Buckingham's letters, which he characterizes as "repulsive," and adds: "James's letters to Buckingham are few and not much less revolting" (60). Moral judgment triumphs in analyzing the letters.

The twentieth century makes major contributions to our understanding of these letters, however, in large measure by editing them. In his 1940 biography of Buckingham, Hugh Ross Williamson provides over 100 pages of Buckingham's letters, although he makes no analysis of them. Ross Williamson entitles chapter 2 "Ganymede," which offers promise, but mainly he avoids the subject of sexual interest between James and Buckingham in this brief chapter. He records James's first encounter with Buckingham at Apthorpe: "And James himself, whose feminine genius for intrigue was at its best in such domestic situations," made arrangements to see more of the young man.[33] Now James exhibits feminine qualities. The author refers to Buckingham as a "pretty, harmless, affable gentleman" (37). In 1984, G. P. V. Akrigg published his magnificent edition of James's letters. His brief introduction tries to situate these letters, which range over a myriad of topics. Akrigg writes on the first page that James was "one of the most complicated neurotics ever to sit on either the English or the Scottish throne."[34] This sweeping claim might need to be altered had we the same amount of letters from other British monarchs. Akrigg touches gingerly on the subject of sexuality but without explanation, as when he writes that Esmé Stuart "opened new worlds for him [James], introducing him to poetry and possibly to homosexuality" (5). Akrigg devotes one paragraph to a consideration of James and his favorites, and he writes: "King James was a man who, in his own twisted fashion, loved profoundly" (19). James "turned chiefly to his male favourites for love." If James exhibits his love in a "twisted fashion," then something must be wrong with it. For Akrigg that means that the love moved in an inappropriate direction. The letters have proved vexing to many commentators, as we have already seen. Philippe Erlanger, for example, puzzlingly complains about the "crumpled, dirty and hastily scrawled letters."[35] Since the letters have been meticulously preserved and appear no more hastily scrawled than others, Erlanger's point sounds misguided at best. He adds: "Most of these letters seem like part of a game which served to amuse a sensitive man prematurely falling into senility" (75). This view reinforces Cammell's, which saw the letters as rhetorical excess, a mere game affording amusement. If we throw in "senility," we have a lethal combination for destroying the seriousness of the letters and their inscribed love.

Two highly influential books sit in the middle of the century and conveniently sum up many of the attitudes about James's sexuality: David Harris Willson's *King James VI and I* (1956) and William McElwee's *The Wisest Fool in Christendom: The Reign of King James I and VI* (1958). Willson's book has in some ways become the standard biography of James. This historian has trouble, however, knowing how to negotiate the matter of James's sexual behavior: he seems understanding at one moment and condemnatory at the next. Like many before him, Willson notes James's presumed public behavior and wonders what went on in private: he "pawed his favourites so fondly in public [that] he was unlikely to restrain himself in private."[36] But, Willson concludes, "The vice was common to many rulers and we need not be too shocked." The "vice" remains unnamed, but Willson sees it as a sign of James's loosening moral fiber. In one breath he can write about the deepening nature of the love shared between James and Buckingham and in the next refer to Buckingham's skillfully pretending to return James's love (385). By combining "masculine strength and feminine delicacy" (385), Buckingham "was a seductive young man, with something of the allurements of both sexes" (384). The matter of Buckingham's effeminacy will not go away, in part because it offers a kind of strange explanation of James's attraction to him; it also plays into stereotypes of homosexuals as effeminate. Willson adds: Buckingham's attractive physical features "must have made him most alluring. Assuming, that is, that one was allured by these things" (385). I sense that Willson nervously catches himself just at the moment that he, too, finds himself attracted to Buckingham. Therefore, the historian beats a hasty retreat: "Assuming, that is, that one was allured by these things." After that close call, Willson adds that Buckingham "allowed himself to be pawed and petted." "These things" heighten distaste and underscore a deep moral revulsion that runs through this analysis. In Willson's last chapter he concludes: "James clung to Buckingham with the excessive fondness of an aged parent for a beloved child. His maudlin letters invoked blessings upon his favourite" (425). This last portrait of James resonates as pathetic.

McElwee has heard quite enough about Buckingham's effeminate appearance: "It has been the fashion to talk of Villiers's effeminate charm, but he was in fact well-built and athletic and his good looks, though startling, were in no way womanish."[37] Buckingham merely had a "boyish charm" and a "frolicsome, adolescent gaiety." No problem here. But Robert Carr is another matter for McElwee: "Carr was a tall, brainless athlete with the slightly effeminate fair-haired good looks most calculated to catch James's eye" (176). McElwee wants to be sure that we appreciate what foolishness James indulged in by caring about such a brainless creature with "effeminate" qualities. Thus, for McElwee, the afternoon that Carr fell from his horse and James expressed concern for him changed everything: "Thus, by James's folly, in one afternoon the whole pattern of English politics and of English history was changed, immeasurably for the worse" (178). We can regard such a statement as more histrionic than historical. McElwee says that "what had already been a little odd in a sixteen-year-old boy when he was worshipping at the shrine of Esmé Stuart, became grotesque in the middle-aged man" (179). He offers this bizarre picture: James "appeared everywhere with his arm round Carr's neck, constantly kissed and fondled him, lovingly feeling the texture of the expensive suits he chose and bought for him, pinching his cheeks and smoothing his hair" (179). In this flight of fantasy James seems very busy indeed. Few at the time, McElwee insists, did not find the pair "ludicrous and unseemly." One might say the same about this historian's rendition, an account calculated to trivialize James's emotions and attraction to his favorites.

Three writers from the 1990s can suggest diverging opinions about James's sexuality. Believing that Shakespeare in a direct way served as James's playwright, Alvin Kernan in 1995 brushes across the issue. He draws a link between James and Octavius in Shakespeare's *Antony and Cleopatra:* "While James-Octavius coolly controls the world, in the course of the play the shabby decadence of the Stuart court and James's domesticated carnalities—'old dad' writing to 'Steenie' about how he misses him—take on liveliness and erotic excitement."[38] And yet, somehow, "Homoeroticism is avoided." What, one wonders, does Kernan have precisely in mind when he alludes to James's "domesticated carnalities?" We may also wonder how *Antony and Cleopatra* can reflect anything about James's relationship with Buckingham since their involvement does not seriously begin until *after* Shakespeare's death. The only example of Stuart decadence that Kernan cites refers to the letters exchanged between king and subject, which obviously Kernan finds repulsive. How can James's writing to Buckingham about how he misses him qualify as a "domesticated carnality"? Would an "undomesticated carnality" be better? Kernan has tacitly accepted the attitude of a host of writers before him, stretching back to the seventeenth century.

But if we turn to Bruce Smith's *Homosexual Desire in Shakespeare's England* (1991), we find quite a different perspective. Smith accepts the king's homosexuality and astutely observes: "In terms of the male power structure of English Renaissance society, James's homosexuality may be the equivalent of Elizabeth's virginity: the erotic seal of men's political transactions with one another."[39] The emphasis on politics leads to Smith's placing James and Buckingham in the "Myth of Master and Minion" for what it reveals "about political exchanges among men" (203). Therefore, their relationship reinforces hierarchical arrangements, all of which deftly underscores power concerns. Mark Kishlansky's *A Monarchy Transformed* (1996), a general history of the Stuart seventeenth century, has little space to explore James's sexuality. Instead, the author accepts the idea that Esmé Stuart, Robert Carr, and Buckingham functioned as James's "lovers"—the term Kishlansky uses.[40] He may support a new era of understanding and acceptance of James's homoerotic desire and behavior, as we also find earlier in Roger Lockyer's excellent biography of Buckingham.[41] After this survey of writers writing about James's sexuality, it might seem perverse or churlish to complain about a historian who accepts the idea of James's lovers; but potential danger also lurks in this position. Not that it is wrong, but it rushes by the issue too quickly. The complex nature of James's relationship with his favorites demands more than a passing reference to his male lovers. Even as we welcome this perspective, freed from moral judgment and not nervously trying to find or invent a way to proclaim James's innocence, we must be on guard that the subject does not become inadvertently trivialized by a too-ready acceptance. That runs the risk of implying that James's homoerotic desire just did not mean very much to him. We know differently. Fortunately, for our sakes and to the consternation of centuries of historians, James left his own written record that demands recognition and documents homoerotic desire. He and his favorites write sexual desire in a compelling and meaningful style.

Writing about love can be found in Esmé's surviving letters and in James's poem *Phoenix*. In December 1581, Esmé states his intention to "give myself up entirely to serve you."[42] A year later, as he readied to depart Scotland, he writes from an anguished heart: "I feel myself to be the most unhappy man in the world" (*CSP Scot* 6: 222) (16 December). He refers to the "pains, torments and vexation which I have suffered for three years"—all of which come about because of his love for James. On 18 December 1582, he writes: "For whatever might happen to me, I shall alwayes be your very faithful servant" (6: 223). He promises eternal fidelity and love, attributes that James could find engraved on his heart. Indeed, as a final sign of his love, he willed that his heart be removed and sent to James upon his death, which it was.

James's letters to Esmé do not survive, although we can infer some of their content from Esmé's to him. But in late 1583 James decided to respond to his deep grief at Esmé's death in the only way left to him: he wrote *Phoenix* (published in 1584), which we can see as a familiar, elegiac verse epistle to Esmé.[43] Here James creates an allegorical fiction about love and desire with the myth of the phoenix bearing an oblique correspondence to the actual relationship of king and cousin. The poem bristles with homoerotic desire as the poet admires unceasingly the bird's beauty and accomplishments and as the bird, under attack, takes refuge between the narrator's legs. Physical desire for the phoenix gains its most explicit expression in the stanzas that focus on the bird's refuge with the narrator. The poem forever links the two cousins in a fiction that adumbrates their personal lives; it recollects with lamentation and consolation the loving relationship with its sharp edge of desire. Although couched as an allegory, the poem provides an outlet for the creative mind of the youthful king. Recalling the lost and dead love, the poet recuperates beauty, wonder, and desire, assuaging his grief by giving it poetic life. In *Phoenix,* I believe, James responds to Esmé's letters that speak of his having hazarded everything in order to serve James. Like the phoenix, Esmé brought color, light, beauty, and love into James's bleak world. They had, in a sense, lived the phoenix myth, and they wrote about it.

Three of James's letters to Carr survive from this period, and they resonate with regret and unrequited love. In the longest and most important of the three letters James writes that the letter flows from the "infinite grief of a deeply wounded heart."[44] The king writes in a startlingly candid and open way about their relationship as he seeks the reformation of Carr's behavior so their love might be restored. This letter contains outbursts of frustration and passion, all ultimately under rhetorical control. James has thought long and hard about this letter. He says early in the letter: "For I am far from thinking of any possibility of any man ever to come within many degrees of your trust with me, as I must ingenuously confess ye have deserved more trust and confidence of me than ever man did: in secrecy above all flesh, in feeling and unpartial respect." One struggles to understand what James can mean about a "secrecy above all flesh." At the least, it implies private intimacy, what he toward the end of the letter refers to as Carr's "own infinite privacy with me."

James calls Carr "an inwardly trusty friend and servant," adding that his "love hath been infinite towards you." If "infinite" toward Carr, where does that leave James's own family? The king insists that he has "many a time prayed for you, which I never did for no subject alive but for you." Out of frustration James includes this bracing comment: "I leave out of this reckoning your long creeping back and withdrawing yourself from lying in my chamber, notwithstanding my many hundred times earnest soliciting you to the contrary." Carr no longer satisfies James's homoerotic desire; sexual frustration governs this letter, which reflects a love relationship that has gone sour. James wants the withdrawing Carr to return to the bedchamber. "All I crave," James writes, "is that in all the words and actions of your life ye may ever make it appear to me that ye never think to hold grip of me but out of my mere love, not one hair by fear." The happy effect that the king hoped to gain from his letters to Carr lost all possibility as the revelations about the Overbury murder destroyed the remnant of their relationship.

The treasure-house of letters exchanged between James and Buckingham helps write James's sexuality. They constitute the largest and most important cache of such personal information for any of James's favorites, and they document love and desire more clearly than any body of kingly correspondence in England's early modern period. The letters simultaneously reflect and create a close and loving relationship; in their writing, James and Buckingham inscribe their love. These letters become sites of homoerotic desire and a collaborative text, as I have argued. Amidst soaring declarations of love and concern for the mundane affairs of life, king and subject find their distinctive, writers' voices.

The letters often demonstrate a self-consciousness about the act and art of letter-writing, from reflection about the nature and purpose of such correspondence to James's careful tallying of how many letters he has written. Although physically separated, both James and Buckingham take delight in the letters, which have been prompted by absence—the cause of most familiar letters. Buckingham writes of being alone in a chamber, reading over and over James's "sweet cordial letters." The delight in this long-distance conversation mitigates the pain of separation. Relaxed playfulness runs through some of the letters, as when Buckingham threatens James that when he "once gets hold of your bedpost again, never to quit it."[45] How James must have enjoyed this threat and contemplated its reality. Writing on 1 September, flush with excitement about returning to England, Buckingham writes: "I cannot now think of giving thanks for friend, wife, or child; my thoughts are only bent of having my dear Dad and master's legs soon in my arms; which sweet Jesus grant me."[46] He reinforces desire by naming the body of the beloved as gathered in an embrace.

James writes to Buckingham, possibly in December 1622: "My only sweet and dear child, I am now so miserable a coward, as I do nothing but weep and mourn; for I protest to God I rode this afternoon a great way in the park without speaking to anybody and the tears trickling down my cheeks, as now they do that I can scarcely see to write."[47] Out of this isolated and sad image James poses the problem: "But alas, what shall I do at our parting?" We do not know the occasion of this expected separation, but we can perceive the depth of James's feelings for Buckingham. The king hits on a strategy: "The only small comfort I can have will be to pry in thy defects with the eye of an enemy, and of every mote to make a mountain, and so harden my heart against thy absence." James knows that he only deceives himself: "But this little malice is like jealousy, proceeding from a sweet root; but in one point it overcometh it, for as it proceeds from love so it cannot but end in love." Mutual love induces a circulation of feeling, proceeding from and returning to love.

In this same letter James implores Buckingham: "Remember thy picture and suffer none of the Council to come here. For God's sake write not a word again and let no creature see this letter." Out of this somewhat puzzling command a physical icon emerges: Buckingham's picture. On 28 February 1623, while Prince Charles and Buckingham are in Spain, James writes to them and includes a simple sentence near the end of the letter: "I have no more to say but that I wear Steenie's picture in a blue ribbon under my waistcoat next my heart."[48] The picture has found a home next to the king's heart. Buckingham responds by writing on 24 March 1623, acknowledging his extraordinary good fortune: "myself is increased in revenue, decreased in expense, my unworthy picture worn next the worthiest heart living, and all this in absence, which word goes down like an ill herb in a good sallett [salad], making the rest not so perfectly well tasted."[49] The picture that binds king and subject gains additional life and force through the letters that underscore its value as symbolizing love.

Writing during Buckingham's trip to Spain, James typically closed the letters with a desire for his return; thus, on 18 April James writes: "I pray the Lord send my sweet Steenie gossip a happy and comfortable return in the arms of his dear dad."[50] On 14 June, James increases this statement of desire: "I care for match nor nothing, so I may once have you in my arms again."[51] James ends his letter of 31 July: "And so God bless thee, my sweet Steenie, and send thee a quick and happy return . . . in the arms of thy dear dad and steward."[52] Interestingly, instead of focusing on Buckingham's body, James thinks of his own, namely his arms receiving and embracing Buckingham. The open arms simultaneously suggest parent, friend, and lover—precisely how James saw himself with regard to Buckingham, his "only sweet and dear child." The embracing arms can connote emotion and intimacy.

Even after Buckingham's return, he and James continued to exchange letters. Probably in December 1623, James wrote an exceptional love letter to Buckingham; it powerfully links kinship and love as it builds on earlier letters. James writes:

> My only sweet and dear child,
>
> Notwithstanding of your desiring me not to write yesterday, yet had I written in the evening if, at my coming out of the park, such a drowsiness had not come upon me as I was forced to sit and sleep in my chair half an hour. And yet I cannot content myself without sending you this present, praying God that I may have a joyful and comfortable meeting with you and that we may make at this Christmas a new marriage ever to be kept hereafter; for, God so love me, as I desire only to live in this world for your sake, and that I had rather live banished in any part of the earth

> with you than live a sorrowful widow's life without you. And so God bless you, my sweet child and wife, and grant that ye may ever be a comfort to your dear dad and husband.[53]

Familial terms raise the relationship to a different level: "marriage," "wife," "husband," as well as the common "child" and "dad." On the basis of this letter we can plausibly infer that James saw himself as married to Buckingham, even as he anticipates a renewal of marriage "at this Christmas." The letter excludes everyone else; James seeks a world made only for Buckingham and him, proof against the vicissitudes of this life and secure against change. James senses no conflict between being both dad and husband to Buckingham; this curious configuration probably strikes him as perfectly logical. In any event, the letter represents James's effort to define their love as it raises marriage to some higher power, earthly yet spiritual. In a letter from late 1623 or early 1624, Buckingham writes that he has experienced more of tenderness from James "than fathers have of children, of more friendship than between equals, of more affection than between lovers in the best kind, man and wife."[54] More than man and wife hints of James's own formulation of their marriage. When he writes in 1624, Buckingham adds that "were not only all your people, but all the world besides, set together on one side, and you alone on the other, I should, to obey and please you, displease, nay despise all them."[55] Collaboratively, James and Buckingham have written a text about love and sexual desire.

Countering the many historians and others who have gone before me, I believe that we must take James's relationships with his male favorites seriously. We should avoid strident and misguided moral judgment, examining the evidence closely and fairly but not creating alternative myths to displace the truth that stares at us. When James refers to himself as Buckingham's "husband," we acknowledge that this concept transcends the usual idea of master-servant or master-minion relationship. Similarly, in the midst of the parliamentary struggles over the Spanish match in March 1624, Buckingham writes succinctly and powerfully to James: I "will live and die a lover of you."[56] We need to open up such statements to interpretation, not shove them into the closet and close the doors. Out of the sometimes complicated, confusing, and even contradictory relationships that James had with Esmé, Carr, and Buckingham an important reciprocal love emerges, which we must accept, analyze, and write about.

Notes

1. Sedgwick.
2. Bergeron. In the discussion that follows, I borrow directly from my book, including direct quotations from other sources. The book examines in detail how James wrote about his sexual desire; this essay offers an abbreviated account of the king's writing on this subject.

3. 1: 249.
4. British Library, Harleian ms. 6987, fol. 214, slightly modernized. All of James's letters cited in this essay can be found in Akrigg, and in ch. 5 of my *King James.*
5. *Calendar of State Papers Venetian* 17: 439.
6. Goodman 1: 92.
7. Oglander 194.
8. Osborne 1: 274–75.
9. Peyton 2: 346.
10. Weldon 87. The book was first published in 1650; it went through five editions from 1650 to 1689, attesting to its popularity. Weldon's tract is also included in Scott's *Secret History* volume.
11. Sparke 4.
12. Wilson 79.
13. Hacket 1: 39. Bishop Hacket died in 1670.
14. Coke 1: 62.
15. Welwood 26.
16. Clarendon 19.
17. Harris 66–74.
18. Macaulay 1: x.
19. Hailes sig. a3v–a4.
20. Hardwicke 1: 464.
21. Raumer 2: 191.
22. Thomson 1: 133.
23. Scott 2: 348–49n.
24. 1: 223n.
25. Jesse 1: 90. Several of the editions carry no publication date; the earliest dated one is 1840, published in London.
26. Gardiner 2: 212.
27. Williams 242.
28. Cammell 84.
29. Mathew, *Jacobean Age* 111.
30. Mathew, *James I* 292.
31. Lee 249.
32. Davies 62.
33. Williamson 33.
34. Akrigg 3.
35. Erlanger 52.
36. Willson 337.
37. McElwee 214.
38. Kernan 124.
39. Smith 75.

40. Kishlansky.
41. Lockyer. Jonathan Goldberg also pointed the way in the 1980s in his important book *James I and the Politics of Literature* (Baltimore: Johns Hopkins UP, 1983), with his analysis of James's relationships with his lovers, especially Buckingham (see 141–46). A book published too late for inclusion in this discussion is Michael B. Young's *King James and the History of Homosexuality* (New York: New York UP, 2000). Young finds convincing the evidence for James's homosexual involvement with several young men.
42. *Calendar of State Papers Relating to Scotland* 6: 104. Esmé's letters will be quoted from these state papers.
43. For a text of *Phoenix,* see James VI and I, *Poems,* vol. 1; and the final section of my *King James.*
44. Lambeth Palace Library ms. 930 (Gibson Papers, vol. 2), Item 90. The letter can be found in Akrigg's edition as well, 335–40.
45. British Library, Harleian ms. 6987, fol. 149. An edition of Buckingham's letters can be found in ch. 5 of my *King James.*
46. British Library, Harleian ms. 6987, fol. 164–65.
47. British Library, Lansdowne ms. 1236, fol. 64.
48. British Library, Harleian ms. 6987, fol. 15.
49. British Library, Harleian ms. 6987, fol. 38.
50. British Library, Harleian ms. 6987, fol. 69.
51. British Library, Harleian ms. 6987, fol. 100.
52. British Library, Harleian ms. 6987, fol. 135.
53. Bodleian Library, Tanner ms. 72, fol. 14. I comment in my book on the important change that James made in the letter as he crossed out the word "master" and replaced it with "husband," presumably finding this word much more appropriate for describing his relationship with Buckingham.
54. National Library of Scotland, Adv. ms. 33.1.7, vol. 22, no. 79.
55. National Library of Scotland, Adv. ms. 33.1.7. vol. 22, no. 88.
56. British Library, Harleian ms. 6987, fol. 200.

Works Cited

Bodleian Library: Tanner ms. 72

British Library: Harleian ms. 6987, Lansdowne ms. 1236

Lambeth Palace Library: ms. 930 (Gibson Papers, vol. 2)

National Library of Scotland: Advocates ms. 33.1.7., vol. 22

Akrigg, G. P. V., ed. *The Letters of James VI and I.* Berkeley: U of California P, 1984.

Bergeron, David M. *King James and Letters of Homoerotic Desire.* Iowa City: U of Iowa P, 1999.

Calendar of State Papers Relating to Scotland and Mary, Queen of Scots. 13 vols. Edinburgh: H. M. General Register House, 1898–1969.

Calendar of State Papers Venetian, 1621–1623. London: H. M. Stationery Office, 1911.

Cammell, Charles Richard. *The Great Duke of Buckingham.* London: Collins, 1939.

Chamberlain, John. *The Letters of John Chamberlain.* Ed. Norman E. McClure. 2 vols. Philadelphia: American Philosophical Society, 1939.

Clarendon, Edward Hyde. *The Characters of Robert Earl of Essex and George Duke of Buckingham.* London, 1706.

Coke, Roger. *A Detection of the Court and State of England during the Reigns of King James I.* 4th ed. 3 vols. London, 1729.

Davies, Godfrey. "The Character of James VI and I." *Huntington Library Quarterly* 5 (1941–42): 33–63.

Erlanger, Philippe. *George Villiers Duke of Buckingham.* Trans. Lionel Smith-Gordon. London: Hodder & Stoughton, 1953.

Gardiner, Samuel R. *History of England from the Accession of James I to the Outbreak of the Civil War, 1603–1642.* 10 vols. 1883–34. Rpt. New York: AMS, 1965.

Goodman, Godfrey. *The Court of King James the First.* Ed. John S. Brewer. 2 vols. London: Richard Bentley, 1839.

Hacket, John. *Scrinia Reserata: A Memorial Offer'd to the Great Deservings of John Williams.* London, 1693.

Hailes, David Dalrymple. *Memorials and Letters Relating to the History of Britain in the Reign of James the First.* Glasgow, 1762.

Hardwicke, Philip Y., ed. *Miscellaneous State Papers from 1501 to 1726.* London, 1778.

Harris, William. *An Historical and Critical Account of the Life and Writings of James the First.* London, 1753.

James VI and I. *Letters.* (See Akrigg.)

———. *The Poems of James VI of Scotland,* ed. James Craigie. 2 vols. Edinburgh: Blackwood, 1955–58.

Jesse, John Heneage. *Memoirs of the Court of England during the Reign of the Stuarts.* 6 vols. Boston: Chester Rice, n. d.

Kernan, Alvin. *Shakespeare, the King's Playwright: Theater in the Stuart Court, 1603–1613.* New Haven: Yale UP, 1995.

Kishlansky, Mark. *A Monarchy Transformed: Britain 1603–1704.* London: Allen Lane, 1996.

Lee, Maurice. *Great Britain's Solomon: James VI and I in His Three Kingdoms.* Urbana: U of Illinois P, 1990.

Lockyer, Roger. *Buckingham: The Life and Political Career of George Villiers, First Duke of Buckingham, 1592–1628.* London: Longman, 1981.

Macaulay, Catherine. *The History of England from the Accession of James I to the Elevation of the House of Hanover.* London, 1766.

Mathew, David. *The Jacobean Age.* London: Longmans, Green, 1938.

———. *James I.* London: Eyre & Spottiswoode, 1967.

McElwee, William. *The Wisest Fool in Christendom: The Reign of James I and VI.* New York: Harcourt Brace, 1958.

Oglander, John. *A Royalist's Notebook: The Commonplace Book of Sir John Oglander.* Ed. Francis Bamford. London: Constable, 1936.

Osborne, Francis. *Traditional Memoirs (1658). Secret History of the Court of James the First,* ed. Scott.

Peyton, Edward. *The Divine Catastrophe of the Kingly Family of the House of Stuarts* (1652). *Secret History of the Court of King James the First,* ed. Scott.

Raumer, Friedrich Ludwig George von. *History of the Sixteenth and Seventeenth Centuries.* 2 vols. London: John Murray, 1835.

Ross Williamson, Hugh. *George Villiers, First Duke of Buckingham: Study for a Biography.* London: Duckworth, 1940.

Scott, Sir Walter. *Secret History of the Court of King James the First.* 2 vols. Edinburgh: Ballantyne, 1811.

Sedgwick, Eve Kosofsky. *Epistemology of the Closet.* Berkeley: U of California P, 1990.

Smith, Bruce R. *Homosexual Desire in Shakespeare's England: A Cultural Poetics.* Chicago: U of Chicago P, 1991.

Sparke, Michael. *The Narrative History of King James for the First Fourteen Years.* London, 1651.

Thomson, Katherine. *The Life and Times of George Villiers, Duke of Buckingham.* 3 vols. London: Hurst & Blackett, 1860.

Weldon, Anthony. *The Court and Character of King James.* London, 1651.

Welwood, James. *Memoirs of the Most Material Transactions in England of the Last Hundred Years.* London, 1702.

Williams, Charles. *James I.* London: Barker, 1934.

Williamson, Hugh Ross. *George Villiers, First Duke of Buckingham: Study for a Biography.* London: Duckworth, 1940.

Willson, David Harris. *King James VI and I.* [1956.] New York: Oxford UP, 1967.

Wilson, Arthur. *The History of Great Britain, being the Life and Reign of King James the First.* London, 1653.

III

Writing and Religion

12

The Making of *Rex Pacificus*: James VI and I and the Problem of Peace in an Age of Religious War

Malcolm Smuts

I know not by what fortune the diction of Pacificus was added to my title at my coming to England; that of the lion, expressing true fortitude, having been my diction before.

James I, A Meditation upon the Lord's Prayer *(1619), 93.*

However it originated, James I's reputation as *Rex Pacificus* has shaped evaluations of his rule ever since the early seventeenth century. For some contemporaries and many later historians, it reflected a fundamental weakness that led to the betrayal of international Protestant interests and the decay of English military power. Other scholars have been more sympathetic, among them James Patterson, who has recently written a book on the king's pursuit of religious reconciliation throughout Europe. But in all the discussion James's intellectual commitment to peace has more often been taken for granted than closely examined. A handful of contemporary anecdotes concerning his fear of violence and aversion to military exercises, repeatedly recycled by modern biographers, has fostered an impression of a monarch viscerally opposed to war under almost any circumstances (Willson 273–74). The possibility that his desire for peace involved more complex considerations—perhaps even amounting to some sort of strategic vision—has never received adequate attention (cf. Parker).

This neglect does not stem from lack of evidence. Few subjects illustrate so well Gordon Donaldson's characterization of this "king who was himself a theologian, the first king about whose thoughts and ideals we are adequately informed through his own writings"(197). James's published discussions of issues relating to religious war and peace began with his earliest prose tracts in the 1580s and continued through to the posthumous edition of his table talk that appeared in 1627 (*Flores Regii*). Since he also enjoyed verbal discussions of religious politics, we can compare his printed works to a stream of oral pronouncements recorded in the correspondence of English courtiers and foreign diplomats. Few other monarchs of the period have left such abundant sources documenting their views on international politics. Queen Elizabeth and Charles I, for example, were both far less voluble.

The chief problem with this evidence is that James's pronouncements on war and peace are scattered, interwoven with discussions of other subjects, and not altogether consistent. The inconsistencies stem partly from the shifting political and polemical contexts in which he wrote and the suppleness of his mind, which was adept at adjusting theoretical positions to meet immediate practical needs. From an early age James had learned to treat intellectual arguments as political tools, which he deployed to attract allies, throw opponents off balance, and probe the attitudes of others with whom he had to deal. He did have fundamental beliefs, and his fondness for sweeping statements of principle sometimes got him into trouble, but he could also be very cagey when discussing contentious issues, often deliberately revealing only one side of a multi-faceted position. This fact makes him a very difficult thinker to pin down, since we need to pay attention not just to the king's words but to the contexts in which he uttered them.

It is well worth attempting to do so, however, not only to understand his own outlook, but because to a considerable extent his views established parameters within which his servants had to operate. There was little point for a Jacobean courtier or diplomat in opposing the king's stated beliefs, whereas a strategy of trying to guide him by appealing to his own convictions and prejudices had a far greater chance of success. It will be argued here that until fairly late in the reign, James's ideas on international religious politics were sufficiently broad and flexible to accommodate a wide spectrum of attitudes toward most policy issues, including firm commitment to international Protestant causes. Only toward the end of his life did his desire for accommodation with Spain during the early phases of the Thirty Years War begin to narrow the range of views that could be advocated within his court with some prospect of success. The result was a sharper polarization of opinion both at court and among the political nation generally.

Thanks in part to Charles McIlwain, discussions of James as a political thinker commonly begin with two treatises of the late 1590s, *The True Law of Free Monarchies* and *Basilikon Doron* (*Political Works of James I*). To understand the evolution of his ideas on religious war, however, we need to start about a decade earlier, with two "meditations" on scriptural texts he published in 1588–89. Both are wartime tracts, written in response to the Spanish Armada and the rising tide of war and confessional violence that engulfed much of northwest Europe in the late 1580s. They also date from the period of James's closest alliance with Presbyterianism, when he was eager to establish his credentials as a godly monarch. They accordingly take a decidedly militant position.

The 1588 *Fruitfull Meditation, Containing a Plaine and Easie Exposition . . . of the vii. viii. ix and x Verses of the 20. chapter of Revelations* advances the standard Protestant argument that the pope is the Antichrist foretold by St. John. This enemy has now placed Scotland under a threefold siege: "spiritually by the heresies of the antichrist"; "corporally . . . as members of that church . . . which . . . they persecute;" and "particularly" by Spain's Armada (*Workes* 80; cf. Parker 186, 191–92). Scots must accordingly "join one with another as warriors in one camp, and citizens of one beloved city, for defense of the good cause God hath clad us with, and in defence of our liberties, native country and lives" (*Workes* 80). A year later the second meditation on a passage from Chronicles followed up with a discussion of Davidic kingship as a model for the alliance James sought to lead in Scotland. David had gone to war against the Philistines accompanied by the elders, the captains, and the priests and Levites of Israel—groups that corresponded, James argued, to the barons and civil magistrates, military commanders, and clergy of Scotland. It had been necessary for David and his people "to fight God's battles, to subdue the enemies of his Church, and to procure by doing so a peaceable kingdom for Solomon his son, who should in peace, as a figure of Christ the Prince of Peace, build the Lord's Temple" (ibid. 84–85). In the same way the people of Britain were obliged to fight an enemy who are "as the Philistines . . . continually the persecutors and we as Israel the defenders of our native soil" (ibid. 88).

An unpublished speech to the Scottish Parliament, preserved among the Cotton manuscripts in the British Library, was even more forceful. God blessed his elect, James argued, by separating them from "bad hypocrites" who might otherwise corrupt their religion. To that end he had permitted "the confederating together of all the bastard Christians (I mean the papists) in a league which they term holy (albeit most unholy in very truth) for the subversion of true religion in all realms throughout the whole world" (British Library Cotton mss., Caligula C IX, fo. 276v). Good Christians had no choice but to resist this oppression. A similar emphasis appears, somewhat incongruously, at the conclusion of James's poem *Lepanto,* celebrating the great naval victory over the Turks by a Catholic fleet in 1571. A "chorus of angels" draws the lesson that since the Almighty has avenged Turkish cruelty even against people who "worship a God of bread" and "bear upon their brow / The mark of Antichrist the whore," he will certainly stand by true Christians when they are persecuted by Catholics. Protestants should therefore take courage and "resist with confidence" (*Lepanto* sig. E3).

James in the late 1580s was far more outspoken in denouncing the papacy and justifying armed Protestant resistance than Elizabeth. This fact would continue to color his reputation for some time. In 1603, for example, Henry IV complained to his ambassador in London of the publication and dissemination in Paris and Bordeaux of an early "confession of faith" by James VI, "full of injurious words against the pope and the mass," which had stirred up Catholic opinion against him (British Library King's mss. 124, fos. 40v–41).

In sharp contrast, the panegyrics that greeted James in England in 1603–4 frequently hailed him as a peacemaker and only rarely betrayed traces of bellicose Protestantism. Ben Jonson, for example, graced the king's first formal entry into London in March of 1604 with a pageant hailing him as a monarch whose:

> Strong and potent virtues have defac'd
> Stern Mars statues, and upon them plac'd
> His and the worlds bless'd blessings. This hath brought
> Sweet peace to sit in that bright state she ought
> Unbloody or untroubled; hath forced hence
> All tumults, fears or other dark portents. (Qtd. in Nichols 1:393; other examples at 1: 122, 127, 133, 271, 275)

Other pageants on this occasion, written by Thomas Dekker, were less overtly pacific, but they did not contain references to godly warfare either. The one significant exception was a pageant sponsored by Dutch merchants, who were rightly worried that James was about to abandon Elizabeth's alliance with their country by signing a separate peace with Spain. This alluded to the English Reformation under Edward VI and Elizabeth I, while employing a vaguely messianic imagery somewhat reminiscent of the King's earlier meditation on Revelations (qtd. in Nichols 1: 349–51; Smuts 2001). Its staunchly Protestant message found no clear echoes elsewhere in the day's pageantry. A short time later James himself boasted to his first Parliament that the chief blessing "which God hath jointly with my person sent unto you, is outward peace: that is, peace abroad with all foreign neighbors. . . . I found the state embarked in a great and tedious war . . . and by the peace in my person, is now amity kept" (*Political Works of James I* 270).

From this perspective James VI and I does indeed begin to look like two very different kings. The discrepancy is largely explained, however, by altered circumstances. By 1603 the military emergency had passed and the long Anglo-Spanish war was visibly drawing to a close. James's accession made it easier to achieve peace since, unlike the case with Elizabeth, the Spaniards did not hold him responsible for more than thirty years of hostile acts against their interests. But most of Elizabeth's ministers, including Robert Cecil, had wanted peace for some time. James was able to take credit for a treaty, signed in March 1604, that owed more to the mutual interests of both belligerents than to his own efforts. Moreover, in pursuing the English throne he had made a number of conciliatory gestures to English recusants, foreign Catholic rulers, and even the pope. There was no point in squandering whatever goodwill he had thereby achieved by antipapal rhetoric. Finally, his smooth succession had come as an enormous relief to contemporaries who feared a violent contest for the Crown following the queen's death. Even after James's arrival in London some observers, like the French ambassador, kept nervously watching for signs of unrest (British Library King's mss. 128, e.g. fos. 6, 30–31, 308). Under these conditions James and his English supporters had every reason to stress his qualities as a guarantor of peace and stability.

Changes in Scottish politics during the 1590s had also stimulated an evolution in the king's thought that continued to influence him in England. The Presbyterian alliance collapsed, leading to far more assertive attempts to bring the Kirk under royal control as well as shrill protests by alienated clergy. James responded by developing a critique of Puritanism as a political force, most clearly articulated in a passage of *Basilikon Doron* describing the Scottish reformation (Wormald "James VI and I"; Mason "George Buchanan"). Unlike the reformations of England, Denmark, and "sundry parts of Germany," this had been achieved "by a popular tumult and rebellion," in the course of which "some fiery spirited men in the ministry . . . begouth to fantasy to themselves a democratic form of government" and feed "themselves with the hope to become *Tribuni plebis*" (*Political Works of James I* 23). They supported every faction that arose to contest royal authority, while simultaneously agitating for "a parity in the ministry" to frustrate efforts to restore order to the church. The external Catholic threat to Scotland's peace and security had come to be balanced, in James's mind, by an internal Presbyterian threat.

Although the immediate context was Scottish, this critique of Presbyterianism closely paralleled arguments deployed by English conformist polemics against Puritanism. Richard Bancroft, for example, had described the Scottish reformation in fairly similar terms in a Paul's Cross sermon of 1588, in which he also praised James for resisting the leveling instincts of Presbyterians (74–75). At the time, James had rejected Bancroft's embrace by defending the Scottish Kirk, and even years later, in England, he never gave unreserved support to the most determined anti-Puritans among the English clergy (Wormald "Ecclesiastical Vitriol"). Yet on many points he had come to share the views of men like Bancroft before ever setting foot in England. Like them he tended to regard puritan agitation as a manifestation of qualities of "Pride, Ambition and Avarice" that had generated heresy throughout the history of the church, while also troubling civil society (*Political Works of James I* 23; Larkin and Hughes 62). As Peter McCullough and Lori Anne Ferrel have shown, sermons by anti-Puritan clergy at James's English court repeatedly sought to exploit this attitude to polemical advantage.

The king's theological understanding of his own role had also become considerably more complex by the time he composed *Basilikon Doron* and *True Law,* which provide the fullest exposition of his concept of divine right monarchy. For James royal divine right was always closely linked to ideas concerning a king's duties to promote God's will by assisting the church, administering justice, and punishing wrongdoing. The primary model remained the Old Testament account of Jewish monarchy in Kings and Chronicles, "wherein," he told Prince Henry, "shall ye see yourself as in a mirror, in the catalogue either of the good or the evil" (*Political Works of James I* 14). But *Basilikon Doron* supplemented scriptural sources through a discussion that drew extensively on Greek and Roman political writers, such as Cicero, Seneca, and Plato, as well as observations gleaned from his own practical experience. A king, James argued, needs to master the laws of his realm, sit in "secret counsel . . . for matters of estate," and read "authentic histories" with an eye toward "applying bypast things to the present." He must learn to judge men and weigh the truth of their reports, and observe carefully the characteristic vices of his people and of each particular rank among them. Only in that way can he learn where reform and discipline is most required. Finally, since people naturally imitate their prince's behavior, he must lead by example (ibid. 39–40, 18).

Although none of these precepts was in the least original, they do indicate how the scripturally based vision of James's early meditations had expanded into a wider and deeper understanding of his role. The emphasis had shifted from rallying Scotland against a foreign religious foe to reforming it internally, by a combination of legislation, more effective law enforcement, and a forceful assertion of personal kingship. Emphasis on a monarch's responsibilities toward his subjects had been especially characteristic of Scottish political thought since the fifteenth century (Burns). James gave this belief, which he shared with Presbyterian opponents like George Buchanan and Andrew Melville, a set of peculiar inflections reflecting his own struggle to reassert royal authority in a kingdom riven by religious and aristocratic factionalism. In addition to suppressing mutinous clergy, a Scottish king needed to humble the nobility's "arrogant conceit of . . . greatness and power" by making it submit "to the laws as precisely as the meanest," while keeping an especially careful eye over hereditary jurisdictions and borough courts that served local interests at the expense of the common good (*Political Works of James I* 24–26). The "barbarous" lords of the Highlands and even more barbarous inhabitants of the Western Isles required still more strenuous discipline, including, in the latter case, colonization by orderly lowlanders, who might in time draw them toward civilization. In short, he must restrain oppression and violence wherever he finds it, while working to extend order, civility, and habits of obedience. By doing so he becomes the living image of God within his kingdom, dispensing justice and mercy in the service of divine law.

In addition a king will sometimes serve more particular providential objectives. James's Calvinist upbringing and interest in the Bible lent his thought an eschatological coloration, sometimes causing him to interpret historical events as part of an unfolding divine plan. His attitude toward the union of England and Scotland provides an especially clear example. "It is manifest that God by his Almighty providence hath ordained it," he told his first English Parliament when advocating a statutory unification of his two kingdoms:

> Hath not God first united these two kingdoms both in language, religion and similitude of manners? Yea hath he not made us all in one island, compassed with one sea, and of itself by nature so indivisible, as almost those that were borderers . . . cannot distinguish . . . their own limits. . . ? And now in the end and fullness of time united, the right and title of both in my person . . . . What God hath joined then, let no man separate. I am the husband and all the whole Isle is my lawful wife. (*Political Works of James I* 271)

As Arthur Williamson has shown, this argument had a lineage going back to John Knox and, behind him, to English propagandists on behalf of Protector Somerset's attempts to conquer Scotland in the 1540s. But as even some English writers acknowledged in the early seventeenth century, Somerset's wars had failed, as had all previous attempts at English conquest, whereas James achieved unification peacefully, as the result of an earlier marriage between the two kingdoms' ruling dynasties. The result was a union "not enforced by conquest and violence . . . but naturally derived from . . . right and title" that both nations freely recognized (Larkind and Hughes 95).

In short, just as an ordinary marriage united the families of bride and groom, God sometimes used royal marriages as a way of incorporating two different peoples into a single body politic. James knew that true unification could only be achieved gradually. Let the work "be brought on with time, and at leisure," he had written in *Basilikon Doron,* "by so mixing through alliance and daily conversation the inhabitants of every kingdom with [the] other, as may make them grow and weld all in one" (*Political Works of James I* 51). But he had no doubt that was what God ultimately wanted. The enforced mixing of English and Scots at his court, along with marriages he arranged between noble families of the two kingdoms, were intended to promote that end.

In this way the concept of peace—in an extended sense, involving the eradication of ancient hatreds and promotion of charity, goodwill, and mutual dependence among nations—became linked to the principle of indefeasible hereditary succession to thrones and the equally fundamental conviction that political allegiance ultimately derives from a *personal* bond between monarchs and their subjects rather than any particular body of local custom. This view had considerable implications for understanding relations between European states. Francis Bacon, for example, speculated that God had brought about the dynastic unification of three great monarchies—Britain, France, and the Spanish empire—so that they might together settle "the affairs of Europe . . . to a more assured and universal peace and concord" (6: 275). It is a mistake to regard James's later pursuit of a dynastic alliance with the Habsburgs as a purely secular policy, in contrast to the religiously charged anti-Spanish militancy of his Puritan subjects. The king's vision of peace was equally rooted in providentialist thinking.

The emphasis on peace in English panegyrics seems perfectly consistent with these attitudes, while James's pursuit of a treaty with Spain also becomes readily intelligible in their light. Once in London he quickly signaled not only his desire for peace but a willingness to acknowledge the legitimacy of Habsburg dynastic rights over the Netherlands. In May a worried French ambassador reported that while dining the king had announced to his entourage that "the soldiers can hang up their arms, that his objective is to have peace with all the world, and the conservation of Ostend [then under siege by a Spanish army] did not concern him at all since that place belonged by right to the Archduke," the Habsburg governor of the Netherlands (British Library King's mss. 123, fos. 135v–36). The publication of a book maintaining the duty of subjects to obey their sovereign sparked another conversation around the king's table in which he "openly condemned" the cause of the rebellious Dutch provinces with whom he was still formally allied, scandalizing their ambassadors, who had recently arrived in London (British Library King's mss. 123 fos. 144 and 160).

It would be a mistake, however, to regard James's support of peace and dynastic rights of sovereignty as the whole story. For he had not entirely forgotten his earlier fears of Catholic "holy leagues." By June of 1603 he was reassuring the French ambassador of his deep mistrust of the "pernicious and ambitious designs" of the Spanish Habsburgs, whose aspiration to become monarchs of all Christendom led them to "continually trouble [other kingdoms] by wars and seditions, employing all their industry to foment revolts and assassinations in neighboring states" (British Library King's mss. 123, fo. 245v). Even if he made peace with Spain, as he insisted his people wanted, he realized the need for continuing cooperation with France against the "perfidious" Spaniards (British Library King's mss. 123, fo. 212). Meanwhile he had discussed with at least one English diplomat the need to prevent the *French* from achieving a closer alliance with the Netherlands (Historical Manuscripts Commission 30). The seeming inconsistency of James's pronouncements led the Venetian ambassador to conclude that he was a monarch who, "having passed all his life in deep dissimulations which have happily succeeded," had now decided to pursue the same strategy in international politics (British Library King's mss. 123, fo. 236).

But the dissimulation served a purpose, since it kept James's options open while he warily sought to assess the intentions of the major

European powers and lay the groundwork for possible future cooperation with each of them. His lingering suspicions of Spain and other Catholic powers probably owed something to religious conviction, since he still regarded the pope as Antichrist. He was less concerned with Catholicism as such, however, than with the danger that confessional differences might give rise to secular disturbances. The single greatest source of unrest in European politics, he told the French ambassador, was "the diversity of opinion in religion that extends through all nations and the interest of the popes in taking advantage of it by inciting wars" (British Library King's mss. 123, fo. 327). The desire for accommodation was balanced not only by fear of Spanish military power, but fear that foreign popish agents might foster religious rebellions or regicidal plots within his own dominions.

A number of developments during James's first decade in England kept these fears alive. Several conspiracies involving recusants, culminating in the Gunpowder Plot of 1605, convinced him that English papists remained dangerous. Even before 1605 the Bye plot—a mysterious episode—had implicated the earl of Northumberland and other leading Catholics in conspiracies against the king. In the wider European arena the assassination of Henry IV in 1610, a disputed succession to the territory of Julich-Cleves that threatened to ignite a German confessional war, and the conclusion of a double marriage alliance between France and Spain all provoked considerable alarm. Ravaillac's crime was not an isolated incident: Henry IV had survived nineteen earlier assassination attempts (Parker 147). Even though Spain was never implicated, the French king's death accentuated fears that Spain and the papacy still regarded political murder as a legitimate tool of policy. The Habsburg-Bourbon marriage treaty raised fears not only of an alliance between the two great military powers of the continent but also a revival of the intolerant pro-Spanish Catholicism that had flourished in France during the wars of religion.

James attempted to counter these dangers in several ways. He concluded an alliance of his own by marrying his daughter Elizabeth to the Elector Palatine, the leading Calvinist prince in Germany. This provided some insurance, should the Franco-Spanish alliance turn aggressive. Meanwhile he attempted to sound out both the French and Spanish courts about their willingness to conclude a match with his eldest son, Prince Henry, or, after Henry's death in 1612, with Prince Charles. He also sought to intervene in French politics by encouraging the princes of the blood and other great nobles to join in opposition to the policies of the regency government of Marie de Medici. To that end he sought to mediate quarrels among the French grandees, while opening direct lines of communication to as many of them as possible. "You shall labor with all earnestness to hasten . . . a sound and perfect reconciliation betwixt the persons of Bouillon and Rohan," James wrote to his ambassador in Paris, Thomas Edmonds, in August of 1612:

> You shall also use all the indirect means you can to win Monsieur de Guise to be of this party, and you may let it come to his ears that you hear that we wonder much that notwithstanding of the message we sent him at Monsieur de Bouillon's departure . . . we have never yet heard from him since. . . . that by the means of the princes of the blood, with the assistance of Bouillon, Desdiguisers and all the body of the [Protestant] religion, together with the house of Guise if they may be won, that pernicious statesman may be first removed, and then this alliance and popish cabal betwixt France and Spain to be quite broken off. (British Library Stow mss. 173, fos. 80–81)

Five years later, when the prince of Condé was arrested for a revolt against the regency government, James wrote a letter in his support that found its way into print (*Lettre*).

Despite his belief in divine right, the king was not above meddling in the affairs of other monarchs when he felt his vital interests were at stake. Although his efforts were conducted mainly through ambassadors and other intermediaries, his own published and unpublished writings also played a role. His reputation as a scholar and author made it easier for him to establish relations with other writers among the political and religious leaders of foreign states, some of whom actively sought his approval. Thus he agreed to accept the dedication of an antipapal treatise by the major Huguenot writer Philipe Du Plessis-Mornay, but he criticized a book by the duke de Bouillon (British Library Stowe mss. 173, fos. 161 [Bouillon]; 43, 119v–20, 163 [Du Plessis Mornay]). James attacked the ideas of the Dutch theologian Vorstius, antagonizing some of the latter's political allies in the Netherlands, and he tried to contain a French theological dispute between Pierre Du Moulin and Daniel Tilenus through personal communications to both protagonists urging restraint (Birch, *Life of Henry* 402; Public Record Office State Papers 14/67/100; Patterson 168–69 and ch. 5). These interventions extended James's role as a peacemaker and promoter of religious reconciliation, but they also served British strategic interests, by preserving the unity of foreign churches that might some day become military allies while enticing Catholic noblemen like Guise into coalitions that spanned confessional boundaries.

James also responded to threats of popish conspiracy and aggression by initiating a polemical campaign against doctrines that justified regicide, rebellion, and confessional warfare. In the aftermath of the Gunpowder Plot the English Parliament passed an Oath of Allegiance that the government might extend to subjects at will, forcing them to swear that they regarded the pope's claim to possess a right to depose monarchs as "impious and heretical." Many English Catholics took the oath, but Pope Pius V issued a breve condemning it, and the prominent Jesuit theologian Cardinal Bellarmine attacked it in print. James personally replied with a pamphlet published in English, French, and Latin, *Triplici nodo triplex cuneus, or an Apologie for the Oath of Allegiance.* This touched off an international controversy that ultimately gave rise to over 150 tracts. The king actively recruited and patronized Protestant and moderate Catholic theologians to support his position and published two more tracts under his own name: *A Premonition to All Most Mighty Monarches, Kings, Free Princes and States of Christendom,* and *A Remonstrance for the Right of Kings, and the Independence of their Crownes* (*Political Works of James I* 71–268).

In these tracts, whose preparation required a substantial investment of his time and energy, he sought to show that the pope's pretended concern for religion was a specious pretext masking a real desire for political power. (For James's preoccupation with the controversy see Public Record Office State Papers 14/14/88; Casaubon 80.) Although Roman apologists claimed that popes would only attempt to depose monarchs for notorious heresy, history proved otherwise. The papacy had repeatedly encouraged rebellions against orthodox kings in the past and refused to repudiate its right to do so in the future. "Let a kingdom fall into some grievous disaster or calamity," James thundered: "let civil wars boil in the bowels of the kingdom . . . who rusheth sooner into the troubled streams than the Pope . . . and all under color of a heart wounded and bleeding for the salvation of souls" (*Political Works of James I* 267). "The pestilent mischief" had taken root because God in his secret judgment had "smitten" Christian rulers "with a spirit of dizziness." But he would soon awaken them from their "slumber," so that popes would no longer be able "to put bits and snaffles in their noble mouths . . . like mighty bulls led about by little children with a small twisted thread" (ibid. 267).

These arguments sought to rally not only Protestants but Catholic *politiques,* many of whom detested the Jesuits and resented clerical attempts to meddle in secular politics. This appeal was especially pertinent in two European contexts that developed while the controversy raged. In Venice a dispute arising in 1606 over the jurisdictional and inheritance rights of the clergy resulted in the city's being placed under a papal interdict (Bouwsma). James eagerly followed the ensuing controversy with the aid of his ambassador Henry Wotton, who forwarded satires, visual lampoons, and more serious tracts—especially the writings of Paolo Sarpi, the Venetian republic's chief defender (Smith 1: 400, 412, 431, 444). English translations of two of Sarpi's lesser treatises were printed in London during the controversy, while his greatest work, *The History of the Counsel of Trent,* appeared in English a few years later from the press of James's official printer (Sarpi, *Full and Satisfactory Answer; Apology; History*). In return, James dispatched a number of Protestant books for Wotton to distribute in Venice, naturally including the Latin edition of his own *Apology* (Smith 416–17, 462, 465–66). The second context was France during a meeting of the Estates General in 1614, in which the Third Estate, representing the people, passed an oath modeled after that of England, which the First (clerical) Estate soon vetoed. James's *Remonstrance for the Right of Kings* attacked the oration of the clergy's leader, Cardinal Du Perron.

Neither intervention succeeded, and several of James's continental allies, including Sarpi, soon grew impatient with him for writing books instead of taking decisive action (Bouwsma 526–27). But James was convinced that ideas mattered in politics. So long as Catholics believed their religion justified disobedience and regicide the peace of Europe would never be safe. Although militant Catholicism no longer represented the kind of immediate threat that it had in the 1580s, while Jesuits and other papal writers continued to support doctrines that encouraged conspiracies like the Gunpowder Plot the danger had not passed. Although James certainly wanted peaceful coexistence with Catholic Europe, he had not let down his guard. Stalwart Protestants, who believed in the need to prepare for a renewal of the wars of religion, consequently had little reason to feel isolated at his court. Even if the king's willingness to entertain Habsburg diplomatic overtures and his reluctance to take stronger action sometimes frustrated such people, the most sensible response was to keep emphasizing the suspicions of Spain, Rome, and domestic popery that he shared with them. This is precisely what Protestant internationalists on the Privy Council, like Archbishop Abbot, kept doing (British Library Trumbull mss., items 6, 12, and 16).

The ultimate outcome of policy discussions remained unclear partly because the early seventeenth century had brought a pause in Europe's wars of religion, without ending the mutual suspicion and hostility of the confessional adversaries. No one could know for certain whether this interval would lead to a gradual amelioration of tensions, a renewed outbreak of conflict, or, in the latter case, precisely what the alignment of forces might be. So long as it was necessary to prepare for a variety of contingencies policies remained somewhat fluid.

But the international situation changed again after 1618, when a Protestant rebellion attempted to transfer the crown of Bohemia from the Habsburgs to James's son-in-law, the Elector Palatine. The Elector's acceptance of this offer precipitated a crisis that escalated, over the next three years, into a confessional war in which Spanish troops helped conquer the Palatinate itself. The king and his Council therefore faced an increasingly stark choice: between entering the war on the Protestant side or maintaining a neutrality that benefited Habsburg interests, in the hope that an Anglo-Spanish marriage alliance might also lead to a negotiated settlement on acceptable terms.

Although many of James's counselors favored military action, he refused to break off negotiations with Madrid (Birch, *Court and Times* 2: 191; Public Record Office State Papers 14/109/157). This policy not only deeply offended Protestant sentiment, it also contradicted James's own earlier published opposition—in *Basilikon Doron*—to a Catholic match for his children (*Political Works of James I* 8). Why had he decided to trust the king of Spain rather than rallying to the defense of his coreligionists? That question can only be fully answered through a more complete study of Jacobean diplomacy in this period, based on European as well as British sources, especially the Spanish archives in Simancas (Pursell).

James's later writings do provide some suggestive indications, however. Even at the height of his polemical campaign against the Jesuits, the king's hostility to Protestant radicalism never abated. As Dudley Carleton remarked at the time and Ferrel has shown in a recent book, many court sermons against the Gunpowder Plot also attacked Puritan disobedience. As Carleton put it, they struck indiscriminately at "Jesuited or Genevated divinity." He found this offensive: "I doubt our good friends, that profess the same as we do, will hold themselves much scandalized" (Birch, *Court and Times* 1: 99). James correctly perceived that Jesuit arguments often closely resembled the ideas of earlier Calvinist resistance theorists, such as François Hotman and his own tutor, George Buchanan. He drew the logical inference: "Jesuits are nothing but Puritan-papists" (*Political Works of James I* 126). The fundamental problem was not popery so much as a willingness to use religion as an excuse for rebellion, which might develop on either end of the confessional spectrum. This attitude cooled his support for European Protestant extremism. So did his reaction to the internal quarrels of foreign reformed churches, especially in the Netherlands. In a treatise justifying his intervention against Vorstius James complained vociferously against "the corrupt seed" that divided the Dutch Republic into religious and political "factions," threatening it with "utter ruin" (*A Declaration Concerning the Proceedings of the States Generall of the United Provinces of the Low Countries in the Cause of D. Conradus Vorstius,* rpt. in *Political Works of James I,* quotation at 355). Worse, "those heretics, or rather atheistical sectaries" had attempted to subvert his own kingdom by arguing that their ideas were agreeable to the doctrines of the Church of England. Suggestively, James thought that heresy and faction were even more of a problem in "Bohemia, where there are such infinite diversities of sects (agreeing in nothing but their union against the Pope)" (ibid. 371). This attitude helps explain his skepticism of the Bohemian cause and his conclusion that Frederick's decision to accept that kingdom's crown was both impolitic and probably unjustifiable (*Political Works* 257–58).

James held an elastic definition of Puritanism that tended to expand or contract to suit his shifting moods and polemical needs. In his more generous moments he exonerated moderate Calvinists, even when they politely criticized aspects of the official liturgy (e.g., *Political Works of James I* 7–8). Comments in his later works suggest a hardening of his attitude, however. In *A Meditation upon the Lord's Prayer* (1619) he repudiated Puritan chiliasts like Thomas Brightman, who "gape after that thousand years of Christ's kingdom," forgetting "that the latter days shall prove the worst and most dangerous days." Since chiliasm was sometimes associated with belief in the imminence of a great religious war that might finally destroy the papal Antichrist, this stance is significant. James criticized divines whose zeal for sermons led them to neglect prayer, a standard complaint of anti-Puritan clergy like Lancelot Andrewes (*Meditation* 40–41; 5–6). He also refused to exonerate moderate Puritans from the sins of the radical Brownists, arguing that "the latter only boldly [put] in practice what the former do teach" (ibid. 14–15). "Trust not that private spirit or holy ghost which our puritans glory in," he warned, "see how . . . once trusting to the private spirit of Reformation, according to our Puritan doctrine, it is easy to fall and slide by degrees into Chaos, filthy sink and farrago of all horrible heresies" (ibid. 18–19). This suspicion of "private spirits" and religious "chaos" must have cooled James's ardor for the fractious politics of German Protestantism.

Equally important, the distrust of demagoguery that James had developed in his confrontation with Scottish Presbyterianism had later broadened out to encompass members of Parliament and country gentlemen who criticized his actions. If the Commons did not do a better job of discouraging irresponsible complaints, he warned in 1610, it "may become a place for pasquils, and at another time such grievances may be cast in amongst you as may contain treason or scandal against me or my posterity" (*Political Works of James I* 314). Six years later he complained of justices of the peace who "cannot be content with the present form of government, but must have a kind of liberty in the people . . . and in every cause that concerns the prerogative give a snatch against monarchy, through their puritanical itching after popularity" (ibid. 340). One reason for wishing to avoid war may well have been that he simply did not trust Parliament or the English political nation to respect his authority, once he had become dependent on supply to meet military needs.

Finally, James's commitment to peace as an ideal also seems to have grown stronger during his English reign. In 1589 the biblical model had been David, a king beset with internal and external enemies. By 1619 it had become Solomon, who presided over an age of peace and plenty. "God would not permit King David to build him a material temple," James wrote, "because of his shedding of blood, but made him leave that work to his son Solomon, who was a king of peace" (*Political Writings* 235). There was a parallel shift in classical paradigms from Julius Caesar, whose writings James had warmly praised in *Basilikon Doron,* to Augustus. "It should not have been fitting," the quoted passage continued, "that the savior of the world, the builder of his Church . . . should have been born but under a King of peace, as was Augustus, and in a time of peace" (ibid.). A number of undated comments in the posthumous edition of James's table talk echo the same message: "No country can be called rich wherein there is war." "Those princes which seek to secure themselves by blood, shall find that the more they kill the more they have needs to kill." "It was never found that blood and too much severity did good in matters of religion, God never loving to plant the Church by violence and bloodshed" (*Flores Regii* 7, 44, 112–13).

For all these reasons James must instinctively have recoiled from the prospect of going to war in support of German Protestants. He had indeed become *Rex Pacificus.* Counselors who wanted a more aggressively Protestant policy accordingly found themselves stymied at every turn, until Prince Charles and the duke of Buckingham grew disillusioned with the Spanish match and came to their rescue in 1623. Even after that date it is by no means clear that James would have permitted the actual commencement of hostilities had he lived a year or two longer.

As this essay has argued, however, it is a mistake to read the king's attitude of the early 1620s back into the earlier years of his reign, assuming that James was always a pro-Spanish pacifist at heart. There is, to be sure, abundant evidence that he *desired* better relations with Madrid from at least 1603 onward and that he was considerably less enthusiastic about militant Protestant causes than *some* of his subjects. The danger lies in exaggerating the king's genuine pacific and irenic instincts to the point at which other attitudes, especially his lingering fear and distrust of militant Catholicism, become obscured. Doing so will distort our view of not only James himself but the circumstances in which his counselors and diplomats tried to shape and implement his policies. Even more seriously, exaggerating James's pacifism can lead us to avoid asking the right questions about just how his attitudes toward European confessional conflict changed over the course of his reign.

The stereotype of James as *Rex Pacificus,* who succeeded the more warlike Queen Elizabeth and dismantled her system of Protestant alliances, is embedded within a larger set of stereotypes of early seventeenth-century politics. It contributes to narratives of the period involving sharply defined contrasts: between the hispanaphile policies of the Stuarts and the patriotic Protestantism which the last Tudor is supposed to have shared with the English people and their parliaments. This image has a lineage dating back to the period itself—especially some of the pamphlets opposing the Spanish match, which evoked Elizabethan memories in order to excoriate the king for negotiating with the former enemy. It can also be supported by citing Jacobean panegyrics and court masques that glorified the King's pacific rule. But if we penetrate beyond the claims of panegyrists and pamphleteers, refusing to read the entire reign from the perspective of the early 1620s, a much more complex story emerges. It is a story that cannot be told entirely in terms of conflicts between fixed ideological positions because it unfolded in a constantly changing international environment, in which intellectual assumptions had to be adjusted to shifting circumstances. Like all statesmen, James never enjoyed the luxury of a purely theoretical approach to the major issues confronting his contemporaries. If he was a royal theologian he was also a working politician trying to thread his way through dangerous political minefields. Certain fundamental beliefs do appear to have shaped his outlook throughout his adult life. These include an abhorrence of atrocities justified by religion, a firm belief in the sacred nature of his royal office, and a commitment to the advancement of the interests of God's church, as he understood them. But his understanding of the meaning of these principles and the strategies needed to achieve them changed fairly drastically over the course of a career that spanned more than forty years. Examined carefully, his writings provide considerable insight into the evolution of his views.

Works Cited

Bacon, Francis. *Works.* Ed. James Spedding. 14 vols. Stuttgart-Bad Cannstatt: G. Holzboog, 1962.

Bancroft, Richard. *A Sermon Preached at Paul's Cross.* London, 1588.

Birch, Thomas, ed. *The Life of Henry, Prince of Wales, Eldest Son of James I.* London: A. Millar, 1760.

———. *The Court and Times of James I.* 2 vols. London: H. Colburn, 1848.

Bouwsma, William. *Venice and the Defense of Republican Liberty: Renaissance Values in the Age of the Counter Reformation.* Berkeley: U of California P, 1968.

British Library (London) Manuscripts Division

Cotton mss. Caligula C IX

King's mss. 124–28

Stowe mss. 173

Trumbull mss. vol. 1

Burns, J. H. *The True Law of Kingship: Concepts of Monarchy in Early-Modern Scotland.* Oxford: Oxford UP, 1996.

Casaubon, Isaac. *Ephemerides.* Oxford: Oxford UP, 1850.

Donaldson, Gordon. *Scotland, James V to James VII.* Edinburgh: Oliver and Boyd, 1971.

Ferrel, Lori Anne. *Government by Polemic: James I, the King's Preachers and the Rhetorics of Conformity, 1603–1625.* Stanford: Stanford UP, 1998.

Guy, John, ed. *The Reign of Elizabeth: Court and Culture in the Last Decade.* Cambridge: Cambridge UP, 1995.

Historical Manuscripts Commission (Great Britain). *Salisbury Manuscripts.* Vol. 11. London: His Majesty's Stationery Office, 1930.

James VI and I. *Flores Regii. Or aphorisms divine and moral.* London, 1627.

———. *Lepanto.* 1603.

———. *Lettre d[u] Roy d'Angleterre. A madame la princesse de Condé.* 1617.

———. *A Meditation upon the Lord's Prayer.* London, 1619.

———. *Political Writings.* Ed. Johann Sommerville. Cambridge: Cambridge UP, 1994.

———. *The Political Works of James I Reprinted from the Edition of 1616.* Ed. Charles Howard McIlwain. Cambridge, Mass.: Harvard UP, 1918.

———. *The Workes of the Most High and Mightie Prince James . . . King of Great Britain.* Ed. James Montague. London, 1616.

Larkin, James F., and Paul L. Hughes, eds. *Stuart Royal Proclamations.* Vol. I *Royal Proclamations of King James I.* Oxford: Oxford UP, 1973.

Mason, Roger. "George Buchanan, James VI and the Presbyterians." Mason, *Scots and Britains.* 112–37.

———. *Scots and Britons: Scottish Political Thought and the Union of 1603.* Cambridge: Cambridge UP, 1994.

McCullough, Peter. *Sermons at Court: Politics and Religion in Elizabethan and Jacobean Preaching.* Cambridge: Cambridge UP, 1998.

Nichols, John, ed. *Progresses of James I.* 4 vols. London, 1828.

Parker, Geoffrey. *The Grand Strategy of Philip II.* New Haven: Yale UP, 1998.

Patterson, W. B. *King James VI and I and the Reunion of Christendom.* Cambridge: Cambridge UP, 1997.

Peck, Linda Levy, ed. *The Mental World of the Jacobean Court.* Cambridge: Cambridge UP, 1991.

Public Record Office (London). *State Papers* 14. N.d.

Pursell, Brennan. "The Constitutional Causes of the Thirty Years War: Friedrich V, the Palatine Crisis, and European Politics, 1618–1632." Diss. Harvard U. 2000.

Sarpi, Paolo. *An apology or apologeticall answere made unto Cardinal Bellarmine.* London, 1607.

———. *A full and satisfactory answer to the late . . . Bull against Venice.* London, 1606.

———. *The History of the Councel of Trent Conteining Eight Books.* Trans. Nathaniel Brent. London, 1620.

Smith, Logan Pearsall. *Life and Letters of Sir Henry Wotton.* 2 vols. Oxford: Oxford UP, 1907.

Smuts, Malcolm, ed. "The Whole Royal and Magnificent Pageant of King James through the City of London." In Taylor (forthcoming).

Taylor, Gary, ed. *The Complete Works of Thomas Middleton.* Oxford: Oxford UP, forthcoming.

Williamson, Arthur. *Scottish National Consciousness in the Age of James VI: The Apocalypse, the Union and the Shaping of Scotland's Public Culture.* Edinburgh: John Donald, 1979.

Willson, David Harris. *James VI and I.* Paperback ed. New York: Oxford UP, 1967.

Wormald, Jenny. "James VI and I, *Basilikon Doron* and *The Trew Law of Free Monarchies:* The Scottish Context and the English Translation." Peck, *Mental World.* 36–54.

———. "Ecclesiastical Vitriol: The Kirk, the Puritans and the Future King of England." Guy, *Reign of Elizabeth.* 171–91.

13

"To Eate the Flesh of Kings": James VI and I, Apocalypse, Nation, and Sovereignty

Daniel Fischlin

I

> And hee cryed out with a loude voyce, saying, *It is fallen, It is fallen, Babylon* that great Citie, and it is made the dwelling place of vncleane spirits, and the habitation of all vncleane and hatefull sowles, *to wit,* it shall be destroyed, and that great Citie, the seate of that Monarchie, shall be desolate for euer, euen as it was prophesied of Ierusalem; Because all nations haue drunke of the Vine of her whoredome, and the kings of the earth haue committed whoredome with her, and the Merchants of the earth are become rich by the great wealth of her delights, in so great a worldly glory and pompe did that Monarchie shine. And I heard another voyce from heauen, *to wit,* the voyce of the holy Spirit, saying, Goe foorth from her my people, *to wit,* all the chosen, lest ye be participants of her sinnes, and of the plagues which are to fall vpon her for them. (*Workes* 57; from James VI and I's *A Paraphrase upon the Revelation of the Apostle S. Iohn;* Rev. 18:2–4)

The above paraphrase of Revelation 18:2–4 by James VI and I exemplifies one strand of the many narrative allegories to be found in Revelation. Here, contestatory visions of the "vncleane" and the "chosen" are arrayed against a backdrop of apocalyptic, national, and sovereign concerns: survival versus destruction; Babylon versus Jerusalem; corrupt monarchy versus those who spurn participation in its sinful practices. In the apocalyptic struggle framed by this passage, corrupt kingship, a metonym for corrupt nationhood, is destroyed, while "another voyce from heauen" offers the hope of a people free from the whoredom and profligacy associated with Babylon. For a late sixteenth-century Scottish audience, the passage would have had particular allegorical potency, if only for its relation to the religious tensions particular to Reformation and Counter-Reformation Scotland and England. Apocalypse figures here as a crucial trope for monarchic decline but also for the hope of something better, presumably an ascendant monarch who will lead the "chosen" from the temptation of Babylonian dissipation. Because of its obvious allegories related to national and sovereign self-interest, the passage encapsulates the ground I wish to cover in this essay, especially in relation to formulating a context for understanding James VI and I's fascination with apocalypse as a literary structure with particular resonances to his historical situation as monarch. In this essay, then, I examine two apocalyptic texts.[1] The first is *A Paraphrase upon the Revelation of the Apostle St. John* (1588?),[2] in which James, through a brash prosopopoeia,[3] takes on the voice of John of Patmos. The second is *A Fruitfull Meditation, Containing a Plaine and Easie Exposition* . . . , first published in Edinburgh in 1588,[4] in which James provides commentary on Revelation 20:8–10. James, only twenty-two when he published the meditation (and probably several years younger when he wrote the Paraphrase)[5] ten years into his reign as James VI of Scotland, saw fit to include these as the first two texts a reader would encounter in his 1616 *Workes*. My argument is that these neglected texts articulate a nascent sense of James's emergent position in the political economy of Europe. Perhaps more importantly, the apocalyptic texts figure his emergent relation to the problematic form of absolute power he was to embody both in his political and literary actions over the next forty-odd years.

As much recent scholarship has been at pains to acknowledge,[6] James had a clear sense of the filiations between writing and governing: "In 1607 he told Parliament . . . 'Here I sit and governe it [Scotland] with my Pen, I write and it is done, and by a Clearke of the Councell I governe Scotland now, which others could not doe by the sword'" (Goldberg 56).[7] Among others, Jonathan Goldberg argues that "James ruled by the word" and that "in 1616, not only did the king publish his *Workes* but Ben Jonson also had the audacity to publish a wholly unprecedented folio" (ibid.). Both James's and Jonson's works are "unprecedented" in inversely significant ways: a monarch showing himself capable of and invested in writerly accomplishment and a commoner deigning to gather his works for public consumption, as if to suggest his own elevated status in the hierarchy of ideological and cultural values with which the production of texts was associated.[8] Both *Workes* hint at sophisticated notions of authority and authorship that were emerging as crucial strategies in early modern attempts to shape the uses of literary representation, and they provide a crucial context for understanding the literary and political function of James's commentaries on Revelation.

James's paraphrases of Revelation, I argue, effectively fetishize the book and, by consequence, bookish culture and the power of writing, thus contributing in critical ways to how James enacts his sovereignty in relation to literary culture.[9] For instance, in Revelation 20:12, a verse James found significant enough to devote an entirely separate meditation to in *A Fruitfull Meditation,* James paraphrastically imagines an eschatological and resurrective vision of the dead standing before God to be judged:

> And the bookes were opened, *to wit,* the counsels, and secrets of all mens hearts; and another booke, *to wit,* the booke of *Life* was opened, to the effect that all those whose names were written into it, *to wit,* predestinated and elected for salvation before all beginnings, might there be selected for eternall Glory: And the dead were iudged out of these things which were written in the bookes, according to their workes; for as God is a Spirit, so iudgeth he the thoughts of man, and so by faith onely iustifies him, which notwithstanding is done according to his workes, because they, as the fruits of faith, cannot be separated from it, and beare witness of the same to men in the earth. (*Workes* 65–66)

The passage puts into play a vision of a bookish God, basing final judgment on what various texts contain, namely "the counsels, and secrets of all mens hearts" and the names of the predestinated. The *Paraphrase* follows the original closely until James launches into the final sentence "for as God is a Spirit."[10] It is clear that up to this point in the *Paraphrase* books are sacred objects imbued with the secret of subjectivity as well as with the names of the elect. This position is not too far removed from that elaborated in the third book of *Basilikon Doron,* in which James affirms to his son Henry that "your writs will remain as true pictures of your mind to all posterities" (Fischlin and Fortier 165). Books contain the "thoughts of man," which, in the circular logic of James's *Paraphrase,* expose the faith that justifies "man" to God, which, in turn, is entirely dependent on man's "workes," the "fruits of faith" that "beare witnesse" to man's faith. Buried in the passage is a valorization of the "*booke*" as object of divine significance and of the "*worke*" as an emblem of the faith that designates the elect. Thanatological and eschatological worth, then, is literally predicated on one's "workes." In the context of such a passage it is not surprising that James's *Workes* begins with the crucial apocalyptic texts, which testify to his faith while highlighting the importance of the book (and, by extension, of the writing the book contains) in relation to his sovereign position as *fidei defensor.*

The capacity to conceive of rule by the word—captured in his famous phrase about governing "with my Pen"—is a crucial aspect of James's significance to early modern political strategies, as were his conciliarist and pacifist strategies[11] of political engagement described in detail by W. B. Patterson. Goldberg, as we have seen, frames James's discursive self-awareness in terms of a political speech made to Parliament *after* his accession to the English throne, but it is worth noting that in a much earlier text, the *Paraphrase* of Revelation, James had already formulated, or perhaps was in the process of formulating, the kind of political animus he would articulate throughout his life. For example, Revelation 2:16 states: "Repent; or else I will come unto thee quickly, and will fight against them with the sword of my mouth." James's paraphrase of the same verse has uncanny resonances with the passage cited from the 1607 speech to Parliament, perhaps functioning as a remote rehearsal for the later comment: "Repent therefore in time, otherwise I will come against thee soone, and I will fight and ouercome them who are amongst you, with the sword of my mouth, *to wit,* by the force of my word" (*Workes* 10).[12] The (s)word is transformed into a trope for the word in James's exegesis, which depends upon a prosopopoetic chain in which the "*Sonne of man*" (*Workes* 8) is given voice by John of Patmos, who in turn is given voice by James's *Paraphrase.* By setting up such linkages in the literary and rhetorical contexts of the *Paraphrase* James insures his association with both divine and vatic empowerment. But at the same time he voices "the force of *my* word" (emphasis mine), the possessive case here becoming a complicated metonym for James's, John's, and Jesus' "word" *as mediated by James.* The *Paraphrase* is noteworthy in this instance for how it uses the apocalyptic mise-en-scène to situate James as the nexus through which these different energies flow by virtue of his control of the exegesis.[13]

Other kinds of textual control are evident in James's apocalyptic writings as published in the 1616 *Workes.* In the case of the *Workes* it has not been customary to comment critically on the literary choices made with regard to placement of the texts chosen for inclusion in the collection. But the topography of the collection—the literary ordering James and his publisher James Montague, bishop of Winchester, saw fit to enact in this early attempt to define authorial integrity and influence through the creation of a monolithic "work"—does bear some thinking. With James, I would suggest that the choices made in deploying a particular sequence of texts in the *Workes* are far from random or unconsidered, especially in opening the grand authorial gesture of a collected works with two arcane readings of apocalyptic texts. My argument is that James converted the theological capital of Revelation into a covert form of secular capital specifically related to his sovereign dominion over the conflicted national contexts of Scotland and England. Figuratively, the Revelation texts allow James to imagine the relations between his role as sovereign and the national interests, religious and otherwise, he advocated.[14] The prominent positioning in the *Workes* of the two Revelation texts as the portals through which a reader passes on the way to subsequent works with more overt ideological and political resonances—*Basilikon Doron, The True Law,* the parliamentary speeches, and so forth—suggests an equally prominent place in the symbolics of James's textual self-presencing. These symbolics are almost invariably (and slyly) aligned with his sovereign relations to the nation.[15] A reader coming to these inaugural and recapitulative texts (inaugural because written early in James's writing career and recapitulative because they return the reader to what James must have felt was an important, perhaps even "originary," moment in his writing career) looking for facile connections between James's sovereign, national interests and his apocalyptic writings must be prepared to understand them not as unsophisticated juvenilia nor as exegetical exercises that bear little relation to James's politics. Rather the apocalyptic texts represent early attempts to link his literary inclinations with the contingencies of sovereign power.

As texts, the apocalyptic paraphrases have been notoriously overlooked by all major commentators on James—with the exception of Arthur H. Williamson's summary remarks—and there are no sustained critical reflections on either of them. As part of a literary strategy of self-empowerment or "self-explication" they have received no attention at all.[16] And yet, to return to their prominent position in the 1616 *Workes,* there seems little question as to their importance in James's strategy of literary self-presentation. After all, on encountering the *Workes,* a reader would first have been exposed to Bishop Winton's (James Montague, bishop of Winchester, dean of the Chapel Royal, and publisher of the 1616 *Workes*) dedicatory epistle to Prince Charles, then to James's "The Epistle to the Whole Church Militant, in Whatsoeuer Part of the Earth," then to "The Argument of this Whole Epistle," and, finally, to the two apocalyptic texts in question. The ordering is strategic for several reasons, not the least of which is to prepare the reader for a sort of literary progress through James's works that align issues of religion with those of divine right political ideology, not to mention the principles of leadership espoused by James. The *Workes* are performative: a staged detailing of the bedrock of James's thought, a record of key speeches made in public, an inditing of underlying principles, and, importantly, a not-so-subtle public recognition that princely authority is enhanced by textual means.

Montague's epistle is significant in that it provides some of the reading context for what follows: after first describing the loss of Henry, Charles's elder brother, Hinton states that Henry's "part" is "falne to your Lot" (*Workes* n.p.). Then Montague reinforces Charles's position as no less important than Henry's by stating a trifle indelicately that: "The rule in Scripture is; that if the first fruits be holy, so is the whole lumpe" (*Workes* n.p.). Montague's remarks suggest that just as Henry received *Basilikon Doron* from James—after the example of Basilius for his son Leo, Constantinus for his son Romanus, Manuell for his son Iohannes, and Charles V for his son Philip—so James is offering his *Workes* to Charles: "To your *Highnes* therefore are these offered, as to the trew Heire and Inheritor of them" (*Workes* n.p.). Besides locating the *Workes* as an important element in the transference of paternal values related to the exercise of James's sovereignty, Montague's remarks seem to provide for the possibility of linking the *Workes* with scriptural exegesis, particularly to the notion that if the "first fruits" are holy, then so is the rest, "the whole lumpe." I note in passing James's use of the adjective "Fruitfull" in the title to his commentary on Revelation 20:8–10, which provides a kind of rhetorical link between James's apocalyptic texts and Montague's comments to Charles. It is not much of a leap from such a connection to the notion that Montague's remarks about "first fruits" may well have been commenting on the textual structure of the *Workes*, beginning in the sacred world of Scriptural exegesis, in which James transmutes himself from early modern sovereign to Christian apocalyptic prophet in a literary act of symbolic self-enhancement. Such a literary transmutation has an important place in the changing politics of textual representation that James had grasped from an early stage in his career as an instrument for manipulating his relations to the putative absolutism he was said to embody.

The importance, then, of the *Workes* as a textual sampler, an exemplary pattern of the literary qualities associated with sovereign self-investiture, should not be underestimated. Nor should the literary ordering of the text be underestimated, with its dependence on the Revelation commentary and paraphrase being a key formal aspect of the *Workes* as a whole. Montague makes this explicit in his closing comments to Charles:

> Let these *Workes* therefore, most Gracious *Prince,* lie before you as a Patterne; you cannot haue a better: Neither doeth the Honour of a good Sonne consist in any thing more, then in immitating the good *Presidents* of a good *Father;* as we may very well perceiue by the Scriptures phrase, where the vsuall *Encomium* of good *Kings* is, that they walked in the wayes of their Fathers. Al men see, how like the Patterne God and *Nature* haue framed the outward *Liniaments:* and who knowes your Highnes wel, knowes also, that the inward *Abilliments* hold in the like proportion. The *Philosophers* say, that Imitation proceeds from Inclination; And trewly, if your future Imitation be answerable to your forward Inclination, in *Religion, Learning* and *Vertue;* your *Highnesse* cannot come farre short of your *Patterne,* nor yet of any of your *Predecessors* that euer went before you. (*Workes* n.p.)

Not only do Montague's comments emphasize the lineal relations that the *Workes* embody in James's setting of a fatherly literary precedent that can be imitated, they also indicate that the *Workes* provides a pattern for Charles's "future Imitation" and "forward Inclination"—a pattern whose sovereign ideals Charles was ultimately incapable of fulfilling, as the events of the Civil War were to demonstrate. Whatever the ironies of Montague's admonitions and hopes for Charles, it is clear that the outward lineaments embodied in the *Workes* are imagined as a mirror to the inward habiliments thought to inhere in Charles.

The place of apocalypse in this discourse so bound up with family history, anxiety over succession, and Stuart dynastic ambitions is notable. Apocalyptic discourse literally "reveals" the site at which an imagined futurity can come into existence by literary means.[17] Apocalyptic futurity, in which the varied elements of apocalyptics—death, rebirth, prophecy, purgation, fantasy, retribution, destiny, and so forth—are evident forms a literary backdrop to conceiving of the self in relation to a future in which that self is no longer present. Apocalypse presumes a sustained genealogy (a genealogy of kings) that makes the end truly apocalyptic, that literally invests the end with the depth of the tradition to which it is invariably bound, however illusively. The loss associated with apocalyptic end-time confirms the sacral nature of that by which it is preceded. This act of confirmation is especially crucial for signifying structures—like the state, nation, monarchic dynasty—that rely for their symbolic authority upon a metaphysical absence for which apocalyptic end-time can be an appropriate metonym.[18]

Moreover, apocalypse carries within its privileged status as Scripture a particular form of self-legitimation. Jacques Chevalier argues that "the New Testament Apocalypse is Christianity's response to cults that dare to assimilate the divine (immaterial, atemporal) to the visible and the tangible—to celestial bodies and the signs of heavenly desire governing the cosmos and the wheels of time. In the Book of Revelation, Christian prophecy superimposes itself on the language of 'pagan' divination, disassembling and recomposing it in such ways as to satisfy the higher rule of Logos" (3). Expressed another way, apocalyptic discourse legitimates the coherence of Christian self-fashioning (its collective dimensions) in opposition to alternative religious discourses associated with paganism. In so doing, the assimilation of the divine to the material takes on the form of the logos, the written word, and, in the particular instance of James, the form of the logos as made manifest by the king's symbolic body (his works) as an emblem of his divine right. Predicated on an oppositional structure in which the collective, as mediated by the logos, is at stake, apocalyptic discourse translates the divine into the word (in a movement parallel to the king's body's subsumption of the divine into the material). At once, then, an anxious narrative of self-legitimation as well as a signifier of a divinity that can be appropriated, apocalyptic had obvious uses in James's immediate historical context, trapped as he was (in the 1580s) between the threatening Scylla of Scottish internal politics and the Charybdis of sweeping religious changes brought on by the Reformation and Counter-Reformation.[19]

At the time of the composition of the commentaries on Revelation, both James's personal future as Scottish sovereign and the larger issues related to religious controversy could barely be ascertained. But, paradoxically, apocalyptic discourse is founded on the certainty of the future, the ability to speak of and to the future, the very precondition of all discourse, even as it imagines a scenario predicated on the end of time, history, self-presence, and so forth. Its invocation, then, in the self-authorizing scenario I am mapping here, has particular resonances in the face of the political and religious instability that had deeply marked James's experience to 1588. Furthermore, apocalyptic texts meld fantasies of the collective to the individual in a way that allows the individual prophetic presence in a pre-apocalyptic world. Revelatory paraphrase, a distinctive early modern subgenre in its own right—witness the work of John Bale, Thomas Mason, John Napier, Thomas Brightman, and William Cowper, to cite only a few examples—stages a particular speaking presence doubly enabled by its reliance on scriptural authority as well as by the scene of authoritative overwriting it presents.

Paraphrastic speech, with its overt meaning of "to say the same thing, but in other words," is deceptive, always deforming the relationship of homology it is supposed to enact. This is especially so in revelatory paraphrasis: the literariness of John's Revelation necessarily leads to allegory and its related hermeneutics based on the *allos* (other) of interpretive positioning. The specificity of historical context, of individual reading practices, and of the particular religious and cultural raisons d'être associated with revelatory paraphrase (a particular literary structure based on a showing forth of a showing forth) all contribute to an auto-legitimation that has collective dimensions, precisely the formula required for absolutist monarchic discourse based on divine right theory. Nation and individual come together through the device of the prophet (the individual who "speaks forth" for all) capable of envisioning an apocalyptic end that has collective consequences. By giving prominence to apocalyptic paraphrase and commentary as the first major texts in the *Workes,* by literally beginning with the imagined end, and by doing so in the context of the historical battle between Reformation and Counter-Reformation forces that were clearly associated with vested state interests—whether Catholic or Protestant—James was reformulating a theological notion of history in which the sovereign, the nation, and the apocalyptic came together as mutually enabling concepts.

II

The base position James stakes out in his interpretations of Revelation is predicated on the notion that "the Booke of the Revelation is most meete for this our last aage, as a Prophesie of the latter times" (*A Fruitfull Meditation* 73). What is interesting about this strategy is not so much the actual co-opting of apocalyptic discourse to describe the secular and religious battles particular to James's historical context.

Rather, what is notable is the arbitrariness of assigning a specific historical context to an apocalyptic text whose very literariness defies categorical interpretation, as the ongoing battles over Revelation as the site of meaningful historical perspective in the context of late twentieth-century millennial anxiety indicate.[20] Watch James's spurious reasoning as he begins the meditation: "As of all Bookes the holy Scripture is most necessary for the instruction of a Christian, and of all the Scriptures, the Booke of the Revelation is most meete for this our last aage" (ibid.): the logic of the passage is an illusion, based on a key assumption about the centrality of Revelation to scriptural interpretation. In historical terms this is a conventional move, largely derived from John Bale, "the key theoretician of the English Reformation." For Bale, "the book of Revelation embodied the sum of scripture: 'not one necessary point of belief is in all the other scriptures, that is not here also [Revelation] in one place or another'" (Williamson viii). James's Baleanism here cannot mask the arbitrariness of the move when examined from a different historical perspective, one perhaps more cynical about the typological relation of Revelation to other scriptural writings. James uses a kind of historical relativism to suggest the adequacy of Revelation as an interpretive key to the historical moment of "our last aage."[21] And this sense of Revelation as key to grasping the historical present suits the larger purposes of James's argument in relation to how it legitimates his historical place by way of a textual gesture, a strategy James would reiterate throughout his twinned careers as writer and absolute monarch.

But at the same time such self-enabling gestures are being enacted, contradictory impulses are undermining the very means by which political legitimacy and agency are achieved through textual means. For instance, James's "The Argument of This Whole Epistle," which introduces his *Paraphrase,* begins with the issue of textual doubt: "This Booke or Epistle of *Revelation,* was called in doubt, aswell for the incertaintie of the Author, as also for the canonicalnesse of the Booke it selfe. . . . So that this doubt onely rests now in men, that this Booke is so obscure and allegorique, that it is in a maner vnprofitable to be taught or interpreted; Whereunto I will shortly make an answere, and then goe forward to set downe the methode of the same" (*Workes* 4). The very premise of James's *Paraphrase* is dependent on the doubt that will be "answer[ed]" in James's interpretation. What is notable about the rhetoric of the passage is the doubleness of the doubt that James describes as a central feature of the reception of Revelation. On the one hand, the doubt grounds the authorial uncertainty and the canonicity of Revelation, making it "obscure and allegorique," precisely the terms that make it a viable literary vehicle for a critical reader and interpreter. James ups the ante by locating the "doubt" that makes the text "vnprofitable to be taught or interpreted" *in men,* not in the text itself. On the other hand, the suggestion that he is capable of responding to that doubt, allaying it with a methodical technique that will produce an "answere" to the textual uncertainty he locates in Revelation, indicates that James is beyond mere human interpreters. Proficient in the ways of allegory, James is empowered literarily even as he is distanced from the "men" not so empowered. Doubt, then, is the necessary, foregrounded condition of his textual authority. The gesture is revealing in its exposition of basic textual principles shaped by doubt, and, though intended as a self-justifying approach to his exegesis, this opening gambit makes James's own reading vulnerable to the possibility of doubt about its veracity and viability. Even as the "maner vnprofitable" of Revelation is turned to profit by James's prophetic insight, the obscurity and allegoricalness of the text—that is, its unyielding literariness—will not be denied as James begins his interpretation.

Furthermore, in "The Epistle to the Whole Church Militant," James performs a rather extraordinary maneuver. Rather than overtly portraying himself as an interpreter blessed with a *donum intellectus,* a special insight facilitated by the divine into the meaning of Revelation, James takes a slightly more subtle tack. He states categorically that he understands the "meaning of this Booke [Revelation]" to be "a speciall cannon against the Hereticall wall of our common aduersaries the Papists" (*Workes* 2). Then, in a carefully worded summary of his approach, he states: "I would wish to know, that in this my *Paraphrase* upon it [Revelation], I haue used nothing of my owne coniecture, or of the authoritie of others, but onely haue interpreted it, in that sense which may best agree with the methode of the Epistle, and not bee contradictorie to it selfe: The meaning whereof I expound, partly by it selfe, and partly by other parts of the Scriptures, as the worke it selfe will beare witnesse" (*Workes* 2). The apposition of these two statements is typically hubristic of James, for he affirms in the first statement a clearly politicized version of his reading, one that brooks little tolerance for different perspectives. Then he confirms the viability of his interpretation by denying that it is a matter of his own conjecture or the authority of others, suggesting instead that the meaning, *his* meaning, is non-contradictorily immanent in the text: the text literally bears witness to itself by virtue of James's interpretation. The contradiction is that James's interpretation, which is not an interpretation—neither based on his own conjecture nor the authority of others—is itself an exegetical strategy with deep roots in the Baleanism I have described earlier. Revelation expounds meaning autonomously or in relation to the "other parts of the Scriptures" that Revelation echoes and synthesizes.

The phrasing of the above passage obfuscates James's manipulation of his interpretive position as the sole credible position because it is entirely consistent with how Revelation bears "witnesse" to itself, unmediated by James's or others' interpretative visions. A crucial erasure of James's exegetical mediation occurs even as that mediation is made visible. Thus James is both present and absent from the process by which meaning inheres in the *Paraphrase.* The rhetorical technique disallows the notion of the interpreter as capable of manipulating Scripture even as such a manipulation occurs, almost by sleight of hand, before the reader's very eyes. Moreover, the technique covertly inscribes James as privy to the *donum intellectus*, privy to the immanence of meaning that his *Paraphrase* will explicate by way of the text's (un)mediated presence. The logic of the technique insures that James achieves hierarchical place in close alignment with the divine by virtue of his presence-absence from the text. Even as he affirms that the method of the epistle "not bee contradictorie to it selfe," he performs the contradiction of his exegetical position as an agent of meaning who has, if we believe the rhetoric of the passage, no agency. The literary strategy is one of simultaneous affirmation and negation in which both enabling and disabling effects may be discerned.

Several lines later, perhaps in an even more dissimulative mode, James affirms the following:

> But of one thing I must forewarne you (Christian Readers) to wit, that yee may understand, that it is for the making of the Discourse more short and facile, that I haue made *Iohn* to be the Speaker in this *Paraphrase;* and not that I am so presumptuously foolish, as to haue meant thereby, that my *Paraphrase* is the onely trew and certaine exposition of this Epistle, reiecting all others: For although through speaking in his person, I am onely bounded and limitted to use one, and not diuers interpretations, of euery seuerall place; yet I condemne not others, but rather allow them to interpret it diuersly. . . . (*Workes* 2)

Here James engages in significant distortions that open up interesting fault lines with regard to the discursive uncertainty and doubt so crucial to how James saw himself in relation to his writing practice. The logic of the passage is founded on James denying that his interventions, his paraphrases, make the "Discourse" any longer, and that he has made John of Patmos the speaker of the *Paraphrase* in order to keep the discourse "short and facile." But the inverse is true. The *Paraphrase* is really a significantly extended commentary on Revelation that is anything but "short and facile," with James's interpolations marked off by the rhetorical device of the "to wit." James's argument that he has made John the speaker of the *Paraphrase* in order to curtail its length rings hollow to any reader who survives the sixty-five succeeding folio pages.

James used the tactic of claiming discursive concision while enacting the very opposite in other writing and speaking situations as well. For instance, in "A Speach to Both the Houses of Parliament, Delivered in the Great Chamber at White-Hall, The Last Day of March 1607," James's opening comments note that "in all great Councels of Parliaments, fewest wordes with most matter doeth become best . . . . [L]ike the garment of a chaste woman, who is onely set forth by her naturall beautie, which is properly her owne: other deckings are but ensignes of an harlot that flies with borrowed feathers" (McIlwain 290). The speech goes on for sixteen pages and is hardly a demonstration of rhetorical brevity. In the case of the passage just cited from the *Paraphrase,* dissimulation, uncertainty, circumlocution, and indirection mask what is at stake: namely, that James is speaking in John's voice, usurping, in a display of exegetical sovereignty, the role of prophetic interlocutor. In fact, by speaking in John's voice and interpolating lengthy commentaries on the substance of John's vision, James has effectively transmuted himself into the "harlot that flies with borrowed feathers." And this, I would argue, accounts for the indirection used to steer readers away from the issue of authorial voice to that of discursive efficacy. The indirection is a crucial fault line running through the exegetical frame James imagines for the ideal reception of the *Paraphrase* by readers. And yet, typically, the passage throws into doubt James's very authority as the agent through whom the interpretation is mediated, even as it struggles to mask the anxiety produced by his effective substitution of his voice for John's.

A second fault line is also evident in the passage under discussion and it has to do with a different anxiety—no less related to James's sense of interpretive method—from that of authorial integrity. Having appropriated John's voice in his prosopopoetic legerdemain, James then denies that having John as the speaker of the *Paraphrase* effectively gives it any authoritative weight: "not that I am so presumptuously foolish, as to haue meant thereby, that my *Paraphrase* is the onely trew and certaine exposition of this Epistle, reiecting all others." The tactic at once legitimates and delegitimates the *Paraphrase:* though it is spoken by John, it is not thereby necessarily the "onely true and certaine exposition." James also uses the possessive case immediately after affirming the speaker in the *Paraphrase* to be John, suggesting in any event that it is "*my* Paraphrase," regardless of whether the speaker in it is John.[22] The passage complicates things further when James argues that "through speaking in his [John's] person" he is limited and bound to one as opposed to "diuers interpretations." The implication seems to be that the singularity of voice adopted by James sets hermeneutic limits on the *Paraphrase.* James uses this singularity to promote the authority of the interpretation he offers, but at the same time he scores the point that interpretation is not only about such singular readings by claiming that "I condemne not others, but rather allow them to interpret it diuersly."

The fault line between singular interpretation and polysemy opens up here even as the prose strains to speak dissimulatively and clearly in the same instance. Having just "craue[d] of our Aduersaries, that they will not refute any part of my Interpretation, till they find out a more probable themselues" (*Workes* 2), James's openness to "diuers interpretations" seems to put considerable stress on his attempt to authorize the singularity, the univocal truth, of his reading.[23] What is at stake are the ways in which interpretation and representation can be manipulated to produce the illusion of such a singular reading in the face of the enormous intertextual pressures brought to bear on any author of a paraphrase, while also admitting to textual realities that produce semic diversity.[24] James is attempting to sustain both versions of the truth about texts: that they are founded on a notion of authorial coherence even though that coherence dissolves in the face of exegetical variation produced by different reception contexts. It is little wonder that the effect of trying to produce a text that simultaneously recognizes the anxieties circulating round both authorial integrity and exegetical diversity should be so conflicted, so contradictory in its own framing devices. For a king who conceived the forms of his sovereign empowerment in relation to his textuality, there are fraught implications to the recognition of such a fault line. That this fault line is carried forward into the literary work performed in James's paraphrase of and meditation on Revelation is not surprising, especially in the larger context of James's writing practices, though it has gone entirely unnoticed by previous scholarship.

I now wish to turn to two examples of the kind of exegetical uncertainty I have been ascribing to James's apocalyptic texts: the first from *A Fruitfull Meditation* and the second from the *Paraphrase*. *A Fruitfull Meditation* functions effectively as a kind of summary statement of the *Paraphrase*. Here the historical moment of 1588 is read as an apocalyptic crisis in which Satan, after being bound a thousand years, breaks "forth loose, and for a space rage[s] in the earth more than euer before: but yet shall in the end be ouercome and confounded for euer" (*Workes* 74). In James's terms, Satan represents both "the Turke the open enemy, and the Pope the couered enemie" (*Workes* 79), a position James was developing in the mid-1580s, as his poem *The Lepanto* (1585) shows, with its apocalyptic imagery based on the Antichrist and the Whore of Babylon.[25] The political purposes of *A Fruitfull Meditation* are clear enough: to undermine papal authority by demonizing the pope as an instrument of Satan, and to thereby consolidate James's position as an oppositional figure of national (and even international) importance who can counter Satan's ability to deceive "the nations vniuersally" (*Workes* 77).[26] The national contexts of *A Fruitfull Meditation* are consistently iterated throughout the text, with direct references to the Turks, the French, the Flemish, and the Germans (*Workes* 78) as national sites in the battle against the spiritual tyranny (78) of the papists. As James reads it, the apocalyptic threat is immanent. He goes so far as to ask: "and what is prepared and come forward against this Ile? Doe we not daily heare, and by all appearance and likelihood shall shortly see?" (78). The strategy, then, is for James as sovereign to formulate his interpretation of Revelation, his meditation, as a response to the national threat posed by papist forces.

The most curious moment in the meditation, a moment in which the fault lines I have been describing open to reveal the textual investments James has in his interpretation, occurs in "The Third Part" of the meditation. Reading the latter part of Revelation 20:9—"but fire came downe from God out of the heauen, and deuoured them [Satan's armies]"—James asserts:

> Seventhly, in the forme of language, and phrase or maner of speaking, of fire comming downe from heauen here vsed, and taken out of the Booke of the Kings, where, at *Elias* his prayers, with fire from heauen were destroyed *Achazias* his souldiers: as the greatest part of all the words, verses, and sentences of this booke are taken and borrowed of other parts of the Scripture, we are taught to vse onely Scripture for interpretation of Scripture, if we would be sure, and neuer swarue from the analogie of faith in expounding, seeing it repeateth so oft the owne phrases, and thereby expoundeth them. (*Workes* 80)

James attempts to establish a typological relation between Revelation 20:9 and 2 Kings 1:9–14, in which the divine power enacted by Elijah against Ahaziah's army is emblematized by "fire from heauen." The moment in Revelation is significant because "the past tense called aorist is used in the original Greek text" (Quispel 110). This grammatical choice suggests that with Gog and his armies surrounding the Christian camp and Jerusalem, the correct translation would not be "fire came downe" but rather "fire *is going to* descend from heaven" (ibid.). The implication of the tense is that the moment can be transposed to an indefinite future in which analogous historical conditions prevail, thus enabling James's reading of the passage in relation to contemporary threats by papists against his national and sovereign interests. In the passage from *A Fruitfull Meditation* just cited, James goes on to make a by now familiar argument, based on Balean principles: namely that "we are taught to vse onely Scripture for interpretation of Scripture."

This is where a significant issue appears in the text, for within the larger interpretive frame of *A Fruitfull Meditation,* James's insistence that Scripture be used to interpret Scripture is wholly misleading in several very different ways. First, *A Fruitfull Meditation* itself, which articulates an exegesis, is not solely dependent on Scripture for its exegetical moves. The point, however seemingly obvious, must be made if only to show how James deviates from the kind of hermeneutic principles he foregrounds in the text. The very fact that he indulges in this metacritical point as he brings the meditation to a close points to the non-scriptural contexts of the exegesis. Secondly, by historicizing the reading of Revelation in a context that is clearly not scriptural, James introduces yet another non-scriptural element, one wholly dependent on the point of view of the interpreter's historical context. James's historical presumption in converting the vision of Revelation into a vision of the chosen nation, the chosen religion, was hardly sustainable. As Arthur Williamson points out, "Whatever the king's claims about leading a British empire and thereby the Protestant world in the struggle against the Antichrist—whatever his yet more cosmic aspirations for a reunited Christendom and the defeat of the Turk—he was at the moment nothing more than the prince of a relatively unimportant realm to which no man could attribute any peculiar apocalyptic significance" (42). Moreover, the very arbitrariness of historical narratives severely undermines the exegetical fixity James is at pains to establish in *A Fruitfull Meditation.* Bernard Capp points out that "James's interest in the exposure of the Antichrist was perhaps dampened when a Catholic reply [entitled 'Balaam's Ass'] to his treatise [*A Premonition*] was discovered at Whitehall in 1613, allegedly claiming that Britain was the seat of Antichrist and that James was Antichrist in person. The author, a Hampshire recusant squire named John Cotton [of Warblington], was arrested on a charge of treason" (103).[27] Treasonous or not, Cotton's treatise effectively demonstrated the arbitrariness of interpretive positionings, the ease with which apparently secure exegeses could be overturned and deconstructed. Thus, the fault line of historical relativism further undermines James's attempt to validate his reading of interpretation as a function of internal typological relations that require no external mediation.

A last fissure that appears in the textual facade James attempts to produce has to do with the structural techniques of James's hermeneutic method. In the passage I have been examining from *A Fruitfull Meditation,* for instance, the use of paraphrase—with all the attendant interpolations—is evident, as is the use of tendentious sidebars, summary epigraphs, metacritical comments, framing literary devices like the epistle to the reader, and so forth. All these techniques lead the reader to a less than objective perspective in line with James's ideology. All of them are also intrusive, though not obviously so, and directly contradict James's claim that "we are taught to vse onely Scripture for interpretation of Scripture." Nothing could be further from the truth, as the contexts and intertexts—whether historical or literary—that conspire to undermine such a position show.

III

In the *Paraphrase* similar fault lines are at work, though in perhaps a subtler way, if only because the blend between Scripture and James's exegetical commentary is more nuanced here, less obviously a separate meditation on a set group of verses. I wish to turn to a striking passage from a climactic moment in the *Paraphrase* (Rev. 19:17–21) that envisions the actual instant when victory over the "Beast" is achieved. As James writes it, the passage is redolent with the sovereign fantasy of a force so absolute as to be capable of eating "the flesh of kings." The latter trope signifies, in James's historical reckoning, the moment of victory (the Day of Judgment) over the forces of the "two Monarches, the one secular [the Turks], the other Ecclesiasticall [the papists]" (*Workes* 30) aligned against

Protestantism and thus against himself as putative defender of Protestant interests. But if apocalyptic is the revelatory mode of historical crisis—its vision being the end beyond which no signification can go—then it is also a pertinent site where the crisis of subjectivity is enacted, if only because imagining the end of history necessarily invokes the end of the individual.

We have seen how James predictably adapts apocalyptic discourse to a larger sense of historical purpose, and I now wish to consider how his apocalyptic mode points to other forms of crisis related to his unstable subject-position in that larger historical context. In the passage in question, the moment when the "King of kings, and Lord of lords" (*Workes* 62) vanquishes the Beast and the nations seduced by his call, the Day of Judgment is signaled by

> an Angel standing in the Sunne, that there he might be seene publikely of all, and that the Whole world might take heed to that which he was to proclaime, and he cried with a loude voice to all the fowles flying through the middest of heauen, *Come* and gather your selues to the supper of the Lord; To eate the flesh of Kings, of Tribunes, of mightie men, of horses and their riders: in short, come eate the flesh of all free-men and slaues, great and small: This was to declare, that the day of Iudgement was come, wherein should that destruction ensue, signified by fowles eating their flesh, (because fowles vse to eate the flesh of dead men vnburied) which should ouerwhelme all sorts of men, excepting alwayes these that were marked, who were sundry times excepted before, as ye heard. (Rev. 19:17–18; *Workes* 62)

The enunciatory scene of the angel, who publicly proclaims a perverse form of the Lord's Supper in which apocalyptic retribution is enacted by "fowles" who "eate the flesh of Kings," is striking in a number of ways. As a literary trope it proleptically stages the death of those still alive and under the sway of the "the false prophet, *or false Church*" (*Workes* 62; the italicized phrase, my emphasis, is James's silent interpolation).[28] Those alive and true to the "false Church" are carrion, whose imminent destruction is ensured by angelic proclamation. Once more the word is converted into the sword of retribution, which in Revelation 19:21 is evoked yet again: "And the rest were slaine by the sword which came out of his mouth, that sate vpon the horse, and the fowles were filled with their flesh" (ibid.).

The metonym for these living dead is "the flesh of Kings," which I want to suggest is a useful trope for thinking through James's fraught relations to what he was enunciating in his apocalyptic writings. As we have seen, James implicitly recognizes that Revelation is the site of interpretive quandaries involving contingent reading practices; this is further complicated by issues of the multiple voices implicit in the paraphrastic mode. Many of these issues are reinforced in Revelation 19, if only because the passage contributes, however unwittingly, to the contradictory structures of sovereign self-affirmation and self-denial that I have been suggesting characterize James's textual strategies. Literally, to envision the militant and total overthrow of the false church, James must accept the revelatory language of the fallen monarch—the monarch whose flesh is eaten by "fowles." His own sovereign status as one of the "excepted" is based on a tenuous and historically contingent reading that places him in a position that excepts him from the same fate. But the basis for such a reading is, as we have already seen, highly arbitrary, the rough equivalent of a heads or tails interpretive toss that is totally dependent on arguable distinctions between who stands for the true or the false church. Thus, embedded in the apocalyptic vision of the end, as paraphrased by James, is a vision of the end of kings, a gesture whose logic suggests that kings are contingent on hermeneutic practices that either validate or destroy them. The literariness of this gesture is noteworthy, for it confirms the importance of text as a means of establishing the symbolic position of the monarch even as it envisions that position to be far from absolute, always contingent on an angelic proclamation that shapes or destroys monarchic status. Control over the metaphysics of divine speech remains at the crux of this poetics of transcendence and betrays the literary and symbolic foundations of an absolute power that is not.

Bernard McGinn has argued that "Most modern scholars . . . view John's Revelation as a cyclical presentation of visions repeating, or recapitulating, the same basic message of present persecution, imminent destruction of the wicked and reward of the just" (525). This generalized pattern is evident in both of James's apocalyptic texts. His *Paraphrase* dramatically transforms the historical vision and context of John of Patmos[29] to suit the particular historical narrative of self-legitimation at stake in his hermeneutics. Diverse conditions feed into James's place in apocalyptic discourse. The first, as Bernard Capp points out, is that James

> quickly replaced Elizabeth as the subject of apocalyptic hopes. Brought up as a Calvinist, James had published in 1588 (the Armada year) a treatise on the papal Antichrist in which he promised the sudden overthrow of the Catholic states at the very height of their power. He returned to these themes in *A Premonition* (1609), offering elaborate proof that the pope was Antichrist, and seeking to persuade the kings of Europe that the papacy was a deadly threat to all royal authority. (102)[30]

The continuity between James's 1588 apocalyptic writings and the later *Premonition* is striking, as are the incidental remarks to be found in texts written in the intervening years.[31] The ligature between papist politics and anxieties about the sustainability of James's own political situation underscores what was at stake in the apocalyptic writings that sought to undermine the Catholic position.

If, as de Certeau suggests, "Christian epistemology links mystic knowledge to language" (114), then James's claims to be privy to exegetical insight into Revelation play a crucial role in aligning the king himself with a divine principle, what de Certeau calls "the principle of a 'concord' between the infinite and language" (115), a concord that is a grounding thematic in Revelation. Apocalyptic discourse—James's ability to navigate the tricky interpretive waters of the crowning moment in Scripture, with its narrative end in an infinity beyond corporeal experience—buttressed his consistent tactic of aligning his textual with his political presence. Goldberg points out that as *lex loquens*, "The authority he claims as king parallels the authoritarian imposition he brings to the text. God's word becomes the king's word, but it is also the king's support" (21). Goldberg's position fails to acknowledge the resistant nature of the text itself, its inversely symmetrical sovereignty in relation to the monarch deploying it for political ends. Admittedly, the authoritarianism of the interpreter parallels the absolutist dream of omnipotence and functions to support such a position. But, to push Goldberg's argument a step further by inverting its key terms, the very textuality that is used as a prop to authoritarian regimes can also serve to subvert the terms by which those regimes enlist textuality in their support. That is, texts have a certain indifference to attempts to fix their meaning (as the history of scriptural hermeneutics shows). They can just as easily produce uncertainty and indeterminacy as they can the fixity used to self-enable the particular form of early modern sovereignty locatable in James's writing practices.

Capp argues that "It was a major step for a reigning monarch to give public endorsement to Protestant apocalyptic teaching" and that "James's writings underlined the special role of kings in God's work" (102). Left out of this formulation is the special role of God in the king's works, where "God" signifies the transcendental absolute that grounds the king's secular interests, regardless of the public religiosity of the king. The use of public expressions of outrage at religiously contrarian positions had its secular dimension, and indeed the dynamic tension between the sacred and the secular is precisely what is at stake in all James's apocalyptic hermeneutics. Capp notes how, to the Scottish antiquarian James Maxwell—part of the "Joachimite tradition, looking for a messianic emperor of the last days and a reforming pope, 'Pastor Angelicus'" (ibid.)—James's "writings could persuade the kings of Europe to reform the Catholic Church and reunite Christendom, while Prince Charles might perhaps be the long-awaited Emperor Charles, destined to destroy the Turks and recapture Constantinople" (103). The investment in this kind of Joachimite and messianic apocalyptic thinking is in the king as a national and even international savior, someone who embodies, literarily and iconographically,[32] the necessary sovereign, national, imperial, and apocalyptic virtues to address significant military and political opposition.

But frequently forgotten in such a view is the inverse position, in which the apocalyptic does not serve greater altruistic and messianic goals by way of the sovereign. Rather the apocalyptic, in its representation of the sovereign as messiah and prophet, plays a self-serving, symbolic role in the textual strategies by which the sovereign achieves a form of self-investiture. As Williamson accurately points out: "But if a messianic emperor whose authority was not securely located within the context of a similarly endowed empire might prove highly dangerous, it would also prove a difficult matter indeed to create an empire *ex nihilo.* However much the reformers were obsessed with the idea of a messianic prince, such a prince could not be divorced from the traditional means of legitimation" (5). The apocalyptic in this latter context is a crucial feature of the illusion of legitimation, the consensual hallucination of absolutism. Support for this view lies in Capp's observation that "James did little to satisfy the hopes placed in him. He made peace and friendship with Spain instead of intensifying Elizabeth's war. He refused to intervene in the Thirty Years War on the Protestant side, preferring—more like [James] Maxwell—to seek harmony through peaceful persuasion. The king ignored Puritan pressure to suppress recusants and his *Premonition* indeed attacked Puritans almost as fiercely as papists" (103).[33]

Thus, despite James's seemingly radical opposition to the sacred and secular forces threatening Protestantism that we have seen in both his apocalyptic texts, complex political realities dictated a subtler course of action. William Robertson, in his summary of the events of 1588 and 1589, suggests that James,

> though firmly attached to the Protestant religion, though profoundly versed in the theological controversies between the Reformers and the Church of Rome, though he had employed himself, at that early period of life, in writing a Commentary on the Revelations, in which he proved the Pope to be Antichrist, had nevertheless adopted, already, those maxims concerning the treatment of the Roman Catholics, to which he adhered through the rest of his life. The Roman Catholics were at that time a powerful and active party in England; they were far from being an inconsiderable faction in his own kingdom. The Pope and King of Spain were ready to take part in all their machinations, and to second every effort of their bigotry. The opposition of such a body to his succession to the Crown of England, added to the averseness of the English from the government of strangers might create him many difficulties. (2: 197)

In such a context, in which balance between strongly opposed parties in the same state had to be negotiated with care, and especially where powerful foreign interests were concerned, James's apocalyptics served a particular secular purpose in assuaging the hardline Protestants within his own government. These hardliners demanded a vigorous opposition to the Catholics, despite James's own sense of himself as a peacemaker in the *Insula pacis* or island of peace that he envisioned in his 1618 treatise *The Peacemaker.* As Peter Lake argues, "From the outset James's ecclesiastical policy had involved the representation at court of a wider range of religious opinions than had ever made it into the inner circles of the Elizabethan régime" (87). One of the effective methods for negotiating the conciliarist positioning that became one of James's key diplomatic goals involved circulating texts that appealed to different factions, militant and otherwise. The apocalyptic writings, then, especially coming so early in his career, may well have been a signal that he was capable of religious propagandizing and controversy (as a prime defender of Protestant religious values), even if the texts in question were also part of an emergent strategy he was developing to shape his sovereignty in relation to his literary output.

Even as a jeu d'esprit, the apocalyptic writings are far from negligible. When read as seminal documents in the formation of a writing strategy that was also a strategy of governance, they are immensely important as early attempts at textual authority through the medium of scriptural hermeneutics. Robertson discusses some of the double strategies James cannily employed to maintain a relative peace within his kingdom while preparing for accession to the English throne:

> In order to avoid these [the aforementioned difficulties], he thought it necessary to soothe, rather than to irritate the Roman Catholics, and to reconcile them to his succession, by the hopes of gentler treatment, and some mitigation of the rigour of those laws, which were now in force against them. This attempt to gain one party by promises of indulgence and acts of clemency, while he adhered with all the obstinacy of a disputant, to the doctrines and tenets of the other, has given an air of mystery, and even of contradiction, to this part of the King's character. (2: 197)

"[I]n order to please both [Protestants and Catholics]," concludes Robertson, "James often aimed at an excessive refinement, mingled with dissimulation, in which he imagined the perfection of government, and of king-craft, to consist" (2: 198). The ideal place in which such a policy of refinement and dissimulation could be articulated was in the texts James produced as a symptom of the contradictory policies he was forced to enact in order to survive. The studied uncertainty, indeterminacy, and ambiguity of which the king was so capable were both reactive and proactive strategies for addressing political and religious tensions that were not likely to disappear.

James's apocalyptic writings are particularly important in the context of conciliarist policies he was seeking to deploy, for as Patterson convincingly argues, "reconciling those who were at enmity by reason of traditional rivalries, conflicts, and feuds had been very much a part of his political program since the mid-1580s" (18–19)—precisely the historical moment in which James was writing his commentaries on Revelation. Patterson notes that James's "*Frvitfvll Meditation* on Revelation 20:7–10, written in 1588, the year of the Armada, to rally his countrymen against attack, developed the view that Christendom had long suffered from the rule of 'the Antichrist and his Clergie.' This rule had largely overcome 'the sincere preaching of the Gospel, the true use of the Sacraments, which are seales and pledges of the promises contained therein, and lawfull exercise of Christian discipline'" (17). As Patterson's study shows so effectively, the crucial point of these passages is not so much James's radical opposition to Catholicism as his adherence to a rhetoric of Christian conciliarism and ecumenicism, in which doctrinal differences vitiate a religious and secular vision that "encompassed both a lasting peace among the European nations and the reuniting of the Church, shattered in the West by the Reformation and the Counter-Reformation" (Patterson 364).

But at the same time as these commentaries addressed specific issues of an emergent religious policy—and, in particular, a topic, papal prerogative, that was to vex James over the length of his career—they enabled him to shape the beginnings of a formidable rhetoric of absolutist self-investiture. His apocalyptic texts mark the site of an early recognition that the alignment between absolutist fantasies of power and authorial fantasies of creation and interpretation had its uses in the struggle to control the imaginary of the reader and, thus, of the political subject. It is no small coincidence that five years after James's death, the king's printer "was 'required' to doe many services in printing for ye advancement of our religion & honor of ye Nation"—one of which involved the printing of "King Iames his woorks alltogeather very faire & Chargeable for Lattine & English" (Greg 258). National self-interest, evident in the anti-papal rhetoric of the apocalyptic commentaries, merges with exegetical command of scriptural documents that envision apocalyptic end-time as a metonymy for the threat by which nation becomes a coherent concept. The apocalyptic texts show that even as such enabling fantasies were being enacted, perhaps to James's sovereign advantage, the forces of contradiction and textual indeterminacy were working to delimit the contingencies of James's textual empowerment. For even as James, via apocalyptic paraphrase, articulated eating "the flesh of Kings," the same vision was working to expose the anxieties circulating round the exercise of absolute power in which such vicarious cannibalism signified the end of time and thus the apocalyptic limits beyond which secular absolutism could have no further meaning.

Notes

1. For more detailed commentaries on the historical context of the apocalyptic traditions in early modern England and Scotland see, among oth-

ers, Norman Cohn, Richard K. Emmerson and Bernard McGinn, Katharine R. Firth, Richard Bauckham, and Arthur H. Williamson. For a brief descriptive summary of *A Paraphrase* see Willson 83–85.

2. James's personal library, as documented by Sir George Warner, contained English and French copies of Heinrich Bullinger's *Hundred Sermons on Revelation* (1557) (Warner xli and lii, the latter mispaginated as ii; using the same source, Firth notes that James collected other important texts from the apocalyptic tradition, including the *Magdeburg Centuries* and *Carion's Chronicle* [132]), which as McGinn points out, was "less interested in drawing correlations with historical events than in creating an evangelical version of the old moralizing Tyconian interpretation" (535). McGinn describes the Tyconian-Augustinian model for interpreting Revelation as one of three available "on the eve of the Reformation," suggesting that it was "recapitulative, moral, and ecclesiological, but resolutely ahistorical and antimillenarian" (534). In his apocalyptic writings James sought to shift from Bullinger's Tyconian-Augustinian ahistoricism to a conventional historicization of Revelation as a description of events leading up to and including the contemporary historical moment. In this last regard, a more likely influence on James would have been Martin Luther's 1530 "Preface to the German Bible," which "offered a brief sketch of the meaning of Revelation that proved central for Protestant interpreters for centuries, both because it identified the papacy with the Antichrist and because this identification was made within the context of a historically progressive reading of the text" (McGinn 529). Firth sees the paraphrase as delivering a message derived from "[John] Knox and the Geneva Bible. [James] took the belief fostered by Knox that prophecies dealt almost exclusively with affairs of state and were therefore of especial necessity to princes. The Apocalypse revealed to [James] the historical identity of Antichrist and his approaching defeat" (131–32). James's Knoxian view of prophetic texts as having state relevance underpins the importance of these texts in relation to James's sovereign self-investiture by textual means.
3. In the sense of "the rhetorical exercise known as the speech in character or impersonation" (Lanham 124).
4. Williamson points out that *Ane Fruitfull Meditatioun contening ane plane and facil expositioun . . . of the 20 Chapter of the Revelatioun in the forme of ane sermon* was printed in French "at La Rochelle [in] 1589. Other editions, in Latin, were subsequently published in various parts of the continent, and only gradually did the *Basilikon Doron* later outstrip it" (40). McIlwain states the various publication dates for *A Fruitfull Meditation* as follows: "Edinburgh, 1588, London, 1603,

1616 . . . in Latin: Basiliae, 1596; Jenae, 1603; Halle, 1603; in French: La Rochelle, 1589" (ciii). According to McIlwain, "These are the basis of James's later view of the Pope as Antichrist, as set forth in his *Premonition*" (ibid.). McIlwain has no such listing for James's paraphrase, and mistakenly gives the impression that *A Fruitfull Meditation* is the sole source of James's apocalyptic views on the pope.

5. Wormald notes that the manuscript of *Basilikon Doron* contains "James's justification for a piece of early writing, his *Paraphrase on Revelations* (1588) [British Library, Royal ms. 18 B xiv, f. 1], which is 'asvell to teache my self as others'" (49). According to Williamson, James's paraphrase served as a prolegomenon to "three major works discussing the *Revelation* and the role of the godly prince" (40). In Williamson's estimation the basis for "James's understanding of secular history—set forth in the paraphrase, in the two meditations written at the time of the Armada, and in his more cautious digression in the preamble to *An Apologie for the Oath of Allegiance* (1609)—was largely unexceptional" (40). The two meditations to which Williamson is referring are *A Fruitfull Meditation* (Edinburgh 1588), dealing with Revelation 20, and *A Meditation* (Edinburgh 1589), dealing with the "*first buke of the chronicles of the Kingis,*" chs. 25–29. There is some confusion as to the precise dating of the paraphrase and its publication history prior to 1616. Wormald dates the paraphrase at 1588 with a different title from that found in the 1616 *Workes;* unfortunately she does not provide documentation regarding her source for the date and the title. Williamson notes that James had written the "massive, line-by-line paraphrase of the *Revelation* 'before he was twenty yeeres of aage'—and there could hardly have been a great many teenagers who had done the same" (40), but he is vague on his source for this information, his footnote stating that it comes from the "*Works,* 'Preface'" (159), with no page indicated. Indeed, James Montague's preface to the *Workes* clearly states that "For this *Paraphrase,* that leades the way to all the rest of his *Maiesties Workes,* was written by his Maiestie before hee was twenty yeeres of aage; and therefore iustly in this Volume hath the first place, the rest following in order according to the time of their first penning" ("The Preface," *Workes* n.p.). The comment establishes a writing chronology for James that originates with the *Paraphrase.* Since no *STC* listing exists for the paraphrase, the primary evidence for dating it comes from the preface to the *Workes,* thus suggesting that Wormald is confusing the date for *A Fruitfull Meditation* with the date for the paraphrase, which seems to have been written at least two or three years prior to the dating for *A Fruitfull Meditation.* A further possible proof for the dating of the *Paraphrase* is to be found in an

obscure reference by Elizabeth I in a letter to James written "about January 1585–6," which states the following: "For your churche matters, I do both admire and reioise to see your wise paraphrase, wiche far excedeth ther texte" (Bruce 26–27). If in fact Elizabeth is referring to James's paraphrase, this would place the work roughly in the period prior to the writing of the letter, assuming some time for the dissemination of the manuscript to Elizabeth. The actual writing of the *Paraphrase,* then, probably occurred somewhat prior to the approximate date of Elizabeth's letter—that is, in James's late teens. A further factor in the question of these texts' genealogies has to do with the Jesuit priest William Creighton and his 1598 "An Apologie and Defence of the K. of Scotland against the infamous libell forged by John Cecill," which states that "manie other Ernest men do well knowe that [James] hath written no books at all of diuinitie, And that the erroneous paraphrase vpon certein numbrs of the Apocalips, was written by Mr Patrique Galloway, one of his Court Ministers, and by the Pollycie of the most cunning of these malicious brethern, published in the Prince his name, to make those imaginations more acceptable to the people, and the supposed author odyous to the Catholique Church, wch his Matie permytted at that time in pollicie" (Law 46). Further work on the publication history of the *Paraphrase* is required.

6. See, for example, recent work by Patterson, Bergeron, and Wormald, not to mention the work of Lee and Akrigg. These evaluations, which acknowledge the fundamental literariness of James and his mode of governance, echo Disraeli's nineteenth-century evaluation of James, who "was a literary monarch at one of the great æras of English literature, and his contemporaries were far from suspecting that his talents were inconsiderable, even among those who have their reasons not to like him . . . . more wit and wisdom have been recorded of James I. than of any one of our sovereigns" (2–3).
7. See McIlwain 301; the passage is from "A Speach to Both the Hovses of Parliament, Delivered in the Great Chamber at White-Hall, The Last Day of March 1607." In the same speech to Parliament James asserts "that *Rex est lex loquens*" (McIlwain 291).
8. Leeds Barroll's discussion of a Spanish pamphlet's description of James's encounter with the constable of Castile puts James's attitude toward being lettered in a particular light: "Complimenting King James, the constable observed what a wonderful thing James's love of the noble pastime of hunting was, especially when this love was coupled with a love of letters—a combination rarely met with among those who are crowned kings. King James, continues this account, promptly replied that it was strange that kings and common men of letters had to

be lumped together like this. For among a group of monarchs only one king might indeed be found who loved hunting *and* learning; yet this one king was certainly one more than could ever be found in any group of common men of letters. Evidently, James assumed that letters did not ennoble him, but he letters" (58). No matter James's predictable sentiments on ennobling letters via royal presence, the fact is that the relationship between sovereignty and writing in James's case was of reciprocal function in distinguishing James as *both* a writer and a monarch.

9. It is no small coincidence, in relation to James's own sense of relation to scriptive and Scriptural culture, that Revelation 5:1 states "And I saw in the right hand of him that sat on the throne a book written within and on the backside, sealed with seven seals" and that the primary iconographic representation of James in the *Workes* involves a similar representation: the frontispiece engraving of James by Simon Pass shows him enthroned and to his right a book titled *Verbum Dei,* perhaps echoing the image as written in Revelation.
10. The original scriptural passage reads: "And I saw the dead, small and great, stand before God; and the books were opened: and another book was opened, which is *the book* of life: and the dead were judged out of those things which were written in the books, according to their works."
11. Richey notes that "James chose to dismiss a crucial aspect of the 'Constantinian' character encoded in contemporary interpretations of the Apocalypse. Putting aside the notion of imperial conquest written into Foxe's *Acts and Monuments* and nearly all commentaries on Revelation, James began to advocate an alternative, pacifistic understanding of prophecy" (4).
12. The passage echoes Revelation 19:13–15, in which, in James's paraphrase, "*The word of God*" (*Workes* 61) prepares to do battle against Babylon and the "false Church" (*Workes* 62): "And from his mouth came foorth a sharpe sword . . . that he might strike the Gentiles therewith; for hee shall rule them with *a rod of yron*" (*Workes* 62). The sword becomes a metonymy for God, truth, and the word by which God's enemies are vanquished, the point of this passage in James's account of his own historical moment presumably being to draw attention to the analogy between the force of God's word in the apocalyptic situation and James's word in the Reformation battle against the papists.
13. Willson notes how "Mendoza, the former Spanish Ambassador in England," after hearing about a public theological debate between James and the Jesuit James Gordon, wrote: "'after the disputation the King said in his chamber that Gordon did not understand the Scripture,

which is a fairly bold thing to say, only that the King has the assurance to translate Revelation and to write upon the subject himself as if he were Amadis de Gaul himself'" (82). The incident reveals the kind of status James was accruing while still in his teens through his literary and scholarly abilities.

14. James's apocalyptic writing strategies confirm *avant la lettre* the Derridean notion that "no one can exhaust the overdeterminations and indeterminations of the apocalyptic stratagems" (Derrida 89), if only because once one reads apocalyptic as a function of specific historical contexts—as James does with regard to Reformation struggles for political and religious supremacy—then apocalyptic becomes contingent upon the over- and indeterminations that make of history such a dense and polysemous signifying field. According to Lois Parkinson Zamora, "Apocalyptic narration responds to its historical context by balancing (in various combinations and degrees) description and prescription, accommodation and revision. Apocalyptic texts dramatize the decisive moment when an old world discovers a believable new world and either reacts against the old system or incorporates it into its new design" (177).
15. Other evidence for the importance James invested in them is to be found in his prefatory comments ("The Author to the Reader") to his translation of Salluste Du Bartas's *The Furies.* James states, "Yea scarslie but at stollen moments, haue I the leasure to blenk [glance] upon any paper, and yet not that, with free and vnuexed spirit. Alwaies, tough and vnpolishede as they are, I offer them vnto thee: Which beeing well accepted, will moue mee to hast the presenting vnto thee, of my APOCALYPS, and also such nomber of the PSALMES, as I haue perfited" (Craigie, *Poems* 1: 99–100).
16. I note Kevin Sharpe's observation that "Perhaps even more regrettably, no study has been made of James's letters, devotional tracts, commentaries on Scripture, and, especially, his poetry as self-examinations and as self-explications of the king's person and concept of office" (81).
17. For Altizer, "Christianity begins with apocalypse, with the proclamation and enactment of the advent of a new eon or new world which can only be the end of an old eon and old creation" (1).
18. Richey suggests, in her discussion of the politics of apocalyptic writings, that they articulate a "poetics of transcendence" and that the "power behind the sermons, lyrics, and pamphlets of the age resides in the writer's ability to refer beyond his or her own material articulations to that transcendent, immaterial voice that can never wholly be contained, a voice that opens human discourse up both to representational innovation and to divine Presence" (14).

19. This scenario, marked by political, religious, and personal anxiety, plays out in relation to Eugen Weber's notion that "For a long time, chiliasm had been an answer to persecution. Belief in the imminence of the end brought comfort in the midst of danger and pain" (33–34).
20. For more on this see Stephen D. O'Leary's book, which focuses on "apocalyptic doctrines as they move, or attempt to move, into the mainstream of public discourse" (225) in a contemporary historical setting.
21. For more on "apocalyptic as a historical movement" (28) see Koch, esp. 28–33. Koch identifies eight apocalyptic motifs that have historical significance: 1) "The writings are dominated by an *urgent expectation* of the impending overthrow of all earthly conditions *in the immediate future*" (28); 2) "The end appears as a vast *cosmic catastrophe*" (29); 3) "The end-time is closely connected with the previous history of mankind and of the cosmos" (29); 4) "In order to explain the course of historical events and the happenings of the end-time, an army of *angels and demons* is mustered, divided into a hierarchy of orders" (30); 5) "Beyond the catastrophe a new *salvation* arises, paradisal in character" (30); 6) "The transition from disaster to final redemption is expected to take place by means of an act issuing from *the throne of God*" (31); 7) "in connection with the ascent of the throne in the end-time, *a mediator with royal functions* is frequently introduced to accomplish and guarantee final redemption" (31); 8) "The catchword *glory* is used wherever the final state of affairs is set apart from the present and whenever a final amalgamation of the earthly and heavenly spheres is prophesied" (32). Koch's motifs all figure significantly in James's apocalyptic writing stratagems; indeed, Koch's seventh motif regarding a royal mediator is a defining (and self-justificatory) tactic evident in James's apocalyptic texts.
22. From the beginning of its narrative in Revelation 1:1 ("The reuelation of IESVS CHRIST, which God gaue vnto him" [Geneva Bible (1560)]), Revelation makes issues of voice a crucial part of its literary and allegorical strategies. The gloss for this passage that appears in the margins of the Geneva Bible exemplifies these issues, stating: "Christ receiued this reuelation out of his fathers bosome as his owne doctrine, but it was hid in respect of vs so that Christ as Lord and God reueiled it to Iohn his seruant by the ministrie of his Angel." Revelation initiates in the "fathers bosome" and is received by Jesus, who in turn transmits it to John via angelic intervention. This paraphrastic comment shows at least four levels of voice enabling the allegory to follow, thus producing the potential for exegetical mystification. Who, after all, is to say that the translation of the "original" text of Revelation has not been corrupted or deformed in the process of translation and transference?

James attempts to lend a certain interpretive stability to this scenario by appropriating revelatory discourse to his own literary and political uses.

23. In a major interpolation to Revelation 22:19, the anxiety about alternative readings returns, James stating: "For whosoeuer in coping or translating this Booke, adulterateth any waies the Originall, or in interpreting of it, wittingly strayes from the trew meaning of it, and from the analogie of Faith, to follow the fantasticall inuention of man, or his owne preoccupied opinions; he I say, that doeth any of these, shalbe accursed as a peruerter of the trewth of God and his Scriptures" (*Workes* 72). James must have recognized that any translation or "coping" was inevitably, *always already* a perversion of the original—that is, that any interpretation necessarily corrupts to the extent that it cannot substitute for the original, thus committing the heresy of paraphrase. Frank Kermode avers that it is "worth remembering that the rise of what we call literary fiction happened at a time when the revealed, authenticated account of the beginning was losing its authority" (67).
24. Revelation was the site of considerable anxiety about interpretation, as evidenced in the numerous paraphrases it underwent in the early modern period. Furthermore, paraphrase was a crucial mode of textual presentation from the first appearance of Revelation in English in the Geneva Bible (1560), which went so far as to publish marginal glosses to clarify particular doctrinal issues associated with problematic passages. The opening letter of Thomas Brightman's *A Reuelation of the Reuelation that is, the Reuelation of St. Iohn,* makes the meta-interpretive nature of Revelation explicit: "Revelation doth still require necessarily a Revelation."
25. The interesting deviation in *The Lepanto* is the way in which it focuses apocalyptic imagery on the Turks in opposition to the forces of the Christian "baptiz'd race" (so named as an agglomerate religious entity and not as a divisive grouping of sects with major doctrinal differences; see Craigie, *Poems* 202). Perhaps this is an early indication of the conciliarist, ecumenical positioning James was to advocate through the length of his career, as detailed by Patterson.
26. Bauckham notes that the "Protestant image of the papal Antichrist was . . . an extraordinary vision of the devil disguising himself as an angel of light. By means of the counterfeit church of papal Rome, Antichrist achieved the supreme blasphemy of usurping the whole office and glory of Christ, and was actually enabled to be worshipped as God in the very temple of God" (104). Lake, in his comments on anti-popery, suggests the importance of the sort of rhetorical stance taken by James

in his apocalyptic writings: "Certainly anti-popery appealed to people's emotions. It did so because it incorporated deeply held beliefs and values and it helped to dramatize and exorcise the fears and anxieties produced when those values came under threat. But that, surely, is what political ideologies do, and it is from their capacity to do it that they derive their ability to motivate and mobilize large numbers of people" (97).

27. See Historical Manuscripts Commission, lxvi, *Ancaster MSS* 362–85.
28. This interpolation is important for how it subtly instructs the reader in a way that previous glosses of the same passage had not. The Geneva Bible gloss, for instance, only states: "This [the angel standing] signifieth [that] the day of iudgement shalbe cleare and euident; so that none shal be hid: for the trumpet shal blowe a lowde & all shal understand it."
29. McGinn notes that "Debate continues about the social setting and ecclesial identity of John of Patmos, but most current scholarship views him as an itinerant Christian prophet of Asia Minor who wrote in the last decade of the first century" (524). McGinn goes on to suggest that "All classic interpreters conceived of Revelation as a literary unity, the work of a single author. The same wave of historical-critical scholarship, largely German in inspiration, that questioned traditional views of authorship also attacked the book's unity, claiming that it was either composed of a variety of sources (frequently seen as Jewish rather than Christian in origin) or was a mélange of different redactions. Though the denial of literary unity won the day among critics at the end of the nineteenth century, it has recently come under increasing fire to the point where most biblical scholars would hold that Revelation is indeed the work of one author, whatever fragments of earlier traditions and materials he might have incorporated" (ibid.).
30. Williamson also locates the "more cautious digression in the preamble to *An Apologie for the Oath of Allegiance* (1609)" (40) as a locus where "James's understanding of sacred history" (ibid.) is set forth. See also Patterson, esp. 75–123.
31. In the second book, seventh chapter of *Daemonologie* (1597), for instance, James uses Epistemon to comment on the "formes of Sathans conuersing visiblie in the world" (Craigie, *Minor Prose* 37), then makes explicit the connections among these "formes of Sathan," Revelation, and "Papistrie": "For of two different formes thereof, the one of them by the spreading of the Euangell, and conquest of the white horse, in the sixt Chapter of the Reuelation, is much hindred and becomes rarer there through, This his appearing to any Christians, troubling of them outwardly, or possessing of them constraynedly. The other of them is be-/come communer and more vsed sensine, I meane by their vnlawfull

artes, wherevpon our whole purpose hath bene. This we finde by experience in this Ile to be true. For as we know, moe Ghostes and spirites were seene, nor tongue can tell, in the time of blind *Papistrie* in these Countries, where now by the contrarie, a man shall scarcely all his time here once of such things" (ibid.).

32. Linda Levy Peck notes that "Although both Elizabeth and James I used Roman motifs James I changed English iconography. James I was the first English monarch to portray himself on his coinage as a Roman Emperor. In his accession medal of 1603 copied perhaps from a miniature by Nicholas Hilliard, he is presented in armour and crowned with a laurel wreath, and lays claim to the title of Emperor in the coin's inscription. Indeed, in the first year of his reign he called himself Emperor of Great Britain which he later dropped as hopes for a 'perfect union' between England and Scotland faded" (5). Such imperial ambitions were clearly not new to James; in his early career he was preoccupied with apocalyptic texts that figured forth a godly prince capable of extraordinary political and theological influence to countervail that of the pope. That these imperial tendencies may have been exacerbated in the years after his coming to the English throne by England's sense of itself as "an apocalyptically elect nation" (McGinn 536), thus leading to the republication of the Revelation paraphrase and meditation, is not surprising. In the Scottish mathematician John Napier's resolutely anti-imperial view, "the effective and *de jure* emperors were the popes: indeed, the popes inherited the imperial robes and insignia [of the Roman emperors] which they continued to possess 'to this day.' That the popes were the heirs to the emperors was manifest in the *Revelation,* as well as in *Daniel* and Paul. The seven kings referred to by St. John (Rev. 17:9–10) were the seven royal governments of Rome: kings, consuls, dictators, triumvirs, tribunes, emperors and popes. When John was writing, the first five had fallen, the emperors were in power, and the popes were yet to come" (Williamson 23). Napier's *A Plaine Discovery of the Whole Revelation of St. John* (1593) was written, like James's meditation on Revelation, "in the wake of that singular historical 'proof' of the Protestant view of history, the defeat of the Armada in 1588" (McGinn 536). It is important to remember that Napier's apocalyptic views, which did not include the notion of Scotland or England as elect nations (Williamson 24) and which associated "kingly power" with "barbaric nations" (Williamson 25), would not have jibed with James's use of apocalyptic texts to justify his politics. For Napier, the Reformation "meant the liberation from empire and universal headship in any guise whatsoever" (ibid.). Firth suggests, somewhat contradictorily, that Napier "joined the ranks of those who

encouraged James to see his duty as a prince in apocalyptic terms" (134). Firth cites a dedicatory passage to James VI from Napier's *A Plaine Discovery of the Whole Revelation of St. John* as support for her position: "Therefore, it is likewise the dutie of God's servants in this age, interpreters of the Prophecies, as well (according to the example of the Prophets) to incourage and inanimate Princes, to be ready against that greate day of the Lords revenge, as also to exhort them generally, to remove all such impediments in their cuntries and commonwealths, as many hinder that work, and prove Gods plagues" (cited in Firth 134).

33. As Capp points out, subsequent apocalyptic hopes of finding a godly prince were linked to various of James's offspring with similar results.

Works Cited

Altizer, Thomas J. J. *History as Apocalypse.* Albany: State U of New York P, 1985.

Bale, John. *The Image of Bothe Churches after the moste wonderfull and heavenly Revelacion of Sainct John the Evangelist, Contayning a very frutefull exposicion or Paraphrase upon the same . . .* (*STC* 1297). London, 1548.

Barroll, Leeds. *Politics, Plague, and Shakespeare's Theater: The Stuart Years.* Ithaca: Cornell UP, 1991.

Bauckham, Richard. *Tudor Apocalypse: Sixteenth Century Apocalypticism, Millenarianism and the English Reformation: From John Bale to John Foxe and Thomas Brightman.* Oxford: Sutton Courtenay P, 1978.

Brightman, Thomas. *A Reuelation of the Reuelation that is, the Reuelation of St. Iohn opened clearely . . .* (*STC* 3755). Amsterdam, 1615.

Bruce, John, ed. *Letters of Queen Elizabeth and King James VI. of Scotland.* London: Camden Society, 1849.

Capp, Bernard. "The Political Dimension of Apocalyptic Thought." *The Apocalypse in English Renaissance Thought and Literature: Patterns, Antecedents and Repercussions.* Eds. C. A. Patrides and Joseph Wittreich. Ithaca: Cornell UP, 1984. 93–124.

Chevalier, Jacques M. *A Postmodern Revelation: Signs of Astrology and the Apocalypse.* Toronto: U of Toronto P, 1997.

Cohn, Norman. *The Pursuit of the Millennium: Revolutionary Millenarians and Mystical Anarchists of the Middle Ages.* London: Pimlico, 1993.

Cowper, William. *Pathmos: or, A Commentary on the Revelation of Saint Iohn . . .* (*STC* 5931). London, 1619.

Craigie, James, ed. *Minor Prose Works of King James VI and I.* Edinburgh: Scottish Text Society, 1982.

———, ed. *The Poems of James VI of Scotland.* Vol. 1. Edinburgh: William Blackwood, 1955.

de Certeau, Michel. *The Mystic Fable.* Vol. 1: *The Sixteenth and Seventeenth Centuries.* Trans. Michael B. Smith. Chicago: U of Chicago P, 1992.

Derrida, Jacques. "Of an Apocalyptic Tone Recently Adopted in Philosophy." Trans. John Leavey, Jr. *Semeia* 23 (1982): 63–98.

Disraeli, Isaac. *An Inquiry into the Literary and Political Character of James the First.* London: John Murray, 1816.

Emmerson, Richard K., and Bernard McGinn, eds. *The Apocalypse in the Middle Ages.* Ithaca: Cornell UP, 1992.

Firth, Katharine R. *The Apocalyptic Tradition in Reformation Britain 1530–1645.* Oxford: Oxford UP, 1979.

Fischlin, Daniel, and Mark Fortier, eds. *James I:* The True Law of Free Monarchies *and* Basilikon Doron. Toronto: Centre for Reformation and Renaissance Studies, 1996.

The Geneva Bible: A Facsimile of the 1560 Edition. Madison: U of Wisconsin P, 1969.

Goldberg, Jonathan. *James I and the Politics of Literature.* Stanford: Stanford UP, 1989.

Greg, W. W., ed. "Burdens of the Office of King's Printer (1630)." *A Companion to Arber Being a Calendar of Documents in Edward Arber's Transcript of the Registers of the Company of Stationers of London 1554–1640.* Oxford: Clarendon P, 1967. 257–58.

The Holy Bible. Authorized King James Version. Grand Rapids, Mich.: Zondervan Bible Publishers, 1983.

James I. *The Peacemaker: or Great Brittaines Blessing Fram'd . . .* (*STC* 14387). London: 1618.

———. *The Workes* (1616). Hildesheim: Georg Olms Verlag, 1971.

Kermode, Frank. *The Sense of an Ending: Studies in the Theory of Fiction.* London: Oxford UP, 1967.

Koch, Klaus. *The Rediscovery of Apocalyptic.* London: SCM Press, 1972.

Lake, Peter. "Anti-popery: the Structure of a Prejudice." *Conflict in Early Stuart England.* Eds. Richard Cust and Ann Hughes. New York: Longman, 1989. 72–106.

Lanham, Richard A. *A Handlist of Rhetorical Terms.* 2nd ed. Berkeley: U of California P, 1991.

Law, Thomas Graves, ed. "Documents Illustrating Catholic Policy, 1596–98." *Publications of the Scottish History Society.* Vol. 15. *Miscellany of the Scottish History Society.* Edinburgh: Edinburgh UP, 1893. 1: 1–70.

Mason, Thomas. *A Revelation of the Revelation . . . Whereby the Pope is most plainely declared and proued to bee Antichrist* (*STC* 17623). London, 1619.

McGinn, Bernard. "Revelation." *The Literary Guide to the Bible.* Eds. Robert Alter and Frank Kermode. Cambridge: Harvard UP, 1987. 523–41.

McIlwain, Charles H., ed. *The Political Works of James I.* New York: Russell and Russell, 1965.

Napier, Iohn. *A Plaine Discouery of the whole Reuelation of Saint Iohn . . .* (*STC* 18354). Edinburgh, 1593.

O'Leary, Stephen D. *Arguing the Apocalypse: A Theory of Millenial Rhetoric.* New York: Oxford UP, 1994.

Patterson, W. B. *King James VI and I and the Reunion of Christendom.* Cambridge: Cambridge UP, 1997.

Peck, Linda Levy. "The Mental World of the Jacobean Court: An Introduction." *The Mental World of the Jacobean Court.* Ed. Linda Levy Peck. Cambridge: Cambridge UP, 1991. 1–17.

Quispel, Gilles. *The Secret Book of Revelation: The Last Book of the Bible.* Trans. Peter Staples. New York: McGraw-Hill, 1979.

Richey, Esther Gilman. *The Politics of Revelation in the English Renaissance.* Columbia: U of Missouri P, 1998.

Robertson, William. *The History of Scotland during the reigns of Queen Mary and of King James VI till his accession to the Crown of England.* 2 vols. London, 1761.

Sharpe, Kevin, "Private Conscience and Public Duty in the Writings of James VI and I." *Public Duty and Private Conscience in Seventeenth-Century England: Essays Presented to G. E. Aylmer.* Eds. John Morrill, Paul Slack, and Daniel Woolf. Oxford: Clarendon P, 1993. 77–100.

Warner, George F., ed. "The Library of King James VI, 1573–1583 from a manuscript in the hand of Peter Young, his tutor." *Publications of the Scottish History Society.* Vol. 15. *Miscellany of the Scottish History Society.* Edinburgh: Edinburgh UP, 1893. 1: xi–lxxv.

Weber, Eugen. *Apocalypses: Prophecies, Cults and Millenial Beliefs through the Ages.* Toronto: Random House, 1999.

Williamson, Arthur H. *Scottish National Consciousness in the Age of James VI: The Apocalypse, the Union and the Shaping of Scotland's Public Culture.* Edinburgh: John Donald, 1979.

Willson, D. H. *King James VI and I.* London: Jonathan Cape, 1962.

Wormald, Jenny. "James VI and I, *Basilikon Doron* and *The Trew Law of Free Monarchies:* The Scottish Context and the English Translation." *The Mental World of the Jacobean Court.* Ed. Linda Levy Peck. Cambridge: Cambridge UP, 1991. 36–54.

Zamora, Lois Parkinson. *Historical Vision in Contemporary U.S. and Latin American Fiction.* Cambridge: Cambridge UP, 1989.

14

James I and King David: Jacobean Iconography and Its Legacy

John N. King

The reputation of James I of England (James VI of Scotland) as Britain's "New Solomon" has long endured.[1] That typological figure fuses the King's own claim to Solomonic wisdom with his self-styled role as *Rex Pacificus.* Indeed, his motto, *Beati Pacifici* ("blessed are the peacemakers"), constitutes a tag from the Sermon on the Mount (Matt. 5:9) that accords with both the peaceful and prosperous reign of the Old Testament monarch and the princely maxim with which the king concludes *ΒΑΣΙΛΙΚΟΝ ΔΩΡΟΝ: Or His Majesties Instructions to His Dearest Son, Henry the Prince* (Edinburgh, 1599): "Parcere subiectis, & debellare superbos."[2] Uttered by Anchises to Aeneas (*Aeneid* 6.1154), those words afford a model for fatherly counsel to a valiant son. James's reign was the only one during the Tudor-Stuart era that endured without foreign war or domestic rebellion. It is no accident, therefore, that the funerary sermon by John Williams, bishop of Lincoln, thus praises the late king: "Every man lived in peace under his vine and his fig tree in the days of Solomon. . . . And so did they in the blessed days of King James."[3]

Despite the importance of Solomon as a precedent for Jacobean majesty, his father, King David, looms as the foremost scriptural model for Jacobean iconography. Indeed, Davidic typology that pervades visual images of the Scottish king of England corresponds to many references to David as a regal exemplar in James's own writings. In *Basilikon Doron,* for example, James holds up David over Solomon as the model for ideal kingship. Indeed, David's warlike behavior constitutes an inverse precedent for Jacobean peace according to the new king's inaugural speech to the Parliament of England on 19 March 1603:

> Yet do I hope by my experience of the by-past [i.e., former] blessings of peace, which God hath so long ever since my birth bestowed upon me, that he will not be weary to continue the same, nor repent him of his grace to me, transferring that sentence of King David's upon his by-past victories of war, to mine of peace, that "that God who preserved me from the devouring jaws of the bear and of the lion, and delivered them into my hands, shall also now grant me victory over that uncircumcised Philistine."[4]

James's writings repeatedly cite David as a model for Jacobean governance. His *True Law of Free Monarchies* thus records a memorable assertion that affords a foundation for the regal claim to authority *jure divino* (by divine right): "Kings are called Gods by the prophetical King David, because they sit upon God his throne in the earth, and have the count of their administration to give unto him." Echoing the Virgilian postscript to *Basilikon Doron,* James continues: "Their office is, 'To minister justice and judgment to the people,' as the same David saith: 'To advance the good, and punish the evil.'"[5] It is no accident, therefore, that *True Law of Free Monarchies* contains an extended commentary on Samuel's declarations concerning the establishment of kingship.[6] Davidic counsel came to mind yet again in James's 9 November 1605 speech to Parliament in thanksgiving for providential deliverance from the Gunpowder Plot: "And here in this place, where our general destruction should have been, to magnify and praise him for our general delivery: that I may justly now say of mine enemies and yours, as David doth often say in the Psalm, Inciderunt in foueam quam fecerunt."[7]

This essay investigates why David assumes primacy over Solomon in Jacobean iconography, despite the former's problematic status as a sinner. Surely David's capacity as the most powerful Hebrew king held out considerable appeal, but his union of the northern and southern kingdoms of Israel and Judah must have attracted the attention of James I, whose 1607 appeal for the union of the realms of England and Scotland failed to persuade the House of Commons. This essay also considers interconnections between Davidic iconography and James's assumption of a regal manner modeled on Jesus Christ, whose advent as the Messiah born of the House of David constitutes a fulfillment of Old Testament prophecies in accordance with Christian tradition. (It was commonplace for medieval and early monarchs to style themselves as types of Christ.[8]) The present inquiry concludes with an examination of the contorted afterlife of Davidic iconography during the reigns of Charles I and II, who succeeded their father and grandfather on the thrones of England and Scotland.

Given the gaps and fissures that fill scriptural accounts of the House of David, notably the story told in 2 Samuel and 1–2 Kings, one may wonder why monarchs ever sought solace in Old Testament prototypes. A profoundly antimonarchic strand counterbalances pro-regal elements in the story of David, which is commonly regarded as an outstanding instance of Hebrew narrative art. After all, the Old Testament records that the Israelites' desire to have a king constituted a mark of infidelity, despite divine consent to that wish (1 Sam. 8). Samuel may have anointed Saul as King, but he twice deposed him for disobeying divine commands. Although David succeeded in uniting the kingdoms of Israel and Judah, disaster fell upon the royal house following his adultery with Bathsheba and murder of her husband Uriah. Application of scriptural typology posed a potential problem for King James, because prophetic reproofs delivered to Saul by Samuel and to David by Nathan might have suggested that clerical authority constitutes a check on regal claims to govern by divine right. After all, some Caroline supporters of *jure divino* episcopacy posited that kings are subordinate to clergy.[9]

Sexual contamination and turmoil at court are dominant concerns in a scriptural narrative filled with incidents of political betrayal, murder, exhibitionism, voyeurism, family discord, rape, and incest. Many of the failures of David and members of his dynasty were applied against kings (and in rare instances their enemies) during the turbulent events of the sixteenth and seventeenth centuries.[10] From the vantage point of the opposition to Charles I, for example, Davidic precedent afforded not an argument for divine right monarchy but a precedent for regicide. Sexual transgression disturbed the Davidic dynasty as the offspring of David's adulterous union died soon after birth; as David's eldest son Amnon raped Tamar, his half-sister; as Tamar's full brother Absalom slew Amnon in revenge; and as Absalom mounted rebellion against David under the influence of the evil counselor Achitophel. Above all, Absalom declared war against David by engaging in sexual intercourse with "his father's concubines in the sight of all Israel" (2 Sam. 16:22). Even though Solomon succeeded in constructing the Temple in Jerusalem, an achievement denied to David because he was tainted by sin, the second son born to Bathsheba marred his greatness by breaking the divine prohibition against marriages to foreign women and failing to suppress rites involving cult prostitution at Canaanite hill shrines.

Despite its inherently conflicted state, Davidic (and Solomonic) iconography represents not a new departure but an important continuity that connects representations of Stuart monarchs with their Tudor predecessors. Scholarship has therefore worked in a vacuum by ignoring sixteenth-century precedents for praise of Stuart monarchs as Davidic (and Solomonic) kings. Critics have instead posited a rupture between the increasing classicization of the cultic images of Queen Elizabeth and the "Roman Style" of James I.[11] In doing so, they ignore the import of texts such as "A Speech in Star Chamber of 20 June 1616," in which James insists upon the Davidic and Solomonic foundation of regal judgment. The king thus construes the opening verse of Psalm 72, "Give thy judgments to the king, O God, and thy righteousness to the king's son": "These be the first words of one of the Psalms of the kingly prophet David, whereof the literal sense runs upon him, and his son Solomon, and the mystical sense upon God and Christ his eternal son. . . . But both senses, as well literal as mystical, serve to kings for imitation, and especially to Christian kings: for kings sit in the throne of God, and they themselves are called gods." James connects just and righteous governance, wherein "true" monarchs imitate God and Christ, to godliness and wisdom that underlie regal justice, wherein they model themselves on David and Solomon.[12]

Davidic and Solomonic typology constitutes an important continuity between Tudor and Stuart iconography. Recognition of the centrality of scriptural narrative in Jacobean monarchic representation does not imply that regal panegyrics were frozen into a hieratic style contingent upon unchanging formulaic repetition.[13] Scriptural types underwent fine shades of variation and modulation through application to the political and life histories of different monarchs. We should therefore note that Henry VIII inherited the Davidic style of his father Henry VII, founder of the House of Tudor.[14] Representations of Edward VI are devoid of comparison to David, however, because the Hebrew king's contamination with sin clashed with Edward's reputation for piety and chastity. Instead, apologists looked to the boy king as a new Solomon, wise in his youth, or a second Josiah, whose commitment to an iconoclastic policy of church reform encouraged millennial expectations for the fulfillment of Christ's kingdom on earth. Henry VII, Henry VIII, Edward VI, and Elizabeth I participated in stylized comparison to Solomon as a type for regal majesty. Even Elizabeth's unique status as England's Virgin Queen constituted no obstacle to comparison with kings tainted with sexual contamination and marriages to foreign queens. Apologists praised her not only as a "New Solomon" but as a type of the queen of Sheba.[15] She received praise as a second David from Protestants who wished to admonish her obliquely to embrace a thoroughgoing program of church reform like that which held sway during the brief reign of her late brother Edward.[16] The absence of such precedents in the iconography of Mary I, the Catholic half-sister to both Edward VI and Elizabeth I, represents a singular exception to a tradition of monarchical praise that dates back at least as far at the Kingdom of the Franks.

Unlike the Tudor monarchs—for whom little evidence indicates that they themselves, as opposed to their apologists, appealed to Davidic precedents—James I invokes King David as a model both for himself and his offspring. Indeed, James employs Psalms 105:15, a hymn attributed to David, as a proof text for the divine right of kings in his personal motto, "Touch not mine Anointed." Inscribed beneath the king's portrait in an engraving by Willem van de Passe (c. 1621), for example, that maxim balances an alternative Jacobean motto, *Beati Pacifici,* which appears at the top of the oval.[17] The king appropriates a divine rebuke originally directed to kings who threatened Hebrew patriarchs and prophets, converting it into a stern warning to advocates of emergent theories of either resistance to monarchical authority or tyrannicide. He thus conflates a psalmic text concerning divine intervention on behalf of Israel with David's execution of the Amalekite who lodged a presumably false claim that he had assented to Saul's appeal for a coup de grâce after the Israelite king's wounding at Mount Gilboa: "And David said to him, 'Your blood be upon your head; for your own mouth has testified against you, saying, 'I have slain the Lord's anointed'" (2 Sam. 1:16). In *The True Law of Free Monarchies,* James further conflates that act of vengeance with David's prior refusal to murder Saul, despite the Benjamite king's yearning for the death of his onetime favorite:

> And David, notwithstanding he was inaugurate in that same degraded King's room, not only (when he was cruelly persecuted, for no offense, but good service done unto him) would not presume, having him in his power, scantly, but with great reverence, to touch the garment of the anointed of the Lord, and in his words blessed him: but likewise, when one came to him vaunting himself untruly to have slain Saul, he, without form of process, or trial of his guilt, caused only for guiltiness of his tongue, put him to sudden death.[18]

James I invokes David and Solomon as models for ideal kingship in *Basilikon Doron* ("The Royal Gift"). Book 1, which addresses "a King's Christian Duty Towards God," offers fatherly counsel that his eldest son and heir apparent, Prince Henry Frederick, follow the Pauline injunction to apply scriptural texts as a spiritual guide (2 Tim. 3:16–17). James singles out texts concerning Hebrew monarchs: "And most properly of any other, belongeth the reading thereof unto kings, since in that part of scripture, where the godly kings are first made mention of, that were ordained to rule over the people of God, there is an express and most notable exhortation and commandment given to them, to read and meditate in the Law of God" (12–13). Among Bible readings suitable to princes, James grants a notable position to wisdom texts attributed to Solomon, whose proverbial sagacity occupies an important place in princely instruction:

> and likewise the books of the Proverbs and Ecclesiastes, written by that great pattern of wisdom Solomon, which will not only serve you for instruction, how to walk in the obedience of the Law of God, but is also so full of golden sentences [i.e., sententia] and moral precepts, in all things that can concern your conversation in the world, as among the profane [i.e., classical] philosophers and poets, ye shall not find so rich a storehouse of precepts of natural wisdom, agreeing with the will and divine wisdom of God. (15)

In addition to the Song of Solomon (i.e., Canticles or the Song of Songs), an ever-problematic allegory, James ignores the Wisdom of Solomon because it is an apocryphal text excluded from the biblical canon by Protestants: "And as to the Apocrphy[al] books, I omit them, because I am no papist, as I said before" (15).

Among distinctively royal scriptures recommended to the Prince of Wales are "especially the books of the Kings and Chronicles, wherewith ye ought to be familiarly acquainted: for there shall ye see yourself, as in a mirror, in the catalogue either of the good or evil kings" (15). The composite Book of Kings contains texts designated in contemporary Bibles as 1–4 Kings (i.e., 1–2 Samuel and 1–2 Kings). Along with Chronicles, they constitute a *speculum principis* in which the princely reader will encounter abundant examples of regal behavior, both positive and negative. Study of David's history, the narrative core of those kingly scriptures, represents an obligation for Christian sovereigns.

Furthermore, James I recommends that the Book of Psalms occupy a special position in the devotional life of Prince Henry, because of its traditional ascription to King David: "And so much the fitter are they for you, than for the common sort, in respect the composer thereof was a king: and therefore best behoved to know a king's wants, and what things were meetest to be required by a king at God's hand for remedy thereof" (*Political Writings* 16). Aside from the Lord's Prayer, Psalms affords the foremost models for prayer: "as of most rich and pure fountains, ye may learn all form of prayer necessary for your comfort at all occasions." Devout application of Psalm texts should enable the prince to strike a middle way between the set observances of ordinary people, who "prayeth nothing but out of books," on the one hand, and the extemporaneous prayer of "vain Pharasaical Puritans," on the other, who "think they rule him [God] upon their fingers: The former way will breed an uncouth coldness in you towards him, the other will breed in you a contempt of him." Above all, princes must honor God as king of kings: "But in your prayer to God speak with all reverence: for if a subject will not speak but reverently to a king, much less should any flesh presume to talk with God as his companion" (16).

The history of King David functions not only as a guide to religious devotion but also as a source of practical advice concerning organization of the courtly establishment. *Basilikon Doron* paraphrases Psalm 101, in particular, as a pledge by David to govern himself through proper ordering of his royal court. In a hymn that may have functioned originally as part of a coronation ritual, the regal speaker promises to fashion a blameless court in which

> No man who practices deceit
> shall dwell in my house;
> no man who utters lies
> shall continue in my presence. (Ps. 101:7)

In advocating that his son "follow good king David's counsel in the choice of your servants, by setting your eyes upon the faithful and upright of the land to dwell with you,"[19] James suppresses murderous intrigue and disorder that flourished at David's court in line with the Deuteronomic thesis that divine punishment follows as a consequence upon unrighteousness. Oppositional readers might therefore discover irony in the father's counsel to his heir:

> as to the government of your court and followers, King David sets down the best precepts, that any wise and Christian king can practice in that point: For as ye ought to have a great care for the ruling well of all your subjects, so ought ye to have a double care for the ruling well of your own servants; since unto them ye are both a politic and economic governor. . . . And therefore in two points have ye to take good heed anent your court and household: first, in choosing them wisely; next in carefully ruling them whom ye have chosen (34).

As a complement to the Davidic ideal, James holds up Solomon as a further model for governance of the royal court:

> And shortly, maintain peace in your court, banish envy, cherish modesty, banish deboshed [debauched] insolence, foster humility, and repress pride: setting down such a comely and honorable order in all the points of your service; that when strangers shall visit your court, they may with the Queen of Sheba, admire your wisdom in the glory of your house, and comely order among your servants. (38)

In the case of Solomon, however, James acknowledges instability inherent in the scriptural model of a wise king whose greatest flaw involved apostasy through participation in ritual cults associated with his many foreign wives. Counseling his son to marry a wife who observes the same religion as he, the father warns against harboring vain hope "that ye will be able to frame and make her as ye please: that deceived Solomon the wisest king that ever was: the grace of perseverance, not being a flower that groweth in our garden" (34–36).

When it comes to the negative side of David's history, James stresses its virtuous outcome. In praising conscience to his son as "the light of knowledge that God hath planted in man," he cites the example of David's "senselessness of sin, through sleeping in a careless security . . . after his murder and adultery, ever till he was wakened by the Prophet Nathan's similitude" (17). Recalling the execution of his own mother, Mary, Queen of Scots, in the preface to *Basilikon Doron,* James counsels against revenge by renouncing "a Davidical testament" (9), thus casting his son (and himself) in the role of an unprecedentedly benevolent Solomon. The reference is to David's dying counsel that his successor settle scores by executing those who had wronged a father incapable of executing his own revenge (1 Kings 2). Oblique analogies to Elizabethan courtiers may infuse James's renunciation of vengeance modeled on the bloodbath that followed David's death, when Solomon ordered the slaughter of Joab, the disloyal nephew who commanded David's army; Shimei, a member of the House of Saul who cursed David as he fled Jerusalem during the rebellion of Absalom; and Adonijah, half-brother to Solomon, whose proposal to wed Abishag, the concubine of his father's deathbed, constituted a treasonous claim to the throne of Israel and Judah. Of course, James had ample cause to rein in hostility as the Elizabethan age was drawing to a close. It was an open question whether the aged queen would name him, her closest living relative, as her successor.

King James was not alone in looking to Psalms as a guidebook for princely conduct. After the untimely death of Prince Henry in 1612, his brother Charles replaced him as heir apparent and Prince of Wales. George Hakewill, a chaplain charged with guarding Prince Charles against Roman Catholicism, published a dozen sermons delivered before Charles as *King David's Vow for Reformation of Himself, his Family, his Kingdom* (1621). Those homilies extract advice concerning the "reformation and government" of the princely "household and State" out of Psalm 101, a royal hymn that underwent paraphrase in *Basilikon Doron* (Av–3r). The engraved title page indicates that princes may comprehend the imperial virtues of justice and mercy by reading the Book of Psalms held in King David's right hand.

James VI and I actually versified Psalm translations—unlike Henry VIII, who limited his imitation of King David to musical rather than metrical composition. Long before James's accession to the English throne, a versification of Psalm 104 out of the psalter of Emanuel Tremellius had appeared as a hymn to God the creator in the king's anonymous *The Essayes of a Prentice in the Divine Art of Poesie.* A late sixteenth-century manuscript contains thirty Psalm translations, many of which are in the king's own hand (British Library, ms. Royal 18 B. XVI).

During his last years, James I husbanded a desire to produce a new version of the Psalms in English. Although death halted that project, Charles I authorized publication of a revision of fifty of his father's Psalms by William Alexander, earl of Stirling; Alexander's own compositions completed that collection. Even though King Charles planned for the King James Psalter to replace the *Whole Book of Psalms* in official use in English and Scottish churches, the Stationers' Company hampered publication in order to protect its monopoly on publishing the Sternhold and Hopkins version.[20] A reproduction of the royal patent that circumvented the Stationers' monopoly faces the engraved title page of *The Psalms of King David Translated by King James,* an elegant duodecimo text that functions as a elite memorial to the late king. A preface composed by King Charles makes it clear that the text appears under royal auspices.[21]

The title page contains flanking portrayals of James I and King David, who bears his lyre at the left hand side (fig. 1). The ancient and modern kings join

FIG. 1. The Psalms of King David Translated by King James (Oxford, 1631). Reproduced by permission of the British Library, shelf mark 3434.b.8.

in holding the Book of Psalms borne by a heavenly hand encircled by clouds. That scene appropriates iconography familiar from the title pages of both the Coverdale Bible of 1535 and the Great Bible of 1539, which link Henry VIII to King David as a transmitter of scripture. The former title page portrays King Henry in the act of handing the first printed version of the complete Bible in English to the bishops at his right-hand side (fig. 2). Beyond them stands the lyre-playing King David, who affords an Old Testament precedent for royal authorization of Bible translation. Inscribed in the intervening banderole is a Davidic text: "O how sweet are thy words unto my throat: Yea more than honey" (Ps. 119:103; Vulg. Ps. 118:103). Loosely modeled on the 1535 woodcut, the title page of the Great Bible portrays Henry VIII both as a disseminator of the English Bible and, in the upper right-hand corner, as a "New David" who utters a prayer from the very same Psalm. It celebrates the power of the Bible as a guide for royal conduct: "Thy word is a lantern unto my feet (Ps. 119:105; Vulg. Ps. 118:105).[22]

The focal image of the book on the title page of King James's Psalter bears a further association with what may be the best-known Jacobean portrait, the frontispiece of the folio edition of *The Workes of the Most High and Mighty Prince, James,* published in 1616 by the king's printers, Robert Barker and John Bill (fig. 3). The king sits enthroned, bearing the regalia of the scepter and orb, before a cloth of estate adorned with his motto, *Beati Pacifici.* Crowded into a

Fig. 2. Hans Holbein, Coverdale Bible (1535), woodcut title page.
By permission of the British Library, shelf mark 132.h.46.

FIG. 3. The Workes of the Most High and Mighty Prince, James, (1616), frontispiece.

niche at the viewer's left are defining symbols of Tudor majesty, the sword and the book, which first appear in Henry VIII's hands in the Coverdale Bible title page (compare fig. 2). The sword's primary signification of justice is traditional, but its proximity to the weapon borne by St. Paul, who stands opposite to David on the Coverdale Bible title page, aligns it with "the sword of the Spirit, which is the word of God" (Eph. 6:17). The sword accordingly rests upon *Verbum Dei,* that is, the Bible.

The King James Psalter became embroiled in the Bishops' Wars (1639–40), which accelerated the long decline in royal authority that culminated in the execution of Charles I on 30 January 1649. Psalms attributed to James I were appended to the ill-fated version of the *Book of Common Prayer* published in 1637 for official use in the Episcopal Church of Scotland just as the Sternhold and Hopkins version had concluded the English prayer book. Musical accompaniment allowed the singing of Psalms in church. Known as "Laud's Liturgy," the Scottish prayer book sparked rioting upon its introduction at St. Giles Cathedral in Edinburgh and in other Scottish churches. Resistance to its adoption contributed to the eradication of Scottish episcopacy during the following year. The failure of royal authority in Scotland, losses in the Bishops' Wars, and ensuing fiscal distress contributed to the convening of the Long Parliament, whose actions eroded Crown authority until the epochal event of Charles's execution.[23]

James I's fatherly recommendation that "the Psalms of David are the meetest schoolmaster" for instruction in the art of prayer (*Political Writings* 16) supplied an immediate model for the occasional prayers and meditations in *ΕΙΚΩΝ ΒΑΣΙΛΙΚΗ: The Portraiture of His Sacred Majesty in His Solitudes and Sufferings.* Publication of that extraordinarily influential piece of royalist propaganda took place within days of Charles's execution on 30 January 1649. Dozens of editions appeared during the first year of publication. This essay will attribute the text to Charles because it is virtually certain that John Gauden, a royal chaplain, constructed the narrative of events leading up to Charles's execution out of the king's personal papers.[24]

Serving as a frontispiece, William Marshall's engraving portrays Charles as a royal martyr who has surrendered the earthly crown at his feet in order to receive the celestial crown upon which he gazes (fig. 4). The scene alludes to 1 Peter 5:4 and scattered verses in Revelation, but *Basilikon Doron* offers a Jacobean model for supplanting an earthly crown with a heavenly diadem: "For a good king (after a happy and famous reign) dieth in peace, lamented by his subjects, and admired by his neighbors; and leaving a reverent renown behind him in earth, obtaineth the crown of eternal felicity in heaven" (*Political Writings* 21). The crown of thorns in Charles's right hand labels him as a Christlike King. The emblems of the palm tree bearing weights and the sea-encircled rock allude to Italian emblems,[25] but they bear a further relationship to similes in the Book of Psalms (e.g., Pss. 18:2, 42:9, 62:2, 71:3, 92:12), thus associating Charles with

Fig. 4. ΕΙΚΩΝ ΒΑΣΙΛΙΚΗ: The Portraiture of His Sacred Majesty in His Solitudes and Sufferings (1649), engraved frontispiece. By permission of the Department of Prints and Drawings, British Museum, 1867-3-9-1712.

Jacobean iconography. The Latin legend for the palm tree indicates that "Virtue Grows Beneath Weight," whereas the motto for the rock claims that is "Triumphing Motionless."

Charles's assumption of a crown of thorns suggests that he emulated his father in providing the program for the allegorical engraving. After all, his father had recommended that figure to him as a symbol for the burdens of kingship in *A Meditation upon the 27th, 28th, and 29th Verses of the 27th Chapter of Saint Matthew, or a Pattern for a King's Inauguration.* In meditating on Christ's torture by means of the crown of thorns as a precedent for his son's coronation, James I dedicated the text to Charles, then Prince of Wales, by means of an analogy to mockery of Christ as king of the Jews (Matt. 27:27–29): "Which appeared to me to be so punctually set down, that my head hammered upon it diverse times after, and specially the Crown of Thorns went never out of my mind, remembering the thorny cares, which a king (if he have a care of his office) must be subject unto, as (God knows) I daily and nightly feel in mine own person."[26] In a meditation on Christian kingship infused with Davidic (and Solomonic) typology, James lodges the claim "that as Christ himself was the son and right heir by lineal descent of King David; so was he born under the first Roman emperor, that ever established the Roman Empire." Like Solomon, a peaceful monarch who constructed the Temple in Jerusalem, Christ as "a king of peace" is the "builder of his Church (whose body was likewise the true Temple represented by that of Solomon)."[27]

King James's dedication makes it clear that contemplation of the crown of thorns in his *Meditation upon Matthew* functions as a sequel to *Basilikon Doron,* the *speculum principis* whose title undergoes reworking in *Eikon Basilike* ("The King's Image"). The chapter addressed "To the Prince of Wales" (later Charles II) near the end of *Eikon Basilike* makes it clear that the text functions as a filial sequel to the *Meditation upon Matthew,* in which Charles I's father claims that Christian kingship assumes a distinctly Davidic cast: "it was necessary that Christ in the time of his passion should approve himself to be lineally descended from David, yea even next heir to the crown of the Jews."[28] In contemplating the stripping of Christ by Roman soldiers, who replaced his garments with a scarlet robe, James discovers a fulfillment of "the prophecy of David, that they 'should cast lots [on] it.'" Replacement of his "prophet's garment" with a "royal robe" affords an allegory for the "indivisible unity of the Church, which I pray God the true Church of Christ would now well remember."[29]

Interpretation of the crown of thorns as a symbol of ideal kingship was well established by the Stuart age. That association is present, for example, in a manuscript in Edward VI's own hand.[30] John Foxe identifies Christian kings rather than popes as "true" imitators of Christ in *Acts and Monuments of These Latter and Perilous Days,* which contrasts the papal tiara or triple "crowns of gold" both with the crowns of emperors and kings deposed by popes and that of Christ, whose "crown . . . was of sharp thorn."[31] *Eikon Basilike* goes to great lengths to fashion an image of regal piety that accords with the conventions of Protestant martyrology popularized by the *Book of Martyrs*—the alternative title of Foxe's text—in particular "the sustaining faith that makes constancy possible and a corresponding peace of mind in the face of persecution and the threat of death." One must recognize, at the same time, that the king defended established religion in a manner antithetical to the disobedience of Foxean martyrs.[32]

The frontispiece to *Eikon Basilike* portrays a chapel-like setting that likens the king's place of imprisonment to the cell of a saintly martyr. Charles rests his foot on a map that delineates the coast of Hampshire, indented by the Solent, and the northwest corner of the Isle of Wight, where the king underwent incarceration at Carisbrooke Castle. The legend "Mundi Calco" (I step upon the world) suggests that the king's image personifies the state upon which his foot treads.[33] The portrait infuses imagery of saintly triumph into a scene that recalls the best-known model for a kneeling king: illustrations of penitent King David in manuscript and printed versions of books of hours, psalters, penitential Psalms, and other devotional manuals.

The doubling of worldly and celestial crowns in the frontispiece to *Eikon Basilike* is related to the title page of *The Workes of the Most High and Mighty Prince, James* (fig. 5), which in turn complements that text's frontispiece portrayal of James I as a "godly" monarch (fig. 3). Crowns are the most prominent iconographical feature on the title page of James's *Workes,* supplying yet another precedent for the Caroline portrait. A celestial crown appears at the apex, held aloft by angels who flourish a banderole that bears the Latin motto, SUPEREST (it rises above). Shaped like the imperial crown of England, but studded with stars rather than diamonds, the divine crown validates the *jure divino* authority of King James, which undergoes representation in the four crowns of England, Scotland, Ireland, and Wales on the obelisk atop the architectural frame of the title page's border. As if in anticipation of his martyred son, James aspires to a distinctly regal variation of the celestial crown, one that surpasses the crown of glory worn by heavenly saints. Crowned lions are paired with regal unicorns atop the entablature, the former supporting the royal coat of arms while the two unicorns respectively support the crowned emblems of the Tudor Rose and Stuart Thistle. Standing in niches at either side of the book's title, personifications of religion and peace allegorize James's two-fold pursuit of religious purity at home and nonintervention abroad. Bearing a cornucopia and olive branch as she tramples upon warlike weaponry, *Pax* corresponds to James's self-styled role as a Christlike "Prince of Peace." More germane to the portrayal of James (and Charles) as a "godly" monarch is the angelic personification of *Religio,* whose emblems of the cross and open book align her with evangelical faith. Her trampling upon the skeletal figure of death identifies the Church of England, under royal governance, with the Christian promise of Resurrection.[34]

Fig. 5. The Workes of the Most High and Mighty Prince, James (1616), title page. Reproduced courtesy of Robert Spencer.

In line with the psalmic elements in the frontispiece of *Eikon Basilike*, the extemporaneous prayers and meditations at the end of each chapter indicate that the text functions as a royal psalter attributed to Charles as the son of Davidic James.[35] An intricate pattern of allusion to 2 Samuel and Psalms affords the basis for dramatizing the king's loss of power and imprisonment as the misfortune of one who, akin to David, suffers insults from "Shimei's tongue" and whose people rebel against him in the manner of an Absalom goaded into action by the false "counsel of Ahithophel." Most significantly, the "Penitential Meditations" near the end of *Eikon Basilike* are modeled broadly on the seven penitential Psalms, thus representing the king as one abjectly penitent for sin: "I come far short of David's piety, yet since I may equal David's afflictions, give me also the comforts and sure mercies of David."[36]

As a proponent of an English republic, John Milton rejected Charles I's comparison of his predicament to that of King David. He therefore challenged an effort initiated by James I to undertake "a large-scale restoration of the archaic symbolism of Davidic sacerdotal kingship and the cosmological empire."[37] Milton's initial rebuke came in *The Tenure of Kings and Magistrates*, published on 13 February 1649, within a fortnight of the king's execution. Milton argues that David explicitly excludes tyrants from protection in Psalm 94:20; he claims instead that Old Testament examples of divine deposition of kings provide ample precedent for the people to depose monarchs.[38] In place of Davidic analogy, Milton substitutes a grisly comparison of Charles to Agag, the Amalekite king whom Samuel, a type for the Puritan opposition, hewed "in pieces before the Lord" (1 Sam. 15:33).[39] Milton's contention that the claim that kings are accountable to God alone represents a misreading of Psalms cannot allude to *Eikon Basilike*. We know this because his pamphlet in defense of tyrannicide must have been in progress before or during the king's trial. Nevertheless, he shrewdly anticipates the king's minimization of David's sin of murdering Uriah the Hittite in order to conceal his adultery with Bathsheba.[40] Charles's confession to the solitary sin of condoning the execution of the earl of Strafford by parliamentary attainder had represented a masterstroke of "perverse genius," because he "offers as his sin one of the few actions Charles performed in 1640 which secured the support of parliamentary opponents."[41]

Milton's *Tenure* presumably found favor with the new regime, because the Council of State offered him appointment as secretary for foreign languages one month after its publication. In all likelihood, he received a commission to reply to *Eikon Basilike* along with the job offer.[42] It took him somewhat more than half a year to produce *ΕΙΚΟΝΟΚΛΑΣΤΗΣ* (6 October or 6 November 1649), his chapter-by-chapter refutation of the "King's Book." Milton's iconoclastic attack against civil idolatry of the kind that informs the frontispiece of *Eikon Basilike* is appropriately devoid of visual imagery; the only decorative element in the first edition of Milton's text consists of the printing of the title page in red and black. The work stridently assaults Davidic precedents that James I and his son Charles I had applied in defense of royal absolutism. Recognizing that the latter "borrows . . . many penitential Verses out of David's Psalms," Milton mocks King Charles's daring application of Psalm 51:4—David's reputed confession to the murder of Uriah—to his own acquiescence to the parliamentary attainder of Strafford. Focusing on unsettling elements in the David story that James had glossed over, Milton challenges the overall strategy of likening royal behavior to Davidic models as a misapplication of Psalms. In particular, Charles has failed to understand that "David was a sinner, and was justly punished."[43] Milton's most telling blow comes when he claims that Charles's habit of constructing prayers and meditations as an unacknowledged pastiche of phrases from Psalms amounts to little more than literary forgery. Were he a better author or a sincere Christian, his wholesale borrowings might be excused as literary imitation: "Had he borrow'd David's heart, it had been much the holier theft. For such kind of borrowing as this, if it be not bettered by the borrower, among good authors is accounted plagiary. However, this was more tolerable then Pamela's prayer, stolen out of Sir Philip."[44] Milton undermines the very claim to Christian piety that Davidic models were chosen to support through the startling discovery that a prayer appended to *Eikon Basilike* is virtually identical to one delivered by Pamela, a pagan heroine in Sidney's *Arcadia.* In his view, more fitting models for Charles's behavior may be found in the actions of royal apostates and enemies of Israel and Judah such as Rehoboam, Ahab, and Pharaoh, whose idolatry resulted in divine punishment. Above all he likens him to Nimrod, whose reputed foundation of monarchy (Gen. 10) made him the first tyrant in Milton's eyes.[45]

Writings by James I had stressed King David's status as a powerful ruler and reputed author of Psalms. What is new is Milton's willingness under a republican regime to subvert such praise. He confines destructive attack to Charles, however, because he never questions the status of David as an ideal monarch in his own right. Royalist writers and their opponents struggled to commandeer scriptural types such as King David in favor of their respective views: "Either literally or metaphorically (and the controversy over Scripture interpretation hinged on just this point), both sides were able to see themselves as reliving biblical episodes."[46] Even Milton stops short of acknowledging that the Hebrew ruler's reputation as a sinful adulterer and murderer contains potential for revolutionary subversion of monarchical authority.

Charles's inheritance of his father's pose as a "New David" underwent radical attack during the Civil Wars of the 1640s as royalists joined Parliamentarians in acknowledging the impotence of a monarch who suffered one battlefield defeat after another. When Samuel Gibson delivered the monthly fast day sermon before the House of Commons on 24 September 1645, on the verge of Parliamentary victory in the First Civil War, he amplified failures of King David that James I had minimized. Most notably, Gibson flaunts the king's adultery with

Bathsheba and its disastrous consequences: "So if one would magnify David for his piety and zeal for the house of God, and for his valor and exploits; some may answer . . . and object to his killing of Uriah."[47]

As a member of the Assembly of Divines and minister pro tempore of the Parliamentary congregation St. Margaret's Church, Westminster, Gibson reversed Jacobean precedent: he cites David's many mistakes and vulnerability to false counselors as reasons for supplanting belief in the divine right of kings with a theory of constitutional monarchy whereby kings must answer to divine and human law (D2r–v). In an extraordinary shift, Gibson cleaves the Davidic paradigm in two by contrasting a feeble David, whose mistakes anticipate the failures of Charles I, with a powerful one, whose successes are assigned to Parliament. Members of the House of Commons therefore function collectively as a second David, who rebels against tyrannical Charles on the precedent of David's own rebellion against Saul. The preacher exults to the members of the House: "Such as were for David, are for you. . . . Wee are for Christ and Sion, they are for Antichrist and Babylon" (D4v–E1v).

Despite their acknowledgment of King Charles's defeat, royalists resorted to the legacy of Jacobean iconography in rejecting Parliamentary claims. Indeed, Humphrey Moseley, the royalist publisher, engaged in a form of "devious cultural subversion" by secretly commissioning a portrait of King David with the face of Charles I as a frontispiece for the 1647 edition of Virgilio Malvezzi's *Il Davide Persequitato: David Persecuted* (fig. 6).[48] William Marshall's engraving adds a polemical twist to the second edition of Robert Ashley's translation, which was devoid of political commentary when it first appeared in 1637. Although the large harp borne by the king is a conventional attribute of David (see figs. 1–2), it bears a close resemblance to the harp of Ireland that James I quartered into the royal arms of England after his accession in 1603 (see fig. 3). Inscriptions from Psalms function as royalist mottoes. Borne by the hand of God extending from heaven, the shield that protects the king from attack declares "The Lord is my shield" (Pss. 33:20, 59:11, 84:9, 11; 91:4; 115:9–11). Words from Psalm 105:15—"Touch not my Anointed, and do my Prophets no harm"—evoke the well-known motto of James I.

A striking reversion to the Jacobean-Caroline iconography of the Davidic kingship took place not long before the Restoration. Published only weeks before Oliver Cromwell's death on 3 September 1658, Edward Gee's *The Divine Right and Original of the Civil Magistrate from God* (July) contains a frontispiece that complements the text's argument in favor of *jure divino* monarchy. Publication of this text suggests that a remarkable degree of press freedom existed during the Second Protectorate (1657–59). The top panel symbolizes the interregnum with an empty throne on a dais, before which a crown, orb, and scepter are placed. Portraits of Cromwell and Charles I respectively symbolize tyranny and divine right monarchy (fig. 7). The sword-wielding figure of the Lord Protector personifies *Αὔτοχειρατχιά*

Touch not my Anointed.
And do my Prophets no harme.
London Printed for Humphrey Mosley

Il Davide Perseguitato

DAVID
Persecuted.

Written in Italian
BY
The Marquesse *Virgilio Malvezzi*:
And done into English
BY
ROBERT ASHLEY
GENT.

LONDON,
Printed for *Humphrey Mosely*, at
the signe of the Princes Armes
in St Pauls Church-Yard.
1647.

FIG. 6. Virgilio Malvezzi, *Il Davide Persequitato: David Persecuted* (1647), frontispiece. By permission of the British Library, shelf mark E.1161.(2.)

or government by one's own hand. By contrast, the late king personifies *Θεοχρατιά* (theocracy) as he receives a Bible *(Verbum Dei)* that descends from heaven borne by the hand of God. That scene recalls the frontispiece of the King James Psalter (fig. 1). The banderole from Charles's mouth applies the Vulgate text of Romans 13:1 ("for all authority comes from God") as a royalist motto. The bottom panels implicitly identify Charles I as a "New David" and Cromwell with rebels against the authority of the Hebrew king. Portrayal of Joab's slaughter of Absalom (2 Sam. 18) at the left side serves as a warning to Cromwell—the favorite "son" who rebelled against his royal "father." An even more grisly admonition is supplied by the scene at the right, which portrays a "wise woman" of Abel-beth-maacah throwing the severed head of Sheba, who rebelled against David after Absalom's death, from the walls of the town (2 Sam. 15–22). This image threatens that decapitation of Cromwell may bring rebellion to an end, just as the severance of King Charles's head marked the beginning of the interregnum.

At the restoration of English and Scottish monarchy in 1660, royalist sermons celebrated the return from exile of Charles II in the manner of King David's

Fig. 7. Edward Gee, *The Divine Right and Original of the Civil Magistrate from God* (1658), title page. By permission of the Department of Prints and Drawings, British Museum, 1868-8-8-3262.

return to Jerusalem following Absalom's rebellion (2 Sam. 19:18–20, 26). They resort to arguments epitomized in writings by James I and in *Eikon Basilike.* Clement Barksdale exults: "He is driven from Jerusalem by Conspiracy and Rebellion, and afterwards returns with victory and honor."[49] Anthony Hulsius utters praise of the "New David" upon the occasion of "the first News of the Proclamation of Charles II, King of Great Britain" on 21 May. Hulsius served as preacher of the Walloon church at the town where Charles issued the Declaration of Breda (4 April), which guaranteed religious toleration and extended pardon to most rebels. His sermon applies a messianic prophecy from Psalm 121 to Charles upon the occasion of his departure to England from the Low Countries.[50]

Despite effusive flattery, many panegyrics acknowledge the flaws of Charles I in a way that demystifies Jacobean-Caroline assertions concerning divine right monarchy. Preached one day after the king's 26th May landing at Dover, a sermon by Francis Gregory alludes to David's murder of Uriah in the course of welcoming the restored king. He exculpates David's sin by way of attack against regicide: "If the blood of Uriah did so torment King David, O How would the blood of David have tormented some poor Uriah? If common blood be precious, how precious is blood Royal?" Continuing in the same vein, he likens the predicament of the rebels to the defeat of Absalom: "David enters upon Uriah's bed, there's his sin; well, Absalom must enter upon David's throne, there's his punishment."[51] Preaching on a psalm of thanksgiving for royal victory in battle (Ps. 18:49), Gilbert Sheldon, archbishop of Canterbury, falls back on the archaic theory that the king possesses "two bodies," one private and natural and the other public and mystical, in arguing that divine punishment of David's manifest sins as a private man provided no warrant for rebellion against his "just and moderate" government. Sheldon's application of biblical typology would have been inconceivable in a sermon preached before James I: "So that if we consider what we have escaped, the miseries of War, and of a Civil War, the worst of all wars; and what we have gained, the blessings of Peace, and Kingly Government the best preserver of them; a gracious PRINCE, and together with him our Laws, Liberties, Properties, the free exercise of Religious Duties, indeed all that is or ought to be dear to a Christian Common-wealth in this world."[52]

Depending upon the political affiliation of authors, heroic poetry of the Restoration applied the Davidic legacy of Jacobean iconography in order to flatter Charles II or blame him covertly, thus anticipating the cleavage between the Tory and Whig parties during the Exclusion Crisis. John Dryden, for example, compares Charles II to David in *Astraea Redux* (1660), a poem that celebrates the Restoration by allusion to the classical goddess of justice, whose return to earth after a period of exile symbolizes the advent of a new golden age. Astraea's longstanding association with imperial majesty had played an important role in the iconography of Queen Elizabeth I.[53] Dryden's unproblematic reversion to the

Jacobean theory of the divine right of kings stigmatizes defeated supporters of the Commonwealth and Protectorate as rebels against God:

Thus banished David spent abroad his time,
When to be God's anointed was his crime,
And when restored made his proud neighbors rue
Those choice remarks he from his travels drew,
Nor is he only by afflictions shown
To conquer others realms but rule his own. (ll. 79–84)[54]

Milton's biblical epics recall Jacobean writing practices. Indeed, James I and Milton were influenced by Guillaume de Salluste Du Bartas, leader of the Christian poetry movement, both through the French text of his *Sepmaines* and through Sylvester's English verse translations.[55] James had translated Du Bartas's *L'Uranie* and *Furies* prior to Sylvester's 1605 publication of *Bartas His Divine Weeks and Works.* In turn, Sylvester dedicated his text to the king, and many copies are decorated with the royal arms (B1r). The muse of *Paradise Lost* recalls Du Bartas' refashioning of Urania as the muse of Christian poetry, his hexameral verse, and his cataloguing of Old Testament tales.

Regardless of the liking for Du Bartas that Milton shares with James I, the revolutionary poet subverts Jacobean-Caroline iconography. *Paradise Lost* (1667) and *Paradise Regained* (1671) subtly contest the status of kings as "God's anointed," a Davidic figure important to James I's alignment of himself and his offspring with Jesus' status as the "Anointed Son of God."[56] Oblique allusions to Charles I and Charles II support the findings of recent critics, who claim that Milton's epics are permeated with politics in ways previously unknown.[57] Given the endurance of Davidic typology as a means of defining English kingship during the sixteenth and seventeenth centuries, it seems inconceivable that archangel Michael's references to David as a type of Christ at the end of *Paradise Lost* omit criticism of Stuart monarchs for their failure to measure up to scriptural prototypes. In discourse with Adam, Michael asserts that evil monarchs are in the majority among immediate successors of David: "Part good, part bad, of bad the longer scroll" (12.336). The archangel's prophecy of conflict among the priests at the Temple, who would break the line of royal succession from David, sets up an enduring antithesis between worldly and spiritual kingship:

. . . at last they seize
The scepter, and regard not David's sons,
Then lost it to a stranger, that the true

Anointed king Messiah might be born

Barred of his right. (12.358–60)

If we apply the *Tenure of Kings and Magistrates* and *Eikonoklastes* as subtexts for Michael's prophecies concerning future history at the end of *Paradise Lost*, that rupture in the line of Davidic succession extends to the reigns of James I and his heirs.

Eikonoklastes affords a model for Jesus' rejection of "Davidic kingship" in *Paradise Regained*, an action that incorporates "a pointed attack against the Stuart monarchy." The temptation of the kingdoms focuses on Jesus' resistance to Satan's repeated offer that the Messiah reverse the course of the history of Israel and Judah and "sit on David's throne" (1.240). In contemporary panegyrics such as *Astraea Redux*, the transfer to Charles II of Jacobean iconography provides an important context for Milton's brief epic. With great irony, Milton's Jesus shatters the precedent that James I, his successors, and their apologists had forged by claiming David—and Jesus for whom he serves as a type—as precedents for *jure divino* authority. Milton directs iconoclastic attack against the Davidic and "Christological pretenses of the Stuart monarchy" at the same time that he takes up a complementary effort to reclaim "these figures and 'purify' them of their royalist associations." In imitation of Pompey's defeat according to Lucan's *Pharsalia*, Milton casts Jesus in the role of "a defeated republican, the loser of the civil war who now considers what form of resistance to pursue against the new Caesarian monarchy."[58] The epic identifies "true kingship" as a spiritual state accessible to all believers, rather than militant values that royalist apologists associated with David's temporal kingship.

In *Paradise Regained*, the Son's definition of "true" kingship as an internal and spiritual phenomenon affords an antithesis to Satan's false display and, by extension, Jacobean (and Caroline) claims to govern *jure divino:*

What if with like aversion I reject

Riches and realms; yet not for that a crown,

Golden in show, is but a wreath of thorns,

Brings dangers, troubles, cares, and sleepless nights

To him who wears the regal diadem.

When on his shoulders each man's burden lies;

For therein stands the office of a king,

His honour, virtue, merit, and chief praise,

That for the public all this weight he bears.

Yet he who reigns within himself, and rules

Passions, desires, and fears, is more a king;

Which every wise and virtuous man attains. (2.457–68)

The allusion to Shakespearean speeches on the burdens of kingship by Prince Hal, later Henry IV,[59] is well-documented, but those Shakespearean passages shed no light on the Son's proleptic alignment of the royal crown with the crown of thorns.

The existence of a highly politicized link to Jacobean iconography went without notice until the present century.[60] Recalling the *imitatio Christi* in James I's *Meditation upon Matthew,* the Son's words sound like a rebuttal to the prayer printed as an "Explanation" of the frontispiece to *Eikon Basilike:*

That splendid, but yet toilsome crown

Regardlessly I trample down.

With joy I take this crown of thorn,

Though sharp, yet easy to be born.

James's *Meditation* supplies the model for assuming the crown of thorns as a monarchical emblem. In *Eikonoklastes* Milton rejects Charles I's claim to wear "our Savior's crown of thorns" on the grounds that his sufferings were the product of his "own gathering" and "twisting" (*CPW* 3:417–18). With reference to the climactic incident in *Paradise Regained,* it is worthy of note that *Eikonoklastes* rejects a conceit in *Eikon Basilike* (B12) that compares Charles I to Jesus as one who is at risk of being cast down from the Temple by a satanic Parliament (*CPW* 3: 405). The epic "attacks the Christological pretences of the Stuart monarchy" as part of an attempt to recuperate commonplace "figures and 'purify' them of their royalist associations."[61]

Dryden enjoyed the final word, however, when he composed *Absalom and Achitophel* as a royalist response to the political crisis provoked by the Whig effort to exclude Charles II's Roman Catholic brother James, duke of York, from the royal succession. The text constitutes a personal attack against Anthony Ashley Cooper, the first earl of Shaftesbury, who led the Parliamentary effort to establish the succession of the king's illegitimate son, the duke of Monmouth, whose Protestantism was acceptable to the Whig opposition to the Crown. The Exclusion Crisis resulted from the inability of Catherine of Braganza to bear offspring to Charles II—in sharp contrast to the fecundity of the king's unions with numerous mistresses, which resulted in a large number of illegitimate children. Charles II clearly violated the counsel of his grandfather James I, whose *Basilikon Doron* recommends that his heir, and presumably his future heirs, "marry one that were fully of your own religion."[62] The failure of three bills of exclusion and Charles's refusal to legitimate Monmouth led the Shaftesbury faction to the verge of rebellion and the king to an unsuccessful effort to convict the earl of high treason. Dryden's poem was published anonymously on 24 November 1681 in an effort to sway public opinion only a week before the treason trial began.

Identifying Absalom and Achitophel as types for a Stuart prince and an unscrupulous adviser who enter into rebellion against a Davidic king, Dryden casts Monmouth as Absalom and Shaftesbury in the role of Achitophel. This cluster of biblical types permeated political tracts throughout the reigns of Charles I and Charles II. Nathaniel Carpenter initiated this vogue in *Achitophel, Or, The Picture of a Wicked Politician,* a set of sermons that associated the evil counselor with the danger of Roman Catholic ascendancy at the royal court. Attacks on Achitophel gained currency among Puritan opponents of the King. In the 1645 sermon in which he attributed David's weaknesses to Charles I and his strengths to the House of Commons, Samuel Gibson declared that "all the enemies of the King and Parliament be as that young man Absalom, and that old Fox Achitophel."[63] Poems appended to *The Princely Pelican* (1649), a collection of meditations attributed to Charles I soon after his execution, attack the regicides who tried and convicted the king as a collection of Achitophels (F3v). Aaron Baker's *Achitophel Befooled,* a Gunpowder Day sermon preached during the Popish Plot of 1678, supplies an immediate context for *Absalom and Achitophel,* even though it reverses Dryden's typology by accusing Roman Catholics of infiltrating the royal court in the manner of Achitophel, a "State Machiavel" and "cunning Politician" (A3v, B4r).

Absalom and Achitophel exemplifies a strategy that accords with James I's testament to his heir, *Basilikon Doron,* but it opposes the minimization of David's sinfulness in *Eikon Basilike.* Although the narrator makes no effort to obscure how the promiscuity of Charles II has plunged England into constitutional crisis by rendering uncertain the line of royal succession, he purges royal excesses of any taint. Indeed, the poem wittily legitimizes royal profligacy by identifying it with David's polygamy: "When Nature prompted, and no law denied / Promiscuous use of Concubine and Bride" (ll. 5–6). He fuses the early Stuart theory of royal absolutism with a daring parody of Genesis 1:26–28, likening the wanton behavior of David, a type for Charles II, with divine creation:

> Then, Israel's Monarch, after Heaven's own heart,
> His vigorous warmth did, variously, impart
> To Wives and Slaves: And, wide as his Command,
> Scattered his Maker's Image through the Land. (ll. 7–10)

Bathsheba is significantly absent; Michal is the only queen present in Dryden's poem, one whose barrenness affords a type for the infertility of Catherine of Braganza. Even Davidic Charles is largely absent from a poem given over to allegorization of rebellion that ensues upon Achitophel's temptation of Absalom (ll. 363–64, 373, 481–82). Despite the traditional view that *Absalom and Achitophel* represents a disinterested call to moderation in the midst of the Exclusion Crisis—an interpretation that derives from praise of Achitophel as a judge (l. 187)—it appears instead that "moderation masks vengeance" in a poem that employs a typological scheme that balances implied endorsement of royal absolutism with a "rhetoric that proclaims balance and moderation."[64] Indeed, the poem ends abruptly when "God-like David" assumes absolute power to supplant mercy with the "Sword of Justice" within a scriptural narrative that implicitly ends with the deaths of Absalom and Achitophel. That conclusion represents a throwback to James's application of Davidic models for regal justice in *Basilikon Doron* and other writings.

James I left as a legacy to his successors a pattern of Davidic iconography that is at least as important as the well-known classical style of the Stuart monarchs. By appropriating and transforming scriptural typology claimed by the Tudor monarchs and their predecessors, James exploited the story of King David and the trope of the psalmist king to afford precedents for divine right monarchy in *Basilikon Doron, True Law of Free Monarchies,* and varied parliamentary addresses. King James possessed better understanding than either his Tudor predecessors or Stuart successors of ambiguities and fissures inherent in Davidic typology. During the reigns of Charles I and II, republican opponents and royalist defenders of kingship exploited inconsistencies in the David story to their own ends. Imitation of his father's practice left Charles I open to the mockery of Milton, for example, who vilified the executed king's cynical politicization of scriptural precedents. Following the death of James I, Stuart monarchs underwent attack because of their emulation of David, whose sins of adultery and murder and impotence in the face of palace intrigue and filial rebellion offset the accomplishments of a legendary king whose stature exceeded that of Solomon, his proverbially wise, wealthy, and powerful son.

Notes

1. Modern usage is followed in quotations from early printed books, and capitalization and italicization are ignored unless they are essential to the sense of passages. The abbreviation sig. is omitted from signature references. Consideration of the legacy of Jacobean iconography builds upon abbreviated presentation of some of the present findings in King, "Davidic Kingship." I gratefully acknowledge research assistance provided by the Center for Medieval and Renaissance Studies, College of Humanities, and Department of English of the Ohio State University.
2. "To spare the defeated and conquer the proud." James VI and I, *Political Works,* ed. McIlwain, 52. Hereafter cited as McIlwain.

3. *Great Britain's Salomon. A Sermon Preached at the Magnificent Funeral, of the Most High and Mighty King James, etc., in A Collection of Scarce and Valuable Tracts* (The Somers Tracts), 2nd ed. (London, 1809), 2: 43. Qtd. in Gordon 35.
4. King James VI and I, *Political Writings,* ed. Sommerville, 134. Hereafter cited as Sommerville. The quotation is from 1 Sam. 17:34–36.
5. Sommerville 64. The extract paraphrases Psalm 101.
6. Sommerville 64–71, and passim.
7. "They have fallen into the pit which they made." Sommerville 151. See Pss. 7:15, 57:6.
8. On the praise of Western European monarchs as anti-types of Christ, see Kantorowicz 16, 49, and passim. See Kipling 158–63 et passim.
9. Lamont 39–41.
10. Anne Lake Prescott concludes that early modern readers who attributed Psalms to David understood them by reference to royal "courts, plots, 'policy,' and political tyranny" (184). See also Schwartz 143–44.
11. E.g., Goldberg 33–50 and passim. On Elizabethan iconography, see Yates 29–87, and passim; Strong, *Cult of Elizabeth* 46–48 and passim; and King, *Tudor Royal Iconography* 182–266.
12. Sommerville 204.
13. See Foucault 141–48 and passim.
14. See King, "Henry VIII as David."
15. King, *Tudor Royal Iconography* 34–36, 73–74, 76–88, 90–93, 114–15, 160, 254–56.
16. Johnson; Hannay 91–95, 105.
17. Hind 2: 291, and pl. 174.
18. Sommerville 70. The reference is to 2 Sam. 1.
19. McIlwain 31. First published in Edinburgh in 1599, *Basilikon Doron* went through eight editions in English, Latin, and Welsh within a year of James's accession to the English throne in 1603.
20. The distinctively regal aspect of the King James Psalter is enhanced by gold lettering of two presentation copies preserved at Lambeth Palace and the Henry E. Huntington Library.
21. On the public dimension of James's Psalms of King David and its reception during the reign of Charles I, see Doelman's essay in the present collection.
22. See King, "Henry VIII as David" 78–82 and fig. 3.
23. See Doelman, "George Wither"; and Maxwell 86.
24. Madan 126–33. See Corns 80–81.
25. Hind 3: 151.

26. Sommerville 229.
27. Sommerville 234–35.
28. Sommerville 246.
29. Sommerville 237. The text refers to Psalm 22:18.
30. "Petit Traité à l'encontre de la primauté du pape," Cambridge University Library ms. Dd. 12, 59, fols. 13v–14. See King, *Tudor Royal Iconography* 6, 48, 88n, 89, 128, 145–46, 166; also Aston 1: 275–77.
31. Foxe 2–2v; also known as the *Book of Martyrs.* See King, *Tudor Royal Iconography* 128, 144–46.
32. Knott 161. The present argument counters belief that woodcuts in Foxe's *Book of Martyrs* exerted no influence on the frontispiece of *Eikon Basilike.* For the counterargument, see Corns 207.
33. The scene bears a relationship to the Ditchley portrait, in which Queen Elizabeth stands upon Ditchley in Oxfordshire on a map of England. See Strong, *Gloriana* 136–37.
34. See Corbett and Lightbown 135–42.
35. See Potter 160–11; and Corns 88–89.
36. Charles I and John Gauden 149. See also 94, 130, 144.
37. Shuger 142.
38. Intro. to *Eikonoklastes* 3: 360. Hereafter cited as *CPW.*
39. *CPW* 3: 193, 215. John Gauden rejected the Puritan equation of Charles to Agag in a 5 January address to Thomas Fairfax that underwent publication as *The Religious and Loyal Protestation of John Gauden Dr. in Divinity* (1648), B1r. Thomas Brooks produced a complicated variation of that topos as a republican precedent when he preached a fast-day sermon before the House of Commons on 26 December 1648. Published as *Gods Delight in the Progress of the Upright* (1649), the sermon warned Commons to avoid Saul's fate by punishing Charles as Agag (C2r). See *CPW* 3: 193n16.
40. *CPW* 3: 205.
41. Corns 89.
42. Parker 1: 542, 360–61.
43. Quint 132.
44. *CPW* 3: 547. See also 373, 381, 446, 543, 547, 553, 571.
45. *CPW* 3: 153 and nn. 11–312, 382, 446, 547, 550, 553–54. See also Charles I and John Gauden, 183n.
46. Potter 131. *In Protestant Poetics and the Seventeenth-Century Religious Lyric,* Barbara K. Lewalski notes that "the pamphlet literature and political poetry of the seventeenth century is studded with correlative types" whereby "Queen Elizabeth is a new Judith, Deborah, Joshua; King James is a new Solomon; Prince Henry is a new Josiah

(full of promise in reforming the Church and dying young); Oliver Cromwell is a new Moses or Gideon or David; Charles II restored is a new David reuniting the tribes after a long warfare" (131).

47. E4r.
48. Potter 161 and fig. 5.
49. A3r.
50. C4r.
51. C3v, D1v.
52. C1r, E4v.
53. See Yates 4, 9–11, 29–38. Christians identified Virgil's prophecy of Astraea's return in the Fourth Eclogue with messianic expectation of the birth of Christ.
54. *Works* 1: 22–31.
55. See Prescott, *French Poets* 172–74, 176–77, 186, 191, 233.
56. See Shuger 144–45.
57. See Hill 354–427; Radzinowicz; Wilding 205–31. References to Milton's poetry are from *The Poems of John Milton,* ed. Carey and Fowler.
58. Quint 128, 130–32, 135–36.
59. Evans et al., eds., *2 Henry IV* 4.5.21–47, *Henry V* 4.1.230–84
60. Gilbert. See also Potter 161–62
61. Quint 131.
62. McIlwain 35.
63. Qtd. in Jones 213; see also 211–12.
64. Zwicker and Hirst 41, 54.

Works Cited

Aston, Margaret. *England's Iconoclasts.* Vol. 1. Oxford: Clarendon P, 1988.

Baker, Aaron. *Achitophel Befooled.* London, 1678.

Barksdale, Clement. *The King's Return. A Sermon Preached at Winchcomb in Gloucestershire Upon The Kings-Day, Thursday, May 24, 1660.* London, 1660.

Carpenter, Nathaniel. *Achitophel, Or, The Picture of a Wicked Politician.* Dublin, 1627.

Charles I (pseud.). *The Princely Pelican.* London, 1649.

Charles I and John Gauden. *Eikon Basilike: The Portraiture of His Sacred Majesty in His Solitudes and Sufferings.* Ed. Philip A. Knachel. Ithaca: Cornell UP for the Folger Shakespeare Library, 1966.

Corbett, Margery, and Ronald Lightbown. *The Comely Frontispiece: The Emblematic Title-page in England 1550–1660.* London: Routledge & Kegan Paul, 1979.

Corns, Thomas N. *Uncloistered Virtue: English Political Literature, 1640–1660.* Oxford: Clarendon P, 1992.

Doelman, James. "George Wither, the Stationers Company and the English Psalter." *Studies in Philology* 90 (1993): 74–82.

Dryden, John. *The Works of John Dryden.* Ed. H. T. Swedenberg, Edward Niles Hooker, Jr., et al. 20 vols. Berkeley and Los Angeles: U of California P, 1959–89.

Evans, G. Blakemore, et al., eds. *The Riverside Shakespeare.* Boston: Houghton Mifflin, 1974.

Foucault, Michel. *The Archaeology of Knowledge and the Discourse on Language.* Trans. A. M. Sheridan Smith. New York: Pantheon, 1972.

Foxe, John. *Acts and Monuments of the English Martyrs.* 2 vols. 2nd ed., rev. and enlarged. London, 1570.

Gauden, John. *The Religious and Loyal Protestation of John Gauden Dr. in Divinity.* London, 1648.

Gee, Edward. *The Divine Right and Original of the Civil Magistrate from God.* London, 1658.

Gibson, Samuel. *The Urine of the Authors and Fomenters of Civil Wares.* London, 1645.

Gilbert, Allan H. "The Wreath of Thorns in *Paradise Regained.*" *Journal of the Warburg and Courtauld Institutes* 3 (1939–40): 156–61.

Goldberg, Jonathan. *James I and the Politics of Literature: Jonson, Shakespeare, Donne, and Their Contemporaries.* Stanford: Stanford UP, 1989.

Gordon, D. J. *The Renaissance Imagination: Essays and Lectures by D. J. Gordon.* Ed. Stephen Orgel. Berkeley: U of California P, 1975.

Gregory, Francis. *David's Return from His Banishment. Set forth in a Thanksgiving Sermon for the Returnee of his Sacred Majesty Charles the II.* Oxford, 1660.

Hakewill, George. *King David's Vow for Reformation of Himself, his Family, his Kingdom.* London, 1621.

Hannay, Margaret. *Philip's Phoenix: Mary Sidney, Countess of Pembroke.* New York: Oxford UP, 1990.

Hill, Christopher. *Milton and the English Revolution.* 1977. 2nd. ed. Harmondsworth: Penguin, 1979.

Hind, Arthur M. *Engraving in England in the Sixteenth and Seventeenth Centuries.* 3 vols. Cambridge: Cambridge UP, 1953–64.

Hulsius, Anthony. *The Royal Joy. Or, A Sermon of Congratulation Upon the five first Verses of Psalm One Hundred and Twenty-one* (23 May 1660).

James VI and I. *ΒΑΣΙΛΙΚΟΝ ΔΩΡΟΝ: Or His Majesties Instructions to His Dearest Son, Henry the Prince.* Edinburgh, 1599.

———. *Essayes of a Prentice in the Divine Art of Poesie.* Edinburgh, 1584.

———. *A Meditation upon the 27th, 28th, 29th Verses of the 27th Chapter of Saint Matthew, or a Pattern for a King's Inauguration.* London, 1620.

———. *The Political Works of James I: Reprinted from the Edition of 1616.* Ed. Charles H. McIlwain. Cambridge: Harvard UP, 1918.

———. *The Psalms of King David, Translated by King James.* Oxford, 1631.

———. *The Workes of the Most High and Mighty Prince, James.* London, 1616.

———. *Political Writings.* Ed. Johann A. Sommerville. Cambridge: Cambridge UP, 1994.

Johnson, Lynn Staley. "Elizabeth, Bride and Queen: A Study of Spenser's April Eclogue and the Metaphors of English Protestantism." *Spenser Studies* 2 (1981): 75–91.

Jones, Richard F. "The Originality of Absalom and Achitophel." *Modern Language Notes* 46 (1931): 211–19.

Kantorowicz, Ernst H. *The King's Two Bodies: A Study in Medieval Political Theology.* Princeton: Princeton UP, 1957.

King, John N. "Davidic Kingship and Reformation Politics: The Iconography of Henry VIII, Charles I, and Charles II." *European Iconography East and West: Selected Papers of the Szeged International Conference June 9–12, 1993.* Ed. György E. Szonyi. Symbola et Emblemata. Zbol. Leiden: E. J. Brill, 1996. 7: 146-58.

———. "Henry VIII as David: The King's Image and Reformation Politics." *Rethinking the Henrician Era: Essays on Early Tudor Texts and Contexts.* Ed. Peter C. Herman. Urbana: U of Illinois P, 1993. 78–92.

———. *Tudor Royal Iconography: Literature and Art in an Age of Religious Crisis.* Princeton: Princeton UP, 1989.

Kipling, Gordon. *Enter the King: Theatre, Liturgy, and Ritual in the Medieval Civic Triumph.* Oxford: Clarendon P, 1998.

Knott, John R. *Discourses of Martyrdom in English Literature, 1563–1694.* Cambridge: Cambridge UP, 1993.

Lamont, William. *Godly Rule: Politics and Religion, 1603–60.* London: Macmillan, 1969.

Lewalski, Barbara Kiefer. *Protestant Poetics and the Seventeenth-Century Religious Lyric.* Princeton: Princeton UP, 1979.

Madan, F. F. *A New Bibliography of the "Eikon Basilike" of King Charles the First.* Publications of the Oxford Bibliographical Society, vol. n.s. 3. Oxford: Oxford UP, 1950.

Malvezzi, Virgilio. *Il Davide Persequitato. David Persecuted.* London, 1647.

Maxwell, William D. *A History of Worship in the Church of Scotland.* Oxford: Oxford UP, 1955.

Milton, John. *Complete Prose Works of John Milton.* Ed. Don M. Wolfe, et al. 8 vols. New Haven: Yale UP, 1953–82.

———. *The Poems of John Milton.* Ed. John Carey and Alastair Fowler. London: Longman, 1968.

Parker, William Riley. *Milton: A Biography.* 2 vols. Oxford: Clarendon P, 1968.

Potter, Lois. *Secret Rites and Secret Writing: Royalist Literature, 1641–1660.* Cambridge: Cambridge UP, 1990.

Prescott, Ann Lake. "Evil Tongues at the Court of Saul: The Renaissance David as a Slandered Courtier." *Journal of Medieval and Renaissance Studies* 21 (1991): 163–86.

———. *French Poets and the English Renaissance: Studies in Fame and Transformation.* New Haven: Yale UP, 1978.

Quint, David. "David's Census: Milton's Politics in Paradise Regained." *Re-membering Milton: Essays on the Texts and Traditions.* Ed. Mary Nyquist and Margaret W. Ferguson. New York: Methuen, 1987. 128–47.

Radzinowicz, Mary Ann. "The Politics of *Paradise Lost.*" *Politics of Discourse: The Literature and History of Seventeenth-Century England.* Ed. Kevin Sharpe and Steven N. Zwicker. Berkeley: U of California P, 1987. 204–29.

Schwartz, Regina. "Nations and Nationalism: Adultery in the House of David." *Critical Inquiry* 19 (1992): 131–50.

Sheldon, Gilbert. *David's Deliverance and Thanksgiving. A Sermon Preached before the King at Whitehall Upon June 28, 1660. Being the Day of Solemn Thanksgiving for the Happy Return of His Majesty.* London, 1660.

Shuger, Debora K. *Habits of Thought in the English Renaissance: Religion, Politics, and the Dominant Culture.* Berkeley: U of California P, 1990.

Strong, Roy. *The Cult of Elizabeth: Elizabethan Portraiture and Pageantry.* London: Thames and Hudson, 1977.

———. *Gloriana: The Portraits of Queen Elizabeth I.* London: Thames and Hudson, 1987.

Wilding, Michael. *Dragons Teeth: Literature in the English Revolution.* Oxford: Clarendon P, 1987.

Yates, Francis A. *Astraea: The Imperial Theme in the Sixteenth Century.* London: Routledge & Kegan Paul, 1975.

Zwicker, Steven N., and Derek Hirst. "Rhetoric and Disguise: Political Language and Political Argument in *Absalom and Achitophel.*" *Journal of British Studies* 21 (1981): 39–55.

15

The Reception of King James's Psalter

James Doelman

King James's versification of the Psalms has largely defied scholarly commentary. When discussed at all, it has been dismissed in an offhand manner. D. H. Willson's comment is typical in presenting the effort as part of the folly of the "wisest fool in Christendom": "He was to fancy himself a David as he rewrote the Psalms in doggerel English verse."[1] Scholarly neglect can partly be explained by the problems with James's status as "author" of the work. First, the king was merely a translator, one of many at the time, and secondly, the published volumes of his Psalms, which finally appeared in 1631 and 1636, were substantially amended and added to by Sir William Alexander. Furthermore, we do not have a static or definitive text to work with: none of the existing manuscripts or published versions likely represent James's work as he left it at his death, and most of his contemporaries did not see it either. Yet the idea of his Psalms was of great significance both in his own reign and in that of his son. For his contemporaries as well, the question of authorship plagued the work: were these the Psalms of King David, King James, or William Alexander? In spite of these problems, a study of "James's Psalms" and the public response to them is useful, for such a study can highlight the dynamics of royal authorship and its reception in the period. With a king's work generally, public reception is of great import, but as a volume that could play a central part in the worship of the Scottish and English churches, the Psalms attracted special attention. They would require a far more involved public response than any other work of James: a new Psalter would entail the participation of every voice in every parish of the church. In reference to the biblical translation of 1611, James wrote, "Whosoever attempteth any thing for the publike (specially if it pertaine to

Religion, and to the opening and clearing of the word of God) the same setteth himselfe upon a stage to be glouted upon by every evil eye, yea, he casteth himself headlong upon pikes, to be gored by every sharpe tongue."[2] This would certainly apply to any Psalms versification as well. James never took that final step of setting his Psalms upon a stage, and only a few of his contemporaries had any first-hand acquaintance with them. In his own time they lived a ghost-like existence, known only by reputation and rumor. After James's death, Charles attempted to give the work a public existence, but the role it eventually played was far from what either the royal father or son had hoped. The envisioned public role of James's Psalter, and the actual reception that followed his death, will be the central concerns of this study.

Among James's earliest poetic endeavors was a versification of Psalm 104, which appeared in *The Essayes of a Prentise* (1584); this psalm is described as "translated out of Tremellius," and being composed in an eight-line stanza it would not have matched any of the common meter tunes then in use with the Psalms:

> To Jehova I all my lyfe shall sing,
> To sound his Name I ever still shall cair:
> It shall be sweit my thinking on that King:
> In him I shall be glaid for ever mair:
> O let the wicked be into no whair
> In earth. O let the sinfull be destroyde.
> Blesse him my soule who name Jehova bair:
> O blesse him now with notts that are enjoyde.

Versification of a psalm was a fairly common poetic exercise at the time, and the 104th, rich in natural imagery, was a popular choice for this. James's tutor George Buchanan produced a Latin version of it that had become famous across Europe. Thus the publication of James's translation of this single psalm was by no means a signal that he intended a complete versification of the Psalter. Such an inclination was only first hinted at in his next collection of poetry, *His Majesties Poeticall Exercises* (1591); if that collection were well received James would be moved "to haste the presenting unto thee, of my APOCALYPS, and also such nomber of the Psalmes as I have perfited: & incourage mee to the ending out of the rest."[3] How far James advanced in these efforts during his Scottish reign is unclear; already in 1591 he would complain that "scarslie but at stollen moments have I the leasure to blenk upon any paper, and yet not that, with free and unvexed spirit."[4] As no further publication of his Psalms was to appear during his lifetime, it is difficult to trace his progress. However, a surviving manuscript, with certain of his Psalms in

Scottish dialect and the signature J. D. R. S.—meaning "Jacobus Dominus Rex Scotia"—seems to indicate that he had completed at least twenty-eight of them while still in Scotland.[5] These versions are completely different from those finally published in 1631; like Psalm 104 from *The Essayes of a Prentise,* they do not conform to the meters usually found in the English and Scottish Psalters. They are most likely early Scottish experiments, which were then abandoned as James turned to forms more appropriate for congregational singing. Unfortunately, no other manuscript with a significant number of his Psalms has come to light. This has encouraged some scholars to conclude that the 1631 and 1636 publications were completely the work of Alexander.

James's ambition to be a David-like poet-king was likely furthered by the English response to his accession, which highlighted his poetic and theological interests. The accession also presented the possibility of a broader scope for his Psalter: it could be a unifying element in all the British churches, or in what James hoped would ultimately be a single British church. Like his sponsorship of a new translation of the Bible, James's work on the Psalms confirmed his role as leader of his churches. Because of their dual biblical and royal origin, James's translation of the Psalms would hold a special place. Ordinary procedures of literary criticism did not apply: William Drummond might think his Psalms superior, but the king was to play both poet and critic. At the same time, the work in question was no ordinary work: as that part of Scripture most used in worship, it had a status beyond even that of the king's work. In this situation—unlike, for instance, his translation of Du Bartas—James was subordinate to his material: readers might feel justified in using the source against the king's treatment of it. A complete versification of the Psalms is a daunting task, one in which the writer is limited not only by his source but also by the metrical forms established for psalmody in the church. Such versification may also be self-effacing: the goal of the versifier is to provide a clear glass through which the divine word may be seen. Anything that attracts attention to the versifier is a sort of failure: the preface to the Bible of 1611 criticized earlier versions in that instead of opening the window, the compilers had replaced it with a variety of other windows—ornate, stained ones with varying degrees of transparency.[6] More than other biblical books, the Psalms presented special challenges, because of the variety of versifications available and the important place in Protestant worship and identity they had achieved in the previous half century.

The English and Scottish Psalters were part of a movement throughout the Calvinist churches to render the Psalms in a metrical form appropriate for congregational song.[7] On the continent the Genevan Psalter, with texts translated by Clément Marot in a variety of meters, was the best-known and most-celebrated of these. The Protestant exiles who returned to England with Elizabeth's accession promoted a similar use of the Psalms, and versifications largely by Thomas Sternhold and John Hopkins became the basis for the Psalter. In Scotland a

Psalter, also based partly on the work of Sternhold and Hopkins, appeared in 1564, and it became the standard in the Scottish Kirk until 1650. These Psalms, while actually based on the work of a number of versifiers, became traditionally known as "Sternhold and Hopkins." They relied heavily on common meter (alternating tetrameter and trimeter lines rhyming *a b c b*) or long meter (tetrameter lines, *a b c b*). The uniformity of meter made it possible for a limited number of familiar tunes to be used for all the Psalms. Since hymns played no part in English or Scottish worship in the sixteenth and seventeenth centuries, these Psalms held an important place.[8] Certain Psalms became strongly associated with militant Protestantism; during James's own reign Psalm 124, which expressed defiant strength in the Lord in the face of persecution, was frequently used in Scotland at events of national significance. Congregational, as opposed to choral, singing of the Psalms was a symbolic part of the Calvinist movement, one which joined the Scots and the English Puritans with their brethren in the Low Countries and Switzerland.

In both England and Scotland a consensus emerged in the early part of the seventeenth century that the old versions of the Psalms were not satisfactory. Even their defenders admitted that as translations they had their defects, and those with an interest in poetry frequently derided them for their barbarous language and "galloping" rhythm. George Wither, for example, lamented "that we make use of the most excelent expressions of the holy ghost in rude, and barbarous Numbers, whilst our own wanton fancies were paynted, & trymed out in the most mooving languag."[9] James found the Scottish Psalter of 1564 unsatisfactory both poetically and biblically. At the Scottish General Assembly of 1601 he "did recite whole verses of the same, showing both the faults of the metre and the discrepance from the text."[10] At that assembly Robert Pont, minister at St. Cuthbert's, was appointed to revise the Psalter, but nothing more is heard of his work.[11] Despite James's objections to the Old Version, he was to draw on it to a limited extent in his own work, at least as it appears in the published versions.[12] Numerous early seventeenth-century poets attempted to supplant this Old Version; by including himself in these attempts, James hoped to fill a role consistent with his larger vision of the king as leader of the church.

While the English Psalter was largely in common meter, the Scottish Psalter used a wider variety of verse forms; this meant that a single Psalter to replace both would have to introduce some new tunes.[13] Common meter was to become the standard one for most attempted replacements, including that of James: any other meter would necessitate the introduction of a new tune as well, and thus make the attempted version less plausible. The best-known Renaissance versification of the Psalms today is that of Mary and Philip Sidney; while unpublished in its own time, it circulated widely in manuscript. However, the Sidney Psalter's use of a variety of relatively complex verse forms made it unlikely that it would become established in the church.[14]

While there was widespread dissatisfaction with both the English and Scottish Psalters, few attempts to replace them actually reached print in the first quarter of the century. Two factors are responsible for this: first, the desire of James himself to be the author of a new version, and secondly, the monopoly that the Stationers' Company enjoyed for the printing of metrical Psalters in England. James had made his intention publicly known, and any attempt at the same task might be perceived as disrespectful. This situation continued until at least 1620. James was still active as a poet in the years leading up to his death, but it is not clear if he continued work on the Psalms at this time.[15] Nevertheless, the public knowledge, or semi-knowledge, that he contemplated such a work cast a shadow over any similar endeavors. When a king himself is a poet, his role as a patron may be diminished. Joseph Hall noted already in 1608 that "Many great wits have undertaken this taske; which yet have either not effected it, or have smothered it in their private desks, and denied it the common light."[16] William Alexander, who was later to complete the king's Psalms, explicitly warned William Drummond of Hawthornden of James's jealousy in the area of the Psalms: "Brother, I received your last letter, with the Psalm you sent, which I think very well done; I had done the same long before it came; but He [King James] prefers his own to all else; tho' perchance, when you see it, you will think it the worst of the three [Alexander's, Drummond's, and the King's?]. No men must meddle with that subject, and, therefore, I advise you to take no more pains therein."[17] Further illustration of the caution exercised by those versifying Psalms is shown by a letter of Sir Robert Kerr, earl of Ancrum, to his son, which accompanied a Psalm versified for the Genevan tunes: "I began thereupon to trye if I could fit them [the Psalms] to their measure, that whilst I was there [in the Low Countries] I might doe as they did, not presuming to introduce them to be used in this Isle, well knowing how they are undertaken to the measure of our own tunes by those that can doe them farre better."[18] If the Psalm translations of James's courtiers were being rejected in such a fashion, it is not surprising that others held back from publication.

James's work was not the only obstacle to other new versions of the Psalms. The Stationers' Company's patent on the printing of psalters, which it had purchased in 1603, led the company to challenge any new versification, which found itself in a legal grey area: was it covered by the Stationers' monopoly? The company claimed that it extended to "all manner of books of that nature"—that is, any collection of Psalms, even if incomplete, in English.[19] As will be explored below, this patent might very well have impeded the establishment of James's Psalter itself. That authorization, either from James or the Stationers' Company, was necessary to proceed with such a publication is clear from the letter of an anonymous respondent to George Wither, perhaps the most dogged versifier of the Psalms in the period: "there are soe many Reverend and learned Men, that have desired to doe the same thing that you doe; but out of respect they had to authoritie would not proceed, except they had bene imployed by publique

Commaund."[20] New versions of the Psalms were written, but publication was difficult and even dangerous. The major English versifiers of Psalms in James's reign were Joseph Hall, Sir John Harington, Henry Dod, and George Wither. Of these, only Dod and Wither produced complete versions that reached print, and both of these had their work printed in Amsterdam in attempts to overcome the monopoly of the Stationers' Company. The fate of Henry Dod's versification illustrates the difficulties faced by any new English Psalter. His first publication, *Certain Psalmes of David* (1603), was merely a sample of a later promised work that was not to appear until 1620. Dod explains that the seventeen-year gap between his initial sample and his complete Psalter is due to his waiting "for the performance of this worthie worke, by some godly learned, whom I hoped wold have donne it in manner better beseemeing the same."[21] After publication, Dod's full Psalter was publicly burned, likely due to its infringement of the Stationers' patent, although it may be that James's attempt made such enforcement of the patent all the more possible.

From George Wither's attempts to publish his Psalter in the 1620s we get the best sense of the combined effect of James's personal desire to compose a Psalter and the Stationers' Company's monopoly. In 1619 Wither published, in lavish form, *A Preparation to the Psalter*, as the harbinger of the Psalms themselves. However, Wither's Psalter was not to appear until 1632, when a cheap version was printed in Holland. Wither describes his change of plans in *The Schollers Purgatory* (1624): "But before I had halfe ended them [the Psalms] I heard that one of much better sufficiency had made a long, and happy progresse into that worke: and thereupon in expectation of his more able performance delayed to proceed with what I had begunne, untill such tyme as I was informed that the other was by the multiplicity of weighty Affayres compelled to give over his laborious Attempt. And then, I thought my selfe engaged agayne, to proceed."[22] Nowhere in this work does Wither make explicit reference to the king, but the details of the latter part of the passage and the date confirm that he is the one referred to.

The situation in Scotland seems to have been somewhat different. There the privilege of publishing Psalms belonged to the king's printer rather than the Stationers' Company, and James allowed a number of new partial versions of the Psalms early in the century. Henry Dod published *Certaine Psalmes of David* in 1603, "Cum Privilegio Regiae Majestatis." Two years later *The Mindes Melodie. Contayning Certayne Psalmes of the Kinglie Prophete David*—long attributed to Alexander Montgomerie—was published, again "Cum Privilegio Regali." In the 1630s and 1640s some Scottish opponents of James's version would refer back to these Psalms as a more suitable revision.

In the last few years of his life James's attitude toward other attempts seems to have changed as he recognized his own inability to finish. The most explicit assertion of this is by Wither in his prefatory letter "To the Reader" in ms.

Eg. 2404, where he refers to "ye late Soveraigne of happie memory: who having worthely begunn ye same taske himself and finding that the multitude of his royall and waightie affaires threatned to prevent his p[er]sonall performance thereof, was lately mooved, through an earnest desire of adding a reformed version of ye metricall Psalmes unto ye translation of ye Bible to hearten on many of those in this undertaking, who had discovered themselves voluntarily enclined thereunto."[23] Wither visited James a few months before the king's death in 1625, and in the preface to his 1632 publication he claims that it was specifically he himself who was thus encouraged by James: "I was commanded to perfect a *Translation* of the *Psalmes,* which he understood I had begunn; & by his encouragment, I finished the same about the tyme of his *Translation* to a better Kingdome." His claim is substantiated by a letter of Joseph Mead from 23 April 1625: "Mr. Withers is come to Cambridge to print his psalms, whereof he showed the old king an hundred in Christmas time, who then told him himself had done fifty, but meant not now to go on."[24] In the preface to the 1632 *Psalms,* Wither once again makes reference to James's work on the Psalms: "I waited long, to see a more exact *performance:* But, none appearing, answerable to the dignitie of our *English-Muses,* I have sent forth my *Essay,* to provoke others, to discover their endeavours, on this *subject;* the best might receive the best Approbation."[25] It would seem that about 1624 James recognized that he himself would not complete a Psalter, and he became more open to others, like Wither, who were attempting to do so. That Francis Bacon and Sir John Davies both published versions of some of the Psalms in that year would support this as well. James's encouragement of others also suggests that he did not foresee that his translations would form any part of a new Psalter after his death.

Just how many Psalms James had completed at the time of his death is unclear. In his sermon for James's funeral, John Williams, bishop of Lincoln, notes that "This translation he was in hand with, when God called him to sing Psalms with the angels. He intended to have finished and dedicated it to the only saint of his devotion—the Church of Great Britain and that of Ireland. This worke was staied in the one and thirty Psalme, Blessed is he whose unrighteousnesse is forgiven, and whose sinne is covered."[26] Whether James completed this number of Psalms or the fifty mentioned by Mead, it is clear that he was far from having produced a complete Psalter. It is not surprising that the king failed to complete his translation: his interest in poetry waned during his English reign, replaced by an increasing interest in theology. His final years were also marked by failing health.

While many knew of James's Psalms during his lifetime, they seem to have circulated very little. A few years after his death Henry Wotton procured some of them as a gift for James's grandson, the Prince of Bohemia, but declares that he was only able to do so "with much adoe."[27] This limited circulation is in contrast to the majority of his works, which were frequently republished and provoked response both in England and abroad. The idea of them, rather than their substance, had the larger effect. Ironically, in the 1630s they became the most public and controversial of his works, at a time when his other writings faded into the background.[28]

Charles and His Father's Psalter

In his epistle dedicating James's *Workes* to Charles, James Montague describes the young prince as "the trew Heire and Inheritor of them."[29] It was certainly in this spirit that Charles accepted his father's Psalms, regardless of how incomplete they stood. The problem of the Psalter in the 1630s seems to have been created by Charles rather than bequeathed to him by his father. From 1626 Charles zealously promoted a work his father had recognized as insufficient, yet he called upon the memory of his father to achieve that success. His motivation in this is far from clear.

Charles began the institution of his father's Psalms in 1626 by dividing the labor of reviewing them into two parts: the Scottish Archbishop John Spottiswoode was to appoint churchmen who were to "confer them [the Psalms] with the originall text and with the most exact translations," and Sir William Alexander, the long-time courtier of James's and Charles' secretary for Scotland, was "to consider and revew the meeter and poesie."[30] Unnoted in this letter is any indication of how large Alexander's role in this would need to be. The object of these reviews was "for the good of all the Churches within his dominions," which clearly suggests that Charles was contemplating James's work as a new Psalter for England, Scotland, and Ireland. John Spottiswood suggests that James himself commissioned Alexander to complete the work: "The revising of the Psalms he made his own labour; and, at such hours as he might spare from the public cares, went through a number of them, commending the rest to a faithful and learned servant, who hath therein answered his Majestie's expectation,"[31] but there is no other evidence for this. Alexander was granted a twenty-one-year patent on the work in January 1628.[32] This patent would have proved to be very lucrative if the Psalter had been successfully established. However, it also raised a potential conflict with the Stationers' Company and their patent on the existing Psalter. The archbishops and bishops of England clearly found themselves in a difficult situation: they had to review the work of the late king in light of the original texts. At the same time, Charles was promoting the work not just on the basis of its quality but as "a perpetuall monument to his [James's] memorie," a phrase that recurs throughout his correspondence promoting the use of the Psalter.[33] No response from the bishops seems to survive.

The joint work finally appeared in 1631 as *The Psalms of King David, Translated by King James;* it was printed by W. Turner at Oxford. The title page shows Kings David and James standing as parallel figures on either side of a Psalter—a reflection of James's lifelong desire to be the godly poet-king in the tradition of David. Alexander's name appears nowhere in the volume. In a preface Charles makes clear his intention that this Psalter become the standard one for church use: "CHARLES R. Haveing caused this Translation of the Psalmes (whereof oure late deare Father was Author) to be perused, and it being found to be exactly and truely done wee doe hereby authorize the same to be Imprinted according to the Patent graunted thereupon: and doe allow them to be song in all the Churches of our Dominiones, recommending them to all oure goode Subjects for that effect."[34] Charles was to find that introducing a new Psalter required more than publication and a printed authorization. A year after the publication he wrote again to the archbishop of Canterbury, encouraging him to promote the use of the Psalter and leaving the means up to Abbot, in consultation with other English bishops. The two possibilities are for them to "be receaved by a generall ordour, or to beginn in some Churches by the particular recommendatioun of everie bischop within his owin dyocie."[35] Neither happened, and from this point it seems that Charles silently abandoned his plans for James's Psalter in England. David Calderwood, in his argument against James's version, suggests that the English bishops rejected the work, but no other evidence has been found to confirm this.[36] I would suggest that the Stationers' Company's tight monopoly on the printing of the Sternhold and Hopkins Psalter discouraged Charles from attempting to introduce the widespread use of his father's Psalter in England. Without their full cooperation the distribution of enough Psalters to the English parishes would have been impossible. That Charles had the first edition of his father's Psalter printed at Oxford, which was to a certain degree beyond the reach of the Stationers' Company, suggests that they would not cooperate in his plans.[37] From 1631 his efforts with the Psalter shifted to Scotland. Ironically, that Charles turned his attention to establishing the new Psalter in Scotland while abandoning the project in England breaks with his usual pattern of moving toward uniformity between the two national churches.

Charles's attempts in Scotland were stymied for close to six years by the slow response of the bishops and clergy. The many delays in the publication and distribution of the Psalter may have reflected the bishops' uncertainty about how to promote a work they knew would arouse the hostility of many within the Scottish church and make the already distrusted bishops even less popular.[38] This is just one instance of Charles's tendency to conduct his Scottish affairs without a full understanding of the complexities of the situation.[39] Shortly before the book went to press, Charles wrote his Scottish Privy Council and the archbishop of St. Andrews, expressing the hope that "the first beginning [of instituting the Psalter in all his churches] may be made in that our ancient kingdome, wher our said dear father, the Authour, was borne."[40] In May 1631 he called a meeting of the bishops and archbishops to consider not only the introduction of the new Psalter but also the place of organ music, surplices and a potential new service book in the Scottish church.[41] John Row reports that in 1631 "There was also brute that the

King wold have the Psalmes translated be his father to be receaved in the Kirk of Scotland; and some of the books wer delyvered to Presbyteries, that Ministers might advyse concerning the goodnes of the translation, or badness, and report their iudgments to the Diocesian Assemblies; but that lay over for a while."[42] On 2 June 1631, Samuel Rutherford, minister at Anwoth in Galloway, wrote to his godly friend Marion McNaught the recent news: "I have received a letter from Edinburgh, certainly informing me that the English service, and the organs, and King James' Psalms, are to be imposed upon our Kirk; and that the bishops are dealing for a General Assembly."[43] He perceives this as a great trial for the Kirk, and from this letter it is possible to see organized opposition to the changes developing.

The fullest expression of the objections was that of the anti-episcopal David Calderwood, in his "Reasons against the reception of King James's metaphrase of the Psalms."[44] He rehearses a large number of reasons for maintaining the present Psalter despite its minor imperfections. While this Scottish divine seems to have been most strongly motivated by a loyalty to the Scottish Psalter and antagonism toward any changes not initiated by the Kirk itself, he gives some further objections to James's Psalter.[45] He argues that such work should be done by clergy rather than "a courteour or commone poet." He recognizes that Alexander was responsible for much of it and notes that "the people call them Menstries Psalmes," after Alexander's manor house, Menstrie.[46] That Alexander stands to gain so substantially from the Psalter also attracts Calderwood's notice, and he suggests that earlier poets had "offered to translate the whole book frielie without anie pryce for their paines, ather frae the public state or privat mens purses."[47] He also objects that the metaphrase, as he calls it, is full of "heathenish libertie and poeticall conceats" and uses too many hard and foreign words. (Scottish Psalm versifiers of the later 1630s and 1640s were to stress the simplicity of their translations.) Calderwood fears that the proposed change will make the Scottish church seem "inconstand and unsetled in our orders." He not only objected to church use of James's Psalter but also to its private use, largely because of fear that this might lead to later public use.[48]

Despite such opposition, Charles broadened his attempt in the spring of the next year, calling on the archbishop of St. Andrews and the Ministerie and Burgh of Edinburgh to assist in seeing that his father's Psalter "might be receaved and sung in the Churches thereof."[49] In a general letter "To the Clergie" of 6 July 1632, Charles urges them "at last to effectuat that which we so much desyre."[50] Between that letter and one written on 13 September to the archbishop of St. Andrews, the clergy responded by arguing that there were not enough copies available.[51] While the bishops may have been prevaricating over a move they were unsure of, it is reasonable that there were legitimate problems with distributing the work. After all, it was only being printed at Oxford, and from there sent to Scotland, and the numbers required to supply the churches of Scotland would be very high.[52] His patience obviously wearing thin, Charles expresses the hope "that the work may be found setled at our comeing, God willing, at the nixt spring of the yeir to that our kingdome."[53] At the same time, Charles does give indications in this letter that he is willing to consider changes to the work, possibly in response to objections raised: he will order the "reformeing or adding to that work what shalbe fund necessarie."

Resistance to the Psalter was part of a broader fear of "innovation" in the Church of Scotland sponsored by Charles or the bishops he appointed.[54] The tension was already palpable in 1630, when William Struther, minister in Edinburgh, wrote to the earl of Airth, gently warning against innovation: "our fire is so great already, that it hath more need of water to quench it, then oile to augment it."[55] Throughout the 1630s Charles was to add further oil to the fire, in the form of liturgical changes. In 1632 Calderwood feared that if the new Psalter was accepted, "Then may they luik for the new service to be recommended to them, the nixt day the organes, &c."[56] Calderwood was not simply engaging in a slippery slope argument; he feared that the usual forms for worship and discipline in the Scottish church, which had always been printed with the Psalter, would be lost.[57] The new Psalter would, in effect, make necessary the introduction of a new Service Book and Book of Canons as well. That Psalter revision could have this effect was clear to those at the General Assembly of 1601, who had specified that any such revision must not include an altering or deletion of the prayers printed with it.[58] If Charles were not aware of these ramifications of replacing the Old Psalter with his father's, his bishops certainly were. Suspicion of innovation was to increase over the next few years, as Charles added a Book of Canons and Prayer Book to the Psalter, and it culminated in the riots of 1637. However, by that point the Service Book as a whole had replaced James's Psalter as the focus of opposition.

Charles misjudged the situation if he believed that the connection of James's name with the Psalter would endear it to the people of Scotland. James had alienated the more Presbyterian members of the clergy by pushing through the Five Articles of Perth in 1621, which many had attacked for their Roman tendencies. While James had never enforced the articles, Charles seemed to go beyond them in his attempts to change the Scottish liturgy.[59] Where James had been content with words, Charles insisted that reform be taken one step further to the active changing of Scottish church life.[60] Ultimately, the different treatments of the Psalter by James and Charles is a further example of the latter's strident determination.

Charles's coronation as king of Scotland did not take place until the summer of 1633, as he had not visited Scotland since his father's death. With his coronation he introduced a completely new English liturgy into the chapel at Holyrood, but it seems that his father's Psalms were not part of this.[61] In May 1635 he approved the revised Book of Common Prayer for Scotland and ordered that James's Psalms be printed with it, to be "receaved and used togidder in the Church of that our Kingdome."[62] An undated letter to the Privy Council of Scotland orders "that no other Psalmes of aney edition whatsoever be aither printed heirafter within that our kingdome, or imported thither, aither bund by themselffs or otherwayes from any forrayne port."[63] Charles's injunction against the publishing in Scotland of the traditional Psalter seems to have been ineffective, yet even if it had been, there was already a great supply of the traditional Psalter throughout Scotland.

James's Psalms reached their final form in 1636, when an edition in two different forms appeared.[64] The octavo has the prose version of the Psalms appearing in the margins, and it includes the music of thirty-six tunes. For Psalms without a tune, it is suggested that one elsewhere in the Psalter be used. This 1636 edition is significantly different from that of 1631, and these differences were noticed by at least one contemporary, John Row, the Presbyterian historian: "In the first impression, thair were some expressions so poeticall, and so farre from the language of Canaan, that all quho had any Religion did dislyke them; as, calling the Sunne 'the Lord of light,' and the Moone 'the pale Ladie of the night,' etc."[65] William McMillan, in his thorough comparison of the two published versions, finds that the majority of terms and phrases objected to by Calderwood were amended in the 1636 edition.[66] Psalm 148:3–10 from the two versions illustrates the extent of the changes:

His praise at length dilate
You flaming Lord of light
And with the starres in state
Pale Lady of the night.
Heavens, heavens him praise
And all you floods;
Enclos'd in cloudes;
His glory raise. (1631)

His praise at length dilate,
Thow Sun that shin'st so bright,
Praise him with stars in state,
Thou moon the lesser light.
Heavens, heavens him praise,

> Ye flouds that move,
>
> The heavens above,
>
> His glory raise. (1636)

That the revised Psalter attracted less direct negative comment than the 1631 edition may have been due to these changes, or to the fact that the new Book of Canons and the Service Book became the foci of opposition. However, as the Psalter was nearly always bound with the new Service Book—in Charles's own words they were to be "receaved and used togidder in the Church"—it had no chance of independent acceptance. Frequently, Scottish opponents of the changes referred simply to the "Service Books," by which they likely meant all three of the Book of Canons, the Prayer Book, and the Psalter. That in Scottish tradition these had always been a unit likely encouraged such perception of the new works.

The controversy came to a crisis in 1637, as Charles became more aggressive in his attempts. On 3 February he sent a letter to the Privy Council of Scotland:

> Whereas the late psalmes have by auctoritie frome ws and clergie of both kingdoms been exactlie revised and approved, we now (according to our pleasure formerlie signified for receaving thame in the church of that kingdome) being fullie resolved to have that worke goe on for the churches good and the authors memorie, it is our expresse will and pleasure that, according as yow sall thinke fitt, yow suffer no further impression to be made of the old psalmes, and that yow give suche order as yow sall find necessarie, and whiche is in your power, for printing and receaving of the new, to be generally receaved, and sung in all the churches of the said kingdome.[67]

The council responded on 14 March 1637, encouraging the archbishop to instruct the printers sternly that no printing or importing of the old Psalters would be allowed.[68] Both the king and the official acts of the Privy Council associated the Psalms with the name of James, but Sir Thomas Hope recorded in a more personal account that Charles had sent an order to the Scottish Privy Council forbidding the use of the old Psalms "and geving command to sing the new of the Erl Stirling."[69] Throughout the spring Charles urged the whole new liturgy, and the Scottish clergy resisted. Finally, on 23 July 1637, the new liturgy was used at a number of Edinburgh churches. The long delays in introducing the new Prayer Book and Psalter had given those opposed to it ample time to organize resistance. The uprisings at St. Giles and other Edinburgh churches on 23 July were less than spontaneous events, but nevertheless they reflected widespread opposition to the new liturgy. This was followed by further violent resistance against the new liturgical works on 17 October.[70] Eventually the resistance led to the Scottish Covenant and the Bishops' War of 1638–39.

Ultimately the content of the Psalter, like that of the Prayer Book, may have been less significant than the way it was introduced. Charles worked solely through the bishops, completely bypassing Parliament and the Assembly of the Church.[71] The Prayer Book was, in Walter Makey's words, "merely the outward manifestation of the system which the bishops had created."[72] The bishops themselves were referred to as "Canterburians" for their close connections to Archbishop Laud and the English court in general.[73] Frequently, later popular history came to see the work as "Laud's Liturgy," stemming from the archbishop's personal desires, but at the time the Scots blamed their own bishops and archbishops.[74] Kevin Sharpe has shown that Charles himself was largely responsible for the religious policy of uniformity and order in the church.[75] The same is true of the Psalter; Laud makes no reference to it in his correspondence, and McMillan suggests that he had grave reservations about it.[76] Also, the attempted imposition of the Psalter and Prayer Book has the hallmarks of Charles's tendency to work by decree rather than consultation or persuasion.[77] According to Gordon Donaldson, "If the Scots suspected the truth—that the principal author and inspirer of the book, outside Scotland, was King Charles himself—they could not directly accuse him as long as the fiction was maintained that 'our sweet prince' had been acting under evil advice."[78] In the same way, the Psalter was attacked not as the work of James but as the work of William Alexander, earl of Stirling. However, in this case the attribution of the work to a non-royal figure did have a strong basis. Charles consistently promoted the work as James's, while its Presbyterian opponents used nothing but such phrases as "Menstries Psalms." Though James may not have been universally loved by the more radical Scottish Presbyterians for his insistence on an episcopal system, his doctrinaire Calvinist theology was useful for the Scotts who accused the new liturgy of Arminianism. They could charge the bishops without rebelling against the sound orthodoxy of the former king. For them to treat it as Charles did—that is, as a memorial to his father—would have made opposition all but impossible. Thus the derision of the work as "Menstrie's Psalms" was very important to their opposition. By 1637 Alexander's name was anathema to the people of Scotland: he had been responsible a few years earlier for the introduction of a new coin, the "Turner," which profited him but played havoc with the Scottish economy. At the death of his son in 1638 the Presbyterian historian Robert Baillie commented: "His father is old and extreamely hated of all the countrey for his alleged briberie, urgeing of the Psalmes and the Books [Service Books] for them [i.e., on account of the Psalms], overwhelming us with his Black money."[79] With such a reputation, the derisive attacks on the Psalter as "Menstrie's Psalmes" had great effect. Later, in the

1640s, the Presbyterian historian John Row could take a more balanced view of the Psalter: "The worke wes comonlie thought to be rather Sir William Alexander's of Menstrie than the King's; howbeit, it is most probable that both hes had a hand in it."[80]

In the 1640s both the English and Scottish churches would consider more moderate emendations of the Old Psalters. Charles's pressing of his father's Psalter had cleared the field, and in the late 1630s and 1640s new versions by William Mure of Rowallan, Zachary Boyd, Francis Rous, and William Barton appeared. Ultimately, through the deliberations of the Westminster Assembly, a new version based substantially on that of Francis Rous was instituted for both England and Scotland. In their Assembly of 1647 the Kirk of Scotland considered the new Psalter prepared in England. They recommended an examination of the work and asked the examiners "to make use of the travels of Rowallen, Master Zachary Boyd, or any other on that subject, but especially of our own Paraphrase, that what they finde better in any of these Works may be chosen."[81] While it failed to take hold in England, from 1650 this work became the new standard Scottish Psalter in the churches. Among those "other[s] on that subject" that were considered was James's work. William McMillan has demonstrated the great irony that the king's Psalms were substantially drawn upon by those who put together the 1650 Psalter. McMillan estimates that as many as 572 lines (of a total of 9,000) are taken directly from James's work, with a further 1,400 lines showing some influence.[82] However, by the late 1640s all such indebtedness had to go unacknowledged: the reputations of James and Alexander and the coupling of their Psalter with the 1637 Prayer Book made it impossible for it to be publicly recognized as influencing the new version. Thus James's ambitions with regard to the Psalms were ultimately partially fulfilled, but in a way that completely eclipsed his image as a latter-day David. Both in his own reign and that of his son, James's "Psalms" were a sort of phantom work; their reality was inconsequential or elusive, while the idea of them played a major role. Subsequently in the Scottish church James's authorship has become the phantom, with his actual lines remaining as the real presence.

Notes

1. 63. The most thorough study to this point has been William McMillan, "The Metrical Psalter of James VI," *Records of the Scottish Church History Society* 8 (1944): 114–33, 184–208. McMillan's detailed work comparing James's Psalter with both previous and later ones cannot be surpassed, but his paper does not consider James's Psalter in England, nor the full ramifications of the work's reception.
2. Preface to AV, 1611, 344.

3. *His Maiesties Poeticall Exercises* 3.
4. Ibid.
5. BL Old Royal ms. 18B. XVI; this includes Psalms 1–7, 9–21, 29, 47, 100, 125, 128, 133, 148, and 150, as well as versifications of Ecclesiastes 12, the Lord's Prayer, and Deuteronomy 32 (the Song of Moses). The manuscript is in a number of different hands, one probably of James and two others of scribes; see Westcott lxxxviii. Ms. Bodl. 165, fol. 58b also includes Psalm 101 as translated by King James. It too is in Scots and different from that appearing in the 1631 and 1636 editions. It is printed by Robert Rait in *Lusus Regius* (London: A. Constable, 1901).
6. Preface to AV, 1611, 349.
7. See Reid 43–53.
8. There seems to be some disagreement about the significance of psalm-singing in the Scottish church of the early seventeenth century. Millar Patrick suggests that the "1564 Psalter cannot at any time have had more than a very restricted use" (79). However, the many references collected by Neil Livingston seem to tell a different story.
9. 1: 37–38.
10. Spottiswoode 3: 98. Spottiswoode's history was first published in 1655.
11. *Acts and Proceedings* 3: 970.
12. McMillan 193.
13. However, McMillan notes that the most popular of the Psalms in Scotland used the common meter (120).
14. A number of the Sidney Psalms were set to the music of the Genevan Psalter and published in *All the French Psalm Tunes with English Words* (1632). See my "Seventeenth-Century Publication."
15. See Craigie, "Poems of King James" and "Last Poems of James VI."
16. "To M. Hugh Cholmley. Ep. V. Concerning the Metaphrase of the Psalms," in *Poems* 271.
17. 18 April 1620, Drummond, *Works* 151. Drummond also sent one of his metrical Psalms to Robert Kerr, earl of Ancrum. See Kerr 2: 520–21.
18. 24 April 1624, *Correspondence* 2: 488. At the time, Kerr was a gentleman of James's bedchamber.
19. *Records of the Court of the Stationers' Company,* 5 September 1631, 231. For further discussion of the Stationers' Company's patent and its effect, see my "George Wither, the Stationers' Company and the English Psalter."
20. BL ms. Add. 18648, fol. 19r. Rpt. Pritchard, "George Wither's Quarrel."
21. sig. 6r.
22. 12–13.
23. sig. 4r. This manuscript of Wither's Psalms is in a scribe's hand and contains a version of the Psalms different from those in the final

printed version of 1632. The preface was also replaced in the printed work. The manuscript likely dates from 1625, when Wither attempted to have the Psalms printed at Cambridge. See Pritchard, "Manuscript of George Wither's *Psalms.*"

24. Rev. Joseph Mead to Sir Martin Stuteville, in Birch 12–13.
25. sig. A6r.
26. 42. The passage that Williams quotes is actually from Psalm 32.
27. "To my most dear and worthy friend, Mr. John Dinely, at the Hague," 12 August 1628; Wotton 558.
28. On the relative neglect of James's works in Charles's reign, see Joseph Marshall's essay in this volume.
29. *Workes, STC* 14344.
30. Letter of Charles to the archbishop of St. Andrews, 25 August 1626; see Alexander 2: 73. Calderwood suggests that "another, if not others, also hath had ane hand in them" (237).
31. 3: 99.
32. "To our right trustie and weelbeloved Cousen and Counseller the Erle of Marleburh, our Thesaurer of England," 28 December 1627; see Alexander 240–41. In this letter Charles asks the earl to make arrangements for the patent. It was actually granted on 21 January 1628 (*CSPD*, 1627–28, 524). In this letter Charles also calls for a bill to be drawn up for Ireland.
33. Letter to the archbishops and bishops, 14 June 1631; see Alexander 2: 538.
34. Opposite title page in James VI and I, *Psalmes of King David, STC* 2732. The same authorization was included with the 1636 edition.
35. 13 March 1632; see Alexander 2: 581.
36. 1: 238. The manuscript in the Advocates Library in which this appears is undated; however, Calderwood's comment that the present Psalms had been in use "thriescoir and eight yeirs" would suggest that he wrote it in 1632.
37. The 1631 edition likely did contravene the Stationers' patent, and to correct this before the edition of 1636 an Order of the King in Council was passed on 9 March 1636, granting Oxford printers limited rights to print Psalters outside the Stationers' Company's domain (*Cal. S. P. D., Charles I, 1636* 281).
38. Since 1625 Charles had appointed a number of new Scottish bishops perceived by their countrymen as creations of the king, little connected to the clergy. See Guthry 10.
39. Sharpe, *Personal Rule* 774–77.
40. See Alexander 2: 815. These letters are undated, but Charles's comment—"sieing we have alreadie gevin ordour for ane Impression of

that Translatioun"—indicates that he is writing just before the 1631 or 1636 edition. The overall tone of the letter is more like that of the others from 1631.

41. Peterkin 1: 50n.
42. 1: 144.
43. 60.
44. This attack on James's Psalter was not published in the seventeenth century, but it survives in manuscript in a number of different versions. Calderwood and the king had clashed as early as James's visit to Scotland in 1617, with the result that Calderwood was imprisoned and then exiled. He returned to Scotland in 1625.
45. In the late 1640s the revised Psalter was brought in with seemingly few objections; this would suggest that Calderwood and the other Presbyterians were most opposed to what James's Psalter represented, rather than a deep-seated loyalty to the Old Psalter.
46. 237.
47. 236.
48. 241.
49. All letters 5 May 1632; see Alexander 2: 591–92. On this day Charles also wrote to James Ussher, the archbishop of Armagh in Ireland, urging the same.
50. Alexander 2: 605.
51. Alexander 2: 621.
52. Calderwood estimated that it would take six hundred thousand psalters to fulfill the need (245); this figure is rightly challenged as ridiculous by McMillan (127–28).
53. Alexander 2: 621.
54. On Charles and the Scottish church, see Donaldson and Lee. For a more particular study of his relations with the Covenanters, see MacInnes.
55. 28 January 1630. Qtd. in *Grievances Given in by the Ministers STC* 22034.
56. 242.
57. Pollard and Redgrave 2: 106–7. The Psalter was always far more than a collection of Psalms: it included prayers, forms for communion, baptism, excommunication, ordination, and so on. Some editions also included an almanac and a calendar of Scottish fairs.
58. *Acts and Proceedings* 6: 124.
59. See Cowan.
60. On the differences between James's and Charles's styles in treating Scotland, see Sharpe, *The Personal Rule of Charles I.*
61. Lee 2.

62. Alexander 2: 855.
63. Alexander 2: 815. A similar letter to the archbishop of St. Andrews appears on the next page. See also *Register of the Privy Council of Scotland* 1635–37: 409–10.
64. *STC* 2736 (folio) was printed in England by Thomas Harper; *STC* 2736.5 (octavo) has no printer identified; *STC* suggests that Harper may have printed this as well, but it seems more likely to have been produced in Scotland.
65. These phrases were also among those which Calderwood had ridiculed.
66. 125.
67. *Register of the Privy Council of Scotland* 6: 409.
68. Ibid.
69. 56. Hope was the king's advocate, but, according to Guthry, he was also a party to the opponents of the new liturgy (23).
70. Hope 66.
71. No General Assembly of the Church of Scotland was called between 1618 and 1638.
72. 16.
73. Horton Davies 2: 341.
74. Donaldson 79–80.
75. *Politics and Ideas* 108–9. See also Julian Davies 36–39.
76. Unfortunately, McMillan provides no source for this.
77. Sharpe has argued that Laud generally preferred to work through persuasion (*Personal Rule* 126).
78. 80.
79. Qtd. in Rogers 1: 173. Rogers also quotes a manuscript satire by Sir James Balfour written shortly after Alexander's own death:

Heir layes a farmer and a miller,

A poet and a Psalme booke spiller,

A purchaser by hoode and crooke,

A forger of ye service booke,

A copper smith who did much evill

A friend to Bischopes and ye Devil. (190)

80. 492.
81. 28 August 1647; see Peterkin 1: 475. This same act also advises them to heed the "animadversions sent from Presbyteries."
82. 192. McMillan also cites an independent study by a Dr. Rorison, who found 516 lines taken from James's Psalter.

Works Cited

Acts and Proceedings of the General Assembly of the Kirk of Scotland. Ed. T. Thomson. 3 vols. Edinburgh, 1845.

Alexander, Sir William. *Earl of Stirling's Register of Royal Letters Relative to the Affairs of Scotland and Nova Scotia from 1615 to 1635.* 2 vols. Edinburgh, 1885.

Birch, Thomas, ed. *Court and Times of James I.* 1848.

Calderwood, David. "Reasons against the reception of King James's metaphrase of the Psalms." *Bannatyne Miscellany.* Vol. 1. Ed. Sir Walter Scott and D. Laing. Edinburgh, 1827.

Cowan, I. B. "The Five Articles of Perth." *Reformation and Revolution.* Ed. D. Shaw. Edinburgh: Saint Andrew P, 1967. 160-77.

Craigie, James. "Last Poems of James VI." *Scottish Historical Review* (1951): 134–42.

———. "Poems of King James I of England and VI of Scotland." *Bodleian Library Record* (Supplement) 3: 1–7.

Davies, Horton. *Worship and Theology in England.* 5 vols. Princeton: Princeton UP, 1975.

Davies, Julian. *The Caroline Captivity of the Church.* Oxford: Oxford UP, 1992.

Dod, Henry. *All the Psalmes of David.* 1620.

Doelman, James. "George Wither, the Stationers' Company and the English Psalter." *Studies in Philology* 90 (1993): 74–82.

———. "A Seventeenth-Century Publication of Three of Sir Philip Sidney's Psalms." *Notes and Queries* n.s. 38 (1991): 162–63.

Donaldson, Gordon. *The Making of the Scottish Prayer Book of 1637.* Edinburgh: Edinburgh UP, 1954.

Drummond, William. *Works.* 1711.

The Grievances Given in by the Ministers before the Parliament Holden in June 1633. 1635.

Guthry, Henry. *Bp. of Dunkeld. Memoires.* Glasgow, 1747.

Hall, Joseph. *Collected Poems.* Ed. Arnold Davenport. Liverpool: Liverpool UP, 1949.

Hope, Sir Thomas. *Diary of the Correspondence.* Ed. T. Thomson. Bannatyne Club. Edinburgh, 1843.

James VI and I. *His Majesties Poeticall Exercises at Vacant Houres.* Edinburgh, 1591.

———. *Lusus Regius.* Ed. Robert Rait. London: A. Constable, 1901.

———. *The Psalmes of King David, Translated by King James.* Oxford, 1631.

———. *The Psalmes of King David, Translated by King James.* Oxford, 1636.

———. *Workes.* London, 1616. Fasc. rpt. New York: George Olms Verlag, 1971.

Kerr, Robert, Earl of Ancrum. *Correspondence.* 2 vols. Edinburgh, 1875.

Lee, Maurice, Jr. *The Road to Revolution: Scotland under Charles I, 1625–37.* Urbana: U of Illinois P, 1985.

Livingston, Neil. *The Scottish Metrical Psalter of* A.D. *1635.* London: Novello, 1935.

MacInnes, Allan I. *Charles I and the Making of the Covenanting Movement, 1625–1641.* Edinburgh: J. Donald, 1991.

Makey, Walter. *The Church of the Covenant, 1637–51: Revolution and Social Change in Scotland.* Edinburgh: John Donald, 1979.

McMillan, William H. "The Metrical Psalter of James VI." *Records of the Scottish Church History Society* 8 (1944): 114–33, 184–208.

Patrick, Millar. *Four Centuries of Scottish Psalmody.* London: Oxford UP, 1949.

Peterkin, Alexander. *Records of the Kirk of Scotland.* Edinburgh, 1838.

Pollard, A. W. *Records of the English Bible 1525–1611.* Oxford: Oxford UP, 1911.

Pollard, A. W., and G. R. Redgrave. *A Short Title Catalogue of Books Printed in England, Scotland, and Ireland . . . 1475–1640.* 2nd ed. 3 vols. London: Bibliographical Society, 1976–81.

Pritchard, Allen. "George Wither's Quarrel with the Stationers: An Anonymous Reply to The Schollers Purgatory." *Studies in Bibliography* 16 (1963): 27–42.

———. "A Manuscript of George Wither's Psalms." *Modern Philology* 77 (1980): 370–81.

Records of the Court of the Stationers Company. Ed. W. W. Greg et al. London: Bibliographical Society, 1930.

Register of the Privy Council of Scotland, 1635–37. 2nd ser. Ed. P. Hume Brown. Edinburgh, 1905.

Reid, W. S. "The Battle Hymns of the Lord: Calvinist Psalmody of the Sixteenth Century." *Sixteenth-Century Essays and Studies* 2 (1971): 43–53.

Rogers, Charles. *Memorials of the Earl of Stirling.* 2 vols. Edinburgh: Paterson, 1877.

Row, John. *Historie of the Kirk of Scotland, 1558–1637.* 2 vols. Edinburgh: Maitland Club, 1842. Rpt. New York: AMS, 1973.

Rutherford, Samuel. *Letters.* Ed. Andrew Bonar. 4th ed. Edinburgh, 1891.

Sharpe, Kevin. *The Personal Rule of Charles I.* New Haven: Yale UP, 1982.

———. *Politics and Ideas in Early Stuart England.* New York: Pinter, 1989.

Spottiswoode, John. *History of the Church of Scotland.* 3 vols. Ed. M. Russell. Edinburgh, 1851.

Williams, John. *Great Britains Salomon.* 1625.

Willson, David Harris. *King James VI and I.* London: Jonathan Cape, 1956.

Wither, George. *Schollers Purgatory* (1624). *Works.* Spenser Society Reprint. New York: Burt Franklin, 1871–72. Rpt. 1967.

Wotton, Henry. *Reliquiae Wottoniae.* 1685.

16

Reading and Misreading King James 1622–42: Responses to the *Letter and Directions Touching Preaching and Preachers*

Joseph Marshall

King James VI and I's instructions to the bishops in 1622, concerning the regulation of politically charged sermons at a time of political crisis, constitute his last major written work. In terms of the critical and intelligent responses it generated in James's readers, the document is among the most important texts of the Stuart period. The king's unsuccessful attempts to control the way his subjects interpreted his words played a major role in the transformation of the politics of reading in the years immediately before the outbreak of the Civil War. This work has always been known to scholars, but a reliance on corrupt texts printed late in the seventeenth century has obscured the extent to which the early printed and manuscript versions reveal a complex series of exchanges between the royal author and his readers.[1]

James's relationship with the public audience for his speeches and printed books was always difficult. Although as a literary artist who was also a king he could be certain that his texts would be read carefully in search of the royal meaning, James found that this did not always mean that his readers produced interpretations of his works that were acceptable to their author. As a good Protestant, James believed that words could perfectly transmit the authorial intention: he was dismayed to see his words quoted in defense of beliefs he did not hold, and the authority of his works invoked to legitimize diverse religious and political positions. James frequently referred to his discourse as a glass revealing his thoughts, and he warned Parliament, on 21 March 1610, not "to soile it with a foule breath, and vncleane hands: I meane, that ye peruert not my words by any corrupt affections, turning them to an ill meaning, like one, who when hee heares the tolling of a Bell, fancies to himselfe, that it speakes those words which are most in his minde."[2] In fact, James's continual emphasis on the transparency and importance of his meaning seems to have encouraged readers to appropriate his works for themselves. Confident that the author's intentions were easily accessible, and eager to find that the all-important will of the king coincided with their own beliefs, readers approached James's texts with the reverence usually reserved for Holy Scripture—and proceeded to take the holy words out of context like any sectarian. James Doelman has shown how readers engaged with and reworked *Basilikon Doron*, seeking to "discover" that, behind the rhetoric, James was really sympathetic to Anabaptism or "High Church" episcopacy.[3] Once James's texts were separated from their author by print, he had few means of preventing readers from making the king's words their own.[4] James tried to regain control by issuing more explanatory texts. There is evidence that his decision to publish his collected *Workes* in 1617 was motivated by the belief that readers were using corrupt versions of his writings to produce extraordinary readings.[5] Yet all this gave readers more royal material to misinterpret.

By the 1620s, James was increasingly aware that he had underestimated the risks inherent in writing as a king. Opening Parliament on 30 January 1621, James announced with much rhetorical flourish that he was determined to end the problem of people turning his words against him.[6] He would, in future, be silent:

> in many sessions of divers Parliaments before this I have made many long discourses, especially to the gentlemen of the House of Commons, and to them I have delivered, as I myself have said, a true mirror of my mind and free thoughts of my heart. But as no man's actions, be he never so good, are free from sin, being a mortal, sinful creature, so some through a spice of envy have made all my speech heretofore turn like spittle against the wind upon mine own face and contrary to my expectation, so that I may truly say with our Saviour, I have often piped unto you, and you have not danced, I have mourned and you have not lamented. This hath made me more fully to resolve that for these few days, if God grant me more, I never mean to weary myself nor you with such tedious discourses as I have done heretofore.[7]

James was not entirely able to repress his love of words; he continued to make lengthy speeches to Parliament, and in April he repudiated the speech cited above, saying that "when I spake formerly it was with apprehension of fear how my speech would be taken."[8] When Parliament insisted on discussing James's foreign and religious policies rather than the issue of supply, James dissolved it, and published a volume containing his exchanges with the leaders of the House of Commons.[9] However, he never issued another edition of his *Workes,* and a volume of poems he seems to have been preparing for publication, with the assistance of Prince Charles, was left in manuscript until this century (British Library ms. Add. 24195).[10] James published only one major work between 1621 and his death in 1625, the *Letter and Directions Touching Preaching and Preachers* of 1622. The fact that the main subject of this work is the problem of people criticizing the king's words makes it an interesting conclusion to a difficult relationship between the royal author and his readers, as well as an immediate response to a critical political situation.

Recent research has drawn attention to the significance of the English political crisis that developed in 1618–24.[11] The outbreak of war in Germany, and the spectacular gains being made by Catholic armies, were of special concern in England as the Protestant Elector Frederick was married to King James's beloved daughter Elizabeth. It was popularly expected that England would intervene, particularly in view of the fact that her historic enemy Spain was one of the main combatants. Even before his accession to the English throne, James had vigorously promoted the apocalyptic myth of the mission of the British kingdoms to uphold the reformed faith, publishing a sonnet in celebration of the defeat of the Armada in 1588.[12] Several of the texts collected in the *Workes* were strongly anti-Catholic and referred to the prophecies in the Apocalypse which he interpreted to mean that the Church of Rome would be overthrown by a coalition of Christian princes. However, in practice James was determined to uphold his motto "Beati Pacifici." In 1618 a work showing clear signs of James's involvement and called *The Peace-Maker: Or, Great Brittaines Blessing* was published to celebrate his fiftieth year as a king.[13] Reluctant to abandon his anti-militaristic policies, James refused to send more than a token contingent of soldiers to Germany, and he opened negotiations with Catholic Spain in the hope that a diplomatic solution could be arranged, probably involving the marriage of Prince Charles to the Spanish Infanta. To many of his subjects, however, James appeared to be proposing to negotiate with Antichrist: it was rumored that he had converted to Roman Catholicism.

This was certainly unfair. In earlier texts, produced in different circumstances, James had been happy to explore the idea that the pope was Antichrist, as the myth seemed a good explanation of the divisions between the churches and made his readers enthusiastic about the established church over which he was supreme governor.[14] In the volatile international situation of the 1620s, the rhetoric of Knox did not seem so appropriate. Anthony Milton describes James's attempts to reinterpret his own anti-papal writings to further the cause of international peace.[15] However, by fixing his words in print and enshrining them in the *Workes,* James had given readers the opportunity to judge his actions against his writings. His texts had been widely interpreted to mean that he seriously believed that the Church of Rome should be destroyed, and unfortunately he had never discouraged this interpretation.[16] Surely the king could no more change his mind expressed in his words than God could repudiate the Bible? The perplexed language of Thomas Scott's *Vox Regis,* which seems to have appeared in 1624, is representative of the whole period. Scott tries to convince himself that the words and works of kings must always be consonant, even if appearances are against them:

> And if their words & works seem to differ, it is to those who ought to be held in suspence. But to their own, their words & works speake one language, and they striue to resemble him whose substitutes they are, *Who spake & it was done.* . . . Whereas therfore his most excellent Maiesty hath referd vs, his poore subiects, to the reading of his bookes for the sincerity of his heart in point of Religion; because some actions of his, either did (as he heard) or might (as he thought) giue occasion of suspicion and iealousie to some, who looked as it were asquint, or with purblind eies vpon them. I doe assure my selfe it can be no presumption in me for my owne and other mens resolution, to obserue his words, and to reade his writings, therby to learn to know him perfectly & to expect without doubt the accomplishment of his promises. For his words and writings are published to this end and called his Works, because they should be turned into workes. For as it implyes weaknesse to haue workes resolued into words: so it expresseth strength to haue words sublimated into works, as the words of potent Princes vse to be, or ought to be.[17]

Scott went on to quote James's *Remonstrance . . . for the Right of Kings* (1615), in which James had commented on the danger of kings making unworthy contracts.[18] Was the Spanish match not such a contract, and did not the people have the right to remind James of what he had said? James had chastised his readers for making his words conform to their personal intentions, but now readers felt they should make the king live up to his words.[19]

After the dissolution of Parliament in January 1622, James made it clear that he intended to continue negotiations with the Catholic powers, even though Protestant strongholds, frequently defended by English volunteers, were in grave danger. Opposition to his policies was increasingly voiced in public, despite proclamations in 1620 and 1621 warning people against such criticism.[20] It was perhaps unfortunate for James that the 1620s saw the birth of the English newspaper, which brought the latest details of Spanish advances to the attention of an excited and horrified reading public; in April 1622 the series of newsbooks organized by Nathaniel Butter and Nicholas Bourne commenced.[21] The situation can hardly have been helped by the circulation of a speech purporting to be by James, in which he declared the Roman Church to be true.[22] The most dangerous criticism, however, came from the established church.[23] Ministers (or "lecturers") with special responsibility for preaching outside normal church services were frequently inclined to the so-called Puritan wing of the church, which emphasized the need for political and social life to be infused with Christian values, and which was bitterly opposed to any compromise with "Roman" doctrine or ceremony.[24] They defied repeated warnings against bringing politics into their sermons and spoke darkly of the horrors of apostasy.

In April a furor was caused by a sermon preached in Oxford by one John Knight, who discussed the question of whether subjects might, in certain circumstances, take up arms against their sovereign; Knight unwisely concluded that they might, leading to his imprisonment.[25] The government made every effort to promote sympathetic preachers, but as the sermon of one such preacher, Walter Curll, admitted, books that "spare not, to spit their poyson in the face of Princes" were becoming increasingly common.[26] Just as the preachers felt James had betrayed the Protestant cause, so James felt that his church was rebelling against its supreme governor. He seems to have been particularly angered by the circumstances in which Marc'Antonio de Dominis, the former Catholic archbishop of Spalatro who had defected to the Church of England, decided to return to Rome in early 1622. Spalatro's motives may have been more materialistic than theological, but his assertion that he could not believe the Anglican Church to be Catholic while the Puritan preachers held sway clearly touched a nerve with James.[27] In May 1622, James took part in a conference with the leading Jesuit, John Percy (also known as Fisher), in which the king explained his main objections to the Church of Rome.[28] This kind of ecumenism was a long way from the days of his writings during the Oath of Allegiance controversy. The proceedings of the conference, which had its immediate origin as a response to the attempts to convert Buckingham and his family to Catholicism, were meant to be kept secret, but one suspects that it contributed to the atmosphere of estrangement between king and people that developed in the summer of 1622.

On 2 August 1622, on James's instructions, the Lord Keeper John Williams wrote to the circuit judges to order the suspension of the recusancy laws, completing a process of gradual relaxation that had been underway ever since the marriage negotiations started.[29] James's reign had seen periods in which Roman Catholics had been less rigorously treated, such as shortly after his accession to the English throne, but never before had England seen anything so close to religious toleration. From the point of view of the marriage negotiators, it was a necessary move, as the pope would only permit a Catholic princess to marry a heretic if she and her servants could attend Mass freely on English soil. Furthermore,

James could hardly appeal to Catholic Spain to preserve Protestant rights in Germany while English law criminalized the practice of the Roman faith. However, James knew that an explosion of protest would follow. On 4 August, James wrote to George Abbot, the archbishop of Canterbury, enclosing some new instructions for regulating preaching that Abbot was to transmit to all the bishops.[30]

The strategies James uses in his letter and directions suggest a keen awareness of the importance to ensure a positive reception of the work. However, he was hampered from the start by his consciousness of the fact that in this text it would not do to make his intentions crystal clear; readers would not accept that he was more committed to international peace than to militant Protestantism. He had to persuade people that he was restricting the preachers in order to protect the reformed religion. James takes great pains to make it appear that these directions are nothing new and that they have nothing whatsoever to do with the current political crisis. His letter begins by invoking a tradition of state control of preaching, declaring that: "the abuses and extravagancies of preachers in the pulpit haue beene in all times repressed in this Realme by some acte of Councell or State with the Advice and resolution of graue and learned prelats." James is trying to prepare the reader to accept his measures by suggesting that they are merely the latest in a long series of interventions by the state to regulate clerical activities. The idea that these interventions take place with the backing of the clergy is designed to win support from the very people who were potentially his most dangerous critics. In a sense, it was true that the directions were not particularly innovative; it was the context of a divided church and the king's possible rapprochement with Rome that made them so threatening.[31] James goes on to explain specifically why preachers need regulation at this time. He states: "at this present diuers yonge students by readinge of late Writers and vngrounded devines, doe broache many times vnprofitable, vnsound, seditious, and daungerous doctrines to the Scandall of this Churche and disquietinge of the State and present gouernment." James attacks those who have criticized his policies by arguing that they, in fact, are the ones introducing new and dangerous ideas.[32]

The six new directions for preachers that follow display the same uneasy combination of conciliatory rhetoric and explosively confrontational argument. The first direction imposes limits on the way preachers expound on their scriptural text; they are not to use any "set discourse or common place" illustration not found in the Thirty-Nine Articles or the Books of Homilies. This essentially bans preachers from commenting on political affairs. The second direction imposes even stricter limitations on the afternoon lectures, which were a focus for so-called Puritans. Preachers are restricted to preaching on the catechism, the Lord's Prayer, the Creed, or the Ten Commandments; moreover, they are strongly encouraged not to preach at all, but to examine children in the catechism instead. The third direction orders that no preacher of lower rank than a dean should "presume to preache in any populary auditory the deepe poynts of *Predestinacon*

Election Reprobacion or of the *vniversality Efficacy Resistabillity or Irresistabillity of gods grace;* but leaue thise theames to be handled by learned men, and that moderately and modestly by way of vse and applicacion, rather then by way of positiue doctrine as beinge fitter for the Schooles and vniuersities then for simple auditories." This is taking a huge swipe at the intellectualism of the Puritan preachers (it is difficult to imagine how anyone could be expected to discuss the *shallow* points of predestination). James was trying to stop preachers from discussing controversial theological issues, as these would inevitably be used to attack the Church of Rome and, by implication, James's policies. The manuscript in the Public Record Office cited here, which appears to be a very early draft, suggests that James paid particular attention to this sensitive section. The words italicized above seem to be in a different hand, possibly that of the king himself.

The fourth direction touches on an issue even closer to James's heart. Preachers are forbidden to discuss

> the power prerogatiue Jurisdicion Authoritie or Duty of Soueraigne princes, or otherwise meddle with theise matters of State, and the references betweene princes and their people, then as they are instructed and presidented in the Homily of Obedience, and in the rest of the homilies set forth as before is mencioned by public Authoritie but rather confine themselues wholly to those 2 heads of Faith and ~~obedience~~ & good leife, which are all the subiect of the auncient sermons and homilies.

Again, the manuscript suggests that James was unhappy about this section; the deleted word "obedience" probably sounded too overbearing. James was clearly very concerned to make his readers believe that the directions proceeded from purely religious motives, not his secular needs for public order. However, this passage fails to conceal the fact that James's dislike of public opposition was greater than his desire for preachers to stick to strictly theological subjects.

The directions become increasingly threatening. In the fifth one, the king orders

> That noe preacher of what title or denominacion soeuer shall causlesly and without invitacion from the Text, fall into any bitter Invectiues and vndecent raylinge speeches against the persons of either Papists or Puritanes, but modestly and grauely when they are occasioned therevnto by the Text of Scripture, free both the Doctrine & Discipline of the Churche of England from the aspersions of either adversary especially where the auditorie is suspected to be tainted with the one or the other infection.

Everyone knew that the critics of the Spanish marriage, against which the fourth direction is clearly aimed, were the Puritan party. In this direction, therefore, when James warns against sermons opposing "either Papists or Puritans," he is really targeting anti-Catholic preaching. The mention of the need to stop preachers attacking the Puritans is merely a token reference, an attempt to preserve the illusion that the directions are a traditional means of checking extremists on both sides of the church.[33] The sixth direction confirms that the conciliatory language of the letter and the earlier directions is essentially window dressing. James explains that all ministers who wish to preach must have a license. They must be recommended by their bishop, and this recommendation must be supported by the archbishop of Canterbury and confirmed by the Great Seal of England. Only then might their application be considered in the Court of Faculties. If these directions were as strictly enforced as James commanded, the preachers who had been delivering Sunday afternoon lectures for years would be silenced.

George Abbot was given the task of officially communicating and explaining these instructions to various leading figures, above all to the bishops, who were to transmit them to the rest of the clergy. It was a neat move to make Abbot responsible for repressing the government's critics, as he was known to be unhappy with the Spanish match and considerably more sympathetic to the "Puritan" lecturers than rising stars like William Laud. Abbot's status within the establishment had been greatly reduced by his notorious accidental shooting of a man while out hunting in 1621; he was an opponent of James's policies, but a weak opponent, and one whom James believed could be dragooned into promoting the new directions.[34] Abbot seems to have initially introduced the king's orders with a short letter, in which he states that the directions are designed to improve the quality of preaching and ensure that sermons take "a religious forme, and not that euery younge man, shall take unto himself an exorbitant libertie to teach what he listeth."[35] This deflects attention from James's evident intentions to suppress the afternoon lectures altogether, and no doubt the king was reasonably satisfied.

However, as the new directions became known during the middle of August 1622, it became clear that many were neither satisfied with the king's text nor with Abbot's explanation. John Chamberlain, writing on 10 August, was one of many to connect the new directions with the suspension of the recusancy laws two days earlier: the king spoke of the need to defend the reformed religion even as he was releasing Roman priests from prison.[36] James had tried to conceal the political reasons for the directions under pious rhetoric: unfortunately people seem to have suspected that it was Roman piety speaking. On 26 August the Venetian ambassador described an extraordinary situation in rather prophetic terms:

> From the enclosed copy your Serenity will see the manner in which his Majesty orders the release of the Catholics, of which I wrote

> before. It was also ordained, although this has not yet been executed, that the archbishop of Canterbury should forbid the preachers here to attack the Roman faith or enlarge upon any disputes and disagreements with the Catholic church. I hear that they also propose to confine to Sundays only the preaching which is now so frequent through the week. Although all these things afford great joy to the Catholics and seem to promise the marriage, they incense the others to a remarkable degree and may possibly sow the seeds of a civil war.[37]

A more sophisticated justification of the directions was needed; again Abbot was called on to write the bishops a more lengthy letter, which appeared in early September.[38] I have not found a holograph of this letter, and the circumstances of its composition are unclear. However, the work has several peculiarities that suggest it is a genuine work by Abbot, written under protest.[39]

The writer says of the directions: "no godly or discreet man cann otherwise then acknowledge that they doe much tend to edificacion if he do not take then vppe vppon report, but doe punctually consider the tenor of the words as they lye and do not giue an ill construccion to that which may receaue a faire interpretation." It is *possible* to give the directions a fair interpretation, but the writer cannot conceal the fact that reports of the directions were causing an uproar. He continues: "some few Churchmen and manie of the people haue sinisterly conceiued, as wee here find, that those instruccions do tend to the restrainte of the exercise of preachinge and doe in some sorte abate the number of Sermons and so consequentlie by degrees, do make a breach to let in ignorance and superstition." Perhaps Abbot is trying to suppress the reading that he himself had made. He then gives a lengthy explanation for James's actions, which is quite different from that given in James's own part of the text:

> his Maiestie being much trouble [sic] and greued at the heart to heare euery day of so many defections from our Religion both to poperie and Anabaptisme, or other points of separacion in some parts of this Kingdome and considering with much admiracion what might be the cause thereof especially in the reigne of such a Kinge, who doeth so constantly professe himselfe an open aduersarie to the superstition of the one and madnesse of the other, his princely wisdome could fall vppon noe one greater probabillitie, than the lightenes, affectedfnes [*sic*] and vnprofitablenes of that kind of preachinge which hath bin of late yeares to much taken vp in Court Vniuersitie Citie and Countrey.

This is much more reasonable and convincing than James's alternate appeals to traditional devotion and warnings against political sedition. Moreover, the aware reader would have noticed an ironic subtext. By describing James as a king "who doeth so constantly professe himselfe an open aduersarie to the superstition of the one," meaning popery, Abbot may be getting a small revenge for James's attempt to make it seem that Abbot was on his side. In fact, James's open hostility toward Catholicism was currently in as much doubt as Abbot's sympathy for the Spanish marriage.

The writer continues the "explanation" by describing the main faults in contemporary preachers:

> The vsuall scope of verie many preachers is noted to be a soaringe vp in points of Diuinity to deepe for the Capacitie of the people or a mustring vp of much reading or displayinge of their owne witt or an ignorant meddling with Ciuill matters, aswell in the priuate of seavrall parishes and Corporacions as in the publique of the Kingdome or a venting of their owne distastes or a smoothing vppe of those idle fancies which in this blessed time of so longe a peace doe boyle in the braines of unaduised people.

The reference to "this blessed time of so longe a peace" is potentially highly satirical; Abbot and many others felt that the time was not blessed but cursed by James's refusal to consider military intervention on the Continent. Many felt that the king's enthusiasm for peace had made the English, who had been frequently at war under Elizabeth, soft and decadent. *Tom Tell Troath,* an important anonymous complaint against James's pusillanimous foreign policy circulating at this time, remarks: "I feare wee have too much cause to complaine of your Majesties unlimited Peace."[40] The writer of the letter is replying to James's argument that preachers were discussing matters that did not directly contribute to the salvation of their flocks by suggesting that James's cowardly policies had given people leisure to think about forbidden things. The vigor of the language, in fact, makes one wonder whether he has James's directions in mind when he criticizes those who tackle matters they do not fully understand.

The writer then gives a reading of the second direction, which clearly intended the suppression of afternoon lectures. He writes: "And so farre are these direccions from abating; that his Maiestie doth expect att our hands, that it should increase the number of sermons by renewinge vppon euery Sunday in the afternoone in all parishes throughout the Kingdome that primitiue and most profitable exposition of the Catechisme." It looks as though Abbot was trying to save the lectures, using his task of defending the directions by producing an interpretation of them that severely restricted James's actions. Perhaps Abbot was obeying James's instruction to perform a favorable interpretation of his text while trying to ensure that the king was consequently tied to a reading which softened the impact of the original directions.

Certainly, Abbot's letter does not seem to have made it any easier for James to impose the directions. Joseph Mead, writing on 14 September, describes how Abbot's second letter had in fact made people more aware of the lack of support for the Spanish match at court:

> There is another letter from the archbishop to all the bishops, concerning both a complaint of the misunderstanding of the former directions for preaching, and an explication and further declaration, both of the occasion and his majesty's intendment by them. It should seem by it, that there had been great talk and strange construction somewhere. Dr. Donne preaches at Paul's tomorrow, either to that purpose, to give satisfaction, or, as the Londoners talk, to teach men how to preach there hereafter; because the two last, Mr. Clayton, of Fulham, and Dr. Sheldon, went beyond the usual limit, as was thought; for which Clayton is in prison, but Sheldon was only checked. Clayton told a tale of a great murrain of sheep in Edward the Sixth's days (I think); the reason whereof was, as he said, the coming of scabbed sheep out of Spain.[41]

The directions, guided by Abbot's interpretation, were having the effect of turning open criticism of James's policies into the more insidious ironic mockery that Mead records here. It was in this climate that John Donne was employed to defend the king's policies at St. Paul's cross.[42] On 15 September, taking a rather obscure text from the Song of Deborah, Judges 5:20, "The stars in their courses fought against Sisera," Donne proceeded to give a defense of the need for the church to engage in spiritual warfare by means of *orderly* preaching.[43] However, his continual references to conflict, the need for an unambiguous defense of the truth, and the foolishness of trying to reconcile good and evil suggested that he was not altogether happy with the directions. Indeed, writing to Sir Thomas Roe in December with a copy of the sermon, Donne suggested his unease at the pro-Catholic policy that had caused the unrest which had made the directions necessary: "many men, measuring public actions with private affections, have been scandalised, and have admitted suspicions of a tepidness in very high places. Some Civil Acts, in favour of the Papists, have been with some precipitation over-dangerously misapplied too."[44] In his sermon Donne insisted that the new orders proceeded, as James had said, from religious motives alone, yet he seems to have tried to communicate a certain distrust of the directions. He quoted Abbot's letter, stating explicitly that it contained James's intentions, in order to argue that there would be no reduction in the number of sermons.[45] He could not resist a few ironic quips, remarking that the spirit of preaching should not be quenched: "Saint

Chrysostome took his example from the lampe that burnt by him, when he was preaching; (It seemes therefore hee did preach in the afternoone)."[46] This witticism reminds the audience that the tradition of lectures outside normal morning services was well-established.

Donne concluded his defense of James's good intentions with an appeal to James's earlier writings: "And when his works shall stand in the Libraries of our Posteritie, amongst the Fathers, euen these Papers, these Directions, & these Reasons shalbe pregnant evidences for his constant zeale to Gods truth, and in the meane time, as arrowes shot in their eyes, that imagine so vaine a thing, as a defection in him, to their superstition."[47] This praise of James was also a warning that the king should be wary of acting in a way that conflicted with the zealously Protestant interpretations which had traditionally been given to his works, and which Donne and Abbot were now trying to apply to the directions for preachers. Appealing to the royal meaning to restrict James's actions was a strategy the king could hardly condemn, especially when the appeal was made in what was superficially a defense of his policy. Yet Donne's sermon seems to have done still more damage to James's plans. Writing on 25 September, John Chamberlain commented:

> On the 15th of this present the Dean of Paules preached at the Crosse to certifie the Kings goode intention in the late orders concerning preachers and preaching, and of his constancie in the true reformed religion, which the people (as shold seeme) began to suspect; his text was the 20th verse of the 5th chapter of the booke of Judges, somwhat a straunge text for such a busines, and how he made yt hold together I know not, but he gave no great satisfaction, or as some say, spake as yf himself were not so well satisfied.[48]

In view of the fact that on 30 September James was to write to Pope Gregory XV to ask for his cooperation in securing a European peace, doubt and suspicion were at least partially understandable.[49] Donne's audience was clearly complicit in his subversion of the king's text.[50] James, presumably feeling that any defense was better than none, ordered the work to be printed. One suspects that even the printers shared Donne's desire to prevent people from taking the sermon at face value; the title page of the first two issues announces a sermon not on Judges 5:20 but on Judges 20:15, a text that describes the outbreak of civil war in Israel following an attack on a priest.[51]

James might have done well to have dropped the matter at this stage; however, he was determined to make one final effort to enforce a positive reception of his work. He seems to have returned to the theory that rumors and corrupt texts had caused people to interpret his works in an unsatisfactory way, and that the solution was to ensure maximum distribution of his writings. Although he had seen this theory fail in practice on numerous occasions, at least it offered him a course of action. In his second letter, Abbot had told the bishops to ensure "that both the former direccions and these reasons of the same be fairely written in euery Registers office to the end that euery preacher of what denomination soeuer may if he be pleased take out Coppies of either of them with his owne hand gratis."[52] Judging by the number of copies of the letter and directions that survive, many copies were made, and these copies were copied themselves. The networks of Jacobean letter writers were at their most active during this period, when printers and preachers were being heavily censored. The British Library alone has more than a dozen contemporary copies of the letter and directions, or of parts of the work. It was also decided to spread the work further by printing James's letter and directions, with Abbot's letters of support. This appears to have been done in Oxford, with the support of Bishop John Howson, who had once been chastised by Abbot for his opposition to doctrinal Calvinism, and who was probably delighted to see Abbot apparently enforcing the repressive policies he had formerly resisted.[53] The work that eventually appeared in print seems to have consisted of two parts. *The Coppie of a Letter sent from my Lords Grace of Canterburie shewing the graue and weighty reasons which induced the Kings Maiestie to prescribe those former directions for Preachers* contained Abbot's second letter, as received by Howson.[54] The other part, headed *To the Minister Church-Wardens,* contains a letter from Howson introducing the work, James's letter to Abbot, Abbot's first letter, the directions themselves, and Howson's conclusions ordering the transmission and enforcement of the directions.[55] The fact that Howson's conclusions are dated "the last of August" may indicate that *Church-Wardens* was printed first and *Coppie* was issued as a supplement when Abbot's second letter became known. There are three surviving copies of *Coppie,* which are all bound with a copy of *Church-Wardens;* the fact that one of the four surviving copies of *Church-Wardens* exists separately adds weight to the possibility that it was originally printed as an independent text.[56]

The decision to transmit the work by print, however, seems to have inspired the most dangerous subversion of James's words yet. There are two surviving copies of an edition or editions of the letter and directions, apparently printed in 1622, which are very different from the official edition printed at Oxford. The copies of *The Kings Maiesties Letter to the Lords Grace of Canterbury, touching Preaching, and Preachers* now in Durham University Library (shelfmark SR.4.C.11/7, reproduced in facsimile here) and Emmanuel College, Cambridge (shelfmark S14.3.10/1) are set differently from each other and have a number of important textual discrepancies.[57] However, they both rearrange the texts found in *The Coppie of a Letter* and *To the Minister Church-Wardens:* the new editions contain James's letter to Abbot, the directions, and Abbot's second letter. Abbot's more unambiguous first letter of support and the explanatory notes by Bishop Howson are omitted altogether. Unlike the other editions, and as the title suggests, this publication places the emphasis firmly on the intentions of King James rather than on the wishes of his prelates.

Most importantly, the text in the Durham and Emmanuel copies changes the words of James's letter to Abbot to make the text seem less provocative and less anti-Puritan. The Durham copy has been annotated by a contemporary reader, who appears to be noting places where it differs from a corrupt manuscript copy of the official version in circulation.[58] Where the official text talks of the English "realm," the unauthorized edition has the more neutral, less kingly word "land." Where the official text states that preaching has traditionally been regulated with the advice of "grave and learned prelates," the unauthorized edition suggests, ironically, that it is in fact "grave and reverend preachers" who have been given the job of regulating preaching.

The most significant change is the omission of a phrase in the first direction. James's text had originally stated that the restrictions on preachers' subject matter were designed "not only for a helpe for the non-preachinge but withall for a patterne & a boundary as it were for the preachinge ministers," and this was followed in the official edition.[59] In the unauthorized edition represented by the Durham copy (although not in the Emmanuel copy), the reference to the non-preaching ministry was not printed. This is highly significant. James's reference to the importance of assisting the non-preaching ministry would have been controversial in 1622. The Puritan party believed that the main function of a minister was to preach God's word. The concept of ministers who did not preach, but whose duties were prayer and the administration of the sacraments, was associated by many with Roman Catholicism. The editor of the unauthorized edition seems to be changing James's words to make it appear that the king was not really an enemy of the Puritans, and thereby to prevent the directions from taking full effect. Like Donne and Abbot, the editor knew it would be futile to attack the directions openly; he probably hoped that the rumors about James's apostasy were false and that by twisting the author's words he could make it more difficult for James's actions to confirm people's worst fears.

However, that one version of James's words could be quoted against another may well have weakened the authority of the royal word more than the editor of the unauthorized edition intended. It is interesting to speculate on what the reader who made the annotations in the Durham copy was thinking. The fact that a royal declaration existed in different forms must have caused considerable surprise and suspicion, especially if the reader was not sure which version represented the official text. By comparing the different texts, the reader's attention would have been drawn to the more extreme passages that had been revised by the editor of the unofficial edition. An atmosphere of growing distrust between royal author and subject readers was not going to be improved by a debate about what James had actually said and meant.

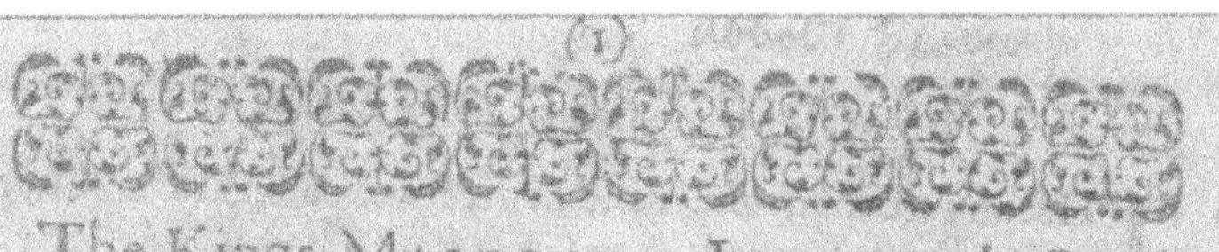

The Kings MAIESTIES Letter to the Lords Grace of *Canterbury*, touching Preaching, and Preachers.

MOst Reuerend Father in God, Right trustie and right intirely beloued Councellour, Wee greet yee well. Forasmuch as the abuse and extravagancies of Preachers in the Pulpit, haue been at all times repressed in this Land by some Act of Councell *or* State, *with the aduise and resolution of Graue and Reuerend Preachers, insomuch as the very licensing of Preachers, had beginning by order in the* Starre-Chamber *the eight day of Iuly in the nineteenth yeare of King* Henry *the eight, Our Noble Predecessor: And whereas at this present diuers young Students, by reading of late Writers and ungrounded Diuines, doe preach many times unprofitable, unseasonable, seditious, and dangerous doctrine, to the scandall of the* Church, *and disquieting of the* State *and present gouernment: Wee, upon humble presentation unto Us of these inconueniencies by your Selfe, and sundry other Graue and Reuerend Prelates of this* Church, *as of Our Princely care and desire, for the extirpation of schisme and dissention growing from these seedes; and for the setling of a religious and peaceable gouernment both of* Church *and* State, *Doe by these Our speciall Letters straightly charge and command you, to use all possible care and diligence, that these limitations and cautions herewith sent you concerning Preachers, be duly and strictly from henceforth obserued and put in practise, by the seuerall Bishops in their seuerall Diocesses within your iurisdiction. And to [illegible] end Our Pleasure is, that you send them forth seuerall copies of these directions, to be by them speedily sent and communicated to euery P[illegible] Vicar and Curate, Lecturer and Minister, in euery Cathedrall and [illegible] Church within their seuerall Diocesses; and that ye earnestly require [illegible] to imploy their utmost indeauours for the performance of this so im[illegible] a businesse: letting them know, We haue a speciall eye to their proce[illegible] and expect a strict accompt thereof both from you and euery of them. [illegible] Our Letter shall be your sufficient warrant and discharge in this [illegible]*

Giuen under Our Signet at Our Castle of Windsor, *the f[illegible] August, in the twentieth yeare of Our Reigne of* England [illegible] *and* Ireland, *and of* Scotland *the fiue and fiftieth.*

Directions concerning Preachers.

1 THat no Preacher, vnder the degree and calling of a Bishop, or Deane of a Cathedrall or Collegiate Church, and they vpon the Kings dayes, and set Festiuals, doe take occasion by the expounding of any text of Scripture whatsoeuer, to fall into any set discourse or Common-place (otherwise then by opening the coherence and diuision of his Text) which shall not be comprehended and warranted, in essence, substance and effect, or naturall inference, within some one of the Articles of Religion set forth 1562. or in some of the Homelies set forth by authoritie in the Church of *England*, not onely for a helpe for the preaching Ministers, and for their further instructions: for the performance hereof, that they forthwith peruse ouer, and read diligently the said Articles, or the two bookes of Homilies.

2 That no Parson, Vicar, Curate, or Lecturer, shall preach any Sermon or Collation vpon Sunday and Holy-dayes in the afternoon, in any Cathedrall or Parish Church throughout the Kingdome, but vpon some part of the Catechisme, or some text taken out of the Creed, tenne Commandements, or Lords Prayer, (funerall Sermons onely excepted) and that those Preachers be most encouraged and approoued of, who spend these afternoone Exercises in examining the children in their Catechisme, and in expounding of the seuerall points and heads of the Catechisme, which is the most auncient and laudable custome of teaching in the Church of *England*.

3 That no Preacher of what title soeuer, vnder the degree of a Bishop or Deane at the least, do from henceforth presume to preach in any populous auditorie, the deepe points of Predestination, Election, Reprobation; of the Vniuersalitie, Efficacie, Resistabilitie, or Irresistabilitie of Gods grace, but leaue those Theames to be handled by the learned men, and that moderately, and modestly, by way of vse and application, rather then by way of positiue doctrine, as being fitter for the Schooles and Vniuersities, then for simple auditories.

4 That no Preacher of what title or denomination soeuer, shall presume from hence forth in any auditorie in this Kingdome, to [illegible] limit, or bound out by positiue doctrine, in any Lecture or Sermon,

Sermon, the Power, Prerogatiue, Iurisdiction, Authoritie, or Duty of Soueraigne Princes; or otherwise meddle with these matters of State, and the references betweene Princes and the People, then as they are instructed and presidented in the Homilie of obedience, and in the rest of the Homilies and Articles of Religion, set forth as is before mentioned by publike authoritie; but rather confine themselues for those two heads, Faith and good Life, which are the subiect of auncient Sermons and Homilies.

5 That no Preacher of what title or denomination soeuer, shall causlesly, and without inuitation from the Text, fall into bitter inuectiues, and vndecent rayling speeches, against the persons of either Papist or Puritan, but modestly, and grauely when they are inuited or occasioned thereunto by their text of Scripture, free both the Doctrine and Discipline of the Church of *England*, from the aspersion of either Aduersarie, especially where the auditorie is suspected to be tainted with the one or the other infection.

6 Lastly, the Archbishops and Bishops of this kingdome (whom his Maiestie hath good cause to blame for their former remisnes) be more warie and choice in licensing Preachers, and reuoke all grants made to any Chancellor, Officiall, or Commissary to licence in this kind. And that all the Lectures throughout the kingdome (a new body seuered from the auncient Clergie of England, as beeing neither Parson, Vicar, nor Curate) be licensed henceforth in the Court of faculties, onely vpon recommendation of the party from the Bishop of the Diocesse, vnder his hand and seale with a *Fiat* from the L. Archbish. of *Canterbury*, and a confirmation of the great seale of *England*: and that such as transgresse any of these directions, bee suspended by the L. Bish. of the Diocesse; in his default by the L. Archbish. of the prouince, *ab Officio & Beneficio*, for a yeare and a day, vntill his Maiestie by aduice of the next Conuocation shall prescribe some further punishment.

The Lord Archbishop of *Canterbury* his letters to the Bishop of the Diocesse of *Norwich*.

MY very good L. I doubt not but before this time you haue receiued from me, the directions of his most excellent Maiesty concerning Preaching and Preachers, which are so graciously set downe, that no godly or discreete man, can otherwise then acknowledge, that they doe much tend to edification, if he doe not take them vpon report, but doe punctually consider the tenor of the words as they lie; and doe not giue an ill construction to that, which may receiue a faire interpretation. Notwithstanding, because some few Churchmen, and many of the people haue sinisterly conceiued (as we doe here find) that those Instructions doe tend to the restraint of the exercise of preaching, and doe in some sort abate the number of Sermons, and so consequently by degrees, doe make a breach to let in ignorance and superstition: His Maiestie in his Princely wisedome hath thought fit, that I should aduertise your Lordship of the graue and waighty reasons which induce his Highnes to prescribe that which is done. You are therefore to know, that his Maiestie beeing much troubled and grieued at the heart, to heare euery day of so many defections from our Religion, both to Popery and Anabaptisme, or other pointes of separation in some partes of this Kingdome, and considering with much admiration, what might be the cause thereof, especially in the Raigne of such a King, who doth so constantly professe himselfe an open Aduersarie to the superstition of the one, and madnes of the other: His Princely wisedome could fall vpon no one greater probability then the lightnes, affectednes, and vnprofitablenesse of that kind of preaching, which hath beene of late yeares too much taken vp in Court, Vniuersitie, Citie, and Country. The vsuall scope of very many Preachers is noted to be a soaring vp in points of Diuinity too high for the capacities of the people, or a mustering of much reading, or displaying of their wit, or an ignorant medling with ciuil matters as well in the priuate of seuerall Parishes and Corporations, as in the publike of the Kingdome: or a venting of their owne distastes, or a smoothering vp of those idle fancies, which in this blessed time of so long a peace, doe boile in the braines of vnaduised people. And lastly by a rude and vndecent

decent rayling, not onely against the doctrine (which when the text shall occasion, the same is not onely approoued, but much commended by his Maiestie) but against the persons of Papists and Puritanes. Now the people bred vp with this kind of teaching, and neuer instructed in the Catechisme and Fundamentall points of Religion, are for all this ayerie nourishment, no better then abrasæ tabulæ, new table-bookes readie to be filled vp, either with the Manualls or Catechismes of Popish Priests, or papers and pamphlets of Anabaptists, Brownists, & Puritans. His Maiesty euer calling to mind the saying of Tertullian, Id verum quod primum, and remembring with what doctrine the Church of England in her first and most happie reformation, did driue out the one, and kept out the other from poysoning and infecting the people of this Kingdome, did finde that the whole scope of this doctrine is contained in the Articles of Religion, the two Bookes of Homilies, the lesse and the greater Catechisme, which his Maiestie doth therefore recommend againe in these directions, as the theames & proper subiect of all sound and edifying Preaching. And so far are these directions from abating, that his M. doth expect from our hands, that it should increase the number of Sermons, by renewing vpon euery Sunday in the afternoone in all Parish Churches throughout the Kingdome, the primitiue and most profitable exposition of the Catechisme, wherwith the people, yea very children may be timely seasoned and instructed in all the heads of Christian Religion. Which kind of teaching (to our amendment be it spoken) is more diligently obserued in all the reformed Churches of Europe, then of late it hath been here in England. I find his Maiestie much moued with this neglect; & resolued, that if we which are his Bishops do not see a reformation hereof (which I trust we shall) to recommend it to the care of the Ciuill Magistrate, so far is he from giuing the least discouragement to solid Preaching, and discreete and Religious Preachers.

To all these I am to adde, that it is his Maiesties Princely pleasure, that both the former directions, and these reasons of the same, bee fairly written in euery Registers Office. To that end, that euery Preacher of what denomination soeuer, may if he be pleased, take out copies of either of them with his owne hand gratis, paying nothing in the name of Fee, or Expedition. But if he doe vse the paines of the Register or his Clerks, then to pay some moderate Fees, to be pronounced in open Court by the Chancellor and Commissaries of the place, taking the direction and approbation of any the Lords the Bishops.

Lastly, that from henceforth a course may be taken, that euery Parson, Vicar, or Curate, or Lecturer, doe make exhibites of these his Maiesties

direct*ions*

for directions and reasons of the same, at the next ensuing Visitation of the Bishops and Archdeacons, paying to the Register by way of Fee two pence onely at the time of the exhibite.

but with And so wishing, and in his Maiesties Name requiring your Lordsh. to haue a speciall and extraordinarie care of the premisses: I leaue you to the Almightie. From Croidon, Sept. 4. 1622.

Your very louing brother,

G. Cant.

With his policies being increasingly undermined, in early 1623 James took the extraordinary step of resorting to writing satirical verses to his subjects, as if he were a discontented citizen rather than an absolute monarch. "The Wiper of the Peoples Teares" seems to have been a direct reply to a vanished document called "The Comons Teares," presumably a work complaining about James's actions.[60] Although there is no surviving holograph, it seems very unlikely that it could have been written by anyone other than the king.[61] Although the poem starts as a tirade against the opponents of James's religious policies, it moves toward an acknowledgment of the problems that his earlier texts had caused for his political strategy in the 1620s. Recognizing that the unwelcome reception of the *Letter and Directions* was not simply a matter of outright insubordination but the product of his subjects' readings and theories of reading, James writes with a fascinating combination of royal anger and thoughtful self-analysis:

why doe you push me downe to hell
by makeinge me an Infidell
Tis true I am a cradle kinge
yet doe remember every thinge
That I have heretofore put out
and yet begin not for to doubt.
O how grosse is your device
change to impute to kings as vice
The wise may change, yet free from fault
though change to worse is ever nought.

James seems to be replying to specific accusations or insinuations that he has apostasized, that he has been king for so long that he has forgotten his initial anti-Spanish fervor, and that he appears to have changed the opinions he recorded in his books. James looks back over his life, acknowledging that his coronation in 1567 was a long time ago, and perhaps acknowledging the mental restrictions imposed by the fact that his whole conscious life had been lived as a king. He recalls all the books he "put out" over the years, and he refuses to "doubt," as Thomas Scott and others were doubting, that his past words preclude his current political strategy. James finally perceives the extent to which his readers have exalted the printed word: they have come to believe that a king should be as immutable as his texts. The absurdity of saying that a king should never change his mind is clear once James voices it, but as an unspoken assumption it was extremely damaging. James's struggle to articulate and criticize the unstudied beliefs about language and meaning that lay behind the conflict between king and people is a landmark in literature and in the development of expressions of royal authority.

John Chamberlain noted that all kinds of verses were circulating in early 1623, some criticizing the king, some purporting to be by him.[62] James Craigie has shown that a great number of manuscript copies of this text survive, much like the *Letter and Directions,* and it seems probable that James permitted such copies to be made.[63] James had certainly degraded the royal word, but he had done so to regain contact with readers who were becoming increasingly alienated from their king. It is interesting to speculate about what might have happened if the Spanish match had proceeded much further. When King Charles found that his words had lost their authority in 1642, he resorted to military force; in 1623 James seems to have been preparing to deal with a comparable situation in a completely different way. Whereas Charles would cling to the image at the expense of the reality, James seems to have deliberately jeopardized the aura of sanctity surrounding the royal word in order to show that the situation was less catastrophic than popular rhetoric suggested.

As it was, the journey of Prince Charles and Buckingham to Madrid in February 1623 suspended the impending conflict. The negotiations there became protracted and eventually failed completely, and the disappointed wooers returned in October, eager to change James's pacific stance and go to war with Spain. Appeasement and ecumenism had failed. Parliament was summoned, and it was made clear to James that he would have to reimpose the recusancy laws and give preachers a free rein to attack papists and Spaniards.[64] Without the support of his son and his best friend, James no longer had the heart to uphold the policies that the *Letter and Directions* had been issued to defend. At the opening of Parliament on 19 February 1624, James made a remark which suggests how far he was aware of the fact that his policies had been wrecked by interpretations of his words: "remembering many misunderstandings between me and you before, I am now brought hither with an earnest desire to do my duty that God hath called me unto, by declaring unto you the verity of this, that God hath put in my heart, and to manifest my actions to be true by my words."[65] It would be rather more normal to speak of proving one's words by one's deeds; as Thomas Scott argued, people had been expecting James's literary works to be turned into action. James's ironic inversion here points at the way in which his words, and particular readings of his words, had come to be exalted over the king and his actions. James tries to erase the memory of the now discredited *Letter and Directions* by giving his audience words that conform to their interpretations of his earlier writings, and that justify his actions:

> One particular I must remember you of, because it hath been much talked of in the country, that I should be slack in my care of religion for other occasions. My Lords, and you Gentlemen all, I pray you judge me charitably, as you would have me to judge you; for I never made public nor private treaties but I always made a direct reservation for the weal public and [the] cause of religion, for the glory of

> God [and] the good of my subjects. I only thought good sometimes to wink and connive at the execution of some penal statutes, and not to go on so rigorously as at other times, but to dispense with any, to forbid or alter any that concern religion, I never promised or yielded; I never did think it with my heart, nor speak it with my mouth.[66]

But despite James's recantation, the *Letter and Directions* remained, in many different versions, both printed and manuscript, as a testimony to the fact that the king had written a work he abandoned under pressure from his readers. The fact that only six printed copies of the work or parts of the work dating from 1622 seem to have survived may suggest that the authorities made a belated attempt to prevent its distribution.[67] Yet it was not forgotten. Like the Armada or the Gunpowder Plot, the wavering of King James in 1622 was inscribed into the national myth of God's intervention to save England's Protestant mission.[68] John Reynolds, in his *Vox Coeli,* a work addressed to the Parliament of 1624 to encourage them to back a holy war with Spain, presented a dramatic debate between various deceased English monarchs on King James's policies.[69] In Reynolds's work, Queen Elizabeth describes how James had been influenced by the Spanish into repressing his people, so that "no cinsere [*sic*] aduise, honest Letter, Religious Sermon, or true picture can point at the King of Spaine, but they are called in; and their Authours imprisoned."[70] Henry VIII reminds her that in such cases the English people would overrule James's mistaken orders: "For (for the good of England) if one pen, or tongue bee commanded to silence, they will occasion and set tenne at libertie to write and speake; as Grasse or Cammomell, which the more it is depressed, the thicker it will spread and grow."[71] The word of the king had become a tool of the Catholics, but God was behind the words of the king's readers.

This remarkable "victory" by the readers of the *Letter and Directions* ensured that the work retained political potency well into the Civil War and after. At the outbreak of the Civil War in 1642, numerous political documents from the Elizabethan and Jacobean periods were reprinted, as people tried to discover how the crisis had arisen and sought guidance from other historical events. Thomas Cogswell and Nigel Smith have shown that the events surrounding the Spanish marriage in the 1620s were seen as closely paralleling the events which had led to the break between Charles and his Parliament.[72] Once again, the king was conducting policies which involved closer links with Catholicism, trying to restrict free speech, and issuing ambiguous and threatening declarations. Those seeking a precedent for resisting or reinterpreting the royal word found it in the *Letter and Directions.*

A new version of the *Letter and Directions* appeared in May 1642, the month in which Charles's attempts to gain control of the arsenal at Hull were leading both sides to refine their intellectual positions and prepare for war.[73] *King James his Letter and Directions to the Lord Archbishop of Canterbury; concerning Preaching and Preachers* contains James's letter to Archbishop George

Abbot, the directions for preachers, and Abbot's two letters in support of the directions.[74] The text is not identical with that in any of the printed editions of 1622, and it seems likely that the editor made use of one of the manuscript copies in circulation. The text appears to be based on a version of the official edition, rather than one of the unofficial editions, but it is worth noting that the way in which the various documents are structured is closer to the format of the unofficial editions.

Particularly interesting is the way in which George Abbot's longer letter, written on 4 or 5 September 1622, is printed before his shorter letter, written on 12 August 1622. As has been said, Abbot's long letter is a complex and critical response to James's directions, unlike Abbot's short letter, written before the scale of public opposition had become known, which is simply a brief note ordering that the directions be obeyed. In the 1642 edition, the long letter is given its accepted date of 4 September 1622, but the short letter that follows it is undated. This gives the impression that the author's attitude is hardening. The title page, in fact, makes use of the short letter, stating that James's letter is printed along with "the Bishop of Canterburies Letter to the Bishop of Lincolne, Lord Keeper, desiring him to put in practise the Kings desires, that none should preach but in a Religious forme. And not that every young man should take to himselfe an exorbitant Liberty, to preach what he listeth, to the offence of his Majesty, and the disturbance and disquiet of the Church and Common-wealth." This is a quotation from Abbot's letter. What were the motives behind this confrontational restructuring?

The work purports to have been printed for Thomas Walkeley, a known royalist bookseller who lost his estates in 1642.[75] It seems most unlikely that he would have published such a work at this time. The dispute between King Charles and Parliament was on the edge of becoming a military conflict; every announcement by anyone in authority was read with great care. It would have been provocative in the extreme for a royalist to remind the world of past actions by monarchs to repress preachers, particularly in view of the recent fall of Archbishop Laud. It is more probable that this edition was printed under Walkeley's name by a Parliamentary sympathizer to make readers think that the royalists subscribed to the extremist position in the letter and directions. By emphasizing the hectoring tone of Abbot's first letter, the editor could link the two archbishops. In 1622 Abbot had resisted the *Letter and Directions,* and his long letter was used by others seeking to resist the text. In 1642, however, the editor finds it more useful to identify Abbot with the work, perhaps to suggest that he seduced James into passing the document, just as Laud had imposed his policies on Charles. In 1622 the continuation of episcopal government in England had not been an issue of serious debate, particularly in view of Abbot's Calvinist views. In 1642, however, the *Letter and Directions* makes very useful propaganda for the reforming party. The new edition might have been intended to suggest that the current crisis would blow over as quickly as the crisis in 1622, and that Charles would repudiate his declarations as rapidly as James had jettisoned the letter and directions. However, the main purpose of the republication seems to be to link King Charles and his supporters to a tradition of repression and hidden agendas, and, equally, to a tradition of royal weakness and inconsistency.

Other editions of texts relating to events in the 1620s seem to confirm this. A work called *The Svpplication of all the Papists of England to King James,* which appeared in June 1642, reprinted the Catholic appeal for toleration made to James at the start of his English reign.[76] The implication is that the papists were treacherous, and the title reminds the reader how soon the Gunpowder Plot followed their petition. However, the text also suggests that James was gullible and too sympathetic to the Catholics. The 1642 republication of the *Svpplication* includes a letter, purportedly written by Archbishop Abbot in 1623, in which he warns James against tolerating the heretical doctrines of Rome. Addressed to King James, this letter begins, "I have beene too long silent, and I am afraid, by my silence I have neglected the duty of the place it hath pleased God to call me unto." The text goes on to attack James's policies:

> Your Majesty hath propounded a tolleration of religion. I beseech You Sir, take into Your consideration what Your act is, what the consequence may be: By Your act You labour to set up that most damnable and hereticall doctrine of the Church of Rome, that whore of Babylon. How hatefull will it be to God, and grievous to Your good Subjects, (the true Professors of the Gospell) that Your Majesty, who hath often disputed and learnedly written against those wicked heresies, should now shew Your selfe a Patron of those doctrines, which Your Pen hath told the world, and Your conscience tels Your Selfe, are superstitious, idolatrous and detestable?[77]

This letter was probably not by Abbot, but it may well have reflected his real discontent with James's proceedings.[78] The suggestion that the king's subjects were "the true Professors of the Gospell" rather than the king himself made very useful propaganda in 1642. The Parliamentary propagandists do not seem to have bothered to agree on a consistent interpretation of Abbot's opinions so long as they could use his words to subvert the authority of the royal word and the royal policies.

Abbot's letters in support of the *Letter and Directions* were published again, with the printed date of 15 July, in a collection of miscellaneous pro-Parliamentary declarations and petitions entitled *Remarkeable Passages,* with the imprimatur of the clerk of the House of Commons.[79] The long letter—which precedes the short letter, as in the 1642 edition of the complete *Letter and Directions*—is introduced as "The Arch-Bishop of Canterburies Letter to the Arch-Bishop of Yorke."[80] Richard A. Christophers is apparently right when he remarks, "This work seems to be a tract of government propaganda, and the title page, significantly, does not mention Abbot. Perhaps the publishers hoped that Laud's name would be understood."[81] Without James's directions, Abbot's ironic subtext is lost, and the writer sounds as though he is promoting a new program of repression. However, the long letter is given its correct date of 4 September 1622.[82] The editor seems to be allowing the reader to interpret the work in two different ways, which would be equally damaging to the "High Church" party. The work could be read as a last attempt by Laud to repress the Puritans or as evidence that the *Letter and Directions,* reprinted in May, is highly relevant to the current crisis. It is significant that the short letter, which is given the ambiguous signature "CANT" (rather than "G. CANT" as with the long letter), is followed by a petition from the distressed Irish Protestants to Charles. Whether the work is understood in relation to James or Charles, Abbot or Laud, the reader is encouraged to feel indignation at the treatment of Protestants.

It seems clear that copies of various parts of the *Letter and Directions* were circulating in manuscript well into the mid-seventeenth century. When the republican historians of the 1650s began to produce their revisionist accounts of James's reign, the *Letter and Directions* featured prominently. Arthur Wilson and John Rushworth reprinted the work with commentary clearly setting the text and its reception in the context of the breakdown in 1642, and they were answered by William Sanderson, Thomas Fuller, and John Hacket, who defended James's actions.[83] These historians print versions of the work that contain an extraordinary number of textual variants: this may indicate that manuscript copies were more readily available than the surviving copies of the official printed edition.

A version of the *Letter and Directions* was clearly used to produce Charles II's *Directions Concerning Preachers,* which was published in 1662 to assist with the enforcement of the restored episcopal system, and this document was republished by James VII and II.[84] The revival of interest in the work at the Restoration may have been the reason why Archbishop William Sancroft began to research the state of the text; as a believer in the divine right of kings, he must have found it disconcerting to see the extent to which James had lost control over his words. Sancroft read and annotated a copy of the 1642 edition of the complete *Letter and Directions,* now in Durham University Library (shelfmark R.37.B.11), and on the first page he wrote "see y[e] 2[d] pt of y[e] Cabbala." In *Scrinia Sacra . . . a Svpplement of the Cabala* (1654), a pro-republican collection of Jacobean documents, a version of the *Letter and Directions* is printed.[85] Was Sancroft comparing the edition of 1642 with the later version? Many of his annotations do correspond to the text in *Scrinia Sacra;* however, there are many differences between the two texts that Sancroft does not mark, and sometimes his marginalia suggest a change to text that is identical in *Scrinia Sacra* and the 1642 text. Sancroft was presumably comparing the 1642 edition to a manuscript copy, perhaps trying to account for the origin of the text in *Scrinia Sacra*.

Sancroft's interest in this confusing multiplicity of texts is further indicated by the fact that one of the two surviving copies of the 1622 unauthorized edition (*STC* 14379.5) is among the books he donated to his college, Emmanuel. Sancroft lists the work, bound in a volume of tracts relating to ecclesiastical history, in a table of contents in his own handwriting. One suspects that he had examined the other copy of *STC* 14379.5, and that its current presence in the library of Durham University is connected to Sancroft's time at Durham in the 1660s.[86] Although his annotations to the Durham copy of the 1642 edition do not relate to either of these two earlier versions, it seems more than likely that he was aware of their existence, and perhaps of their significance as subversive reworkings of King James's words. The fact that the *Letter and Directions* could still command this level of interest in the 1650s and 1660s suggests that its republication in 1642 was not an event of minor significance.[87]

The misinterpretations of James's writings prior to 1622 had weakened the authority of the king's word, but because they were largely individualistic responses, the damage had been limited. The *Letter and Directions* of 1622, however, was understood according to widely accepted readings of James's other works, which it appeared to contradict. Readers engaged with James's text to show that it was an imperfect expression of the royal will, and through various strategies they succeeded in transforming a repressive text into a vehicle for expressing popular thought and sentiment. Detached from the author who had been forced to abandon it, the work retained its power to alarm and excite for many years, even though it was increasingly difficult to establish what James had actually said, let alone what he had meant. The memory of the work's initial reception allowed it to retain its political potency well into the Civil War and after. The *Letter and Directions* that exists today, in manuscripts and annotated copies, paraphrases and explanations, is not just the product of King James in 1622, but the product of the activity of the subjects and readers who made the king's word their own.

Notes

This essay is a substantially revised version of a paper delivered at the Scottish Renaissance Seminar in Edinburgh in February 1998. It is placed in the broader context of the reception of King James's writings as ch. 2 of my doctoral thesis, "Reading King James VI and I in the Civil War." In citations I have modernized long "s" and expanded contractions, but spelling and punctuation are otherwise unaltered.

1. The best modern edition of the text is Fincham, *Visitation Articles and Injunctions* 1: 211–15, based on the text in Abbot's Register (Lambeth Palace Library) ii, fos. 199r–200v. An incomplete text is to be found in Kenyon 145–46.
2. *The Kings Maiesties Speach* sig. I1r–v; also in Sommerville 203.
3. See Doelman.
4. See Helgerson.
5. See James's letter of 25 June 1616, in Jackson 356–57. For the probable appearance of the *Workes,* whose title page bears the date 1616, in early 1617, see Sommerville xi, and Craigie, "The Latin Folio" 20.
6. For the Parliament, see Zaller.
7. Notestein, Relf, and Simpson 2: 2.
8. Ibid. 2: 303.
9. *His Maiesties Declaration.* Also in Sommerville 250–67.
10. Craigie, *Poems* 2: xxii–xxiii.
11. See Cogswell, *Blessed Revolution* and "England and the Spanish Match"; Patterson esp. 293–338. Still useful is Gardiner.
12. In *Ane Meditatiovn* sig. Biv^{v}. See Craigie, *Poems* 164, 250.
13. *Peace-Maker.*
14. For the development of apocalyptic myth, particularly in creation with the new imperial British state, see the writings of Williamson, *Scottish National Consciousness* and "Scotland, Antichrist and the Invention of Great Britain."
15. James's change of mind is noted in Simon Adams's excellent essay, "Foreign Policy and the Parliaments of 1621 and 1624," esp. 148. See also Milton 108.
16. Parallel to the tendency of readers to manipulate James's words seems to have been the tendency to take them too seriously; see Wormald, esp. 54.
17. Scott sig. π2r–v.
18. Scott sig. B2v. The relevant passage in the *Remonstrance* is in McIlwain 261.
19. There is an interesting discussion of Scott in Lake, esp. 815–18.
20. Larkin and Hughes 1: 495–96, 519–21.
21. See Dahl; Bennett 186–87; and Cust.
22. *Ragionamento Fatto dal Re* (1622). This subversive work is in Italian, and claims to have been printed in Bologna for Nicolò Tebaldini, having been translated from a Spanish version of the English original published in London for "Hercule Francese." However, Francese is otherwise unknown, and such a complex publishing history seems improbable. This may have been printed in London at the instigation of the Spanish embassy to create unrest, which would

hamper James's attempts to resolve the crisis on the continent, or possibly concocted by the pro-war "Puritan" party to stir up anger at the way James was being deceived into Romanist opinions. My thanks go to Professor Jon Usher of the department of Italian at the University of Edinburgh for his assistance with this text, on which I am planning an article. See *Calendar of State Papers, Domestic Series* (hereafter *CSPD*) 345.

23. See Davies, esp. 9. Bennett (108–9) argues that Davies underestimates the number of sermons.
24. See Seaver.
25. See *CSPD* 379, 380, 396, 404–5, 418, 426–27.
26. Curll sig. C2r.
27. See W. B. Patterson, "Peregrinations."
28. See *Answere vnto the Nine Points of Controuersy;* also Wadkins.
29. PRO SP 14/132/84.
30. PRO SP 14/132/85, from which subsequent citations are taken. For the possibility that clerics such as William Laud or John Williams had a hand in writing the directions, see Heylyn sig. O1r–2r; and John Hacket, *Scrinia Reserata,* sig. N1r.
31. Peter White seems to take at face value James's presentation of the *Directions* as a traditional and moderate document, but he does not really analyze the specific context that made its implications so radically disturbing; see White 210–14.
32. There was some basis for James's argument, in view of the controversies resulting from the Synod of Dort (see W. B. Patterson 281–82), but the directions were clearly a response to immediate political events.
33. See Calderwood 7: 562.
34. The standard biography of Abbot is by Welsby; Abbot's role in this crisis is briefly discussed at 107–9. Welsby's account needs to be read in conjunction with Fincham, "Prelacy and Politics," which uses new evidence that reveals more clearly Abbot's sympathy for doctrinal Calvinist preachers, and his belief in popish conspiracies. See also Heinemann, esp. nn. on 157, 276.
35. PRO SP 14/132/93. *CSPD* 440 suggests that this was written on 12 August.
36. McClure 2: 449. See Cogswell, *Blessed Revolution* 32–33.
37. *Calendar of State Papers . . . Venice* 397.
38. In most early versions, like British Library ms. Add. 3694 f.23–24, the letter is dated 4 September, but in Lambeth Palace ms. Tenison 669/108—which I am using here to indicate the diversity of the versions that survive in different locations, and from which subsequent citations are taken—it is dated 5 September.

39. Abbot's second letter contains many arguments similar to those used by King James in his letter to the Scottish Privy Council of 31 October 1622, in which he insisted that the *Directions* would not lead to a toleration of popery; see Masson 13: 79–81.
40. sig. [A4r]. See *CSPD* 332.
41. In Birch 2: 329–30.
42. See Shami, "'Stars in their Order,'" and Kearney 74–100.
43. *Sermon;* also in Potter and Simpson 4: 178–209.
44. Gosse 2: 174; for Donne's later thought on the *Letter and Directions,* see Shami, "Donne's 1622 Sermon."
45. sig. [I4r–v].
46. sig. F2v.
47. sig. K1r.
48. McClure 2: 451.
49. Akrigg 383–85, using Bodleian Library Tanner ms. 73, f. 236.
50. See Annabel Patterson 97–99.
51. See Keynes 31–35.
52. Lambeth Palace ms. Tenison 669/108.
53. See Cranfield and Fincham. Howson was accused, among other things, of having said that James had not written the *Apologie* or the *Premonition* (336). James, characteristically, did not uphold Abbot's charges, but he advised Howson to preach against popery to prove his orthodoxy.
54. *Coppie of a Letter.*
55. *To the Minister Church-Wardens.*
56. Of the three copies of *The Coppie of a Letter,* all bound with *To the Minister Church-Wardens,* one is in the British Library, shelfmark 1608/1117, and two are in the library of Corpus Christi College, Oxford, shelfmarks **Φ**.A.I.10 (3–4) and **Φ**.A.I.10 (11–12). In the first two copies, *Coppie* precedes *Church-Wardens,* but in the third copy the order is reversed. *Church-Wardens* exists separately in the Bodleian Library, shelfmark Wood 516.8. Madan (117) claims that *Church-Wardens* is simply part of *Coppie.* My thanks are due to the library staff at Corpus Christi for allowing me to see their copies.
57. Despite the differences, they share the single reference *STC* 14379.5. University Microfilms has not helped the bibliographical confusion surrounding this work by cataloguing the film of the Emmanuel copy of *STC* 14379.5 as "*STC* 33."
58. It seems unlikely that the reader was comparing his work with the official *printed* edition, as a few of his marginal corrections do not correspond with the text in *STC* 33/13880; for example, on sig. A3r, he inserts the word "haue" where *STC* 13880 sig. [*3v] reads instead

"pass," which is also the reading in PRO SP 14/132/85. Presumably he was using one of the manuscript copies, based on PRO SP 14/132/85, distributed among the clergy. I have not found any version, either printed or manuscript, which corresponds exactly to these annotations: any further information on this matter would be gratefully received.

59. *STC* 13880, sig. [*2v].
60. Two texts are printed in Craigie, *Poems* 182–91; I am using Craigie's printing of British Library ms. Harley 367, fol. 151r–152v. My interpretation of this poem differs from that in Goldberg 18–21, 140–41, which is more cynical about James's strategies for regaining control of his readers.
61. See Craigie, "Last Poems."
62. McClure 2: 473, 478.
63. Craigie, *Poems* 262–65n.
64. Nicholas Tyacke notes the fact that Calvinist sermons resumed at St. Paul's Cross in 1624, and he concludes that the *Directions* "seem to have been largely inoperative." See Tyacke 103.
65. Kenyon 48.
66. Kenyon 49.
67. Fincham draws attention to the fact that the *Letter and Directions* was sometimes mentioned as an authoritative document in visitation articles of the 1620s and 1630s (*Visitation Articles* 2: xviii, 15, 60–61). It would be interesting to know what tendencies connected those bishops who continued to think the *Letter and Directions* useful although it no longer commanded the support of its author. My thanks to Dr. Fincham for his helpful suggestions.
68. For more information see Cressy.
69. This and related pamphlets are summarized in Wright.
70. sig. H1r.
71. Ibid.
72. Cogswell, "England and the Spanish Match" 110–11, 130; Smith 31.
73. For the dating of this, and subsequently for all pamphlets in the Thomason collection, unless otherwise stated, see Fortescue.
74. Wing J139.
75. See Plomer 187; *CSPD* [1641–3] 426–27.
76. *Svpplication of all the Papists of England,* Thomason E. 151 (19). The original text is reproduced in an early Protestant response by Powel.
77. sig. [A4r].
78. On the debate over the authenticity of this letter, see [Oldys] 35–37; also Christophers 86; Cust 72–73.
79. (f. W. G., Wing R922), Thomason E. 155 (17).

80. sig. [A1v].
81. Christophers 38.
82. sig. [A3r].
83. Wilson sig. [2C3v–2C4v]; Rushworth sig. I3v–K2r; Sanderson, which is usually found as the second part of William Sanderson, *A Compleat History* (f. Humphrey Moseley, Richard Tomlins & George Sawbridge, 1656, Wing S647), sig. 4a2r–[4a3r]; Fuller sig. 4O2v–[4O4r]; Hacket sig. N1r–v.
84. Charles II. There are particularly striking similarities between the first direction (sig. [A2v]) and the fourth direction of the 1622 version. This was republished by James VII and II, *To the most Reverend Fathers in God.* There were several other editions in 1686, Wing J390, J391, J391A.
85. *Scrinia Sacra* sig. 2A2r–[2A3v].
86. My thanks to the staff of Durham University Library and Emmanuel College, Cambridge, for their patience and courtesy in helping to work through these intricacies.
87. The 1642 edition of the complete *Letter and Directions,* Wing J139, seems to have had an unusually high print run, judging by the number of copies that survive today.

Works Cited

Adams, Simon. "Foreign Policy and the Parliaments of 1621 and 1624." *Faction and Parliament: Essays on Early Stuart History.* Ed. Kevin Sharpe. London: Methuen, 1985. 139–71.

Akrigg, G. P. V., ed. *Letters of King James VI & I.* Berkeley: U of California P, 1984.

Answere vnto the Nine Points of Controuersy, proposed by our late Soueraygne. St. Omer: English College Press, 1625. *STC* 10911.

Bennett, H. S. *English Books & Readers 1603 to 1640: Being a Study in the History of the Book Trade in the Reigns of James I and Charles I.* Cambridge: Cambridge UP, 1970.

Birch, Thomas, ed. *The Court and Times of James the First.* London: f. Henry Colburn, 1849.

Calderwood, David, ed. *Thomas Thomson, The History of the Kirk of Scotland.* Vol. 7. Edinburgh: Wodrow Society, 1845.

Calendar of State Paper, Domestic Series, 1619–1623. Ed. M. A. E. Green. London: Longman, Brown, Green, Longmans, and Roberts, 1858.

Calendar of State Papers . . . Venice, 1621–1623. Ed. Allen B. Hinds. London: His Majesty's Stationery Office, 1911.

Charles II. *To the most Reverend Father in God, William.* London: b. John Bill & Christopher Barker, 1662. Wing C3613.

Christophers, Richard A. *George Abbot: A Bibliography.* Charlottesville: Bibliographical Society of the U of Virginia, 1966.

Cogswell, Thomas. "England and the Spanish Match." *Conflict in Early Stuart England—Studies in Religion and Politics 1603–1642.* Ed. Richard Cust and Ann Hughes. London: Longman, 1989. 107–33.

———. *The Blessed Revolution: English Politics and the Coming of War, 1621–1624.* Cambridge: Cambridge UP, 1989.

Coppie of a Letter. Oxford: b. Iohn Lichfield & Iames Short, 1622. *STC* 33.

Craigie, James. "Last Poems of James VI." *Scottish Historical Review* 29 (1950): 134–42.

———. "The Latin Folio of King James's Prose Works." *Edinburgh Bibliographical Society Transactions* 3 (1948): 17–30.

———, ed. *The Poems of James VI. of Scotland.* Vol. 2. Edinburgh: Scottish Text Society, 1958.

Cranfield, Nicholas, and Kenneth Fincham, eds. "John Howson's Answers to Archbishop Abbot's Accusations at his 'Trial,' before James I at Greenwich, 10 June 1615." *Camden Miscellany* 29 (1987): 319–41.

Cressy, David. *Bonfires and Bells: National Memory and the Protestant Calendar in Elizabethan and Stuart England.* London: Weidenfeld & Nicolson, 1989.

Curll, Walter. *A Sermon . . . 28. of April.* London: b. John Bill, 1622. *STC* 6132.

Cust, Richard. "News and Politics in Early Seventeenth-Century England." *Past and Present* 112 (1986): 60–90.

Dahl, Folke. *A Bibliography of English Corantos and Periodical Newsbooks 1620–1642.* London: Bibliographical Society, 1952.

Davies, Godfrey. "English Political Sermons, 1603–1640." *Huntington Library Quarterly* 3 (1939): 1–22.

Doelman, James. "'A King of Thine Own Heart': The English Reception of King James VI and I's *Basilikon Doron.*" *Seventeenth Century* 9 (1994): 1–9.

Donne, John. *A Sermon.* London: f. Thomas Jones, 1622. *STC* 7054.

Fincham, Kenneth. "Prelacy and Politics: Archbishop Abbot's Defence of Protestant Orthodoxy." *Bulletin of the Institute of Historical Research* 61 (1988): 36–41.

———, ed. *Visitation Articles and Injunctions of the Early Stuart Church.* Vols. 1 & 2. London: Church of England Record Society, 1994, 1998.

Fortescue, G. K. *Catalogue of the Pamphlets.* Vol. 1. London: British Museum, 1908.

Fuller, Thomas. *The Church-History of Britain.* London: f. John Williams, 1655. Wing F2416.

Gardiner, Samuel R. *History of England.* Vol. 4. London: Longmans, Green, 1886.

Goldberg, Jonathan. *James I and the Politics of Literature: Jonson, Shakespeare, Donne, and Their Contemporaries.* Stanford: Stanford UP, 1989.

Gosse, Edmund. *The Life and Letters of John Donne.* Vol. 2. London: William Heinemann, 1899.

Hacket, John. *Scrinia Reserata.* London: Edw. Jones f. Samuel Lowndes, 1693. Wing H171.

Heinemann, Margot. *Puritanism and Theatre: Thomas Middleton and Opposition Drama under the Early Stuarts.* Cambridge: Cambridge UP, 1980.

Helgerson, Richard. "Milton Reads the King's Book: Print, Performance, and the Making of a Bourgeois Idol." *Criticism* 29 (1987): 1–25.

Heylyn, P[eter]. *Cyprianus Anglicus.* London: f. A. Seile, 1668. Wing H1699.

Jackson, William A., ed. *Records of the Court of the Stationers' Company 1602 to 1640.* London: Bibliographical Society, 1957.

James VI and I. *His Maiesties Declaration, Touching his proceedings.* London: b. Bonham Norton and John Bill, 1621 [1622]. *STC* 9241.

———. *King James his Letter and Directions to the Lord Archbishop of Canterbury; concerning Preaching and Preachers.* London: "f. Thomas Walkeley," 1642. Wing J139.

———. *Kings Maiesties Letter to the Lords Grace of Canterbury, touching Preaching, and Preachers.* n.p., n.d. *STC* 14379.5.

———. *The Kings Maiesties Speach.* London: b. Robert Barker, 1610. *STC* 14396.

———. *Ane Meditatiovn vpon the xxv, xxvi, xxvii, xxviii, and xxix verses of the xv Chapt. of the first buke of the Chronicles.* Edinburgh: b. Henrie Charteris, 1589. *STC* 14380.

———. *The Peace-Maker: Or, Great Brittaines Blessing.* London: b. Thomas Purfoot, 1618. *STC* 14387.

James VII and II. *To the most Reverend Fathers in God.* London: b. Charles Bill, Henry Hills & Thomas Newcomb, 1685/6. Wing J389.

Kearney, Jillian. "Donne's *Devotions* in the Context of his Early Sermons." Diss. Oxford, 1995.

Kenyon, J. P. *The Stuart Constitution 1603–1688.* Cambridge: Cambridge UP, 1966.

Keynes, Geoffrey. *A Bibliography of Dr. John Donne.* 4th ed. Oxford: Clarendon P, 1973.

Lake, P. G. "Constitutional Consensus and Puritan Opposition in the 1620s: Thomas Scott and the Spanish Match." *Historical Journal* 25 (1982): 805–25.

Larkin, James F., and Paul L. Hughes, eds. *Stuart Royal Proclamations.* Vol. 1. Oxford: Clarendon P, 1973.

Madan, Falconer. *The Early Oxford Press.* Oxford: Clarendon P, 1895.

Masson, David, ed. *The Register of the Privy Council of Scotland.* Vol. 13. Edinburgh: Her Majesty's Stationery Office, 1896.

McClure, Norman Egbert, ed. *The Letters of John Chamberlain.* Vol. 2. Philadelphia: American Philosophical Society, 1939.

McIlwain, Charles Howard, ed. *The Political Works of James I: Reprinted from the Edition of 1616.* Cambridge, Mass.: Harvard UP, 1918.

Milton, Anthony. *Catholic and Reformed: The Roman and Protestant Churches in English Protestant Thought 1600–1640.* Cambridge: Cambridge UP, 1995.

Notestein, Wallace, Frances Helen Relf, and Hartley Simpson. *Commons Debates 1621.* Vol. 2. New Haven: Yale UP, 1935.

[Oldys, William.] *The Life of Dr. George Abbot.* Guildford: f. & s. b. J. Russell, 1777.

Patterson, Annabel. *Censorship and Interpretation.* Madison: U of Wisconsin P, 1984.

Patterson, W. B. *King James VI and I and the Reunion of Christendom.* Cambridge: Cambridge UP, 1997.

———. "The Peregrinations of Marco Antonio de Dominis 1616–24." *Religious Motivation: Biographical and Sociological Problems for the Church Historian.* Ed. Derek Baker. Oxford: Basil Blackwell f. Ecclesiastical History Society, 1978. 241–57.

Plomer, Henry. *A Dictionary of the Booksellers and Printers.* London: Bibliographical Society, 1907.

Potter, George R., and Evelyn M. Simpson, eds. *The Sermons of John Donne.* Vol. 4. Berkeley: U of California P, 1959.

Powel, Gabriel. *The Catholikes Supplication.* London: b. F. Kyngston f. E. Weaver, 1603. *STC* 20141.

Ragionamento Fatto dal Re. Bologna: f. Nicolò Tebaldini, 1622.

Remarkeable Passages. London: f. W. G., 1642. Wing R922.

Reynolds, John. *Vox Coeli.* "Printed in Elisium," 1624. *STC* 20946.7.

Rushworth, John. *Historical Collections.* London: b. Tho. Newcomb f. George Thomason, 1659. Wing R2316.

Sanderson, William. *The Reign and Death of King James.* London: b. Henry Hills, 1655. Not in Wing.

Scott, Thomas. *The Workes,* Utrick, 1624. *STC* 22064. Rpt. Amsterdam: Theatrvm Orbis Terrarvm, 1973.

Seaver, Paul S. *The Puritan Lectureships: The Politics of Religious Dissent 1560–1662.* Stanford: Stanford UP, 1970.

Scrinia Sacra. London: f. G. Bedel & T. Collins, 1654. Wing C184.

Shami, Jeanne. "Donne's 1622 Sermon on the Gunpowder Plot: His Original Presentation Manuscript Discovered." *English Manuscript Studies 1100–1700* 5 (1995): 63–86.

———. "'The Stars in their Order Fought Against Sisera': John Donne and the Pulpit Crisis of 1622." *John Donne Journal* 14 (1995): 1–58.

Smith, Nigel. *Literature and Revolution in England 1640–1660.* New Haven: Yale UP, 1994.

Sommerville, J. P., ed. *King James VI and I: Political Writings.* Cambridge: Cambridge UP, 1994.

Svpplication of all the Papists of England to King James. London: b. E. Griffin, 1642. Wing S6189.

Tom Tell Troath. n.p., n.d. *STC* 23868.

To the Minister Church-Wardens. [Oxford: b. John Lichfield & James Short,] 1622. *STC* 13880.

Tyacke, Nicholas. *Anti-Calvinists: The Rise of English Arminianism c. 1590–1640:* Oxford: Clarendon P, 1987.

Wadkins, Timothy H. "King James I meets John Percy S.J. . . . : An Unpublished Manuscript." *Recusant History* 19 (1988): 146–54.

Welsby, Paul A. *George Abbot: The Unwanted Archbishop 1562–1633.* London: Society for the Promotion of Christian Knowledge, 1962.

White, Peter. *Predestination, Policy and Polemic: Conflict and Consensus in the English Church from the Reformation to the Civil War.* Cambridge: Cambridge UP, 1992.

Williamson, Arthur H. *Scottish National Consciousness in the Age of James VI: The Apocalypse, the Union and the Shaping of Scotland's Public Culture.* Edinburgh: John Donald, 1979.

———. "Scotland, Antichrist and the Invention of Great Britain." *New Perspectives on the Politics and Culture of Early Modern Scotland.* Ed. John Dwyer, Roger A. Mason, and Alexander Murdoch. Edinburgh: John Donald, 1982. 34–58.

Wilson, Arthur. *The History of Great Britain.* London: f. Richard Lownds, 1653. Wing W2888.

Wormald, Jenny. "James VI and I, *Basilikon Doron* and *The Trew Law of Free Monarchies:* The Scottish Context and the English Translation." *The Mental World of the Jacobean Court.* Ed. Linda Levy Peck. Cambridge: Cambridge UP, 1991. 36–54.

Wright, Louis B. "Propaganda against James I's 'Appeasement' of Spain." *Huntington Library Quarterly* 6 (1942–43): 149–72.

Zaller, Robert. *The Parliament of 1621: A Study in Constitutional Conflict.* Berkeley: U of California P, 1971.

Index